COMPLETE POEMS

EDGAR ALLAN POE
By Samuel Stillman Osgood
New-York Historical Society

Edgar Allan Poe

COMPLETE POEMS

EDITED BY

THOMAS OLLIVE MABBOTT

UNIVERSITY OF ILLINOIS PRESS

Urbana and Chicago

First Illinois paperback, 2000
© 1969 by the President and Fellows of Harvard College
Reprinted by arrangement with Harvard University Press
All rights reserved
Manufactured in the United States of America
⊗ This book is printed on acid-free paper.

Previously published as *Collected Works of Edgar Allan Poe*,
volume 1: *Poems*

Library of Congress Cataloging-in-Publication Data
Poe, Edgar Allan, 1809–1849.
[Poems]
Complete poems / Edgar Allan Poe ; edited by
Thomas Ollive Mabbott. — 1st Illinois pbk.
p. cm.
Originally published as v. 1 of: Collected works of
Edgar Allan Poe. Cambridge, Mass. : Belknap Press of
Harvard University Press, 1978.
Includes bibliographical references and index.
ISBN 0-252-06921-8 (alk. paper)
1. Fantasy poetry, American. I. Mabbott, Thomas Ollive, 1898–1968.
II. Poe, Edgar Allan, 1809–1849. Works. 1969. III. Title.
PS2605.A1   2000
811'.3—dc21   00-038639

P 5 4 3 2

TO
H. MOTT BRENNAN
1898–1968
My lifelong friend

ACKNOWLEDGMENTS

In more than forty years of study, I have been indebted to a great many librarians and other scholars, as well as to booksellers and collectors, whose help on special points I have usually acknowledged in the appropriate notes. But a few people to whom I have been indebted in a more general way, during the early years, should be named here. Among librarians were Belle da Costa Greene of the Pierpont Morgan Library, Clarence Saunders Brigham of the American Antiquarian Society, Nelson Nichols and Harry N. Lydenberg of the New York Public Library (both pupils of the great bibliographer, Wilberforce Eames), and Alexander J. Wall of the New-York Historical Society, all of whom were my teachers in method. Among booksellers were Oscar Wegelin and Dr. A. S. W. Rosenbach; among collectors Oliver Barrett of Chicago and William Koester of Baltimore. Among teachers should be mentioned my preceptor, William Peterfield Trent, and my friends and correspondents, George Saintsbury, George Edward Woodberry, and Killis Campbell.

In George N. Shuster I found a college president who understood the problem of a scholar engaged on a project that produced results only after long years. I should also like to express my appreciation to William S. Dix and the staff of the library of Princeton University for the warm hospitality accorded my work on the Poe edition during the summers of the last fifteen years; and to record a working scholar's sincere gratitude to Chancellor Harry Ransom and the University of Texas for their generosity in providing reproductions of manuscripts in the Koester Collection, acquired by them in 1966. I am grateful to H. Bradley Martin and Colonel Richard Gimbel for permission to use materials in their splendid collections, and for the general help and advice received from James Holly Hanford, the late John Gordan, and especially Kenneth Murdock and Floyd Stovall.

Patricia Edwards Clyne has not only typed the manuscripts

ACKNOWLEDGMENTS

but read the proof and helped in many generous ways. Finally I should like to thank Dr. George E. Hatvary who for the last three years has been my editorial assistant.

T. O. M.

St. John's University
May 1, 1968

At the time of Mr. Mabbott's death on May 15, 1968, the present volume was all but finished. The printer's copy for the texts of the poems and for the accompanying apparatus had been read and approved by him. He had completed recent revisions of the preface and the introduction to the poems, of all the appendixes, and of the "Annals," as he called his outline of Poe's biography and career as a writer. He had also corrected ninety five galleys more than half — of the proofs of the poems and commentary.

This edition of the poems has been seen through the press by Maureen C. Mabbott, who served as an assistant to her husband during the many years of his research, and by Eleanor D. Kewer, Chief Editor for Special Projects of the Harvard University Press. Both have been fully cognizant of Mr. Mabbott's methods of work, and their final efforts loyally and expertly carry out his wishes.

CLARENCE GOHDES
ROLLO G. SILVER
November 1968

CONTENTS

CONTENTS

CONTENTS

CONTENTS

CONTENTS

ILLUSTRATIONS

EDGAR ALLAN POE
Portrait by Samuel Stillman Osgood. Reproduced by permission of The New-York Historical Society

FOLLOWING PAGE 352

TO OCTAVIA, 1827
From the album of Octavia Walton, dated in Octavia's hand. Reproduced by permission of the Columbia University Libraries

A PAGE OF THE WILMER MANUSCRIPT, 1828
The last stanza of "Dreams" and the first stanza of "The Lake." From Poe's manuscript collection of his poems long in the possession of his friend Lambert A. Wilmer. Reproduced by permission of the Trustees of the Pierpont Morgan Library

THE FIRST PAGE OF *POLITIAN*, 1835
Reproduced by permission of the Trustees of the Pierpont Morgan Library

EARLY CORRECTIONS FOR "THE RAVEN," 1845
Within a week of the poem's first publication Poe corrected the bad rhyme in the eleventh stanza, sending the changes to his friend John Augustus Shea for the *New-York Tribune*. The poem, with the corrections, was printed in the *Tribune* for February 4, 1845. Reproduced by permission of the Trustees of the Pierpont Morgan Library

VALENTINE FOR FRANCES SARGENT OSGOOD, 1846
The copy sent to Miss Lynch's Valentine party. Poe misspelled Mrs. Osgood's middle name. This manuscript is reproduced through the courtesy of the Harvard College Library

VALENTINE FOR MARIE LOUISE SHEW, 1847
HM 2513: the manuscript given to Mrs. Shew. Reproduced through the courtesy of the Henry E. Huntington Library

ANNABEL LEE, 1849
The first three stanzas of the poem, from the manuscript given to Rufus W. Griswold. Reproduced through the courtesy of the Harvard College Library.

· X V ·

ILLUSTRATIONS

POE'S FOUR VOLUMES OF HIS POETRY

Paper wrapper of *Tamerlane and Other Poems* (1827), reproduced through the courtesy of the Berg Collection, The New York Public Library.

Title page of *Al Aaraaf, Tamerlane, and Minor Poems* (1829), reproduced from the copy in the Aldis Collection, by courtesy of the Yale University Library.

Title page of *Poems* (1831), reproduced through the courtesy of the Harvard College Library

Paper wrapper of *The Raven and Other Poems* (1845), reproduced through the courtesy of the Harvard College Library.

TEXT ILLUSTRATIONS

PREFACE TO *THE RAVEN AND OTHER POEMS* (1845)

Corrections in the Lorimer Graham copy, now at the University of Texas. In the photographs supplied through the courtesy of the Miriam Lutcher Stark Library, Poe's faintly penciled changes were barely discernible; this reproduction is therefore made from the facsimile edition (1942), by permission of Columbia University Press.

Page 15 of the Lorimer Graham copy of *The Raven* . . . showing Poe's alterations. From the facsimile, through the courtesy of the University of Texas and Columbia University Press.

THE BEGINNING OF AN EARLY POETRY COLLECTION

A heading and two lines of verse, on a sheet later used by John Allan for some figuring. From the Ellis and Allan Papers, by courtesy of the Library of Congress.

PREFACE TO THE PROJECTED EDITION

Edgar Allan Poe's position as a major author of poetry, fiction, and criticism is generally recognized. There has long been a need for a complete collection of his writings. The last and only previous attempt to present an unabridged edition was made more than sixty years ago. Since then the corpus of Poe's known works has increased considerably.

The earliest collection, *The Works of the Late Edgar Allan Poe*, brought out in four volumes between 1850 and 1856 by Rufus Wilmot Griswold, was professedly a selection, but remained the basis of all subsequent editions for the prose [1] — the poems fared somewhat better — until 1902. In that year James A. Harrison edited *The Complete Works of Edgar Allan Poe* in seventeen volumes. The title was used with some propriety, yet a fair number of articles mentioned in Harrison's bibliography were not included in his text.

My edition was planned after a discussion with Killis Campbell some forty years ago, and from it nothing surely authentic is to be intentionally excluded. Since 1902 scholars have recovered, from old periodicals and from manuscripts, many compositions inaccessible to Harrison. The bulk of Poe's writings here to be presented has been increased about twenty per cent. The inspiration of Harrison is gratefully acknowledged,[2] but this edition will not be a mere revision of his work. It will be a complete recension of the text, based on all accessible manuscripts and known printings by Poe. As I see it, the chief duties of an editor are to present

---

[1] In their once celebrated edition of Poe's *Works* (1895), Edmund Clarence Stedman and George Edward Woodberry "collected and edited" only the poetry independently. The introduction to different sections of the present edition will describe the few accretions to the prose in that and other nineteenth-century editions.

[2] The chronological arrangement (within categories) is based on Harrison's; but the order of some compositions is changed in the light of new information, and I have placed among the "Tales and Sketches" a few items Harrison classified as essays.

PREFACE TO THE EDITION

what an author wrote, to explain why he wrote it, to tell what he meant when he wrote it (if that be in any way now obscure), and to give a history of its publication. In addition, some evaluation of the more important works may be desirable.

The canon is established on the basis of both external and internal evidence. Almost unexceptionally, Poe's imaginative works were published at some time with his name. Unsigned works, chiefly critical, can be assigned to him on the basis of his own acknowledgments in manuscript or in print, by the statements of contemporaries in a position to know the facts, and by cross references. Poe's habit of repeating himself, especially in his "Marginalia," is well known. Nevertheless, the authorship of some few compositions remains in doubt. My editorial policy is to include (with a caveat) imaginative works for which there is considerable evidence of Poe's authorship, even if it is short of absolute proof. In the case of articles that are not imaginative, only those considered certainly to have been written by Poe will be given. The reasons for the ascription of unsigned items will be explained in every instance.[3]

The introductions to the sections of the miscellaneous contributions to periodicals will explain the few omissions; it does not seem necessary to include whole chapters of books quoted by Poe as "specimens of the author's style" but not the subject of analytic comment, nor to reprint more than once in the same volume favorite poems by Poe's friends which he quoted in full again and again.[4] Besides reviews, Poe sometimes wrote notices that amount to no more than records of the receipt of books. These will be reprinted only if they are specifically acknowledged.

The text may be fairly called conservative. The problems confronting the editor of Poe's writings are of some complexity, since no collected edition appeared during his lifetime; and the posthumous edition of Rufus Wilmot Griswold, his literary executor (*de facto* and perhaps *de jure*), was a selection, somewhat hastily

[3] These reasons have been discussed with my advisors, but final decisions are necessarily my responsibility. No two men presumably would agree on every item, but instances of serious disagreement are few.

[4] Notably "Unseen Spirits" by N. P. Willis and "The Forsaken" by Mrs. Sarah Anna Lewis.

made, and not representing Poe's final intentions in the case of some compositions. Hence, each poem and each prose article must be considered in the light of what is known of the merits of the documents we have today. Let it be said at once that we do have excellent sources in a large majority of instances. It is usually possible to find a document that certainly is the best in representing the latest intentions of the author, which should and can be reproduced with no alterations at all. This is not true for a small minority of documents; and in such cases "correct" texts will be presented, insofar as possible.

Where changes are made, editorial policy will be guided by rules — maxims rather than Median laws — to be described below. These depend on the nature of the surviving documents in every case. For Poe we have most of the kinds of sources to be expected for an American author of the second quarter of the nineteenth century.

The *original manuscripts* include drafts — both preliminary notes and hastily written versions not carefully revised — as well as carefully finished manuscripts prepared by the author as fair copy for the printer. All these are holographs. Poe did not dictate to amanuenses or employ copyists. A few manuscripts were written as autographs in albums or otherwise for collectors.[5]

There are *printed texts* of two kinds: some read in proof by the author, others which he did not so read.

There are also *revised printed texts* — both of book and of periodical printings — with later manuscript alterations made by Poe with a view to future republications.

We do not have any specimens of corrected proof, although some must once have existed. It may be confidently asserted that Poe did not stop the presses to make changes either for his books or for separate articles.

Lastly, we have a few *transcripts* of now lost manuscript and printed texts, made when they still existed or long afterward from memory by people who knew the poet.

Poe's handwriting changed much over the years. In his youth

---

[5] We have specimens of Poe's manuscripts from every period of his career, but relatively few of those used by his printers survive. It was the custom in his day to throw away manuscripts after the text was set up and proofread, unless the author requested their return or an editor or printer kept one for a special reason.

it was generally rather large and flowing. Later, in the early 'thirties, he wrote pieces meant for publication in an imitation of print (it would now be called "script"), and then he turned to a plain hand which, as the years advanced, became more and more designedly calligraphic. It is, of course, specimens of this that are familiar to most students from illustrations in popular books. Poe's hand is never hard to read, but he was old-fashioned in writing capital *I* and *J* without differentiation, his capital *P* and *T* often look alike, and the diphthongs *æ* and *œ* can be distinguished (at least by me) only from the sense. These often bewildered his printers, and I will print them correctly. Poe did sometimes employ an ampersand, which will always (save in the names of firms and "&C") be printed as "and" without comment. I am unwilling to call these emendations.[6]

Actual verbal emendations will be confined to the correction of sure misprints (typographical errors) and of obvious slips of the pen. The former are infrequent after 1827; Poe's first printer, Calvin Thomas, was an inexperienced beginner. Later Poe always had the services of competent compositors, and usually was on friendly terms with them. The slips of the pen were extremely rare but they exist.[7] No "improvement" of Poe's grammar will be attempted in any case; slight errors may be found in his English and certainly there are wrong genders in his Greek and French.

He was an almost impeccable speller but not a consistent one. Fashions changed during his lifetime, and he sometimes used forms curious to our eyes. He wrote words like *honour* and *honor* indifferently, although late in life he preferred the American forms. But it should be remembered that in his day *visiter, headach*, and even *it's* (possessive) were tolerated as correct, and I shall preserve them.

Poe strove to improve his punctuation in 1835, and later wrote in his "Marginalia" (number 196) of the importance of dashes;

[6] I have at one time or another seen in the original or in a mechanical facsimile every known manuscript of a poem or story. This, of course, is not true of all the critical prose or of all the letters.

[7] All authorized versions of the tale "Thou Art the Man" twice give the name of one character where sense demands another, and in this case the surviving manuscript proves the slips were the author's own.

of these he was extremely fond, as he was of italics. But it was not so much logical as rhetorical punctuation, a guide to the pauses in reading aloud.

Finally there are accents. In English they are given as Poe gave them, except for an addition of a diaeresis for the name *Irenë*, where modern Americans do not sound the final letter and their ancestors a century ago did, as is still the custom in Britain. Poe usually wrote French accents correctly, and these are all given *selon les règles*. For Greek, editorial policy may puzzle readers. Poe usually did not write the accents, and his printers rarely printed them. After discussion with advisors, I have decided, in an American text of the second quarter of the nineteenth century, to follow copy and use accents only if they appear in the original.

When the best text of an item has been chosen, it will be presented according to the methods just described. Poe often rewrote poems and even stories completely; and he constantly made minor revisions in reprinting them. Hence it is sometimes desirable to give full texts of earlier versions in addition to what is regarded as the best. Significant minor changes will be recorded as variants. For the imaginative works, the collection of verbal changes will be as complete as possible.

The annotation will be as nearly exhaustive as possible. In an introductory note to each item I plan to give the history of its composition and an account of Poe's major sources if they are certainly known or plausibly suggested. The history of publication which follows will include a list of all authorized versions of the item now known. In the case of articles that neither Poe nor his literary executor collected, record will be made of first publication in periodicals and of first inclusion in books.

In the commentary I will give the sources of Poe's direct and indirect quotations and explanations of his references and allusions that may not be clear to a reader of today. These notes are "a modified variorum." There will be a full discussion of cruces, but record will usually be omitted of views outmoded in the light of present knowledge and of explanations withdrawn or abandoned by their proponents.

PREFACE TO THE EDITION

Credit is given to my predecessors, I hope with some thoroughness. I am also indebted to my students and to friends for unprinted suggestions given to me directly,[8] which I have tried to acknowledge and for which I express my sincere thanks.

Purely aesthetic criticism will be deliberately kept to a minimum. It will usually be confined to pointing out the merits of widely recognized masterpieces and to evaluation of pieces less well known. Something will be said of the estimates of his work (not always favorable) that stem from Poe himself. Of Poe's vast influence on his contemporaries and on those who have come after him even less will be said, but mention will be made of all known reprints in Britain before 1850, and of translations made on the Continent during his lifetime.

THOMAS OLLIVE MABBOTT

[8] Some have come from master's essays I directed, from papers written for my classes, and from discussions with my students and other friends, verbally or in correspondence. I have, after consultation, decided to read no unprinted doctoral dissertations, save at the request of their writers.

INTRODUCTION TO THE POEMS

Poe was by choice a poet. He began to be one in boyhood, and continued to write verse to the end of his life. His actual product is small, but the proportion of excellence is surprisingly high, and, as is not always true of lyric poets, his powers never waned; they increased. His first book, published at eighteen, contained at least one very fine poem, "The Lake." When he was twenty-two he gave us "Israfel," even in its unrevised version a masterpiece, and in his last year he composed "Annabel Lee."

Recognition came early from those close to him, and the world was to know him as "Mr. Poe the poet" from 1845, when "The Raven" appeared. There has never been even a temporary decline of his popularity among general readers. Among critics there was disagreement from the start.

In the *American Review* of March 1850, George W. Peck replied to early unfavorable criticism. To those who complained of Poe's "lack of moral and religious principle . . . elevated and generous sentiment," he answered: "It is not Poe's province to deal in sentiment, but he could give expression to elevated emotion . . . he did not undertake to write sermons. His poetry and prose are full of pure beauties; he could . . . express those affections . . . which only gentle hearts can feel."

Little need be added to that, save that Poe tended to overstate his antididactic attitude. He really opposed only the bald insertion of a moral in a work of art, not its subtle introduction. We have the noble instance of "Eldorado."

That Poe valued pure beauty of sound and image is indisputable, but this is the business of a lyric poet. Where his poems are obscure it is usually because he sought for a vague effect. How deliberately he did this can be seen by comparing "The Valley Nis" of 1831 with the final version, called "The Valley of Unrest," of 1845.

INTRODUCTION TO THE POEMS

THE CANON OF THE POEMS

For a complete edition of Poe's works it seems better to disregard his famous aesthetic definition of poetry as "the rhythmical creation of beauty" and to adopt one that is purely arbitrary: every formally versified composition is regarded here as a poem. Each is treated as a separate entity. I give them in chronological order, with appropriate introductions and bibliographical and explanatory notes. In an appendix I have collected Poe's known collaborations.

A great many poems have been ascribed to Poe without complete authentication, by good, bad, and indifferent "authorities." A few items which can not yet be positively accepted, although a good case can be made out for their authenticity, I have placed in the main body of the work, with a caveat. The rest are listed under the heading "Apocrypha." More than one hundred of these are certainly not Poe's. But there are a few cases where my reasons for rejection are not wholly decisive; I give full texts for such "doubtfully rejected" items.

POETIC STYLE

The vocabulary of the poems is not large — it is said to comprise about eighteen hundred words, relatively few of them unusual. Neologisms are very rare, and, of the few words Poe is now thought to have coined or used in a novel sense, almost all are proper nouns such as Nesace, Ulalume, and Yaanek.[1]

Most of Poe's later poetry is written in the ordinary speech of ordinary men, even to its word order. He consciously sought to reproduce the rhythms of conversation. What is elaborate is the metrical form; that grew more complex with the years, while Poe's prose tended to be increasingly simple, straightforward, and less ornamented. Early in his career, he experimented with the refrain, alliteration, cross-alliteration, and the partial repetition of whole lines.

[1] See Bradford A. Booth and Claude E. Jones, *A Concordance of the Poetical Works of Edgar Allan Poe* (Baltimore, 1941). As a name of a sea creature, *sidrophel* may be new; use of *scoriac* prior to Poe's will, I think, be found in time.

INTRODUCTION TO THE POEMS

SCANSION

Poe was greatly interested in scansion. In a letter of October 8, 1835, he mentions having made a careful study of the later works of Alexander Pope. He published his views first in "Notes Upon English Verse" in 1843, and in 1846 he wrote the highly technical "Rationale of Verse." We have in addition an unpublished leaf of notes made in 1849 for revising the latter. His views changed somewhat over the years. But he finally held that English verse was quantitative, accent making for quantity, and that we had, besides long and short syllables, some which are very short and some which are very long.[2]

It has been debated whether Poe wrote his poems and then theorized about them, or vice versa. The dates of the documents make me accept the former view. Poe composed "Ulalume" after the "Rationale," and the late notes indicate that the poem led him to modify his classification of English metrical feet.

RHYME

Poe sought for perfect rhyme, as some of his comments on Elizabeth Barrett's work reveal.[3] But he composed for his own pronunciation; we can reconstruct to a degree what it would have been. He lived chiefly in Richmond and Baltimore until he was twenty-eight, thereafter in Philadelphia and New York. He spoke with a slight Southern drawl. Hence he rhymed *sister* and *vista*, *ha'nted* and *enchanted*. A joke in "The Gold-Bug" suggests that he said *tin* for *ten*. One of his very rare misspellings, in a letter of 1847, is *lenth* for *length*, but his comment on rhymes shows that Poe did not drop the final letter of words like *hunting*.

[2] Poe pronounced Latin in the English fashion, for he thought "qualis" and "quail is" a good pun. His ignorance of the Romans' pronunciation led him to write incorrectly about their meter. But this error does not invalidate his ideas about English. His theories about accent in our language can be (to some extent) confirmed in the laboratory today.

[3] The list of "bad rhymes" in his review in the *Broadway Journal* of January 11, 1845, is very important. The rhyme of *abjure* and *nevermore* in early versions of "The Raven" Poe soon emended. He expressed, in the *Broadway Journal* of July 19, 1845, his disapproval of conscious imitation by Americans of British speech.

INTRODUCTION TO THE POEMS

Lyric poetry is perhaps the most timeless of all arts; its themes are happiness and sorrow, which are alike the world over. Yet the commonplace that Poe's poetry is "out of space, out of time" is an overstatement. He applied this phrase himself only to the land of dreams, and no artist lives altogether in an imaginary world, nor can he be wholly oblivious of his background and immediate surroundings. Poe lived in the first half and worked in the second quarter of the nineteenth century — a time far more different from the hundred years succeeding than is often remembered. A new era followed the Civil War.

Poe was classically educated, and knew about Greek literature in general, but showed no deep interest in much of it save Homer and perhaps the *Anacreontea*. He was not enthusiastic about Greek tragedy and probably read little in the original, although that is all uncertain. In Latin he certainly read much of Vergil, and he shows familiarity with Horace, whom he probably preferred. He read little Italian, though the poem "To One in Paradise" is, as he revealed, a free adaptation of some lines of Politian. Poe knew Dante's *Inferno* in Cary's translation, which he quoted.[4] He read a good deal in French, but it had little influence on his poetry, much on his prose.

Poe knew the English Bible well and quoted it often.[5] He shows much familiarity with the giants of English literature, Shakespeare and Milton. Indeed, he made a careful study of both, and two leaves of brief handwritten extracts, from the former's tragedies and comedies and the latter's minor poems, survive.[6] They show chiefly a concern for verbal felicity. Poe constantly alludes to both these greatest authors, and his play *Politian* is

[4] Poe's friend Stella — Sarah Anna Lewis — in her sonnet "Beneath the Elms" says Poe at Fordham discussed with her Homer, Vergil, and Dante's "Hell." Her verses, originally printed in the New York *Home Journal* of February 11, 1880, are reprinted in "Appendix D" in all issues of John H. Ingram's *Edgar Allan Poe* (1880).

[5] See William Mentzel Forrest, *Biblical Allusions in Poe* (New York, 1928), an exhaustive study.

[6] The Milton extracts were published by Thomas P. Haviland, "How Well Did Poe Know Milton?" *PMLA* (September 1954). The Shakespeare material has not yet been printed. I am inclined to date the manuscript pages about 1829.

"Shakespearean," but in later years he disapproved of modern imitations of Shakespeare.[7] Poe disliked epics and says little of Spenser, but I suspect he read more of him than may be often supposed. Poe's acquaintance with other English poets who wrote before 1700 was sketchy, and he shows no interest in Chaucer at all.

Poe was naturally under the influence of eighteenth-century poetry. Admiration of Alexander Pope was fashionable when Poe was growing up, and he did not cease from it when it became unfashionable. Both poets had a passion for correct use of meter and language. A satire in Pope's manner is Poe's earliest work of any bulk, and his first volume carries a motto from Cowper. Poe did not worship Robert Burns, but he named "Tam O'Shanter" in a list of about a dozen "examples of entire poems of the purest ideality." [8]

The *Lyrical Ballads* (1798) of Wordsworth and Coleridge were reprinted in America in 1802. Although they included the "Ancient Mariner," which Poe later praised, it is uncertain how much interest he took in the poems until after 1830. He rejected Wordsworth's didacticism but admired some of his work. The extent of Coleridge's influence on Poe is much disputed. I simply cannot regard Poe as in any way or at any time a disciple of Coleridge.[9]

Poe as a very young man was an imitator of Byron, but he wrote on May 29, 1829, "I have long given up Byron as a model." Obviously he had become a disciple of Thomas Moore; after "Al

---

[7] Lambert A. Wilmer, in his "Recollections" (reprinted by me with his *Merlin* in 1941), p. 31, says that Poe held "Milton [and] Shakspeare . . . in great contempt," but Edward M. Alfriend, in the *Literary Era* for August 1901, says that Poe thought Shakespeare the greatest dramatist of all time. I think Poe's contempt was for the use of the great poets as models.

[8] Review of Joseph Rodman Drake and Fitz-Greene Halleck in the *Southern Literary Messenger*, April 1836. Poe's reference to Burns in the *Broadway Journal* of September 6, 1845, occurs in a review of a book by a Scottish author whose adulation of Burns was excessive. Poe admired James Macpherson's "translations" of Ossian, but their influence is seen rather in Poe's prose poems like "Shadow" than in his formal verse.

[9] Poe listed among the ideal poems referred to just above "The Ancient Mariner," "Christabel," and "Kubla Khan." He wrote to J. R. Lowell on July 2, 1844, "I am profoundly excited by . . . Coleridge (occasionally)." In a review in the *Broadway Journal*, August 30, 1845, he scoffed at Leigh Hunt's "absurd eulogies on Coleridge's 'Pains of Sleep.' "

Aaraaf" his affection waned but never completely disappeared — the last book he read was Moore's *Irish Melodies*.

Poe did not show much interest in Thomas Campbell, though he certainly knew his work, nor in Robert Southey, although he did not dislike his. Poe says little of Henry Kirke White, the youthful poet whom Southey edited, but no bibliographer can suppose that our author completely escaped the influence of this mild religious poet, who enjoyed incredible popularity in America and inspired "Thanatopsis" — the only poem by Bryant with which Poe showed early familiarity.

There was one earlier American poet whose work he certainly knew. Edward Coote Pinkney's little volume, *Poems*, was published in Baltimore in 1825. The author was acquainted with Poe's brother Henry, and it is at least possible that he met Edgar Poe. Pinkney's melody is distinctive,[10] but the close kinship of his lyrics to Poe's is not fortuitous. In his "Poetic Principle" Poe revealed that he thought Pinkney should have been recognized as "the first" of American lyrists.

The Galignani edition (Paris, 1829) of Coleridge, Keats, and Shelley reached America in due time, and Poe was obviously familiar with those poets before he finished his own *Poems* (1831), a collection in which "Israfel" and perhaps some other poems are in Shelley's manner.[11]

Poe expressed unbounded enthusiasm for Tennyson, but does not seem to have mentioned him before 1840. For some time before that, Poe was nobody's disciple in a general way. But part of his creative method was to write poems, as well as stories, "in the manner" of other authors. Sometimes he replied to a work with which he disagreed. Sometimes he seized on a rhythmical form

[10] See his *Life and Works* (New York, 1926) edited by myself and Frank Lester Pleadwell. The book includes all of Pinkney's poetry, well worth reading for itself and essential for a real understanding of Poe as a part of his own time and surroundings.

[11] A few selections from Shelley had appeared in Richmond newspapers earlier. One of them, in the *Examiner* of April 2, 1824, was from "The Sensitive Plant." Poe's appreciative later references to that poem may be nostalgic. See Agnes M. Bondurant, *Poe's Richmond* (1942), p. 108. A notion that Poe knew of Keats before 1830 rests only on evidence now unacceptable.

that interested him. Occasionally he actually reworked a piece that he thought he could greatly improve.

This practice might be termed "plagiarism" by some critics, and Poe used that word so much himself that something must be said about his attitude.[12] He seems to have regarded imitation as reprehensible only if the copyist failed to make something better than his model. Like Shakespeare and Molière, Poe took his own where he found it, and unfailingly improved upon his sources. In a few cases, perhaps, he was not conscious of his debts, but he acknowledged that possibility to Mrs. Browning. How greatly he could excel may be readily seen by comparing "The Haunted Palace" with its source in a trifle by John Wolcot (quoted in my notes on Poe's poem, below). Some of his sources are in the works of even lesser poets.

In such matters Poe depended to some extent on the literary climate in which he lived, the school (he disliked the term, but it is familiar) to which he belonged. It is well to remember that he was not really a Romantic, or a Victorian, but of "the curious group . . . sometimes called the 'Intermediates,' who in a manner bridge the gap of the twenty–forties and to whom 'E.B.B.' certainly does belong with Darley, Beddoes, Miss Landon ('L.E.L.') . . . and others,"[13] among whom Mrs. Hemans and Thomas Hood may be named.[14]

So much has been said of literary influences that we must not forget that Poe, like all real poets, was at last his own best teacher, as personal experience deepened his feelings and heightened his art. It is a far cry from "Imitation" of 1827 to "A Dream within a Dream," into which he turned it two decades later. Since we

[12] He especially used the term in speaking of Longfellow, but he discusses the subject in a more moderate tone in the "Literati" article on the obscure George Hill, pointing out that "plagiarism" is often an unconscious result of great appreciation, and that it is common among truly poetic authors.

[13] George Edward Saintsbury in *The Dial*, May 1929, in a review of my *Selected Poems of Edgar Allan Poe* (New York, 1929). In his essay, Saintsbury approved my emphasis on Poe's position in the group mentioned.

[14] Poe took an interest in all of them save perhaps in Beddoes. The Irish poet James Clarence Mangan might be added, for his work is much like Poe's and has been thought to have been an inspiration to him, but it is unlikely that Poe saw the Dublin magazines in which Mangan's work appeared.

know much of his life, we cannot wholly neglect that personal element, but we should not unduly emphasize it. "For Annie" is autobiographical, but it would be hard to find a less personal poem than "The City in the Sea." Poe surely wanted posterity to read his poetry as closely akin to music, the purpose chiefly to arouse our best emotions by contemplation of beauty and power. This the poems have accomplished during more than a century for his countless admirers. One can suppose with reason that of his "voice in echoing hearts the sound will long remain."

EARLIEST POEMS

1820–1827

EARLIEST POEMS
1 8 2 0 – 1 8 2 7

We know that Poe wrote verses as a schoolboy, but the exact date when he began the practice is uncertain. George Edward Woodberry in his *Edgar Allan Poe* (1885, p. 19), and in *The Life of Edgar Allan Poe* (1909), I, 23, wrote as if he believed that Poe "made his first trials at verse and kept the manuscripts" before he left England in June 1820, but no document supports this conjecture. The surviving verses of his boyhood are collected here, together with descriptions of early pieces no longer preserved about which we have definite information.

[LINES TO RICHMOND SCHOOLGIRLS]

Poe certainly wrote poetry while at the school of Joseph H. Clarke in Richmond, in the years 1820 to 1823. Clarke lived to be very old, remained a lifelong friend of his distinguished pupil, and attended the unveiling of his monument in 1875. To Eugene L. Didier he wrote on April 16, 1876 (the letter is in the Wendell Collection at Harvard), that Poe's "imaginative powers seemed to take precedence of all his other faculties, he gave proof of this, in his juvenile compositions addressed to his young female friends." William Fearing Gill (*Life of Edgar Allan Poe*, 1878, p. 28) says that the boy Poe "wrote poems, chivalrously inscribed to his girl playmates, and . . . prepared them for the press, and handed them to Mr. Allan for publication." Gill adds that it was "due to the judicious advice of Professor Clarke that the verses were not published." Richard Henry Stoddard ("Life," p. xxvii) says the work was "a manuscript volume" and that "Mr. Allan . . . retained his admiration for Master Edgar's poetry, which he was in the habit of reading to his friends." Father John B. Tabb had heard that Mrs. Mackenzie, to whom Poe submitted his juvenile poems, called them "worthless imitations of Byron blended with some original nonsense." [1]

Susan Archer Talley Weiss (*The Home Life of Poe*, 1907, p. 37) says that when Poe was about fifteen he used to have his sister Rosalie carry candy, letters, and "original poetry" to her schoolmates at Miss Jane Mackenzie's. These "verses were sometimes compared by their fair recipients, and found to be alike, with the exception of slight changes appropriate to each; a practice which he kept up in after years." Not one of these poems addressed to schoolgirls has been preserved.

[EPISTOLA AD MAGISTRUM]

When Poe's schoolmaster Joseph H. Clarke was about eighty years old, he talked with a newspaper reporter in Baltimore. A clipping about this interview, unfortunately undated, was given to a Richmond newspaperman in 1892 by Clarke's son, and was used by Mrs. Weiss in her *Home Life of Poe*, p. 24. Mr. Clarke "spoke with pride of Edgar as a student, especially in the classics. He and Nat Howard on one vacation each wrote him a complimentary letter in Latin, both equally excellent in point of scholarship; but Edgar's was in verse, which Nat could not write."

Although Clarke had his students play at capping verses, he seems not to have followed the English fashion of making them compose them. It is possible that Poe had been given instruction in this "art" by his earlier teacher, the Reverend John Bransby at Stoke Newington. Schoolboy Latin verses are commonly, as the reader of *Tom Brown's School-Days* will recall, at best little more than centos, poems made up of lines from other poems.

One regrets the loss of Poe's Latin verses, presumably (like the *Epistolae* of his favorite Horace) in dactylic hexameters. Poe

[1] Stoddard's "Life" is quoted from *Selected Works of Edgar Allan Poe* (1880). Father Tabb is quoted from a manuscript of "Recollections" collected by the poet-priest from people who had known Poe; see the Ingram List (*John Henry Ingram's Poe Collection at the University of Virginia: A Calendar*, by John Carl Miller, 1960), no. 361.

is not known to have composed anything else in verse save in English. The probable date is summer of 1822.

[AN EARLY SATIRE]

A schoolmate at Clarke's about 1823, Colonel John T. L. Preston, long afterward wrote "Some Reminiscences of Edgar A. Poe as a Schoolboy" (see Sara Sigourney Rice, *Edgar Allan Poe, A Memorial Volume,* 1877, p. 41). Preston says:

> Not a little of Poe's time, in school and out of it, was occupied with writing verses. As we sat together he would show them to me, and even sometimes ask my opinion, and now and then my assistance. I recall at this moment his consulting me about one particular line, as to whether the word *groat* would properly rhyme with such a word as *not.*

Poe could hardly have used the word "groat" in any save a satirical poem. This satire is not one of the three satires dealt with below.

[FAREWELL TO MASTER CLARKE]

Charles Marshall Graves, in "Landmarks of Poe in Richmond" (*The Century Magazine,* April 1904), tells us that when Joseph H. Clarke stopped teaching in 1823, "Poe was selected by the boys to deliver the farewell ode, and did so with grace and with satisfaction to all." Graves was using local traditions; the story probably comes from Clarke.

POETRY

This is from the earliest known manuscript of the poet, and the couplet is probably his earliest surviving composition. The leaf on which it was written was later used for "commercial calculations" by the thrifty John Allan, who was figuring out that he had some $30,000 "available for any emergency."

The document was discovered by Hervey Allen among the Ellis and Allan papers at the Library of Congress, in the file for

November 1824, and the verses were first published by Allen in his *Israfel* (1926), in which he also published a facsimile. From our reproduction facing page 582 below (among the descriptions of Poe's own collections in the list of sources), it will be seen that the poet was already calling himself Edgar A. Poe and that he was apparently planning to number his pieces as he did the "Minor Poems" in his volume of 1829.[1]

Frances Winwar, in *The Haunted Palace* (1959), p. 75, points out that the scrap "uncannily foreshadowed the mood of the first two lines of 'The Raven,' even to the use of the word 'weary.' "

In printing the lines here I have corrected the spelling and punctuation. The sixth word — in the manuscript, an ampersand — has sometimes been read as "by."

POETRY

Last night, with many cares and toils oppress'd,
Weary, I laid me on a couch to rest —

[SATIRE ON THE JUNIOR DEBATING SOCIETY]

While Poe was at William Burke's school in Richmond, he wrote a satire. All that is known of this poem comes from an extract from a manuscript letter signed "R. C. Ambler," dated " 'The Dell' Fauquier County, Va. Dec. 14th '74," mailed on May 18, 1875, by Edward V. Valentine, the sculptor, to John H. Ingram and now at the University of Virginia (Ingram List, number 228). Richard Carey Ambler, M.D., had been at school with Poe. He wrote:

I remember to have heard some verses of his, in the shape of a satire upon the members of a debating society to which he belonged. This society held its meetings in a house known as the Harris Building, situated at the corner of Main and 11th Streets, if I recollect it aright. I cannot recall a line of those verses.

Agnes M. Bondurant, in *Poe's Richmond* (1942), p. 142, tells

[1] The leaf is now Item 130 in the E. A. Poe Volume, Ellis and Allan Papers, Manuscript Division, Library of Congress.

us that the societies that celebrated Benjamin Franklin's centenary in 1827 were the Jefferson and Junior Debating societies. Poe must have belonged to the latter in 1825.

[DON POMPIOSO]

The following, by Charles Marshall Graves, is based on a reminiscence of Dr. John F. Carter (who saw much of Poe in 1849):

> Dr. Carter tells me the story of "Don Pompioso", one of the early poems, now lost. A young man had hurt Poe's feelings. He held himself too high to associate with the son of an actress and a pauper, and let the high-strung boy understand it. Soon a poem appeared on the street ridiculing this young man unmercifully. The girls at Mrs. MacKenzie's school, then at No. 506 East Franklin street, got hold of the poem and were laughing over it and wondering who its author was. That evening about dusk Poe dropped in at the school, where his sister lived . . . A number of young people were in the parlor, and one of the girls asked him to read the poem aloud. This he did by the fading light, reading with a readiness that one could not possibly have shown without really repeating it from memory. "You wrote it!" they all cried, and he did not deny it. When the young man who had drawn the fire appeared on the street, he was peppered with allusions from the poem, with jests and gibes, and at length he was driven from the city.[1]

This account is, of course, at third hand, but Dr. Carter was alive at the time of the publication and had known intimately the Mackenzie family of Richmond, into which Rosalie Poe had been taken. Graves himself was of good family in Richmond.

Mrs. Weiss tells this story with little variation,[2] but gives the title as "Don Pompiosa."

Jay B. Hubbell, discussing "Oh, Tempora! Oh, Mores!" [3] argued against the identification of that satire with "Don Pompioso," because the clerk lampooned in the surviving satire was not pompous. I incline to agree, but absolute certainty is impossible.

[1] *Century Magazine*, April 1904, p. 917.
[2] *Home Life of Poe* (1907), p. 34.   [3] See below.

OH, TEMPORA! OH, MORES!

These verses are a typical imitation of the eighteenth century satires, and the earliest of Poe's compositions of any length to survive. The original manuscript probably was burned during the Civil War, but a transcript was preserved in the Mackenzie family and was at one time owned by Poe's sister Rosalie.[1] From her, I believe, John R. Thompson obtained a copy, which he made available for publication to Henry Rives Pollard, who edited *Southern Opinion* in Richmond, 1867–1869.[2] Thompson supplied the introduction, signed "J.R.Y.," an obvious misprint for "J.R.T."

Later, Eugene L. Didier obtained a transcript of the satire (apparently without knowing it had ever been published), and printed a text in the first number of his own *No Name Magazine*, dated October 1889, as a "new" poem by Poe.[3] Didier's text omitted two words, but is obviously closer to Poe's than Pollard's.

Thompson said Pitts, who was lampooned in Poe's verses, was a clerk in the "leading fashionable dry goods store" of Richmond. Pitts was paying court to a youthful belle of the period. She later married a man who went to Congress, and she possibly flirted a little with Edgar Poe. Pitts boarded at the same house as a number of Virginia legislators, and Poe's use of legal terms may be explained by his desire to ridicule the clerk among them.

The young man whom Poe delighted to honor with this bitter attack has been identified, at my request, by Mrs. Ralph Catterall

---

[1] Professor Jay B. Hubbell, who discovered the first publication of the poem, has discussed it with scholarly acumen and completely established its authenticity (" 'O, Tempora! O, Mores!' A juvenile poem by Edgar Allan Poe," *Elizabethan Studies and Other Essays in Honor of George F. Reynolds*, University of Colorado Studies, ser. B, Studies in the Humanities, vol. 2, no. 4, pp. 314–321, October 1945). J. H. Whitty's statement to Mary E. Phillips, recorded in *Edgar Allan Poe the Man* (1926), II, 1595, that Thompson arranged for Rosalie Poe to be paid ten dollars for the poem I think preserved the right tradition.

[2] Pollard was apparently a *laudator temporis acti* whose form sheet required spellings like "authour" and "logick." He also seems to have "corrected" the poem to suit his ideas of grammar, and printed "Vester's" for Vestris. Hubbell reprinted Pollard's text.

[3] See J. H. Whitty, ed., *Complete Poems of Edgar Allan Poe* (1911), pp. 161–165. Didier wrote Whitty that his introductory note came from Thompson. Whitty copied Didier's text.

of the Valentine Museum in Richmond. Both printed versions give his name as "Job," but this must be an error for Bob (or Rob), since Robert Pitts was a clerk in a dry goods store. He worked for the firm of Robert & Hall Neilson & Co., located on the north side of Main Street, between 13th and 14th, and afterward for Hall & Moore, whose store was next door. He receipted a bill for the latter firm for John Adams Smith (1802–1864), a son of Governor George William Smith; and two letters from Pitts to young Smith, dated September 19, 1824, and March 3, 1825, are preserved in the Valentine Museum. These show that the clerk was on terms of friendship with members of the best families.

TEXTS

(A) Poe's original manuscript (1825?), now lost; (B) transcript, possibly existing, but now inaccessible; (C) *Southern Opinion* (Richmond), March 7, 1868; (D) *No Name Magazine* (Baltimore), October 1889.

Both of the early printed texts contain obvious errors. My text is based on Didier's (D) with emendations in lines 13, 21, 36, and 68.

OH, TEMPORA! OH, MORES!   [D]

Oh Times! Oh Manners! It is my opinion
That you are changing sadly your dominion —
I mean the reign of manners hath long ceased,
For men have none at all, or bad at least;
5   And as for times, although 'tis said by many
The "good old times" were far the worst of any,
Of which sound doctrine I believe each tittle,
Yet still I think these worse than them a little.

I've been a thinking, isn't that the phrase?
10   — I like your Yankee words and Yankee ways —
I've been a thinking, whether it were best
To take things seriously or all in jest;
Whether with grim Heraclitus of yore
To weep, as he did, till his eyes were sore,
15   Or rather laugh with him, that queer Philosopher,

Democritus of Thrace, who used to toss over
The page of life and grin at the dog-ears,
As though he'd say, "Why who the devil cares?"

This is a question which, oh Heaven, withdraw
20   The luckless query from a Member's claw!
Instead of two sides, Bob has nearly eight,
Each fit to furnish forth four hours debate.
What shall be done? I'll lay it on the table,
And take the matter up when I'm more able,
25   And in the meantime, to prevent all bother,
I'll neither laugh with one or cry with t'other,
Nor deal in flattery or aspersions foul,
But, taking one by each hand, merely growl.

Ah growl, say you, my friend, and pray at what?
30   Why, really, sir, I almost had forgot —
But damn it, sir, I deem it a disgrace
That things should stare us boldly in the face,
And daily strut the street with bows and scrapes,
Who would be men by imitating apes.
35   I beg your pardon, reader, for the oath,
The monkey's made me swear, though something loath;
I'm apt to be discursive in my style,
But pray be patient: yet a little while
Will change me, and as politicians do
40   I'll mend my manners and my measures too.

Of all the cities, and I've seen no few —
For I have travelled, friend, as well as you, —
I don't remember one, upon my soul,
But take it generally upon the whole,
45   (As Members say they like their logic taken
Because divided it may chance be shaken)
So pat, agreeable, and vastly proper
As this for a neat, frisky counter-hopper;
Here he may revel to his heart's content,

50 Flounce like a fish in his own element,
    Toss back his fine curls from his forehead fair
    And hop o'er counters with a Vestris air,
    Complete at night what he began A.M.
    And having cheated ladies, dance with them;
55 For at a ball what fair one can escape
    The pretty little hand that sold her tape,
    Or who so cold, so callous to refuse
    The youth who cut the ribbon for her shoes!

    One of these fish, par excellence the beau,
60 God help me, it has been my lot to know,
    At least by sight, for I'm a timid man
    And always keep from laughing when I can;
    But speak to him, he'll make you such grimace,
    Lord! to be grave exceeds the power of face.
65 The hearts of all the ladies are with him,
    Their bright eyes on his Tom and Jerry brim
    And dove-tailed coat, obtained at cost; while then
    Those eyes won't turn on anything like men.

    His very voice is musical delight,
70 His form once seen becomes a part of sight,
    In short his shirt-collar, his look, his tone is
    The "beau ideal" fancied for Adonis.
    Philosophers have often held dispute
    As to the seat of thought in man and brute,
75 For that the power of thought attend the latter
    My friend, the beau, hath made a settled matter,
    And spite all dogmas current in all ages,
    One settled fact is better than ten sages.

    For he does think, although I'm oft in doubt
80 If I can tell exactly what about.
    Ah yes! his little foot and ancle trim,
    'Tis there the seat of reason lies in him;
    A wise philosopher would shake his head,

He then, of course, must shake his foot instead.
85   At me in vengeance shall that foot be shaken —
Another proof of thought, I'm not mistaken —
Because to his cat's eyes I hold a glass
And let him see himself a proper ass?
I think he'll take this likeness to himself,
90   But if he won't *he shall*, the stupid elf,
And lest the guessing throw the fool in fits,
I close the portrait with the name of *Pitts*.

[1825?]

VARIANTS

13   grim [*added from C, as required by the meter*]
21   Bob [*my emendation*]/Job (*C, D*)
26   or/nor (*C*)
36   The monkey's made [*my emendation*]/The monkeys make (*C*); The monkey made (*D*)

52   Vestris/Vester's (*C*)
62   when I can/if I can (*C*)
68   eyes [*added from C, as required by the meter*]
75   attend/attends (*C*)
79   although I'm/though I am (*C*)
90   the stupid elf/a stupid elf (*C*)

NOTES

Title   Poe, of course, knew that the opening of the first *Catilinarian Oration* of Cicero is followed by the famous "O tempora! o mores!" Indeed he was studying Cicero with Joseph Clarke in 1824.

4   Apparently originally from the lost *Oeneus* of Euripides, and quoted in Aristophanes, *Frogs*, line 72: "For there are none, but those there are, are bad."

13   Heraclitus of Ephesus was known as the "weeping philosopher."

16   Democritus of Abdera in Thrace was the "laughing philosopher" because he thought good humor part of the "summum bonum."

28   Poe does not name but means Diogenes the Cynic — whose school of philosophy took its name from the Greek word for dog, and so growled.

52   Vestris was the name of a remarkable family of dancers acclaimed in Europe for at least three generations. Gaetano (1729–1808), progenitor of the clan, was born in Italy but won fame in France. Marie Auguste (1760–1842) had enormous success in England and, as Miss Helen Willard has pointed out, was the subject of a popular engraving depicting him in a fantastic leap. Auguste Armand (d. 1825), ballet master at the King's Theatre in London, married in 1813 Lucia Elisabetta Bartolozzi (1797–1856), who as Madame Vestris was internationally famous as a singer, actress, and theatre manager. Among other members of the family was Charles, who with his wife Maria Ronzi Vestris contributed greatly to the success of the Bowery Theatre in New York for several seasons after their debut there in 1828. (Charles Francis

Adams saw them in Boston on December 12 of that year and commented that their performance was "astonishingly fascinating." See his *Diary*, ed. A. and D. Donald, 1964, II, 321.)

64 Compare Pope's "Epistle to Dr. Arbuthnot," line 36: "to be grave, exceeds all pow'r of face."

66 The "Tom and Jerry brim" refers to a style of hat, like our high silk hats, with the top a trifle expanded and the brim a little rolled up. These hats can be seen in George Cruikshank's illustrations for the elder Pierce Egan's *Life in London; or the Days and Nights of Jerry Hawthorn, Esq. and his Elegant Friend Corinthian Tom* (1821). The book, dedicated by permission to George IV, was extremely popular and was the basis of at least three stage plays, some performed in America. John Camden Hotten tells us, at page 10 of his reprint of 1869, that "tailors, bootmakers, and hatters recommended nothing but Corinthian shapes and Tom and Jerry patterns." The book is lively, but is now hard to read, because so much of it is in forgotten slang. The memory of Tom and Jerry chiefly survives in a drink named for them, of which Bob Cratchit and the reformed Scrooge partook, at the end of Dickens' *Christmas Carol*. This is a concoction of egg, sugar, spices, and rum.

81 The spelling "ancle" was tolerated in 1825.

82 This seems to allude to the heel of Achilles, in which lay not his reason but his life.

[TRANSLATION FROM TASSO]

In *The Independent*, September 13, 1900 (reprinted by James A. Harrison in *The Complete Works of Edgar Allan Poe*, I, 45–47), there are given the reminiscences of Poe drawn up in 1869 by William Wertenbaker, Librarian of the University of Virginia, a classmate of Poe's there in 1826. Wertenbaker wrote:

> On one occasion Professor Blaettermann requested his Italian class to render into English verse a portion of the lesson in Tasso, which he had assigned them for the next lecture. He did not require this of them as a regular class exercise, but recommended it as one from which he thought the students would derive benefit. At the next lecture on Italian the Professor stated from his chair that Mr. Poe was the only member of the class who had responded to his suggestion, and paid a very high compliment to his performance.

We have no clue to what passage was translated. The date must fall within the few months after February 14, 1826, when Poe was at Charlottesville.

[EXPERIMENTAL VERSES]

On July 20, 1875, Edward V. Valentine wrote John H. Ingram from Richmond (Ingram List, no. 239): "I will give you . . . some extracts from a letter written me by Mr. Thomas Bolling, Willow Bank, Nelson County, Virginia." Bolling, a fellow student of Poe's at the University, after telling of the poet's interest in athletics and drawing, adds:

> In his room when conversing with him, when with pencil he would be scratching something on paper . . . he gave as a reason . . . he was only trying to see if he could divide his mind, carry on conversation and write sense on a different subject. Several times on such occasions he handed me some verses he had written, and all that I remember about them they rhymed pretty well.

Ingram told the story, but I give the above from the original manuscript, transcribed by Professor John C. Miller at the University of Virginia.

Another fellow student, Miles George, wrote in 1880 that when at Charlottesville Poe read to his friends "poetic productions of his own," which were admired, and he mentions Poe turning quickly from writing poems to making sketches but says nothing of his trying to do more than one thing at a time. See A. H. Quinn, *Edgar Allan Poe* (1941), p. 108.

TO MARGARET

This is a parodic cento, made up of lines from other poets, deliberately misquoted for humorous effect. It is in Poe's handwriting, and must have been composed hastily, since two of the sources of the quotations were given inaccurately.

The piece was written and signed "E.A.P." in the album of Miss Margaret Bassett of Baltimore. The book has an inscription from her father, January 1, 1827. It contains nothing dated later than 1828, and includes a poem, "Woman," dated September 11, 1827, and signed by W. H. Poe.

EARLIEST POEMS

Margaret Bassett was noted for her beauty; and her social position — as a descendant of Richard Bassett, a signer of the United States Constitution, and a governor of Delaware — made her the center of an admiring circle. It included a judge, a bishop, and a publisher, as well as the Poes and their friend Lambert Wilmer, who also wrote in her album.

In 1833 Margaret Bassett went to reside in Huntsville, Alabama, with her brother John, a distinguished physician.[1] She gave the album to his granddaughter, Lenore, who parted with it when it was auctioned by the Walpole Galleries, on March 30, 1930. A facsimile of the poem by Edgar Poe is in the catalogue (lot 76). By permission of Mrs. Turnbull, director of the Galleries, I saw the original in the salesroom, and printed texts of both the Poes' poems in *Notes and Queries* (London), November 28, 1931. Edgar's poem was collected in the Introduction to my facsimile edition of *Tamerlane and Other Poems* (1941), page xvii. The album is now in the Josiah K. Lilly Collection in the Library of Indiana University, where it is accompanied by several documents, upon which the foregoing discussion is based.[2]

TO MARGARET

Who hath seduced thee to this foul revolt	Milton Par. Lost. Bk. I
From the pure well of Beauty undefiled?	Somebody
So banished from true wisdom to prefer	
Such squalid wit to honourable rhyme?	Cowper's Task, Book I
To write? To scribble? Nonsense and no more?	Shakespeare
I will not write upon this argument	do. Troilus & Cressida
To write is human — not to write divine.	Pope Essay on Man

NOTES

The verses quoted parodically by Poe are:
1 *Paradise Lost*, I, 33: "Who first seduced them to that foul revolt?"

[1] Sir William Osler paid a high tribute to Dr. Bassett in *An Alabama Student* (1896).

[2] The documents include a typescript account by a Miss Allison, who had recently interviewed Lenore Bassett, sent to Mr. Lilly on October 3, 1930, by the bookseller Harry Stone. The papers were made accessible to me by my friend David A. Randall, head of the Lilly Library at Bloomington.

2 Spenser, *Faerie Queene*, IV, ii, 32: "Dan Chaucer, well of English undefiled."

3-4 Cowper, *The Task*, I, 578f. (of gypsies): "Self-banished from society, prefer / Such squalid sloth to honorable toil."

5 *Hamlet*, III, i, 65f.: "To die — to sleep — / To sleep — perchance to dream."

6 *Troilus and Cressida*, I, i, 95: "I cannot fight upon this argument."

7 Pope, *Essay on Criticism*, II, 525: "To err is human; to forgive divine."

TO OCTAVIA

This original poem, unsigned, is written in Edgar Poe's hand in the album of Octavia Walton, to whom it is addressed. She was the daughter of George Walton, Secretary of West Florida under Governor William P. Duval. Her grandfather was Governor George Walton of Georgia, who had signed the Declaration of Independence. After her marriage to M. LeVert they built Château LeVert, near Augusta, where she was a celebrated hostess. The date of the poem, "May the 1st, 1827," is in Octavia's hand.

The poem has always been known as Edgar Poe's. He also wrote in the album eight lines (in quotation marks) from the first chapter of Voltaire's *Princesse de Babylone*. The principal evidence for Poe's visit to Baltimore has been cited in the discussion of "To Margaret" above. Octavia Walton's visit to Baltimore is argued by the fact that her path can hardly have crossed Poe's anywhere else. The similarity of their social backgrounds certainly suggests that Miss Bassett and Miss Walton would have met.

The album was obtained by the late August William Dellquest from the administrator of the estate of Colonel D. B. Dyer, who, in 1868, bought Château LeVert after Mme. LeVert's death. Her grandson, George Walton Reab, authenticated the contents of the album. The history is complete, for the album was inherited by Mr. Dellquest's son, Augustus Wilfred Dellquest, now of Los Angeles. Through his courtesy, in 1941 I was able to print the text of the poem from a copy, in the introduction of my facsimile reprint of *Tamerlane and Other Poems,* at page xiv. The title is mine. Mr. Dellquest showed me the actual album at my home in the summer of 1953. It is now at Columbia University.

[TO OCTAVIA]

When wit, and wine, and friends have met
And laughter crowns the festive hour
In vain I struggle to forget
Still does my heart confess thy power
    And fondly turn to thee!

But Octavia, do not strive to rob
My heart, of all that soothes its pain
The mournful hope that every throb
    Will make it break for thee!

POEMS PUBLISHED IN 1827

POEMS PUBLISHED IN 1827

Poe's *Tamerlane and Other Poems. By a Bostonian* was published by Calvin F[rederick] S[tephen] Thomas, of 70 Washington Street, Boston, in 1827, when the author was eighteen years old. The volume was on sale about July, in time to be noticed as received in the Boston *United States Review and Literary Gazette* of August. It is mentioned in the *North American Review* of October of the same year and in Samuel Kettell's "Catalogue of American Poetry" in his *Specimens of American Poetry* (Boston, 1829). No review, however, has been found. The little volume was reprinted by Richard Herne Shepherd (London, 1884) and, subsequently, by six other persons. My edition, made for the Facsimile Text Society (New York, 1941), has a long introduction dealing with bibliographical problems, the biography of the printer, and so forth.

The title page bears a quotation from Cowper's "Tirocinium," lines 444–445:

> Young heads are giddy, and young hearts are warm,
> And make mistakes for manhood to reform.

The preface follows, beginning with a statement of doubtful accuracy — like all Poe's statements about dates — and ending with a quotation from Martial (Bk. 13, Epigram 2, line 8) meaning, freely, "I myself know the unimportance of all this."

PREFACE

The greater part of the Poems which compose this little volume, were written in the year 1821–2, when the author had not completed his fourteenth year. They were of course not intended for publication; why they are now published concerns no one but himself. Of the smaller pieces very little need be said: they perhaps savour too much of Egotism; but they were written by one too young to have any knowledge of the world but from his own breast.

In Tamerlane, he has endeavoured to expose the folly of even *risking* the best feelings of the heart at the shrine of Ambition. He is conscious that in this there are many faults, (besides that of the general character of the poem) which he flatters himself he could, with little trouble, have corrected, but unlike many of his predecessors, has been too fond of his early productions to amend them in his *old age*.

He will not say that he is indifferent as to the success of these Poems — it might stimulate him to other attempts — but he can safely assert that failure will not at all influence him in a resolution already adopted. This is challenging criticism — let it be so. *Nos haec novimus esse nihil.*

TAMERLANE

Poe's first published book begins with the earlier of his two long narrative poems. Its Byronic inspiration was admitted when, on May 29, 1829, he wrote to John Allan, "I have long given up *Byron* as a model." "Tamerlane" is not a great poem, but there are flashes of true fire, even in the unpolished but never greatly improved first version. A fair critic must consider that, if Pope and Chatterton had done better before they were nineteen, Byron, Shelley, and even Keats had not.

R. H. Stoddard remarked in his "Life of Edgar Allan Poe" [1] that Poe's attention may have been called to Tamerlane by a passage in Byron's *The Deformed Transformed* (1824), I, i, 313ff:

> I ask not
> For valour, since deformity is daring.
> It is its essence to o'ertake mankind
> By heart and soul, and make itself the equal —
> Ay, the superior of the rest. There is
> A spur in its halt movements, to become
> All that the others cannot, in such things

[1] For full titles see the list of Other Sources Frequently Cited, below.

TAMERLANE

As still are free to both, to compensate
For stepdame Nature's avarice at first.
They woo with fearless deeds the smiles of fortune,
And oft, like Timour the lame Tartar, win them.

The Tamerlane of history (1336–1405) was called in Turkish Timur Beg and in Persian Timur-i-Leng "Timur the Lame." In youth he was highly educated and of a gentle nature, but he turned warrior. He was never a shepherd or a brigand. He did conquer the Turkish sultan Bajazet (or Bayazet) in a battle near Angora (modern Ankara) about 1402, suppressed numerous rebels, and beautified his capital, Samarkand, like Poe's hero; and although he came of a distinguished family, his detractors spread stories of his low birth. He had a royal horoscope and married Tumaan, daughter of the Emir Musa, through whose influence he obtained the government of Casch, near his birthplace, a day's journey from Samarkand. He also married two Chinese princesses (unnamed in histories), but made no wife his queen. Tamerlane was publicly an orthodox Mahometan, but rumors of his interest in Christianity occur. (See *The Encyclopedia of Islam* and Herbelot's *Bibliothèque Orientale*.) Tamerlane's "low birth" is discussed by Sir Thomas Browne, *Vulgar Errors,* VII, xvi, 5. He believed Tamerlane was supposed to have been a simple shepherd because his ancestors called themselves Shepherd Kings.

SOURCES

Poe's choice of Tamerlane as a romantic hero may seem strange to modern readers familiar with Marlowe's *Tamburlaine*. But a century ago Marlowe's play was never performed and rarely read. Poe showed no acquaintance with it. Traditions about the Oriental conqueror are of very different kinds, and the more pleasant stories were gathered up by the biographer Ali Yazdi, called Sharifu'd Din, under the patronage of Tamerlane's grandson, Ibrahim Soltan. Upon these, Nicholas Rowe wrote a drama Poe must have known about.

Rowe's play *Tamerlane* (1702) long held the stage in England, being acted annually until 1815 on November 5, the anniversary

of the landing of William III. In this play Bajazet represents
Louis XIV, and Tamerlane, a kindly and tolerant ruler who
conquers enemies only when provoked by their bad faith, is
meant for William III. He has no queen, for Dutch William
became a widower in 1694. Rowe's hero is reproached by fanatical
enemies for his kindness to Christians. Thus even Poe's friar is
not too inappropriate a friend for Tamerlane as the hero was
usually thought of in 1827.

There are other plays about Tamerlane, one by Charles
Saunders (1681) and one by Matthew Gregory ("Monk") Lewis
(1811). The latter, a horse-spectacle, was presented in Richmond
on July 12, 1822, and repeated on July 17 and October 25. Poe
may well have seen it and surely must have heard about it as
Martin Shockley suggests in *PMLA* (December 1941).

PLOT

Poe took little from historic and dramatic sources; his poem
is largely a personal allegory, based on his unhappy love for his
Richmond sweetheart, Sarah Elmira Royster. Engaged, at least
privately, to Miss Royster, Poe went off to the University of
Virginia — poetically "to conquer the world." Elmira's father
intercepted their letters, and Poe "came home" to find the lady
affianced to Alexander Shelton — poetically "dead" to Poe.

HISTORY OF THE TEXT

The textual history of "Tamerlane" is complicated. The au-
thor completely reworked his poem three times after its first
publication, and on other occasions made minor changes. The
four major forms are given in full below.

The first form of the poem (*A*) consists of 406 lines. It is
badly printed, and requires at least fourteen emendations, most
of which have been made by my predecessors. Since my reprint
of the original volume, issued in 1941, is easily available, it suffices
to list them here: (25) hated / hatred; (66) crush / crash; (74)
steep / sleep; (109) [was] *added*; (119) *interrogation mark added*;
(152) Dwelt / Dwell; (184) *comma deleted after* aching; (190)

were / wore; (244) *comma added*; (350) too / to; (Note 5) think / thnik; (361) long-abandon'd / long—abandon'd; (371) list / lisp; (373) *numeral for note added.*

I have also substituted parentheses for square brackets after line 189. These are obviously vagaries of the printer who had run out of parentheses. A few commas are indistinguishable from periods in the facsimile, but in such cases the two originals in the Berg Collection confirm my readings. Poe's notes, on pages 37–40 at the end of the original volume, are here given as footnotes.

The second form of "Tamerlane," presumably written in 1828, is now incompletely preserved in the holograph manuscript (*B*) given to Lambert A. Wilmer, and still in the possession of his family when the verbal variants were listed in the Stedman and Woodberry edition of Poe's *Works*, X (1895), 201–211. The manuscript later entered the Wakeman Collection and was purchased by J. P. Morgan. It is now first published here by permission of the Trustees of the Pierpont Morgan Library. Since it is the first publication, I give what amounts to a type facsimile — preserving punctuation and spelling (even ampersands) exactly. Several words, clearly not part of the text, are scribbled on the pages; but I have concluded these are mere trials of the pen, and do not record them. The two surviving fragments comprise 157 lines. The numeration of the lines is based on the version of 1827 (*A*). It can be seen that Poe had already dropped lines 182–188 and 256–326. He had thoroughly reworked 150–153, 221–223, 245–246, 250–256, 334–338. Minor changes were made in lines 68, 90–91, 98, 145, 154, 164, 173, 176, 189–190, 193–194, 219, 244, 247, 330, 332, 339, 342–343, and 346.

Late in 1829 Poe shortened the poem to 243 lines for publication in his volume *Al Aaraaf, Tamerlane, and Minor Poems* (*C*). This was to be practically its final form, for in 1845 it was set up from a copy of the 1829 volume with slight corrections (*G*), none verbal. Only two lines (40 and 57) were changed in proof for *The Raven and Other Poems* (*H*).

There are slight changes in extracts printed in the *Yankee* for December 1829 (*E*); and one (in line 187) in a presentation copy of the 1829 volume sent John Neal (*D*) which was discovered in 1966. Most of them are abortive.

In 1831 there was another revision for the *Poems* (*F*). This time the poem was expanded by the incorporation of "The Lake" and "To — —" beginning "Should my early life seem . . ." All these changes save two (in lines 40 and 57) were abandoned in 1845. See also lines 73–75, 77, 81–82, 86, 106, 110, 112, 119–120, 128–138, 151–152, 164–176, 181, 194, 202, 207–221, 235, and 243. The comma in line 81 is demanded by sense, and I emend the period of the original, and add an apostrophe in line 238.

In 1850 Griswold (*J*) followed the 1845 volume (*H*) closely.

TEXTS

(*A*) *Tamerlane and Other Poems* (Boston, 1827), pp. 5–21, notes, pp. 37–40; (*B*) Wilmer manuscript (fragments), 1828, now in the Pierpont Morgan Library; (*C*) *Al Aaraaf, Tamerlane, and Minor Poems* (Baltimore, 1829), pp. 43–54; (*D*) John Neal's presentation copy of *Al Aaraaf* . . . , with manuscript change in line 187; (*E*) *The Yankee and Boston Literary Gazette*, December 1829 (1:297–298), extracts; (*F*) *Poems* (New York, 1831), pp. 111–124; (*G*) Elizabeth Herring's copy of *Al Aaraaf* . . . with manuscript changes, 1845; (*H*) *The Raven and Other Poems* (New York, 1845), pp. 74–82; (*J*) *Works* (New York, 1850), II, 96–104.

TAMERLANE [*A*]

I.

I have sent for thee, holy friar; [1]
But 'twas not with the drunken hope,
Which is but agony of desire
To shun the fate, with which to cope
5   Is more than crime may dare to dream,

[1] Of the history of Tamerlane little is known; and with that little, I have taken the full liberty of a poet. — That he was descended from the family of Zinghis Khan is more than probable — but he is vulgarly supposed to have been the son of a shepherd, and to have raised himself to the throne by his own address. He died in the year 1405, in the time of Pope Innocent VII.

How I shall account for giving him "a friar," as a death-bed confessor — I cannot exactly determine. He wanted some one to listen to his tale — and why not a friar? It does not pass the bounds of possibility — quite sufficient for my purposes — and I have at least good authority on my side for such innovations. [Poe's note]

That I have call'd thee at this hour:
Such father is not my theme —
Nor am I mad, to deem that power
Of earth may shrive me of the sin
10 Unearthly pride hath revell'd in —
I would not call thee fool, old man,
But hope is not a gift of thine;
If I *can* hope (O God! I can)
It falls from an eternal shrine.

II.

15   The gay wall of this gaudy tower
Grows dim around me — death is near.
I had not thought, until this hour
When passing from the earth, that ear
Of any, were it not the shade
20 Of one whom in life I made
All mystery but a simple name,
Might know the secret of a spirit
Bow'd down in sorrow, and in shame. —
Shame said'st thou?
              Aye I did inherit
25 That hated portion, with the fame,
The worldly glory, which has shown
A demon-light around my throne,
Scorching my sear'd heart with a pain
Not Hell shall make me fear again.

III.

30   I have not always been as now —
The fever'd diadem on my brow
I claim'd and won usurpingly —
Aye — the same heritage hath giv'n
Rome to the Caesar — this to me;
35 The heirdom of a kingly mind —
And a proud spirit, which hath striv'n

Triumphantly with human kind.
   In mountain air I first drew life;
The mists of the Taglay have shed [2]
40   Nightly their dews on my young head;
And my brain drank their venom then,
When after day of perilous strife
With chamois, I would seize his den
And slumber, in my pride of power,
45   The infant monarch of the hour —
For, with the mountain dew by night,
My soul imbib'd unhallow'd feeling;
And I would feel its essence stealing
In dreams upon me — while the light
50   Flashing from cloud that hover'd o'er,
Would seem to my half closing eye
The pageantry of monarchy!
And the deep thunder's echoing roar
Came hurriedly upon me, telling
55   Of war, and tumult, where my voice
My *own* voice, silly child! was swelling
(O how would my wild heart rejoice
And leap within me at the cry)
The battle-cry of victory!

          *   *   *   *   *

IV.

60   The rain came down upon my head
But barely shelter'd — and the wind
Pass'd quickly o'er me — but my mind
Was mad'ning — for 'twas man that shed
Laurels upon me — and the rush,
65   The torrent of the chilly air
Gurgled in my pleas'd ear the crush
Of empires, with the captive's prayer,

[2] The mountains of Belur Taglay are a branch of the Immaus, in the southern part of Independent Tartary. They are celebrated for the singular wildness, and beauty of their vallies. [Poe's note]

The hum of suitors, the mix'd tone
Of flatt'ry round a sov'reign's throne.

70   The storm had ceas'd — and I awoke —
Its spirit cradled me to sleep,
And as it pass'd me by, there broke
Strange light upon me, tho' it were
My soul in mystery to steep:
75   For I was not as I had been;
The child of Nature, without care,
Or thought, save of the passing scene. —

V.

My passions, from that hapless hour,
Usurp'd a tyranny, which men
80   Have deem'd, since I have reach'd to power
My innate nature — be it so:
But, father, there liv'd one who, then —
Then, in my boyhood, when their fire
Burn'd with a still intenser glow;
85   (For passion must with youth expire)
Ev'n *then*, who deem'd this iron heart
In woman's weakness had a part.

I have no words, alas! to tell
The lovliness of loving well!
90   Nor would I dare attempt to trace
The breathing beauty of a face,
Which ev'n to *my* impassion'd mind,
Leaves not its memory behind.
In spring of life have ye ne'er dwelt
95   Some object of delight upon,
With steadfast eye, till ye have felt
The earth reel — and the vision gone?
And I have held to mem'ry's eye
One object — and but one — until

100 Its very form hath pass'd me by,
But left its influence with me still.

VI.

'Tis not to thee that I should name —
Thou can'st not — would'st not dare to think
The magic empire of a flame
105 Which ev'n upon this perilous brink
Hath fix'd my soul, tho' unforgiv'n
By what it lost for passion — Heav'n.
I lov'd — and O, how tenderly!
Yes! she [was] worthy of all love!
110 Such as in infancy was mine
Tho' then its *passion* could not be:
'Twas such as angel minds above
Might envy — her young heart the shrine
On which my ev'ry hope and thought
115 Were incense — then a goodly gift —
For they were childish, without sin,
Pure as her young examples taught;
Why did I leave it and adrift,
Trust to the fickle star within?

VII.

120 We grew in age, and love together,
Roaming the forest and the wild;
My breast her shield in wintry weather,
And when the friendly sunshine smil'd
And she would mark the op'ning skies,
125 I saw no Heav'n, but in her eyes —
Ev'n childhood knows the human heart;
For when, in sunshine and in smiles,
From all our little cares apart,
Laughing at her half silly wiles,
130 I'd throw me on her throbbing breast,
And pour my spirit out in tears,

She'd look up in my wilder'd eye —
There was no need to speak the rest —
No need to quiet her kind fears —
135   She did not ask the reason why.

The hallow'd mem'ry of those years
Comes o'er me in these lonely hours,
And, with sweet lovliness, appears
As perfume of strange summer flow'rs;
140   Of flow'rs which we have known before
In infancy, which seen, recall
To mind — not flow'rs alone — but more
Our earthly life, and love — and all.

VIII.

Yes! she was worthy of all love!
145   Ev'n such as from th' accursed time
My spirit with the tempest strove,
When on the mountain peak alone,
Ambition lent it a new tone,
And bade it first to dream of crime,
150   My phrenzy to her bosom taught:
We still were young: no purer thought
Dwelt in a seraph's breast than *thine*; (3)
For passionate love is still divine:
I lov'd her as an angel might
155   With ray of the all living light
Which blazes upon Edis' shrine.(4)
It is not surely sin to name,
With such as mine — that mystic flame,
I had no being but in thee!
160   The world with all its train of bright

(3) I must beg the reader's pardon for making Tamerlane, a Tartar of the four-teenth century, speak in the same language as a Boston gentleman of the nineteenth: but of the Tartar mythology we have little information. [Poe's note]

(4) A deity presiding over virtuous love, upon whose imaginary altar, a sacred fire was continually blazing. [Poe's note]

And happy beauty (for to me
All was an undefin'd delight)
The world — its joy — its share of pain
Which I felt not — its bodied forms
165   Of varied being, which contain
The bodiless spirits of the storms,
The sunshine, and the calm — the ideal
And fleeting vanities of dreams,
Fearfully beautiful! the real
170   Nothings of mid-day waking life —
Of an enchanted life, which seems,
Now as I look back, the strife
Of some ill demon, with a power
Which left me in an evil hour,
175   All that I felt, or saw, or thought,
Crowding, confused became
(With thine unearthly beauty fraught)
Thou — and the nothing of a name.

IX.

The passionate spirit which hath known,
180   And deeply felt the silent tone
Of its own self supremacy, —
(I speak thus openly to thee,
'Twere folly *now* to veil a thought
With which this aching breast is fraught)
185   The soul which feels its innate right —
The mystic empire and high power
Giv'n by the energetic might
Of Genius, at its natal hour;
Which knows (believe me at this time,
190   When falsehood were a ten-fold crime,
There *is* a power in the high spirit
To *know* the fate it will inherit)
The soul, which knows such power, will still
Find *Pride* the ruler of its will.

195   Yes! I was proud — and ye who know
      The magic of that meaning word,
      So oft perverted, will bestow
      Your scorn, perhaps, when ye have heard
      That the proud spirit had been broken,
200   The proud heart burst in agony
      At one upbraiding word or token
      Of her that heart's idolatry —
      I was ambitious — have ye known
      Its fiery passion? — ye have not —
205   A cottager, I mark'd a throne
      Of half the world, as all my own,
      And murmur'd at such lowly lot!
      But it had pass'd me as a dream
      Which, of light step, flies with the dew,
210   That kindling thought — did not the beam
      Of Beauty, which did guide it through
      The livelong summer day, oppress
      My mind with double loveliness —

*   *   *   *   *

X

      We walk'd together on the crown
215   Of a high mountain, which look'd down
      Afar from its proud natural towers
      Of rock and forest, on the hills —
      The dwindled hills, whence amid bowers
      Her own fair hand had rear'd around,
220   Gush'd shoutingly a thousand rills,
      Which as it were, in fairy bound
      Embrac'd two hamlets — those our own —
      Peacefully happy — yet alone —

*   *   *   *   *

      I spoke to her of power and pride —
225   But mystically, in such guise,

That she might deem it naught beside
The moment's converse, in her eyes
I read (perhaps too carelessly)
A mingled feeling with my own;
230   The flush on her bright cheek, to me,
Seem'd to become a queenly throne
Too well, that I should let it be
A light in the dark wild, alone.

XI.

There — in that hour — a thought came o'er
235   My mind, it had not known before —
To leave her while we both were young, —
To follow my high fate among
The strife of nations, and redeem
The idle words, which, as a dream
240   Now sounded to her heedless ear —
I held no doubt — I knew no fear
Of peril in my wild career;
To gain an empire, and throw down
As nuptial dowry — a queen's crown,
245   The only feeling which possest,
With her own image, my fond breast —
Who, that had known the secret thought
Of a young peasant's bosom then,
Had deem'd him, in compassion, aught
250   But one, whom phantasy had led
Astray from reason — Among men
Ambition is chain'd down — nor fed
(As in the desert, where the grand,
The wild, the beautiful, conspire
255   With their own breath to fan its fire)
With thoughts such feeling can command;
Uncheck'd by sarcasm, and scorn
Of those, who hardly will conceive
That any should become "great," born [5]

[5] Although Tamerlane speaks this, it is not the less true. It is a matter of the

260 In their own sphere — will not believe
That they shall stoop in life to one
Whom daily they are wont to see
Familiarly — whom Fortune's sun
Hath ne'er shone dazzlingly upon
265 Lowly — and of their own degree —

XII.

I pictur'd to my fancy's eye
Her silent, deep astonishment,
When, a few fleeting years gone by,
(For short the time my high hope lent
270 To its most desperate intent,)
She might recall in him, whom Fame
Had gilded with a conquerer's name,
(With glory — such as might inspire
Perforce, a passing thought of one,
275 Whom she had deem'd in his own fire
Wither'd and blasted; who had gone
A traitor, violate of the truth
So plighted in his early youth,)
Her own Alexis, who should plight ⁽⁶⁾
280 The love he plighted *then* — again,
And raise his infancy's delight,
The bride and queen of Tamerlane —

XIII.

One noon of a bright summer's day
I pass'd from out the matted bow'r

---

greatest difficulty to make the generality of mankind believe that one, with whom they are upon terms of intimacy, shall be called, in the world, a "great man." The reason is evident. There are few great men. Their actions are consequently viewed by the mass of people thro' the medium of distance. — The prominent parts of their character are alone noted; and those properties, which are minute and common to every one, not being observed, seem to have no connection with a great character.

Who ever read the private memorials, correspondence, &c., which have become so common in our time, without wondering that "great men" should act and think "so abominably"? [Poe's note]

⁽⁶⁾ That Tamerlane acquir'd his renown under a feigned name is not entirely a fiction. [Poe's note]

285 Where in a deep, still slumber lay
My Ada. In that peaceful hour,
A silent gaze was my farewell.
I had no other solace — then
T' awake her, and a falsehood tell
290 Of a feign'd journey, were again
To trust the weakness of my heart
To her soft thrilling voice: To part
Thus, haply, while in sleep she dream'd
Of long delight, nor yet had deem'd
295 Awake, that I had held a thought
Of parting, were with madness fraught;
I knew not woman's heart, alas!
Tho' lov'd, and loving — let it pass. —

XIV.

I went from out the matted bow'r,
300 And hurried madly on my way:
And felt, with ev'ry flying hour,
That bore me from my home, more gay;
There is of earth an agony
Which, ideal, still may be
305 The worst ill of mortality,
'Tis bliss, in its own reality,
Too real, to *his* breast who lives
Not within himself but gives
A portion of his willing soul
310 To God, and to the great whole —
To him, whose loving spirit will dwell
With Nature, in her wild paths; tell
Of her wond'rous ways, and telling bless
Her overpow'ring loveliness!
315 A more than agony to him
Whose failing sight will grow dim
With its own living gaze upon
That loveliness around: the sun —

The blue sky — the misty light
320   Of the pale cloud therein, whose hue
Is grace to its heav'nly bed of blue;
Dim! tho' looking on all bright!
O God! when the thoughts that may not pass
Will burst upon him, and alas!
325   For the flight on Earth to Fancy giv'n,
There are no words — unless of Heav'n.

XV.

*   *   *   *   *

Look 'round thee now on Samarcand,[7]
Is she not queen of earth? her pride
Above all cities? in her hand
330   Their destinies? with all beside
Of glory, which the world hath known?
Stands she not proudly and alone?
And who her sov'reign? Timur he [8]
Whom th' astonish'd earth hath seen,
335   With victory, on victory,
Redoubling age! and more, I ween,
The Zinghis' yet re-echoing fame [9]
And now what has he? what! a name.
The sound of revelry by night
340   Comes o'er me, with the mingled voice
Of many with a breast as light,
As if 'twere not the dying hour
Of one, in whom they did rejoice —
As in a leader, haply — Power
345   Its venom secretly imparts;
Nothing have I with human hearts.

[7] I believe it was after the battle of Angoria that Tamerlane made Samarcand his residence. It became for a time the seat of learning and the arts. [Poe's note]
[8] He was called Timur Bek as well as Tamerlane. [Poe's note]
[9] The conquests of Tamerlane far exceeded those of Zinghis Khan. He boasted to have two thirds of the world at his command. [Poe's note]

XVI.

When Fortune mark'd me for her own,
And my proud hopes had reach'd a throne
(It boots me not, good friar, to tell
350   A tale the world but knows too well,
How by what hidden deeds of might,
I clamber'd to the tottering height,)
I still was young; and well I ween
My spirit what it e'er had been.
355   My eyes were still on pomp and power,
My wilder'd heart was far away,
In vallies of the wild Taglay,
In mine own Ada's matted bow'r.
I dwelt not long in Samarcand
360   Ere, in a peasant's lowly guise,
I sought my long-abandon'd land,
By sunset did its mountains rise
In dusky grandeur to my eyes:
But as I wander'd on the way
365   My heart sunk with the sun's ray.
To him, who still would gaze upon
The glory of the summer sun,
There comes, when that sun will from him part,
A sullen hopelessness of heart.
370   That soul will hate the ev'ning mist
So often lovely, and will list
To the sound of the coming darkness (known
To those whose spirits hark'n) (10) as one
Who in a dream of night *would* fly
375   But cannot from a danger nigh.
What though the moon — the silvery moon
Shine on his path, in her high noon;
Her smile is chilly, and *her* beam

---

(10) I have often fancied that I could distinctly hear the sound of the darkness, as it steals over the horizon — a foolish fancy perhaps, but not more unintelligible than to see music —

         "The mind the music breathing from her face."   [Poe's note]

In that time of dreariness will seem
380   As the portrait of one after death;
A likeness taken when the breath
Of young life, and the fire o' the eye
Had lately been but had pass'd by.
'Tis thus when the lovely summer sun
385   Of our boyhood, his course hath run:
For all we live to know — is known;
And all we seek to keep — hath flown;
With the noon-day beauty, which is all.
Let life, then, as the day-flow'r, fall —
390   The trancient, passionate day-flow'r,[11]
Withering at the ev'ning hour.

XVII.

I reach'd my home — my home no more —
For all was flown that made it so —
I pass'd from out its mossy door,
395   In vacant idleness of woe.
There met me on its threshold stone
A mountain hunter, I had known
In childhood but he knew me not.
Something he spoke of the old cot:
400   It had seen better days, he said;
There rose a fountain once, and *there*
Full many a fair flow'r raised its head:
But she who rear'd them was long dead,
And in such follies had no part,
405   What was there left me *now*? despair —
A kingdom for a broken—heart.

[1827]

[11] There is a flow'r, (I have never known its botanic name,) vulgarly called the day flower. It blooms beautifully in the day-light, but withers towards evening, and by night its leaves appear totally shrivelled and dead. I have forgotten, however, to mention in the text, that it lives again in the morning. If it will not flourish in Tartary, I must be forgiven for carrying it thither. [Poe's note]

TAMERLANE [B]

[5]

65 [. . . . .]
Gurgled in my pleas'd ear the crush
    Of empires, with the captive's prayer
The hum of suitors & the tone
Of flatt'ry 'round a sov'reign's throne.

6

70 The storm had ceas'd & I awoke —
    Its spirit cradled me to sleep,
And as it pass'd me by there broke
        Strange light upon me, tho' it were
    My soul in mystery to steep:
75 For I was not as I had been —
        The child of Nature, without care,
Or thought save of the passing scene.

7

My passions, from that hapless hour
    Usurp'd a tyranny which men
80 Have deem'd since I have reach'd to power
        My innate nature — be it so:
    But, father, there liv'd one who then,
Then, in my boyhood, when their fire
        Burn'd with a still intenser glow
85 (For passion must with youth expire)
Ev'n *then* who deem'd this iron heart
In woman's weakness had a part.

8

I have no words, alas! to tell
The loveliness of loving well!
90 Nor would I now attempt to trace
The more than beauty of a face

Which, ev'n to this impassion'd mind,
Leaves not its memory behind.
In spring of life have ye ne'er dwelt
95   Some object of delight upon
With steadfast eye, till ye had felt
    The earth reel, & the vision gone?
So have I held to Memory's eye
    One object, and but one, until [. . . . .]

11

Yes! she was worthy of all love —
145   Such as I taught her from the time
My spirit with the tempest strove
        When, on the mountain peak alone,
        Ambition lent it a new tone,
    And bade it first to dream of crime.
150 There were no holier thoughts than thine.
    I lov'd thee as an angel might,
155   With ray of the all-living light
Which blazes upon Edis' shrine —
It is not surely sin to name
With such as mine that mystic flame.
I had no being but in thee —
160   The world, with all its train of bright
And happy beauty — (for to me
    All was an undefin'd delight.)
The world — its joy — its share of pain
    Unheeded then — its bodied forms
165 Of varied being which contain
    The bodiless spirits of the storms,
The sunshine, & the calm — th' ideal
    And fleeting vanities of dreams
Fearfully beautiful — the real
170   Nothings of mid-day waking life —
    Of an enchanted life, which seems,
    Now as I look back, the strife

Of an ill demon with a power
Which left me in an evil hour —
175 All that I felt, or saw, or thought,
    Crowding confusedly became
(With thine unearthly beauty fraught —)
    Thou — & the nothing of a name.

12

    The passionate spirit which hath known
180 And deeply felt the silent tone
    Of its own self-supremacy —
189 Which knows (believe! for now on me
190 Truth flashes thro' Eternity,
    There *is* a power in the high spirit
    To *know* the fate it will inherit)
    The soul which feels such power will still
    Find Pride the ruler of its will.

13

195 Yes! I was proud & ye who know
        The magic of that meaning word
    So oft perverted, will bestow
        Your scorn perhaps when ye have heard
    That the proud spirit had been broken,
200   The proud heart burst in agony
    At one upbraiding word or token
        Of her, that heart's idolatry!
    I was ambitious — have ye known
        The fiery passion? ye have not —
205 A cottager, I mark'd a throne
    Of half the world as all my own
        And murmur'd at such lowly lot;
    But it had pass'd me as a dream
        Which, of light step, flies with the dew
210 (That kindling thought) — did not the beam
        Of Beauty, which did guide it thro'

The live-long summer day, oppress
My mind with double loveliness!

14

We walk'd together on the crown
215   Of a high mountain which look'd down
Afar from its proud natural towers
  Of rock & forest on the hills;
The dwindled hills, whence, amid bowers
    Her magic hand had rear'd around
220   Gush'd shoutingly a thousand rills,
    Encircling with a glitt'ring bound
Of diamond sunshine & sweet spray
Two mossy huts of the Taglay.

15

I spoke to her of power & pride,
225   But mystically, in such guise,
That she might deem it nought beside
  The moment's converse: in her eyes
I read, perhaps too carelessly,
  A mingled feeling with my own —
230 The flush on her bright cheek to me
  Seem'd to become a queenly throne
Too well that I should let it be
  A light in the dark wild alone.

16

There, in that hour, a thought came o'er
235 My mind it had not known before —
To leave her while we both were young:
To follow my high fate among
The strife of nations, & redeem
The idle words which, as a dream,
240 Now sounded to her heedless ear —
I held no doubt, I knew no fear

Of peril in my wild career —
To gain an empire & throw down
As nuptial dowry a queen's crown
245 The undying hope which now oppress'd
A spirit ne'er to be at rest.

17

Who that had known the silent thought
Of a young peasant's bosom then
Had deem'd him, in compassion, aught
250   But one whom Phantasy had thrown
Her mantle over? among men
    Lion Ambition is chain'd down,
And crouches to a keeper's hand —
Not so in deserts where the grand
The wild, the terrible conspire
255 With their own breath to fan his fire.

18

327 Look 'round thee now on Samarcand!
    Is she not queen of earth? her pride
Above all cities? in her hand
330   Their destinies? in all beside
Of glory which the world hath known
Stands she not nobly & alone?
And who her sov'reign? Timur — he
    Whom the astonish'd people saw
335 Striding o'er empires haughtily
    A diadem'd outlaw!
More than the Zinghis in his fame —
And now what has he? even a name.

19

The sound of revelry to night
340   Comes o'er me, with the mingled voice
Of many with a breast as light

TAMERLANE [*F*]

As if 'twere not their parting hour
From one in whom they did rejoice —
As in a leader, haply; Power
345 Its venom secretly imparts —
And I have naught with human hearts. [. . . .]
[1827–1828]

TAMERLANE [*F*]

I.

Kind solace in a dying hour!
Such, father, is not (now) my theme:
I will not madly think that power
Of earth may shrive me of the sin
5 Unearthly pride hath revell'd in —
I have no time to dote or dream:
You call it hope — that fire of fire!
It is but agony of desire —
If I can hope (O God! I can)
10 Its fount is holier — more divine —
I would not call thee fool, old man,
But such is not a gift of thine.

II.

Hear thou the secret of a spirit
Bow'd from its wild pride into shame.
15 O yearning heart! (I did inherit
Thy withering portion with the fame,
The searing glory which hath shone
Amid the jewels of my throne,
Halo of Hell! and with a pain
20 Not Hell shall make me fear again)
O craving heart for the lost flowers
And sunshine of my summer hours!
The undying voice of that dead time,

With its interminable chime
25   Rings in the spirit of a spell,
Upon thy emptiness, — a knell.
Despair, the fabled vampire-bat,
Hath long upon my bosom sat,
And I would rave, but that he flings
30   A calm from his unearthly wings.

III.

I have not always been as now:
The fever'd diadem on my brow,
I claim'd and won usurpingly —
Hath not the same heirdom given
35   Rome to the Cæsar — this to me?
The heritage of kingly mind
And a proud spirit which hath striven
Triumphantly with human kind.

IV.

On mountain soil I first drew life —
40   The mists of the Taglay have shed
Nightly their dews upon my head,
And I believe the winged strife
And tumult of the headlong air
Hath nestled in my very hair.

V.

45   So late from Heaven — that dew — it fell
(Mid dreams of an unholy night)
Upon me with the touch of Hell,
While the red flashing of the light
From clouds that hung, like banners, o'er,
50   Appear'd to my half-closing eye
The pageantry of monarchy,
And the deep trumpet thunder's roar
Came hurriedly upon me, telling

Of human battle, where my voice,
55   My *own* voice, silly child, was swelling
(O how my spirit would rejoice
And leap within me at the cry!)
The battle cry of victory.

VI.

The rain came down upon my head,
60   Unshelter'd, and the heavy wind
Was giant-like — so thou, my mind!
It was but man, I thought, who shed
Laurels upon me — and the rush,
The torrent of the chilly air,
65   Gurgled within my ear the crush
Of empires, with the captive's prayer,
The hum of suitors, and the tone
Of flattery, round a sovereign's throne.

VII.

My passions from that hapless hour
70   Usurp'd a tyranny which men
Have deem'd, since I have reach'd to power,
My innate nature — be it so:
But, father, there liv'd one who then —
Then in my boyhood when their fire
75   Burn'd with a still intenser glow,
(For passion must with youth expire)
Ev'n then who knew that as infinite
My soul — so was the weakness in it.

VIII.

For in those days it was my lot
80   To haunt of the wide world a spot
The which I could not love the less,
So lovely was the loneliness
Of a wild lake with black rock bound,

And the sultan-like pines that tower'd around!
85 But when the night had thrown her pall
Upon that spot as upon all,
And the black wind murmur'd by,
In a dirge of melody;
My infant spirit would awake
90 To the terror of that lone lake.
Yet that terror was not fright —
But a tremulous delight —
A feeling not the jewell'd mine
Could ever bribe me to define,
95 Nor love, Ada! tho' it were thine.
How could I from that water bring
Solace to my imagining?
My solitary soul — how make
An Eden of that dim lake?

IX.

100 But then a gentler, calmer spell,
Like moonlight on my spirit fell,
And O! I have no words to tell
The loveliness of loving well!
I will not now attempt to trace
105 The more than beauty of a face
Whose lineaments upon my mind
Are shadows on the unstable wind.
I well remember having dwelt,
Pages of early lore upon,
110 With loitering eye till I have felt
The letters with their meaning melt
To fantasies with — none.

X.

Was she not worthy of all love?
Love as in infancy was mine —
115 'Twas such as angel minds above

Might envy — her young heart the shrine
On which my ev'ry hope and thought
Were incense — then a goodly gift —
For they were childish and upright —
120   Pure — as her young example taught:
Why did I leave it and adrift
Trust to the fire within for light?

XI.

We grew in age and love together,
Roaming the forest and the wild,
125   My breast her shield in wintry weather,
And when the friendly sunshine smil'd,
And she would mark the opening skies,
I saw no Heaven but in her eyes.

XII.

Young Love's first lesson is — the heart:
130   For mid that sunshine and those smiles,
When from our little cares apart,
And laughing at her girlish wiles,
I'd lean upon her gentle breast,
And pour my spirit out in tears,
135   There was no need to speak the rest,
No need to quiet any fears
Of hers — who ask'd no reason why,
But turn'd on me her quiet eye.

XIII.

I had no being but in thee:
140   The world and all it did contain,
In the earth — the air — the sea,
Of pleasure or of pain —
The good, the bad, the ideal,
Dim vanities of dreams by night,
145   And dimmer nothings which were real,

(Shadows and a more shadowy light)
Parted upon their misty wings,
And so, confusedly, became
Thine image and a name — a name!
150 Two separate yet most intimate things.

XIV.

We walk'd together on the crown
Of a high mountain which look'd down
Afar from its proud natural towers
Of rock and forest on the hills —
155 The dwindled hills! begirt with bowers
And shooting with a thousand rills.

XV.

I spoke to her of power and pride,
But mystically, in such guise
That she might deem it nought beside
160 The moments' converse — in her eyes
I read — perhaps too carelessly —
A mingled feeling with my own —
The flush upon her cheek to me,
Seem'd fitted for a queenly throne,
165 Too well that I should let it be,
Light in the wilderness alone.

XVI.

I wrapp'd myself in grandeur then
And donn'd a visionary crown —
Yet it was not that Fantasy
170 Had thrown her mantle over me,
But that among the rabble men,
Lion ambition is chain'd down,
And crouches to a keeper's hand,
Not so in deserts where the grand,

175 The wild, the terrible, conspire
With their own breath to fan its fire.

*   *   *   *   *   *

XVII.

Say, holy father, breathes there yet
A rebel or a Bajazet?
How now! why tremble, man of gloom,
180 As if my words were the Simoom!
Why do the people bow the knee,
To the young Tamerlane — to me!

XVIII.

O human love! thou spirit given
On earth of all we hope in Heaven!
185 Which fallest into the soul like rain
Upon the Syroc-wither'd plain,
And failing of thy power to bless,
But leavest the heart a wilderness!
Idea which bindest life around,
190 With music of so strange a sound,
And beauty of so wild a birth —
Farewell! for I have won the earth.

XIX.

When hope, the eagle that tower'd, could see
No cliff beyond him in the sky,
195 His pinions were bent droopingly,
And homeward turn'd his soften'd eye.

XX.

*   *   *   *   *   *

'Twas sunset: when the sun will part,
There comes a sullenness of heart
To him who still would look upon

200   The glory of that summer sun.
       That soul will hate the evening mist,
       So often lovely, and will list
       To the sound of the coming darkness (known
       To those whose spirits harken) as one
205   Who in a dream of night would fly,
       But cannot from a danger nigh.

XXI.

       What tho' the moon — the white moon —
       Shed all the beauty of her noon,
       Her smile is chilly, and her beam
210   In that time of dreariness will seem
       (So like you gather in your breath)
       A portrait taken after death.

       *   *   *   *   *   *

XXII.

       I reach'd my home — what home? above,
       My home — my hope — my early love,
215   Lonely, like me, the desert rose,
       Bow'd down with its own glory grows.

XXIII.

       Father, I firmly do believe —
       I *know* — for death, who comes for me
       From regions of the blest afar,
220   Where there is nothing to deceive,
       Hath left his iron gate ajar,
       And rays of truth you cannot see,
       Are flashing thro' eternity:
       I do believe that Eblis hath
225   A snare in every human path —
       Else how when in the holy grove,
       I wander'd of the idol, Love,

TAMERLANE [*H*]

Who daily scents his snowy wings
With incense of burnt offerings,
230   From the most undefiled things;
Whose pleasant bowers are yet so riven
Above with trelliced rays from Heaven,
No mote may shun — no tiniest fly
The lightning of his eagle eye —
235   How was it that Ambition crept,
Unseen amid the revels there,
Till growing bold, he laugh'd and leapt
In the tangles of Love's very hair?

XXIV.

If my peace hath flown away
240   In a night — or in a day —
In a vision — or in none —
Is it, therefore, the less gone?
I was standing 'mid the roar
Of a wind-beaten shore,
245   And I held within my hand
Some particles of sand —
How bright! and yet to creep
Thro' my fingers to the deep!
My early hopes? no — they
250   Went gloriously away,
Like lightning from the sky —
Why in the battle did not I?

[1827–1831]

TAMERLANE [*H*]

Kind solace in a dying hour!
   Such, father, is not (now) my theme —
I will not madly deem that power
   Of Earth may shrive me of the sin

Title: *Before this is* TO/JOHN NEAL/   THIS POEM/IS RESPECTFULLY
DEDICATED. (*C*)

5   Unearthly pride hath revell'd in —
      I have no time to dote or dream:
      You call it hope — that fire of fire!
      It is but agony of desire:
      If I *can* hope — Oh God! I can —
10   Its fount is holier — more divine —
      I would not call thee fool, old man,
          But such is not a gift of thine.

      Know thou the secret of a spirit
          Bow'd from its wild pride into shame.
15   O yearning heart! I did inherit
          Thy withering portion with the fame,
      The searing glory which hath shone
      Amid the Jewels of my throne,
      Halo of Hell! and with a pain
20   Not Hell shall make me fear again —
      O craving heart, for the lost flowers
      And sunshine of my summer hours!
      The undying voice of that dead time,
      With its interminable chime,
25   Rings, in the spirit of a spell
      Upon the emptiness — a knell.

      I have not always been as now:
      The fever'd diadem on my brow
          I claim'd and won usurpingly —
30   Hath not the same fierce heirdom given
          Rome to the Cæsar — this to me?
          The heritage of a kingly mind,
      And a proud spirit which hath striven
          Triumphantly with human kind.

35   On mountain soil I first drew life:
          The mists of the Taglay have shed
          Nightly their dews upon my head,

---

29 claim'd/claimed (*E*)

And, I believe, the winged strife
And tumult of the headlong air
40   Have nestled in my very hair.

So late from Heaven — that dew — it fell
    ('Mid dreams of an unholy night)
Upon me with the touch of Hell,
    While the red flashing of the light
45   From clouds that hung, like banners, o'er,
      Appeared to my half-closing eye
      The pageantry of monarchy,
And the deep trumpet-thunder's roar
    Came hurriedly upon me, telling
50   Of human battle, where my voice,
    My own voice, silly child! — was swelling
        (O! how my spirit would rejoice,
And leap within me at the cry)
    The battle-cry of Victory!

55   The rain came down upon my head
      Unshelter'd — and the heavy wind
      Rendered me mad and deaf and blind.
It was but man, I thought, who shed
    Laurels upon me: and the rush —
60   The torrent of the chilly air
Gurgled within my ear the crush
    Of empires — with the captive's prayer —
The hum of suitors — and the tone
Of flattery 'round a sovereign's throne.

65   My passions, from that hapless hour,

---

40 Have/Hath (*C, E*)
42 an/one (*E*)
46 Appeared/Seem'd then (*E*)
50–51 Of human battle (near me swelling.) (*E*)

57 Was giantlike — so thou my mind (*C, E*)
64 sovereign's throne/sovereign-throne (*E*)

· 5 5 ·

Usurp'd a tyranny which men
Have deem'd, since I have reach'd to power,
My innate nature — be it so:
But, father, there liv'd one who, then,
70   Then — in my boyhood — when their fire
Burn'd with a still intenser glow
(For passion must, with youth, expire)
E'en *then* who knew this iron heart
In woman's weakness had a part.

75   I have no words — alas! — to tell
The loveliness of loving well!
Nor would I now attempt to trace
The more than beauty of a face
Whose lineaments, upon my mind,
80   Are —— shadows on th' unstable wind:
Thus I remember having dwelt
Some page of early lore upon,
With loitering eye, till I have felt
The letters — with their meaning — melt
85   To fantasies — with none.

O, she was worthy of all love!
Love — as in infancy was mine —
'Twas such as angel minds above
Might envy; her young heart the shrine
90   On which my every hope and thought
Were incense — then a goodly gift,
For they were childish and upright —
Pure —— as her young example taught:
Why did I leave it, and, adrift,
95   Trust to the fire within, for light?

We grew in age — and love — together —
Roaming the forest, and the wild;
My breast her shield in wintry weather —
And, when the friendly sunshine smil'd,

100 And she would mark the opening skies,
    I saw no Heaven — but in her eyes.

Young Love's first lesson is —— the heart.
    For 'mid that sunshine, and those smiles,
When, from our little cares apart,
105   And laughing at her girlish wiles,
I'd throw me on her throbbing breast,
    And pour my spirit out in tears —
There was no need to speak the rest —
    No need to quiet any fears
110 Of her — who ask'd no reason why,
    But turn'd on me her quiet eye!

Yet *more* than worthy of the love
My spirit struggled with, and strove,
When, on the mountain peak, alone,
115 Ambition lent it a new tone —
I had no being — but in thee:
    The world, and all it did contain
In the earth — the air — the sea —
    Its joy — its little lot of pain
120 That was new pleasure —— the ideal,
    Dim, vanities of dreams by night —
And dimmer nothings which were real —
    (Shadows — and a more shadowy light!)
Parted upon their misty wings,
125   And, so, confusedly, became
    Thine image and — a name — a name!
Two separate — yet most intimate things.

I was ambitious — have you known
    The passion, father? You have not:
130 A cottager, I mark'd a throne
Of half the world as all my own,

---

111 turn'd/turned (*E*)

And murmur'd at such lowly lot —
But, just like any other dream,
Upon the vapor of the dew
135   My own had past, did not the beam
Of beauty which did while it thro'
The minute — the hour — the day — oppress
My mind with double loveliness.

We walk'd together on the crown
140   Of a high mountain which look'd down
Afar from its proud natural towers
Of rock and forest, on the hills —
The dwindled hills! begirt with bowers
And shouting with a thousand rills.

145   I spoke to her of power and pride,
But mystically — in such guise
That she might deem it nought beside
The moment's converse; in her eyes
I read, perhaps too carelessly —
150   A mingled feeling with my own —
The flush on her bright cheek, to me
Seem'd to become a queenly throne
Too well that I should let it be
Light in the wilderness alone.

155   I wrapp'd myself in grandeur then
And donn'd a visionary crown ——
Yet it was not that Fantasy
Had thrown her mantle over me —
But that, among the rabble — men,
160   Lion ambition is chain'd down —
And crouches to a keeper's hand —
Not so in deserts where the grand —
The wild — the terrible conspire
With their own breath to fan his fire.

165　　Look 'round thee now on Samarcand! —
　　　　　Is she not queen of Earth? her pride
　　　　Above all cities? in her hand
　　　　　Their destinies? in all beside
　　　　Of glory which the world hath known
170　　Stands she not nobly and alone?
　　　　Falling — her veriest stepping-stone
　　　　Shall form the pedestal of a throne —
　　　　And who her sovereign? Timour — he
　　　　Whom the astonished people saw
175　　Striding o'er empires haughtily
　　　　　A diadem'd outlaw!

　　　　O, human love! thou spirit given,
　　　　On Earth, of all we hope in Heaven!
　　　　Which fall'st into the soul like rain
180　　Upon the Siroc-wither'd plain,
　　　　And, failing in thy power to bless,
　　　　But leav'st the heart a wilderness!
　　　　Idea! which bindest life around
　　　　With music of so strange a sound
185　　And beauty of so wild a birth —
　　　　Farewell! for I have won the Earth.

　　　　When Hope, the eagle that tower'd, could see
　　　　　No cliff beyond him in the sky,
　　　　His pinions were bent droopingly —
190　　　And homeward turn'd his soften'd eye.
　　　　'Twas sunset: when the sun will part
　　　　There comes a sullenness of heart
　　　　To him who still would look upon
　　　　The glory of the summer sun.
195　　That soul will hate the ev'ning mist
　　　　So often lovely, and will list
　　　　To the sound of the coming darkness (known

187　When towering Eagle-Hope could   see (*D*)

To those whose spirits harken) as one
Who, in a dream of night, *would* fly
200   But *cannot* from a danger nigh.

What tho' the moon — the white moon
Shed all the splendor of her noon,
Her smile is chilly — and *her* beam,
In that time of dreariness, will seem
205   (So like you gather in your breath)
A portrait taken after death.
And boyhood is a summer sun
Whose waning is the dreariest one —
For all we live to know is known
210   And all we seek to keep hath flown —
Let life, then, as the day-flower, fall
With the noon-day beauty — which is all.

I reach'd my home — my home no more —
For all had flown who made it so.
215   I pass'd from out its mossy door,
    And, tho' my tread was soft and low,
A voice came from the threshold stone
Of one whom I had earlier known —
    O, I defy thee, Hell, to show
220   On beds of fire that burn below,
    An humbler heart — a deeper wo.

Father, I firmly do believe —
    I *know* — for Death who comes for me
    From regions of the blest afar,
225   Where there is nothing to deceive,
    Hath left his iron gate ajar,
    And rays of truth you cannot see
    Are flashing thro' Eternity ——
I do believe that Eblis hath
230   A snare in every human path —
Else how, when in the holy grove

TAMERLANE

I wandered of the idol, Love,
Who daily scents his snowy wings
With incense of burnt offerings

235   From the most unpolluted things,
Whose pleasant bowers are yet so riven
Above with trellic'd rays from Heaven
No mote may shun — no tiniest fly —
The light'ning of his eagle eye —

240   How was it that Ambition crept,
    Unseen, amid the revels there,
Till growing bold, he laughed and leapt
In the tangles of Love's very hair?

[1827–1828/45]

NOTES

The poem is thoroughly Byronic, and even more parallels than those here noted could probably be found to Byron's works. Earlier commentators have noticed resemblances to Wordsworth and Coleridge, but none striking enough to convince me that Poe knew much of those authors in 1827. Line references are to the version of 1845, unless specifically marked otherwise.

1–12 Compare Byron's *Manfred*, III, i, 154–158:

      Old man! I do respect
Thine order, and revere thine years; I deem
Thy purpose pious, but it is in vain:
Think me not churlish; I would spare thyself,
Far more than me . . .

Killis Campbell, *The Poems of Edgar Allan Poe* (1917), p. 149, cites also *Manfred*, III, i, 66–78.

15 (1827) There is a tower on the stage in Lewis's *Timour the Tartar* according to Martin Shockley, "*Timour the Tartar* and Poe's *Tamerlane*," *PMLA*, December 1941 (56:1104–1105).

16–20 Compare Goldsmith's *Traveller*, line 436, for "Luke's iron crown" — a reference to the Hungarian rebel named George Dózsa, upon whose head a red-hot iron crown was placed in 1514. (Goldsmith confused him with his brother Luke, and Poe quoted Goldsmith's line as Pope's in a review of Bryant's *Poems* in the *Southern Literary Messenger*, January 1837.)

29–30 (1831) Compare Edward C. Pinkney, "Lines from the Portfolio of H——," I, 75–76, "An ancient notion, that time flings / Our pains and pleasures from his wings . . ."

---

235 unpolluted/undefiled (*E*)   243 very/brilliant (*E*)
237 trellic'd/trelliced (*E*)

30–34 This may allude to the royal horoscopes of Augustus Caesar and Tamerlane. Both had Saturn in the ascendant in Capricorn, and all the other planets in favorable aspects.

39 (1827) Note 2 Poe's exact source is unknown, but Mr. Francis Paar tells me that the mountains (the Pamirs) are a branch of the Himalayas in a part of Turkestan ruled by native khans in Poe's day. Johann Jakob Egli, *Nomina Geographica* (Leipzig, 1893), gives the forms *Bolor-Tagh*, *Bélut-tagh*, and Turkish *Bulyt-tagh*, meaning cloud mountains. Ancient geographers call the Himalayas Imaus, as does Milton, *Paradise Lost*, III, 431.

43 (1827) Manfred was saved from suicide by a chamois hunter.

44 (1827) Sir Walter Scott has the phrase "in pride of power" in *The Lay of the Last Minstrel*, Introduction, line 43.

79–99 (1831) These lines are a version of "The Lake."

81 Poe's hero in "Berenice" says, "To muse for long unwearied hours with my attention riveted to some frivolous device on the margin, or in the typography of a book."

84 (1831) Sultan-like pines are thought of as turbaned; compare the "serangs" in "Irenë."

88–89 The envy of the angels appears again in "Annabel Lee," and is cited as evidence by those who would connect that poem with Elmira Royster. Poe in 1827 wrote in the album of Octavia Walton, "The following lines are fr[om] Voltaire's story styled 'The Princess of Babylon,'" and copied a passage ending "l'univers sera jaloux de lui." L. A. Wilmer in *Merlin* (1827), III, iv, 1–2, speaks of "a joy that human kind can feel / And angels envy." This is probably the earliest borrowing from Poe.

101 Poe wrote to Annie Richmond on November 16, 1848, of looking "deep into the clear Heaven of your eyes."

102 Compare Byron, *Don Juan*, IV, x, 8, "Alas! There is no instinct like the Heart."

116 Compare Byron, "The Dream," line 51, "He had no breath, no being, but in hers."

122–127 Poe wrote much of daydreams, and he has a passage in "Morella" on the intimate connection between a thing or a person and its name.

135–138 Richard Wilbur, *Poe: Complete Poems* (1959), p. 119, explains that Tamerlane's ambition for himself was mingled with a desire to make his beloved the queen.

136–143 (1827) In 1849 Poe told Miss Susan Ingram that the perfume of orris root reminded him of his foster mother, who kept it with her linen. See the *New York Herald*, February 19, 1905, quoted by Woodberry, *Life*, II, 332. In "Berenice" the hero dreams "away whole days over the perfume of a flower," and in "The Pit and the Pendulum" writes of one "who ponders over the perfume of some novel flower."

139–140 Compare "Fairy-land," lines 16–17, "its centre on the crown / Of a mountain's eminence," and "Serenade," line 12, "on the spectral mountain's crown."

139–141 Compare Edward C. Pinkney, *Rodolph*, I, 10–12:

> To Rodolph's proud ancestral towers,
> Whose station from its mural crown
> A regal look cast sternly down.

156 (1827) Note 4 Edis is probably from Latin *aedis*, a small temple.

178 (1831) Bajazet was the Turkish sultan captured by Tamerlane.

178 (1827) Compare Byron, "Churchill's Grave," line 43, "The Glory and the Nothing of a Name."

180 The Siroc (sirocco) and the simoom are hot winds from the desert. Both are mentioned in the 1831 version (lines 180, 186), and the simoom appears in "Al Aaraaf," II, 165.

191 Campbell (*Poems*, p. 153) compares the opening of Byron's "Monody on Sheridan":

> When the last sunshine of expiring day
> In summer's twilight weeps itself away,
> Who hath not felt the softness of the hour
> Sink on the heart, as dew along the flower?
> With a pure feeling which absorbs and awes
> While Nature makes that melancholy pause,
> Her breathing moment on the bridge where Time
> Of light and darkness forms an arch sublime;
> Who hath not shared that calm, so still and deep,
> The voiceless thought which would not speak but weep.

199–200 See Poe's review of Harrison Ainsworth's *Guy Fawkes* in *Graham's Magazine* for November 1841, for a "dream . . . in which the sufferer, although making . . . efforts to *run*, finds a walk or a crawl" alone possible.

203 Poe refers to the coldness of the moon also in "Evening Star," "Al Aaraaf," II, 151, and "Ulalume."

207–212 Wilbur (*Poe*, p. 118) says, "The villain of the piece is . . . Time" which cuts the hero off from his boyhood with complete imaginative power, to seek real power as a man.

212 Compare *King Lear*, V, ii, 11, "Ripeness is all."

213–215 See Byron's *Don Juan*, III, lii, 1–4:

> He entered in the house — his home no more,
>   For without hearts there is no home; — and felt
> The solitude of passing his own door
>   Without a welcome . . .

229 Eblis is Mahomet's name for the prince of jinns and evil spirits.

239–251 (1831) These are a version of "To — —" ("Should my early life seem").

243 Compare Milton's *Lycidas*, line 69, "the tangles of Neaera's hair."

259 (1827) Note 5 The words "so abominably" are quoted from *Hamlet*, III, ii, 39.

275–276 (1827) See *All's Well That Ends Well*, IV, ii, 5, "If the quick fire of youth light not your mind."

279 (1827) Alexis is a conventional shepherd's name, used in Vergil's second *Eclogue* and Pope's second *Pastoral*.

286 (1827) Byron's line in *Childe Harold*, III, i, 2, "Ada! sole daughter of my house and heart," was extremely familiar in Poe's day, and his heroine is surely a namesake of Byron's only legitimate child. Byron wrote John Murray, on October 8, 1820, that the name had been used in his family in Plantagenet times, that it was that of Charlemagne's sister, and (probably) the same as Adah, wife of Lamech in Genesis 4:19. Poe omitted it in 1829, but used it in line 95 of 1831.

311 (1827) Poe echoes the opening of Bryant's "Thanatopsis":

> To him who in the love of Nature holds
> Communion with her visible forms, she speaks
> A various language.

This form was in the version of 1821 and later. Compare also the first lines of Poe's own "Stanzas" (1827) below.

337 (1827) Zinghis is Genghis Khan, a reputed ancestor of Tamerlane. See also Poe's own first note on his poem.

339 (1827) Despite the absence of quotation marks, most of this line is taken verbatim from Byron's *Childe Harold*, III, xxi, 1. In the Wilmer manuscript version of 1828 it was retained with a change of "by night" to "tonight."

347 (1827) Compare Gray's "Elegy," "Melancholy mark'd him for her own."

355 (1827) Compare Poe's "Coliseum," line 3, "buried centuries of pomp and power."

373 (1827) Note 10 Poe quotes from Byron, *The Bride of Abydos*, I, vi, 22. See also "Marginalia," number 32, for Poe's fancy of a relation, which he thought might be mathematical, between a ray of orange light and the buzzing of a gnat.

389 (1827) Note 11 The dayflower is any member of the genus *Commelina*; the flowers last only a day. In this country members of the genus *Tradescantia* are also called dayflowers.

402 Compare Gray's "Elegy," "Full many a flower is born to blush unseen."

SONG
("I saw thee on thy bridal day")

This poem follows "Tamerlane" immediately in the volume of 1827, and I think it, too, concerns Elmira Royster. In the *Literary Era*, August 1901, Edward M. Alfriend wrote of her:

> She told me that when Poe left Richmond, before her marriage to Mr. Shelton, she and Poe were engaged to be married; that her father intercepted their letters, and both she and Poe became convinced that each had forgotten the other, and that she, urged by her father, and in a spirit of spite, determined to marry Mr. Shelton; thàt Poe returned to Richmond on the day of the night of her marriage, came to her home while the wedding party was going on, not knowing of her marriage, . . . and asked her to dance with him; — she then told him of her marriage, and he was so grief stricken that he left the house at once, and she did not dance again that evening; but Poe remained long enough for each to tell the other of the intercepted letters and for each to learn of the other's love and loyalty.

This story is not strictly true, for the Sheltons were not married until December 6, 1828, when Poe was not in Richmond. But I do not think Alfriend invented it. He was the last editor, in 1864, of the *Southern Literary Messenger*, and he and his father, Thomas M. Alfriend, knew Poe, the Allans, and the Sheltons socially. The father was a regular visitor at the Shelton home. It is my conjecture that the party was to celebrate Elmira Royster's engagement — and that later the lady's memory was confused, or perhaps (in her character of "Annabel Lee") she made the story more romantic. She was demonstrably inconsistent in her statements about the poet. There is a reference to the hero seeing his beloved on her bridal day in W. H. Poe's story "The Pirate": " 'Miss Rose is to be married in half an hour!' . . . a wealthy suitor had been . . . accepted . . . an interview . . . was impossible, but if I would stand in the passage I might see her as she passed to the room." (See Allen and Mabbott, *Poe's Brother* [1926], p. 58.)

TEXTS

(*A*) *Tamerlane and Other Poems* (1827), p. 25; (*B*) Wilmer manuscript, 1828, on the recto of "To the River —"; (*C*) *Al Aaraaf, Tamerlane, and Minor Poems* (1829), p. 61; (*D*) John Neal's presentation copy of *Al Aaraaf* . . .

with manuscript change in line 4; (E) Herring copy of *Al Aaraaf* . . . changed in line 7 in 1845; (F) *The Raven and Other Poems* (1845), p. 90; (G) *Broadway Journal*, September 20, 1845 (2:166); (H) *Works* (1850), II, 110.

The text given is *F*, verbally identical with *E, G*, and *H*. I saw the Wilmer manuscript (*B*), described by Stedman and Woodberry, *The Works of Edgar Allan Poe* (1894–95), X, 230, in the collection of Oliver Barrett in Chicago. The copy of *Al Aaraaf* Poe presented to John Neal (*D*) was cut down in rebinding, and Poe's abortive change is damaged. The volume was shown me in 1966 by a Boston bookseller.

SONG [F]

I saw thee on thy bridal day —
   When a burning blush came o'er thee,
Though happiness around thee lay,
   The world all love before thee:

5   And in thine eye a kindling light
   (Whatever it might be)
Was all on Earth my aching sight
   Of Loveliness could see.

That blush, perhaps, was maiden shame —
10   As such it well may pass —
Though its glow hath raised a fiercer flame
   In the breast of him, alas!

Who saw thee on that bridal day,
   When that deep blush *would* come o'er thee,
15   Though happiness around thee lay,
   The world all love before thee.   [1827–1845]

VARIANTS

Title: To — — (*A*); In an Album. To — (*B*)
1 thy/the (*A*)
4 *Beside this line in D, Poe wrote* As heedless [as (?)] *probably as a substitution for the beginning of the line.*
5 a/the (*A*)

5–8 *Not in B, where Poe wrote* 4 lines omitted see last page *but the page is now lost.*
6 Of young passion free (*A*)
7 aching/chain'd (*A*); fetter'd (*C*)
8 could/might (*A*)
9 perhaps/I ween (*A*)
13 thee/*misprinted* the (*A*)

DREAMS

SONG: NOTES

Title   The 1827 title read "To — —." The blanks probably stand for "Elmira Royster." The lines may also have been written later in another lady's album, as the title "In an Album" suggests.

1   The opening line and some of the rest of the poem were found by Whitty to be very similar to a poem in the Philadelphia *Saturday Evening Post* of July 15, 1826, by John Lofland, the "Milford Bard," who reprinted it in his volume, *The Harp of Delaware* (1828), pp. 27–28. Of the original text Mr. Bunford Samuel sent me a copy, which is used here. The firm of Ellis and Allan owned a file of the *Post* for 1826, and Poe may well have had in mind the opening that follows:

THE BRIDE

I saw her on the bridal day
In blushing beauty blest.
Smiles o'er her lips were seen to play
Like gilded gleams at dawn of day,
The fairest of the guest . . .
And now a tear stole from her eye,
And mingled with her softer sigh;
Now wish'd it not, now wish'd it here,
And blush'd to think the hour so near.

2   Compare Poe's tale "The Assignation": "Why *should* the lady blush! . . . what other possible reason could there have been for her so blushing?"

4   Compare *Paradise Lost*, XII, 646: "The world was all before them." Nelson Adkins in *Notes and Queries* (London), July 21, 1934, p. 67, compares also the opening of a poem by Fitz-Greene Halleck in *The Croakers* (1819), "To * * * * *":

The world is bright before thee,
Its summer flowers are thine;
Its calm blue sky is o'er thee,
Thy bosom pleasure's shrine.

DREAMS

The poem is obviously early, and in a Byronic mood. Killis Campbell (*Poems*, pages 157–158) cites two passages possibly reflected: "The Dream," I, 19–21,

. . . The mind can make
Substance, and people planets of its own
With beings brighter than have been . . .

and *Childe Harold*, III, xiv, 1–3,

> Like the Chaldean, he could watch the stars,
> Till he had peopled them with beings bright
> As their own beams . . .

also connected with lines 6–7 of Poe's "Imitation":

> . . . waking thought
> Of beings that have been.

TEXTS

(A) *Tamerlane and Other Poems* (1827), pp. 26–27; (B) Baltimore *North American*, October 20, 1827; (C) manuscript (1828).

The manuscript (C) in Edgar Allan Poe's hand, and once owned by Lambert A. Wilmer, is the latest text and is followed, by permission of the Trustees of the Pierpont Morgan Library. The second version (B) was initialed "W.H.P." by Edgar's brother, but (although complete) is headed "Extract," presumably as a disclaimer of authorship.

DREAMS [C]

Oh! that my young life were a lasting dream!
My spirit not awak'ning till the beam
Of an Eternity should bring the morrow:
Yes! tho' that long dream were of hopeless sorrow,
5   'Twere better than the dull reality
Of waking life to him whose heart shall be,
And hath been ever, on the chilly earth,
A chaos of deep passion from his birth!

But should it be — that dream eternally
10 Continuing — as dreams have been to me
In my young boyhood — should it thus be given,
'Twere folly still to hope for higher Heaven!
For I have revell'd, when the sun was bright
In the summer sky; in dreamy fields of light,
15 And left unheedingly my very heart
In climes of mine imagining — apart
From mine own home, with beings that have been
Of mine own thought — what more could I have seen?

DREAMS

'Twas once and *only* once and the wild hour
20   From my remembrance shall not pass — some power
Or spell had bound me — 'twas the chilly wind
Came o'er me in the night and left behind
Its image on my spirit, or the moon
Shone on my slumbers in her lofty noon
25   Too coldly — or the stars — howe'er it was
That dream was as that night wind — let it pass.

I have been happy — tho' but in a dream.
I have been happy — and I love the theme —
Dreams! in their vivid colouring of life —
30   As in that fleeting, shadowy, misty strife
Of semblance with reality which brings
To the delirious eye more lovely things
Of Paradise and Love — and all our own!
Than young Hope in his sunniest hour hath known.

[1827–1828]

VARIANTS

5 dull/cold (*A*, *B*)
6 shall be/must be (*A*)
7 And hath been still, upon the lovely earth (*A*, *B*)
14 In the summer sky, in dreams of living light (*A*, *B*) [*except that the first word is from broken types in A*

and may be meant for I']
15 And loveliness — have left my very heart (*A*, *B*)
16 Inclines of mine imaginary apart (*A*)
20 remembrance/remembering (*B*)
27 tho' but/tho' (*A*)

NOTES

19 The language reminds one of the opening line of the late poem "To Helen Whitman": "I saw thee once — once only" — and of a passage in the tale "Eleonora": "Once — oh, but once only, I was awakened from a slumber . . . by the pressing of spiritual lips upon my own."

19–26 These lines, Richard Wilbur (*Poe*, pp. 119–120) suggests, answer the question of the preceding line. The poet has once — but only once — had a mystic experience, becoming aware of the reality of his visions. Campbell (*Poems*, p. 158) thought the reference was to the moment when Poe realized his poetic genius.

30 The description is of a daydream, according to Wilbur as cited above.

SPIRITS OF THE DEAD

In this poem, says Woodberry (1909, I, 44), "the treatment of landscape is wholly Poe's own . . . it affords the first glimpse of that new tract of Acheron . . . which he revealed" — a place "out of space, out of time."

On the surface the poem merely says that one who visits a churchyard communes through memory with the departed. But I share Campbell's idea (*Poems*, p. 158) that the poem is inspired by the long incantation at the end of the first scene of Byron's *Manfred*, which is believed to refer to the last unsuccessful attempt at a reconciliation with Lady Byron. Poe's poem may be meant to say to Elmira Royster merely, "You never can quite forget the person you wronged." The most significant lines from *Manfred* are:

> And the meteor on the grave,
>   And the wisp on the morass; . . .
> And the silent leaves are still
> In the shadow of the hill,
> Shall my soul be upon thine,
> With a power and a sign. . . .
> There are shades which will not vanish,
> There are thoughts thou canst not banish;
> By a Power to thee unknown,
> Thou canst never be alone . . .
> And to thee shall Night deny
> All the quiet of her sky . . .

The version of Poe's poem in his volume of 1827 contained two obvious misprints: "ferver" in line 17, which in text *A* below I have corrected to "fever" because of the rhyme, and "wish" in line 24, usually corrected to "mist" from the later versions, but here changed to "wisp," which is in the Byronic source and is a less radical change from "wish." About 1828 Poe made a number of changes in a manuscript version retitled "Spirits of the Dead." (This manuscript, once in the possession of Lambert A. Wilmer, is, *pace* Woodberry, in Poe's own hand.) In 1829 he published the poem, still further revised, in his second little volume. In 1839 it was used as an unsigned filler in *Burton's Gentleman's Magazine*. Griswold did not collect it, but it was pointed out as a new poem by Poe in the little periodical of the Washington Sanitary Fair, the *Roll Call*, of March 12, 1864. E. L. Didier collected it in *The Life and Poems of Edgar Allan Poe* in 1877.

TEXTS

(*A*) *Tamerlane and Other Poems* (1827), pp. 27–28; (*B*) Wilmer manuscript, 1828, now owned by H. Bradley Martin; (*C*) *Al Aaraaf, Tamerlane, and Minor Poems* (1829), pp. 65–66; (*D*) *Burton's Gentleman's Magazine*, July 1839 (5:51).

VISIT OF THE DEAD [*A*]

* * * *

Thy soul shall find itself alone —
Alone of all on earth — unknown
The cause — but none are near to pry
Into thine hour of secrecy.
5   Be silent in that solitude,
Which is not loneliness — for then
The spirits of the dead, who stood
In life before thee, are again
In death around thee, and their will
10 Shall then o'ershadow thee — be still:
For the night, tho' clear, shall frown:
And the stars shall look not down
From their thrones, in the dark heav'n;
With light like Hope to mortals giv'n,
15 But their red orbs, without beam,
To thy withering heart shall seem
As a burning, and a fever
Which would cling to thee forever.
But 'twill leave thee, as each star
20 In the morning light afar
Will fly thee — and vanish:
— But its *thought* thou can'st not banish.
The breath of God will be still;
And the wisp upon the hill
25 By that summer breeze unbrok'n

Shall charm thee — as a token,
And a symbol which shall be
Secrecy in thee.   [1827]

SPIRITS OF THE DEAD [D]

I

Thy soul shall find itself alone
'Mid dark thoughts of the gray tomb-stone —
Not one, of all the crowd, to pry
Into thine hour of secrecy:

II

5   Be silent in that solitude,
       Which is not loneliness — for then
    The spirits of the dead who stood
       In life before thee are again
    In death around thee — and their will
10 Shall overshadow thee: be still.

III

    The night — tho' clear — shall frown —
    And the stars shall look not down,
    From their high thrones in the heaven,
    With light like Hope to mortals given —
15 But their red orbs, without beam,
    To thy weariness shall seem
    As a burning and a fever
    Which would cling to thee for ever.

IV

    Now are thoughts thou shalt not banish —
20 Now are visions ne'er to vanish —
    From thy spirit shall they pass
    No more — like dew-drop from the grass.

EVENING STAR

V

The breeze — the breath of God — is still —
And the mist upon the hill

25 Shadowy — shadowy — yet unbroken,
Is a symbol and a token —
How it hangs upon the trees,
A mystery of mysteries! —   [1827–39]

VARIANTS

Title: The Spirits of the Dead (B)
  5 that/thy (B)
10 overshadow/then o'ershadow (B)
18 *After this B adds:*

But 'twill leave thee as each star
With the dewdrop flies afar.
19 shalt/can'st (B)
21–22 *Transposed in B*

NOTES

5–10 Compare "Dream-Land," lines 31–38.

6 Campbell *(Poems,* p. 159) has a long note on the proverb "Never less alone than when alone," which has been traced back to Cicero, and, in English, to Shakespeare — and was used by Byron.

23 Compare "The City in the Sea," lines 38–41, and "The Valley of Unrest," lines 11–19.

26 See "Stanzas" (1827), line 24, for "a symbol and a token."

EVENING STAR

The chief interest of this poem lies in its foreshadowing of "Ulalume." The Evening Star thought of as warm is, of course, the planet Venus, the Lady of Love, the crescent Astarte of the later poem.

Campbell *(Poems,* pp. 160–161) suggests what may be accepted as sure, that Poe had in mind the opening lines of one of Thomas Moore's *Irish Melodies,* "While Gazing on the Moon's Light":

> While gazing on the moon's light,
>   A moment from her smile I turn'd,
> To look at orbs, that, more bright,
>   In lone and distant glory burn'd.
>   But *too* far
>   Each proud star,

For me to feel its warming flame;
　　Much more dear
　　That mild sphere,
Which near our planet smiling came.

Poe, who commented on the coldness of the moon in "Tamer-lane," "Dreams," "Al Aaraaf," and "Ulalume," wrote "Evening Star" as a reply to Moore's verses. Similar replies by Poe to poems of other authors are "Sonnet — Silence" and "Eulalie."

TEXT

Tamerlane and Other Poems (1827), pp. 28–29, is the text here followed. There are no variants, for Poe printed the poem only once, and no manuscripts are known.

EVENING STAR

'Twas noontide of summer,
　　And mid-time of night;
And stars, in their orbits,
　　Shone pale, thro' the light
5　Of the brighter, cold moon,
　　'Mid planets her slaves,
Herself in the Heavens,
　　Her beam on the waves.
　　I gaz'd awhile
10　　On her cold smile;
Too cold — too cold for me —
　　There pass'd, as a shroud,
　　A fleecy cloud,
And I turn'd away to thee,
15　　Proud Evening Star,
　　In thy glory afar,
And dearer thy beam shall be;
　　For joy to my heart
　　Is the proud part
20　Thou bearest in Heav'n at night,
　　And more I admire
　　Thy distant fire,
Than that colder, lowly light.　　[1827]

IMITATION

"Imitation," in the 1827 volume and "To —— ——" ("Should my early life seem") of 1829 have usually been treated as variants of "A Dream Within a Dream" (1849). But they have so little in common that I treat them here as three separate poems under their proper years. The second poem uses but one line (4) unaltered from the first, and the third none at all. For the general meaning of the poem see the 1827 version of "Tamerlane," lines 160ff.

TEXT

There is only one text, *Tamerlane and Other Poems* (1827), pp. 29–30, which Poe surely did not see in proof. I emend two sure misprints: "on" to "of" in line 12 and "sight" to "sigh" in line 18, and change the comma in line 8, for sense, to a period. The spelling "controul" in line 13 was probably tolerated in 1827.

IMITATION

A dark unfathom'd tide
Of interminable pride —
A mystery, and a dream,
Should my early life seem;
5   I say that dream was fraught
With a wild, and waking thought
Of beings that have been,
Which my spirit hath not seen.
Had I let them pass me by,
10   With a dreaming eye!
Let none of earth inherit
That vision of my spirit;
Those thoughts I would controul,
As a spell upon his soul:
15   For that bright hope at last
And that light time have past,
And my worldly rest hath gone
With a sigh as it pass'd on:
I care not tho' it perish
20   With a thought I then did cherish.   [1827]

NOTES

Title: The imitation is of Byron. Compare lines 6–10 with "The Dream," I, 7: "They leave a weight upon our waking thoughts . . ." and I, 21: "With beings brighter than have been . . ." and *Manfred*, I, i, 212–213: "Though thou seest me not pass by, / Thou shalt feel me with thine eye."

9–10   The lines express a wish.

19–20   Byron's "Dream" is about Mary Chaworth, whom that poet failed to win, as Poe failed to wed Elmira Royster. In his youth Poe probably loved Elmira deeply. But his plate article in the *Columbian Magazine* for December 1844, "Byron and Miss Chaworth," makes it clear that in middle life Poe took a cool view of early love.

STANZAS

This poem is one of the most difficult Poe ever wrote; the explanation by Wilbur (*Poe*, p. 122) may be synopsized. In youth the author communed with nature, especially the sun and stars, but did not understand the "power" (1–8). He questions if it be madness (9–10) — but believes it is visionary (11–16). Intuitively he finds profound meaning in common things (17–24). Beauty, foreshadowing Heaven, draws him by the grace of God away from a fall threatened by his pride (25–32).

The motto inexactly quoted from Byron, *The Island*, II, xvi, 13–16 (published June 26, 1823), is a good commentary on the poem, in conjunction with two remarks of Poe. On July 2, 1844, he wrote James Russell Lowell: "There are epochs when . . . nothing yields me pleasure but solitary communion with the 'mountains and the woods' — the 'altars' of Byron. I have . . . rambled and dreamed . . ." To his friend Thomas M. Alfriend he said, probably in the summer of 1849: "Nature rests me, I always find a calm with nature that I seek in vain everywhere else, and no matter how great my perturbation, she never fails to bring me peace." The remark is recorded by Alfriend's son, Edward, in the *Literary Era*, August 1901.

TEXT

The only original form is that of *Tamerlane and Other Poems* (1827), pp. 30–32, untitled, which presents three incorrect readings. In line 7, I have

STANZAS

changed "knew — not" to "knew not —"; in line 10 "ferver" may be for "fever" (as the rhyme shows it is in "Visit of the Dead" line 18), but, since here the intention may be "fervor," I forbear emendation; line 24 closes with what looks like a period, but might be a broken comma; since sense demands the latter, I print a comma. The title "Stanzas" was given the poem by Stedman and Woodberry, in *Works*, X, 122.

[STANZAS]

How often we forget all time, when lone
Admiring Nature's universal throne;
Her woods — her wilds — her mountains — the intense
Reply of HERS to OUR intelligence!

1

In youth have I known one with whom the Earth
In secret communing held — as he with it,
In day light, and in beauty from his birth:
Whose fervid, flick'ring torch of life was lit
5 From the sun and stars, whence he had drawn forth
A passionate light — such for his spirit was fit —
And yet that spirit knew not — in the hour
Of its own fervor — what had o'er it power.

2

Perhaps it may be that my mind is wrought
10 To a ferver by the moon beam that hangs o'er,
But I will half believe that wild light fraught
With more of sov'reignty than ancient lore
Hath ever told — or is it of a thought
The unembodied essence, and no more
15 That with a quick'ning spell doth o'er us pass
As dew of the night-time, o'er the summer grass?

3

Doth o'er us pass, when, as th' expanding eye
To the loved object — so the tear to the lid

· 7 7 ·

Will start, which lately slept in apathy?
20 And yet it need not be — (that object) hid
From us in life — but common — which doth lie
Each hour before us — but *then* only bid
With a strange sound, as of a harp-string broken
T'awake us — 'Tis a symbol and a token,

4

25 Of what in other worlds shall be — and giv'n
In beauty by our God, to those alone
Who otherwise would fall from life and Heav'n
Drawn by their heart's passion, and that tone,
That high tone of the spirit which hath striv'n
30 Tho' not with Faith — with godliness — whose throne
With desp'rate energy 't hath beaten down;
Wearing its own deep feeling as a crown.   [1827]

NOTES

1–2 Compare the opening of Bryant's "Thanatopsis," quoted in the note on "Tamerlane" of 1827, lines 311ff.

13–14 Compare "To Marie Louise," line 12: "Unthoughtlike thoughts that are the souls of thought."

17–25 Campbell (*Poems,* pp. 164–165) compares this with *Childe Harold,* IV, xxiii:

> And slight withal may be the things which bring
> Back on the heart the weight which it would fling
> Aside forever: it may be a sound —
> A tone of music — summer's eve — or spring —
> A flower — the wind — the ocean . . .

23 See note on "The Coliseum," line 36, for an explanation of the statue which greeted the dawn with the weird sound of a breaking harpstring. The sound was emitted also by the stone on which Apollo placed his lyre at the building of the walls of Megara; E. C. Pinkney refers to this in "A Picture Song," lines 21–22, "Apollo placed his harp, of old, a while upon a stone,/ Which has resounded since, when struck, a breaking harp-string's tone." The story is in Ovid's *Metamorphoses,* VIII, 14f.

24 "A symbol and a token" is also in "Spirits of the Dead," line 26.

27–28 Compare "Al Aaraaf" (1829), II, 263–264: "Heaven to them no hope imparts/ Who hear not for the beating of their hearts."

A DREAM

The poem seems to refer to the loss of Mrs. Jane Stith Craig Stanard ("Helen") and of Elmira Royster; the canceled first stanza suggests that it was composed after Poe left the Allan home in Richmond.

It is partly, as Wilbur observed in his *Poe* (1959), pages 122–123, based on Byron's "I would I were a Careless Child," lines 21–24:

> Once I beheld a splendid dream,
> A visionary scene of bliss!
> Truth! — wherefore did thy hated beam
> Awake me to a world like this?

TEXTS

(A) *Tamerlane and Other Poems* (1827), pp. 32–33; (B) *Al Aaraaf, Tamerlane, and Minor Poems* (1829), p. 67; (C) Herring copy of *Al Aaraaf . . .* with manuscript changes, 1845; (D) *Broadway Journal*, August 16, 1845 (2:85); (E) *The Raven and Other Poems* (1845), p. 83; (F) *Works* (1850), II, 105.

The text used here is E, which like D was set up from C.

A DREAM [E]

In visions of the dark night
   I have dreamed of joy departed —
But a waking dream of life and light
   Hath left me broken-hearted.

5   Ah! what is not a dream by day
   To him whose eyes are cast
On things around him with a ray
   Turned back upon the past?

    That holy dream — that holy dream,
10   While all the world were chiding,
Hath cheered me as a lovely beam
   A lonely spirit guiding.

What though that light, thro' storm and night,
   So trembled from afar —
15   What could there be more purely bright
   In Truth's day-star?   [1827–1845]

VARIANTS

Title: *Untitled in A*

1 *Before this A inserts:*
   A wilder'd being from my birth
   My spirit spurn'd control,
   But now, abroad on the wide earth,
   Where wand'rest thou my soul?

5 Ah!/And (*A, B*)
13 storm and night/misty night (*A*)
14 trembled from/dimly shone (*A*)

NOTES

2 Compare the second version of Burns's "The Banks o' Doon": "Thou minds me o' departed joys,/ Departed — never to return!" Also compare *Politian*, IV, 66.

3–4 Compare *The Troubadour* by Letitia E. Landon (1825), I, 138–141:

   He dreams a dream of life and light,
      And grasps the rainbow that appears
   Afar all beautiful and bright,
      And finds it only form'd of tears.

Poe in *Graham's* for August 1841 writes nostalgically of Miss Landon ("L.E.L."), an English poetess popular at the time, "all who have loved, in other days, the poetry of this sweet writer"; he mentioned her affectionately also in his acrostic "Elizabeth." His appreciation of her work was real if indulgent, and her influence may be found even in Poe's *Poems* of 1831.

16 "Day-star" is the sun, as in "Lycidas," line 168.

THE HAPPIEST DAY

The poem is not easy to interpret, and includes one crux. There is no doubt that it is personal, but there is less certainty that it concerns Elmira Royster. The "happiest day" may have been that on which the poet realized his genius and also divined that, in the long run, men of genius are often unhappy. It may be the day he left Richmond for the University of Virginia, with high hopes of success and of his lady's love, but not without vague forebodings. Or it may have been the day of his return to Richmond, when his high hopes were dashed to earth by the discovery that Elmira was lost to him. It is also suggested that he had the mystic experience in mind.

However personal, the piece, like its author at the time, is Byronic. W. P. Trent was reminded of Byron's famous lines on his thirty-sixth birthday (1824).

A few months after its first publication, the poem was printed, with a number of changes, in the Baltimore *North American*. There it is headed "Original" but signed "W.H.P.," the mark of Poe's brother — who may well have been the reviser, in view of the tame quality of the new lines. The piece received no title from either Poe. There is a facsimile of the Baltimore text in Allen and Mabbott, *Poe's Brother*, page 43.

TEXTS

(*A*) *Tamerlane and Other Poems* (1827), pp. 33–34; (*B*) Baltimore *North American*, September 15, 1827.

[THE HAPPIEST DAY] [*A*]

The happiest day — the happiest hour
　　My sear'd and blighted heart hath known,
The highest hope of pride, and power,
　　I feel hath flown.

5　　Of power! said I? Yes! such I ween
　　But they have vanish'd long alas!
The visions of my youth have been —
　　But let them pass.

And, pride, what have I now with thee?
10　　Another brow may ev'n inherit
The venom thou hast pour'd on me —
　　Be still my spirit.

The happiest day — the happiest hour
　　Mine eyes shall see — have ever seen

15   The brightest glance of pride and power
        I feel — have been:

     But were that hope of pride and power
        Now offer'd, with the pain
     Ev'n *then* I felt — that brightest hour
20   I would not live again:

     For on its wing was dark alloy
        And as it flutter'd — fell
     An essence — powerful to destroy
        A soul that knew it well.   [1827]

VARIANTS

2 hath/has *(B)*
3 highest hope/brightest glance *(B)*
4 hath/has *(B)*
6 they have/it has *(B)*
10 ev'n/e'en *(B)*
12 *After this line, B gives a new stanza:*

  The smile of love — soft friendship's charm —
  Bright hope itself has fled at last,
  'Twill ne'er again my bosom warm —
  'Tis ever past.

16 have/has *(B)*
17–24 *Omitted from B.*

NOTES

2 Compare Byron's "Fare thee well," line 59, "Sear'd in heart, and lone, and blighted," also echoed in "Tamerlane" (1827), line 28, and *Politian*, VII, 28.

10–11 This is the crux; Campbell (*Poems*, page 167) saw in the word "inherit" an allusion to a new heir for John Allan, a theory combated by the fact that his first wife was alive in 1827. If the poem concerns Elmira Royster, it is a reproach that a woman who was cruel to her first fiancé might prove so to her husband. Compare the severity of "To [Elmira]" ("The bowers whereat, in dreams, I see"). A more general idea may be that Pride, renounced by the poet, may find another genius, equally unwise, to injure.

21–24 Compare "Romance," lines 11–27.

23 Campbell (*Poems*, page 167) compared this to *Manfred*, I, i, 233: "An essence which hath strength to kill."

THE LAKE

This is the best of Poe's early poems. It comes last in his first volume, and even in its first form shows maturity and power.

THE LAKE

It is founded on fact, recording a visit near sunset to a place reputedly haunted by the ghosts of two lovers, neither unfriendly nor truly unhappy. The place is the Lake of the Dismal Swamp. That strange body of water is not really rockbound, but the driftwood on its shores, when wet, looks like black rock, and the water was believed to be poisonous. The identification was made by Professor Robert Morrison in the *Explicator*, December 1948, after he had visited the spot. It may be firmly accepted, for no other lake Poe is likely to have known, so closely fitting his description, has been discovered by commentators.[1]

Thomas Moore visited the place in 1803, and then, at nearby Norfolk, Virginia, wrote "A Ballad: The Lake of the Dismal Swamp," with a quoted anonymous foreword: "They tell of a young man who lost his mind upon the death of a girl he loved, and who, suddenly disappearing from his friends, was never afterwards heard of. As he had frequently said, in his ravings, that the girl was not dead, but gone to the Dismal Swamp, it is supposed he had wandered into that dreary wilderness, and . . . been lost."

In the poem Moore says that the "deadly vine doth weep/Its venomous tear" and goes on —

> But oft, from the Indian hunter's camp
> This lover and maid so true
> Are seen at the hour of the midnight damp
> To cross the Lake by a fire-fly lamp,
> And paddle their white canoe!

Moore does not mention the blackness of the shores, but Poe had seen them, as he indicated in the poem. We have no other reference to a visit to Norfolk before 1827, but E. M. Alfriend in the *Literary Era*, August 1901, tells of Poe's visits, alone, to the wild islands in the James River between Richmond and Manchester, among beds of great granite rocks, over which the river

---

[1] Prior to Morrison's discussion in 1948, students were much puzzled by the poem. C. W. Kent and R. M. Hogg sought for such a tarn in Scotland, but there the rocks are not black or the waters poisoned. Nor is Poe's scene a place like Patrick's Purgatory in Donegal, about which Moore has a song, "I wish I was by that dim lake," in *Irish Melodies*, which Poe praised in "The Poetic Principle."

leaps and bounds, where he spent "hours amid wild and beautiful localities, musing with nature."

The poet, recalling his visits, shares imaginatively the delusion of the lover who found in the waves a heaven for his beloved, and now haunts the lake in her company.

The poem, with some changes, was reprinted in *Al Aaraaf, Tamerlane, and Minor Poems* (1829). A cut and much altered version was inserted in the 1831 version of "Tamerlane," where the lines are put into the mouth of the hero and — some of them — addressed to the heroine, Ada. The poem was again collected under its own title in *The Raven and Other Poems* (1845) and by Griswold in *Works* (1850).

Meanwhile, toward the end of 1845 it was published in *The Missionary Memorial* for 1846. This text seems definitely earlier than that in *The Raven and Other Poems*. It was the custom to reprint gift books from stereotype plates with new dates and titles on occasion. During Poe's lifetime the compilation published in 1845 as *The Missionary Memorial* appeared with the title *Christ's Messengers: or the Missionary Memorial*, issued at New York as of 1847 and 1848. *The Missionary Offering, a Memorial*, Auburn, New York, dated 1850, possibly appeared while Poe was still alive. See Ralph Thompson, *American Literary Annuals* (1936), page 141, for six other reprints.

TEXTS

(*A*) *Tamerlane and Other Poems* (1827), p. 34; (*B*) Wilmer manuscript, 1828, now in the Pierpont Morgan Library; (*C*) *Al Aaraaf, Tamerlane, and Minor Poems* (1829), pp. 64–65; (*D*) *Poems* (1831), pp. 115–116 (in "Tamerlane" as lines 79–99); (*E*) *The Missionary Memorial* for 1846, pp. 324–325; (*F*) *The Raven and Other Poems* (1845), p. 89; (*G*) *Works* (1850), II, 109.

Texts *A* and *F* are given in full, *D* above at pp. 47–48.

THE LAKE [*A*]

In youth's spring, it was my lot
To haunt of the wide earth a spot
The which I could not love the less;

THE LAKE

So lovely was the loneliness
Of a wild lake, with black rock bound,
And the tall trees that tower'd around.
But when the night had thrown her pall
Upon that spot — as upon all,
And the wind would pass me by
In its stilly melody,
My infant spirit would awake
To the terror of the lone lake.
Yet that terror was not fright —
But a tremulous delight,
And a feeling undefin'd,
Springing from a darken'd mind.
Death was in that poison'd wave
And in its gulf a fitting grave
For him who thence could solace bring
To his dark imagining;
Whose wild'ring thought could even make
An Eden of that dim lake.

[1827]

THE LAKE — TO —— [F]

In spring of youth it was my lot
To haunt of the wide world a spot
The which I could not love the less —
So lovely was the loneliness
Of a wild lake, with black rock bound,
And the tall pines that towered around.

But when the Night had thrown her pall
Upon that spot, as upon all,
And the mystic wind went by
Murmuring in melody —
Then — ah then I would awake
To the terror of the lone lake.

Yet that terror was not fright,
But a tremulous delight —
15 A feeling not the jewelled mine
Could teach or bribe me to define —
Nor Love — although the Love were thine.

Death was in that poisonous wave,
And in its gulf a fitting grave
20 For him who thence could solace bring
To his lone imagining —
Whose solitary soul could make
An Eden of that dim lake.   [1827–1845]

VARIANTS

1 In youth's spring it was my lot (B, C, E)
2 world/earth (B)
6 towered/tower'd (C, E)
9 mystic wind went/wind would pass me (B); black wind murmur'd (C); ghastly wind went (E)
10 Murmuring in/In a stilly (B); In a dirge of (C); In a dirge-like (E)
11 My boyish spirit would awake (B); My infant spirit would awake (C)

12 the lone/that lone (E)
15 And a feeling undefined (B); A feeling not the jewell'd mine (C, E)
16 Springing from a darken'd mind (B); Should ever bribe me to define (C)
17 Nor Love — altho' the Love be thine: (C)
18 poisonous/poison'd (B, C, E)
19 gulf/depth (E)

NOTES

Title: The Lake of the Dismal Swamp was formerly called Drummond's Pond; now it is usually Lake Drummond. The blank of the dedication cannot now be filled in; it did not appear during the lifetime of Poe's foster mother, in whose company he might have visited Norfolk.

1 Compare *Childe Harold*, III, iii, 1: "In my youth's summer I did sing of One."

18–19 Compare *Manfred*, I, ii, 103: "such would have been for me a fitting tomb." John Phelps Fruit, *The Mind and Art of Poe's Poetry* (1899), p. 18, thought the poem contained a hint of suicide. But this is precluded by the publication of "The Lake" in a religious annual, and by identification of the lake.

23 "Eden" here and in "To Frances," like "Aidenn" in "The Raven," means Heaven or Paradise. For the notion of spirits dwelling in the "heaven of a lake" see also "Irenë," lines 43–59.

POEMS COLLECTED
IN 1829

POEMS FIRST COLLECTED IN 1829

Al Aaraaf, Tamerlane, and Minor Poems. By Edgar A. Poe (Baltimore: Hatch and Dunning, 1829), came out late in the year. The negotiations for its production are discussed in my introduction to the title poem, "Al Aaraaf," and at p. 540, below. The publishers were two young men from New York; the printers, Matchett and Woods, named on the verso of the title page, brought out the Baltimore City Directory for fifty years. My reproduction of Poe's volume was published for the Facsimile Text Society by Columbia University Press, New York, in 1933.

The book has no preface but includes three playful introductory quotations:

Entiendes, Fabio, lo que voi deciendo?
Toma, si, lo entendio: — Mientes, Fabio.[1]

What has night to do with sleep?
COMUS.[2]

DEDICATION.
Who drinks the deepest? — here's to him.
— CLEVELAND.[3]

Following the major poems there is a half-title, MISCELLANEOUS POEMS, and on its verso there are two mottoes:

My nothingness — my want —
My sins — and my contrition —
SOUTHEY E PERSIS.[4]

And some flowers — *but no* bays.
MILTON.

[1] Lame Spanish from an unidentified play, meaning: "Fabio, do you understand what I tell you?" — "Yes, Thomas, I understand it" — "Fabio, you lie."

[2] Line 22 of Milton's masque.

[3] Line 36 of "A Song of Sack" in *The Works of John Cleveland* (1687). Poe probably saw it in an anthology, and would have cared little that its ascription is now doubted.

[4] From an epigram beginning "Four things not in thy treasury I bring before

POEMS COLLECTED IN 1829
SONNET—TO SCIENCE

This fine sonnet is used as an introduction to "Al Aaraaf" in all complete versions, and in 1841 was altered to serve as motto of the prose fantasy "The Island of the Fay." In his sonnet Poe proclaims his intention to disregard scientific fact when fantasy better suits his purpose.

The source of inspiration for Poe's sonnet is a passage in the *Études de la Nature* of Jacques-Henri Bernardin de Saint-Pierre, which in the notes to "Al Aaraaf" Poe quotes directly from Henry Hunter's translation. In the Philadelphia edition of 1808, *Studies of Nature* (II, 248), in a section on the "Pleasures of Ignorance," I find the idea that Poe put in verse at the end of his sonnet: "It is Science which has dragged down the chaste *Diana* from her nocturnal car: she has banished the Hamadryads from the antique forests, and the gentle Naiads from the fountains." [5]

TEXTS

(*A*) *Al Aaraaf, Tamerlane, and Minor Poems* (1829), p. 11; (*B*) Philadelphia *Saturday Evening Post*, September 11, 1830; (*C*) *The Casket*, October 1830 (5:480); (*D*) *Poems* (1831), p. 81; (*E*) *Southern Literary Messenger*, May 1836 (2:366); (*F*) *Graham's Magazine* for June 1841 (18:253), in "The Island of the Fay"; (*G*) Philadelphia *Saturday Museum*, March 4, 1843; (*H*) *Broadway Journal*, August 2, 1845 (2:54); (*J*) *The Raven and Other Poems* (1845), p. 55; (*K*) *Works* (1850), II, 77.

Text *J*, identical with *H*, is used here. *C* is from *B*'s type, left standing and reused. A version in *The Casket* for May 1831 is a reprint from *D*. The prospectus of *The Casket* in the *Post*, December 27, 1825, said that the monthly was to be made up of reprints of the best contributions to the weekly paper.

thee, / Lord, with my petition," contributed by Robert Southey to *The Bijou for 1828*, as "Imitation from the Persian." The original of the famous distich by the poet Souzeni may be seen with French translation in Herbelot's *Bibliothèque Orientale* (1697), page 830. The epigram is referred to by Voltaire in his *Poème sur le destruction de Lisbonne*, where Southey, deeply interested in Portugal, probably found it. The second motto, credited to Milton, is deliberately altered from "An Epitaph on the Marchioness of Winchester," line 57, "And some flowers and some bays."

[5] This source seems to have been first noticed in print by Palmer C. Holt in the *Bulletin* of the New York Public Library (November 1959). Far less close parallels in Keats' "Lamia" (I, 9–14; II, 229ff), cited by earlier commentators, may now be disregarded. It is not probable that Poe read Keats before 1830.

POEMS COLLECTED IN 1829

SONNET — TO SCIENCE [*J*]

Science! true daughter of Old Time thou art!
　　Who alterest all things with thy peering eyes.
Why preyest thou thus upon the poet's heart,
　　Vulture, whose wings are dull realities?
5　How should he love thee? or how deem thee wise,
　　Who wouldst not leave him in his wandering
To seek for treasure in the jewelled skies,
　　Albeit he soared with an undaunted wing?
Hast thou not dragged Diana from her car?
10　And driven the Hamadryad from the wood
To seek a shelter in some happier star?
　　Hast thou not torn the Naiad from her flood,
The Elfin from the green grass, and from me
The summer dream beneath the tamarind tree?

[1829–1843]

VARIANTS

Title:　*None* (*A, D, F*); Sonnet (*B, C, E*)
1　true/meet (*A, B, C, D, E*)
2　peering/piercing (*B, C*)
3　preyest/prey'st (*A, B, C, D, E, F, G, H*); the/thy (*B, C*)
5　should/shall (*B, C*)
7　jewelled/jewell'd (*A, B, C, D, E*)
8　soared/soar (*A, B, C, D, E*); he/be (*misprint F*)
9　dragged/dragg'd (*A, B, C, D, E*)
10　driven/driv'n (*A, D, E*)
11　To seek for shelter in some happier star (*B, C*); Hast thou not spoilt a story in each star (*F*)
12　The gentle Naiad from her fountain-flood (*A, D, E*); The gentle Nais from the fountain flood (*B, C*)
13　green grass/greenwood (*B, C*)
13–14　The elfin from the grass? — the dainty *fay*, The witch, the sprite, the goblin — where are they? (*F*)
14　summer/summer's (*B, C*); tamarind tree/shrubbery (*A, B, C, D, E*)

NOTES

12　(1830) "Nais" is good Greek, although the more usual form is "Naias"; Ausonius uses the shorter form in his *Mosella*, line 82, and Keats has it in his *Endymion*, III, 899.

13–14　With the version of 1841 compare "The Domain of Arnheim": "the phantom handiwork, conjointly, of the Sylphs, of the Fairies, of the Genii, and of the Gnomes."

14　The tamarind tree (*Tamarindus indica*), tall and spreading, has yellow flowers striped with red, and produces pods which are the source of a spice used in medicine and cookery. Originally from the Orient, whence the name from Arabic, "date of India," the tamarind grew widely in both the East and West Indies by Poe's time, and his reference is no doubt to its fragrance.

AL AARAAF

In May 1829 Poe wrote to Isaac Lea, of the publishers Carey, Lea & Carey:

I send you, for your tenderest consideration, a poem . . .

Its title is "Al Aaraaf" — from the Al Aaraaf of the Arabians, a medium between Heaven & Hell where men suffer no punishment, but yet do not attain that tranquil & even happiness which they suppose to be the characteristic of heavenly enjoyment . . .

I have placed this "Al Aaraaf" in the celebrated star discovered by Tycho Brahe which appeared & disappeared so suddenly — It is represented as a messenger star of the Deity, &, at the time of its discovery by Tycho, as on an embassy to our world. One of the peculiarities of Al Aaraaf is that, even after death, those who make choice of the star as their residence do not enjoy immortality — but, after a second life of high excitement, sink into forgetfulness, & death — This idea is taken from Job — "I would not live always — let me alone" . . . I have imagined some well known characters of the age of the star's appearance, as transferred to Al Aaraaf — viz Michael Angelo — and others — of these Michael Angelo as yet, alone appears.

"Al Aaraaf" is the most difficult of Poe's poems, as well as the longest. A. H. Quinn (p. 161) remarked well that Poe was not trying primarily to present his story clearly, but experimenting "in the translation of feeling into harmony . . . neither words nor feeling alone, but a blending of both." Many lovers of poetry have read it with pleasure, for the sake of those "happy and melodious passages" in which, J. H. Ingram pointed out, "it abounds." [1] Poe himself wrote to John Neal, sometime in October or November 1829: "Al Aaraaf has some good poetry and much extravagance which I have not had time to throw away."

The poem as a whole has baffled so many readers — including such sympathetic lovers of Poe as E. C. Stedman and Charles W. Kent [2] — that it may be well to say at once that it has a definite, if

---

[1] Ingram, *Edgar Allan Poe: His Life, Letters and Opinions* (1885), p. 64.

[2] Stedman in *Works*, ed. Stedman and Woodberry, X, xx; Kent in *Complete Works*, ed. Harrison, VII, xvii.

not a well-told, story. This students of Poe have discovered — though hardly at first reading — to be *not* past finding out. The following scenario tells the story in plain prose.

PLOT

Part I. The ethereal beauty of the "wandering star" is described (1–15). The ruling angel Nesace bathes in the light of four suns (16–29) and prepares to pray (30–41). Her silent, hence spiritual, prayers are borne to heaven by the odors of the many flowers catalogued by the poet (42–81). The prayer expresses the angels' obedience to God in seeking only beauty, not truth, which belongs to a higher heaven. His form is unknown, although man is made in His image in being intellectual (82–117). Nesace awaits in silence a divine command, through the music of the spheres, to visit other stars (133–150), which she prepares to obey (151–158).

Part II. A temple on a mountain is described (1–39), which Nesace enters (40–59) to sing a charm that summons her subjects (60–67). She invokes Ligeia, the music of Nature, to arouse the sleeping population of Al Aaraaf (68–155). The spirits assemble (156–173), save for two lovers (174–181). One of these, Angelo, on earth Michelangelo Buonarroti,[3] looks at his native planet (182–197) and tells his beloved Ianthe that he half wishes to return there (198–226). Ianthe (probably from another planet) says that the beauty of their present home and love should compensate him (227–230). Angelo seems to think that Earth was destroyed just after he left it (231–244), but Ianthe explains that it merely trembled (245–260). Ignoring Nesace's orders, the inattentive lovers sleep forever (261–264).

The action definitely takes place in 1574, the year in which Tycho's star faded from the ken of humanity, but Poe's locale is

---

[3] Poe distinctly says, both in the introduction to the extract from his poem in the Baltimore *Gazette* of May 18, 1829, and in his letter to Isaac Lea quoted above, that Angelo is the spirit of Michelangelo. The material in the *Gazette* was first pointed out by the late Kenneth Rede in "Poe Notes," *American Literature* (March 1933); the letter to Lea was quoted later in the same year, on the same point, in my "Bibliographical Note" in the facsimile reprint of Poe's volume of 1829. Prior to 1933 no student of Poe seems even to have guessed a connection of Poe's hero with the painter-sculptor.

a place that is not meant to fit into any system of cosmology save one that he imagined.

This, of course, is merely the story on the surface, like the "Arguments" which old-time authors sometimes provided for their epics. Poe's poem is not primarily didactic or allegorical, for it surely has no carefully planned and consistent parallel meanings such as we seek in Dante or Spenser.

Nevertheless, it is not intended to be wholly without a message. Few will disagree with Vincent Buranelli, who calls Poe's Al Aaraaf a dream world, the spiritual home of the poet, where the Platonic idea of absolute beauty is known directly instead of through earth's imperfections.[4] Floyd Stovall argues, I think convincingly, that in "Al Aaraaf" Poe shadows forth a doctrine of poetry to which he adhered to the end.[5] The divine is known through beauty and power, best understood through the imagination.

To sum up briefly: Beauty is the sole object of poetry. Nesace is Beauty, Ligeia is Harmony, and through them the Will of God, or Truth, is imaginatively communicated to us, who are lacking in the complete knowledge given only to angels. True passion is too mundane for true poetry, and the intrusion of even the noble passion of love is fatal to the human spirits of Al Aaraaf. The poet also rejects an anthropomorphic idea of God, emphasizes His vastness and power (not merely in minor things like tempests), and His omnipresence. The doctrine at least verges on pantheism; spirit fills happy flowers, and even inanimate sculptures have flown in spirit to the new star.

Much of this appears again fancifully in the story of "The Fall of the House of Usher" in 1839. It has also been remarked that "Al Aaraaf" in a way foreshadows *Eureka* of 1848, but there Poe attempted to make his ideas conform to current scientific ideas, as he understood them.

[4] *Edgar Allan Poe* (1961), p. 97.

[5] See Stovall's important articles, "An Interpretation of Poe's 'Al Aaraaf'" and "Poe as a Poet of Ideas," *Studies in English*, no. 9 (University of Texas Bulletin, 1929) and no. 11 (1931). The earlier literature is largely synopsized there. Serious students should not neglect John Phelps Fruit, *Mind and Art of Poe's Poetry*, pp. 23ff., where Poe's Platonism is first discussed, and the pioneer work of William B. Cairns, "Some Notes on Poe's 'Al Aaraaf,'" *Modern Philology* (May 1915).

AL AARAAF

SOURCES

When on May 29, 1829, Poe wrote John Allan to ask for money to subsidize the publication of his poem, he said that he no longer was a follower of Byron. It is plain enough that he now had two masters, an incongruous pair, John Milton and Thomas Moore. Poe's poem has the obscurity of the first and more than the diffuseness of the second. The echoes are numerous from each, and the notes below might be increased by the citation of less striking parallels. These probably are not all unconscious; Poe was not yet so worried about such borrowings as he became later on. But he less often imitated Moore's verses in *Lalla Rookh* and *Loves of the Angels* than he versified Moore's footnotes. His own footnotes are modeled on those of Moore, and like them are sometimes more entertaining than the verses they accompany.

Poe also seems to have had in mind Vergil's *Georgics*, IV, 221–227, where it is said that God pervades all things, earth, sea, and sky — that from Him men and animals draw life, and that when they die, He remakes their spirits — that there is no annihilation, but "they mount up each into his own order of star, and take their appointed seat in the heavens." The direct quotation is from the motto used by Sarah Helen Whitman for a version of her poem "To Arcturus" in *Graham's Magazine* for June 1850. In that poem she says that Poe chose

> *Thee*, bright Arcturus ! for our spirit home —
> Our trysting star, where, while on earth's cold clime,
> Our mingling souls might meet in dreams sublime.

This is clearly based on some of Poe's romantic fancies in conversing with his "Helen of a thousand dreams." She removed the lines from later versions of the poem.

Poe presumably consulted Sale's English version of the Koran, first published in 1734 and cited frequently by Moore in *Lalla Rookh*. The seventh chapter is called "Al Ârâf" and reads in part:

And between the blessed and the damned there shall be a veil; and men shall stand on al Ârâf, who shall know everyone of them by their marks; and shall call unto the inhabitants of paradise, saying, Peace be upon you; yet they shall not enter therein, although they earnestly desire it. And when they shall turn their eyes towards the companions of hell fire, they shall say, O Lord, place us not with the ungodly people!

Sale comments at length in his "Preliminary Discourse" and says there is

a wall or partition . . . between (Heaven) and Hell . . . They call it al Orf . . . in the plural al Araf, from . . . arafa . . . to distinguish between things or to part them; some . . . give another reason for the . . . name, because, say they, those who stand on this partition will know and distinguish the blessed from the damned . . . and others say the word . . . intends anything . . . *high* raised or elevated . . . The Mahometan writers . . . differ as to the persons . . . on al Araf. Some imagine it to *be a sort of limbo,* for the patriarchs and prophets, or for the martyrs, and those . . . most eminent for sanctity, *among whom they say there will be also angels in the form of men.* Others place here such *whose good and evil works are so equal that they exactly counterpoise each other, and therefore deserve neither reward nor punishment* and will, on the last day be admitted to paradise, after they perform an act of adoration, which will . . . make the scale of their good works to overbalance.

The italics are mine, and show what little Poe adopted. Poe's Al Aaraaf is very different from what he found in Sale — it is not a wall between heaven and hell; it is not a place of sorrow, but contentment; its inhabitants are almost wholly amoral.

Poe also seems to have read up (probably in an encyclopedia) on Tycho Brahe and his new star. Tycho first noticed it on November 11, 1572, and published a book about it, *De Nova Stella* (Copenhagen, 1573). The star appeared near a rectangle of four stars in the constellation of Cassiopeia. It was already brighter (some thought) than Venus, and was at first white, then yellow, then red, and lastly of a leaden hue. It was visible for sixteen months, until in 1574 it faded away completely from human sight. The nova caused great excitement and, especially in its red phase, terror. Tycho, like almost all the old astronomers, was also an astrologer, and regarded it as of bad omen. Some of his contemporaries thought it a warning of the end of the world.

All this Poe treated almost as freely as he did his sources in the Koran and Sale. He takes from the historical record dates of the new star's visit, its location in Cassiopeia, its colors, and the fear it aroused. The rest is almost [6] pure fancy, as the introductory

[6] There is a correct astronomical passage in "Al Aaraaf," II, 1–10; however, it

sonnet should warn us. The notion that the nova was guided by a spirit is pretty surely taken from an idea entertained by Sir Isaac Newton that *comets* were so directed. But Tycho, who took much interest in comets, did not believe his nova was one.

Poe presumably composed "Al Aaraaf" while in the army. He turned up with it in Baltimore, and William Gwynn inserted an "Extract from 'Al Aaraaf' an Unpublished Poem" in his paper, the *Baltimore Gazette and Daily Advertiser*, of May 18, 1829. Poe also submitted the manuscript to William Wirt, who read it at a sitting and wrote him a polite letter on May 11, 1829. Obviously the biographer of Patrick Henry was baffled by the poem. He assured the young author that he was himself of too old-fashioned taste to appreciate it, but that it would please the younger sort; Wirt called the notes "useful." He recommended Poe to Robert Walsh, editor of the *American Quarterly Review* in Philadelphia, and to Joseph Hopkinson, who had written the lyrics of "Hail Columbia" in Washington's time (1798).

Apparently Poe was recommended also to Isaac Lea of the firm of Carey, Lea & Carey, and wrote him a long letter (undated but docketed as answered on May 27), with a copy of the poem. Poe's description of the plot of the poem is quoted above, but the following belongs here: "I send you parts 1^{rst}, 2^d, & 3^d. I have reasons for wishing not to publish the 4th at present — for its character depends in a measure upon the success or failure of the others." This passage led Quinn, whose handling of "Al Aaraaf" is generally admirable, to say (p. 144), "This shows that we do not have all of 'Al Aaraaf.' " While Poe's syntax is not clear, surely the fourth part to which he refers is something not yet written. The reference to a third part may be explained by the fact that, in the poem as it stands, Part II is much longer than Part I; there are breaks at II, 156, and II, 174, either one of which may have marked the beginning of a new part. Hence I believe none of "Al Aaraaf" is lost.

---

describes a situation not peculiar to Nesace's home, but something that can be seen by an untrained observer under proper conditions here on earth.

The upshot of it all, which may be followed in Poe's correspondence, was that the Philadelphia publishers offered to bring the book out, *if* a guarantee of a hundred dollars were forthcoming; Poe tried to get the money from John Allan, who rebuffed him, not unexpectedly; and *Al Aaraaf, Tamerlane, and Minor Poems* was finally issued, without subsidy, very late in 1829 by Hatch and Dunning in Baltimore.

"Al Aaraaf," from which a few lines, as we have seen, had been published in May 1829, was revised carefully before its appearance in book form late in the year. Poe made a few changes, almost all abortive, for the edition of 1831. In 1845 he sent as copy to the printers of *The Raven and Other Poems* a slightly revised version of the 1829 volume; a very few new changes were made in proof. The text printed in *The Raven . . .* was essentially the final version, though three or four special alterations were made for a reading of the poem in October 1845 and in illustrating meter in "The Rationale of Verse" about 1847.

My text is based on the text in *The Raven and Other Poems* (1845). I have added two accents (I, 114 and II, 20) and three or four minor corrections of spelling in Poe's notes. Poe's inconsistent spelling of words like "favo[u]r" has not been changed, nor have slightly incorrect forms of words found in his known sources. Poe marked his notes with printer's signs, but I have used superscript numbers in parentheses. The copy of the Baltimore *Gazette* I have used is in the Maryland Historical Society; that of the *Saturday Museum* at the University of North Carolina; and that of the *Portland Advertiser* in the Library of Congress.

In addition to the texts mentioned in the list below, Poe made brief quotations from "Al Aaraaf" in the tale "Siope" (the first version of "Silence — A Fable"), published in the *Baltimore Book* for 1838; and in a review of Thomas Ward's *Passaic* in *Graham's Magazine* for March 1843. These show no verbal variations from our text.

TEXTS

(A) *Baltimore Gazette*, May 18, 1829 (extracts); (B) *Yankee and Boston Literary Gazette*, December 1829 (1:296–297), extracts; (C) *Al Aaraaf, Tamer-*

AL AARAAF

lane, and Minor Poems (1829), pp. 13–38; (D) letter to John Neal, December 29, 1829 (extract, not in the fragment of the letter at the University of Texas), first published in Portland Daily Advertiser, April 26, 1850; (E) Poems (1831), pp. 83–108; (F) Philadelphia Saturday Museum, March 4, 1843 (extracts in H. B. Hirst's sketch of Poe); (G) Graham's Magazine for February 1845 (27:51), extract in J. R. Lowell's sketch of Poe; (H) Broadway Journal, May 24, 1845 (1:330), extract in a review of William W. Lord's Poems; (J) manuscript changes in Elizabeth Herring's copy of Al Aaraaf . . . made in 1845 as printer's copy for K; (J2) another set of manuscript changes made for Poe's reading at Boston, October 16, 1845; (K) The Raven and Other Poems (1845), pp. 56–73; (L) manuscript fragment of "The Rationale of Verse" seen in the collection of Oliver Barrett (extract); (M) Southern Literary Messenger, October 1848 (14:585), extract in "The Rationale of Verse"; (N) manuscript of "A Reviewer Reviewed" owned by H. Bradley Martin (extracts); (P) Works (1850), II, 78–95; (Q) Works (1850), II, 235 (extract in "The Rationale of Verse").

The extracts of A consist of II, 194–201, 214–220, 237–260 and footnotes 28 and 29; of B, I, 126–132 and II, 11–39; of D, I, 128–129; of F, I, 66–67, 70–79, 82–101, 126–129, and II, 20–21, 24–27, 52–55, 56–59, 68–135; of G, II, 100–111; of H, I, 50–56; of L, M, Q, II, 253–256; of N, II, 20–21 and 172–173.

The text followed is that of Poe's volume of 1845 (K).

AL AARAAF [1] [K]

PART I

O! nothing earthly save the ray
(Thrown back from flowers) of Beauty's eye,
As in those gardens where the day
Springs from the gems of Circassy —
5   O! nothing earthly save the thrill

[1] A star was discovered by Tycho Brahe which appeared suddenly in the heavens — attained, in a few days, a brilliancy surpassing that of Jupiter — then as suddenly disappeared, and has never been seen since.

Introductory Note: Al Aaraaf, among the Arabians, a medium between Heaven and Hell, is supposed to be located in the celebrated star discovered by Tycho Brahe, which burst forth in one night upon the eyes of the world, and disappeared as suddenly. — Michael Angelo is represented as transferred to this star, and speaking to the "lady of his unearthly love" of the regions he had left. (A)

A star was discovered by Tycho Brahe which burst forth, in a moment, with a splendor surpassing that of Jupiter — then gradually faded away and became invisible to the naked eye. (C, E)

1–15 Twenty-nine lines, subsituted in 1831 (E), are given below at pages 159–160 as "Mysterious Star."

Of melody in woodland rill —
Or (music of the passion-hearted)
Joy's voice so peacefully departed
That like the murmur in the shell,
10   Its echo dwelleth and will dwell —
Oh, nothing of the dross of ours —
Yet all the beauty — all the flowers
That list our Love, and deck our bowers —
Adorn yon world afar, afar —
15   The wandering star.

     'Twas a sweet time for Nesace — for there
Her world lay lolling on the golden air,
Near four bright suns — a temporary rest —
An oasis in desert of the blest.
20   Away — away — 'mid seas of rays that roll
Empyrean splendor o'er th' unchained soul —
The soul that scarce (the billows are so dense)
Can struggle to its destin'd eminence —
To distant spheres, from time to time, she rode,
25   And late to ours, the favour'd one of God —
But, now, the ruler of an anchor'd realm,
She throws aside the sceptre — leaves the helm,
And, amid incense and high spiritual hymns,
Laves in quadruple light her angel limbs.

30   Now happiest, loveliest in yon lovely Earth,
Whence sprang the "Idea of Beauty" into birth,
(Falling in wreaths thro' many a startled star,
Like woman's hair 'mid pearls, until, afar,
It lit on hills Achaian, and there dwelt)
35   She look'd into Infinity — and knelt.
Rich clouds, for canopies, about her curled —
Fit emblems of the model of her world —
Seen but in beauty — not impeding sight

---

11   Oh/With (*C*); Ah! (*J*)   19   An oasis/A garden-spot (*C, E, J*)
15   wandering/Messenger (*J2*)   34   Achaian/Archaian (*C*)

Of other beauty glittering thro' the light —
40   A wreath that twined each starry form around,
And all the opal'd air in color bound.

    All hurriedly she knelt upon a bed
Of flowers: of lilies such as rear'd the head
(2) On the fair Capo Deucato, and sprang
45   So eagerly around about to hang
Upon the flying footsteps of —— deep pride —
(3) Of her who lov'd a mortal — and so died.
The Sephalica, budding with young bees,
Uprear'd its purple stem around her knees:
50   (4) And gemmy flower, of Trebizond misnam'd —
Inmate of highest stars, where erst it sham'd
All other loveliness: its honied dew
(The fabled nectar that the heathen knew)
Deliriously sweet, was dropp'd from Heaven,
55   And fell on gardens of the unforgiven
In Trebizond — and on a sunny flower
So like its own above that, to this hour,
It still remaineth, torturing the bee
With madness, and unwonted reverie:
60   In Heaven, and all its environs, the leaf
And blossom of the fairy plant, in grief
Disconsolate linger — grief that hangs her head,
Repenting follies that full long have fled,
Heaving her white breast to the balmy air,
65   Like guilty beauty, chasten'd, and more fair:

(2) On Santa Maura — olim Deucadia.
(3) Sappho.
(4) This flower is much noticed by Lewenhoeck and Tournefort. The bee, feed-
ing upon its blossom, becomes intoxicated.

---

43   rear'd/rear (*C, E*)   50–56 *These lines are condensed thus in*
50   misnam'd/misnamed (*C, E*)   *H:*
                         —————— a gemmy flower,
                  Inmate of highest stars, where erst it shamed
                  All other loveliness: — 'twas dropped from Heaven
                  And fell on gardens of the unforgiven
                  In Trebizond.
62   head/he (*broken type E*)

Nyctanthes too, as sacred as the light
She fears to perfume, perfuming the night:
[5] And Clytia pondering between many a sun,
While pettish tears adown her petals run:
70   [6] And that aspiring flower that sprang on Earth —
And died, ere scarce exalted into birth,
Bursting its odorous heart in spirit to wing
Its way to Heaven, from garden of a king:
[7] And Valisnerian lotus thither flown
75   From struggling with the waters of the Rhone:
[8] And thy most lovely purple perfume, Zante!
Isola d'oro! — Fior di Levante!
[9] And the Nelumbo bud that floats for ever
With Indian Cupid down the holy river —
80   Fair flowers, and fairy! to whose care is given
[10] To bear the Goddess' song, in odors, up to Heaven:
"Spirit! that dwellest where,
    In the deep sky,
The terrible and fair,
85   In beauty vie!
Beyond the line of blue —
The boundary of the star
Which turneth at the view

[5] Clytia — The Chrysanthemum Peruvianum, or, to employ a better-known term, the turnsol — which turns continually towards the sun, covers itself, like Peru, the country from which it comes, with dewy clouds which cool and refresh its flowers during the most violent heat of the day. — *B. de St. Pierre.*

[6] There is cultivated in the king's garden at Paris, a species of serpentine aloes without prickles, whose large and beautiful flower exhales a strong odour of the vanilla, during the time of its expansion, which is very short. It does not blow till towards the month of July — you then perceive it gradually open its petals — expand them — fade and die. — *St. Pierre.*

[7] There is found, in the Rhone, a beautiful lily of the Valisnerian kind. Its stem will stretch to the length of three or four feet — thus preserving its head above water in the swellings of the river.

[8] The Hyacinth.

[9] It is a fiction of the Indians, that Cupid was first seen floating in one of these down the river Ganges — and that he still loves the cradle of his childhood.

[10] And golden vials full of odors which are the prayers of the saints. — *Rev*[.] *St. John.*

77   Isola/I sola (*misprint C*)   88   Which/That (*F*)
82–101   *These lines have a special title:*
SPIRITS INVOCATION (*F*)

Of thy barrier and thy bar —
90   Of the barrier overgone
     By the comets who were cast
     From their pride, and from their throne
     To be drudges till the last —
     To be carriers of fire
95   (The red fire of their heart)
     With speed that may not tire
     And with pain that shall not part —
     Who livest — *that* we know —
     In Eternity — we feel —
100 But the shadow of whose brow
     What spirit shall reveal?
     Tho' the beings whom thy Nesace,
     Thy messenger hath known
     Have dream'd for thy Infinity
105 (11) A model of their own —
     Thy will is done, Oh, God!
     The star hath ridden high
     Thro' many a tempest, but she rode

(11) The Humanitarians held that God was to be understood as having really a human form. — *Vide Clarke's Sermons*, vol. 1, page 26, fol. edit.

The drift of Milton's argument, leads him to employ language which would appear, at first sight, to verge upon their doctrine; but it will be seen immediately, that he guards himself against the charge of having adopted one of the most ignorant errors of the dark ages of the church. — *Dr. Sumner's Notes on Milton's Christian Doctrine.*

This opinion, in spite of many testimonies to the contrary, could never have been very general. Audeus, a Syrian of Mesopotamia, was condemned for the opinion, as heretical. He lived in the beginning of the fourth century. His disciples were called Anthropomorphites. — *Vide Du Pin.*

Among Milton's minor poems are these lines: —

   Dicite sacrorum præsides nemorum Deæ, &c.
   Quis ille primus cujus ex imagine
   Natura solers finxit humanum genus?
   Eternus, incorruptus, æquævus polo,
   Unusque et universus exemplar Dei. — And afterwards,
   Non cui profundum Cæcitas lumen dedit
   Dircæus augur vidit hunc alto sinu, &c.

---

95   red fire/fire (*E*)
104 dream'd/dreamed (*E*)

105 Note 11 Sumner's/Summers' (*misprint E*); *two errors in all old texts,* Andeus *and* anthropmorphites *are corrected editorially.*

Beneath thy burning eye;
110 And here, in thought, to thee —
In thought that can alone
Ascend thy empire and so be
A partner of thy throne —
(12) By wingéd Fantasy,
115 My embassy is given,
Till secrecy shall knowledge be
In the environs of Heaven."

She ceas'd — and buried then her burning cheek
Abash'd, amid the lilies there, to seek
120 A shelter from the fervour of His eye;
For the stars trembled at the Deity.
She stirr'd not — breath'd not — for a voice was there
How solemnly pervading the calm air!
A sound of silence on the startled ear
125 Which dreamy poets name "the music of the sphere."
Ours is a world of words: Quiet we call
"Silence" — which is the merest word of all.
All Nature speaks, and ev'n ideal things
Flap shadowy sounds from visionary wings —
130 But ah! not so when, thus, in realms on high
The eternal voice of God is passing by,
And the red winds are withering in the sky!

(13) "What tho' in worlds which sightless cycles run,
Link'd to a little system, and one sun —
135 Where all my love is folly and the crowd
Still think my terrors but the thunder cloud,

(12) Seltsamen Tochter Jovis
Seinem Schosskinde
Der Phantasie. — *Goethe.*
(13) Sightless — too small to be seen — *Legge.*

---

114 wingéd/wing'd (*E*)
114 Note 12 Goethe/Göethe (*K*) *corrected from C and E*
126 *Before this* — Silence is the voice of God — (*B*)

127 merest/veriest (*F*)
128 All/Here (*B, C, E, F*), There (*D*); ev'n/even (*D, F*)
130 thus, in/in the (*B*)
131 passing/moving (*B*)

· 104 ·

The storm, the earthquake, and the ocean-wrath —
(Ah! will they cross me in my angrier path?)
What tho' in worlds which own a single sun
140   The sands of Time grow dimmer as they run,
Yet thine is my resplendency, so given
To bear my secrets thro' the upper Heaven.
Leave tenantless thy crystal home, and fly,
With all thy train, athwart the moony sky —
145   (14) Apart — like fire-flies in Sicilian night,
And wing to other worlds another light!
Divulge the secrets of thy embassy
To the proud orbs that twinkle — and so be
To ev'ry heart a barrier and a ban
150   Lest the stars totter in the guilt of man!"

Up rose the maiden in the yellow night,
The single-mooned eve! — on Earth we plight
Our faith to one love — and one moon adore —
The birth-place of young Beauty had no more.
155   As sprang that yellow star from downy hours
Up rose the maiden from her shrine of flowers,
And bent o'er sheeny mountain and dim plain
(15) Her way — but left not yet her Therasæan reign.

PART II

High on a mountain of enamell'd head —
Such as the drowsy shepherd on his bed
Of giant pasturage lying at his ease,
Raising his heavy eyelid, starts and sees,
5   With many a mutter'd "hope to be forgiven"
What time the moon is quadrated in Heaven —

(14) I have often noticed a peculiar movement of the fire-flies: — they will collect in a body and fly off, from a common centre, into innumerable radii.
(15) Therasæa, or Therasea, the island mentioned by Seneca, which, in a moment, arose from the sea to the eyes of astonished mariners.

---

145   Note 14   fire-flies/firefly (C, E)

Of rosy head, that towering far away
Into the sunlit ether, caught the ray
Of sunken suns at eve — at noon of night,
10 While the moon danc'd with the fair stranger light —
Uprear'd upon such height arose a pile
Of gorgeous columns on th' unburthen'd air,
Flashing from Parian marble that twin smile
Far down upon the wave that sparkled there,
15 And nursled the young mountain in its lair.
(16) Of molten stars their pavement, such as fall
Thro' the ebon air, besilvering the pall
Of their own dissolution, while they die —
Adorning then the dwellings of the sky.
20 A dome, by linkéd light from Heaven let down,
Sat gently on these columns as a crown —
A window of one circular diamond, there,
Look'd out above into the purple air,
And rays from God shot down that meteor chain
25 And hallow'd all the beauty twice again,
Save when, between th' Empyrean and that ring,
Some eager spirit flapp'd his dusky wing.
But on the pillars Seraph eyes have seen
The dimness of this world: that greyish green
30 That Nature loves the best for Beauty's grave
Lurk'd in each cornice, round each architrave —
And every sculptur'd cherub thereabout
That from his marble dwelling peeréd out,
Seem'd earthly in the shadow of his niche —
35 Achaian statues in a world so rich?

(16) Some star which, from the ruin'd roof
Of shak'd Olympus, by mischance, did fall. — *Milton*

---

12 unburthen'd/unburthened (B)
20 dome/*so first written, changed to*
chain, *then changed back to* dome (N);
linkéd [*accent added from F, since
Poe's intention is clearly a dissyllable*]/
linked *in all texts save* F
23 Look'd/Looked (E)

27 his/a (B)
31 Lurk'd/Lurked (B)
32 every/ev'ry (C, E)
33 peeréd/ventured (B, C); peered
(E)
34 Seem'd/Seemed (B)
35 Achaian/Archaian (B, C)

[17] Friezes from Tadmor and Persepolis —
From Balbec, and the stilly, clear abyss
[18] Of beautiful Gomorrah! O, the wave
Is now upon thee — but too late to save!

40   Sound loves to revel in a summer night:
Witness the murmur of the grey twilight
[19] That stole upon the ear, in Eyraco,
Of many a wild star-gazer long ago —
That stealeth ever on the ear of him
45   Who, musing, gazeth on the distance dim.
And sees the darkness coming as a cloud —
[20] Is not its form — its voice — most palpable and loud?

But what is this? — it cometh — and it brings
A music with it — 'tis the rush of wings —
50   A pause — and then a sweeping, falling strain
And Nesace is in her halls again.

[17] Voltaire, in speaking of Persepolis, says, "Je connois bien l'admiration qu'inspirent ces ruines — mais un palais erigé au pied d'une chaine des rochers sterils — peut il être un chef d'œuvre des arts!"

[18] "Oh! the wave" — Ula Deguisi is the Turkish appellation; but, on its own shores, it is called Bahar Loth, or Almotanah. There were undoubtedly more than two cities engulphed in the "dead sea." In the valley of Siddim were five — Adrah, Zeboin, Zoar, Sodom and Gomorrah. Stephen of Byzantium mentions eight, and Strabo thirteen, (engulphed) — but the last is out of all reason.

It is said, (Tracitus, Strabo, Josephus, Daniel of St. Saba, Nau, Maundrell, Troilo, D'Arvieux) that after an excessive drought, the vestiges of columns, walls, &c. are seen above the surface. At *any* season, such remains may be discovered by looking down into the transparent lake, and at such distances as would argue the existence of many settlements in the space now usurped by the 'Asphaltites.'

[19] Eyraco — Chaldea.

[20] I have often thought I could distinctly hear the sound of the darkness as it stole over the horizon.

---

36 Note 17 *In C Poe added at end*   37 the/thy (E, J)
Voila les argumens de M. Voltaire!   38 Of/Too (E, J)
He omitted the whole note in E   40 in/near (C, E, *changed in* J)
37-39 *There are seven lines in B:*
      From Balbec and the stilly, clear abyss
      Of beautiful Gomorrah! — oh! the wave
      Is now upon thee — but too late to save!
      Far down within the crystal of the lake
      Thy swollen pillars tremble — and so quake
      The hearts of many wanderers who look in
      Thy luridness of beauty — and of sin.

From the wild energy of wanton haste
    Her cheeks were flushing, and her lips apart;
And zone that clung around her gentle waist
55   Had burst beneath the heaving of her heart.
Within the centre of that hall to breathe
She paus'd and panted, Zanthe! all beneath,
The fairy light that kiss'd her golden hair
And long'd to rest, yet could but sparkle there!

60   (21) Young flowers were whispering in melody
To happy flowers that night — and tree to tree;
Fountains were gushing music as they fell
In many a star-lit grove, or moon-lit dell;
Yet silence came upon material things —
65   Fair flowers, bright waterfalls and angel wings —
And sound alone that from the spirit sprang
Bore burthen to the charm the maiden sang:
" 'Neath blue-bell or streamer —
    Or tufted wild spray
70   That keeps, from the dreamer,
      (22) The moonbeam away —
Bright beings! that ponder,
    With half closing eyes,
On the stars which your wonder
75   Hath drawn from the skies,
Till they glance thro' the shade, and
    Come down to your brow
Like —— eyes of the maiden
    Who calls on you now —
80   Arise! from your dreaming
    In violet bowers,

(21) Fairies use flowers for their charactery. — *Merry Wives of Windsor.*

(22) In Scripture is this passage — "The sun shall not harm thee by day, nor the moon by night." It is perhaps not generally known that the moon, in Egypt, has the effect of producing blindness to those who sleep with the face exposed to its rays, to which circumstance the passage evidently alludes.

---

53 cheeks were/cheek was (*C, E, F*)   58 fairy/brilliant (*F*)
54 around/about (*F*)   77 Come/And come (*F*)
56 that/this (*F*)

To duty beseeming
   These star-litten hours —
And shake from your tresses
85   Encumber'd with dew
The breath of those kisses
   That cumber them too —
   (O! how, without you, Love!
    Could angels be blest?)
90 Those kisses of true love
   That lull'd ye to rest!
Up! — shake from your wing
   Each hindering thing:
The dew of the night —
95   It would weigh down your flight;
And true love caresses —
   O! leave them apart!
They are light on the tresses,
   But lead on the heart.

100 Ligeia! Ligeia!
   My beautiful one!
Whose harshest idea
   Will to melody run,
O! is it thy will
105   On the breezes to toss?
Or, capriciously still,
   [23] Like the lone Albatross,
Incumbent on night
   (As she on the air)
110 To keep watch with delight
   On the harmony there?

Ligeia! wherever

[23] The Albatross is said to sleep on the wing.

---

92 wing/wings (*F*)
93 Each hindering thing/All hindering things (*F*)
95 would/will (*F*)
99 lead/hang (*C, E*)
104 O!/Say (*F, G*)

Thy image may be,
No magic shall sever
1 1 5   Thy music from thee.
Thou hast bound many eyes
In a dreamy sleep —
But the strains still arise
Which *thy* vigilance keep —
1 20   The sound of the rain
Which leaps down to the flower,
And dances again
In the rhythm of the shower —
(24) The murmur that springs
1 25   From the growing of grass
Are the music of things —
But are modell'd, alas! —
Away, then my dearest,
O! hie thee away
1 30   To springs that lie clearest
Beneath the moon-ray —
To lone lake that smiles,
In its dream of deep rest,
At the many star-isles
1 35   That enjewel its breast —
Where wild flowers, creeping,
Have mingled their shade,
On its margin is sleeping
Full many a maid —
1 40   Some have left the cool glade, and
(25) Have slept with the bee —
Arouse them my maiden,
On moorland and lea —

(24) I met with this idea in an old English tale, which I am now unable to obtain
and quote from memory: — "The verie essence and, as it were, springeheade and
origine of all musiche is the verie pleasaunte sounde which the trees of the forest
do make when they growe."
(25) The wild bee will not sleep in the shade if there be moonlight.
The rhyme in this verse, as in one about sixty lines before, has an appearance

113 Thy/Thine (*F*)   121 Which/That (*F*)
117 In a/In a deep (*F*)   134 many/myriad (*F*)

Go! breathe on their slumber,
145 All softly in ear,
The musical number
  They slumber'd to hear —
For what can awaken
  An angel so soon
150 Whose sleep hath been taken
  Beneath the cold moon,
As the spell which no slumber
  Of witchery may test,
The rhythmical number
155 Which lull'd him to rest?"

Spirits in wing, and angels to the view,
A thousand seraphs burst th' Empyrean thro',
Young dreams still hovering on their drowsy flight —
Seraphs in all but "Knowledge," the keen light
160 That fell, refracted, thro' thy bounds, afar
O Death! from eye of God upon that star:
Sweet was that error — sweeter still that death —
Sweet was that error — ev'n with *us* the breath
Of Science dims the mirror of our joy —
165 To them 'twere the Simoon, and would destroy —
For what (to them) availeth it to know
That Truth is Falsehood — or that Bliss is Woe?
Sweet was their death — with them to die was rife
With the last ecstasy of satiate life —
170 Beyond that death no immortality
But sleep that pondereth and is not "to be" —
And there — oh! may my weary spirit dwell —
(26) Apart from Heaven's Eternity — and yet how far
  from Hell!

---

of affectation. It is, however, imitated from Sir W. Scott, or rather from Claud
Halcro — in whose mouth I admired its effect:
   O! were there an island,
    Tho' ever so wild
   Where woman might smile, and
    No man be beguil'd, &c.
(26) With the Arabians there is a medium between Heaven and Hell, where men

What guilty spirit, in what shrubbery dim,
175 Heard not the stirring summons of that hymn?
But two: they fell: for Heaven no grace imparts
To those who hear not for their beating hearts.
A maiden-angel and her seraph-lover —
O! where (and ye may seek the wide skies over)
180 Was Love, the blind, near sober Duty known?
(27) Unguided Love hath fallen — 'mid "tears of
perfect moan."

He was a goodly spirit — he who fell:
A wanderer by moss-y-mantled well —
A gazer on the lights that shine above —
185 A dreamer in the moonbeam by his love:
What wonder? for each star is eye-like there,
And looks so sweetly down on Beauty's hair —
And they, and ev'ry mossy spring were holy
To his love-haunted heart and melancholy.
190 The night had found (to him a night of wo)
Upon a mountain crag, young Angelo —
Beetling it bends athwart the solemn sky,
And scowls on starry worlds that down beneath it lie.
Here sate he with his love — his dark eye bent
195 With eagle gaze along the firmament:
Now turn'd it upon her — but ever then
It trembled to the orb of EARTH again.

suffer no punishment, but yet do not attain that tranquil and even happiness which
they suppose to be characteristic of heavenly enjoyment.

> Un no rompido sueno —
> Un dia puro — allegre — libre
> Quiera —
> Libre de amor — de zelo —
> De odio — de esperanza — de rezelo. — *Luis Ponce de Leon.*

Sorrow is not excluded from "Al Aaraaf," but it is that sorrow which the living love
to cherish for the dead, and which, in some minds, resembles the delirium of opium.
The passionate excitement of Love and the buoyancy of spirit attendant upon intox-
ication are its less holy pleasures — the price of which, to those souls who make
choice of "Al Aaraaf" as their residence after life, is final death and annihilation.
(27) There be tears of perfect moan
Wept for thee in Helicon. — *Milton.*

183 moss-y-mantled/mossy-mantled (*E*)   197 the orb of Earth/one constant star
196 turn'd/turned (*A*)   (*A, C, E*)

"Ianthe, dearest, see! how dim that ray!
How lovely 'tis to look so far away!
200   She seem'd not thus upon that autumn eve
I left her gorgeous halls — nor mourn'd to leave.
That eve — that eve — I should remember well —
The sun-ray dropp'd, in Lemnos, with a spell
On th' Arabesque carving of a gilded hall
205   Wherein I sate, and on the draperied wall —
And on my eye-lids — O the heavy light!
How drowsily it weigh'd them into night!
On flowers, before, and mist, and love they ran
With Persian Saadi in his Gulistan:
210   But O that light! — I slumber'd — Death, the while,
Stole o'er my senses in that lovely isle
So softly that no single silken hair
Awoke that slept — or knew that he was there.

The last spot of Earth's orb I trod upon
215   (28) Was a proud temple call'd the Parthenon —
More beauty clung around her column'd wall
(29) Than ev'n thy glowing bosom beats withal,
And when old Time my wing did disenthral
Thence sprang I — as the eagle from his tower,
220   And years I left behind me in an hour.
What time upon her airy bounds I hung
One half the garden of her globe was flung
Unrolling as a chart unto my view —
Tenantless cities of the desert too!
225   Ianthe, beauty crowded on me then,
And half I wish'd to be again of men."

(28) It was entire in 1687 — the most elevated spot in Athens.
(29) Shadowing more beauty in their airy brows
    Than have the white breasts of the Queen of Love. — *Marlowe.*

---

201 mourn'd/mourun'd (*misprint* E)	215 Note 28 spot/building (*A*)
205 draperied/drapried (*C, E*)	216 column'd/columned (*A*)
213 he/it (*C, E*)	217 ev'n/even (*A*)
214 Earth's/her (*A*)	219 sprang/sprung (*A*)
215 proud temple call'd the/fair tem-ple called (*A*)	226 wish'd/wished (*E*)

"My Angelo! and why of them to be?
A brighter dwelling-place is here for thee —
And greener fields than in yon world above,
230　And woman's loveliness — and passionate love."

"But, list, Ianthe! when the air so soft
(30) Fail'd, as my pennon'd spirit leapt aloft,
Perhaps my brain grew dizzy — but the world
I left so late was into chaos hurl'd —
235　Sprang from her station, on the winds apart,
And roll'd, a flame, the fiery Heaven athwart.
Methought, my sweet one, then I ceased to soar
And fell — not swiftly as I rose before,
But with a downward, tremulous motion thro'
240　Light, brazen rays, this golden star unto!
Nor long the measure of my falling hours,
For nearest of all stars was thine to ours —
Dread star! that came, amid a night of mirth,
A red Dædalion on the timid Earth.

245　"We came — and to thy Earth — but not to us
Be given our lady's bidding to discuss:
We came, my love; around, above, below,
Gay fire-fly of the night we come and go,
Nor ask a reason save the angel-nod
250　*She* grants to us, as granted by her God —
But, Angelo, than thine grey Time unfurl'd
Never his fairy wing o'er fairier world!
Dim was its little disk, and angel eyes
Alone could see the phantom in the skies,

(30) Pennon — for pinion. — *Milton.*

237　my sweet one/Ianthe (*A*); ceased/
ceas'd (*A, C, E*)
243　a/their (*A*)
245　and to thy earth/my Angelo (*A*)

250　grants to us, as granted/gives to
us as given (*A*)
251　Angelo, than thine/truly, Angelo
(*A*)
253　angel/seraph (*A*)

AL AARAAF

255   When first Al Aaraaf knew her course to be
Headlong thitherward o'er the starry sea —
But when its glory swell'd upon the sky,
As glowing Beauty's bust beneath man's eye,
We paus'd before the heritage of men,
260   And thy star trembled — as doth Beauty then!"

Thus, in discourse, the lovers whiled away
The night that waned and waned and brought no day.
They fell: for Heaven to them no hope imparts
Who hear not for the beating of their hearts.

[1829–1845]

NOTES

Title: *Al* is the Arabic definite article. *Aaraaf* is the way some scholars in Poe's day transliterated what usually is now written *Ârâf*. It is trochaic in II, 255, but Poe's pronunciation is not recorded. Whether his idea of placing his spirit home in the star was entirely his own is not quite certain.

Part I.

4   Circassy, or Circassia, the region of the Caucasus whence came the blonde beauties so much admired in Turkey, was also believed to be rich in precious stones. See also the opening of the 1831 version of "Al Aaraaf," I, 14.

16   Nesace (Nēsakē) means "lady of an island" (*nēsos*) and, although not actually recorded from any ancient text, is a possible form. A learned colleague points out such parallels as *skiakos* (shadowy) and *Korinthiakos*. Moore remarks in a note on his *Loves of the Angels* that "a belief that the stars are either spirits, or the vehicles of spirits, was common to all the religions and heresies of the East." Nesace is the presiding spirit of a star; her realm is compared to an island (Therasaea) in "Al Aaraaf," I, 158. It is just possible that a pun on Latin *necesse* may also be intended. Older suggestions, that Nesace is "a form of Nausicaa" or "an anagram of Seneca," may now be dismissed; neither had any point.

17–30   The "four bright suns" and "quadruple light" (line 29) refer to the rectangle of four stars in Cassiopeia near which Tycho's nova appeared. Poe's heavenly body is treated here as if it were a planet and (in line 30) is actually called "yon lovely Earth."

---

255 Al Aaraaf knew her course/ Tophet-Nour knew her course (*J*2); the phantom's course was found (*L, M, Q*)
256 thitherward/hitherward (*L, M, Q*)

260 *This line, the last in **A**, is followed by* MARLOW *which has been taken for a signature, but was merely misplaced by the printer from the end of note 29.*

26–27   The metaphor is of Al Aaraaf as a ship anchored, at rest and not traveling, the captain of which, Nesace, ceases for a time to steer it.

31   The poet here seems to imply that his Al Aaraaf is the home of Plato's "ideal" beauty.

34   "Achaian," from Achaea in the Peloponnesus, is used for "Hellenic." In the edition of 1829 the word, here and at II, 35, is spelled "Archaian." That word means ancient and may have been the poet's intention.

42–47   Poe uses the familiar legend that the lyric poet Sappho leapt into the sea for love of Phaon, told in Ovid's fifteenth *Epistle*, translated by Alexander Pope as "Sappho to Phaon," and recounted in Thomas Moore's *Evenings in Greece*, I, 131ff. and the notes thereon. (Actually the leap from the Leucadian cliff, 114 feet into deep water, was not always fatal. It was made by the lyre player Sappho of Mitylene. The poet, although a resident of Mitylene, was properly Sappho of Eresus, her birthplace. The statements of Suidas in his *Lexicon* s.v. Sappho. Phaon, are confirmed by the coins of Eresus.)

42–43   Moore (citing William Goodisson, *A Historical . . . Essay upon the Islands of Corfu, Leucadia . . . the Ionian Islands*, London, 1822) says (lines 147–151) that there are

> . . . scented lilies found
> Still blooming on that fearful place —
> As if call'd up by Love, to grace
> The immortal spot, o'er which the last
> Bright footsteps of his martyr pass'd!

That they sprang up to restrain her seems to be Poe's own addition to the legend.

44   Note 2: Santa Maura was the Italian name, used for centuries, of the island off the western coast of Greece called by the ancients from its white cliffs Leucas or Leucadia and now Levkadi. The Italian name for the southern promontory of the island was Capo Ducato; it is now called Akra Deucaton. Poe's spellings Deucato and Deucadia are obviously possible variants, but his exact source for them has not been found.

46   The "deep pride" lay in self-immolation for love.

47   The poetess Sappho is referred to by Plato and Plutarch as the "tenth muse" and so herself is a goddess. Poe makes allusion in "Israfel" to the seventh of the Pleiades, who lost her immortality by loving a mortal. Clearly Poe, like most of the ancient and modern poets from Ovid to Moore, accepted the fable that the great lyric poetess was the Sappho who leaped from the Leucadian cliff.

48   In a note to *Lalla Rookh*, Moore quotes Sir William Jones ("Botanical Observations on Select Indian Plants," in his *Works* [London, 1807], V, 72f.): "My Pandits assure me that the plant before us (the Nilica) is their Sephalica, thus named because the bees are supposed to sleep on its blossoms."

50–59   In another note to *Lalla Rookh*, Moore "quotes" Tournefort: "There is a kind of Rhododendros about Trebizonde, whose flowers the bee feeds upon, and the honey thence drives men mad." Moore's source is Joseph Pitton de Tournefort (1656–1708), *A Voyage into the Levant* (London, 1741), III, 66f. The work of this great French botanist was originally published at Lyons in 1717. Poe's surely secondary source for the interest of Anton van Leeuwenhoek (1632–1723), the inventor of the microscope, has not yet been found. The plant is the *Azalea pontica*; animals feeding upon it go temporarily mad, and honey made from it is poisonous.

55–56   The city of Trebizond (in ancient times Trapezus) and the district on the Black Sea named for it were famous for gardens, but it is regrettable that Poe gave no note on "the unforgiven," who is admittedly obscure. I think the allusion is to the wily Mithradates Eupator, King of Pontus, whose dominions included Trapezus; he took an interest in magic, had reputedly made himself immune to poisons, and was certainly unforgiven by his archenemies, the Romans, who finally suppressed him in 63 B.C.

66   Moore has a footnote to *Lalla Rookh* about "The sorrowful nyctanthes, which begins to spread its rich odour after sunset." The sephalica (see line 48) is, according to Sir William Jones, a species of nyctanthes. Jones also says that Linnaeus designates the sephalica as the "sorrowful nyctanthes." It is also mentioned in Poe's "Letter to B—."

68, 70   Notes 5, 6: Both notes come almost verbatim from Henry Hunter's translation of Bernardin de Saint-Pierre's *Études de la Nature* (*Studies of Nature*, Philadelphia, 1808), II, 71.

74   Note 7: This is quoted more freely from the same Study (the eleventh), page 146 in the translation. Poe preserves the incorrect spelling of Vallisnerian as he does in his "1002nd Tale of Scheherezade."

76–77   Poe is here using a passage in Chateaubriand's *Itinéraire de Paris à Jérusalem*, which he read in F. Shoberl's translation, *Travels in Greece, Palestine, Egypt, and Barbary* (Philadelphia edition, 1813, p. 62): "I subscribe to its appellations of *Isola d'oro* and *Fior de Levante* . . . The hyacinth came from Zante, and . . . this island received its name from the flower." Poe used the material more fully in 1836 in his sonnet "To Zante." The Italian phrases mean "Island of gold" and "Flower of the Levant." See the notes on "To Helen" and on "Irenë" for Poe's references to several stories about hyacinths.

78   Note 9: Moore has a note on *Lalla Rookh*: "The Indians feign that Cupid was first seen floating down the Ganges on the Nymphaea Nelumbo. See Pennant." Thomas Pennant (1726–1798), a Welsh naturalist and antiquarian, used an old-fashioned scientific name but clearly meant the sacred lotus. Poe almost surely also knew a poem by Letitia E. Landon — "Manmadin, the Indian Cupid, riding down the Ganges" — in which she says, "Pillow'd on a lotus flower/ . . . Rides he o'er the mountain wave." Modern authorities write of Manmatha ("confusing") as an attributive name of Camdeo or Kamadeva ("god of desire"), which is the Indian equivalent of the Greeks' Eros, the Cupido of the Romans.

81   Note 10: The slightly inaccurate quotation is from Revelation 5:8.

90–95 The comets here are fallen angels, punished by having to carry fire in their hearts. The exact source of the idea in "Al Aaraaf" has not been found.

98–99 Killis Campbell (*Poems*, page 178) compares Byron's *Manfred*, III, iv, 125–126: "Thou hast no power upon me, *that* I feel;/ Thou never shalt possess me, *that* I know."

100–101 The question expects a negative answer.

104 Wilbur, *Poe* (1959), page 126, thinks Nesace apologizes for poets (perhaps Milton in particular) who meddle with theology and seem to give God a human appearance.

105 Note 11: Poe quotes the first two paragraphs from Charles R. Sumner's notes on Milton's *Treatise of Christian Doctrine*, I, 22 of the Boston edition (1825). The reference to the sermons of the Reverend Samuel Clarke is given by Sumner from the edition of Clarke's *Works* (1738) in four volumes, folio. The Sumner references to Clarke were quoted again by Poe in a review of John Gardiner Calkins Brainard in *Graham's Magazine* for February 1842, where Poe remarked that "bestowing upon Deity a human form is . . . low and most unideal."

Audaeus, a Mesopotamian by birth, founded his sect in Syria about A.D. 338. He died during the reign of Valentinian I. Louis-Ellies DuPin (1657–1719) was a Frenchman who wrote most voluminously on ancient and modern history. I doubt that Poe used him at first hand.

Cowper renders the lines from "De idea platonica" thus:

> Ye sister powers, who o'er the sacred groves
> Preside . . . inform us who is He,
> That great original, by nature chosen
> To be the archetype of human kind,
> Unchangeable, immortal, with the poles
> Themselves coëval, one, yet everywhere
> An image of the god who gave him being? . . .
>
> Never the Theban seer, whose blindness proved
> His best illumination, him beheld
> In secret vision.

106 Compare "Thy will be done" in the Lord's Prayer.

107 Note 23: Poe's source is a note in Moore's *Lalla Rookh*.

112–113 The allusion is to Revelation 3:21: "To him that overcometh will I grant to sit with me in my throne."

114 Note 12: The German is from Goethe's "Meine Goettin" (written September 15, 1780), lines 7–9. It is given in George Bancroft's "Life and Genius of Goethe" in the *North American Review* for October 1824. Bancroft rendered Goethe's lines rather freely, "Dearest in her father's eye,/ Jove's own darling, Phantasy." Poe used the German quotation again in 1842 as a motto on the manuscript title page of his planned collection of stories, PHANTASY-PIECES. See Quinn, p. 338, for a facsimile.

AL AARAAF

115 Here "embassy" means "message," as in *Paradise Lost,* III, 658.

118–120 Neither mortals nor angels can bear the effulgence of the countenance of God. The idea is extremely common, and it seems unnecessary to repeat the passages from Moore cited by Killis Campbell, *Poems* (1917), page 180, since they are not verbally very much like what Poe wrote. Mahomet himself, Moore remarks, quoting Sale, could not look directly at the angel Gabriel when the latter appeared in his true form.

123ff. See I Kings 19:11–12: "The Lord passed by, and a great and strong wind rent the mountains . . . but the Lord was not in the wind . . . And . . . a fire; but the Lord was not in the fire: and after the fire a still small voice."

125 Compare a canceled phrase in "Irenë" (version of 1836): "Like music of another sphere." The singular in the phrase is unusual, but in a fragment beginning, "If far from me the Fates remove," Henry Kirke White wrote, ". . . with Plato's ravish'd ear/ I list the music of the sphere." Poe's line is an Alexandrine, correct as the second line of an heroic couplet.

127 Killis Campbell (*Poems,* page 180) compared this to Byron's *Manfred,* III, i, 9–11: "Philosophy/ . . . The merest word that ever fooled the ear."

133 Note 13: *The Century Dictionary and Cyclopedia* (New York, 1895) gives as an obsolete meaning "not appearing to sight; invisible" and cites *Macbeth,* I, vii, 23: "The sightless couriers of the air." Edward Legge (1767–1827), Bishop of Oxford, who published a sermon or two, is probably the man Poe had in mind.

140 Compare *Politian,* VI, 41: "The sands of time are changed to golden grains."

143 The sphere of the fixed stars was sometimes called "crystalline," a concept to which Poe alludes in "Ulalume," line 63.

145 Note 14: Did Poe (as I have done) observe the fireflies after reading a line in Wordsworth's *Ecclesiastical Sonnets* (III, v, 10): "Apart like glowworms on a summer night"? There is no "plagiarism" here, for, surprisingly, Poe is more nearly correct. The mature male glowworm, which alone has wings, has little luminosity.

150 Poe seems to mean that a planet may be incidentally destroyed when God punishes its people; Cowper in *The Task,* VI, 257, says, "And earth be punished for its tenants' sake." See also Pope's *Essay on Man,* I, vii, 247ff.:

> And if each system in gradation roll,
> Alike essential to th' amazing Whole,
> The least confusion but in one, not all
> That system only, but the Whole must fall.
> Let earth unbalanced from her orbit fly,
> Planets and stars run lawless thro' the sky;
> Let ruling angels from their spheres be hurl'd,
> Being on being wreck'd, and world on world;
> Heav'n's whole foundations to their centre nod,

And Nature tremble to the throne of God!
All this dread order break — for whom? for thee?
Vile worm! — O madness! pride! impiety!

158 Note 15: Seneca's account of the new island is in *Questiones naturales*, VI, xxi. Actually it was not named as Poe says, but arose *near* the islands of Thera (Thira or Santorini) and Therasia (Thirasia) in the Cyclades. Pliny, *Natural History*, IV, xxiii, gives the name of the new island as Automate, Hiera, or Thia.

Part II

1–10 I have received from Dr. Stanley P. Wyatt, Professor of Astronomy at the University of Illinois, analysis of this passage. "Eve" means after the sun has set. The moon is "quadrated" when ninety degrees from the sun. "Noon of night" is when the moon is at the zenith, as may occur at sunset (at sea level) only at the first quarter. "Drowsy" is heavy with sleep.

The shepherd awakens from a nap late in the afternoon; it is deep twilight where he lies, but he sees far off to the northwest (or southwest) a mountain's peak that catches the light of the sun sinking below the horizon (at sea level) in the west. The most prominent things seen are the two lights, those of the moon and the mountain top. These are like partners in a dignified dance, such as a minuet. The pious shepherd prays whenever he awakes from sleep. No commentator seems to have explained the passage, but it was so understood by Frederick W. Hulme in his illustration for Poe's *Poetical Works* (London, 1852), p. 152.

1 Killis Campbell (*Poems*, page 182) compared this to *Paradise Lost*, II, 1–2: "High on a throne . . . which far / Outshone the wealth of Ormus."

2–4 Compare James Thomson's *Seasons*, "Summer," lines 284–285: "Or drowsy shepherd as he lies reclin'd, / With half-shut eyes, beneath the floating shade . . ." Also compare Milton's "Elegia," V, 41–42: "Forte aliquis scopuli recubans in vertice pastor/ Roscida cum primo sole rubescit humus," which Cowper translated, "Now haply says some shepherd, while he views/ Recumbent on a rock, the reddening dews." There is also a pertinent passage in Moore's *Lalla Rookh*:

> The boy had started from his bed
> Of flowers, where he had lain his head,
> And down upon the fragrant sod
> Kneels.

Moore decorates this with a long note about the Turkish custom of praying wherever one happens to be at the proper time.

10 "The fair stranger light" is the unusual reflection of the rays of the sunken sun, stranger than moonlight.

13 Parian marble from Mount Paros, near Athens, is of the finest kind and was used for the Parthenon.

16 Note 16: The verses are inaccurately quoted from Milton's ode "On the Death of a Fair Infant," lines 43–44.

17 Compare "To—" ("The bowers whereat"), line 8: "Like starlight on a pall."

20 Poe sometimes omitted the accent on "linkéd," but the word must have two syllables; in the *Yankee*, December 1829, p. 296, John Neal, in a footnote, sagely remarked, "To say link-ed light would be queer . . . but to say link'd-light would spoil the rhythm." In his unfinished satiric fantasy of 1849, "A Reviewer Reviewed," Poe pointed out his own source in Pope's version of the *Iliad*, VIII, 25–26: "Let down our golden everlasting chain,/Whose strong embrace holds Heaven and Earth and Main."

29 Compare "The Domain of Arnheim," where Poe says, "The chiselled stone has the hue of ages."

31 Poe probably had in mind *Paradise Lost*, I, 713–719:

> Built like a temple, where pilasters round
> Were set, and Doric pillars overlaid
> With golden architrave; nor did there want
> Cornice or frieze, with bossy sculptures grav'n,
> The roof was fretted gold. Not Babylon,
> Nor great Alcairo such magnificence
> Equal'd in all their glories.

35 On "Achaian" see note on I, 34.

36–37 In his tale, "MS. Found in a Bottle," Poe writes of "the shadows of fallen columns at Balbec, and Tadmor, and Persepolis." The three places are among the most famous of ruined cities.

"Tadmor in the wilderness" was one of the cities built by Solomon, according to I Kings 9:18 and II Chronicles 8:4. It is also called Tamar, "place of palms," and was the classical Palmyra. It was partially destroyed by the Roman Emperor Aurelian in A.D. 272, after the revolt of its queen, Zenobia, who had boldly assumed the purple as Septimia Zenobia Augusta. She is referred to in Poe's tale, "How to Write a Blackwood Article."

Persepolis was the capital of the ancient kingdom of Persia; the great palace there was burned by Alexander the Great in 330 B.C.

Ba'albek, the "city of the god," seems to have been a great center of the worship of the Sun from early times. The Greeks called it Heliopolis, and the Romans made it a colony. Two huge temples at the place were finished in the third century of our era. The buildings were much damaged before they were visited by European travelers in the sixteenth century, but in Poe's day they were in extremely ruinous condition after an earthquake of 1759. In recent times, they have been to some extent restored. In the earliest version of his tale, "Silence—a Fable," Poe laid the scene at Balbec.

36 Note 17: The passage inexactly quoted from Voltaire is from the fifth chapter of his *Essai sur les mœurs et l'esprit des nations* (1742). It means, "I know well what admiration those ruins inspire—but can a palace built at the foot of a chain of barren cliffs be a masterpiece of art?"

38f. This passage was longer in the earliest text, that of *The Yankee*; it later was the basis of Poe's poem "The City in the Sea."

38 Note 18: The long note is abridged from a passage in Chateaubriand's *Itinéraire*. American editions of Shoberl's translation were published at Philadelphia in 1813 and at New York in 1814. Both contain the misprint "deguisi" for "degnisi"; it is at page 264 in the New York edition, at 277 in the Philadelphia one. "Ula degnisi" is Chateaubriand's own lame Turkish; I have allowed "Deguisi" to stand in our text, since it is what Poe found in Shoberl and shows the source. (See the notes on "Ulalume" for Poe's possible later use of the word *ula*.) The Turks, I am told, sometimes speak of *Ölü deniz*, meaning "Dead Sea," but more usually call it *Lut denizi*, "Lot's sea." For this, the Arabic form is *Bahar Loth*, now usually written *Bahr Lut* ("Sea of Lot"). Another Arabic name for the sea is *Al-Buhairah Al-Muntinah*, the second element from the root *ntn*, "to stink." "Almontanah" is presumably what Chateaubriand thought he heard during his visit.

Siddim (a plural form) means "the large plain." The towns accepted are Sodom ("burning"), Gomorrah ("sunken"), Zoar ("littleness"), Zeboim ("place of hyenas, gazelles, or roes"), and Admah (variously interpreted as "earth," "fortress," or "fruitful place"). Strabo, XVI, ii, 44, mentions the local tradition "that there were once thirteen inhabited cities in that region of which Sodom was the metropolis"; Stephen of Byzantium, *s.v.* "Sodoma," mentions ten, not eight.

The authorities named were probably not all consulted by Chateaubriand, let alone Poe, who probably did look up the first and third. The references are (1) Tacitus, *Historiae*, V, vii; (2) Strabo, *Geographia*, XVI, ii; (3) Josephus, *Bellum judaicum*, IV, viii, 4; (4) Daniel, Abbot of St. Saba (a monastery near the Dead Sea), was not an author, but a friend and informant of (5) Michel Nau, *Voyage de la Terre Sainte* (Paris, 1702), page 378; (6) Henry Maundrell, *A Journey From Aleppo* (1697), under date "March 30" (there are several editions of the book); (7) Franz Ferdinand von Troilo, *Orientalische Reise* (Dresden, 1676), page 345; (8) the Chevalier Lambert d'Arvieux, *Mémoires* (Paris, 1735), chapter xxxviii. I have seen only a later translation of this last, and find that the author said he saw the ruins. Lacus Asphaltites is the Latin name of the Dead Sea.

40f. With the *Yankee* text compare "Eleonora": "We called it the River of Silence . . . No murmur arose from its bed . . . we loved to gaze far down within its bosom."

42 Compare a canceled line in the 1836 text of "Irenë" ("The Sleeper"): "Which stole within the slumberer's ear."

42–43 Eyraco is obviously an old-fashioned name for Iraq, which embraces ancient Babylonia and Chaldea. Compare "The Coliseum," lines 15–16: "O charms more potent than the rapt Chaldee/ Ever drew down from out the quiet stars!"

54 A zone is a girdle, an emblem of maidenhood.

57 Zanthe, whose name is another that derives from the hyacinth, is merely a woman addressed by the poet.

60 Note 21: The full reference is to *Merry Wives of Windsor*, V, v, 77, also

quoted by Poe in a review of the *Poems* of William W. Lord, in the *Broadway Journal*, May 24, 1845.

60–64 Compare E. C. Pinkney's "To —," beginning "'Twas eve," lines 19–24:

> The low strange hum of herbage growing,
> The voice of hidden waters flowing,
> Made songs of nature, which the ear
> Could scarcely be pronounced to hear;
> But noise had furled its subtle wings,
> And moved not through material things.

67 "Charm" is from the Latin *carmen,* which may be a song, lyric poem, or rhymed spell; here Poe means all three.

68f. Killis Campbell (*Poems,* p. 185) cites as the probable model an incantation to the spirit of Achilles in the opening scene of Byron's *Deformed Transformed*:

> Beautiful shadow
>   Of Thetis's boy!
> Who sleeps in the meadow
>   Whose grass grows o'er Troy . . .

71 Compare "Dreams," lines 23–25: "the moon/Shone on my slumbers in her lofty noon/Too coldly."

71 Note 22: Psalms 121:6 is what Poe has in mind. The full moon is widely credited with dangerous power; our word "lunacy" comes from *Luna,* the moon. Poe's source for the moon blindness of Egypt has not yet been found; one supposes that the symptom is of brief duration.

72f. Compare "The Island of the Fay": "As thus I mused, with half-shut eyes," and "The Murders in the Rue Morgue": "To look at a star by glances — to view it in a side-long way . . . is to behold the star distinctly . . . its lustre . . . grows dim . . . as we turn our vision fully upon it."

80–83 Campbell (*Poems,* page 186) cites for comparison Byron's *Deformed Transformed,* I, 158–161:

> Shadows of beauty!
>   Shadows of power!
> Rise to your duty —
>   This is the hour!

85 Compare "Eleonora": "dark eye-like violets . . . were ever encumbered with dew."

88–91 Compare Lambert A. Wilmer, *Merlin* (1827), III, iv, 42–45:

> And O thus forever
> Shall true love be blest,
> Then lovers be constant,
> And fear not the rest.

Wilmer's play is based on the story of Poe and Elmira Royster.

100 "Ligeia (a Greek word signifying canorous, or high-sounding) is intended as a personification of music," wrote Henry B. Hirst in the *Saturday Museum,*

March 4, 1843, in his sketch of Poe, which certainly had the poet's own approval. Poe gave the name also to the heroine of his story "Ligeia," whose speech he wrote was "melody more than mortal." The word is Homeric, and Vergil mentions Ligea as a nymph in *Georgics*, IV, 336.

107 Note 23: Moore in a note to *Lalla Rookh* says of the albatross, "These birds sleep in the air. They are most common about the Cape of Good Hope."

108 Compare *Paradise Lost*, I, 226: "Aloft, incumbent on the dusky air."

112–113 Compare the opening of Byron's "Stanzas for Music":

> There be none of Beauty's daughters
> With a magic like thee;
> And like music on the waters
> Is thy sweet voice to me . . .

124 Note 24: The tale has not been identified.

124–125 Compare E. C. Pinkney's lines quoted in note on lines 60–64, above.

127 John Phelps Fruit, *Mind and Art of Poe's Poetry*, p. 28, thinks "modell'd" means to be regarded as mundane copies of heavenly realities; if so, the idea is Platonic.

132 Compare "The Sleeper," lines 13–14: ". . . the lake/ A conscious slumber seems to take."

134 Killis Campbell (*Poems*, p. 188) compares this to Byron's *Island*, II, xi, 14–15: ". . . the studded archipelago,/O'er whose blue bosom rose the starry isles."

141 Note 25: Poe quotes the fourth stanza of a song called "Mary," from Scott's *Pirate*, chapter xii. The source of the story about the bees has not been found.

159 Here the poet, who is elsewhere careless about the ranks of heavenly beings, uses "Seraphs" exactly. The four seraphim guard the throne of God, have six wings each, veiling their faces with one pair and their feet with another, and they rejoice in *knowledge*. These stories go back to a work called *The Celestial Hierarchy*, ascribed to Dionysius the Areopagite but now supposed to date from the fifth century of our era and cited usually as the work of "Pseudo-Dionysius."

161–171 This passage is admittedly obscure, and has puzzled commentators. "The eye of God" seems to be something different from what is meant in Ezra 5:5. I take it that although death in the form of an eternal sleep was the penalty for love on Al Aaraaf, one should not regret that Angelo and Ianthe found love. It was better than knowledge that would have given them protracted existence without the "last ecstasy of satiate life." I reject the interpretation that there is a reference here to the death that admitted souls to Al Aaraaf, for Ianthe and Angelo did not encounter that together.

165 The simoom, the destructive wind from Africa, is also mentioned in the 1831 version of "Tamerlane," line 180; in the tale, "MS Found in a Bottle"; and in a canceled passage in "Siope" (later called "Silence — a Fable").

167 Compare Gray's famous phrase in his "Ode on . . . Eton College," "Where ignorance is bliss, 'tis folly to be wise," and the statement that "Reason is Folly, and Philosophy a Lie" in Poe's tale, "Loss of Breath."

171 The reference is to the famous soliloquy, beginning "To be or not to be," in *Hamlet*.

172 In "A Reviewer Reviewed" Poe points out the parallel in Moore's *Lalla Rookh*: ". . . to dwell/Full in the sight of Paradise/Beholding Heaven, yet feeling Hell."

173 Note 26: The quotation is from the *Poesías* (Madrid, 1790), p. 2, of the great Spanish mystic poet, Fray Luis Ponce de León (1527–1591). It is abridged cleverly and slightly misquoted by Poe. See Quinn, p. 143. One could translate it: "A dream interrupted, a day pure, happy, free — Seek; free from passion, zeal, hatred, hope, and jealousy." Poe quoted this passage in his letter to Isaac Lea in 1829.

176–177 These lines are repeated with slight variation as the conclusion of the poem; compare Poe's letter, October 18, 1848, to Mrs. Sarah Helen Whitman: "I could scarcely hear my own voice for the passionate throbbings of my heart."

181f. Killis Campbell (*Poems*, page 191) thinks that Poe's model was "The First Angel's Story" in Moore's *Loves of the Angels* (1823). Poe wrote several prose dialogues between angels or happy departed spirits: "The Power of Words," "The Conversation of Eiros and Charmion," and "The Colloquy of Monos and Una."

181 Note 27: Slightly misquoted from Milton's "Epitaph on the Marchioness of Winchester," lines 55–56.

191 Angelo is the spirit of Michelangelo Buonarroti (see above, p. 93). In the temporary paradise on Tycho's star, Angelo enjoys renewed youth.

197 The version of 1829 (see VARIANTS) is here reminiscent of Shakespeare's *Julius Caesar*, III, i, 60: "I am constant as the northern star."

198 Ianthe, the heroine, has a name meaning hyacinth. She had never lived on Earth, but presumably had dwelt on some other planet, since a child could hardly be born on Poe's Al Aaraaf, where passionate love meant destruction. "Ianthe" was the name Byron used for Lady Charlotte Harley when he dedicated *Childe Harold* to her in 1812; see the discussion of "To One in Paradise."

201–215 The action is hard to understand, unless we assume that the poet discarded historical truth here as part of Science, something he indicated in his introductory sonnet that he would discard in his poem when he liked. Michelangelo actually died on February 18, 1563/4, at Rome. In the poem, he died in his sleep on the Greek isle of Lemnos (see next note), and his spirit wandered about, visiting beautiful scenes, the last being the Parthenon, whence he winged his way to the Messenger Star, in 1572.

203–204 Lemnos (modern Limnos), an island off the west coast of Turkey, is the place upon which Vulcan is said to have fallen when hurled from Olympus by Jove. In the text of 1831 Poe put the word "Arabesq" (*sic*) in quotation marks, as inappropriate to a Grecian isle, but in 1574 the island had been under Turkish dominion.

209 Sādi, the bard of Shiraz, a leading poet of Persia, was born about A.D. 1184 and is said to have lived to be 110 years old. Even if these were lunar years, he lived over a century. He was noted for piety, elegance, and wit, and wrote voluminously, his best-known work being the *Gulistan*, or "Rose Garden," a medley of prose and verse, which has been often translated. Poe may have known the English version of 1823 by James Ross.

210–214 Killis Campbell (*Poems*, page 191) compared these lines to Moore's *Loves of the Angels*:

> Can you forget how gradual stole
> The fresh-awakened breath of soul
> Throughout her perfect form?

215 Note 28: Poe borrows his peculiar phraseology from the Shoberl version of Chateaubriand's *Itinéraire* (New York edition, p. 147), where it is said that the Parthenon "existed entire in 1687" — the year during which it was badly damaged by an explosion of the powder stored in it by the Turks, when it was hit by a shot fired by the Venetians besieging Athens.

217 Note 29: The lines are from Marlowe's *Doctor Faustus*, I, 150f., and were quoted with approval in Poe's review of Charles Lamb's *Specimens of English Dramatic Poets* in the *Broadway Journal* for November 15, 1845. Poe probably knew an early edition of Lamb's work, which was first published in 1808, as his quotation is from Lamb's slightly modernized version from the Marlowe quarto of 1616.

219 Perhaps this is an allusion to the flight of the eagle released from the top of the tower-like pyre of an emperor, in order to carry his spirit to heaven during the ceremonies of his consecration and enrollment (by the Roman Senate's decree) among the gods.

222–236 Compare in "Hans Pfaall" the entries for April 4–17 for a more gradual but somewhat similar change in the appearance of the earth with increasing distance of the beholder.

232 Note 30: See *Paradise Lost*, II, 933: "Flutt'ring his pennons, vain, plumb down he drops."

244 "Daedalion" is a proper noun formed from the singular neuter form of the adjective derived from Daedalus, the "cunning" artificer of wings, who had a descriptive name. The Messenger Star, Al Aaraaf, was a carefully designed artifact of the Supreme Artist, God. The red phase of Tycho's star occasioned great terror of the wrath of God.

253f. Compare here Milton's *Comus*, lines 5–6, ". . . this dim spot/Which men call Earth," and Henry Kirke White's "Lines Written in Wilford Churchyard," lines 28–31:

> . . . if heavenly beings may look down
> From where, with cherubim inspired, they sit,
> Upon this little dim-discover'd spot,
> The earth.

255　In the Herring copy of his volume of 1829, from which he read his poem at Boston in 1845 (see p. 559, below). Poe changed the name of his star to "Tophet-Nour," a word which is a mixture of Hebrew and Arabic, meaning "Light of Hell" or "burning light."

262　Campbell (*Poems*, p. 192) compared to this Byron's "Darkness," line 6, "Morn came and went — and came, and brought no day." In "The Fall of the House of Usher" Poe says: "The hours waned and waned away."

ROMANCE

This fine poem, first published under the title "Preface" in *Al Aaraaf, Tamerlane, and Minor Poems* in 1829, is a declaration of the poet's dedication to Romance, in the voice of Nature, "at once the source, and end, and test of Art." The poet hears this voice speaking through a paroquet, of whom he sees but a reflection and whom he identifies with a mark at which a skilled archer aims.

Killis Campbell, in *Poems* (1917), p. 193, suggested that Poe was answering Byron's "To Romance," in which the noble author "professed to abjure romance and to swear allegiance thenceforward to truth." There are no close verbal parallels; but Poe says that for him Romance *is* Truth.

Poe thought highly of the poem. Writing of his new book to John Neal on December 29, 1829, he said, "the best thing . . . is the small piece headed 'Preface' . . . I am certain these lines have never been surpassed," and quoted lines 11–15.

In 1831 Poe incorporated the two stanzas of the poem into a much longer poem, "Introduction," for his *Poems* of that year. He never reprinted the expanded version.

TEXTS

(*A*) *Al Aaraaf, Tamerlane, and Minor Poems* (1829), p. 57: (*B*) manuscript (lines 11–15 only), December 29, 1829, in a letter to John Neal now in the Koester Collection; (*C*) *Poems* (1831), pp. 33–36 (in "Introduction," pp. 156–158, below); (*D*) Philadelphia *Saturday Museum*, March 4, 1843; (*E*) Herring copy of *Al Aaraaf* . . . , with revisions made in 1845; (*F*) *Broadway Journal*, August 30, 1845 (2:119); (*G*) *The Raven and Other Poems* (1845), p. 84; (*H*) *Works* (1850), II, 106; (*J*) *Portland Daily Advertiser*, April 26, 1850 (lines 11–15 only).

Text *G* is given. *J* is merely the first publication of *B*.

ROMANCE [G]

Romance, who loves to nod and sing
With drowsy head and folded wing,
Among the green leaves as they shake
Far down within some shadowy lake,
5 To me a painted paroquet
Hath been — a most familiar bird —
Taught me my alphabet to say —
To lisp my very earliest word
While in the wild wood I did lie,
10 A child — with a most knowing eye.

Of late, eternal Condor years
So shake the very Heaven on high
With tumult as they thunder by,
I have no time for idle cares
15 Through gazing on the unquiet sky.
And when an hour with calmer wings
Its down upon my spirit flings —
That little time with lyre and rhyme
To while away — forbidden things!
20 My heart would feel to be a crime
Unless it trembled with the strings.

[1829–1845]

VARIANTS

(For variants in C, see lines 1–10 and 35–45 of the 1831 version, pp. 156–157 below.)
Title: Preface (A, changed in E); none (B, D, J)
12 Heaven/air (A, B, J); Heavens (E, F)
14 I have no time for idle/I hardly have had time for (A, B, J); I scarcely have had time for (D changed in E)
15 the unquiet/th' unquiet (A, B but not J)
18 time/hour (D)
21 Unless it trembled/Did it not tremble (A changed in E)

NOTES

4 The poet sees only the reflection of the bird; compare his use of mirror images in "To the River —" and in the tales, "Mystification," and "The Fall of the House of Usher."

5 Here the author connects his bird with the carved and painted figure of a

bird, in Scotland locally called a papingo, hung from a pole outside a church tower to be shot at by archers. The custom was kept up from the fifteenth century until 1868 at Kilwinning Abbey at Irvine in Ayrshire, where Poe stayed for a time as a boy. It is clearly referred to in his story, "The Bargain Lost," published in 1832, where it is said of a character wearing brightly colored garments, "the paroquet, upon a certain cathedral, resembled nothing so much as Pedro." The passage is not included in the several later versions of the story called "Bon-Bon." Miss Phillips, I, 385ff, acknowledges indebtedness to R. M. Hogg of Irvine and gives two illustrations of the Kilwinning popinjay (to use the English word for such a target).

7 A suggestion has been made (I believe by J. H. Whitty) that Poe knew a parrot that could say the alphabet. This, without any early evidence, must seem too fanciful, but perhaps the poet imagined one. The idea of the unreasoning speech of parrots long interested Poe, and he said, in "The Philosophy of Composition," that this notion had a part in the genesis of "The Raven."

10 Compare Poe's tale "Morella": "the wisdom or the passions of maturity I found hourly gleaming from [infancy's] full and speculative eye."

11 The condors, the largest birds of prey, are noted for voracity; Poe refers to them also in "The Conqueror Worm." The Norse demon Hresvelger, who, in the form of an eagle, caused storms by flapping his wings, may have been known by Poe, from a mention in the "Ode Addressed to H. Fuseli" by the once widely read poet Henry Kirke White.

11f. Compare the last stanza of "The Happiest Day."

14 "Cares" are here "concerns" rather than "sorrows," as Wilbur in *Poe* (1959), p. 131, remarks.

16–17 Compare E. C. Pinkney's "Lines From the Port Folio of H—," no. I, 75–77:

> Time flings
> Our pains and pleasures from his wings
> With much equality.

16–21 Compare Byron's "Well! Thou Art Happy." lines 25–27:

> Yet was I calm: I knew the time
>   My breast would thrill before thy look;
> But now to tremble were a crime.

18–21 See also "Israfel" (version of 1841), lines 20–21: "That trembling living lyre/Of those unusual strings . . ."

TO——

("Should my early life seem")

It is uncertain who the lady addressed is: possibly Elizabeth

Rebecca Herring, Poe's cousin. The chief image is unusual, that of sands running through the fingers rather than in an hourglass.

Usually this poem is treated as an early version of "A Dream Within a Dream" of 1849, but here, because of the great extent of the revision, we take it up as a separate entity. This 1829 version uses little from the 1827 "Imitation"; only one line is unaltered. The late version of 1839 retains no line of 1827 and very little of the 1829 version.

TEXTS

(*A*) Manuscript, about 1829, once in the possession of Lambert A. Wilmer, described by Stedman and Woodberry, *Works*, X, 228–229; (*B*) *Yankee and Boston Literary Gazette*, December 1829 (p. 298), lines 13–26; (*C*) *Al Aaraaf, Tamerlane, and Minor Poems* (1829), pp. 59–60; (*D*) *Poems* (1831), pp. 123–124, where lines 13–26 are incorporated in "Tamerlane" as section XXIV.

The text given here is C. Version D is given above at page 53, but the variants are also recorded below. In the Herring copy of the volume of 1829, sent to the printer of *The Raven and Other Poems* in 1845, the whole poem is marked for deletion.

TO — — [*C*]

1

Should my early life seem,
(As well it might,) a dream —
Yet I build no faith upon
The king Napoleon —
5   I look not up afar
For my destiny in a star:

2

In parting from you now
Thus much I will avow —
There are beings, and have been
10   Whom my spirit had not seen
Had I let them pass me by
With a dreaming eye —
If my peace hath fled away

In a night — or in a day —
15   In a vision — or in none —
Is it therefore the less gone? —

3

I am standing 'mid the roar
Of a weather-beaten shore,
And I hold within my hand
20   Some particles of sand —
How few! and how they creep
Thro' my fingers to the deep!
My early hopes? no — they
Went gloriously away,
25   Like lightning from the sky
At once — and so will I.

4

So young? ah! no — not now —
Thou hast not seen my brow,
But they tell thee I am proud —
30   They lie — they lie aloud —
My bosom beats with shame
At the paltriness of name
With which they dare combine
A feeling such as mine —
35   Nor Stoic? I am not:
In the terror of my lot
I laugh to think how poor
That pleasure "to endure!"
What! shade of Zeno! — I!
40   Endure! — no — no — defy.

[1829]

VARIANTS

Title: *omitted* (B, D)
6 For/To (A)
13 If my peace hath flown away (B, D)
16 Is it the less gone? (A)

17 am/was (D)
18 weather-beaten/wind-beaten (D)
19 hold/held (D)
21 How bright! and yet to creep (D)
26 Why in the battle did not I? (D)

NOTES

1 Identical with line 4 of "Imitation."

4 Among Napoleon Bonaparte's titles were those of King of Italy (1805) and, finally, King of Elba (1814). The latter is perhaps alluded to here. His beliefs in his star and in himself as a man of destiny are famous.

9–12 Compare "Imitation" (1827), lines 7–10.

39 Zeno of Citium in Cyprus, founder of the Stoic philosophy, is mentioned in Poe's album verses, "Elizabeth [Rebecca]," also apparently of 1829. Zeno's chief doctrine was of endurance.

TO [ELMIRA]

Killis Campbell thought (*Poems,* page 194) that these lines refer to Elmira Royster Shelton and that lines 11 and 12 may refer to the wealth of her successful suitor and husband, Alexander Barret Shelton, who later left her fifty thousand dollars. See my notes on "The Happiest Day" of 1827.

TEXTS

(A) *Al Aaraaf, Tamerlane, and Minor Poems* (1829), p. 62; (B) the Herring copy of *Al Aaraaf . . .* with revisions, 1845; (C) *Broadway Journal,* September 20, 1845 (2:164); (D) *The Raven and Other Poems* (1845), p. 87; (E) *Works* (1850), II, 104.

Text *D,* not verbally different from *C* and *E,* is used.

TO — [D]

The bowers whereat, in dreams, I see
 The wantonest singing birds,
Are lips — and all thy melody
 Of lip-begotten words —

5   Thine eyes, in Heaven of heart enshrined
 Then desolately fall,
O God! on my funereal mind
 Like starlight on a pall —

Thy heart — *thy* heart! — I wake and sigh,

10   And sleep to dream till day
Of the truth that gold can never buy —
Of the baubles that it may.

[1829–1845]

VARIANTS

Title: To — — (*A, B*)   12   baubles/trifles (*A*)
11   the truth/truth (*A*)

NOTES

1–3   Probably this conceit is influenced by E. C. Pinkney's famous "Health," quoted in Poe's essay, "The Poetic Principle":

> Her every tone is music's own, like those of morning birds,
> And something more than melody dwells ever in her words;
> The coinage of her heart are they, and from her lips each flows
> As one may see the burthened bee forth issue from the rose.

In *Titus Andronicus*, III, i, 85, Lavinia's tongue is compared to "a sweet melodious bird."

4   The implication is of falsity, *mere* words.

8   Compare "Al Aaraaf," II, 16–17: ". . . stars . . . besilvering the pall."

11–12   Wilbur, *Poe* (1959), p. 131, questions whether the poem is about a "priceless" dead love or an untruthful lady. The poem seems to me definitely to reproach the person addressed.

TO THE RIVER [PO]

This charming little poem in the author's playful manner, of which "Fairyland" is a better example, long puzzled commentators. In all the versions he wrote or printed himself, Poe left the name of the river a blank, probably thinking that readers would see that "Po" — a pun on his own name — was intended. Apparently Dr. Thomas Holley Chivers saw the joke, for he wrote Poe on February 21, 1847, of composing a "Song to the River Po," which does not seem to be preserved.[1] Killis Campbell (*Poems*, p. 195) noticed an echo of a quatrain in Byron's "Stanzas to the Po":

[1] See *The Complete Works of Thomas Holley Chivers*, edited by E. L. Chase and L. F. Parks, I (1957), 70.

What if thy deep and ample stream should be
A mirror of my heart, where she may read
The thousand thoughts I now betray to thee,
Wild as thy wave, and headlong as thy speed!

But the pun escaped Campbell and all other annotators until in 1945 Mr. Richard J. Lord, my student at Hunter College, pointed out to me what must be meant. Poe, incidentally, chose to think of his river in a calmer mood than Byron's, and may also have had in mind a brief piece by William Cowper:

ANOTHER [COMPARISON] — ADDRESSED TO A YOUNG LADY

Sweet stream, that winds through yonder glade,
Apt emblem of a virtuous maid —
Silent and chaste she steals along,
Far from the world's gay busy throng;
With gentle yet prevailing force,
Intent upon her destined course;
Graceful and useful all she does,
Blessing and blest where'er she goes,
Pure-bosom'd as that watery glass,
And heaven reflected in her face.

TEXTS

(A) Wilmer manuscript, 1828, on the verso of "To — —" ("I saw thee on the bridal day"); (B) Al Aaraaf, Tamerlane, and Minor Poems (1829), p. 63; (C) Burton's Gentleman's Magazine, August 1839 (5:99); (D) Philadelphia Saturday Museum, March 4, 1843; (E) Herring copy of Al Aaraaf . . . with manuscript corrections, 1845; (F) Broadway Journal, September 6, 1845 (2:131); (G) The Raven and Other Poems (1845), p. 88; (H) Works (1850), II, 95.

The text used is G. The Wilmer manuscript was first described by Stedman and Woodberry, Works (1895), X, 230.

TO THE RIVER —— [G]

Fair river! in thy bright, clear flow
Of crystal, wandering water,
Thou art an emblem of the glow
Of beauty — the unhidden heart —
5   The playful maziness of art
In old Alberto's daughter;

But when within thy wave she looks —
Which glistens then, and trembles —
Why, then the prettiest of brooks
10   Her worshipper resembles;
For in his heart, as in thy stream,
Her image deeply lies —
His heart which trembles at the beam
Of her soul-searching eyes.   [1829–1845]

VARIANTS

Title: In an Album. — To the River —— (*A*)
2 crystal, wandering/labyrinth-like (*A, B, C*)
10 My pretty self resembles (*A*)
11 in his/in my (*A, B, C, F*); in thy/

first written on thy *but altered* (*A*)
12 deeply/lightly (*A*)
13 His/The (*A, B, C, F*)
14 The scrutiny of her eyes (*A, B, C, changed to present reading in E*)

NOTES

3–6 These lines long baffled commentators, who could find no well-known daughter of "old Alberto." But Richard J. Lord pointed out what Poe must have had in mind: a charmingly playful young widow who did not hide her heart when she learned of the fatherly love borne her by an elderly physician named Alberto, but returned that love. The story is in the tenth novella of the first day of Boccaccio's *Decameron*.

TO M—
("I heed not")

Called "Alone" in the earliest version, "To M—" in the 1829 volume, and "To —" in a late manuscript, the poem is extremely personal — and, in the final version, worthy of the term "perfect." The allusions will be patent to anyone acquainted with the early life of Poe.

The identities of the ladies addressed, however, are quite uncertain. "M—" cannot be Mary Starr, whom Poe did not know so early as 1829. And it is quite unthinkable that Poe called Mrs. Clemm by her first name, Maria (in the early nineteenth century!), nor was she yet "Muddy" to him. Nor could "M—" have been

POEMS COLLECTED IN 1829

Poe's cousin Mary Estelle Herring (Elizabeth Herring's half-sister), a small child in 1829. Could Mary Winfree have met and mentioned Elmira to Poe earlier than 1834, and be addressed in this poem of 1829?

The presence of the late manuscript (which is signed "E.A.P.") in the Griswold Collection suggests that Frances Sargent Osgood may have been addressed in the final version, for Griswold was literary executor of both Poe and Mrs. Osgood.

TEXTS

(*A*) Manuscript, about 1828, once in the possession of Lambert A. Wilmer (described by Stedman and Woodberry, *Works*, X, 193–194); (*B*) *Al Aaraaf, Tamerlane, and Minor Poems* (1829), pp. 68–69; (*C*) Herring copy of *Al Aaraaf* . . . , with changes of 1845; (*D*) manuscript 1845–1849, from the papers of R. W. Griswold, facsimile in Woodberry, *Life*, II, 328; (*E*) *Works* (1850), II, 51. The texts given are *B* and *D* (verbally like *E*) in full. The first eight lines were not marked for deletion in *C*, but did not appear in the volume of 1845.

TO M — [*B*]

1

O! I care not that my earthly lot
Hath — little of Earth in it —
That years of love have been forgot
In the fever of a minute —

2

5   I heed not that the desolate
Are happier, sweet, than I —
But that you meddle with my fate
Who am a passer-by.

3

It *is* not that my founts of bliss
10   Are gushing —strange! with tears —
Or that the thrill of a single kiss
Hath palsied many years —

4

'Tis not that the flowers of twenty springs
Which have wither'd as they rose
15   Lie dead on my heart-strings
With the weight of an age of snows.

5

Nor that the grass — O! may it thrive!
On my grave is growing or grown —
But that, while I am dead yet alive
20   I cannot be, lady, alone.   [1828–1829]

VARIANTS

Title: Alone (*A*)
9–12 *This stanza stood thus in A:*
  I heed not that my founts of bliss
  Be gushing, oh! with tears

  That the tremor of one kiss
    Hath palsied many years —
9–20 *Marked for deletion in C*
19 yet/and (*A*)
20 lady/love (*A*)

TO — [*D*]

I heed not that my earthly lot
Hath — little of Earth in it —
That years of love have been forgot
In the hatred of a minute: —
I mourn not that the desolate
Are happier, sweet, than I,
But that *you* sorrow for *my* fate
Who am a passer by.   [1828–1849]

NOTES

3–4 Compare Dryden's *All for Love*, IV, 520f.: "And thus one minute's feigning has destroyed/My whole life's truth."

19 John H. Hewitt thought the line offensive, and said so (in the Baltimore *Minerva and Emerald*) in a review of *Al Aaraaf*, to which he refers in his autobiographic *Shadows on the Wall* (1877), p. 43. But the meaning is clear enough: the poet is alive, though dead to certain friends of his past. Poe in his "Selections from Milton" quotes Sonnet XIV, "this earthly load/Of death called life." See Thomas P. Haviland in *PMLA*, September 1954.

20 Compare, on the desire to be alone, Poe's late, unfinished tale "The Lighthouse," as well as passages in "Metzengerstein" and "The Man of the Crowd."

FAIRYLAND [I]

In "A Few Words About Brainard," in *Graham's* for February 1842, Poe has a passage that may be given as his comment on his own "Fairyland." In this article, he puts forth a theory of the relations of poetry and humor. Both occasionally use rhyme, for different reasons. But he says that one "branch of humor . . . blends so happily with the ideal," that the combination is legitimate poetry. "We allude to what is termed '*archness*' — a trait with which popular feeling, which is unfailingly poetic, has invested . . . the whole character of the fairy."

This poem is pure fantasy, in a vein of arch humor, about fairies using tents of moonglow. Poe gave line 33 a footnote in 1829: "Plagiarism — see the works of Thomas Moore — passim." That suggests that he was consciously plagiarizing something in Moore, and Killis Campbell (*Poems*, p. 197) refers to *Lalla Rookh* for a description of Shadukiam in Jinnistan:

> . . . that City of Delight
> In Fairyland, whose streets and towers
> Are made of gems and light and flowers; . . .
>
> Such miracles and dazzling sights,
> As Genii of the Sun behold,
> At evening, from their tents of gold
> Upon th' horizon — where they play
> Till twilight comes, and, ray by ray,
> Their sunny mansions melt away.

This may have partly inspired Poe, but he hardly plagiarized anything here. Actually I think his footnote applies only to the similes: "Like almost anything/Or a yellow albatross." The joke is that Moore compared anything to almost anything else, real or unreal. The very name of the albatross implies what is true of all the species; they are black and white. Nothing is more unreal than a yellow one!

FAIRY-LAND

How successful Poe was in his poem is a matter of opinion. N. P. Willis of the *American Monthly* not only rejected the piece in 1829 but boasted of burning the manuscript. But John Neal, editor of *The Yankee*, admired it, calling it "though nonsense, rather exquisite nonsense." Woodberry (*Life*, I, 65) says appreciatively that it is the only poem of 1829 bearing the mark of Poe's originality, and that the "unique character in this imagery . . . makes it linger in the memory." Frances Winwar (*The Haunted Palace*, p. 116) praises the poem's "lightness and whimsicality . . . the eeriness of the fantasy and the variation in the music," and greets it "as much with delight as surprise." Wilbur (*Poe*, p. 132), says it reflects "Poe's most successful lighter moments," and that the self-mockery enhances rather than endangers "the lyrical charm." Edward H. Davidson, *Poe: A Critical Study* (1957), pages 30–31, sees in the piece an apocalyptic vision, but there is no terrible element in any version of the poem.

A few lines of the poem were quoted by John Neal in a note "To Correspondents" in *The Yankee* for September 1829, and N. P. Willis quoted a few lines in his note on bad poetry in the *American Monthly* for November, but the first complete version — the basis for all save one that Poe later printed — appeared in *Al Aaraaf, Tamerlane, and Minor Poems* (1829), near the end of the year. Poe altered some lines and added considerably to the original text for *Poems* (1831), making virtually a new poem of it, but he did not retain the new material in subsequent printings.

In *Burton's Gentleman's Magazine* of August 1839 Poe had a note: "The Fairyland of our correspondent is not orthodox. His description differs from all received accounts of the country — but our readers will pardon the extravagance for the vigor of the delineation."

TEXTS

(*A*) *The Yankee and Boston Literary Gazette*, September 1829 (lines 1–4, 19–28); (*B*) *American Monthly Magazine*, November 1829 (lines 35–38); (*C*) *Al Aaraaf, Tamerlane, and Minor Poems* (1829), pp. 69–71; (*D*) review from an unidentified Baltimore paper, 1829 or 1830, reprinted in *Virginia Cavalcade*, Summer 1955, p. 7 (lines 1–28); (*E*) *Poems* (1831), pp. 57–58, included in "Fairy Land" [II]; (*F*) *Burton's Gentleman's Magazine*, August 1839 (5:70); (*G*) Herring copy of *Al Aaraaf* . . . with revisions of 1845; (*H*) *The Raven*

and Other Poems (1845), pp. 85–86; (*J*) *Broadway Journal*, October 4, 1845
(2:193–194); (*K*) *Works* (1850), II, 107–108.

Since the extract (*D*) has a reading in line 13 that was adopted in Poe's
latest texts, the unknown reviewer presumably used a copy of Poe's volume
(*C*) with an author's change. My text is from Poe's volume of 1845 (*H*),
which is like Griswold's (*K*). The *Broadway Journal* form (*J*) was printed
after Poe's book appeared, but in line 12 retains "filmy" in italics from older
texts *C* and *F*.

FAIRY-LAND [*H*]

Dim vales — and shadowy floods —
And cloudy-looking woods,
Whose forms we can't discover
For the tears that drip all over.
5   Huge moons there wax and wane —
Again — again — again —
Every moment of the night —
Forever changing places —
And they put out the star-light
10   With the breath from their pale faces.
About twelve by the moon-dial
One more filmy than the rest
(A kind which, upon trial,
They have found to be the best)
15   Comes down — still down — and down
With its centre on the crown
Of a mountain's eminence,
While its wide circumference
In easy drapery falls
20   Over hamlets, over halls,
Wherever they may be —
O'er the strange woods — o'er the sea —
Over spirits on the wing —
Over every drowsy thing —
25   And buries them up quite
In a labyrinth of light —
And then, how deep! — O, deep!

Is the passion of their sleep.
In the morning they arise,
30 And their moony covering
Is soaring in the skies,
With the tempests as they toss,
Like — almost any thing —
Or a yellow Albatross.
35 They use that moon no more
For the same end as before —
Videlicet a tent —
Which I think extravagant:
Its atomies, however,
40 Into a shower dissever,
Of which those butterflies,
Of Earth, who seek the skies,
And so come down again
(Never-contented things!)
45 Have brought a specimen
Upon their quivering wings. [1829, 1845]

VARIANTS

Title: Heaven (*A*); *none* (*B*); Fairyland
(*C, F, J*)
7 Every/Ev'ry (*C, F*)
13 kind/sort (*C, F, changed in D and
G*)
20 over halls /and rich halls (*C, F*)
23–24 O'er spirits on the wing
O'er every drowsy thing (*A*)

33–34 *Canceled in G but retained in
H, J, K*
33 *Footnote*: Plagiarism — see the works
of Thomas Moore — passim — Edr.
(*C, canceled in G*)
44 Never-contented/The unbelieving
(*C, F*)

NOTES

1–4 These lines are used with slight changes in "Dreamland," lines 9–12.

1–2 Compare with this Andrew Marvell, "Upon Appleton House," lines 79–80: "In fragrant gardens, shady woods,/Deep meadows, and transparent floods," and "hollow vales and hanging woods" in the thirty-eighth chapter of Gilbert White's *Natural History . . . of Selborne* (1789).

10 Probably this echoes *King Henry IV, Part I*, I, iii, 202: "To pluck bright honour from the pale-faced moon."

16–17 Compare "Tamerlane," line 139: "on the crown of a high mountain," and "Serenade," line 12: "on the spectral mountain's crown."

35–38 Lucretius, *De rerum natura*, V, 731–736, refers to an old notion that a moon was created and destroyed each day. "It seems wasteful to use a perfectly good moon only once," says Richard Wilbur in his *Poe* (1959), p. 132.

41f.   Compare *Midsummer Night's Dream*, III, i, 175–176: "Go pluck the wings from painted butterflies,/To fan the moonbeams from his sleeping eyes." The Greeks portrayed the soul as a butterfly; they had one name for both: "psyche," to which Poe has a reference in "How to Write a Blackwood Article." Floyd Stovall is probably right in saying that the butterflies symbolize artists, who, "seeking heaven, catch on their wings fragments of those dissolving moons which, settling over earth at night, transform its daylight reality to a fairyland of beauty." See *Studies in English*, no. 11 (University of Texas Bulletin, 1931), p. 59.

FUGITIVE VERSES

1829–1831

ALONE

This remarkably fine poem was written without title, but marked "Original" and signed "E. A. Poe," in the album of Lucy Holmes, who later became the wife of Judge Isaiah Balderston of Baltimore. In the album is another poem, "I have gazed on woman's cheek," "By W. H. Poe — copied at his request by E. A. Poe." Edgar Poe's striking verses have been in print since 1875, but the manuscript was first thoroughly discussed by Irby Bruce Cauthen, Jr. (*Studies in Bibliography*, Charlottesville, 1950–51, III, 284–291), who examined the album. It is now in the possession of the first owner's granddaughter, Mrs. Emma D. Welbourn of Catonsville, Maryland. The manuscript is holographic and the doubts expressed about it in the past are to be firmly dismissed.[1]

The metrical structure of the verses, with the many run-on lines, is one of Poe's earliest bold experiments and a most successful one.

Cauthen sees the influence of Byron's *Manfred*, II, ii, 50–56:

> From my youth upwards
> My Spirit walked not with the souls of men,
> Nor looked upon the earth with human eyes;
> The thirst of their ambition was not mine,
> The aim of their existence was not mine;
> My joys — my griefs — my passions — and my powers,
> Made me a stranger.

There is also a pertinent passage in "The Prisoner of Chillon," X, 44–49:

[1] The doubts arose because of the way the poem was given to the world by Eugene L. Didier. He found the piece in the album owned by Mrs. Dawson, daughter of Lucy Holmes Balderston, and arranged to publish the poem in *Scribner's Monthly* for September 1875. There he gave a facsimile made from a photograph which he retouched by adding a title — and a conjectural date line, "Baltimore, March 17, 1829." J. H. Ingram denounced it as a bold forgery. Pique perhaps played a part in this, but we must remember that Ingram was wholly unfamiliar with Poe's early handwriting. Readers interested in the defunct controversy can find a great deal about Ingram's doubts in the Ingram List, and even in Killis Campbell, *The Mind of Poe and Other Studies* (1933), p. 204.

Lone — as a solitary cloud,
 A single cloud on a sunny day,
While all the rest of heaven is clear,
A frown upon the atmosphere,
That hath no business to appear
 When skies are blue, and earth is gay.

But although in so early a poem echoes of Byron are not un-likely, the experiences are those any imaginative youth who knew his Byron might actually have. In any case, Poe's vision is strik-ingly his own.

TEXTS

(A) Manuscript, about 1829, in an album; (B) *Scribner's Monthly* for Sep-tember 1875 (10:608); (C) Eugene L. Didier's *Life and Poems of . . . Poe* (1877), p. 248. The text used here is from the manuscript (A); but Didier's title (B) is accepted.

[ALONE] [A]

From childhood's hour I have not been
As others were — I have not seen
As others saw — I could not bring
My passions from a common spring —
5 From the same source I have not taken
My sorrow — I could not awaken
My heart to joy at the same tone —
And all I lov'd — *I* lov'd alone —
Then — in my childhood — in the dawn
10 Of a most stormy life — was drawn
From ev'ry depth of good and ill
The mystery which binds me still —
From the torrent, or the fountain —
From the red cliff of the mountain —
15 From the sun that 'round me roll'd
In its autumn tint of gold —
From the lightning in the sky
As it pass'd me flying by —
From the thunder, and the storm —

20   And the cloud that took the form
             (When the rest of Heaven was blue)
             Of a demon in my view —

                      [1829]

NOTES

8 Poe wrote the word "alone" four times on the Wilmer manuscript of "Tamerlane" and used "Alone" as title for the earliest (1828?) version of "To ——" ("I heed not"). See the note on line 20 of that poem.

22 A demon is powerful, but not necessarily evil.

TO ISAAC LEA

This was written, probably impromptu, in a letter to the publisher Isaac Lea, not long before May 27, 1829, when it was docketed as answered. It was published in transcript with a photographic facsimile by A. H. Quinn in his *Edgar Allan Poe* (1941), pages 138–143. The "cause" is poetry, and the language of the marriage service of the Church of England is echoed in the verses. Lea (1792–1886) was the son-in-law and partner of the noted publisher Matthew Carey, and the letter concerned a plan (which came to nothing) to have the firm of Carey and Lea publish the *Al Aaraaf* volume.

        It was my choice or chance or curse
        To adopt the cause for better or worse
        And with my worldly goods and wit
        And soul and body worship it.

                      [1829]

ELIZABETH [REBECCA]

These acrostic verses were written in the album of Poe's cousin, Elizabeth Rebecca Herring. She married Arthur Turner Tutt on December 2, 1834, and was soon a widow. Later she married Edmund Morton Smith. In 1845 she lent Poe the exemplar of his 1829 volume (*Al Aaraaf, Tamerlane, and Minor Poems*) to be used, with other material, as "printer's copy" for *The Raven and Other Poems*. She visited the Poes at Fordham during Virginia's last illness, in 1846. She is said to have been very beautiful. Her portrait in later years (Phillips, II, 1502) confirms this judgment. She lived until October 17, 1889.

TEXTS

(*A*) Manuscript signed "Edgar" about 1829, described and lines 1–4 quoted in Catalogue of the Harold Peirce Sale, Philadelphia, May 6, 1903, lot 959, and facsimiled in the Yale List (1959), number 17; (*B*) *Complete Poems*, ed. J. H. Whitty (1911), p. 140. The original manuscript (*A*), now owned by H. Bradley Martin, is followed. I change square brackets to parentheses in lines 2 and 15, and correct the erroneous spelling "persuing" in line 7.

ELIZABETH [*A*]

Elizabeth — it surely is most fit
(Logic and common usage so commanding)
In thy own book that *first* thy name be writ,
Zeno [1] and other sages notwithstanding;
5 And *I* have other reasons for so doing
Besides my innate love of contradiction;
Each poet — *if* a poet — in pursuing
The muses thro' their bowers of Truth or Fiction,
Has studied very little of his part,
10 Read nothing, written less — in short's a fool
Endued with neither soul, nor sense, nor art,
Being ignorant of one important rule,
Employed in even the theses of the school —
Called — I forget the heathenish Greek name —
15 (Called any thing, its meaning is the same)
"Always write *first* things uppermost in the heart."

[1] It was a saying of this philosopher "that one's own name should never appear in one's own book."

[About 1829]

· 148 ·

NOTES

The initials of the lines spell out the lady's given names.

4   The saying ascribed by Poe to the Stoic philosopher Zeno has not yet been traced. See another reference to him in "To — —" ("Should my early life seem"), line 39.

6   Compare on contradiction Poe's story, "The Imp of the Perverse."

14   The "Greek name" is the rhetorical term *prolepsis*.

15   Compare *Romeo and Juliet*, II, ii, 43–44: "That which we call a rose,/ By any other name would smell as sweet."

16   In an article on Longfellow in the *Broadway Journal*, March 29, 1845, Poe quoted from the first sonnet of Sir Philip Sidney's *Astrophel and Stella* the famous line, " 'Foole,' said my Muse to me, 'looke in thy heart and write!' "

AN ACROSTIC

("Elizabeth, it is in vain")

This is a companion piece to the foregoing, written on another page of Elizabeth Herring's album. Poe surely did not plan to print it. He took unusual poetic license in misspelling a name in order to gain an initial, and in confusing the story of Endymion.

TEXTS

(*A*) Manuscript signed "E. A. P." about 1829, described, and lines 1–2 quoted, in the Catalogue of the Harold Peirce Sale, Philadelphia, May 6, 1903, lot 960; (*B*) complete text in Anderson's Catalogue, May 19, 1905, lot 366; (*C*) *Complete Poems*, ed. J. H. Whitty (1911), p. 141. The manuscript (*A*), owned by H. Bradley Martin, is followed.

AN ACROSTIC   [*A*]

Elizabeth it is in vain you say
"Love not" — thou sayest it in so sweet a way:
In vain those words from thee or L. E. L.
Zantippe's talents had enforced so well:
Ah! if that language from thy heart arise,
Breathe it less gently forth — and veil thine eyes.

Endymion, recollect, when Luna tried
To cure his love — was cured of all beside —
His folly — pride — and passion — for he died.

[1829?]

NOTES

The initials of the lines spell Elizabeth.

3. "L. E. L." was the signature of Letitia Elizabeth Landon. See note on "A Dream," lines 3-4.

4 "Zantippe" is of course Xanthippe, the shrewish wife of Socrates; emendation would spoil the acrostic.

8-9 Compare the following from the first of Moore's *Evenings in Greece*, lines 139-140: "And dying quenched the fatal fire/ At once of both her heart and lyre." According to the usual legend, Endymion was not killed, but put to sleep in a cave on Mount Latmos, where the virgin moon-goddess could kiss him nightly. Poe refers to him again in "Serenade" (1833).

LINES ON JOE LOCKE

These untitled lines are the only specimen that survives of Poe's humorous verses written at West Point. In the sketch of Poe by Henry B. Hirst, in the Philadelphia *Saturday Museum* of March 4, 1843 — an article that Poe surely saw before it was published — we are told that at the Military Academy Poe "amused himself . . . Pasquinading the Professors. There was . . . Joseph Locke, who had made himself especially obnoxious, through his pertinacity in *reporting* the pranks of the cadets . . . Mr. Poe . . . wrote a long lampoon against this Mr. Locke, of which the following are the only stanzas preserved." That Poe really wrote them during his sojourn at West Point is corroborated by the probably inaccurate quotation of one of them from memory in the reminiscences of a fellow cadet, Thomas W. Gibson, in 1867. It is known from tradition that cadets who subscribed for Poe's *Poems* of 1831 were disappointed in finding none of his local squibs in it.

Lieutenant Joseph Lorenzo Locke (1808-1864) was assistant instructor of military tactics at the academy, and his duty as

FUGITIVE POEMS

Inspector, from 1829 to 1831, was to report infractions of rules. Miss Phillips, I, 371, gives his portrait and an account of his later life. He left the army, edited the *Savannah Republican*, and was a major in the Confederate Army when he died. Poe had probably known Locke first when the poet was an enlisted soldier, before encountering him at West Point.

TEXTS

(*A*) Philadelphia *Saturday Museum*, March 4, 1843; (*B*) Philadelphia *Saturday Courier*, October 20, 1849, in Hirst's obituary of Poe; (*C*) *Harper's New Monthly Magazine* for November 1867 (35:754), lines 5–8, in reminiscences by Gibson; (*D*) W. F. Gill, *Life* (1877), p. 53.

The text is *A*, from Hirst's article in the *Saturday Museum*, because Poe undoubtedly approved it. Gill's text is merely the first inclusion in a book and is based on the *Saturday Museum*.

> As for Locke, he is all in my eye,
>   May the d——l right soon for his soul call.
> He never was known to lie —
>   In bed at a *reveillé* "roll call."
>
> John Locke was a notable name;
>   Joe Locke is a greater; in short,
> The former was well known to fame,
>   But the latter's well known "to report."
>   [1830–1831]

VARIANTS

5   was/is (*B*); notable/very great (*C*)   8   But the/The (*B, C*); latter's/latter (*C*)

POEMS OF 1831

POEMS OF 1831

Poems by Edgar A. Poe . . . Second Edition (New York, 1831) was published by Elam Bliss. The printing was done by Henry Mason of 64 Nassau Street. The book appeared in time to be reviewed briefly but favorably, probably by George P. Morris, in the *New York Mirror*, May 7, 1831, and very briefly (by L. A. Wilmer?) in the Philadelphia *Saturday Evening Post*, May 2. The *Post* review was reprinted in *The Casket* for May 1831. Killis Campbell supervised a reprint of the book for the Facsimile Text Society in 1936.

The prefatory matter of the little volume includes a title-page motto, "Tout le monde a raison — Rochefoucault";[1] a dedication, "To the U.S. Corps of Cadets this volume is respectfully dedicated"; the following quotation:

> Tell wit how much it wrangles
> In fickle points of niceness —
> Tell wisdom it entangles
> Itself in overwiseness
>   *Sir Walter Raleigh*[2]

and a long critical essay headed "Letter to Mr. ——," of which only the first paragraph is given here:

West Point, —— 1831

Dear B———.

Believing only a portion of my former volume to be worthy a second edition — that small portion I thought it as well to include in the present book as to republish by itself. I have, therefore,

[1] Not from Rochefoucauld, but from a play, *Le Gouvernante*, I, iii, 64, issued in 1747, by Pierre-Claude Nivelle de La Chaussée. See his *Œuvres* (Paris, 1763), III, 84. The full quotation is "Quand tout le monde a tort, tout le monde a raison" — "When everybody is wrong, everybody is right." Regis Messac, *Influences françaises dans l'œuvre d'Edgar Poe* (Paris, 1929), p. 23, points out that Isaac D'Israeli spelled the name Rochefoucauld with a final "t," as Poe did.

[2] Sir Walter Raleigh's verses are in his poem "The Lie," which Poe probably got from the 1813 edition of Sir Samuel Egerton Brydges, where "fickle" is the reading for the more probable "tickle."

herein combined Al Aaraaf and Tamerlane with other Poems hitherto unprinted. Nor have I hesitated to insert from the "Minor Poems," now omitted, whole lines, and even passages, to the end that being placed in a fairer light, and the trash shaken from them in which they were imbedded, they may have some chance of being seen by posterity.[3]

INTRODUCTION

This poem, published by its author in this form only once — in *Poems* (1831), pages 33–36 — incorporates as lines 1–10 and 35–45 the two stanzas of the poem called "Preface" in *Al Aaraaf, Tamerlane, and Minor Poems* (1829) and later called "Romance" (see page 128, above). The thirty-six new lines have great merit, but are extremely personal. Perhaps that is why Poe never reprinted them.

INTRODUCTION

Romance, who loves to nod and sing,
With drowsy head and folded wing,
Among the green leaves as they shake
Far down within some shadowy lake,
5   To me a painted paroquet
Hath been — a most familiar bird —
Taught me my alphabet to say —
To lisp my very earliest word
While in the wild-wood I did lie
10   A child — with a most knowing eye.

Succeeding years, too wild for song,
Then roll'd like tropic storms along,

---

[3] The "Letter to Mr. ——" will appear in full in a later volume with Poe's other critical essays. The two blanks and the initial B certainly suggest Poe's publisher Elam Bliss; but General George W. Cullum, who had been with Poe at West Point, is quoted in *Harper's Magazine*, November 1872 (45:561) as believing Bulwer was intended.

Where, tho' the garish lights that fly
Dying along the troubled sky,
15   Lay bare, thro' vistas thunder-riven,
The blackness of the general Heaven,
That very blackness yet doth fling
Light on the lightning's silver wing.

For, being an idle boy lang syne,
20   Who read Anacreon, and drank wine,
I early found Anacreon rhymes
Were almost passionate sometimes —
And by strange alchemy of brain
His pleasures always turn'd to pain —
25   His naivete to wild desire —
His wit to love — his wine to fire —
And so, being young and dipt in folly
I fell in love with melancholy,
And used to throw my earthly rest
30   And quiet all away in jest —
I could not love except where Death
Was mingling his with Beauty's breath —
Or Hymen, Time, and Destiny
Were stalking between her and me.

35   O, then the eternal Condor years
So shook the very Heavens on high,
With tumult as they thunder'd by;
I had no time for idle cares,
Thro' gazing on the unquiet sky!
40   Or if an hour with calmer wing
Its down did on my spirit fling,
That little hour with lyre and rhyme
To while away — forbidden thing!
My heart half fear'd to be a crime
45   Unless it trembled with the string.

But *now* my soul hath too much room —

Gone are the glory and the gloom —
The black hath mellow'd into grey,
And all the fires are fading away.

50 My draught of passion hath been deep —
I revell'd, and I now would sleep —
And after-drunkenness of soul
Succeeds the glories of the bowl —
An idle longing night and day
55 To dream my very life away.

But dreams — of those who dream as I,
Aspiringly, are damned, and die:
Yet should I swear I mean alone,
By notes so very shrilly blown,
60 To break upon Time's monotone,
While yet my vapid joy and grief
Are tintless of the yellow leaf —
Why not an imp the greybeard hath,
Will shake his shadow in my path —
65 And even the greybeard will o'erlook
Connivingly my dreaming-book.

[1829–1831]

NOTES

For notes on lines 1–18 and 35–45, see "Romance," above.

20–23 "Anacreon rhymes" are obviously Moore's translations of the *Anacreontea*, but selections from these simple poems in the original language were read in beginning Greek classes in Poe's day. Some commentators have felt the reference to wine here to be connected with actual drinking. But while the youth of Poe's era probably did sometimes accompany the singing of Moore's Anacreon with actual potations, it is not Poe's but the ancient poet's wine that "turned to fire." Note also a passage in "Shadow — A Fable": "We sang the songs of Anacreon — which are madness."

31–34 There seems to me no reason to give these lines any save the simplest meaning: "It was my luck to fall in love only with women from whom age, death, and marriage to others separated me." The allusions are to his "Helen" (Jane Stith Stanard, the mother of his schoolmate), who died early, and to

Elmira Royster, from whom he was separated by her marriage to Alexander Shelton. In the *Explicator* (vol. 20, no. 1, September 1961), David M. Rein, taking "love" in the wider sense of "have deep affection for," would add Poe's real and foster mothers.

47 Campbell (*Poems*, p. 193) compares to this the lines from Wordsworth's ode, "Intimations of Immortality": "Whither is fled the visionary gleam?/ Where is it now, the glory and the dream?" and Moore's *The Loves of the Angels*: "Or, if they did, their gloom was gone, / Their darkness put a glory on!"

54–55 Compare Andrew Marvell's "Nymph Complaining for the Death of her Faun," lines 37–40:

> Thenceforth I set my self to play
> My solitary time away,
> With this: and very well content,
> Could so mine idle Life have spent.

Poe quoted other lines from this poem with enthusiasm in a review of S. C. Hall's *Book of Gems* in the *Southern Literary Messenger*, August 1836, and again in the *Broadway Journal*, May 17, 1845.

61–62 Compare *Macbeth*, V, iii, 23–24: "My way of life/ Is fallen into the sere, the yellow leaf," and Byron's echo of this in "On this Day I complete my Thirty-Sixth Year," line 5: "My days are in the yellow leaf."

MYSTERIOUS STAR!
(A new introduction to "Al Aaraaf")

In the volume of 1831, Poe substituted for the first fifteen lines of "Al Aaraaf" a different and longer introductory passage, retaining only two and a half lines of the earlier version unchanged. This has enough unity to justify its collection as a separate composition. The author never reprinted it; hence the only text, that of *Poems* (1831), is used here.

> Mysterious star!
> Thou wert my dream
> All a long summer night —
> Be now my theme!
> By this clear stream,
> Of thee will I write;

5

Meantime from afar
Bathe me in light!

      Thy world has not the dross of ours,
10   Yet all the beauty — all the flowers
      That list our love, or deck our bowers
      In dreamy gardens, where do lie
      Dreamy maidens all the day,
      While the silver winds of Circassy
15   On violet couches faint away.

      Little — oh! little dwells in thee
      Like unto what on earth we see:
      Beauty's eye is here the bluest
      In the falsest and untruest —
20   On the sweetest air doth float
      The most sad and solemn note —
      If with thee be broken hearts,
      Joy so peacefully departs,
      That its echo still doth dwell,
25   Like the murmur in the shell.
      Thou! thy truest type of grief
      Is the gently falling leaf —
      Thou! thy framing is so holy
      Sorrow is not melancholy   [1831]

NOTES

2–3 The reader will naturally think of Shakespeare's title for his play *A Midsummer Night's Dream*, a great favorite of Poe's. ("Al Aaraaf" was probably planned in the summer of 1828.)

20–21 Killis Campbell (in *Poems*, p. 175) compared Shelley's "To a Skylark," line 90: "Our sweetest songs are those that tell of saddest thought." Poe is believed to have read Shelley and Keats in 1830.

22ff. Campbell (see previous note) compared "Al Aaraaf," Poe's note 26: "Sorrow is not excluded from 'Al Aaraaf,' but it is that sorrow which the living love to cherish for the dead . . ."

23f. Compare Poe's story "Berenicë" for "the spirit of a departed sound . . . seemed to be ringing in my ears." The sound one hears when one holds a conch shell to the ear is commonly said to be the "echo of the sea" — at least children are told so.

FAIRY LAND [II]

Because the first forty lines and four of the last five are entirely new, this "Fairy Land" in *Poems* (1831) is virtually a new poem, with an effect of its own. Lines 41–50 repeat almost verbatim lines 1–10 of "Fairyland" (1829), and lines 51, 52–54, 55–56, 57–59, and 63 use lines 12, 15–17, 27–28, 18–20, and 22, respectively, of the earlier poem, with a few changes. Poe printed the new poem only once.

FAIRY LAND

Sit down beside me, Isabel,
Here, dearest, where the moonbeam fell
Just now so fairy-like and well.
Now thou art dress'd for paradise!
5   I am star-stricken with thine eyes!
My soul is lolling on thy sighs!
Thy hair is lifted by the moon
Like flowers by the low breath of June!
Sit down, sit down — how came we here?
10   Or is it all but a dream, my dear?

You know that most enormous flower —
That rose — that what d'ye call it — that hung
Up like a dog-star in this bower —
To-day (the wind blew, and) it swung
15   So impudently in my face,
So like a thing alive you know,
I tore it from its pride of place
And shook it into pieces — so
Be all ingratitude requited.
20   The winds ran off with it delighted,
And, thro' the opening left, as soon
As she threw off her cloak, yon moon
Has sent a ray down with a tune.

· 1 6 1 ·

And this ray is a *fairy* ray —
25 Did you not say so, Isabel?
How fantastically it fell
With a spiral twist and a swell,
And over the wet grass rippled away
With a tinkling like a bell!
30 In my own country all the way
We can discover a moon ray
Which thro' some tatter'd curtain pries
Into the darkness of a room,
Is by (the very source of gloom)
35 The motes, and dust, and flies,
On which it trembles and lies
Like joy upon sorrow!
O, *when* will come the morrow?
Isabel! do you not fear
40 The night and the wonders here?
Dim vales! and shadowy floods!
And cloudy-looking woods
Whose forms we can't discover
For the tears that drip all over!

45 Huge moons — see! wax and wane
Again — again — again —
Every moment of the night —
Forever changing places!
How they put out the starlight
50 With the breath from their pale faces!

Lo! one is coming down
With its centre on the crown
Of a mountain's eminence!
Down — still down — and down —
55 Now deep shall be — O deep!
The passion of our sleep!
For that wide circumference
In easy drapery falls
Drowsily over halls —

TO HELEN

60   Over ruin'd walls —
          Over waterfalls,
          (Silent waterfalls!)
          O'er the strange woods — o'er the sea —
          Alas! over the sea!

[1829–1831]

NOTES

1   Isabel (Isabella) is a most appropriate name for a friend of a discoverer of an unknown land.

9–10   Compare "A Dream Within a Dream" (1849), lines 23–24, "Is *all* that we see or seem/ But a dream within a dream?"

12   The phrase "what d'ye call it" and its several kindred forms are called colloquial by the lexicographers. Obviously Poe here merely means he is not quite sure the "enormous flower" is a rose.

13   "A dog-star" is here used to mean a cynosure, without direct reference to Sirius.

17   "Pride of place" is from *Macbeth*, II, iv, 12; Poe does not seem to have had in mind here the technical meaning: "at the highest point of a falcon's flight."

22–23   Compare "Irenë" (1831), line 25: "Thus hums the moon within her ear."

29   Compare the abortive ending of one version of "The Valley of Unrest," printed in the *American Review* in April 1845:

> They wave; they weep; and the tears, as they well
> From the depth of each pallid lily-bell,
> Give a trickle and a tinkle and a knell.

33   In a review in *Burton's*, September 1839, and in "Marginalia," number 39, Poe praised a line, "I see the summer rooms, open and dark," from page 13 of *The Bride of Fort Edward*, a book published anonymously by Delia Bacon.

39–40   Compare "The Sleeper," lines 30–31: "Oh, lady dear, hast thou no fear? / Why and what art thou dreaming here?"

(For annotation on lines 41–64, see pp. 138–142.)

TO HELEN

"To Helen" is often regarded as the finest of Poe's lyrics. It includes the incomparable phrases that sum up classical civilization: "the glory that was Greece,/And the grandeur that was Rome." It was a remarkable poem when it first appeared in 1831, but Poe took twelve years to perfect it. The two most famous lines, first published in 1843, are among those Poe changed with consummate art.

Of "To Helen" James Russell Lowell wrote that "there is a little dimness in the filling up," but added that in it "all is limpid and serene," and that it "seems simple, like a Greek column, because of its perfection." [1]

The poem is based on a personal experience of the poet in youth — a memory of Mrs. Jane Stith Stanard at her home in Richmond. But the poem also has a universal meaning. It is spiritual love that leads us to beauty, a resting place from sorrow and the homeland of all that is sacred in our being. Beauty is the lasting legacy of Greece and Rome, and its supreme symbol is the most beautiful of women, Helen, daughter of Zeus, who brings the wanderer home and inspires the poet.

In a letter of October 1, 1848, to Helen Whitman, Poe called the poem "the lines I had written, in my passionate boyhood, to the first, purely ideal love of my soul — to the Helen Stannard [sic] of whom I told you." There is no good reason to doubt the essential truth of this identification. Poe's habit of giving names he liked to women for whose real names he did not care amply accounts for his substitution of "Helen" for "Jane." Of the poet's deep affection for the mother of his schoolmate Robert Stanard there need be no doubt. On March 10, 1859, Mrs. Clemm wrote to Mrs. Whitman:

When Eddie was unhappy at home (which was often the case) he went to [Mrs. Stanard] for sympathy, and she always consoled and comforted him — you are mistaken when you say that you believe he saw her but once in her home. He visited there for years. He only saw her once when she was ill . . . Robert has often told me of his and Eddie's visits to her grave.[2]

The statement repeated from time to time that the poem was composed when Poe was only fourteen years of age is absurd. It is possible, even probable, that Poe wrote something about his

[1] Pages 373–374 of Lowell's sketch of Poe, reprinted from *Graham's Magazine* for February 1845 in Harrison's *Complete Works* (1902), I, 367–383. Actually some critics regard the rhyming of *roam* and *Rome* as a fault.

[2] The letter, now in the Lilly Collection at Indiana University, is quoted by Quinn and Hart, p. 41. A suggestion, by a writer in *Modern Language Notes* (May 1949), that Poe's foster mother shared in the inspiration of "To Helen" is not supported by any document or tradition.

friend when he was fourteen. But the mature and masterly style of "To Helen," even in the earliest version we now have, belies a very early date, as does the author's failure to print it (or anything at all like it) before 1831.[3]

TEXTS

(A) *Poems* (1831), p. 39; (B) *Southern Literary Messenger*, March 1836 (2:238); (C) *Graham's Magazine* for September 1841 (19:123); (D) Philadelphia *Saturday Museum*, March 4, 1843; (E) *Graham's Magazine* for February 1845 (27:51), in James Russell Lowell's "Edgar A. Poe"; (F) *The Raven and Other Poems* (1845), p. 91; (G) *The Lover's Gift* (Hartford, 1848), p. 108; (H) copy of *The Raven* given to Mrs. Whitman by Poe, with one manuscript change; (J) *Works* (1850), I, ix, in Lowell's "Edgar A. Poe."

The text of the 1845 volume (F) is used. The copy given Mrs. Whitman (H) is inscribed "To Mrs. Sarah Helen Whitman — from the most devoted of her friends. Edgar A. Poe." It was described in the Catalogue of the Thomas J. McKee Sale, New York, November 22, 1900, lot 602. The gift book was edited by Poe's friend, Elizabeth Oakes Smith, and the text (G) may be authorized. The copy inscribed to Helen Whitman is owned by Mr. H. Bradley Martin.

TO HELEN [F]

Helen, thy beauty is to me
Like those Nicéan barks of yore,
That gently, o'er a perfumed sea,

[3] It should be recalled that Poe whimsically regarded his birth date as a movable feast. When he enlisted in the Army, he made himself older; when he went to West Point, he grew younger (on this occasion with more motive than whim); and in the last year of his life, Poe, again "younger," wrote Griswold that he had been born in 1813. A tradition reaches me from Baltimore that a lady of that city insisted that Poe was misdated in biographies, for she had met him, and her birth date was mentioned. Poe said that was the very day he was born!

The story that he wrote "To Helen" at fourteen first turned up in Hirst's highly romantical *Saturday Museum* biography, in 1843. Poe was perhaps surprised that his claim was believed. See p. 559 for Poe's statement that he wrote "Al Aaraaf" at ten, and his jest in the *Broadway Journal*, December 6, 1845, that he had a poem "written at 7 months." Poe stated in *The Raven and Other Poems* (1845) in a footnote before his "Poems Written in Youth" — a statement easily disproved by comparison of the texts — that he was reprinting them verbatim. He placed "To Helen" among these youthful efforts, although the rest are from the volumes of 1827 and 1829. In that same footnote Poe also speaks of "plagiarism." Obviously he was anxious to have his little masterpiece accepted as a very early composition. Perhaps this was to emphasize his claims to precocious genius, but he may have wished to head off comparison with the poems of Pike and Shea (both published in 1830), cited as probable "sources" in the notes on lines 2–4 and 9–10.

The weary, way-worn wanderer bore
5   To his own native shore.

On desperate seas long wont to roam,
Thy hyacinth hair, thy classic face,
Thy Naiad airs have brought me home
To the glory that was Greece,
10   And the grandeur that was Rome.

Lo! in yon brilliant window-niche
How statue-like I see thee stand,
The agate lamp within thy hand!
Ah, Psyche, from the regions which
15   Are Holy-Land!

[1831–1843]

VARIANTS

Title: To Helen Stannard (H). *The half-title before the poem is merely* Helen (A)

2 Nicéan/Nicean (A, B, J)

3 perfumed/perfum'd (A, B)

9 glory that was/beauty of fair (A, B)

10 And the grandeur that was/And the grandeur of old (A, B); To the grandeur that was (C)

11 yon brilliant/that little (A, B); that shadowy (C)

13 agate lamp/folded scroll (A, B, C); agate book (G)

14 Ah, Psyche/A Psyche (A)

NOTES

1 There are many stories about Helen of Troy. All agree that she was a daughter of Zeus and the most beautiful of women, but there is disagreement about her adventures and character. Poe alludes only to those legends that present her in the most favorable light. Our earliest document about the wholly good Helen consists of a few lines quoted in Plato's *Phaedrus*, 243a, from the "Palinode" of Stesichorus, who must have had access to far older legends, such as those used by Euripides in his *Helena*.

In a panegyric called *Helen*, the orator Isocrates about 370 B.C. argued that Helen went to Troy only to fulfill the will of the gods, and after their deaths, she, as daughter of Zeus, raised her husband Menelaus to her own divine rank. Furthermore, Helen, in a dream, commanded Homer to compose the *Iliad*, that those who died fighting for her might be envied by living men. Helen thus inspired poetry.

She could appear as a third light with those (now called "St. Elmo's fire") of her twin brothers, Castor and Pollux, to help mariners. See Euripides, *Orestes*, lines 1635–1636.

TO HELEN

At her dream oracle, near Sparta, people consulting Helen slept on the floor of the shrine, and, if she appeared, she took the form of each person's first love. This fits in with Poe's poem about his first love. I take this story from an essay by Andrew Lang on "Helen of Troy"; Lang surely had ancient or medieval authority but unhappily did not name it. For Helen's ability to mimic the voice of each man's beloved, see *Odyssey*, IV, 279.

2 Killis Campbell, *Poems*, page 200, compared Coleridge's "Youth and Age," line 12: "Like those trim skiffs, unknown of yore."

"Nicean" is a good English adjective meaning "victorious," properly formed from *Nike*, the Greek name of Victory. The regular transliteration, *Nice*, in both Latin and English, is often seen in the eighteenth and nineteenth centuries. Although lexicographers have failed to cite the English adjective prior to 1831, it had actually been in print for decades. In John and William Langhorne's standard translation of Plutarch (1770), the life of Nicias (*Lives*, III, 372 and 385), contains two pertinent passages: to the phrase "a general with a name derived from victory," the translator appends a footnote, "That is Nicias. *Nice* signifies *victory*," and later we read the Athenians "ascribed the peace to Nicias . . . It is therefore called the Nicean peace to this day." (See Palmer C. Holt, in *Bulletin of the New York Public Library*, November 1959.)

Another meaning of "Nicean" is "pertaining to Nicea [a city]." Of the many ancient cities named Nicea, one was especially connected with Dionysus. He was revered at Nicea in Bithynia (now Iznik) as a founder (*ktistes*), and its eponymous nymph Nicea was a member of his train. One may consult Photius' synopsis of the historian Memnon, or the *Dionysiacá* of Nonnus. Some coins of the city of Roman times show Bacchus "assis dans un petit barque." How much of this Poe could have known is questionable.

The idea that the word has *no* meaning has certainly been entertained, but hardly by anyone aware of schoolmaster Clarke's statements about his Academy's classical education. No man "first or second in his class" studying Homeric Greek in school is unacquainted with the word for victory.

3–5 These lines still present four cruces. Whence came the barks, where was the perfumed sea, who was the wanderer, and what was his native shore? These problems were discussed in a masterly article, "Poe's Nicean Barks," by Edward D. Snyder, in the *Classical Journal* (Chicago), February 1953 (48:159–169). Snyder gave full references to the literature before 1953, and took up the answers in the order in which they were proposed. I discuss them in a descending order of acceptability, judged by the consistency with Poe's text.

I. Only one entirely consistent explanation has been put forward. In *Notes and Queries*, April 25, 1885 (11:323), W. M. Rossetti proposed Bacchus as the wanderer. He cited *Paradise Lost*, IV, 275–279:

> . . . That Nyseian isle
> Girt with the river Triton, where old Cham,
> Whom Gentiles Ammon call, and Libyan Jove,
> Hid Amalthea, and her florid son
> Young Bacchus . . .

POEMS OF 1831

In *American Literature*, January 1945 (16:342), Frank M. Durham pointed out that in *Paradise Lost*, IV, 301, there is a reference to "hyacinthin locks."

In some editions (1898, for example) of *A Dictionary of Phrase and Fable*, by the Reverend E. Cobham Brewer, the following explanation of "Nicéan barks" was given:

"The way-worn wanderer was Dionysos or Bacchus, after his renowned conquests. His native shore was the Western Horn, called the Amalthēan Horn. And the Nicean barks were vessels sent from the island Nysa, to which in infancy Dionysos was convened to screen him from Rhea. The perfumed sea was the sea surrounding Nysa, a paradisal island."

In the Boston *American Monthly Magazine*, November 1830, Albert Pike published his "Hymn to Bacchus," where there are the lines:

> Where art thou, *conqueror* — before whom fell
> The jewelled kings of Ind . . .
>
> . . . when thou didst check
> Thy tigers and thy lynxes at the *shore*
> Of the broad *ocean* — and didst still the roar,
> Pouring a sparkling and a pleasant wine
> Into its waters — when the dashing brine
> Tossed up new *odors, and a pleasant scent*
> Upon its breath, and many who were spent
> With *weary* sickness, breathed of life anew,
> When wine-inspired breezes on them blew.

The italics are mine. This even accounts for "wayworn," for Dionysus journeyed by land but had to sail to his island home. Pike's verses were unknown to Rossetti, Brewer, and Campbell, who accepted Bacchus as the wanderer before I found the lines in "To Bacchus," no. VI of the once very well known *Hymns to the Gods*, which were reprinted in *Blackwood's Magazine* in June 1839 (45:827). Bacchus and Helen are not too remotely connected; both were children of Zeus and both became gods.

II. A second suggestion (mine) is that the wanderer is Menelaus. According to a story told by Stesichorus and used by Euripides in *Helena*, the gods sent a phantom to Troy with Paris, while the faithful queen of Sparta remained a fugitive in Egypt. Thence, after many years, she was rescued by her husband and returned with him to their native shore. This does not account for the perfumed sea, and Euripides says that the victorious ship was from Sidon, but this explanation connects the wanderer most closely with Helen.

III. My preceptor, Professor W. P. Trent, in his *Raven . . . and Other Poems and Tales* (1897), p. 24, advanced somewhat tentatively the suggestion that Poe had Ulysses in mind but changed Phaeacian to Nicean "intentionally or unintentionally." In *Modern Language Notes*, March 1916 (31:185), Herbert Edward Mierow asserted confidently that "Poe meant not *Nicean* but *Phaeacian*." But why should such a change have been made on purpose? And the mistake — if it were one — could hardly have been overlooked during the many years in which Poe labored over the poem. In his Preface to the *Poems of 1831*, Poe alluded to the "nine-titled Corcyra." This refers to a passage in Chateaubriand's *Itinéraire*, which gives as other names of the home of Al-

TO HELEN

cinoüs and Nausicaa — Argoa, Cassiopea, Ceraunia, Drepanum, Ephisa, Macria, Phaeacia, and Scheria.

In combating the idea that by "Nicean" Poe meant "Phaeacian," some students have dismissed Trent's view completely. The word can mean merely "victorious," without reference to a place. In that case Ulysses is not impossible as the wanderer. Richard Wilbur, *Poe* (1959), page 135, says he would wish it were the Ithacan king, "protected . . . by Athene, . . . rowed in 'a deep and delicious sleep' to his . . . homeland." For most readers Ulysses is the first Greek wanderer who comes to mind. But the "perfumed sea" is without meaning, and Poe's method is not always to use the commonplace.

IV. A suggestion by an unidentified commentator signing himself "A Galwegian," in the London *Notes and Queries*, January 23, 1863 (3 ser., 3:8), is that the wanderer is Alexander the Great, who, according to Strabo (XV, i, 29) built a fleet at Nicaea on the Hydaspes in India, and might have sailed over a sea perfumed from the spice trees of India and Arabia. Alexander was victorious, but he never got home to his native shore at all. He died at Babylon and was entombed at Alexandria in Egypt. This, the earliest explanation propounded, is that preferred by Quinn, p. 179, who credits it to a remark made to him by John C. Rolfe.

V. Snyder's own tentative second suggestion (*Classical Journal*, 48:168) — "Everyman," any weary wanderer coming home — though regarded by him as unlikely, is by no means to be dismissed altogether.

VI. The suggestion of F. V. N. Painter, in *Poets of the South* (1903), p. 217, that Poe was thinking of Nicaea (now Nice) in France and of the Ligurian Sea, deserves notice, but Painter does not identify the wanderer.

VII. An interpretation that would see Catullus as the wanderer was put forward in *Notes and Queries*, May 30, 1914 (11 ser., 9:426–427), by an excellent scholar, Vernon Rendall, and has been independently advanced by at least two American professors, J. J. Jones and Arthur H. Weston, who cite Catullus, poems 4, 29, and 46. The reference would be to Nicea in Bithynia, whence the poet returned to his beloved home, Sirmio. But Catullus refers to his bark (*phasellus*) as of Amastris, not of Nicea; the ship was not victorious, nor the sea perfumed.

VIII. In *Classical Weekly* for April 12, 1943 (36:248–249), E. A. Havelock argued (to me unconvincingly) for a combined interpretation with three motifs, Helen with her power to draw men to Troy and home, the wanderings of Ulysses, and the voyage of Catullus.

IX. A friend once questioned whether the poem linked Christian and Greek traditions. There is a wanderer who fits well: St. Athanasius (whose name means "deathless"), for he returned victorious from Nicea in Bithynia, after the formulation of the Nicene creed; the perfume might be the odor of sanctity. There is no connection with Helen.

6–8   This may be an allusion to Helen's share in what is now called St. Elmo's fire.

6   The line brings to mind the "magic casements, opening on the foam/ Of perilous seas" in the "Ode to a Nightingale" of Keats, which Poe probably read about 1830.

7 It is not too likely that Poe knew it, but Sir Philip Sidney in the first book of *Arcadia* mentions the "jacinth locks of Queen Helen of Corinth." In Pope's version of the *Odyssey*, VI, 231, which Poe almost surely did know, we read of the "hyacinthine locks" of Ulysses; Milton, in *Paradise Lost*, IV, 301, gave Adam "Hyacinthin Locks," and Byron, in *The Deformed Transformed*, I, i, 397–398, has his Stranger, conjuring up a phantom of Achilles, command, "Let these hyacinth boughs / Be his long flowing hair." In his story "Ligeia" Poe says his heroine had "the raven-black, the glossy, the luxuriant and naturally-curling tresses, setting forth the full force of the Homeric epithet 'hyacinthine.' "

References could be multiplied, and this kind of hair can be seen on the Hermes of Praxiteles, and on the statues and coins made in honor of Hadrian's friend Antinoüs. Poe has in mind the shape, not the color, of the flower, for he gives it here to Jane Stanard, whose hair was medium brown with highlights of light brown, according to Mr. Koester, owner of her portrait by James Worrell. The illustration in Quinn's *Edgar Allan Poe* (1941), p. 86, is not in color.

7–12 Wilbur, *Poe* (1959), page 134, compares a passage in Poe's "Assignation," which reminds one of both the epithets "hyacinth" and "Statue-like":

"Her hair . . . clustered . . . round and round her classical head, in curls like those of the young hyacinth . . . and no motion in the statue-like form itself, stirred even the folds of that raiment of very vapor which hung around it as the heavy marble hangs around the Niobe."

The statue here in our author's mind is part of a celebrated group at Florence, thought to have been copied from an original by Praxiteles or, more probably, by Scopas.

8 Naiads are nymphs associated with fresh water, as contrasted with "desperate seas." My student Barbara Johnson sees here a reference to the idea that "Heaven is our home."

9–10 In the Boston *Ariel* of May 1, 1830, there is a lyric called "The Ocean," by John Augustus Shea (1802–1845), of which lines 37–38 are: "The glory of Athens, / The splendor of Rome." In the posthumous volume of Shea's *Poems* (New York, 1846), "Memoir," page 10, his son George said that the lines were composed at West Point, where, although he had no connection with the Academy, it is sure that Shea knew Poe. "The Ocean" was very popular; it was reprinted by Shea himself in volumes of 1831, 1836, and 1843 and often copied in newspapers of the time. Shea died on August 15, 1845. In an obituary in the *Broadway Journal*, August 23, Poe remarked that Shea's "Ocean" was "one of the most spirited Lyrics ever published."

Campbell pointed out in his *Mind of Poe*, p. 156, a line from Wordsworth's "Stanzas: Composed in the Simplon Pass" (1822), "The beauty of Florence, and the grandeur of Rome." Whether the inspiration came from another writer or not, the magic is Poe's own.

10 The architecture of Poe's youth was largely that of the Classic Revival, and there is an old saying that "Richmond is built on seven hills, like Rome." Exact parallels to fact are not unexpected from the author of "The Haunted Palace."

ISRAFEL

11–14 In 1920 the celebrated bibliophile, William A. White, wrote me that the agate lamp would not give a remarkably "brilliant" light, and that the earlier "shadowy" was preferable. The lady was perhaps standing before a window with a light outside. Campbell (*Poems*, p. 203) saw possible echoes of Byron, the most striking being of *Childe Harold*, IV, lxxix, of Rome, "The Niobe of nations! there she stands,/ . . . An empty urn within her withered hands." Poe probably saw Mrs. Stanard holding a letter, but later changed the scroll for a lamp, because Psyche wakened Cupid, or Love, with a drop of oil from hers. The heroine of "The Spectacles" has a "chiselled contour like that of the Greek Psyche." The Psyche *par excellence* is the head and torso at Naples.

The agate is named for "fidus Achates," the *faithful* friend of Aeneas in Vergil. The significant word first appeared in the final revision of 1843.

14 In Greek, Psyche means soul. In a review of Francis Lieber's *Reminiscences of . . . Niebuhr, the Historian* in the *Southern Literary Messenger*, January 1836 (2:125), Poe refers, jocularly, to a medieval monk who, "speaking of the characters in the Iliad," said, "Helen represents the Human Soul — Troy is Hell," and so forth. Poe seems to have based this on the chapter "Introduction to the Iliad" in Henry Nelson Coleridge's *Introductions to . . . Greek Classic Poets* (London, 1830). It is characteristic of Poe to use humorous material with a serious turn, and vice versa, in his imaginative works. See "Poe and H. N. Coleridge's *Greek Classic Poets*" by Palmer C. Holt in *American Literature*, March 1962 (34:8–30).

15 Greece is the Holy Land of art, Richmond the Holy Land of the poet's heart. Poe possibly also knew of the association of Bacchus with Palestine. One of the many places called Nysa where Bacchus was especially revered is in that land, although it is not a seaport.

ISRAFEL

This poem is one of Poe's great accomplishments. It may justly be called a masterpiece, for even in its first version it shows the power of his original genius.

"Israfel" presents no problem of interpretation. The poet acknowledges the superiority of the angel to a man, but says that, in his own proper sphere, the mortal poet is doing very well. The sentiments set forth by Poe in the poem are underlined by his quotation in a review of Lord Brougham's *Critical and Miscellaneous Writings*, in *Graham's Magazine* for March 1842, repeated in the "Marginalia" of the *Southern Literary Messenger* of June 1849 (our number 229): " 'He that is born to be a man,' says

Wieland in his 'Peregrinus Proteus,' 'neither should nor can be anything nobler, greater, or better than a man.' The fact is, that in efforts to soar above our nature, we invariably fall below it." This comment is in a London translation of Christoph Martin Wieland's *Private History of Peregrinus Proteus* (1796), I, 43, but Poe probably picked it up from Bulwer, who used it as a motto for chapter iv of Book V of *Ernest Maltravers* (1837), a favorite source of wit and wisdom for Poe.

Inspiration for "Israfel" obviously comes from Thomas Moore's *Lalla Rookh*, where there are two passages concerning the angel. The first has a note, " 'The angel Israfil, who has the most melodious voice of all God's creatures.' — *Sale*." Poe made this the motto for the first version of his poem. But there is another passage, very near the end of *Lalla Rookh*, with a footnote cross reference to the earlier note, and it is this that, I think, inspired Poe:

> The Georgian's song was scarcely mute,
>   When the same measure, sound for sound,
> Was caught up by another lute,
>   And so divinely breath'd around,
> That all stood hush'd and wondering,
>   And turn'd and look'd into the air,
> As if they thought to see the wing,
>   Of Israfil, the Angel, there; —
> So pow'rfully on ev'ry soul
>   That new, enchanted measure stole.
> While now a voice, sweet as the note
>   Of the charm'd lute, was heard to float
> Along its chords, and so entwine
>   Its sounds with theirs, that none knew whether
> The voice or lute was most divine,
>   So wondrously they went together.

There may also be an echo in Poe's poem of "A Song for St. Cecilia's Day, 1687" by John Dryden, lines 17, 21–23:

> When Jubal struck the corded shell, . . .[1]
> Less than a god they thought there could not dwell
>   Within the hollow of that shell
>   That spoke so sweetly and so well.

[1] Jubal was, according to Genesis 4:19–21, a son of Lamech and Adah, and "the father of all such as handle the harp and organ." See also Mark Van Doren, *The Poetry of John Dryden* (New York, 1920), p. 333.

ISRAFEL [A]

Poe presumably also knew of a reference to "Israfil" in *Amir Khan* (New York, 1829), by the once famous child poet, Lucretia Maria Davidson. Poe's spelling suggests his use of at least one source besides those named.

It has become customary to identify Poe with his angel; the name is the title of Hervey Allen's biography. The practice probably began with Mrs. Osgood's "Echo Song," published in the *Broadway Journal* of September 6, 1845.[2] The transfer of the name, however, is unfortunate, since it disregards the main point made in the poem, the excellence of Man.

TEXTS

(A) *Poems* (1831), pp. 43–45; (B) *Southern Literary Messenger*, August 1836 (2:539); (C) *Graham's Magazine* for October 1841 (19:183); (D) Philadelphia *Saturday Museum*, March 4, 1843; (E) *Broadway Journal*, July 26, 1845 (2:41); (F) *The Raven and Other Poems* (1845), pp. 16–17; (G) J. Lorimer Graham copy of *The Raven* . . . ; (H) R. W. Griswold, *Poets and Poetry of America*, 10th ed. (1850), p. 421; (J) *Works* (1850), II, 46–47.

The first version (A) and the last to be authorized (G) are given. B shows only three variants from A. The change in G is only the insertion of a hyphen in line 25, "grown-up." For clarity I print the introductory quotation as a motto, although all early texts treat it as a footnote to the title.

ISRAFEL [A]

And the angel Israfel who has the sweetest voice of all God's creatures — KORAN.

I

In Heaven a spirit doth dwell
Whose heart-strings are a lute —
None sing so wild — so well
As the angel Israfel —
5   And the giddy stars are mute.

II

Tottering above
In her highest noon
The enamoured moon
Blushes with love —

[2] See p. 234, below.

· 1 7 3 ·

10 While, to listen, the red levin
 Pauses in Heaven.

III

And they say (the starry choir
And all the listening things)
That Israfeli's fire
15 Is owing to that lyre
With those unusual strings.

IV

But the Heavens that angel trod
Where deep thoughts are a duty —
Where Love is a grown god —
20 Where Houri glances are —
— Stay! turn thine eyes afar! —
Imbued with all the beauty
Which we worship in yon star.

V

Thou art not, therefore, wrong
25 Israfeli, who despisest
An unimpassion'd song:
To thee the laurels belong
Best bard, — because the wisest.

VI

The extacies above
30 With thy burning measures suit —
Thy grief — if any — thy love
With the fervor of thy lute —
Well may the stars be mute!

VII

Yes, Heaven is thine: but this
35 Is a world of sweets and sours:
Our flowers are merely — flowers,

ISRAFEL [G]

And the shadow of thy bliss
Is the sunshine of ours.

VIII

If I did dwell where Israfel
40   Hath dwelt, and he where I,
He would not sing one half as well —
One half as passionately,
And a stormier note than this would swell
From my lyre within the sky.

[1831]

VARIANTS

21 *Omitted (B)*   43 stormier/loftier *(B)*
23 yon/a *(B)*

ISRAFEL [G]

And the angel Israfel, whose heart-strings are a lute, and who has the sweetest voice of all God's creatures. — KORAN.

In Heaven a spirit doth dwell
  "Whose heart-strings are a lute;"
None sing so wildly well
As the angel Israfel,
5   And the giddy stars (so legends tell)
Ceasing their hymns, attend the spell
  Of his voice, all mute.

Tottering above
  In her highest noon,
10   The enamoured moon
Blushes with love,
  While, to listen, the red levin
  (With the rapid Pleiads, even,
  Which were seven,)
15   Pauses in Heaven.

And they say (the starry choir
 And the other listening things)
That Israfeli's fire
Is owing to that lyre
 By which he sits and sings —
The trembling living wire
Of those unusual strings.

But the skies that angel trod,
 Where deep thoughts are a duty —
Where Love's a grown-up God —
 Where the Houri glances are
Imbued with all the beauty
 Which we worship in a star.

Therefore, thou art not wrong,
 Israfeli, who despisest
An unimpassioned song;
To thee the laurels belong,
 Best bard, because the wisest!
Merrily live, and long!

The ecstasies above
 With thy burning measures suit —
Thy grief, thy joy, thy hate, thy love,
 With the fervour of thy lute —
 Well may the stars be mute!

Yes, Heaven is thine; but this
 Is a world of sweets and sours;
 Our flowers are merely — flowers,
And the shadow of thy perfect bliss
 Is the sunshine of ours.

If I could dwell
Where Israfel
 Hath dwelt, and he where I,

ISRAFEL [G]

> He might not sing so wildly well
> A mortal melody,
> While a bolder note than this might swell
> From my lyre within the sky.

50

[1831–1845]

VARIANTS

Motto: And the angel Israfel, or Israfeli, whose heart-strings are a lute, and who is the most musical of all God's creatures. KORAN. (C); [D and E read like G but credit the motto to Sale's Koran.]

10 enamoured/enamour'd (D, H)
15 *Transferred to follow 12 in C*
19 owing to/due unto (C)
21 That trembling living lyre (C)
22 Of/With (C)
23 skies/Heavens (C)
25 Where/And (D, E); Love's a grown-up/Love is a grown (C)

26 Where/And (D, E); the Houri/Houri (C)
28 a/the (C) *which also inserts after the line another line*: The more lovely, the more far!
29 Therefore, thou art not/Thou art not, therefore (C, D, E)
31 unimpassioned/unimpassion'd (D, H)
43 thy perfect/thy (C)
45 could/did (C)
48 so wildly/one half so (C)
49 A mortal melody/One half so passionately (C)

NOTES

Motto: That Poe was using Moore is confirmed by the fact that, as Campbell observed *(Poems,* p. 203), Poe's motto is not in the Koran itself but in George Sale's "Preliminary Discourse" to his translation of the Koran, which Moore quoted in his notes.

A lute is actually shaped like a heart (the anatomical, not the playing-card variety). Poe may have had in mind the lines from Letitia E. Landon's "Eastern King" in *The Golden Violet* (1827), page 141:

> And my own heart is as the lute
> I now am waking;
> Wound to too fine and high a pitch
> They both are breaking.

A similar conceit is in some lines from "Le Refus" by Béranger, which Poe added as a motto to "The Fall of the House of Usher" in 1845. It is improbable that Poe could have seen them before 1841, hence Campbell's suggestion that they were a source for "Israfel" may be dismissed. See the notes on Poe's story in the Tales and Sketches.

2–21 Wilbur *(Poe,* page 136) compares "Romance," lines 20–21: "My heart would feel to be a crime / Unless it trembled with the strings."

3 Philip Pendleton Cooke, writing of Poe in the *Southern Literary Messenger* for April 1846 (12:200), calls attention to "an unconscious appropriation" from Byron's *Bride of Abydos,* II, xxviii, 41: "He sings so wild and well!"

9–10 Compare these lines with lines 67–68 of *Il Penseroso*: "To behold the wandering moon,/ Riding near her highest noon."

12 "Levin" is an obsolete word for lightning, revived by Scott.

13–14 The star cluster called the Pleiades is mentioned in Job 9:9. It is situated in Taurus, and consists of seven stars. One of them became fainter, within the memory of man, and two thousand years ago was thought invisible. It has become brighter again and can now be seen by sharp eyes in clear weather. The stars were said by the Greeks and Romans to be sisters, the daughters of Pleionë, translated to the skies. According to one of the classic stories related by Ovid (*Fasti*, IV, 170ff.), one of the sisters loved a mortal and, as the price of willingly sharing his mortality, faded from sight.

There are poems on the subject by many writers of Poe's time, including a favorite of his youth, Letitia E. Landon ("The Lost Pleiad," published in *The Venetian Bracelet*, 1829, p. 69). But Poe did not add the Pleiades to his poem until 1841; he may have noticed George Hill's poem about them, which had a long introductory note, in the *New-Yorker* of May 25, 1839 (7:152). In it Ovid's words (actually *Quae septem dici, sex tamen esse solent*) are quoted as *quae septem — sex*, the terseness of which is as effective as Poe's magical phrase.

18 "Israfeli" means grammatically "my Israfel," but Dr. John L. Mish tells me the usage is almost unknown, and Poe's note, which suggests that he thought "Israfeli" a variant nominative, makes one feel that here Poe builded better than he knew.

20 The houris are the nymphs of the Mahometan paradise; the name comes through the French from the Persian *huri*, and is derived from an Arabic word referring to the dark eyes of these ladies, like those of a gazelle.

21 Charles Henry Watts II, *Thomas Holley Chivers* (1956), p. 162, cites the doctor's "God Dwells in Light," later part of "The Song of Seralim":

> From thy celestial lyre, . . .
> In concert with each golden wire,
> Pour forth the living tide of song —
> The sweetest, holiest hymn
> That ever Angel sung!

This appeared in the *Magnolia* for January 1843. Poe first used "wire" in his poem in the *Saturday Museum* text, presumably prepared late in February of the same year. This is the only "borrowing from Chivers" by Poe that seems to me at all likely.

23 Wilbur (*Poe*, p. 136) complains of the line as defective, the tense being changed to get a rhyme, and the word order inverted (something rare with Poe) — but great emphasis on "skies" is effective here.

37 Campbell (*Poems*, p. 206) compares Edmund Waller, "On a Girdle," "My joy, my grief, my hope, my love."

39 Harry T. Baker in *Modern Language Notes*, March 1910, compares these lines to Coleridge's *Ancient Mariner*, V, 74–75: "And now it is an angel's song, / That makes the heavens be mute."

42 Compare Wordsworth, "Peter Bell" (which Poe ridiculed in his "Letter to B——"), I, 58–60:

A primrose by a river's brim
A yellow primrose was to him,
And it was nothing more.

45–51   Campbell (*Poems*, p. 207) compares the last stanza of Shelley's "To a Skylark," but there are no close verbal parallels.

50   Compare "The Poetic Principle": "We are often made to feel, with a shivering delight, that from an earthly harp are stricken notes which *cannot* have been unfamiliar to the angels."

51   In the earlier versions Poe wrote as if the lute and the lyre were identical, but later corrected this mistake. He may have observed Thomas Moore's note on his Twenty-third Ode of Anacreon, where a similar error by Madame André Dacier is discussed.

IRENË and THE SLEEPER

The poem published in 1831 as "Irene" [1] was given considerable revision in 1836 and 1837. In 1841 Poe revised it again and changed its title to "The Sleeper." He continued to work on it — he made minute changes in 1849 — but nothing was radically altered after March 1843. The differently titled versions have too much in common to be regarded as wholly distinct compositions.

Poe himself was well pleased with "The Sleeper." He named it first in a list of his best poems in a letter of July 2, 1844, to J. R. Lowell. On December 15, 1846, he wrote to George W. Eveleth: "In the higher qualities of poetry, it is better than 'The Raven' — but there is not one man in a million who could be brought to agree with me in this opinion." Killis Campbell (*Poems*, p. 212) quoted J. T. Trowbridge, who in *My Own Story* (1902), page 184, considered Poe's poem "The Sleeper" to be "the most strikingly beautiful of all the productions of that aberrant genius." But Poe's most sincere admirers find only particular passages to praise.[2]

Poe's interest in the death of beautiful women is too well

[1] Irene (*Eirēnē*) is the Greek personification of Peace. Although modern Americans who bear the name often rhyme it with Eileen, it is properly trisyllabic, as Poe makes it, and as it is pronounced in England. The *Saturday Chronicle* text of 1841 had an accent on the final *e* as well as an accent on the final *e* of Lethe. I have therefore felt justified in adding a diaeresis in our texts.

[2] E.g., Quinn, pp. 184–185, who praises lines 12, 22, and 23, and says that "no defense can be made" for line 47.

known to need much comment. "Irenë" and "The Sleeper" are based in part on a commonplace of romantic subject matter, the fair lady who will never awaken. It seems probable that the poem was inspired by the verses of an extremely minor contemporary. In 1826 there appeared a little volume, *Rufiana* (New York, G. & C. Carvil), by William Rufus of Charleston, a decidedly obscure person. The chances that Poe, when he was at Fort Moultrie in 1827, would have seen a work issued only a year before by a local bard are very great. In the Rufus volume at pages 27–29 there is the following poem:

OH LADY, LOVE AWAKE!
A ROMANCE

His lady's name he breath'd in vain —
No signal could the Knight obtain —
    And, pointing to the lake,
He wildly swept his lute again,
And sang a more appealing strain,
    His lady, love, to wake.

"Oh, lady, from yon gloomy tower
The bell hath chim'd the midnight hour,
    The moon sleeps on the lake;
Long have I loitered near thy bower
To free thee from thy tyrant's power,
    Oh, lady, love, awake!

"The skiff awaits us in the bay,
The flapping sail reproves our stay
    The steeds are o'er the lake;
Oh hear you not their distant neigh,
Impatient at our long delay?
    Oh lady, love, awake!

"No taper from thy casement beams,
Nor snowy 'kerchief lightly streams
    In signal t'wards the lake;
Oh, hark! the dismal night-bird screams
To rouse thee from thy lengthen'd dreams —
    Oh, lady, love, awake!"

Nor lover's voice, nor flapping sail,
Nor neighing steeds, nor night-bird's wail,
    The lady's dream can break,
Cold in her shroud, and ghastly pale,
She sleeps within the charnel rail,
    No more on earth to wake!

These verses are mellifluous enough to have pleased Poe, and the poem is verbally closer to the earliest form of "Irenë" than to later texts.

With this commonplace story Poe combined that of the nucta, or magic drop that comes from the moon. He pretty surely took this from a note in Moore's *Lalla Rookh*: "The Nucta, or Miraculous Drop, which falls in Egypt precisely on St. John's Day, in June, and is supposed to have the effect of stopping the plague." The circumstance is ironic; the lady died before St. John's Day, the twenty-fourth of June, ere the healing drop could save her.

Beneficent as the drop may be, it can also be harmful. There is a prominent allusion to this in *Macbeth*. William B. Hunter, Jr., argues convincingly in *American Literature*, March 1948 (20:55–57) that Shakespeare's passage is recalled in "The Sleeper," which has the same metrical form as the scene (III, v, 23–29) where Hecate chants:

> *Upon the corner of the moon*
> *There hangs a vap'rous drop profound.*
> I'll catch it ere it comes to ground;
> And that, distill'd by magic sleights,
> Shall raise such artificial sprites
> As by the strength of their illusion
> Shall draw him on to his confusion.[3]

Another source of the poems about Irenë has recently been found by the scholarly bookseller, J. J. Cohane, who has generously communicated it for use in the present edition. In an annual, *The Anniversary; or, Poetry and Prose for MDCCCXXIX*, edited by Allan Cunningham, issued in London and Philadelphia, there is a rather long poem called "Edderline's Dream," by Professor [John] Wilson (the "Christopher North" of *Blackwood's Magazine*), which describes a fair sleeper who has a terrible dream (pp. 32–43). The more pertinent passages follow; Poe practically quoted some of the phraseology.

[3] Many editions of *Macbeth* carried the note, originally by George Steevens in his 1793 edition: "This vaporous drop seems to have been meant for the same as the *virus lunare* of the ancients, being a foam which the moon was supposed to shed on particular herbs, or other objects, when strongly solicited by enchantment." Steevens refers to Lucan's *Pharsalia*, VI, 666, where the Fury Erictho uses this poison when it is shed during an eclipse.

Therein is a lonesome room,
Undisturbed as some old tomb
That, built within a forest glen,
Far from feet of living men,
And sheltered by its black pine trees
From sound of rivers, lochs, and seas,
Flings back its arched gateway tall,
At times to some great funeral!

    . . . . .

Breathless as a holy shrine,
When the voice of psalms is shed!
And there upon her stately bed,
While her raven locks recline
O'er an arm more pure than snow . . .
There sleeps in love and beauty's glow,
The high-born Lady Edderline.

    . . . . .

Another gleam! how sweet the while,
Those pictured faces on the wall . . .

    . . . . .

Is the last convulsion o'er?
And will that length of glorious tresses,
So laden with the soul's distresses,
By those fair hands in morning light,
Above those eyelids opening bright,
Be braided nevermore?
No, the lady is not dead . . .

    . . . . .

"O, Lady, this is ghastly rest!
"Awake! awake, for Jesus' sake!"

The scene of the action is Castle Oban. The last couplet quoted is especially striking, and it will be noticed that Poe in later versions of the poem removed the echo. Poe's vast improvement in his use of what he took from the rather long and mediocre poem of Wilson hardly needs comment.

TEXTS

Irenë

(*A*) *Poems* (1831), pp. 61–64; (*B*) *Southern Literary Messenger*, May 1836 (2:387–388); (*C*) manuscript, early 1837. This text (*C*) is the first piece written in the album of the Reverend Dr. John Collins McCabe, a minor poet of Richmond and a friend of Poe. On the verso of the printed title page of the album, McCabe wrote: "To/Original Contributors *only* — Those whose/writings are identified with the literature/ of their Country, and whose Claims are/recognized by the Scholar, the Poet and/the Public — is this volume open/for Contributions./ The Owner/1837." Since Poe left Richmond around the beginning of February of that year, the manuscript can be closely dated. A copy of this version was printed in Armistead C. Gordon's *Memories and Memorials of William Gordon McCabe* (Richmond, 1925), I, 20–21; but a photocopy of the actual manuscript, made available by the courtesy of Mrs. William Gordon McCabe Jr., has now been collated. The earliest version (*A*) is followed, with the addition of diaereses in lines 13 and 24.

The Sleeper
(*D*) Philadelphia *Saturday Chronicle*, May 22, 1841; (*E*) R. W. Griswold, *The Poets and Poetry of America* (1842), p. 388; (*F*) Philadelphia *Saturday Museum*, March 4, 1843; (*G*) *Broadway Journal*, May 3, 1845 (1:278); (*H*) *The Raven and Other Poems* (1845), pp. 9–11; (*J*) J. Lorimer Graham copy of *The Raven* . . . with corrections (1849); (*K*) *Works* (1850), II, 37–39. Poe's latest revision (*J*) is followed, with the addition of diaereses in lines 13 and 17.

IRENĖ [*A*]

'T is now (so sings the soaring moon)
Midnight in the sweet month of June,
When winged visions love to lie
Lazily upon beauty's eye,
5   Or worse — upon her brow to dance
In panoply of old romance,
Till thoughts and locks are left, alas!
A ne'er-to-be untangled mass.

An influence dewy, drowsy, dim,
10   Is dripping from that golden rim;
Grey towers are mouldering into rest,
Wrapping the fog around their breast:
Looking like Lethë, see! the lake
A conscious slumber seems to take,
15   And would not for the world awake:
The rosemary sleeps upon the grave —
The lily lolls upon the wave —
And million bright pines to and fro,
Are rocking lullabies as they go,
20   To the lone oak that reels with bliss,
Nodding above the dim abyss.

All beauty sleeps: and lo! where lies

With casement open to the skies,
Irenë, with her destinies!
25   Thus hums the moon within her ear,
"O lady sweet! how camest thou here?
"Strange are thine eyelids — strange thy dress!
"And strange thy glorious length of tress!
"Sure thou art come o'er far-off seas,
30   "A wonder to our desert trees!
"Some gentle wind hath thought it right
"To open thy window to the night,
"And wanton airs from the tree-top,
"Laughingly thro' the lattice drop,
35   "And wave this crimson canopy,
"Like a banner o'er thy dreaming eye!
"Lady, awake! lady awake!
"For the holy Jesus' sake!
"For strangely — fearfully in this hall
40   "My tinted shadows rise and fall!"

The lady sleeps: the *dead* all sleep —
At least as long as Love doth weep:
Entranc'd, the spirit loves to lie
As long as — tears on Memory's eye:
45   But when a week or two go by,
And the light laughter chokes the sigh,
Indignant from the tomb doth take
Its way to some remember'd lake,
Where oft — in life — with friends — it went
50   To bathe in the pure element,
And there, from the untrodden grass,
Wreathing for its transparent brow
Those flowers that say (ah hear them now!)
To the night-winds as they pass,
55   "Ai! ai! alas! — alas!"
Pores for a moment, ere it go,
On the clear waters there that flow,
Then sinks within (weigh'd down by wo)
Th' uncertain, shadowy heaven below.

IRENĖ [A]

* * * * * *

60   The lady sleeps: oh! may her sleep
As it is lasting so be deep —
No icy worms about her creep:
I pray to God that she may lie
Forever with as calm an eye,
65   That chamber chang'd for one more holy —
That bed for one more melancholy.

Far in the forest, dim and old,
For her may some tall vault unfold,
Against whose sounding door she hath thrown,
70   In childhood, many an idle stone —
Some tomb, which oft hath flung its black
And vampyre-winged pannels back,
Flutt'ring triumphant o'er the palls
Of her old family funerals.

[1831]

VARIANTS

Title: Irene, the Dead (*C*)
1 'T is now (so sings/I stand beneath (*B*); We stand beneath (*C*)
2 Midnight in the sweet/At midnight in the (*B, C*)
3–8 *Omitted* (*B, C*)
10 that/yon (*B*); her (*C*)

18 bright pines/cedars (*B, C*)
20 reels with bliss/nodding hangs (*B, C*)
21 Above yon cataract of Serangs (*B, C*)
23 With/Her (*C*)
23–24 *Transposed* (*C*)
25 *For this is substituted in B, C:*

And hark! the sounds so low yet clear,
(Like music of another sphere)
Which steal within the slumberer's ear,
Or so appear — or so appear!

35 this/the (*C*); *after this line is added in B and C:* So fitfully, so fearfully
36 Like/As (*B*); *three added lines follow in B and C:*

That o'er the floor, and down the wall,
Like ghosts the shadows rise and fall —
Then, for thine own all radiant sake

In this passage the manuscript C has:
That thro' the floors
and: own beloved sake.

37 Lady awake! awake! awake! (*B*); Lady awake! — lady awake! (*C*)

38 *Omitted* (*B, C*)
39–59 *Omitted* (*B*)
39–40 *Omitted* (*C*)
43 Entranc'd/Entranced (*C*)
48 Its way to Heav'n — and sorrow forsake (*C*)
49–59 *Omitted* (*C*)
65 chang'd/changed (*B*)
72 vampyre-winged/vampire-wing-like (*B, C*)
73 Flutt'ring/Fluttering (*B, C*)

NOTES

13 Lethe is the river of Hades, to drink of which brings forgetfulness.

21 The *Messenger* variant (*B*) needs comment. A serang is a boatswain of a crew of lascars, hence a turbaned Eastern chief. In the 1831 version of "Tamerlane" Poe spoke of "sultan-like" pine trees.

25 The moon is not often thought of as humming. One suspects that Poe had in mind a Shakespearean parallel, though it is not about the moon. In *Macbeth*, III, vi, 41–42, a lord says: "The cloudy messenger turns his back / And hums, as who should say, 'You'll rue the time.' "

29 Compare "The City in the Sea," line 39: "some far-off happier sea," and "To F[rances]," lines 9–10: "far-off isle / In some tumultuous sea."

45–46 This recalls Pope's "Elegy to the Memory of an Unfortunate Lady," lines 55–58:

> What tho' no friends in sable weeds appear,
> Grieve for an hour, perhaps, then mourn a year,
> And bear about the mockery of woe
> To midnight dances, and the public show?

47–49 For the idea of departed spirits dwelling in the clear water, compare Poe's early poem, "The Lake."

53–55 The Greeks fancied they could see AI AI, the usual expression of wailing, on the flower that sprang from the blood of the beautiful Spartan youth Hyacinthus, after he was accidentally slain by Apollo. The story is told by Ovid, *Metamorphoses*, X, 162–219, and is familiar from the reference in Milton's "Lycidas" to "that sanguine flower inscribed with woe." Poe used a different story about the hyacinth in "Al Aaraaf," "To Helen," and "To Zante."

59 Some have compared a passage quoted by Coleridge, *Biographia Literaria*, chapter xx, from Wordsworth's *Prelude*, V, 387–388: "that uncertain heaven, received / Into the bosom of the steady lake."

62 Campbell (p. 213) calls attention to Byron's *Giaour*, lines 945ff:

> It is as if the dead could feel
> The icy worm around them steal,
> And shudder, as the reptiles creep.

71–72 Compare the phrase in "The Bargain Lost": "a black, heavy and curiously-pannelled door." Hervey Allen, *Israfel* (1926), I, 220–221, says that these and the following lines recall "some of the great family tombs on the plantations about Charleston, with the semi-feudal pomp that surrounds them." He mentions as typical that at Middleton Gardens, near Charleston.

THE SLEEPER [*J*]

At midnight, in the month of June,
I stand beneath the mystic moon.

THE SLEEPER [J]

An opiate vapour, dewy, dim,
Exhales from out her golden rim,
And, softly dripping, drop by drop,
Upon the quiet mountain top,
Steals drowsily and musically
Into the universal valley.
The rosemary nods upon the grave;
The lily lolls upon the wave;
Wrapping the fog about its breast,
The ruin moulders into rest;
Looking like Lethë, see! the lake
A conscious slumber seems to take,
And would not, for the world, awake.
All Beauty sleeps! — and lo! where lies
Irenë, with her Destinies!

Oh, lady bright! can it be right —
This window open to the night?
The wanton airs, from the tree-top,
Laughingly through the lattice drop —
The bodiless airs, a wizard rout,
Flit through thy chamber in and out,
And wave the curtain canopy
So fitfully — so fearfully —
Above the closed and fringéd lid
'Neath which thy slumb'ring soul lies hid,
That, o'er the floor and down the wall,
Like ghosts the shadows rise and fall!
Oh, lady dear, hast thou no fear?
Why and what art thou dreaming here?
Sure thou art come o'er far-off seas,
A wonder to these garden trees!
Strange is thy pallor! strange thy dress!
Strange, above all, thy length of tress,
And this all solemn silentness!

The lady sleeps! Oh, may her sleep,
Which is enduring, so be deep!

Heaven have her in its sacred keep!
40 This chamber changed for one more holy,
This bed for one more melancholy,
I pray to God that she may lie
Forever with unopened eye,
While the pale sheeted ghosts go by!

45 My love, she sleeps! Oh, may her sleep,
As it is lasting, so be deep!
Soft may the worms about her creep!
Far in the forest, dim and old,
For her may some tall vault unfold —
50 Some vault that oft hath flung its black
And wingéd pannels fluttering back,
Triumphant, o'er the crested palls,
Of her grand family funerals —
Some sepulchre, remote, alone,
55 Against whose portal she hath thrown,
In childhood, many an idle stone —
Some tomb from out whose sounding door
She ne'er shall force an echo more,
Thrilling to think, poor child of sin!
60 It was the dead who groaned within.

[1831–1845]

VARIANTS

11 fog about its/mist about their (D);
mist about its (E)
12 Grey towers are mouldering into
rest (D)
13 Lethë/Lethé (D, F) [The diaeresis
in our text is added editorially.]
16 Followed by: With casement open
to the skies (D, E); (Her casement
open to the skies) (F, G, H, K)
17 Irenë, with/Irené and (D); Irene
and (E); Irené, with (F) [The diaeresis
in our text is added editorially.]
19 window/lattice (D, E, F)
20-21 Omitted from D, E, F
26 fringéd/fringed (G, H, K)
33 these/our (E)

35 Stranger thy glorious length of tress
(D, E)
36 this/thine (D)
39 Interchanged with 47 (E)
40 chamber/bed being (D, E); changed
/chang'd (F)
41 bed/room (D, E)
43 unopened/uncloséd (D, E) [Poe
wrote Griswold April 19, 1845, asking
that in the new edition of Poets and
Poetry of America this word be
changed to unopen'd but since his
text was stereotyped no change was
made.]; unopen'd (F, G)
44 pale/dim (F, G, H, K); line omitted (E)

47 *Interchanged with 39 (E)*
49, 50 vault/tomb (D, E)
51 wingéd/wing-like (D, E); winged (G, H, K)
54 Some vault all haughtily alone (D)

57 From out whose hollow-sounding door (D); Some vault from out whose sounding door (E)
59 Thrilling/Nor thrill (D, E)
60 groaned/groan'd (E)

NOTES

7–10 These lines and 22–29 were praised for "spirituality" in the London *Foreign Quarterly Review*, January 1844 (32:322).

20–29 In a review, "Longfellow's Poems," in the *Aristidean* for April 1845, Poe cites what he thinks (less improbably than usual) was a borrowing in "Footsteps of Angels":

> And, like *phantoms* grim and tall,
> Shadows from the fitful fire-light
> *Dance upon the parlor wall.*

26 Campbell (*Poems*, p. 212) compared to this *The Tempest*, I, ii, 407: "The fringed curtains of thine eye."

30–31 Compare "Fairy Land" (version of 1831), lines 39–40: "Isabel! do you not fear / The night and the wonders here?"

47 The line was significantly changed in later versions from its earlier form (compare "Irenë," line 62), perhaps to make the worm a mystic symbol of immortality. Nevertheless, the reviewer in the London *Literary Gazette* of January 1846 (p. 237) complained of it as "morbid," as I think it is. See Edward H. Davidson, *Poe* (1957), p. 39, for a defense.

59 Doctrinally, we are all "children of sin," for the sin of Adam and Eve makes us subject to mortality. No personal allusion seems probable here. See Genesis 3:3 and 19.

THE VALLEY OF UNREST

This poem is a great achievement in a kind Poe made peculiarly his own, the imaginary landscape. In the series of unfinished notes for the introduction to a book he planned to call "The Living Writers of America," he discussed what he thought the most suitable themes for the artist. "Distant subjects," said he, are "in fact the most desirable . . . The true poet is less affected by the absolute contemplation than the imagination of a great landscape." [1] In the present poem and its companion piece, "The City

---

[1] The quotation is from the original manuscript of 1846 to 1848, now in the Pierpont Morgan Library.

in the Sea," he had exemplified his theory much earlier. The landscapes are bathed in "the light that never was on land or sea," and call to mind the scenes painted by the artists of the Hudson River School, to whom he was closely akin in spirit. But Poe was less a follower than a leader, and the reader may well be reminded of later impressionists.

The first form of the poem was published in *Poems* (1831). In 1836 Poe revised it, changing the last twenty lines very considerably but retaining the original title. In 1845 he revised it again, omitting nearly half and changing the title to "The Valley of Unrest." It was published three times in 1845, with minor variations. The vagueness of the final version is intentional; the poet's revisions removed some of the clearer allusions and eliminated almost all of the story. Surely the reader may choose to regard the poem as a picture of dreams alone.[2] Yet Poe did not put his valley entirely "out of space" — a reference to the Hebrides remains in every form of the poem. The underlying ideas are not wholly concealed, but they are more readily understood from the early versions called "The Valley Nis."

The Scottish antiquarian, R. M. Hogg, found the poems to be based on memories of things seen and heard by Poe during his brief stay with his foster parents at Irvine in 1815.[3] Hogg suggests that "Nis" was the way Poe wrongly heard the Gaelic word for island, *innis*, which forms part of such place names as Innisfallen. (Poe omitted the name in the late versions of his poem, as might be expected had he learned of an error.) There *is* a "Syriac tale" about the Isle of Skye, told in Boswell's *Journal of a Tour to the Hebrides,* under the date of September 17, 1773. The Reverend Mr. Donald M'Queen told the amused and incredulous Dr. Johnson that he believed some local stone ruins to be those of an ancient temple of the Syrian goddess Anaïtis. Another local story is that on the island of Fuiday a Norse maiden told her Gaelic

[2] The final version may indeed be, as Edgar Lee Masters told me he thought it, an *allegory* of *this* world.

[3] See Phillips, I, 397–410. Hogg's hobby was Poe in Scotland, and he rode it hard. He did not present his case well in the matter of "The Valley Nis," mingling fact and fancy in so forbidding a way that his remarks have been practically ignored since 1926.

lover that Norsemen were powerless after sunset. He invaded the island by night and exterminated the Norsemen who had not gone to the wars in Ireland. The stars did not watch faithfully.

The nameless grave — note the change from the earlier "forgotten grave" — is very well known locally. It is near Boston Cottage, which Mr. Hogg said was a regular halting stage on the old road from Glasgow to Edinburgh, over which Poe journeyed with the Allan family in 1815. The story is that a farmer, Adam Sanderson of Black Hill, on November 28, 1666, tried to help a dying Covenanter, fatally wounded at the battle of Rullion Green. The man, without revealing his name, died in the arms of Sanderson, saying at the last, "Bury me in the sight of the Ayrshire Hills." Sanderson carried him to the top of Black Hill and buried him, marking the spot with a small cairn. It is hard to believe that Poe did not know this touching story, nor is it surprising that he used it in his poem. In recent times an inscribed monument has been erected at the nameless grave, above which "the blue bells of Scotland weep."

TEXTS

(A) *Poems* (1831), pp. 73–75 (as "The Valley Nis"); (B) *Southern Literary Messenger,* February 1836 (2:154) (as "The Valley Nis"); (C) *American Review,* April 1845 (1:392); (D) *Broadway Journal,* September 6, 1845 (2:135); (E) *The Raven and Other Poems* (1845), p. 6; (F) *Works* (1850), II, 34 (verbally like E). The texts given are the first (A) and final version (E).

THE VALLEY NIS [A]

Far away — far away —
Far away — as far at least
Lies that valley as the day
Down within the golden east —
5   All things lovely — are not they
Far away — far away?

It is called the valley Nis.
And a Syriac tale there is

Thereabout which Time hath said
10   Shall not be interpreted.
Something about Satan's dart —
Something about angel wings —
Much about a broken heart —
All about unhappy things:
15   But "the valley Nis" at best
Means "the valley of unrest."

Once it smiled a silent dell
Where the people did not dwell,
Having gone unto the wars —
20   And the sly mysterious stars,
With a visage full of meaning,
O'er the unguarded flowers were leaning:
Or the sun ray dripp'd all red
Thro' the tulips overhead,
25   Then grew paler as it fell
On the quiet Asphodel.

Now the *unhappy* shall confess
Nothing there is motionless:
Helen, like thy human eye
30   There th' uneasy violets lie —
There the reedy grass doth wave
Over the old forgotten grave —
One by one from the tree top
There the eternal dews do drop —
35   There the vague and dreamy trees
Do roll like seas in northern breeze
Around the stormy Hebrides —
There the gorgeous clouds do fly,
Rustling everlastingly,
40   Through the terror-stricken sky,
Rolling like a waterfall
O'er th' horizon's fiery wall —
There the moon doth shine by night

With a most unsteady light —
45   There the sun doth reel by day
"Over the hills and far away."

[1831]

VARIANTS

6 Far away—/One and all, too (*B*)   22 the unguarded/th' unguarded (*B*)
17 smiled/smil'd (*B*)   24 the tulips/tall tulips (*B*)

[*For lines 27–46 B substitutes a new conclusion:*]

Now each visiter shall confess
Nothing there is motionless:
Nothing save the airs that brood
30   O'er the enchanted solitude,
Save the airs with pinions furled
That slumber o'er that valley-world.
No wind in Heaven, and lo! the trees
Do roll like seas, in Northern breeze,
35   Around the stormy Hebrides —
No wind in Heaven, and clouds do fly,
Rustling everlastingly,
Thro' the terror-stricken sky,
Rolling, like a waterfall,
40   O'er th' horizon's fiery wall —
And Helen, like thy human eye,
Low crouched on Earth, some violets lie,
And, nearer Heaven, some lilies wave
All banner-like, above *a grave*.
45   And one by one, from out their tops
Eternal dews come down in drops,
Ah, one by one, from off their stems
Eternal dews come down in gems!   [1836]

NOTES

Title: While it seems clear that Poe had Hebridean stories in mind, the name Nis as yet cannot be explained with complete certainty. Mr. R. M. Hogg's explanation is given in the commentary above. Another explanation has been offered me by Professor DeLancey Ferguson. The old word *nis,* meaning "is not," is familiar from Chaucer and Spenser. This would accord with the idea that Poe's poem is an allegory of the world — a place of unreality or illusion. A combination of ideas in Poe is not to be dismissed lightly, and he certainly on occasion remarked on life as a dream. Only these two explanations seem to me likely. But the word is a crux, hence all other important suggestions should be given. These are as follows:

Killis Campbell in *Poems*, p. 217, mentions that the phrase *ha nis* occurs in some ancient texts of Jeremiah 48:44 — usually corrected to *ha nâs*, "those who flee." In Norse mythology a *Nis* is a water spirit — usually feminine. In Latin *nis'* is a contraction for *nisi*, "unless." An old city in Serbia, a place of many battles, is Nis, pronounced Nish. Nis might be a misspelling for [Loch] Ness in Scotland.

Many readers notice that Nis is Sin backwards. This pleased Quinn, p. 184; and Frances Winwar in *The Haunted Palace*, p. 133, would see a reference to the lover's circle in the fifth canto of Dante's *Inferno*. Poe did not elsewhere use this kind of anagram in serious poetry. There are also other suggestions. The Wilderness of Sin ("marsh" or "clay") is mentioned in Exodus 16–17; in Ezekiel 30:15–16 is a curse on a city Sin, probably Pelusium; Sîn is a Semitic moon-god for whom Mount Sinai may be named; the twenty-first letter of the Hebrew alphabet is *sin* or *shin* (sometimes a sacred symbol); and finally, in Scottish dialect *sin* is the sun.

5–6 Compare from the 1841 version of "Israfel": ". . . the beauty/Which we worship in a star/ The more lovely the more far."

11–13 See the introductory note. The dart may be the bullet that fatally wounded the Covenanter; the angel wings, those that bore him to heaven; his heart was broken by his inability to return to his native Ayrshire.

24 Poe may have had in mind a note by Letitia E. Landon, in *The Golden Violet* (1827), p. 310: "The tulip symbol . . . bears the allegorical construction of eternal separation in the beautiful language of Eastern flowers."

26 The asphodel, among the ancients, was a plant of the lily family, with light gray and yellow flowers, thought to be of a corpselike color and hence sacred to Proserpine as a symbol of death. In the tales "Berenice" and "Eleonora" Poe uses asphodels with different symbolic meanings.

29 "Helen" seems here to refer to a living person, the poet's present inspiration, rather than to the beloved Jane Stith Stanard.

29–30 In "Eleonora" Poe wrote of "dark eye-like violets." See also, in a song from Scott's *Lord of the Isles*, I, iii: "The dew that on the violet lies/ Mocks the dark lustre of thine eyes." Violets are symbols of purity, but some of the flowers do look like eyes.

32 For the "forgotten" or "nameless" (line 24, version of 1845) grave, see the introductory commentary.

34 In Edward Young's *Night Thoughts*, IX, 1981, we are told that Night "weeps perpetual dews."

35–42 Compare Poe's "Silence — A Fable": "There, like the waves about the Hebrides, the low underwood is agitated continually. But there is no wind throughout the heaven. And the tall primeval trees rock eternally hither and thither with a crashing and mighty sound. And from their summits, one by one, drop everlasting dews. And . . . overhead, with a rustling and loud noise, the gray clouds rush westwardly forever, until they roll, a cataract, over the fiery wall of the horizon." See also "Arthur Gordon Pym," chapter xxv: "The range of vapor . . . I can liken to nothing but a limitless cataract rolling silently into the sea from some immense and far distant rampart in the heaven." There are also parallels in "Fairyland" and "The Sleeper."

36–37 Compare Wordsworth's "Solitary Reaper":
> Breaking the silence of the seas
> Among the farthest Hebrides.
> Will no one tell me what she sings? —
> Perhaps the plaintive numbers flow
> For old, unhappy, far-off things,
> And battles long ago.

37 Milton in "Lycidas" refers to the "stormy Hebrides," and the epithet has become the stock one.

38–42 Compare "The Island of the Fay": "There passed down noiselessly into the valley a rich golden and crimson waterfall from the sunset fountains of the sky."

46 The old song, "Over the Hills and Far Away," is best known from being mentioned in the nursery rhyme, "Tom, Tom, the Piper's Son." The melody and refrain are used in John Gay's *Beggar's Opera*, I, xiii.

THE VALLEY OF UNREST [*E*]

Once it smiled a silent dell
Where the people did not dwell;
They had gone unto the wars,
Trusting to the mild-eyed stars,
5 Nightly, from their azure towers,
To keep watch above the flowers,
In the midst of which all day
The red sun-light lazily lay.
Now each visiter shall confess
10 The sad valley's restlessness.
Nothing there is motionless.
Nothing save the airs that brood
Over the magic solitude.
Ah, by no wind are stirred those trees
15 That palpitate like the chill seas
Around the misty Hebrides!

Ah, by no wind those clouds are driven
That rustle through the unquiet Heaven
Uneasily, from morn till even,
20   Over the violets there that lie
In myriad types of the human eye —
Over the lilies there that wave
And weep above a nameless grave!
They wave: — from out their fragrant tops
25   Eternal dews come down in drops.
They weep: — from off their delicate stems
Perennial tears descend in gems.

[1831–1845]

VARIANTS

18   rustle/rustles (*misprint, C*)
19   Uneasily/Unceasingly (*C, D*)
27   *After this C has three more lines:*

They wave; they weep; and the tears, as they well
From the depths of each pallid lily-bell,
Give a trickle and a tinkle and a knell.

NOTES
(See also notes to the first version.)

22   Lilies are symbols of purity and the Resurrection; compare lines 43–44 of version *B*.

28–30   (text *C*) Compare the following from Shelley's "Sensitive Plant," I, 25–28:

And the hyacinth purple, and white, and blue;
Which flung from its bells a sweet peal anew
Of music so delicate, soft, and intense,
It was felt like an odor within the sense.

Poe refers more than once to that poem of Shelley, with unexpected and perhaps nostalgic admiration; he may have suppressed his own lines because he thought them too imitative. Part of Shelley's poem was reprinted in the *Richmond Enquirer*, April 2, 1824, according to Agnes Bondurant, *Poe's Richmond* (1942), p. 108.

THE CITY IN THE SEA

This poem is a companion piece to "The Valley of Unrest." Unsurpassed for power in its final form, it contains no line that one could wish away. It moves unfaltering from beginning to end. Poe's contemporaries probably did not find the subject obscure for legends about the ruins of the cities sunken in the Dead Sea were a favorite theme with the poets of his time, although none of them, perhaps, treated it as well as he.

The poem is an amplification of the passage in the version of "Al Aaraaf" sent to John Neal, which was quoted in *The Yankee and Boston Literary Gazette* (December 1829, p. 296), thus:

> . . . the stilly, clear abyss
> Of beautiful Gomorrah! oh! the wave
> Is now upon thee — but too late to save!
> Far down within the crystal of the lake
> Thy swollen pillars tremble — and so quake
> The hearts of many wanderers who look in
> Thy luridness of beauty — and of sin.

In the slightly later text of his volume of 1829, Poe shortened the passage but added a long footnote to line 38 (page 107, above).

Here, as in the case of "Al Aaraaf," Poe used F. Shoberl's version of Chateaubriand's *Itinéraire*. It is most probable that of the sources given there Poe did look up Josephus, whose works were in every clergyman's and many a layman's library a century ago. Josephus says in *The Wars of the Jews*, IV, viii, 4, in the standard English version of William Whiston, first printed in 1737:

> The nature of the lake Asphaltitis [the Dead Sea] is also worth describing . . . The change of the colour of this lake is wonderful, for it changes its appearance thrice every day; and as the rays of the sun fall differently upon it, the light is variously reflected . . . and the traces (or shadows) of the five cities are still to be seen.

Poe may also have used encyclopedias and Biblical commentaries on Genesis 19, the story of Lot. The legends, ancient and modern, are that the ruins of the Cities of the Plain are close to the surface at ordinary times, and in very dry weather the tops of walls and columns may be seen above the water. Everything in the poem fits this interpretation. The Dead Sea is in earthquake country, and the poem prophesies that some day an earthquake will tumble down the ruins still standing sunken within the sea.

Poe cannot have missed the passage in Edward Coote Pinkney's *Rodolph*, II, 26–28:

> Gleams, as of drowned antiquity
> From cities underneath the sea
> Which glooms in famous Galilee.

A volume called *The Cities of the Plain* had appeared in 1828 from the pen of the American poet, Sumner Lincoln Fairfield, now remembered (if at all) for his poem of the next year, *The Last Night of Pompeii*, which probably had some influence on Bulwer. Other contemporaries of Poe wrote on the subject: Spencer Wallace Cone has a poem on "The Dead Sea" in *The Proud Ladye* (1840); and in Vision I of *Somnia* (1848), Lambert A. Wilmer has a long passage on the legend. Instances could be multiplied.

Whitty (*Complete Poems*, 1911, page 220) cited the lines of "Al Aaraaf" as printed in *The Yankee* as the earliest form of "The City in the Sea." This obvious indication of the city Poe had in mind had been curiously disregarded.[1]

The original version of 1831 was reprinted with a change of title and a few other minor alterations in 1836. In 1841, in his tale "The Island of the Fay" (*Graham's* for June), Poe quoted lines 40–41, changed to read:

> So blended bank and shadow there
> That each seemed pendulous in air.

In 1845 he revised the poem again for the *American* (Whig) *Review* and still again for the *Broadway Journal* and *The Raven and Other Poems*. These new versions he called "The City in the Sea."

---

[1] R. M. Hogg (Phillips, I, 400) referred to Rocabi, the twilight city of the Highland Gaels, and to Ys in Brittany. There are many cities in history as well as legend that are sunk in the oceans, and one is the undeniably wicked pirate stronghold of Port Royal, Jamaica. Yet some commentators propose cities that are not in the sea at all (despite lines 31–32 of the first version)! Maxwell V. Z. W. Morton (*A Builder of the Beautiful*, 1928, p. 43) found an analogue in "The City of the Dead" (devastated by pestilence) in the London *New Monthly Magazine* of April 1826. Unexpectedly inept was Killis Campbell's choice of Babylon as Poe's city (*Poems*, p. 208). The ruins of Babylon are a mound far distant from any sea — and how could "Babylon-like walls" be at Babylon? Yet in *American Literature* (March 1934 and March 1936) I find that Louise Pound accepted Campbell's strange notion.

THE CITY IN THE SEA [A]

TEXTS

(A) Poems (1831), pp. 49–51; (B) Southern Literary Messenger, August 1836 (2:552); (C) American Review, April 1845 (1:393); (D) Broadway Journal, August 30, 1845 (2:123); (E) The Raven and Other Poems (1845), pp. 21–22; (F) J. Lorimer Graham copy of The Raven . . . ; (G) R. W. Griswold, The Poets and Poetry of America, 10th ed. (1850), p. 418; (H) Works (1850), II, 35–36.

A and H (the latter verbally like D, E, and F) are here given in full. In H the change is only the correction of a misprinted comma in line 51.

THE DOOMED CITY [A]

Lo! Death hath rear'd himself a throne
In a strange city, all alone,
Far down within the dim west —
And the good, and the bad, and the worst, and the best,
5   Have gone to their eternal rest.

There shrines, and palaces, and towers
Are — not like any thing of ours —
O! no — O! no — *ours* never loom
To heaven with that ungodly gloom!
10   Time-eaten towers that tremble not!
Around, by lifting winds forgot,
Resignedly beneath the sky
The melancholy waters lie.

A heaven that God doth not contemn
15   With stars is like a diadem —
We liken our ladies' eyes to them —
But there! that everlasting pall!
It would be mockery to call
Such dreariness a heaven at all.

20   Yet tho' no holy rays come down
On the long night-time of that town,
Light from the lurid, deep sea
Streams up the turrets silently —

Up thrones — up long-forgotten bowers
25 Of sculptur'd ivy and stone flowers —
Up domes — up spires — up kingly halls —
Up fanes — up Babylon-like walls —
Up many a melancholy shrine
Whose entablatures intertwine
30 The mask — the viol — and the vine.

There open temples — open graves
Are on a level with the waves —
But not the riches there that lie
In each idol's diamond eye,
35 Not the gaily-jewell'd dead
Tempt the waters from their bed:
For no ripples curl, alas!
Along that wilderness of glass —
No swellings hint that winds may be
40 Upon a far-off happier sea:
So blend the turrets and shadows there
That all seem pendulous in air,
While from the high towers of the town
Death looks gigantically down.

45 But lo! a stir is in the air!
The wave! there is a ripple there!
As if the towers had thrown aside,
In slightly sinking, the dull tide —
As if the turret-tops had given
50 A vacuum in the filmy heaven:
The waves have now a redder glow —
The very hours are breathing low —
And when, amid no earthly moans,
Down, down that town shall settle hence,
55 Hell rising from a thousand thrones
Shall do it reverence,
And Death to some more happy clime
Shall give his undivided time.   [1831]

THE CITY IN THE SEA [*H*]

VARIANTS

Title: The City of Sin (*B*)
4 And/Where (*B*)
14–19 *Not in B*
20 Yet tho' no holy rays/No holy rays
from heaven (*B*)

22 But light from out the lurid sea
(*B*)
55 Hell rising/All Hades (*B*)

THE CITY IN THE SEA [*H*]

Lo! Death has reared himself a throne
In a strange city lying alone
Far down within the dim West,
Where the good and the bad and the worst and the best
5   Have gone to their eternal rest.
There shrines and palaces and towers
(Time-eaten towers that tremble not!)
Resemble nothing that is ours.
Around, by lifting winds forgot,
10   Resignedly beneath the sky
The melancholy waters lie.

No rays from the holy heaven come down
On the long night-time of that town;
But light from out the lurid sea
15   Streams up the turrets silently —
Gleams up the pinnacles far and free
Up domes — up spires — up kingly halls —
Up fanes — up Babylon-like walls —
Up shadowy long-forgotten bowers
20   Of sculptured ivy and stone flowers —
Up many and many a marvellous shrine
Whose wreathéd friezes intertwine
The viol, the violet, and the vine.

Resignedly beneath the sky
25   The melancholy waters lie.

So blend the turrets and shadows there
That all seem pendulous in air,
While from a proud tower in the town
Death looks gigantically down.

30　There open fanes and gaping graves
Yawn level with the luminous waves;
But not the riches there that lie
In each idol's diamond eye —
Not the gaily-jewelled dead
35　Tempt the waters from their bed;
For no ripples curl, alas!
Along that wilderness of glass —
No swellings tell that winds may be
Upon some far-off happier sea —
40　No heavings hint that winds have been
On seas less hideously serene.

But lo, a stir is in the air!
The wave — there is a movement there!
As if the towers had thrust aside,
45　In slightly sinking, the dull tide —
As if their tops had feebly given
A void within the filmy Heaven.
The waves have now a redder glow —
The hours are breathing faint and low —
50　And when, amid no earthly moans,
Down, down that town shall settle hence,
Hell, rising from a thousand thrones,
Shall do it reverence.　　　　[1831–1845]

VARIANTS

Title: The City in the Sea. A Prophecy
(C)
1　reared/rear'd (G)
3　Far off in a region unblest (C)
25　The melancholy/Around the
mournful (C)

28–35　*These lines do not appear in C*
34　gaily-jewelled/gayly-jewell'd (G)
36　For no/No murmuring (C)
39　some/a (C)
41　On oceans not so sad-serene (C)

THE CITY IN THE SEA [*H*]

(Keyed to H; parentheses enclose references to A or identification of the text if the line appears in only one of those reproduced.)

3 (3) The Dead Sea is "far down" below sea level, and is thought of here as approached from the east. The west is the place of sunsets, and symbolizes finality.

4 (4) The dead include people who died before the destruction of the Cities of the Plain. Birsha, King of Gomorrah, is not described as wicked in Genesis 14:2.

9 (11) A. G. Newcomer, in *Poems and Tales of Edgar Allan Poe* (Chicago, 1902), p. 300, calls attention to lines near the opening of "Absalom," by N. P. Willis (1827):

> The willow leaves,
> With a soft cheek upon the lulling tide,
> Forgot the lifting winds.

12-29 (20-30) Compare Shelley's "Ode to the West Wind," lines 33-34: "and saw in sleep old palaces and towers / Quivering within the wave's intenser day."

14-15 (22-23) The light is phosphorescence. Chateaubriand said that the cities were built of "combustible stones." Henry M. Belden in *American Literature*, November 1935 (7:332-334), saw a parallel to Dante's *Inferno*, VIII, 68ff., where the City of Dis is thus described in Henry Francis Cary's translation:

> "The minarets already, Sir!
> There certes in the valley I descry,
> Gleaming vermilion as if they from fire
> Had issu'd." He replied: "Eternal fire,
> That inward burns, shows them with ruddy flame
> Illum'd . . ."

Poe's city is not otherwise much like Dis.

18 (27) Babylon-like walls are "doomed to fall," said William Lander Weber, in *Selections from the Southern Poets* (1901), p. 195. This simple and obviously right interpretation seems to have been overlooked by all other commentators.

21 (*H*) The locution "many and many a" first appeared in Poe's poem in 1845; he quoted it from an early version of Wordsworth's "Guilt and Sorrow" in 1837, in reviewing William Cullen Bryant, and later used it in "Annabel Lee."

23 (*H*) This was Ernest Dowson's favorite line of poetry. See Isaiah 14:11: "Thy pomp is brought down to the grave, and the noise of thy viols," a passage Campbell (*Poems*, p. 210) thought to have been in Poe's mind when Poe wrote this.

28 (*H*) Compare *Paradise Lost*, V, 907: "those proud towers to swift destruction doom'd"; and "Tamerlane," lines 140-141: "a high mountain which look'd down, / Afar from its proud natural towers."

30-31 (31-32) Campbell (*Poems*, p. 210) compares Byron's "Darkness," (see lines 73f., but Byron's lines concern the end of the world, and only 78 and 80 are pertinent: "The waves were dead; the tides were in their grave . . . The winds were withered . . ."

32–33 (33–34) In his notes on *Lalla Rookh*, Moore quotes Jean-Baptiste Tavernier's *Voyages*: "The idol of Juggernaut has two fine diamonds for eyes." The idol referred to is an image of Jagganath which was carried in procession at Puri in Orissa.

37 (38) Compare Revelation 4:6: "before the throne there was a sea of glass like unto crystal," and 15:2: "I saw . . . a sea of glass mingled with fire."

43–54 (45–56) See Revelation 16:18–19: "And there were voices, and thunders, and lightnings; and there was a great earthquake . . . and the cities of the nations fell"; and 20:14: "death and hell were cast into the lake of fire."

48 (51) See the quotation from Josephus in the introductory comment, above. The authorities consulted say nothing of the redness of the Dead Sea. However, Drummond's Pond in the Dismal Swamp is said to have blood-red waters. Poe did not use this detail in "The Lake," but perhaps he did recall it when he composed "The Doomed City."

52–53 (55–56) Compare Isaiah 14:9: "Hell from beneath is moved for thee to meet thee at thy coming: it stirreth up the dead for thee . . . it hath raised up from their thrones all the kings of the nations." Poe pointed out in his unfinished story "A Reviewer Reviewed" (1849) the following from Mrs. Sigourney's "Musing Thoughts," lines 45–46, in *The Token for 1829*: "Earth slowly rising from her thousand thrones/ Did homage to the Corsican." There are stories that locate Hell directly under the Dead Sea, but I have not found one in the sources named by Chateaubriand. They are very old, however, and are mentioned by the Russian pilgrim, Daniel, Bishop of Surviev.

57 (A) The poem, although echoing apocalyptic phrases in the Bible, does not concern the end of the whole world but the future inevitable destruction of the ruins of Gomorrah by an earthquake. Observe the final couplet of the first version; Death will lose this particular throne.

A PAEAN

This is certainly the weakest piece in Poe's *Poems* of 1831, and has usually been treated as a version of "Lenore," of which it is indeed a kind of preliminary draft. The chief source has recently been found by J. J. Cohane in *The Anniversary for 1829*, mentioned above in comment on "The Sleeper." The annual (pp. 72–75) contains a poem called "The Wedding Wake," by George Darley.[1] It is about the grief of a young bridegroom at the fu-

[1] "The Wedding Wake" was not found by Ramsay Colles, whose edition of

A PAEAN

neral of his bride-to-be, and consists of seventeen quatrains. The
more significant lines follow:

> Dead Beauty's eye is beamless all . . .
>
> Like a dark stream, her raven hair
>   Wanders adown her brow;
> Look how the weetless, reckless air
>   Moves its dead tresses now!
>
> Stain not, O deeply bending Youth!
>   Her sweet cheek with a tear.
>
> Coffin her up, and on the pall
>   Lay one white virgin plume . . .
>
> The pale rose, the dim azure bell,
>   And that lamenting flower,
> With Ai! Ai! its eternal knell,
>   Shall ever-bloom her bower . . .
>
> The bed is laid, the toll is done,
>   The ready priest doth stand;
> Come, let the flowers be strown! be strown!
>   Strike up, ye bridal band!
>
> Forbear, forbear that cruel jest;
>   Be this the funeral song:
> Farewell, the loveliest and the best
>   That ever died so young!

The poem seems to have impressed Poe deeply; there is an echo
also in "Irenë" and new reminiscences appear in "Lenore."

TEXTS

(A) *Poems* (1831), pp. 67–70; (B) *Southern Literary Messenger*, January
1836 (2:71). The revised version (B) is given.

A PÆAN [B]

How shall the burial rite be read?
  The solemn song be sung?
The requiem for the loveliest dead,
  That ever died so young?

Darley's *Poetical Works* is the only one approaching completeness. In 1897 James S.
Cotton wrote J. H. Ingram of a resemblance of Darley's poem to "Lenore" — see the
Ingram List, no. 400.

5   Her friends are gazing on her,
         And on her gaudy bier,
       And weep! — oh! to dishonor
         Her beauty with a tear!

       They loved her for her wealth —
10   And they hated her for her pride —
       But she grew in feeble health,
         And they *love* her — that she died.

       They tell me (while they speak
         Of her "costly broider'd pall")
15   That my voice is growing weak —
         That I should not sing at all —

       Or that my tone should be
         Tun'd to such solemn song
       So mournfully — so mournfully,
20   That the dead may feel no wrong.

       But she is gone above,
         With young Hope at her side,
       And I am drunk with love
         Of the dead, who is my bride.

25   Of the dead — dead — who lies
         All motionless,
       With the death upon her eyes,
         And the life upon each tress.

       In June she died — in June
30   Of life — beloved, and fair;
       But she did not die too soon,
         Nor with too calm an air.

       From more than fiends on earth,
         Helen, thy soul is riven,

A PAEAN

35   To join the all-hallowed mirth
Of more than thrones in heaven —

Therefore, to thee this night
I will no requiem raise,
But waft thee on thy flight,
40   With a Pæan of old days.

[1831–1836]

VARIANTS

8   Her/Dead (*A*)
26   motionless/perfum'd there (*A*)
28   each tress/her hair (*A*)
29–32   *A has two quatrains:*
Thus on the coffin loud and long
   I strike — the murmur sent
Through the grey chambers to my song,
   Shall be the accompaniment.

Thou died'st in thy life's June —
   But thou did'st not die too fair:
Thou did'st not die too soon,
   Nor with too calm an air.
34   Thy life and love are riven (*A*)
35   all-hallowed/untainted (*A*)

NOTES

Title: A paean is a song of rejoicing or praise, usually, but not necessarily, in honor of Apollo. Euripides speaks of a dirge (*Iphigenia in Tauris*, line 184) as a "hymn unlike paeans."

14   The words are quoted because they are said by the "mourners." Compare, in Poe's tale "King Pest": "a richly embroidered black silk-velvet pall."

23   Thomas Moore, in a note to the Thirteenth Ode of Anacreon, quotes and translates an Italian imitation of the Sixth Ode with the phrases "ebro d'Amore" and "drunk with love."

34   Since the second version of "A Paean" mentions "Helen," the poem may be connected with Mrs. Stanard, if with anyone in particular; although it has been suggested (Phillips, I, 327) that the piece was "in memory of Mrs. Allan."

36   Here, as in Colossians 1:16 and *Paradise Lost*, II, 430, "thrones" are angels of high rank.

POEMS OF 1832-1835

EPIGRAM
[From Pulci]

In "The Bargain Lost" (a draft for Poe's well-known tale "Bon-Bon"), published in the Philadelphia *Saturday Courier*, December 1, 1832, Poe mentions "a line from Pulci, thus happily translated by a modern satirist." No translation of the *Morgante Maggiore* in the meter used has been found, nor anything close in sentiment in the Italian original. It is to be suspected that the "translator" was Poe himself. The couplet reads:

> Brethren, I come from lands afar
> To show you all what fools you are.

[1831?]

TO ONE IN PARADISE

This is always considered one of Poe's more important poems. Miss Winwar, in *The Haunted Palace* (p. 163), says it is "among the most musical of his rare love poems" and that it has "yet a sense of irremediable loss." Philip Pendleton Cooke wrote to Poe (Woodberry, *Life*, II, 205): "The closing stanza . . . is the perfection of melody."

In his tale "The Visionary" (later "The Assignation"), Poe gave the poem as the composition of the protagonist — obviously modeled on Lord Byron — who finds his beloved married to an older nobleman. Poe apparently had in mind an incident related in Thomas Moore's biography of Byron,[1] which was pointed out by Roy P. Basler in *American Literature*, May 1937. On the eve of the wedding of Byron's early love Mary Chaworth to John Musters, the bard wrote in her copy of the *Letters of Madame*

---

[1] In *Letters and Journals of Lord Byron, with Notices of His Life* (2 vols. London, 1830), I, 57.

de Maintenon the lines (ascribed by Moore to Eliza Dorothea, Lady Tuite):

> Oh Memory, torture me no more,
>   The present's all o'ercast;
> My hopes of future bliss are o'er,
>   In mercy veil the past.
> Why bring those images to view
>   I henceforth must resign?
> Ah! why those happy hours renew,
>   That never can be mine?
> Past pleasure doubles present pain,
>   To sorrow adds regret,
> Regret and hope are both in vain,
>   I ask but to — forget.

Poe told the story of "Byron and Miss Chaworth" in the *Columbian Magazine* for December 1844; and the only personal name in any version of Poe's poem is "Ianthe," a name Byron used for young Charlotte Harley when he dedicated *Childe Harold* to her.

The connections with Byron of Poe's hero and the poem given in Poe's tale are so striking that interpretations running counter to them deserve little attention. Two may be mentioned, however: J. H. Whitty (see Phillips, I, 179) felt that there was a connection with a garden in Richmond, now called Linden Square, where Colonel Thomas Ellis, son of John Allan's partner, said that Poe and Elmira Royster used to stroll; and Killis Campbell (*Poems*, p. 221) thought that the final stanza of the version used in the tale suggests a connection with Elmira.

Poe himself acknowledged a literary source of his poem. He says, as narrator in "The Visionary" (I quote the earliest version):

In turning over a page of Politian's beautiful tragedy, the "Orfeo," which lay near me upon an Ottoman, I found a passage underlined in pencil. It is a passage near the conclusion of the third act — a passage of heart-stirring pathos — a passage which, divested of its impurity, no man could read without a thrill — no maiden without a sigh . . . upon the opposite interleaf were the following lines . . .

Poe's verses, without title, follow. The only passage to which this reference can apply is *Orfeo*, II, 19–26, which may be translated:

Now I lament, Oh lyre disconsolate, because the usual song no more seems right. Let's weep as heaven spins upon its poles, and nightingale give place to our lament. Oh heaven! oh earth! oh sea! oh dire fate! How can I suffer so much misery? My beautiful Euridice, oh, my life, Without you, it's wrong that I stay in this world.[1]

There is no impurity here, but Poe knew the epigram cited in the note to line 5, below, and may have supposed that there was some possible indelicacy in the lament. He hardly can have had a text before him, his indebtedness is so slight.

The poem must have been written before the end of 1833, since it appears in "The Visionary," which was published in *The Lady's Book* for January 1834. This version includes a fifth stanza, which is retained in all versions of the tale and its revision, "The Assignation," but is omitted in the separately published versions of the poem. The earliest text preserved is probably that of a manuscript published in a supplement to the London *Spectator* of January 1, 1853 — following the appearance of an English edition of Poe's poems — with the amazing claim by one "G.D.B." that the American editor or Poe himself had put his name to a poem by Tennyson. On January 20 the Laureate wrote a letter, published in the issue of January 22, vindicating Poe's integrity as author of the verses. The manuscript seems to have been authentic, but it has not been traced during the past century.

There are two other manuscripts of which I give readings. The first (*J*) is an abridged version written in the album of Poe's little cousin, Mary Estelle Herring, in Philadelphia about 1841. It was reproduced in *The American Collector* for December 1926 by Kenneth Rede, who found it (detached from the album) in the collection of Dr. Thomas S. Cullen of the Johns Hopkins University. The second manuscript (*Z*), first described by J. H. Whitty in *Complete Poems* (1917), p. 323, as having been "discovered within the past year," has no history and is not above suspicion. The readings suggest that, if genuine, it is of 1844 or later.

[1]   Ora piangiamo, o sconsolata lira;
        Che più non ci convien l'usato canto:
        Piangiam mentre che 'l ciel ne' poli aggira:
        E Filomena ceda al nostro pianto.
        Oh cielo! oh terra! oh mare! oh sorte dira!
        Come soffrir potrò mai dolor tanto?
        Euridice mia bella, o vita mia,
        Senza te non convien che al mondo stia.

TEXTS

(A) Manuscript, about 1833 (now lost), published in the Supplement to Vol. 26 of the London *Spectator*, January 1, 1853 (p. 5); (B) *The Lady's Book* for January 1834 (8:42), in "The Visionary"; (C) *Southern Literary Messenger*, July 1835 (1:639–640), in "The Visionary"; (D) *Burton's Gentleman's Magazine*, July 1839 (5:49); (E) *Tales of the Grotesque and Arabesque* (1840), II, 206–207, in "The Visionary"; (F) George P. Morris's *American Melodies* (copyrighted 1840), pp. 186–187; (G) Philadelphia *Saturday Evening Post*, January 9, 1841; (H) Philadelphia *Saturday Museum*, March 4, 1843; (J) manuscript in the album of Mary E. Herring, about 1841 (lines 1–6, 21–26); (K) *Broadway Journal*, May 10, 1845 (1:295); (L) *Broadway Journal*, June 7, 1845 (1:359), in "The Assignation"; (M) *The Raven and Other Poems* (1845), p. 23; (N) J. Lorimer Graham copy of *The Raven . . .*, lines 1 and 23 revised (1849); (P) Rufus W. Griswold, ed., *Poets and Poetry of America*, 10th edition (1850), pp. 422–423; (Q) *Works* (1850), I, 378–379, in "The Assignation"; (R) *Works* (1850), II, 33; (Z) manuscript in the Henry E. Huntington Library.

The J. Lorimer Graham version (N) is followed. The *Post* printing (G) was probably not authorized.

TO ONE IN PARADISE [N]

Thou wast that all to me, love,
   For which my soul did pine —
A green isle in the sea, love,
   A fountain and a shrine,
5   All wreathed with fairy fruits and flowers,
   And all the flowers were mine.

Ah, dream too bright to last!
   Ah, starry Hope! that didst arise
But to be overcast!
10   A voice from out the Future cries,
"On! on!" — but o'er the Past
   (Dim gulf!) my spirit hovering lies
Mute, motionless, aghast!

For, alas! alas! with me
15   The light of Life is o'er!
No more — no more — no more —
   (Such language holds the solemn sea
   To the sands upon the shore)

TO ONE IN PARADISE

Shall bloom the thunder-blasted tree,
20   Or the stricken eagle soar!

And all my days are trances,
    And all my nightly dreams
Are where thy grey eye glances,
    And where thy footstep gleams —
25   In what ethereal dances,
    By what eternal streams

[1833–1849]

VARIANTS

Title: *None* (*A, B, C, E, J, L, Q*); To Ianthe in Heaven (*D, F*); To One Beloved (*G*); To One Departed (*Z*)

1 that all/all (*A*); all that (*K, M, P*)

5 wreathed/wreath'd (*D, P*); with fairy fruits and/round with wild (*B*); around about with (*A, C, D, E, F, G*)

6 all the flowers/the flowers — they all (*A, C, D, E, F, G*)

7 But the dream — it could not last (*A, B, C, D, E, F, G*)

7–20 *Omitted from J*

8 And the star of life did rise (*A*); Young Hope! thou did'st arise (*B*); And the star of Hope did rise (*C, D, E, F, G*); Oh starry Hope! thou did'st arise (*H*)

9 But/Only (*A*)

11 "On! on!" — but/"Onward!" while (*A, B, C, D, E, F, G*); "Onward!" — but (*L, Q, Z*)

13–16 *Omitted from A*

14–20 *Omitted from Z*

15 Ambition — all — is o'er (*B, C, D, E, F, G*)

16 *Omitted from K*

17–18 Like the murmur of the solemn seas [*sic*] / To sands on the sea-shore, / A voice is whispering unto me, / "The day is past"; and never more (*A*)

17 solemn/breaking (*B*)

21 And/*Now* (*J*); Now (*L, Q*); my/mine (*A*); days/hours (*A, B, C, D, E, F, G, J, L, Q*)

22 nightly/nights are (*A*)

23 Are/Of (*A*); thy grey/thy dark *in all other texts except*: thy blue (*J*); the dark (*Q*)

24 In the maze of flashing dances (*A*)

26 what eternal/the slow Italian (*A*); far Italian (*B*); what Italian (*C, E, G, L, Q*); what Elysian (*Z*)

After line 20 there is an additional stanza in B:

Alas! for that accursed time
    They bore thee o'er the billow
From me— to titled age and crime,
    And an unholy pillow —
From Love, and from our misty clime
    Where weeps the silver willow!

This also appears, with "me" and "Love" interchanged (*C, E, G, L, Q*).

NOTES

3 If anything beyond an actual green isle is referred to, it may be that Poe is thinking of the old belief that blessed spirits dwelt in green isles of the ocean. In the Welsh Triads, it is said that Green Islands of Ocean are "the abode of the Fair Family, or souls of the virtuous Druids," according to a note

by Felicia Hemans on her poem "The Green Isles of Ocean" (*Works*, Edinburgh and London, 1854, IV, 221). These isles seem to have been well known in Poe's day. Compare the second stanza of "To F[rances]," and "To Zante."

5–6 In "Pinakidia" (Number 140) in the *Southern Literary Messenger*, August 1836 (2:580), Poe wrote: "Politian, the poet and scholar, was an admirer of Alessandra Scala, and addressed to her this extempore:

> To teach me that in hapless suit
> I do but waste my hours,
> Cold maid, when e'er I ask for fruit
> Thou givest me naught but flowers."

This is the Thirty-second Greek Epigram of Politian (Angelo Poliziano). Where Poe got his translation is not yet known. Flowers are symbols of Platonic, fruits suggest carnal love.

10–11 Thomas Moore in the song "One Bumper at Parting" says: "But Time, like a pitiless master,/Cries 'Onward!' and spurs the gay hours."

13 My student Elizabeth McNeil compared to this Byron's "Prisoner of Chillon," lines 249–250: "A sea of stagnant idleness,/Blind, boundless, mute, and motionless."

14–20 In the *New York Times Saturday Review of Books* for January 23, 1909, W. H. Babcock rebuked a critic who had quoted "as Poe's utterance *in propria persona* what Poe put into the mouth of a broken-hearted man just before . . . self-inflicted death. Read in view of that and with the context, the lines quoted become not unworthy. And the stanza just following [lines 21–26] is not to be matched for its wild, mystical ecstasy, like the best mocking-bird music heard under the moon."

15 See St. John 8:12 for "the light of life."

17–18 In "The Poetic Principle" Poe wrote of the "surf that complains to the shore."

23 The unique reading of Mary Herring's album reveals that the fair owner had blue eyes. The final reading "grey" is possibly a compliment to the gray eyes of Mrs. Annie Richmond. Annie, as described in "Landor's Cottage," had "eyes of spiritual gray."

26 Compare to this a passage in "Metzengerstein": ". . . dames of days gone by, floated away in the mazes of an unreal dance to the strains of imaginary melody."

HYMN

This little poem was originally sung by the heroine of the tale "Morella," who was obviously a practitioner of black magic. As such she still appropriately prayed to the Blessed Virgin, since compacts with the Devil do not involve renunciation of the

Mother of God, and medieval story included accounts of Her rescue of repentant witches who could not pray to God. "Hymn" has echoes of the great prayer, "Ave Maria, gratia plena . . . Sancta Maria . . . ora pro nobis."

In 1845 Poe twice published a briefer version of Morella's prayer as a separate poem of his own, with the title "Catholic Hymn." In the J. Lorimer Graham copy of *The Raven and Other Poems* the poet struck out the word "Catholic" — a sign (a passage in "For Annie" is another) that he himself revered Our Lady.

Some critics would minimize the idea that the poem shows religious feeling, but George W. Peck says in the *American Review* of March 1850 (n.s. 5:315) that "one need not be of the Roman faith to feel a loftier aspiration" in the "Hymn."

In 1842, preparing printer's copy of "Morella" for inclusion in the projected PHANTASY-PIECES, Poe canceled the whole poem, and it was omitted from subsequent versions of the tale.

TEXTS

(A) Manuscript of "Morella," about 1833, in the H. E. Huntington Library; (B) *Southern Literary Messenger*, April 1835 (1:449), in "Morella"; (C) *Burton's Gentleman's Magazine*, November 1839 (5:265), in "Morella"; (D) *Tales of the Grotesque and Arabesque* (1840), I, 13, in "Morella"; (E) PHANTASY-PIECES (exemplar of D with manuscript revisions, 1842), in "Morella"; (F) *Broadway Journal*, August 16, 1845 (2:88); (G) *The Raven and Other Poems* (1845), p. 15; (H) J. Lorimer Graham copy of *The Raven* . . . with Poe's revisions (1849); (J) *Works* (1850), II, 13.

The version of J, verbally like H, is used here.

HYMN [J]

At morn — at noon — at twilight dim —
Maria! thou hast heard my hymn!
In joy and wo — in good and ill —
Mother of God, be with me still!
5   When the Hours flew brightly by,
And not a cloud obscured the sky,
My soul, lest it should truant be,
Thy grace did guide to thine and thee;
Now, when storms of Fate o'ercast

10 Darkly my Present and my Past,
    Let my Future radiant shine
    With sweet hopes of thee and thine!

[1833–1849]

VARIANTS

Title: [*in context*] a Catholic hymn (*A, B, C, D*); Catholic Hymn (*F, G,* changed in *H*); the whole poem is canceled in *E*

1 *Before this A and B have:*
  Sancta Maria! turn thine eyes
  Upon the sinner's sacrifice
  Of fervent prayer and humble love,
  From thy holy throne above.

This stanza is also in C and D, but they have a sinner's *for the* sinner's
5 the Hours flew brightly/my hours flew gently (*A, B, C, D*)
6 not a cloud obscured/no storms were in (*A, B, C, D*)
8 grace/love (*A, B, C, D*)
9 storms/clouds (*A, B, C, D*)
10 Darkly/All (*A, B, C, D*)

LATIN HYMN

This poem is found in the tale called first "Epimanes" and later "Four Beasts in One." It concerns the freaks of the Seleucid king of Syria, Antiochus IV (175–164 B.C.), about whom there is much in Polybius, Livy, Athenaeus, and in Maccabees. He captured Jerusalem, and impiously entered the Holy of Holies in the Temple there. He assumed the title Epiphanes ("Illustrious"), but was called Epimanes ("Madman"), because of his strange conduct, according to Athenaeus, X, 53, following Polybius. From the account of his celebration of games at the grove of Daphne, one judges that he was not quite sane, or at least was rarely sober. Poe has the rabble singing a Latin hymn in his honor less absurdly than may be supposed. Epiphanes was brought up in Rome as a hostage, and admired all things Roman.

Poe took the Latin song from the biography of the Roman emperor Aurelian (A.D. 270–275) in the *Scriptores historiae augustae VI*, ascribed to Flavius Vopiscus of Syracuse. The text he gives follows verbally the edition of the *Scriptores historiae augustae* of Claudius Salmasius, issued at Paris in 1620, p. 211, except that the last two words there are "fudit sanguinis," suggesting that Poe followed a secondary source or quoted from memory. This was

· 2 1 8 ·

pointed out in the Stedman and Woodberry edition of Poe's *Works*, IV, 292. The Latin song may be translated: "We, one man, have beheaded a thousand. [Long] live he who slew a thousand. Nobody has as much of wine, as he has spilt of blood."

In all versions of his story, Poe explained, in a footnote, that the Latin song celebrated Aurelian's exploit of killing, with his own hand, 950 of the enemy during the Sarmatic War.

TEXTS

(*A*) Manuscript sent in a letter, May 4, 1833, to "Messrs. Buckingham, Editors of the N. England Magazine, Boston," containing the tale "Epimanes," owned by Mr. H. Bradley Martin; (*B*) *Southern Literary Messenger*, March 1836 (2:237), in "Epimanes"; (*C*) *Tales of the Grotesque and Arabesque* (1840), II, 12, in "Epimanes"; (*D*) *Broadway Journal*, December 6, 1845 (2:334), in "Four Beasts in One"; (*E*) *Works* (1850), II, 469, in "Four Beasts in One," verbally like *D*. Our text is based on *D*.

[LATIN HYMN]   [D]

Mille, mille, mille,
Mille, mille, mille,
Decollavimus, unus homo!
Mille, mille, mille, mille, decollavimus!
Mille, mille, mille,
Vivat qui mille mille occidit!
Tantum vini habet nemo
Quantum sanguinis effudit!

A thousand, a thousand, a thousand,
A thousand, a thousand, a thousand,
We, with one warrior have slain!
A thousand, a thousand, a thousand, a thousand,
5   Sing a thousand over again!
Soho! — let us sing
Long life to our King,
Who knocked over a thousand so fine
Soho! — let us roar,
10   He has given us more
Red gallons of gore
Than all Syria can furnish of wine!

[1833]

POEMS OF THE EARLY 1830's

SONG OF TRIUMPH

This poem, like the preceding "Latin Hymn," is found in the tale "Epimanes." The title is from the context. The earliest text, the manuscript (*A*), has been chosen exceptionally for use here. In all later versions Poe changed the third and fourth lines to read:

> Who is king but Epiphanes?
> Bravo! — bravo!

and in *B* and *C* repeated the first four lines at the end.

Surely the changes were made to please Mrs. Grundy, who might find the king's assertion of his own divinity shocking. But the change spoils the point of the "Song of Triumph," which is intentionally bathetic but in character for the monarch in whose mouth Poe put it. The Seleucid kings, like their predecessor Alexander the Great, claimed divinity, and more than one assumed the title *Theos*. The official style of Antiochus IV was Basileus Antiochos Theos Epiphanes: "King Antiochus, divine, illustrious" or "god manifest." Augustus Caesar permitted himself to be worshiped, but never when he was present. Antiochus IV, like his fellow madman Caligula, is represented here as having no such scruples. The texts are like those listed for the "Latin Hymn."

[SONG OF TRIUMPH]   [*A*]

Who is king but Epiphanes?
Say do you know?
Who is God but Epiphanes?
Say do you know?
There is none but Epiphanes
No — there is none:
So tear down the temples
And put out the sun!

[1833]

ENIGMA
[on Shakespeare]

This poem appeared, marked *"For the Baltimore Visiter"* and signed "P.," in the *Baltimore Saturday Visiter* of February 2, 1833. It is the only item so initialed in the file of that year. I examined it by courtesy of the then owner, Miss Elizabeth Cloud Seip, in 1918, and use the poem here by permission of Mr. William H. Koester. I have inserted the word "make" in line 15, as required for sense and meter.

The answers to the puzzles are: 1, Spenser; 2, Homer; 3–4, Aristotle; 5–6, Kallimachos; 7–8, Shelley; 9, Pope; 10, Euripides; 11, Mark Akenside, author of *Pleasures of the Imagination*; 12, Samuel Rogers, author of *Pleasures of Memory*; 13–14, Euripides again; 15–16, Shakespeare.

In the *Literary Era* for August 1901, Edward M. Alfriend relates that in 1849 Poe said to his father, Thomas M. Alfriend, of Shakespeare: "If all the dramatists of antiquity, Aeschylus, Sophocles, Euripides, Plautus, Terence were combined in one, they would not be worthy to touch the hem of his garments." According to her "Recollections" in the *Home Journal* of July 21, 1860, Poe talked to Mary Elizabeth Bronson at Fordham about 1847 of how "sensible" Pope was. And some of Shelley's opinions must have horrified our poet. Callimachus is mentioned in Poe's early tale "A Decided Loss."

In 1833 Poe wrote for the *Visiter* under his own name and the pseudonym "Tamerlane," as can be seen immediately below. How many Baltimoreans given to writing graceful enigmas, to the occasional use of "P." as a signature, and holding the same opinions as Poe of both Shakespeare and Pope, were contributing to the *Visiter* in 1833? I assign the poem confidently to Poe.

ENIGMA

The noblest name in Allegory's page,
The hand that traced inexorable rage;
A pleasing moralist whose page refined,
Displays the deepest knowledge of the mind;
5   A tender poet of a foreign tongue,
(Indited in the language that he sung.)
A bard of brilliant but unlicensed page
At once the shame and glory of our age,

The prince of harmony and stirling sense,
10   The ancient dramatist of eminence,
       The bard that paints imagination's powers,
       And him whose song revives departed hours,
       Once more an ancient tragic bard recall,
       In boldness of design surpassing all.
15   These names when rightly read, a name [make] known
       Which gathers all their glories in its own.

                                                    [1833]

SERENADE

This was printed as "by E. A. Poe" in the *Baltimore Saturday Visiter* of April 20, 1833, after its receipt from "E.A.P." had been acknowledged in the issue of April 13. It was completely forgotten until in 1917 Professor John C. French located a file of the paper for 1833 in the hands of Miss Elizabeth Cloud Seip. He reprinted "Serenade" in the *Dial* for January 31, 1918 (64:121), and again in *Modern Language Notes*, May 1918 (33:257–258). Killis Campbell inserted a text in the second issue of his *Poems* at page 137. In line 12, I change the sure misprint "mountains," to "mountain's" but otherwise follow the original printing.

SERENADE

       So sweet the hour — so calm the time,
       I feel it more than half a crime
       When Nature sleeps and stars are mute,
       To mar the silence ev'n with lute.
5   At rest on ocean's brilliant dies
       An image of Elysium lies:
       Seven Pleiades entranced in Heaven
       Form in the deep another seven:
       Endymion nodding from above
10   Sees in the sea a second love:
       Within the valleys dim and brown,

And on the spectral mountain's crown
The wearied light is lying down:
And earth, and stars, and sea, and sky
15   Are redolent of sleep, as I
Am redolent of thee and thine
Enthralling love, my Adeline.
But list, O list! — so soft and low
Thy lover's voice tonight shall flow
20   That, scarce awake, thy soul shall deem
My words the music of a dream.
Thus, while no single sound too rude,
Upon thy slumber shall intrude,
Our thoughts, our souls — O God above!
25   In every deed shall mingle, love.   [1833]

NOTES

5   The spelling "dies" for "dyes" was tolerated in 1833.

7   Here Poe seems to know that all seven Pleiades are visible. See notes on "Israfel," line 14.

9   See the notes on "An Acrostic" ("Elizabeth it is in vain"), above, for Poe's use of a different story about the beloved of the Moon. Athenaeus (XIII, xvii), citing a lost work of Licymnius of Chios, says that Endymion sleeps with open eyes.

11f.   Compare Poe's motto for his tale, "Silence — a Fable," which he takes from Alcman and freely translates, "The mountain pinnacles slumber; valleys, crags and caves are silent." The original fragment may be seen in any collection of the Greek lyric poets.

12   Compare to this "Tamerlane," line 139, in the versions of 1829 and 1845: "We walk'd together on the crown/Of a high mountain," and "Fairyland" (1829) lines 16–17: ". . . on the crown/Of a mountain's eminence."

14f.   Compare Poe's tale "The Sphinx": "The very air from the South seemed to me redolent of death."

17   No lady of Poe's acquaintance named Adeline has been found; the word means "of noble birth."

TO ——
("Sleep on")

This poem appeared in the *Baltimore Saturday Visiter* of May 11, 1833, signed "Tamerlane." I cannot think another Baltimore poet in 1833 used that name, and I regard the ascription to Poe as sure, like that of the companion piece, "Fanny," which followed in the next week. John C. French reprinted the pieces in *Modern Language Notes* for May 1918 (33:265–266).

Nothing is known of the lady to whom the poem is addressed. Miss Phillips (I, 456), suggested that Poe's foster mother was here "etherealized" — but the poem is obviously addressed to a living person, if anyone. It is not impossible that the poet addressed it to Mary Starr, but it is surely not the lost "reproachful" poem discussed below at page 232.

TO ——

Sleep on, sleep on, another hour —
  I would not break so calm a sleep,
To wake to sunshine and to show'r,
  To smile and weep.

5   Sleep on, sleep on, like sculptured thing,
  Majestic, beautiful art thou;
Sure seraph fans thee with his wing
  And fans thy brow —

We would not deem thee child of earth,
10   For, O, angelic is thy form!
But that in heav'n thou had'st thy birth,
  Where comes no storm

To mar the bright, the perfect flow'r,
  But all is beautiful and still —
15   And golden sands proclaim the hour
  Which brings no ill.

Sleep on, sleep on, some fairy dream
  Perchance is woven in thy sleep —
But, O, thy spirit, calm, serene,
20   Must wake to weep.   [1833]

15 Compare *Politian*, VI, 41: "The sands of time are changed to golden grains."

19–20 The ending is very like two lines in Shelley's "Mutability" (1821): "Dream thou — and from thy sleep,/Then wake to weep."

FANNY

This poem, like the preceding "To ——" beginning "Sleep on," was signed "Tamerlane" when published in the *Baltimore Saturday Visiter* on May 18, 1833, a week after "To ——." It was first reprinted, with the other poem, by the discoverer, John C. French, in *Modern Language Notes* for May 1918 (33:266). The verses are surely Poe's, written, presumably, for a lady's album, but the lady addressed has not been plausibly identified. Poe's foster mother was named Frances, but she did not disdain him.

The text is that of the *Visiter*, but two misprints, "Sing's" in the second line and "alter" in the seventeenth, are corrected.

FANNY

   The dying swan by northern lakes
      Sings its wild death song, sweet and clear,
   And as the solemn music breaks
      O'er hill and glen dissolves in air;
5   Thus musical thy soft voice came,
   Thus trembled on thy tongue my name.

   Like sunburst through the ebon cloud,
      Which veils the solemn midnight sky,
   Piercing cold evening's sable shroud
10   Thus came the first glance of that eye;
   But like the adamantine rock,
   My spirit met and braved the shock.

   Let memory the boy recall
      Who laid his heart upon thy shrine,

15 When far away his footsteps fall,
   Think that he deem'd thy charms divine;
  A victim on love's altar slain,
  By witching eyes which looked disdain. [1833?]

NOTES

1 Stories of the swan song abound in literature, and are not wholly fabulous. Dr. Robert G. Murphy refers me to the *Handbook of British Birds* (1939), III, 169, which says that the final expulsion of air from the long convoluted windpipe of the whooper swan (*Cygnus cygnus*) produces a wailing, slow, and flutelike sound. This is not true of the mute swan, another species, better known in England and America.

7–8 The simile is unusually incorrect for Poe.

THE COLISEUM

This poem is a major effort, but somewhat atypical of Poe's work. It was almost surely composed for submission in a prize contest, and probably in haste. It is extremely rhetorical, perhaps calculated to please judges more likely to admire rhetoric than subtler kinds of art. The form, blank verse, was new to Poe, and one in which he was never, I think, at home.

The subject is commonplace, for everyone knows the Coliseum, at least from pictures. Poe was well acquainted with Byron's descriptions in *Manfred*, III, iv, 10–41 and *Childe Harold*, IV, cxlii–cxlv. Poe, however, answers Childe Harold, who saw in the ruins only the fall of Rome and her impotence.[1] The American, like Manfred, sees a memorial of the source of our civilization, by no means impotent but even now an inspiration. Richard Wilbur (*Poe*, p. 138) compares "MS. Found in a Bottle": "I have been all my life a dealer in antiquities, and have imbibed the shadows of fallen columns . . . until my very soul has become a ruin."

[1] See *Edgar Allan Poe, Representative Selections* . . . by Margaret Alterton . . . and . . . Hardin Craig (New York, 1935), p. 495. Poe on several occasions wrote answers to poetry by others. Byron's lines were indebted not only to observation of the ruins, but to a discussion of them in the seventy-first chapter — the last — of Gibbon's *Decline and Fall of the Roman Empire*. With this too Poe was very probably acquainted. Maxwell Morton in *A Builder of the Beautiful* (1928), p. 47, quotes a "parallel" from a poem by "E.B.B." in the London *New Monthly* for July 1821 (2:59), but the verses concern the Acropolis and the analogy is remote.

THE COLISEUM

In the issue of the *Baltimore Saturday Visiter* for June 15, 1833, Charles Ferree Cloud and William P. Pouder (pronounced "Pooder"), the proprietors, announced premiums of "50 dollars for the best Tale and 25 dollars for the best Poem, not exceeding one hundred lines." The judges of the contest, John P. Kennedy, John H. B. Latrobe, and Dr. James H. Miller, met early in October at Latrobe's home, 11 West Mulberry Street, and in the *Visiter* of the twelfth announced the awards — for the story to Poe, and for a poem to "Henry Wilton." Kennedy and Latrobe told Poe he had won both prizes, but the "award was . . . altered" — these are Poe's own words in a letter of July 20, 1835, to Thomas W. White.

Poe's tale, "MS. Found in a Bottle," appeared in the *Visiter* for October 19, 1833, and his poem "The Coliseum" on the twenty-sixth. "Henry Wilton" turned out to be John H. Hewitt (1802–1890), then editor of the *Visiter*. His verses, "The Song of the Wind," printed in the *Visiter* of October 19, may be found in his *Miscellaneous Poems* (Baltimore, 1838) and in his autobiographic *Shadows on the Wall* (Baltimore, 1877), pp. 157–159. The Hewitt piece was also printed by George C. Perine in *The Poets and Verse-Writers of Maryland* (Cincinnati, 1898), pp. 47–49; it is there recorded (p. 43), on the authority of William M. Marine, that on one occasion Poe and Hewitt came to blows.

"The Coliseum" was incorporated as a soliloquy in the eleventh and last scene of Poe's tragedy *Politian*. J. P. Kennedy revealed in a letter of April 13, 1835, to T. W. White, printed in Griswold's "Memoir," p. xiii, that Poe was working on his play at that time. The readings of the last lines in the *Visiter* text were never repeated, hence that version is obviously earlier than the one in the play. Winning the *Visiter* prize really launched Poe on his career as a professional man of letters.

TEXTS

(A) *Baltimore Saturday Visiter*, October 26, 1833; (B) manuscript of *Politian*, scene XI (1835); (C) *Southern Literary Messenger*, August 1835 (1:706); (D) manuscript in the album of Mary Estelle Herring (1841?); (E) *Saturday Evening Post*, June 12, 1841; (F) *The Poets and Poetry of America*, ed. R. W. Griswold (1842), pp. 387–388; (G) Philadelphia *Saturday Museum*, March 4,

1843; (H) *Broadway Journal*, July 12, 1845 (2:14); (J) *The Raven and Other Poems* (1845), pp. 12–13; (K) *The Poetry of the Sentiments* (Philadelphia, 1845), pp. 53–54; (L) J. Lorimer Graham copy of *The Raven . . .* with one correction (1849); (M) *Works* (1850), II, 15–16.

Griswold's text (M) is used; in it line 24 has superior readings. Variants of the *Politian* manuscript (B) are recorded only for "The Coliseum," not for the lines that tie it into the play. The Mary Herring manuscript was facsimiled by Kenneth Rede in the *American Collector* of December 1926 (3:100–102) — the original is now in the Koester Collection at the University of Texas. The poem appeared in the first nine editions of *The Poets and Poetry of America*, but was dropped from the tenth. *The Poetry of the Sentiments* (K) was stereotyped, reissued in 1846, and occasionally after 1850; its supposed publication of 1842 does not exist.

THE COLISEUM [M]

Type of the antique Rome! Rich reliquary
Of lofty contemplation left to Time
By buried centuries of pomp and power!
At length — at length — after so many days
5 Of weary pilgrimage and burning thirst,
(Thirst for the springs of lore that in thee lie,)
I kneel, an altered and an humble man,
Amid thy shadows, and so drink within
My very soul thy grandeur, gloom, and glory!

10 Vastness! and Age! and Memories of Eld!
Silence! and Desolation! and dim Night!
I feel ye now — I feel ye in your strength —
O spells more sure than e'er Judæan king
Taught in the gardens of Gethsemane!
15 O charms more potent than the rapt Chaldee
Ever drew down from out the quiet stars!

Here, where a hero fell, a column falls!
Here, where the mimic eagle glared in gold,
A midnight vigil holds the swarthy bat!
20 Here, where the dames of Rome their gilded hair
Waved to the wind, now wave the reed and thistle!
Here, where on golden throne the monarch lolled,

Glides, spectre-like, unto his marble home,
Lit by the wan light of the hornéd moon,
25 The swift and silent lizard of the stones!

But stay! these walls — these ivy-clad arcades —
These mouldering plinths — these sad and blackened shafts —
These vague entablatures — this crumbling frieze —
These shattered cornices — this wreck — this ruin —
30 These stones — alas! these gray stones — are they all —
All of the famed, and the colossal left
By the corrosive Hours to Fate and me?

"Not all" — the Echoes answer me — "not all!
"Prophetic sounds and loud, arise forever
35 "From us, and from all Ruin, unto the wise,
"As melody from Memnon to the Sun.
"We rule the hearts of mightiest men — we rule
"With a despotic sway all giant minds.
"We are not impotent — we pallid stones.
40 "Not all our power is gone — not all our fame —
"Not all the magic of our high renown —
"Not all the wonder that encircles us —
"Not all the mysteries that in us lie —
"Not all the memories that hang upon
45 "And cling around about us as a garment,
"Clothing us in a robe of more than glory."

[1833–1843]

VARIANTS

Title: *None* (*B*); The Coliseum. A Prize
  Poem (*C, E*); Coliseum (*F, K*)
1 *Before this* Lone amphitheatre!
  Grey Coliseum! (*A*)
6 lore/love (*misprint, A*)
7 kneel/stand (*B*); altered/alter'd (*F,
  G, H, K*)
8 Amid/Within (*D, F, K*); Among (*E*)
10 Eld/old (*K*)
12 *Before this*: Gaunt vestibules and
  phantom-peopled aisles (*A, B, C, D*)
14 Gethsemane/Gethsemané (*E, G*)

15 charms/spells (*B*)
19 midnight/secret (*B*)
20 gilded/yellow (*A, B, C, D*)
21 Waved/Wav'd (*A, C*)
21 *After this*: Here where on ivory
  couch the Caesar sate (*A, B, C*);
  changed to ivory throne (*D*), golden
  throne (*F, K*)
22 *Before this*: On bed of moss lies
  gloating the foul adder (*A, B, C, D,
  F, K*)

· 2 2 9 ·

22 golden throne/golden couch (*D*); ivory couch (*F, K*); lolled/loll'd (*A, C, F, G, H, K*)

24 wan light/wanlight (*misprint J, corrected L*); wan-light (*H*); hornéd/horned (*A, B, C, H, J, K, L*)

26 These crumbling walls; these tottering arcades (*A, B, C, D*); But hold! — these dark, these perishing arcades (*F, K*)

27 mouldering/mould'ring (*G, H*); blackened/blacken'd (*A, C, F, G, H, K*)

28 crumbling/broken (*A, B, C, D, F, K*)

29 shattered/shatter'd (*F, G, H, K*)

31 famed/great (*A, B, C, D*); grand (*E*); proud (*F, K*); fam'd (*G, H*)

35 unto/to (*F. K*)

36 melody from/in old days from (*A, C, D*); from the granite (*B, over a canceled word*)

39 impotent/desolate (*A, B, C, D*)

45 as a garment/now and ever (*A*); like a garment (*E*)

46 Clothing/And clothe (*A*)

NOTES

Title: The Coliseum is the great Flavian Amphitheater at Rome, begun by Vespasian and finished and dedicated by his son Titus in A.D. 80. In the eighth century the Venerable Bede said of it (as Byron put it in *Childe Harold*, IV, cxlv, 1–3, pointing out that he merely translated a remark he found in the last chapter of Gibbon):

> 'While stands the Coliseum, Rome shall stand;
> 'When falls the Coliseum, Rome shall fall;
> 'And when Rome falls — the World.'

The name may have come from its proximity to a colossal statue; hence some modern writers prefer a "more learned" spelling, Colosseum. The Venerable Bede called it Colyseus; but Gibbon and Byron the Coliseum, and Poe follows them.

1 Gibbon says "the most liberal of the pontiffs, Benedict the Fourteenth . . . consecrated [the Coliseum] a spot which persecution . . . had stained with blood of so many Christian martyrs."

2–3 Byron in *Childe Harold*, IV, cxxviii, 7–8, calls the Coliseum "This long-explored but still exhaustless mine/Of contemplation."

3 Compare Gray's "Elegy": "The boast of heraldry, the pomp of power," echoed also in the 1827 version of "Tamerlane," line 355: "My eyes were still on pomp and power."

4 There may be a reminiscence of Keats' "Eve of St. Agnes," stanza 38:

> Ah, silver shrine, here will I take my rest
> After so many hours of toil and quest,
> A famish'd pilgrim . . .

9 "Grandeur, gloom and glory" seems to me a rhetorical phrase needing no special inspiration, although a striking parallel is "Of life's extremes the grandeur and the gloom," in Thomas Campbell's once widely read *Gertrude of Wyoming*, I, vii, 2.

13–14 At first sight this seems to be an allusion to Our Lord's agony in the garden of Gethsemane. But the word "king" is not capitalized, nor is it quite correct to call His teachings "spells." Solomon is the only Jewish king greatly famed, even in legend, for magic, but was he connected with Gethsemane?

15 The Chaldeans, priests among the Babylonians and Assyrians, were great students of astrology. Poe alludes to them in "Al Aaraaf," II, 43.

17–25 Killis Campbell points out the triple use of "Here, where" in *Childe Harold* (IV, cxlii, 1, 2, 5) and compares *Manfred*, III, iv, 22–26:

> Where the Caesars dwelt,
> And dwell the tuneless birds of night, amidst
> A grove which springs through levelled battlements,
> And twines its roots with the imperial hearths,
> Ivy usurps the laurel's place of growth.

Also striking are lines from Lydia H. Sigourney's "Rome": " 'Mid Nero's house of gold, with clustering bats,/ And gliding lizards," and Gray's "Impromptu," lines 13–14: "Here mouldering fanes and battlements arise,/Turrets and arches nodding to their fall."

18 The reference is probably simply to the aquila, the principal standard of each Roman legion. It was an image of an eagle, sometimes made of gold and usually at least of gilded metal, carried on a pole. It was a symbol of victorious Jove. The eagles were themselves objects of worship among the Romans. See Poe's "Marginalia," number 228.

20 Poe changed "yellow hair" to "gilded hair" to be correct. Few Roman ladies were natural blondes, but many used a dye, a plant called *lysimachia,* which Pliny the Elder (*Natural History*, XXVI, xciii) said imparted a blonde tint to the hair.

29 Campbell (*Poems*, p. 220) again cites *Childe Harold*, IV, cxlv, 8: "Rome and her Ruin past Redemption's skill."

32 The striking phrase "corrosive hours" recurs in Poe's "Colloquy of Monos and Una" (1841), and the rest of the line recalls Gray's "Elegy": "And leaves the world to darkness and to me."

36 According to ancient Greek legends Memnon was the son of Tithonus and Eos, the Dawn. He was said to have been the ruler of Ethiopia and of Egypt and, according to Homer, was an ally of Priam during the Trojan War. Near Thebes in Egypt there are twin colossal statues, the more easterly of which, in Greco-Roman times, gave out, when struck by the rays of the morning sun, a sound like the breaking of a harpstring. It was heard by Strabo, and the Emperor Hadrian, but ceased in the third century. It was said that the statue was that of Memnon, saluting his mother. Actually, it represents King Amenophis III. The colossus is made of gritstone or breccia, repaired with sandstone. Poe in *Politian* called it the "granite Memnon" but abandoned the reading, for correctness.

37 Compare *Manfred*, III, iv, 40–41: "The dead, but sceptred, Sovereigns, who still rule/Our spirits from their urns."

45 There seems to be an echo here of Wordsworth's "Ode: Intimations of Immortality": "trailing clouds of glory," and of that poet's sonnet "Composed Upon Westminster Bridge": "This City now doth, like a garment, wear/The beauty of the morning." The latter probably alludes to Psalm 104:2, "Who coverest thyself with light as with a garment."

[TO MARY STARR]

This is a lost poem. While residing with Mrs. Clemm at 3 Amity Street in Baltimore, about 1834, Poe met a girl named Mary Newman. She introduced him to Mary Starr, daughter of a Philadelphia engraver. This Mary lived on Essex Street near Fayette at the home of her mother's brother, James Devereaux, whose surname she used socially. She had a fair complexion and long blonde hair. Poe and Mary Starr fell in love, but her family disapproved, and there was a quarrel — the young lady refused to receive a letter from the poet brought to her by Virginia Clemm. Long afterwards, according to her nephew, Mary said: "Mr. Poe . . . published . . . in a Baltimore paper a poem of six or eight verses [probably meaning stanzas], addressed 'To Mary.' The poem was very severe, and spoke of fickleness and inconstancy. All my friends and his knew whom he meant. This also added to my uncle's indignation."

The quarrel may have been violent; but later, after Mary had married a merchant tailor named Jenning, who had a store in New York City and a home in New Jersey, the friendship was revived. Poe probably called on Mary in 1842. She and her husband visited the Poe family at Fordham in 1846, and in 1847 helped to pay for the funeral of Virginia Clemm Poe. Mrs. Jenning stayed with the poet during that ceremony. She later moved to Detroit, where she died, aged seventy-one, in 1887.

My information about Mary Starr comes largely from her granddaughter, as well as from incomplete printed and manuscript sources used by previous scholars. On January 15, 1935, I interviewed Minnie Aletha Jenning, who assured me that the article by Mary Starr's nephew, Augustus Van Cleef, "Poe's Mary," in *Harper's New Monthly Magazine* for March 1889 (78:634–640) was basically true but probably overcolored. There are also letters referring to Mary Starr from Marie Louise Shew Houghton and her daughter, Dora, described in the Ingram List, numbers 197 and 209. Some students refer to Miss Starr as "Baltimore Mary," or Mary Devereaux.

Since the poem was reproachful, all attempts to identify it

with poems that are not must be wrong. These include "To Mary," signed "P." in the Boston *New England Magazine* for January 1832; "Lines to Mary" by "H. T." in the *Baltimore Saturday Visiter*, November 3, 1832; Poe's own "To Mary" (later retitled "To F[rances]") in the *Southern Literary Messenger* for July 1835; and "Woman's Heart" in the *Baltimore Times*, June 16, 1832. (See Woodberry, *Life*, II, 414; Campbell, *Mind of Poe*, p. 235; and Phillips, *Edgar Allan Poe the Man*, I, 435.) I feel sure Poe's poem existed, but has not been found because of the imperfection of the files of several Baltimore papers.

TO FRANCES S. OSGOOD

These graceful lines of compliment were probably inspired by a line "Ah! may'st thou always be what now thou art" in Byron's dedication of *Childe Harold* to "Ianthe." [1]

Poe's poem can be addressed to almost any lady, and he inscribed it to several friends in turn. The first was his cousin, Elizabeth Rebecca Herring, for whom he wrote it in her album at some time prior to her marriage in 1834. This version was not published until 1917.

Poe first printed the piece himself in the *Southern Literary Messenger*, September 1835, addressed to an Eliza who was generally then understood to be Eliza White, the eighteen-year-old daughter of the proprietor of the magazine. She was "a slender, graceful blonde, with deep blue eyes . . . a great student, and very . . . intelligent. She was said to be engaged to Poe. . . . It was soon broken off on account of his dissipation." [2] She never married, and lived until 1888, being noted in later years for brilliant Shakespearean readings. [3]

In the summer of 1839, Poe again printed the poem — this time

---

[1] See Killis Campbell, *Complete Poems* (1917), p. 227.

[2] See Weiss, *Home Life of Poe* (1907), p. 79. Ingram's statement, *Edgar Allan Poe* (1880), I, 130, that Poe wrote the lines in Eliza White's album seems to be based merely on the title of the first printed version.

[3] See Phillips (1926), II, 1183.

as a filler addressed to nobody in particular — in *Burton's Gentleman's Magazine.* And a year or two later it was written out in the album of Mary Estelle Herring (younger half-sister of Elizabeth Rebecca) and signed by Virginia E. Poe.[4]

The poem served the author again in 1845, when it was addressed — in two forms — to Mrs. Osgood. The first quatrain appeared as "To F——" in the *Broadway Journal,* September 13, 1845, as a reply to her "Echo Song" beginning:

> I know a noble heart that beats
>   For one it loves how "wildly well!"
> I only know for *whom* it beats;
>   But I must never tell! [5]

Very soon thereafter the whole appeared, plainly dedicated "To F——s S. O——d" in *The Raven and Other Poems.*

Nor was this quite all. There is a signed manuscript, certainly genuine, specially written for a very young lady. I think she may have been Mary Neal (daughter of Poe's old friend John Neal) who asked for Poe's autograph on April 25, 1846.[6]

TEXTS

(*A*) Manuscript in the album of Elizabeth Rebecca Herring (*ca.* 1833), printed by J. H. Whitty in *Complete Poems* (1917), p. 324; (*B*) *Southern Literary Messenger,* September 1835 (1:748); (*C*) *Burton's Gentleman's Magazine,* August 1839 (5:75); (*D*) manuscript written and signed by Virginia E. Poe in the album of Mary Estelle Herring (*ca.* 1841), now in the Koester Collection at the University of Texas, facsimiled by Kenneth Rede in the *American Collector,* December 1926 (3:102); (*E*) *Broadway Journal,* September 13, 1845 (2:148), lines 1–4; (*F*) *The Raven and Other Poems* (1845), p. 25; (*G*) *The Lover's Gift* (Hartford, 1848), p. 99; (*H*) *Works* (1850), II, 32; (*J*) manuscript of uncertain date in the Chapin Library of Williams College.

I give *A, F* (exactly like *H*), and *J* in full. Variants from the other texts are given against *F.*

---

[4] Poe himself wrote out "The Coliseum" and "To One in Paradise" in Mary's album. See Kenneth Rede in *American Collector,* December 1926.

[5] Printed in the *Broadway Journal* of September 6; obviously, with its quotation from "Israfel," meant for Poe.

[6] See her letter to Mrs. Osgood, quoted by W. M. Griswold in *Passages from the Correspondence . . . of Rufus W. Griswold* (1898), pp. 203–204: "I guess I *do* want a lock of Mr. Poe's hair . . . but I also want a line of his writing . . . I will enclose in this letter a note for him."

TO FRANCES S. OSGOOD

TO ELIZABETH [*A*]

Would'st thou be loved? then let thy heart
From its present pathway part not —
Be every thing which now thou art
And nothing which thou art not:

So with the world thy gentle ways,
And unassuming beauty
Shall be a constant theme of praise,
And love — a duty.

[1833?]

TO F——s S. O——d. [*F*]

Thou wouldst be loved? — then let thy heart
From its present pathway part not!
Being everything which now thou art,
Be nothing which thou art not.
So with the world thy gentle ways,
Thy grace, thy more than beauty,
Shall be an endless theme of praise,
And love — a simple duty.

[1833?–1845]

TO — — [*J*]

Thou wouldst be loved? — then let thy heart
From its present pathway part not.
Being everything which now thou art,
Be nothing which thou art not.
So, with the world, thy winning ways,
Thy truth, thy youth, thy beauty,
Shall be a daily theme for praise,
And love, no more than duty.

[1833?–1846?]

VARIANTS

Title: Lines Written in an Album (*B*); To — (*C, D, G*); To F — (*E*)
1 Eliza! — let thy generous heart (*B*); Fair maiden, let thy generous heart (*C*); Beloved, let thy generous heart (*D*)
3 everything/every thing (*B, C, D, G*)
5–8 *Not in E*

6 Thy unassuming beauty (*B, C*); Thy virtue, grace, and beauty (*D*)
7 Shall be an endless/And truth shall be a (*B*); Thy truth — shall be a (*C*); Shall be a constant (*D*)
8 Forever — and love a duty (*B, C*); And love of thee — a duty (*D*)

TO FRANCES

This poem when first printed in the summer of 1835 was headed "To Mary." She was, according to tradition, Miss Mary Winfree, of Chesterfield, Virginia, a close friend of Elmira Shelton. She called upon Poe in Baltimore, and informed him that Elmira's marriage was less than happy.[1]

Poe revised the poem slightly for use as a filler in *Graham's Magazine* in 1842, treating it impersonally.[2] Finally, during his romantic association with Frances Sargent Osgood in 1845, he addressed it to her by the initial of her first name.

TEXTS

(*A*) *Southern Literary Messenger*, July 1835 (1:636); (*B*) *Graham's Magazine* for March 1842 (20:137); (*C*) Philadelphia *Saturday Museum*, March 4, 1843; (*D*) *Broadway Journal*, April 26, 1845 (1:260); (*E*) *The Raven and Other Poems* (1845), p. 25; (*F*) *Works* (1850), II, 53.
The text used is *E* (verbally like *D* and *F*).

TO F—— [*E*]

Beloved! amid the earnest woes
That crowd around my earthly path —

[1] "Mary" was identified by Charles Marshall Graves, in *Selected Poems and Tales of Poe* (1906), p. 146. Graves was of an old Richmond family, and hence a reliable witness, although his statement that Miss Winfree "rejected Poe's proffered love" may be a romantic accretion. Hervey Allen heard more about Mary, who had literary interests, from some relative of hers who did not wish to have his name revealed, as is recounted in *Israfel* (1926), I, 367–368; new edition (1934), p. 296. Allen has some conjectures not based on his Richmond informant, which can be disregarded. There should be no confusion between Mary Winfree and Mary Starr.

[2] Campbell, *Poems* (1917), pp. 224–225, records some fanciful identifications, which have nothing to commend them to anyone aware of the Winfree tradition.

TO FRANCES S. OSGOOD

(Drear path, alas! where grows
Not even one lonely rose) —
5   My soul at least a solace hath
In dreams of thee, and therein knows
An Eden of bland repose.

And thus thy memory is to me
    Like some enchanted far-off isle
10   In some tumultuous sea —
Some ocean throbbing far and free
    With storms — but where meanwhile
Serenest skies continually
    Just o'er that one bright island smile.

[1835–1845]

VARIANTS

Title: To Mary (*A*); To One De-
parted (*B, C*)
1–7 *Placed after 14* (*B, C*)
1 Mary, amid the cares — the woes (*A*);
For 'mid the earnest cares and woes
(*B, C*)
2 That crowd/Crowding (*A*)

3 Drear/Sad (*A, B, C*)
4 even/ev'n (*A, C*)
7 bland/sweet (*A*)
8 And thus/Seraph (*B, C*)
11 Some lake beset as lake can be (*A*);
Some ocean vexed as it may be (*B, C*)

NOTES

7 Poe uses Eden for heaven also in "The Lake" and "The Raven."

8 Wilbur (*Poe*, p. 139) remarks that this line implies that the lady is dead or at a distance — not necessarily great.

8–10 Poe wrote in his "Byron and Miss Chaworth" in the *Columbian Magazine* for December 1844: "She to him was . . . Aphrodite that sprang . . . from the bright foam upon the storm-tormented ocean of his thoughts." Compare also "To One in Paradise," line 3: "A green isle in the sea," and my note on it.

9–14 The variants of "lake" and "ocean" suggest that Poe had no particular locale in mind, merely a clear place in the center of a storm, often seen in nature. It has been suggested by H. E. Mierow in *Classical Weekly* (November 1918) that Poe had in mind Aeaea, where Ulysses sojourned with Circe, daughter of the Sun — but a comparison to that formidable enchantress seems out of place in a young lady's album. Less unlikely is a story mentioned by Pliny the Elder (*Natural History*, II, xcvii) that in ancient times, at Paphos in the island of Cyprus, there was a shrine of Venus where no rain ever fell.

POLITIAN

1835

POLITIAN

Politian is Poe's sole attempt to write a play for the stage, and indeed his only effort of any kind at a drama in verse.[1] His abandonment of it must have been deliberate, for while the play is unfinished, the conclusion was obviously planned; the play needed only a few lines to be completed.

Poe, indeed, seems never to have been happy about his play. It simply did not meet the high artistic standards he set for himself. He published five scenes in the *Southern Literary Messenger* in 1835–36 almost surely because the magazine needed copy, and his letter of September 10, 1845, to E. A. Duyckinck makes it clear that the scenes were republished in *The Raven and Other Poems* somewhat against the author's will and only "to fill a book." That he did not plan ever to print the other scenes of the play was implied when to George W. Eveleth, who had asked him about them, Poe laconically replied on December 15, 1846, "There *is* no more of 'Politian.'"

If Poe rightly concluded that his forte was not in the composition of dramas for the stage, he nevertheless preserved most of his manuscript. And today one may well wish to read the sole effort at a full-length play by the author of that masterly prose monodrama, "The Tell-Tale Heart." *Politian* never was finished, and some of what was written has been lost. But it is still almost complete, since the lost lines are demonstrably less than one hundred and the general plan of the final scene is obvious. It can be and indeed has been performed and found acceptable by audiences.[2]

Full discussion of the history of the parts Poe did not print be-

[1] For a probably unreliable story that Poe once had a sketch of a scenario of a tragedy to be worked out with Dr. R. Montgomery Bird, see Phillips, I, 835, citing Howard Paul in *Munsey's Magazine*, August 1892. Paul's statements are notoriously undependable.

[2] It had its *première* on January 19, 1933, when given by the Virginia Players at the University at Charlottesville, and was reviewed by James Southall Wilson in the college annual of the year, *Corks and Curls* (46:351). There were a few later performances elsewhere in Virginia.

longs in the bibliographical and textual notes below. But it should be said at once that a major portion of the manuscript was preserved by Poe's patroness, Sarah Anna Lewis, who gave one leaf to an obscure collector, and the rest later to John H. Ingram.[3] Ingram's portion entered the famous collection of Stephen H. Wakeman, bought *en bloc* by the first J. P. Morgan in 1909.

In 1917, when I was an undergraduate, Miss Belle da Costa Greene, director of the Pierpont Morgan Library, suggested that I edit the play; and in 1923 *Politian, An Unfinished Tragedy* was published at Richmond.[4] This is the first edition, and as such is now followed for the conventional arrangement of speakers' names and stage directions. The text given below is based on very careful re-examination of the manuscript [5] and of all the printings by Poe of parts of the play. The annotation has been brought up to date, and also reduced by the omission of some peripheral material.

SOURCES OF THE PLOT

Poe's source lies in the celebrated "Kentucky Tragedy," the killing of Colonel Solomon P. Sharp in 1825 by Jereboam O. Beauchamp.[6] The grim story follows. Sharp, a politician, seduced a girl of good family, Ann Cook or Cooke. Their child died, and Sharp refused to marry his inamorata, who thereafter lived in retirement, much given to reading. Beauchamp, though much younger than she, became romantically interested in her, made her acquaintance, and sought her hand. She asked him to avenge her; and Beauchamp (who was also interested in politics) tried to challenge Sharp to a duel. The latter refused to fight because he was in the wrong. The lady now got what Beauchamp called a "true womanish whim" to be her own avenger, and practiced

---

[3] Ingram published brief extracts in 1875 and 1888; a New York dealer printed a transcript of the last leaf in 1912.

[4] The edition was my doctoral dissertation, directed by William Peterfield Trent, but also read before publication by George Edward Woodberry, James Howard Whitty, and Killis Campbell.

[5] Both the original and a photocopy have been used; some minutiae are clearer in each than in the other.

[6] The name is pronounced "Beecham." The historical basis of the play is mentioned briefly in Ingram's *Edgar Allan Poe* (1880), p. 90. The biographer presumably learned of it from Mrs. Lewis, whose informant was probably Poe.

pistol shooting. In June 1824, Beauchamp and Ann Cook were married, and they decided to let the husband do the killing. He called Sharp to the door at "2 *A.M.* on the night of November 6" (the morning of the seventh), 1825, and stabbed him to death. Sharp had recently resigned the attorney generalship of the state to run for Congress from Franklin County.

It was a time of great political unrest in Kentucky, and Beauchamp was convicted, probably because the jury thought the crime had a political motive. His confession convinces me that it had not, but it should be recalled that Kentucky killings were rarely caused by quarrels about women. Beauchamp and his wife attempted suicide; she died, but the husband recovered and was hanged on July 7, 1826. They were buried in one grave at Bloomfield, Kentucky, with a monument on which is engraved the epitaph in verse composed by Mrs. Beauchamp.[7]

It is more than probable that Poe's attention was called to the case by an account of it in chapter xxxiv of Charles Fenno Hoffman's *Winter in the West*, where it was remarked: "Incidents like these . . . seem from the . . . romantic rashness they betray, as belonging to a bygone age . . . All combine to make up a drama of real life which can never be forgotten . . . where it was enacted." Hoffman's work bears the date 1835 on its title page, but it came out in time to be reviewed in the New York *American Monthly Magazine* for December 1834. From Hoffman's words Poe probably took the idea of *drama set in another age*. A brief notice of Hoffman's book in the *Southern Literary Messenger*, April 1835, is probably Poe's. It does not refer to Sharp and Beauchamp. There is reason to believe that Poe began work on his play early in 1835 [8] and did not spend many weeks on it, for on April 13 J. P. Kennedy wrote to T. W. White that Poe had been "at work upon a tragedy, but I have turned him to drudging upon whatever may make money." [9]

---

[7] The stone is still to be seen. The text of the poem was first printed in a newspaper of Frankfort, Kentucky, *The Spirit of '76*, July 14, 1826, and has been often reprinted.

[8] "The Coliseum," first printed in October 1833, was revised before Poe inserted it in the eleventh scene of his play.

[9] See Griswold's "Memoir," p. xxix.

POLITIAN

The case had attracted great attention in the newspapers of 1825 and 1826 and has ever since been the subject of many factual works, stories, and songs. There is no evidence, however, that Poe used as sources anything beyond Hoffman's account and two of the pamphlets. *Politian* does reflect the author's familiarity with these publications. The pamphlets are: (1) *The Confession of Jereboam O. Beauchamp* . . . (Bloomfield, Kentucky, 1826), which includes some poems by both Beauchamp and his wife; the authenticity of the work was brought out in testimony in a lawsuit against Beauchamp's uncle, and it is still our chief source of knowledge of the affair. (2) *Letters of Ann Cook, late Mrs. Beauchamp, to her Friend in Maryland* (Washington, 1826), published by one "W—— R———n" of Charles County, Maryland, who said the letters were addressed to his wife Ellen; they are obviously authentic, and Poe seems to echo some of their phraseology, in his seventh scene especially. He had no need to go back to the newspapers of the time of the murder and the trial. Nor can I think that he used any of the other factual pamphlets on the crime,[10] or imaginative works based on it written before his own.[11]

Of the many later treatments of the "Kentucky Tragedy," [12] Poe took notice of only two. Reviewing *Beauchampe*, by William Gilmore Simms, in *Graham's* for May 1842, Poe said that the

---

[10] See my *Politian* (1923), p. 53, for fuller discussions. A supposedly unique broadside, *From the Louisville Public Advertiser. Confession of Jereboam Beauchamp. (Senator from Washington County)*, which I recently gave to the library of the University of Kentucky, was printed prior to 1825, and concerns only a political caucus, unrelated to Sharp.

[11] Isaac Starr Clason, actor and Byronic poet of New York, wrote a long poem on the subject in 1833, which was never printed, according to Duyckinck's *Cyclopedia of American Literature* (1856), II, 263. The play *Conrad and Eudora . . . Founded on the Murder of Sharp* . . . was printed in Philadelphia by Thomas Holley Chivers in 1834, before he had any acquaintance with Poe; it bears no publisher's name, and only one copy is known — that in the Harris Collection at Brown University, which I have read. It is as unlike Poe's play as anything on the same subject could be. Chivers retained the scene in Kentucky; and his backwoods politicians, spouting blank verse, have the merit of unintentional laughability. Chivers rewrote the play as *Leoni, or the Orphan of Venice* in 1838, but did not print it until 1851. After he met Poe, Chivers sometimes referred to his friend as "Politian." See *Complete Works of . . . Chivers* (1957), I, 1–2, and *passim*.

[12] These include folksongs, plays, and novels — one is by Robert Penn Warren, *World Enough and Time* (1950). See *The Beauchamp Tragedy* (1963), edited by Jules Zanger; as well as my edition of *Politian* (1923), pp. 54f.

tragedy itself was romantic and thrilling, but he feared "too little has been left for invention." Of the same book, Poe said in the *Broadway Journal* of October 4, 1845, "Historical truth has somewhat hampered . . . the artist"; this was in a review of *The Wigwam and the Cabin* by Simms. More interesting is a comment on Charles Fenno Hoffman's *Greyslaer* (1840) in Poe's notice of Hoffman in *Godey's* for October 1846: "The facts . . . would put to shame the skill of the most consummate artist . . . The incidents might be better woven into a tragedy."

THE PRESENT TEXT

The text of Poe's play is necessarily a composite, since the scenes that he printed include many lines no longer available in the now imperfect manuscript, which is our only source for the rest. The texts of scenes III, VI, VII, and IX here given are based on *The Raven and Other Poems* (1845); that of scene IV on the Lorimer Graham copy of that book as marked by Poe; and the rest on the manuscript in the Pierpont Morgan Library. The Trustees have kindly granted permission for its use in this edition. Poe himself twice saw through the press the parts he printed. The manuscript, however, is not in final form, but something just short of it. The author must have planned to go over it once again, or have expected his printers to give it finishing touches, as was customary at the time. On June 22, 1835, Poe wrote T. W. White that he would give more care to his punctuation in the future. The manuscript of *Politian* was written before that letter.

Poe never published the play as an entity and never decided finally on the division into acts. Therefore, as in the first edition of 1923, the scenes here are numbered from I to XI, and uniformity has been introduced by printing all speakers' names in capital letters in full (whether Poe abbreviated them or not) and all stage directions in italics within *parentheses*.

Poe's inconsistent spelling I have retained throughout when he used tolerated forms. The only word actually spelled incorrectly ("neice") he checked, and it has been corrected. Poe usually wrote forms like "I've" with the apostrophe; on the rare occasions when it is surely or apparently omitted, I regard the omission as like a failure to dot an *i* or cross a *t*, and supply it. The few ampersands are expanded, as is "sh'd" in II, 35–36.

The punctuation of the scenes Poe printed is reproduced exactly. In the scenes from manuscript, periods are placed at the ends of some complete sentences where nothing can be seen. Commas, dashes, and periods, like semicolons and exclamation points, can sometimes only be distinguished by the context.

Editorial emendation for the scenes Poe printed consists of placing parentheses around some directions and supplying (in square brackets) the name of a speaker accidentally omitted at IV, 35. For the material from manuscript, certain emendations have been made in square brackets: In scene VIII two words are retained which were marked by Poe in pencil as unsatisfactory but for which he made no substitutions; stage directions and speakers' names omitted or lost by imperfection of the original have been added; and the date of the action, about which the author made no final decision, has been assigned to the sixteenth century, as in the first edition of 1923.

TEXTS

Of the texts listed below, only *A* through *G* are authoritative. Texts *H* to *N* are merely first printings and first publications in books; they are of no independent authority, and all are inaccurate. Stovall's text (*P*) is based on *A* and *B*. He divides the play into acts and presents the scenes in a new order, thus: Act First, my I, II, IV; Act Second, my III, V, VI; Act Third, my VII, IX; Act Fourth, my VIII, X, and XI. This he believes to have been the author's plan. In view of the imperfect state of the admittedly unfinished manuscript, I have not felt justified in changing the order of the scenes therein, which is certainly that of composition. That scene IV comes after scene III seems to me confirmed by the order adopted by Poe in his volume of 1845. There is no reason to think (with Ingram) that any part of the play save the opening lines of scenes V and X has been lost. The last leaf of the manuscript (*A*), unlike the others, has writing only on the recto.

(*A*) Manuscript, 1835, originally written in ink on thirteen leaves of which ten are in the Pierpont Morgan Library, one (the last) is in the William H. Koester Collection at the University of Texas, and two (the fifth and eleventh), now are lost; all scenes are complete save IV, V, IX, and X. (*A2*) Changes in pencil on *A* (later than *B*), verbal only at VI, 63, and VIII, 3, 14, 41, and 55; a few italicizations elsewhere. (*B*) *Southern Literary Messenger*, December 1835 and January 1836 (2:13–16, 106–107), scenes IV, VI, VII, and III, IX; (*C*) *Broadway Journal*, March 29, 1845 (1:197), scene IV, lines 5–27 and 56–111, in Poe's article, "Imitation — Plagiarism". (*D*) *The Raven and Other*

SCENE I [A]

Poems (1845), pp. 31–51, scenes III, IV, VI, VII, IX. (*E*) J. Lorimer Graham copy of *The Raven . . .*, with three slight changes on p. 34, in scene IV. (*F*) *Works* (1850), II, 54 (scenes III, IV, VI, VII, and IX from *D*). (*G*) *Works* (1850), III, 328 (scene IV, 5–27, 56–111 from *C*, in Poe's article "Mr. Longfellow and Other Plagiarists").

(*H*) Baltimore *Southern Magazine* for November 1875, about forty scattered lines from scenes I, II (including the rhymed song), V and X, quoted in J. H. Ingram's article "Poe's Politian," of which there was a simultaneous publication in the first number of the *London Magazine of Light Literature*, also dated November 1875. (*J*) *The Poetical Works of Edgar A. Poe* (London and New York, 1888), edited by J. H. Ingram for "Chandos Classics" (scene V); (*K*) *Complete Poems*, ed. J. H. Whitty (Boston, 1911), pp. 227–230, from *H*; (*L*) *The Autograph*, New York, November–December 1912, XI, 15–64, a poor transcript by Patrick F. Madigan from *A*; (*M*) *Complete Poems*, ed. Whitty (second ed., 1917, pp. 327–328), XI, 15–32; (*N*) *Politian*, ed. Thomas Ollive Mabbott (Richmond, 1923), from versions *A*, *D*, and *E*, but XI, 15–64, from *L*; (*P*) *The Poems of Edgar Allan Poe*, ed. Floyd Stovall (Charlottesville, 1965), pp. 301–340.

In the textual notes and variants on the following pages, the symbol *Av* indicates an insertion by Poe in the manuscript, *Ax* indicates a cancellation by Poe in the manuscript, and *A2x* or *A2v* indicates a pencil change by Poe in the manuscript — a change later than text *B*.

POLITIAN [A]

A Tragedy

Scene — Rome in the [16th] century.
Characters.

LALAGE, an orphan ward of Di Broglio.

ALESSANDRA, niece of Di Broglio, and betrothed to Castiglione.

JACINTA, servant maid to Lalage.

DUKE DI BROGLIO.

CASTIGLIONE, his son and heir.

SAN OZZO, companion of Castiglione.

POLITIAN.

Title: *Above scene IV, the first to be published, Poe wrote in the manuscript*: Scenes from Politian. An Unpublished Drama, by Edgar A. Poe. *But in B there was printed*: Scenes from an Unpublished Drama, by Edgar A. Poe. *In D the title is*: Scenes from "Politian;" an Unpublished Drama.

Cast: *After the word* orphan *the manuscript has* (canceled) of illustrious family, last of her race, and; *after* San Ozzo *canceled* a; *and after* Politian *canceled* a young and noble Roman.

POLITIAN

BALDAZZAR his friend.

A MONK.

UGO ⎫
BENITO ⎬ Servants in the family of Di Broglio.
RUPERT ⎭

I. [*A*]

An apartment in the Palazzo of Di Broglio. Traces of a protracted revel. On a wine-table some candles burnt to the socket. Masks, a lute, a lady's slipper, cards and broken bottles are strewn about the floor and on the table. Enter BENITO *meeting* UGO *intoxicated.*

UGO.   Oh! is that you Benito (hiccup) are they gone?

BENITO.   Faith that's a question, Ugo, hard to answer,
But are the bottles empty? — then they're gone.
As for the Count San Ozzo who knocked me down

5   Just now on the staircase as I came up hither,
I can with more precision speak of him —
He's gone, I'm sure of that — pretty far gone.

UGO.   Is the bravo gone? (hiccup) where is the buffo-singer?
Did you say his Excellency had departed?

10   Are all the fiddlers off (hiccup) the devil go with them!
I'm positively stupid for want of sleep!

BENITO (*eyeing him.*)   Oh you are right — quite right —
being as you say
Ugo, a most confounded stupid man.

UGO.   Sirrah! I said not so, or else I (hiccup) lied.

15   BENITO.   I have no doubt, good Ugo, that you lied
Being, as you observe, a most notorious liar —
(UGO *sits, and helps himself to wine. Enter* RUPERT.)
Well, master Rupert what have you done with the
count?

RUPERT.   What should I do with any drunken man?
I pulled him from under the table where he lay
And tumbled him into bed.

Heading: Act I, Scene I (*A*)

SCENE I [A]

20 BENITO.   I say, good Rupert!
    Can it be the Duke di Broglio is acquainted
    With these untimely revels of his son?
    It is a pity in so proper a man
    Is't not a pity in so young a man
25   And of so gentle blood? Here is a change
    I had not look'd to see — he is sadly altered!
  UGO.   He is drunk, Benito, — did you not say so, Rupert?
    Most men are sadly altered when they're drunk
    Oh, I am sadly altered when I'm (hiccup) drunk.
30 RUPERT (*to* BENITO.) You think the Count Castiglione
       altered —
    I think so too. He was, not long ago,
    Barring some trivial improprieties,
    A very nobleman in heart and deed.
  BENITO.   Now I've no faith in him, poor Lady Lalage!
    So beautiful and kind.
35 RUPERT.   Truly Benito
    His conduct there has damned him in my eyes.
    O villain! villain! she his plighted wife
    And his own father's ward. I have noticed well
    That we may date his ruin — so I call it —
40   His low debaucheries — his gambling habits
    And all his numerous vices from the time
    Of that most base seduction and abandonment.
  BENITO.   We may: the sin sits heavy on his soul
    And goads him to these courses. They say the Duke
45   Pardons his son, but is most wroth with her
    And treats her with such marked severity
    As humbles her to the dust.
  RUPERT.   She sits alone
    Continually in her chamber with clasped hands
    (Jacinta tells me this).
  BENITO.   Ah Noble lady!

---

49 (Jacinta tells me this)/*Originally
the passage was longer*:
(Jacinta tells me this) and listens
  aghast

To the frightful sounds of merriment
below
Which she must never more share in.
  (*Ax*)
49 Ah (*Av*)

50 I saw her yester eve thro' the lattice-work
Of her chamber-window sobbing upon her knees
And ever and anon amid her sobs
She murmured forth Castiglione's name
Rupert, she loves him still!

RUPERT.   How will she bear
55 Think you, the consummation of these nuptials?
Tomorrow week are they not?

BENITO.   Most true! they are.
Tomorrow week Castiglione weds
His cousin Alessandra. She was the friend
The bosom friend of the fair lady Lalage
60 Ere this mischance. I cannot bear to think
On the despair of the young lady Lalage.

UGO.   This wine's not bad! gentlemen why d'ye blame
My master in this matter? very good (hiccup) wine!
Who is my lady Lalage? God knows!
65 I don't, a super(hiccup)ciliary somebody
Who play'd on the guitar! most excellent wine!
And pride should have a fall. The count's a rake
Or was, that very sure, but he's reforming
And drinks none but the very (hiccup!) best of wine.

70 RUPERT.   Let us to bed! the man is steeped in liquor.
(to BENITO.)   Come let us to bed (Exeunt RUPERT and
BENITO.)

UGO (arousing.)   What did they say? to bed!
Is it so late? is it all gone? very well!
I will to bed anon (Enter JACINTA) ah! bless my eyes!
Jacinta! is it you?

JACINTA.   Why, yes it is
75 And yet it isn't, Ugo, there's a riddle!
I was Jacinta yesternight, but now
Madam Jacinta if you please, Sir Ugo!

UGO.   Sweetheart, I fear me (hiccup!) very much (hiccup!)
that you
Have been at the bottle — a pretty madam truly!

80 JACINTA.   You may well say that Sir Ugo — very pretty!

SCENE I [*A*]

At all events the Count Castiglione
Tells me I'm pretty — drunken dolt look here! (*Showing
    some jewels*)

Ugo.   (Hiccup!) where?

Jacinta.   Here! — look here!

Ugo.   Jacinta! (hiccup!) why, Jacinta!
You do not mean to say the count my master
Gave you those jewels!

85 Jacinta.   What if he did friend Ugo?
What if he did?

Ugo.   Look here! — I'll take my oath
I saw that very ring upon the finger
The middle — the fore — no on the little finger
Of the Count. I'm (hiccup!) done with You Jacinta!

90 O you vile wretch! I'll (hiccup!) not have you Jacinta!
I'm in despair! I'll (hiccup!) do some desperate deed!
I'm desperate!

Jacinta.   You're drunk!

Ugo.   I'm going to cut —

Jacinta.   Your throat! O Heaven!

Ugo.   To cut you altogether!
I'm gone Jacinta. (*going.*)

Jacinta (*pulling him back.*)   Stop! you snivelling fool!

95 Will you not see the jewels — look you here!
This broach — these pearls — these rubies — don't you
    see?

Ugo (*sulkily.*)   I see.

Jacinta.   These emeralds and this topaz! — *won't* you see?

Ugo.   I see.

100 Jacinta.   You see! you see! can I get nothing more
Out of your ugly mouth but "I see, I see"? —
Dolt I'm not sure you see — or if you see
You certainly see double. Here's a cross
A cross of rubies, you oaf! a cross of rubies!

---

83 Here!/Here! here! (*A*x)   94 gone/going (*A*x)
86 Look *written over an illegible*   98 this (*A*v)
word (*A*x)

105   D'ye hear — a cross which never cost a zecchin
          Less than five thousand crowns!
    UGO.   I see, oh I (hiccup!) see it all. (*looking knowing.*)
    JACINTA.   You see it all!
          You do not see it all. Heaven grant me patience!
          You do not see it all (*mocking him*) you do not see
110   That I'm the richest waiting maid in Rome
          The richest vintner's daughter owning these jewels!
          You do not see, I say, that my mistress Lalage
          Who gave them to me, d'ye hear? who gave them to me
          As a free gift, and for a marriage present
115   (All of her jewels! — every one of them!)
          Is certainly gone mad!
    UGO.   The lady Lalage
          Gave you the jewels! How (hiccup!) came you by the
             ring?
    JACINTA.   The count Castiglione, your sweet master
          Gave it her as a token of his love
120   Last year — she gave it to me — d'ye see?
    UGO.   Jacinta! (*with a leer.*)
    JACINTA.   Ugo! (*returning it.*)
    UGO.   What dear Jacinta?
    JACINTA.   Do you see?
    UGO.   Oh, nonsense, sweet Jacinta, let me look
          Again (hiccup!) at the jewels!
    JACINTA.   D'ye see?
    UGO.   Pshaw! — let me look!
    JACINTA.   D'ye see? (*going and holding up the jewels.*)
125 UGO.   Sweet, dear, Jacinta! madame Jacinta.
    JACINTA.   Oh I see. (*Puts them up and exit followed by* UGO
          staggering.)

II. [*A*]

Castiglione's dressing-room. CASTIGLIONE (*in dishabille*)
and SAN OZZO.

---

112   **my mistress/the lady** (*Ax*)   Heading: **Scene 2d** (*A*)

SAN OZZO.　An excellent joke! I' faith an excellent joke!
　　Ha! ha! ha! ha! — a most superlative joke!
　　I shall die, Castiglione, I shall die!
　　Ha! ha! ha! ha! — Oh, I shall die of laughing!
　　I shall die, I shall die.

5　CASTIGLIONE (*sullenly.*)　I meant it for no joke.

SAN OZZO.　Oh no! oh no! — you meant it for no joke.
　　Not you! — ha! ha! ha! ha! — I'll die, I'll die!
　　It's a very serious business I assure you
　　To get drunk — a very serious business — excellent!

10　So you've turned penitent at last — bravo!
　　Why, Cas! I've got a string of beads at home
　　(I'll send them to you) — a bundle of paternosters
　　(You shall have them all) a robe of sackcloth too
　　I used at a masquerade, you shall have it — you shall
　　　　have it!

15　And I'll go home and send you in a trice
　　A tub of excellent ashes!

CASTIGLIONE.　　　　San Ozzo! have done for — (*hesitating.*)

SAN OZZO.　Oh! I am — I am done for — completely done
　　for — I'll die!
　　I shall die of laughing — yes! I'm done for — I'm done
　　　　for!

CASTIGLIONE (*sternly.*)　San Ozzo!

SAN OZZO.　Sir?

CASTIGLIONE.　I am serious.

SAN OZZO.　I know it — very!

20　CASTIGLIONE.　Why then do you worry me with these ribald
　　　　jests
　　I've the headach, and besides I am not well
　　Either in body or soul. When saw you last
　　The lady — Lalage?

SAN OZZO.　　　　　　Not for eleven months.
　　What could have put that creature in your head?

CASTIGLIONE (*fiercely.*)　San Ozzo!

SAN OZZO (*calmly.*)　Sir?

25　CASTIGLIONE (*after a pause.*)　Nothing. When did you say
　　You spoke to the Lady Lalage?

San Ozzo   Sir Count,
 I have not seen her for eleven months.
 The Duke your father, as you very well know,
 Keeps her secluded from society
30 And, between you and I, he's right in it:
 Ha! ha! you understand?
Castiglione.   Not I, San Ozzo!
 I do not understand.
San Ozzo.   Well! well! no matter (*sings.*)
  Birds of so fine a feather
   And of so wanton eye
35 Should be caged — should be caged
  Should be caged in all weather
   Lest they fly!
Castiglione. San Ozzo! you do her wrong — unmanly
  wrong
 Never in woman's breast enthroned sat
40 A purer heart! If ever woman fell
 With an excuse for falling it was she!
 If ever plighted vows most sacredly
 Solemnly sworn perfidiously broken
 Will damn a man, that damnéd villain am I!
45 Young, ardent, beautiful, and loving well
 And pure as beautiful, how could she think —
 How could she dream, being herself all truth
 Of my black perfidy? Oh that I were not
 Castiglione but some peasant hind
50 The humble tiller of some humble field
 That I might dare be honest!
San Ozzo.   Exceeding fine!
 I never heard a better speech in my life.
 Besides you're right — Oh! honesty's the thing!
 Honesty, poverty, and true content,
55 With the unutterable extacies
 Of butternuts, gingerbread, and milk and water!
Castiglione (*trying to suppress a smile.*) San Ozzo you are
  a fool!

SAN OZZO.   He's right again. My lord, I'm going home,
Ere I be tainted with your wisdomship.
60   Good day! — I crave your patronage however
When you become a cardinal: meantime
I'll take the opportunity of sending
The sackcloth and the ashes.   (*Exit.*)
CASTIGLIONE.   Get you gone
You merry devil! ha! ha! he makes me laugh
65   Spite of myself. One can't be angry with him
For the life of one. After all I don't see why
I should so grieve about this little matter
This every-day occurrence. Marry her — no!
Castiglione wed him with a wanton!
70   Never! — oh never! — what would they say at the club?
What would San Ozzo think? I have no right
Had I the will, to bring such foul disgrace
Upon my family — Di Broglio's line
Di Broglio's haughty and time-honoured line!
75   No right at all to do it. Am I not bound too
By the most sacred ties of honor bound
To my cousin Alessandra? Honor's the thing!
I can not pawn my honor! and Lalage
Is lowly born — I can not pawn my honor.
80   My honor — my honor. Pshaw! Pshaw! 'tis but the
  headach —
The consequence of yestereve's debauch —
Gives me these qualms of conscience. Be a man!
A man, Castiglione, be a man!
A glass of wine will put you all to rights.
Ugo! — do you hear there? — wine!
(*Enter* UGO, *bearing a bundle and a basket full of bottles.*)
85   What the devil's that?
UGO (*hesitatingly.*)   My lord!
CASTIGLIONE.   What's that I say? — where is the wine?
UGO.   My lord! — the wine? — here is some wine my lord —
A dozen bottles, my lord.

---

80   Pshaw! (*Av*)

CASTIGLIONE. A dozen fools!
    Bring me a *glass* of wine!
UGO. A dozen bottles
90   So please you, Sir, of best Salermo brand
    Sent as a present by his reverence
    The Count San Ozzo.
CASTIGLIONE. Really I'm much obliged
    (*smiling*) To his reverence — did you not say his reverence?
    Uncork a bottle, Ugo, and let me see
    What it is made of.
95 UGO. No, Sir, you can't have any.
CASTIGLIONE. How, Sir! — not have it? — what do you mean
    by that?
UGO. Not a drop, Sir, — not a drop.
CASTIGLIONE. And why? you ass.
UGO. Why, Sir, you see, the servant who brings it says
    You're not to have the wine, only your choice.
CASTIGLIONE. What does the idiot mean?
100 UGO. There's another present
    Down in the hall, Sir, — you're to have your choice
    Of the wine or of that.
CASTIGLIONE. Blockhead! why don't you bring
    The other present in?
UGO. Eh? — Sir?
CASTIGLIONE. Dolt! dunderhead! why don't you bring me
    up
    The other present and let me see it?
105 UGO. I can't.
CASTIGLIONE. You can't! you villain? I'll try and make you
    then!
    (*in a passion*) Scoundrel bring it up! What's that you have
    on your shoulder?
UGO. Sir? — it's the sackcloth, and that down below
    (*throwing down the bundle*) 'S a monstrous tub of ashes —
    I can't lift it.

---

104 *Before this* I say *is deleted (Ax)*   108 that/that there *(Ax)*
107 *Before this line* Ugo *is deleted*
(Ax)

110 CASTIGLIONE.   A monstrous tub of ashes! San Ozzo's a fool!
Ha! ha! ha! ha! too bad upon my soul!
A tub of ashes! too bad! I can't be angry
If I should die for it — to have my choice
The wine or the ashes! Ugo, send word to the Count
115 Ha! ha! ha! ha! — Ugo send word to the Count
I'll keep the wine, and he may have the ashes.
Stay! — tell him I've been thinking — I've been thinking
Of what he said — he knows — and that I'll meet him
At the masquerade, and afterwards crack a bottle
(*Exit* UGO)
120 With him and the buffo-singer. Ha! ha! ha!
Only to think of that! a tub of ashes!
Ha! ha! ha! ha! I *can't* be angry with him!
He's a fine fellow after all, San Ozzo! (*Exit.*)

III.   [D]

ROME. — *A Hall in a Palace.* ALESSANDRA *and* CASTIGLIONE.
ALESSANDRA.   Thou art sad, Castiglione.
CASTIGLIONE.   Sad! — not I.
Oh, I'm the happiest, happiest man in Rome!
A few days more, thou knowest, my Alessandra,
Will make thee mine. Oh, I am very happy!
5 ALESSANDRA.   Methinks thou hast a singular way of showing
Thy happiness! — what ails thee, cousin of mine?
Why didst thou sigh so deeply?
CASTIGLIONE.   Did I sigh?
I was not conscious of it.   It is a fashion,
A silly — a most silly fashion I have
10 When I am *very* happy. Did I sigh?   (*sighing.*)
ALESSANDRA.   Thou didst. Thou art not well. Thou has
indulged

---

113   it/it — and I (*Ax*)
117   *The second* I've *is inserted* (*Av*)
Heading: Scene 3rd (*Ax*); Act 2d Sc. 1st
  (*A*); I. *of the second installment* (*B*);
  I. (*D*). *In both B and D the place*

Rome *is given, but it is needless in
the complete play.*
2   *Followed by a line:* Oh! I am very
happy! — sad? — not I (*A*)
4   *Direction at end of line* (sighs heav-
ily) (*A*)

Too much of late, and I am vexed to see it.
Late hours and wine, Castiglione, — these
Will ruin thee! thou art already altered —
15   Thy looks are haggard — nothing so wears away
The constitution as late hours and wine.

CASTIGLIONE (*musing*.)   Nothing, fair cousin, nothing — not
    even deep sorrow —
Wears it away like evil hours and wine.
I will amend.

ALESSANDRA.   Do it! I would have thee drop
20   Thy riotous company, too — fellows low born —
Ill suit the like with old Di Broglio's heir
And Alessandra's husband.

CASTIGLIONE.   I will drop them.

ALESSANDRA.   Thou wilt — thou must. Attend thou also
    more
To thy dress and equipage — they are over plain
25   For thy lofty rank and fashion — much depends
Upon appearances.

CASTIGLIONE.   I'll see to it.

ALESSANDRA.   Then see to it! — pay more attention, sir,
To a becoming carriage — much thou wantest
In dignity.

CASTIGLIONE.   Much, much, oh much I want
In proper dignity.

30 ALESSANDRA (*haughtily*.)   Thou mockest me, sir!

CASTIGLIONE (*abstractedly*.)   Sweet, gentle Lalage!

ALESSANDRA.   Heard I aright?
I speak to him — he speaks of Lalage!
Sir Count! (*places her hand on his shoulder*)   what art
    thou dreaming? he's not well!
What ails thee, sir?

CASTIGLIONE (*starting*.)   Cousin! fair cousin! — madam!
35   I crave thy pardon — indeed I am not well —
Your hand from off my shoulder, if you please.

---

23 Thou wilt — thou/Thou (*A, B*);   26 I'll/I will (*Ax*)
  more/somewhat more (*A2x*)   31 gentle/gentle humble (*Ax*)
24 dress and equipage/habiliments (*Ax*)   35 thy/your (*Ax*)

SCENE III [D]

This air is most oppressive! — Madam — the Duke!

(*Enter* DI BROGLIO.)

DI BROGLIO.   My son, I've news for thee! — hey? — what's
the matter? (*observing* ALESSANDRA.)
I' the pouts? Kiss her, Castiglione! kiss her,
40   You dog! and make it up, I say, this minute!
I've news for you both. Politian is expected
Hourly in Rome — Politian, Earl of Leicester!
We'll have him at the wedding. 'Tis his first visit
To the imperial city.

ALESSANDRA.   What! Politian
Of Britain, Earl of Leicester?
45   DI BROGLIO.   The same, my love.
We'll have him at the wedding. A man quite young
In years, but grey in fame. I have not seen him,
But Rumour speaks of him as of a prodigy
Pre-eminent in arts and arms, and wealth,
50   And high descent. We'll have him at the wedding.

ALESSANDRA.   I have heard much of this Politian.
Gay, volatile and giddy — is he not?
And little given to thinking.

DI BROGLIO.   Far from it, love.
No branch, they say, of all philosophy
55   So deep abstruse he has not mastered it.
Learned as few are learned.

ALESSANDRA.   'Tis very strange!
I have known men have seen Politian
And sought his company. They speak of him
As of one who entered madly into life,
60   Drinking the cup of pleasure to the dregs.

CASTIGLIONE.   Ridiculous! Now *I* have seen Politian
And know him well — nor learned nor mirthful he.
He is a dreamer and a man shut out
From common passions

DI BROGLIO.   Children, we disagree.

---

39   I'/In (*A*); Castiglione *is followed by*
you dog (*Ax*)
40   You dog/Kiss her (*Ax*)
46   A man quite/Politian's (*Ax*)
47   fame/reputation (*Ax*); have not
seen / never saw (*A*)

· 2 5 9 ·

65   Let us go forth and taste the fragrant air
       Of the garden. Did dream, or did I hear
       Politian was a *melancholy* man?   (*exeunt.*)

IV. [*E*]

A Lady's apartment, with a window open and looking into
a garden. LALAGE, *in deep mourning, reading at a table on*
which lie some books and a hand mirror. In the background
JACINTA (*a servant maid*) *leans carelessly upon a chair.*

LALAGE.   Jacinta! is it thou?
JACINTA (*pertly.*)   Yes, Ma'am, I'm here.
LALAGE.   I did not know, Jacinta, you were in waiting.
    Sit down! — let not my presence trouble you —
    Sit down! — for I am humble, most humble.
JACINTA (*aside.*)   'Tis time.
(JACINTA *seats herself in a side-long manner upon the chair,*
    resting her elbows upon the back, and regarding her
    mistress with a contemptuous look. LALAGE *continues to*
    read.)
5   LALAGE.   "It in another climate, so he said,
    "Bore a bright golden flower, but not i' this soil!"
    (*pauses — turns over some leaves, and resumes.*)
    "No lingering winters there, nor snow, nor shower —
    "But Ocean ever to refresh mankind
    "Breathes the shrill spirit of the western wind."
10   Oh, beautiful! — most beautiful! — how like
    To what my fevered soul doth dream of Heaven!
    O happy land! (*pauses.*) She died! — the maiden died!
    O still more happy maiden who couldst die!
    Jacinta!

Heading: *This was first headed* Act 2nd
  Scene 1st, *then* Scene 4th (*Ax*), *then*
  Scene 3rd (*A*). *It is numbered* I *of the*
  first installment (*B*), *and* II (*D*). *In B*
  and D the place Rome *is given, but*
  this was deleted in E.
Directions: with . . . garden (*Av*); Ja-
  cinta (a servant maid)/Jacinta (*A, C*);

upon/upon the back of (*A*); on the
  back of (*C*)
1–4 *and 4 lines of directions omitted*
  (*C*)
4   'Tis/It's (*A*)
5 *Direction before this line:* Lalage
  reading. (*C*)
6 *Direction:* and/and then (*C*)

SCENE IV [*E*]

(JACINTA *returns no answer, and* LALAGE *presently resumes.*)
Again! — a similar tale

15   Told of a beauteous dame beyond the sea!
    Thus speaketh one Ferdinand in the words of the play —
    "She died full young" — one Bossola answers him —
    "I think not so — her infelicity
    "Seemed to have years too many" — Ah luckless lady!

20   Jacinta! (*still no answer.*)
Here's a far sterner story

    But like — oh, very like in its despair —
    Of that Egyptian queen, winning so easily
    A thousand hearts — losing at length her own.
    She died. Thus endeth the history — and her maids

25   Lean over her and weep — two gentle maids
    With gentle names — Eiros and Charmion!
    Rainbow and Dove! — Jacinta!

JACINTA (*pettishly.*)   Madam, what *is* it?

LALAGE.   Wilt thou, my good Jacinta, be so kind
    As go down in the library and bring me
    The Holy Evangelists.

JACINTA.   Pshaw!   (*exit.*)

30 LALAGE.   If there be balm
    For the wounded spirit in Gilead it is there!
    Dew in the night time of my bitter trouble
    Will there be found — "dew sweeter far than that
    Which hangs like chains of pearls on Hermon hill."
    (*re-enter* JACINTA, *and throws a volume on the table.*)

35 [JACINTA]   There, ma'am, 's the book. Indeed she is very
    troublesome.   (*aside.*)

LALAGE (*astonished.*)   What didst thou say, Jacinta? Have I
    done aught
    To grieve thee or to vex thee? — I am sorry.
    For thou hast served me long and ever been
    Trust-worthy and respectful. (*resumes her reading.*)

---

14 Again/La! again (*Ax*)   24–111 *now missing from A*
15 beyond the sea/in Albion (*Ax*)   27 (*second part*) *not included in C*
16 one (*Av*); in/i' (*C*)   28–55 *not included in C*
20 Here's/This is (*Ax*)

JACINTA.   I can't believe

40   She has any more jewels — no — no — she gave me all.
          (*aside.*)

LALAGE.   What didst thou say, Jacinta? Now I bethink me
          Thou hast not spoken lately of thy wedding.
          How fares good Ugo? — and when is it to be?
          Can I do aught? — is there no farther aid
          Thou needest, Jacinta?

45   JACINTA.   Is there no *farther* aid!
          That's meant for me. (*aside*) I'm sure, Madam, you
            need not
          Be always throwing those jewels in my teeth.

LALAGE.   Jewels! Jacinta, — now indeed, Jacinta,
          I thought not of the jewels.

JACINTA.   Oh! perhaps not!

50   But then I might have sworn it. After all,
          There's Ugo says the ring is only paste,
          For he's sure the Count Castiglione never
          Would have given a real diamond to such as you;
          And at the best I'm certain, Madam, you cannot

55   Have use for jewels *now*. But I might have sworn it.
          (*exit.*)
          (LALAGE *bursts into tears and leans her head upon the*
           table — after a short pause raises it.)

LALAGE.   Poor Lalage! — and is it come to this?
          Thy servant maid! — but courage! — 'tis but a viper
          Whom thou hast cherished to sting thee to the soul!
          (*taking up the mirror.*)
          Ha! here at least's a friend — too much a friend

60   In earlier days — a friend will not deceive thee.
          Fair mirror and true! now tell me (for thou canst)
          A tale — a pretty tale — and heed thou not
          Though it be rife with woe. It answers me.
          It speaks of sunken eyes, and wasted cheeks,

65   And Beauty long deceased — remembers me
          Of Joy departed — Hope, the Seraph Hope,

---

56 *In C the preceding direction reads:*   certain jewels, insults her mistress
(Jacinta finally in a discussion about   who bursts into tears.)

SCENE IV [*E*]

Inurned and entombed! — now, in a tone
Low, sad, and solemn, but most audible,
Whispers of early grave untimely yawning
70   For ruined maid. Fair mirror and true! — thou liest not!
Thou hast no end to gain — no heart to break —
Castiglione lied who said he loved —
Thou true — he false! — false! — false!

    (*while she speaks, a monk enters her apartment, and
      approaches unobserved.*)

MONK.   Refuge thou hast,
Sweet daughter! in Heaven. Think of eternal things!
75   Give up thy soul to penitence, and pray!
LALAGE (*arising hurriedly.*) I *cannot* pray! — My soul is at
    war with God!
The frightful sounds of merriment below
Disturb my senses — go! I cannot pray —
The sweet airs from the garden worry me!
80   Thy presence grieves me — go! — thy priestly raiment
Fills me with dread — thy ebony crucifix
With horror and awe!
MONK.   Think of thy precious soul!
LALAGE.   Think of my early days! — think of my father
And mother in Heaven! think of our quiet home,
85   And the rivulet that ran before the door!
Think of my little sisters! — think of them!
And think of me! — think of my trusting love
And confidence — his vows — my ruin — think — think
Of my unspeakable misery! —— begone!
90   Yet stay! yet stay! — what was it thou saidst of prayer
And penitence? Didst thou not speak of faith
And vows before the throne?
MONK.   I did.
LALAGE.   'Tis well.
There *is* a vow were fitting should be made —
A sacred vow, imperative, and urgent,
A solemn vow!

---

76 *In C the direction is placed at the end of the line.*

95 MONK.   Daughter, this zeal is well!

LALAGE.   Father, this zeal is anything but well!
Hast thou a crucifix fit for this thing?
A crucifix whereon to register
This sacred vow? (*he hands her his own.*)
        Not that — Oh no! — no! — no! (*shuddering.*)

100 Not that! Not that! — I tell thee, holy man,
Thy raiments and thy ebony cross affright me!
Stand back! I have a crucifix myself, —
I have a crucifix! Methinks 'twere fitting
The deed — the vow — the symbol of the deed —

105 And the deed's register should tally, father!
    (*draws a cross-handled dagger and raises it on high.*)
Behold the cross wherewith a vow like mine
Is written in Heaven!

MONK.   Thy words are madness, daughter,
And speaks a purpose unholy — thy lips are livid —
Thine eyes are wild — tempt not the wrath divine!

110 Pause ere too late! — oh be not — be not rash!
Swear not the oath — oh swear it not!

LALAGE.   'Tis sworn!

V. [*A*]

[*A room in the palace of* DI BROGLIO. DI BROGLIO *and* CASTIGLIONE.]

[CASTIGLIONE --]
    Undoubtedly.

DUKE.   Why do you laugh?

CASTIGLIONE.   Indeed
I hardly know myself. Stay! was it not
On yesterday we were speaking of the Earl?
Of the Earl Politian? Yes it was yesterday.

---

99 This sacred/A vow — a (*B*); A pious (*C*)

105 *In C the direction is placed after the end of Lalage's speech in line 107.*

The beginning of this scene is lost with the fifth leaf of the manuscript. It is estimated that from twenty to thirty lines are now missing.

5   Alessandra, you and I, you must remember!
       We were walking in the garden.

DUKE.   Perfectly
       I do remember it — what of it? — what then?

CASTIGLIONE.   O nothing — nothing at all.

DUKE.   Nothing at all!
       It is most singular now that you should laugh
       At nothing at all!

10 CASTIGLIONE.   Most singular — singular!

DUKE.   Look you, Castiglione, be so kind
       As tell me, Sir, at once what is't you mean.
       What are you talking of?

CASTIGLIONE.   Was it not so?
       We differed in opinion touching him.

DUKE.   Him! — whom?

15 CASTIGLIONE.   Why, Sir, the Earl Politian.

DUKE.   The Earl of Leicester! — yes! — is it he you mean?
       We differed indeed. If I now recollect
       The words you used were that the Earl you knew
       Was neither learned nor mirthful.

CASTIGLIONE.   Ha! ha! — now did I?

20 DUKE.   That did you, Sir, and well I knew at the time
       You were wrong — it being not the character
       Of the Earl — whom all the world allows to be
       A most hilarious man. Be not, my son,
       Too positive again.

CASTIGLIONE.   'Tis singular!

25   Most singular! I could not think it possible
       So little time could so much alter one!
       To say the truth about an hour ago
       As I was walking with the Count San Ozzo
       All arm in arm we met this very man

30   The Earl — he with his friend Baldazzar
       Having just arrived in Rome. Ha! ha! he *is* altered!
       Such an account he gave me of his journey!

---

7   What of it/decidedly (*A*x)

'Twould have made you die with laughter — such tales
he told
Of his caprices and his merry freaks
35   Along the road — such oddity — such humour
Such wit — such whim — such flashes of wild merriment
Set off too in such full relief by the grave
Demeanour of his friend — who to speak the truth
Was gravity itself.

DUKE.   Did I not tell you?

40   CASTIGLIONE.   You did — and yet 'tis strange! but true as
strange.
How much I was mistaken! I always thought
The Earl a gloomy man.

DUKE.   So, So, you see.
Be not too positive. Whom have we here?
It cannot be the Earl?

CASTIGLIONE.   The Earl! oh, no!
45   'Tis not the Earl — but yet it is — and leaning
Upon his friend Baldazzar. Ah! welcome, Sir!
        (*Enter* POLITIAN *and* BALDAZZAR.)
My Lord! a second welcome let me give you
To Rome — his Grace the Duke of Broglio.
Father! this is the Earl Politian, Earl
50   Of Leicester in Great Britain, (POLITIAN *bows haught-
ily*) this his friend
Baldazzar, Duke of Surrey. The Earl has letters,
So please you for your Grace.

DUKE.   Ah — ha! most welcome
To Rome and to our palace Earl Politian!
And you most noble Duke! am glad to see you!
55   I knew your father well, my lord Politian.
Castiglione! call your cousin hither
And let me make the noble Earl acquainted
With your betrothed. You come, Sir, at a time
Most seasonable. The wedding —

POLITIAN.   Touching those letters, Sir,

---

39 itself/himself (*Ax*)

60   Your son made mention of — (your son is he not?)
             Touching those letters, Sir, I wot not of them.
             If such there be, my friend Baldazzar here —
             Baldazzar! — ah! — my friend Baldazzar here
             Will hand them to your Grace. I would retire.
        DUKE.   Retire! — so soon?
65   CASTIGLIONE.   What ho! Benito! Rupert!
             His lordship's chambers — show his lordship to them!
             His lordship is unwell!   (*Enter* BENITO.)
        BENITO.   This way my lord! (*Exit followed by* POLITIAN.)
        DUKE.   Retire! — unwell!
        BALDAZZAR.   So please you, Sir, I fear me
             'Tis as you say — his lordship is unwell.
70   The damp air of the evening — the fatigue
             Of a long journey — the — indeed I had better
             Follow his lordship. He must be unwell.
             I will return anon.
        DUKE.   Return anon!
             Now this is very strange! Castiglione!
75   This way, my son, I wish to speak with thee.
             You surely were mistaken in what you said
             Of the Earl, mirthful indeed! — which of us said
             Politian was a melancholy man?   (*Exeunt.*)

VI.   [*D*]

An apartment in a palace. POLITIAN *and* BALDAZZAR.

        BALDAZZAR.   —————— Arouse thee now, Politian!
             Thou must not — nay indeed, indeed, thou shalt not
             Give way unto these humours. Be thyself!
             Shake off the idle fancies that beset thee,
             And live, for now thou diest!
5   POLITIAN.   Not so, Baldazzar!
             Surely I live.

---

68   me/me very much (*Ax*)
Heading: Scene 2nd (*Ax*); Scene 3rd
(*A*); II *of the first installment* (*B*); III
(*D*).

Directions: An apt. in the Palace. Poli-
tian and Baldazzar (*A*) ROME. An
apartment in a palace. Politian and
Baldazzar, his friend. (*B*)
6 Surely/I live — (*A, B*)

BALDAZZAR.   Politian, it doth grieve me
To see thee thus.

POLITIAN.   Baldazzar, it does grieve me
To give thee cause for grief, my honoured friend.
Command me, sir! what wouldst thou have me do?

10 At thy behest I will shake off that nature
Which from my forefathers I did inherit,
Which with my mother's milk I did imbibe,
And be no more Politian, but some other.
Command me, sir!

BALDAZZAR.   To the field then — to the field —
To the senate or the field.

15 POLITIAN.   Alas! alas!
There is an imp would follow me even there!
There is an imp *hath* followed me even there!
There is — what voice was that?

BALDAZZAR.   I heard it not.
I heard not any voice except thine own,
And the echo of thine own.

20 POLITIAN.   Then I but dreamed.

BALDAZZAR. Give not thy soul to dreams: the camp — the
  court
Befit thee — Fame awaits thee — Glory calls —
And her the trumpet-tongued thou wilt not hear
In hearkening to imaginary sounds
And phantom voices.

25 POLITIAN.   It *is* a phantom voice!
Didst thou not hear it *then*?

BALDAZZAR.   I heard it not.

POLITIAN. Thou heardst it not! — Baldazzar, speak no more
To me, Politian, of thy camps and courts.
Oh! I am sick, sick, sick, even unto death,

30 Of the hollow and high-sounding vanities
Of the populous Earth! Bear with me yet awhile!
We have been boys together — school-fellows —
And now are friends — yet shall not be so long —
For in the eternal city thou shalt do me

35 A kind and gentle office, and a Power —
  A Power august, benignant and supreme —
  Shall then absolve thee of all farther duties
  Unto thy friend.

BALDAZZAR.   Thou speakest a fearful riddle
  I *will* not understand.

POLITIAN.   Yet now as Fate

40 Approaches, and the Hours are breathing low,
  The sands of Time are changed to golden grains,
  And dazzle me, Baldazzar. Alas! alas!
  I *cannot* die, having within my heart
  So keen a relish for the beautiful

45 As hath been kindled within it. Methinks the air
  Is balmier now than it was wont to be —
  Rich melodies are floating in the winds —
  A rarer loveliness bedecks the earth —
  And with a holier lustre the quiet moon

50 Sitteth in Heaven. — Hist! hist! thou canst not say
  Thou hearest not *now*, Baldazzar?

BALDAZZAR.   Indeed I hear not.

POLITIAN. Not hear it! — listen now — listen! — the faintest
   sound
  And yet the sweetest that ear ever heard!
  A lady's voice! — and sorrow in the tone!

55 Baldazzar, it oppresses me like a spell!
  Again! — again! — how solemnly it falls
  Into my heart of hearts! that eloquent voice
  Surely I never heard — yet it were well
  Had I *but* heard it with its thrilling tones
  In earlier days!

60 BALDAZZAR.   I myself hear it now.
  Be still! — the voice, if I mistake not greatly,
  Proceeds from yonder lattice — which you may see
  Very plainly through the window — it belongs,

---

57 that eloquent/that voice — that (*A*, *B*)
58 Surely I/I surely (*A*, *B*); were/had been (*Ax*)

62 which you may see/this way you can see it (*Ax*)
63 it/that lattice (*A*, *B*)

Does it not? unto this palace of the Duke.

65 The singer is undoubtedly beneath
The roof of his Excellency — and perhaps
Is even that Alessandra of whom he spoke
As the betrothed of Castiglione,
His son and heir.

POLITIAN.   Be still! — it comes again!

70   *Voice*   "And is thy heart so strong
(*very faintly.*)   As for to leave me thus
Who hath loved thee so long
In wealth and wo among?
And is thy heart so strong

75 As for to leave me thus?

                     Say nay — say nay!"

BALDAZZAR.   The song is English, and I oft have heard it
In merry England — never so plaintively —
Hist! hist! it comes again!

     Voice   "Is it so strong

80 (*more loudly.*)   As for to leave me thus
Who hath loved thee so long
In wealth and wo among?
And is thy heart so strong
As for to leave me thus?

85   Say nay — say nay!"

BALDAZZAR.   'Tis hushed and all is still!

POLITIAN.   All *is not* still.

---

79   *Since Poe avoided imperfect lines, the first line of the song is counted as part of line 79.*

79–115   *Originally the scene ended more briefly; Poe pasted a piece of paper over the earlier shorter ending, and proceeded with an expanded version, before beginning Scene VII. The canceled passage reads:*
            'Tis hush'd and all is still!
     Pol: What didst thou say?
            That all is still? Alas, all is not still!
     Bal.   Let us go down — for it is getting late
            And they wait for us below — Politian give
            These fancies to the winds. Remember, pray
            Your bearing lately savoured much of rudeness
            Unto the Duke — Arouse thee! and remember!   Exit.
     Pol: Remember. I do—I do—lead on!—remember! (*Ax*)

BALDAZZAR.   Let us go down.

POLITIAN.   Go down, Baldazzar, go!

BALDAZZAR.   The hour is growing late — the Duke awaits
us, —
Thy presence is expected in the hall
90   Below. What ails thee, Earl Politian?

Voice   "Who hath loved thee so long,
(*distinctly.*)   In wealth and wo among,
And is thy heart so strong?
Say nay — say nay!"

BALDAZZAR.   Let us descend! — 'tis time. Politian, give
These fancies to the wind. Remember, pray,
Your bearing lately savoured much of rudeness
Unto the Duke. Arouse thee! and remember!

POLITIAN.   Remember? I do. Lead on! I *do* remember.
(*going.*)
100   Let us descend. Believe me I would give,
Freely would give the broad lands of my earldom
To look upon the face hidden by yon lattice —
"To gaze upon that veiled face, and hear
Once more that silent tongue."

BALDAZZAR.   Let me beg you sir,
105   Descend with me — the Duke may be offended.
Let us go down, I pray you.
(*Voice loudly.*)   *Say nay! — say nay!*

POLITIAN (*aside.*)   'Tis strange! — 'tis very strange — me-
thought the voice
Chimed in with my desires and bade me stay!
(*approaching the window.*)
Sweet voice! I heed thee, and will surely stay.
110   Now be this Fancy, by Heaven, or be it Fate,
Still will I not descend. Baldazzar, make
Apology unto the Duke for me;
I go not down tonight.

BALDAZZAR.   Your lordship's pleasure
Shall be attended to. Good night, Politian.

115   POLITIAN.   Good night, my friend, good night.

---

100 Believe me/Baldazzar! Oh (*A, B*)

POLITIAN

VII. [D]

The gardens of a palace — Moonlight. LALAGE *and* POLITIAN.

LALAGE.   And dost thou speak of love
  To *me*, Politian? — dost thou speak of love
  To Lalage? — ah wo — ah wo is me!
  This mockery is most cruel! — most cruel indeed!
5 POLITIAN.   Weep not! oh, sob not thus! — thy bitter tears
  Will madden me. Oh mourn not, Lalage —
  Be comforted! I know — I know it all,
  And *still* I speak of love. Look at me, brightest,
  And beautiful Lalage! — turn here thine eyes!
10 Thou askest me if I could speak of love,
  Knowing what I know, and seeing what I have seen.
  Thou askest me that — and thus I answer thee —
  Thus on my bended knee I answer thee. (*kneeling.*)
  Sweet Lalage, *I love thee — love thee — love thee;*
15 Thro' good and ill — thro' weal and wo I *love thee.*
  Not mother, with her first born on her knee,
  Thrills with intenser love than I for thee.
  Not on God's altar, in any time or clime,
  Burned there a holier fire than burneth now
20 Within my spirit for *thee.* And do I love? (*arising.*)
  Even for thy woes I love thee — even for thy woes —
  Thy beauty and thy woes.
LALAGE.   Alas, proud Earl,
  Thou dost forget thyself, remembering me!
  How, in thy father's halls, among the maidens
25 Pure and reproachless of thy princely line,

Heading: *This was headed Act 3rd Sc.* [3d] *in A; the number of the scene is now obliterated in the manuscript but may be restored from "Scene 3d" originally written at the bottom of the preceding leaf, before Poe made the preceding scene longer. The scene is numbered III of the first installment in B,* and IV *in D.* [Directions] Lalage and Politian *not in A.*
5 sob/weep (*A, B*)
6 mourn/weep (*A, B*)
9 — turn here thine eyes/and listen to me! (*A, B*)
16 knee/bosom (*Ax*)
20 spirit/soul (*A*); love/love thee (*A*)

SCENE VII [D]

Could the dishonoured Lalage abide?
Thy wife, and with a tainted memory —
My seared and blighted name, how would it tally
With the ancestral honours of thy house,
30 And with thy glory?
POLITIAN.   Speak not to me of glory!
I hate — I loathe the name; I do abhor
The unsatisfactory and ideal thing.
Art thou not Lalage and I Politian?
Do I not love — art thou not beautiful —
35 What need we more? Ha! glory! — now speak not of it!
By all I hold most sacred and most solemn —
By all my wishes now — my fears hereafter —
By all I scorn on earth and hope in heaven —
There is no deed I would more glory in,
40 Than in thy cause to scoff at this same glory
And trample it under foot. What matters it —
What matters it, my fairest, and my best,
That we go down unhonoured and forgotten
Into the dust — so we descend together.
45 Descend together — and then — and then perchance ——
LALAGE.   Why dost thou pause, Politian?
POLITIAN.   And then perchance
Arise together, Lalage, and roam
The starry and quiet dwellings of the blest,
And still —
LALAGE.   Why dost thou pause, Politian?
50 POLITIAN.   And still *together — together.*
LALAGE.   Now Earl of Leicester!
Thou *lovest* me, and in my heart of hearts
I feel thou lovest me truly.
POLITIAN.   Oh, Lalage! (*throwing himself upon his knee.*)
And lovest thou *me?*
LALAGE.   Hist! hush! within the gloom
Of yonder trees methought a figure past —
55 A spectral figure, solemn, and slow, and noiseless —

---

30 to me/ — speak not (*A, B*)   54 figure/spectre (*Ax*)

· 2 7 3 ·

POLITIAN

Like the grim shadow Conscience, solemn and noiseless.
(*walks across and returns.*)
I was mistaken — 'twas but a giant bough
Stirred by the autumn wind. Politian!

POLITIAN.   My Lalage — my love! why art thou moved?
60   Why dost thou turn so pale? Not Conscience' self,
Far less a shadow which thou likenest to it,
Should shake the firm spirit thus. But the night wind
Is chilly — and these melancholy boughs
Throw over all things a gloom.

LALAGE.   Politian!
65   Thou speakest to me of love. Knowest thou the land
With which all tongues are busy — a land new found —
Miraculously found by one of Genoa —
A thousand leagues within the golden west?
A fairy land of flowers, and fruit, and sunshine,
70   And crystal lakes, and over-arching forests,
And mountains, around whose towering summits the winds
Of Heaven untrammelled flow — which air to breathe
Is Happiness now, and will be Freedom hereafter
In days that are to come?

POLITIAN.   O, wilt thou — wilt thou
75   Fly to that Paradise — my Lalage, wilt thou
Fly thither with me? There Care shall be forgotten,
And Sorrow shall be no more, and Eros be all.
And life shall then be mine, for I will live
For thee, and in thine eyes — and thou shalt be
80   No more a mourner — but the radiant Joys
Shall wait upon thee, and the angel Hope
Attend thee ever; and I will kneel to thee
And worship thee, and call thee my beloved,
My own, my beautiful, my love, my wife,

---

58 Stirred/Moved (*Ax*)
60 turn so pale/tremble thus (*Ax*)
63 boughs/bowers (*A*)
64 gloom/shade (*Ax*)

65 speakest/spokest (*A*)
66 With which all tongues are busy/of which all tongues are speaking (*A*)

85   My all; — oh, wilt thou — wilt thou, Lalage,
          Fly thither with me?
LALAGE.   A deed is to be done —
          Castiglione lives!
POLITIAN.   And he shall die!   (*exit.*)
LALAGE (*after a pause.*) And — he — shall — die! —— alas!
          Castiglione die? Who spoke the words?
90   Where am I? — what was it he said? — Politian!
          Thou *art* not gone — thou art not *gone*, Politian!
          I *feel* thou art not gone — yet dare not look,
          Lest I behold thee not; thou *couldst* not go
          With those words upon thy lips — O, speak to me!
95   And let me hear thy voice — one word — one word,
          To say thou art not gone, — one little sentence,
          To say how thou dost scorn — how thou dost hate
          My womanly weakness. Ha! ha! thou *art* not gone —
          O speak to me! I *knew* thou wouldst not go!
100   I knew thou wouldst not, couldst not, *durst* not go.
          Villain, thou *art* not gone — thou mockest me!
          And thus I clutch thee — thus! —— He is gone, he is
            gone —
          Gone — gone. Where am I? —— 'tis well — 'tis very well!
          So that the blade be keen — the blow be sure,
105   'Tis well, 'tis *very* well — alas! alas!   (*exit.*)

VIII. [*A*]

    A street near a Palace. Bells ringing and shouts heard in
the distance. Several persons cross and recross the stage rapid-
ly. Enter BENITO *walking quickly, and followed by* RUPERT
at the same pace.
RUPERT.   What ho! Benito! did you say to-night?
       Is it to night — the wedding?
BENITO.   To night I believe.   (*Exeunt.*)
       (*Enter* JACINTA *fantastically dressed, and bearing a*

Heading: Sc.2d (*Ax*) Act 4th Sc.1 (*A*).
Directions: near a/near the (*Ax*)

flat band-box. She enters at first quickly — then saunter-
ingly — and finally stops near the middle of the stage,
and is lost in the contemplation of the jewels upon one
of her hands, which is ungloved. She at length sets down
the band-box and looks at a watch hanging by her side.)

JACINTA.   It is not late — o no! it is not late —
What need is there of hurry? I'll answer for it
5   There's time enough to spare — now let me see!
The wedding is to be at dark, and here
The day is not half done, — stay I can tell
To a minute how many hours there are between
This time and dark — one, two, three, four, five, six!
10   Six hours! why I can very easily do
The whole of my errands in two hours at farthest!
Who'd be without a watch? — these are pretty gloves!
I will not walk myself to death at all —
I won't — I'll take my time.

(*Seats herself on a bank and kicks the bandbox to and*
fro with an air of [nonchalance]. BENITO *recrosses the*
stage rapidly with a bundle.)

                                Look you Benito!
15   Benito! I say — Benito! — don't you hear?
The impudent varlet not to answer me!
The wretch not even to deign to condescend
To see me, as I sit upon the bank
Looking so like a lady! *I'm* a lady!
20   I am indeed! — but after all I think
There is a difference between some ladies
And others — the ignorant, stupid, villain! —
Between my former mistress, Lalage,
For instance, and my present noble mistress
25   The lady Alessandra. I made a change
For the better I think — indeed I'm sure of it —
Besides, you know it was impossible

---

3 o no! *preceded by* (turns back the   (*A2x*) *but retained here since nothing*
watch) (*A2x*)   *was substituted.*
14 [*directions*] nonchalance *canceled*   24 instance/example (*Ax*)

When such reports have been in circulation
To stay with her now. She'd nothing of the lady
30   About her — not a tittle! One would have thought
She was a peasant girl, she was so humble.
I *hate* all humble people! — and then she talked
To one with such an air of condescension.
And she had not common sense — of that I'm sure
35   Or would she, now — I ask you now, Jacinta,
Do you, or do you not suppose your mistress
Had common sense or understanding when
She gave you all these jewels?

    (RUPERT *recrosses the stage rapidly and without
noticing* JACINTA.)

                    That man's a fool
Or he would not be in a hurry — he would have
    stopped —
40   If he had not been a *fool* he would have stopped —
[Took] off his hat, and, making a low bow,
Said "I am most superlatively happy
To see you, *Madam* Jacinta." Well I don't know
Some people are fools by nature — some have a talent
45   For being stupid — look at that ass now, Ugo,
He thinks I'll have him — but oh no! — I couldn't.
He might as well, for all the use he makes of it,
Have been born without a head. Heigho! what's this?
Oh! it's the paper that my lady gave me,
50   With the list of articles she wants — ten yards
Of taffeta — sixteen of gold brocade —
And ten of Genoa velvet — one, two, three,

    (*As she counts, she tears a slip from the paper at each
number, and arranges it on the floor in an abstracted
manner.*)

Four, five, six, seven — that's it — now eight, nine, ten,
Ten yards — I can't forget it now — ten yards —

---

38 these/them (*Ax*)
41 [Took] *canceled* (*A2x*) *but retained
here since nothing was substituted.*

54 — ten yards/— ten yards of velvet
(*A2x*)

55 Ten yards of velvet — I must try and get me
A dress of Genoa velvet — 'tis becoming.
And I would look so like my lady in it!
Methinks I see her now — Oh! she's a lady
Worth serving indeed — oh she has airs and graces
60 And dignity — yes! she has dignity.
(*Arises and struts affectedly across the stage.*)
And then she has a voice. Heavens! what a voice!
So loud, so lady-like, and so commanding!
"Jacinta, get me this" — "D'ye hear? — bring that"
"And tell the Count Castiglione I want him."
65 Then "yes ma'am" I reply, and curtsey thus
Meekly and daintily thus. Oh! I'm a maid
One in a thousand for a dainty curtsey.
But when I get to be a lady — when
I wed the apothecary — oh then it will be
70 A different thing — a different thing indeed!
I'll play my lady to a T, that will I.
I'll be all dignity, and I'll talk thus
"Ugo, you villain!" (Ugo shall be my servant)
(*During this part of the soliloquy* Ugo *enters unper-*
ceived and in his astonishment treads upon the band-
box, and remains with his foot in it, as if stupified.)
"Ugo you villain! — look you here, you rascal!
75 "You good-for-nothing, idle, lazy scoundrel!
"What are you doing here? Begone you ugly
"You silly, sulky, dirty, stupid ideot!
"Begone I say this minute — get out you viper.
"Get out you jackass! — out you vagabond!"
80 And *then* if he's not gone in half a moment
I'll turn about and let him have it (*seeing* Ugo *whom*
she encounters in turning round) — who's this
It's he, by all that's good, it is himself!
I'll turn about and let him have it so — (*striking him.*)
It's as well now as any other time —
85 Thus — thus — I'll let him have it thus — thus — thus.

83 so/thus (*Ax*)

SCENE IX [D]

You wretch! what are you doing with your foot
Stuffed in that bandbox? I'll let him have it thus
Thus — thus — (*Exit* Ugo *followed by* Jacinta *who
throws the bandbox after him.*)

IX. [D]

The suburbs. Politian *alone.*

POLITIAN.   This weakness grows upon me. I am faint,
And much I fear me ill — it will not do
To die ere I have lived! — Stay — stay thy hand,
O Azrael, yet awhile! — Prince of the Powers
5   Of Darkness and the Tomb, O pity me!
O pity me! let me not perish now,
In the budding of my Paradisal Hope!
Give me to live yet — yet a little while:
'Tis I who pray for life — I who so late
10   Demanded but to die! — what sayeth the Count?
                              (*Enter* Baldazzar.)
BALDAZZAR.   That knowing no cause of quarrel or of feud
Between the Earl Politian and himself,
He doth decline your cartel.
POLITIAN.   *What* didst thou say?
What answer was it you brought me, good Baldazzar?
15   With what excessive fragrance the zephyr comes
Laden from yonder bowers! — a fairer day,
Or one more worthy Italy, methinks
No mortal eyes have seen! — *what* said the Count?
BALDAZZAR.   That he, Castiglione, not being aware
20   Of any feud existing, or any cause
Of quarrel between your lordship and himself
Cannot accept the challenge.
POLITIAN.   It is most true —
All this is very true. When saw you, sir,

When saw you now, Baldazzar, in the frigid
25   Ungenial Britain which we left so lately,
A heaven so calm as this — so utterly free
From the evil taint of clouds? — and he did *say?*
BALDAZZAR.   No more, my Lord, than I have told you, sir:
The Count Castiglione will not fight,
Having no cause for quarrel.
30 POLITIAN.   Now this is true —
All very true. Thou art my friend, Baldazzar,
And I have not forgotten it — thou'lt do me
A piece of service; wilt thou go back and say
Unto this man, that I, the Earl of Leicester,
35   Hold him a villain? — thus much, I prythee, say
Unto the Count — it is exceeding just
He should have cause for quarrel.
BALDAZZAR.   My lord! — my friend! ——
POLITIAN (*aside.*) 'Tis he — he comes himself! (*aloud.*)
    thou reasonest well.
I know what thou wouldst say — not send the message —
40   Well! — I will think of it — I will not send it.
Now prythee, leave me — hither doth come a person
With whom affairs of a most private nature
I would adjust.
BALDAZZAR.   I go — to-morrow we meet,
Do we not? — at the Vatican.
POLITIAN.   At the Vatican.   (*exit* BALDAZZAR.)
    (*Enter* CASTIGLIONE.)
45 CASTIGLIONE.   The Earl of Leicester here!
POLITIAN.   I *am* the Earl of Leicester, and thou seest,
Dost thou not? that I am here.
CASTIGLIONE.   My lord, some strange,
Some singular mistake — misunderstanding —
Hath without doubt arisen: thou hast been urged
50   Thereby, in heat of anger, to address
Some words most unaccountable, in writing

---

44 *After this A and B add:*   In the Vatican — within the holy walls
If that we meet at all, it were as well   Of the Vatican.
That I should meet him in the Vatican —

SCENE IX [D]

To me, Castiglione; the bearer being
Baldazzar, Duke of Surrey. I am aware
Of nothing which might warrant thee in this thing,

55   Having given thee no offence. Ha! — am I right?
'Twas a mistake? — undoubtedly — we all
Do err at times.

POLITIAN.   Draw, villain, and prate no more!

CASTIGLIONE.   Ha! — draw? — and villain? have at thee then
       at once,
Proud Earl!   (draws.)

POLITIAN (drawing.)   Thus to the expiatory tomb,

60   Untimely sepulchre, I do devote thee
In the name of Lalage!

CASTIGLIONE (letting fall his sword and recoiling to the ex-
tremity of the stage.)
                     Of Lalage!
Hold off — thy sacred hand! — avaunt I say!
Avaunt — I will not fight thee — indeed I dare not.

POLITIAN.   Thou wilt not fight with me didst say, Sir Count?

65   Shall I be baffled thus? — now this is well;
Didst say thou darest not? Ha!

CASTIGLIONE.   I dare not — dare not —
Hold off thy hand — with that beloved name
So fresh upon thy lips I will not fight thee —
I cannot — dare not.

POLITIAN.   Now by my halidom

70   I do believe thee! — coward, I do believe thee!

CASTIGLIONE.   Ha! — coward! — this may not be!
(clutches his sword and staggers toward POLITIAN, but
his purpose is changed before reaching him, and he falls
upon his knee at the feet of the Earl.)
                     Alas! my lord,

55-93 Now missing (A)
58 then at once/— have at thee then
(B)
61 [Directions] letting fall/dropping
(B)
62 thy sacred/hold off thy (B)
63 indeed I dare not/I dare not — dare
not (B)

65 After this B has another line:
Exceeding well! — thou darest not
fight with me?
70 After this B adds a short line:
Thou darest not!
71 my lord/alas! (B)

· 281 ·

It is — it is — most true. In such a cause
I am the veriest coward. O pity me!
POLITIAN (*greatly softened.*)   Alas! — I do — indeed I pity
    thee.
CASTIGLIONE.   And Lalage ——
75 POLITIAN.   *Scoundrel! — arise and die!*
CASTIGLIONE.   It needeth not be — thus — thus — O let me
    die
Thus on my bended knee. It were most fitting
That in this deep humiliation I perish.
For in the fight I will not raise a hand
80 Against thee, Earl of Leicester. Strike thou home —
                   (*baring his bosom.*)
Here is no let or hindrance to thy weapon —
Strike home. I *will not* fight thee.
POLITIAN.   Now s'Death and Hell!
Am I not — am I not sorely — grievously tempted
To take thee at thy word? But mark me, sir!
85 Think not to fly me thus. Do thou prepare
For public insult in the streets — before
The eyes of the citizens. I'll follow thee —
Like an avenging apirit I'll follow thee
Even unto death. Before those whom thou lovest —
90 Before all Rome I'll taunt thee, villain, — I'll taunt
    thee,
Dost hear? with *cowardice* — thou *wilt not* fight me?
Thou liest! thou *shalt*!   (*exit.*)
CASTIGLIONE.   Now this indeed is just!
Most righteous, and most just, avenging Heaven!

X. [*A*]

[*The Hall of Di Broglio's Palace.* UGO *and* SAN OZZO.]

[UGO --]
SAN OZZO.   D - - d if he does that's flat! why — yes, that's flat.

---

73 the veriest/— I am — a (*B*)   *The opening of Scene X is now lost*
92 indeed/ — now this (*B*)   *with the antepenultimate leaf of Poe's*

SCENE X [A]

Extremely flat, and candid, and so forth

50 And sociable, and all that kind of thing
Damned if you do? — look you, you ignoramus
What is it you mean? is it your fixed intention
To lie all day in that especial manner
If so pray let me know!

Ugo.   I'll let you know

55 Nothing about it, and for the best of reasons
In the first place, Sir, I did not hear a word
Your honour said, and in the second, Sir,
I cannot talk at all. It's very strange
You can't perceive I'm dead!

San Ozzo.   It's very strange

60 I can't perceive you're dead? soho! I see!
(aside)   I've heard before that such ideas as these
Have seized on human brains, still not believing
The matter possible. Ha! ha! I have it!
I wish to see the Count — he'll not admit me —

65 Being in the dumps about this little matter
Touching Politian, who in the public streets
Called him a coward on yesterday forenoon,
Set him a laughing once, and he'll forget
Both the Earl and himself. I'd bet a trifle now

70 I'll make this idiot go and tell the Count
That he's deceased — if so the game is up.
(aloud)   So — so — you're dead eh? come now — come now,
        Ugo!
Be candid with me — is it indeed a fact
And are you really dead?

Ugo.   Not, Sir, exactly

75 Dead, so to say, but having just committed
Felo de se, I'm what they call deceased.

San Ozzo.   Ah! I perceive — it's positively so

---

manuscript. At the end of the scene Poe wrote 135 which (from a similar notation at the end of the scene that follows it) I judge to be the number of lines of verse it contained when complete. The missing lines must have numbered forty-seven, of which the last contained the phrase of Ugo, That's flat uttered with a curse. No changes occur in the surviving lines.

Poor soul he's gone! But now I think of it
Deceased is not the word. What say you, Ugo?
80   Deceased is not the proper word to express
Your case with due exactitude. Perhaps
Defunct would suit it better.

UGO.   Sir! — I'm defunct.

SAN OZZO.   Ah — very well! — then I shall tell your master
That you're defunct — or stop suppose I say —
85   I think there would be more of dignity
In saying "Sir Count, your worthy servant Ugo
Not being dead, nor yet to say deceased,
Nor yet defunct, but having unluckily
Made way with himself — that's felo de se you know —
90   Hath now departed this life."

UGO.   Say that, Sir, say that!
For now, upon consideration, I think
I have — departed this life.

SAN OZZO.   I will — I'll say it!
I will inform the Count — but not so fast —
I'm wrong — I must not do it — it were against
95   All rules of etiquette. This is a matter
Demanding due consideration, Ugo,
One of the last importance. Do you not think
(You see I yield unto your better judgment)
Do you not think it were more fitting, Sir,
100   More decorous, you know, — you understand me?
More delicate, more proper, and all that —
That you should tell the circumstance yourself
Unto the Count — ha! — do you take me Sir!
'Tis the better plan, is it not?

UGO.   Why yes, it is.

105 SAN OZZO.   Undoubtedly — it is — you are right — get up!
And lose no time about it — be quick — get up!

UGO.   Get up? I can't — Sir, I've been dead an hour
And am stiff as you perceive.

SAN OZZO.   Well, yes, I do.
You are a little — stiff — all very true.

110 I most sincerely pity you — but, Sir,
Could you not, think you, by a desperate effort,
Contrive to stir a little? let me help you?
Paugh! this will never do! — why, bless me, Sir,
Perhaps you're not aware that — that — in short
115 The day is very sultry — and that a corpse
In very hot weather won't — keep, you take me, Sir?
My nose is delicate, and to be plain
You smell, Sir, yes you smell — come now be quick!
Indeed I cannot will not answer for
120 The consequence of any longer stay
Sir, you may drop to pieces!

UGO.   Good God! that's true!
Lend me your hand, Sir, do!

SAN OZZO.   Ah that is well!
Extremely well attempted! — Sir I am glad
To see you on your legs, — a little stiff
125 No matter! — not ungraceful in a corpse.
Now Sir, this leg — a little farther — that's it!
Most excellent! — ah! that is exquisite!
Now Sir the left — you have a genius, Ugo,
For putting out a leg! Pray Sir proceed!
130 Superlative! — now that's what I call walking!
Magnificent! — a little farther, Sir!
Farewell! — now recollect you tell
The Count as I directed — you've departed
This life — you're dead, deceased, defunct,
135 And all that sort of thing — ha! ha! ha! ha!

XI.   [A]

Interior of the Coliseum. POLITIAN *entering from behind
— moonlight.*

POLITIAN.   Shall meet me here within the Coliseum!

Heading: *Scene XI is headed* Scene 3rd
(A), *and has, added by Poe, at the end,
the numeral* 64 *which is the number of*   *lines counted metrically and not the
lines required in printing.*

POLITIAN

Type of the antique Rome — rich reliquary
Of lofty contemplation left to Time
By buried centuries of pomp and power!
5   At length at length after so many days
Of weary pilgrimage, and burning thirst
(Thirst for the springs of lore that in thee lie)
I stand, an altered and an humble man
Amid thy shadows, and so drink within
10   My very soul thy grandeur, gloom and glory!
She comes not, and the spirit of the place
Oppresses me!
Vastness and Age and Memories of Eld
Silence and Desolation and dim Night
15   Gaunt vestibules, and phantom-peopled aisles
I feel ye now — I feel ye in your strength!
O spells more sure than e'er Judæan king
Taught in the gardens of Gethsemane
O spells more potent than the rapt Chaldee
20   Ever drew down from out the quiet stars!
She comes not and the moon is high in Heaven!
Here where a hero fell, a column falls
Here where the mimic eagle glared in gold
A secret vigil holds the swarthy bat
25   Here where the dames of Rome their yellow hair
Waved to the wind, now wave the reed and thistle:
Here where on ivory couch the Cæsar sate
On bed of moss lies gloating the foul adder:
Here where on golden throne the monarch lolled
30   Glides spectre-like unto his marble home
Lit by the wan light of the horned moon
The swift and silent lizard of the stones.
These crumbling walls — these tottering arcades
These mouldering plinths — these sad and blackened shafts
35   These vague entablatures: this broken frieze

2–53 *For variants of "The Coliseum"*   23 *After this line was first written line*
as a separate poem see pp. 229–230.   *28 (Ax)*
12 me!/me! with awe. Ye Memories!
(Ax)

SCENE XI [*A*]

These shattered cornices, this wreck, this ruin,
These stones, alas! these grey stones are they all
All of the great and the colossal left
By the corrosive hours to Fate and me?
40   Not all the echoes answer me — not all:
Prophetic sounds and loud arise forever
From us and from all ruin unto the wise,
As from the granite Memnon to the sun.
We rule the hearts of mightiest men: we rule
45   With a despotic sway all giant minds.
We are not desolate we pallid stones,
Not all our power is gone — not all our Fame
Not all the magic of our high renown
Not all the wonder that encircles us
50   Not all the mysteries that in us lie
Not all the memories that hang upon
And cling around about us as a garment
Clothing us in a robe of more than glory.
                (*Enter* LALAGE *wildly*).
She comes.
[LALAGE.]   I come. And now the hour is come
55   For vengeance or will never. So! the priest
Is standing by the altar — the robed priest!
And by him the bride — so beautiful — the bride
And in a bride's array! and by the bride
The bridegroom — where art thou?
[POLITIAN]   'Tis true where am I?
60   Not where I should be? — By the God of Heaven
I'll mar this bridal if at the altar's foot
The bridegroom dies.   (*Exit*)
[LALAGE]   Away — Away — farewell!
Farewell Castiglione and farewell
My hope in Heaven!   (*Exit*)
                        [1835]

---

43 from the/*written over an erasure now illegible* (*A*)
55 So!/*written above* Behold (*Ax*)
59 where art thou?/gets this night hence! (*Ax*)

61 bridal/wedding (*Ax*)
63 Castiglione [*apparently written* Castiglioni *but not certainly so* (*A*); *hence the correct form is printed.*]

POLITIAN

Stage directions: I added "16th" in the edition of 1923. Poe left the century blank, being apparently uncertain about just what year should be chosen. It has been objected that Lalage's reading is anachronistic, but the play is certainly not laid in the nineteenth century, and Lalage quotes something first published in 1822! The one remark in the play that to an attentive member of an audience would suggest a date for the action is Lalage's reference, in VII, 67, to the recent discovery of America. Very late fifteenth century might be preferred, but it seems to me better to retain the date used in the first edition.

Cast of Characters: The characters in Poe's play are given names that might have been borne in Renaissance Italy, but it is easier to say for whom they are named than why those names were chosen. None of the names is appropriate in any high degree; Poe merely took most of them from some not yet identified book on the history and literature of the Renaissance, which he also used in his "Pinakidia," and the rest are merely fancy names.

Lalage is best known as the name given by Horace to a fair lady in *Odes*, I, xxii. She is sung by the poet in the famous "Integer vitae," when the wolf fled from him in the Sabine forest, as "dulce ridentem" and "dulce loquentem." Poe's Lalage speaks — at any rate she sings — beautifully, but smiles little in the play. She represents Ann Cook, who in her *Letters*, page 27, wrote of the loss of her father and brothers. Quinn, *Edgar Allan Poe*, page 233, says that Poe's "Lalage is . . . hopeless; her humility . . . and her constant weeping . . . remove her from sympathy."

Alessandra is named for Alessandra di Bartolomeo Scala, famed for her beauty and learning. She preferred to the Italian Politian as a suitor another scholar, Michael Marullus (of Greek origin), and thus caused enmity between the two men. After her husband's death in 1500, she entered a convent, and died in 1506. See Poe's "Pinakidia," number 140, and the notes on "To One in Paradise," line 5, for an epigram Politian addressed to her before her marriage. In Poe's play, Alessandra represents Miss Eliza T. Scott, who became Mrs. Sharp, in the real Kentucky tragedy. In the epigram mentioned, Politian calls Alessandra "cold maid," but Poe's character and the real ladies have little else in common.

Jacinta has a name derived from Poe's favorite flower, the hyacinth. It is borne by a maidservant in "Slawkenbergius's Tale" in Lawrence Sterne's *Tristram Shandy*, book IV. "Jacinta" is the title of a poem by William Rufus of Charleston, in *Rufiana* (1826), pages 49–51; another poem in that book may be a source for Poe's poem "The Sleeper." The character has no counterpart in the real story.

The Duke di Broglio is almost surely named for the famous French ducal family of de Broglie, which was of Italian descent and originally called Broglio. A "Neapolitan Duke di Broglio" is a character in Poe's tale "William Wilson." Di Broglio has no counterpart in the Kentucky story.

Baldassare Castiglione (1478–1529), author of *The Courtier* (1528), was a friend of the real Politian, and is mentioned in "Pinakidia," number 44, and "Marginalia," number 60. He gives his two names to two of Poe's characters.

Castiglione in the play represents Colonel Sharp in the real story. Poe treats his character with compassion (unlike other writers of works based on the Kentucky killing), and this is the one most original and interesting aspect of the play. A good actor, I think, could make much of the part, but it is not an easy one.

San Ozzo (we learn later he is a count) is a common Tuscan diminutive or nickname, usually written as one word. He is purely imaginary, and an amusing fellow — his is a good part for a comedian.

Politian's name is that of an important Italian scholar and poet, born Angelo Ambrogini at Montepulciano in Tuscany in 1454 and called, from his birthplace, Politianus or Poliziano (anglicized as Politian). He was noted for his work on ancient Greek and Latin authors, and wrote some poetry in "the vulgar tongue." Poe says a beautiful passage in Politian's *Orfeo* inspired his own poem "To One in Paradise." His life was quiet; a professor who was the master of many professors, avoiding politics, he never married. Poetry and his love for Alessandra aside, little of the romantic hero is told of him save that grief for the death of his patron, Lorenzo the Magnificent, is supposed to have hastened his own end in 1494. He had nothing, save perhaps a taste for composing verses, in common with the violent Jereboam Beauchamp of Kentucky, whom Politian in Poe's play represents. His English title is from that of Robert Dudley, favorite of Queen Elizabeth, patron of Spenser, and a leading character in Scott's *Kenilworth* (1821).

Baldazzar takes his name from the given name of Baldassare Castiglione, discussed above. He is an imaginary figure. His English title is from that of the Tudor poet, Henry Howard, Earl of Surrey.

Ugo may have been named for Ugo Foscolo (1778–1827), the Italian author long resident in England, whom Killis Campbell — so he told me — considered the best-known Ugo in Poe's day. Campbell also felt that Benito and Rupert are too commonplace for us to seek for namesakes; Campbell's earlier comments and mine are withdrawn.

The Monk is given no personal name in the play. He has a remote counterpart in the real story, for Ann Cook's correspondent, "Mrs. Ellen R——n," remonstrated against the vengeful ideas of her friend in Kentucky.

There have been, of course, those who have sought something of Poe's personality in the characters of his play. Their efforts seem to me fruitless. (See my thesis, p. 61. William Little Hughes said something of this in his *Contes inédits d'Edgar Poe*, 1862, p. 263, in a note on his translation, the first in French, of the scenes from *Politian* Poe printed. There is more in Emile Lauvrière, *Edgar Poe*, 1904, p. 370, where Sharp and Beauchamp are mentioned in a footnote.) Admitted that "Politian is a melancholy man," by which the author makes it clear he means one of varying moods, and that Poe often chose such men as his protagonists, for he was such a person himself. Admitted that "most men are sadly altered when they're drunk" may apply to the author as well as to his Castiglione. But to find much more of the author is to ignore his source in a true story of real people from a background wholly different from Poe's, or even from that of anyone he probably ever knew. They are of the Kentucky frontier in the first decades of the nineteenth century, true children of that "dark and bloody ground." They were not without culture; both Beauchamp and his wife wrote Byronic poetry. But they lived amidst scenes of violence. Duels to the death and bloody brawls were of constant occurrence, and unbridled passions were familiar to all.

Scene I

1ff. The opening conversation between the servants is extremely conventional. Poe commenting on Mrs. Mowatt's new comedy, *Fashion*, in the *Broadway Journal*, March 29, 1845, said: "The *dénouement* should in all cases be full of *action* and nothing else. Whatever cannot be explained by such action should be communicated at the opening of the play."

8 A buffo-singer is here a singer of burlesque songs.

43 Compare William Chamberlayne's *Love's Victory*, I, 273: "Yet though the grief sits heavy on our souls." This play, printed in 1658 and reprinted with the same author's *Pharronida* in 1820, Poe seems to have known, for his motto for "William Wilson" is remotely borrowed from it.

43–44 Possibly a reminiscence of Vergil's *Aeneid*, VI, 100–101: "ea frena furenti/concutit et stimulos sub pectore vertit Apollo," which may be translated, "Apollo shakes the reins on the inspired one, and turns the goad 'neath her heart."

47ff. Compare two passages from Beauchamp's *Confession*, pages 9, 10, about Miss Cook: "She sternly refused to make any acquaintances or even to receive the society or visits of her former acquaintances . . . and she said she could never be happy in society again."

49 In the canceled passage (see variants, p. 249, above) there occurs what may be Poe's first use of "nevermore."

53–54 Miss Cook wrote after her betrayal, in *Letters*, page 60, of suffering "my heart to be irrecoverably lost and blighted by one so little to be trusted — so little worthy of my affections. But whom I yet love."

67 This is condensed from Proverbs 16:18: "Pride goeth . . . before a fall."

97, 99 Ugo's two brief speeches are prose, not parts of the metric lines.

105 The zecchin, zecchino, or sequin was a gold coin first minted at Venice under the Doge Giovanni Dandolo between 1280 and 1289 and issued there and elsewhere in Italy down to the last century. The value was about twelve gold francs.

Scene II

30 "Between you and I" may be intentional because San Ozzo is a "fellow low-born." Poe in "Epimanes," the early form of "Four Beasts in One," wrote "like you and I," but later corrected that vulgarism.

33 "Birds of a feather" usually connotes bad companions and is traced to the seventeenth century.

38 Compare Beaumont and Fletcher's *Maid's Tragedy*, I, ii, 70f.: "You do me wrong,/A most unmanly wrong."

74 In "The Fall of the House of Usher," Poe writes of "The Usher race, all time-honored as it was."

75–80 See *King John*, III, i, 316, "His honor; O, thine honor, Lewis, thine honor!"

90 "Salermo" is clear in the manuscript, but Poe must refer to Salerno, an Italian city famed for its wine.

119 To "crack a bottle" is Shakespearean; see *King Henry the Fourth*, Part II, V, iii, 66: "you'll crack a quart together."

Scene III

23ff. The similarity to the speech of advice to Laertes from Polonius in *Hamlet*, I, iii, is perhaps not accidental.

35–36 Note a similar clash of "thou" and "you" in Scene VI, 97–98.

45ff. Poe's Politian has much in common with the hero of his story "The Assignation," who was also an Englishman, wealthy, of "unexpected eccentricity of . . . address and manner," and known for the rapid change of his moods, like Byron.

54–55 The heroine of Poe's story "Ligeia" had mastered "the most abstruse of the boasted erudition of the Academy" and had "traversed, and successfully, *all* the wide areas of moral, physical, and mathematical science."

67 The line is identical with the last of scene V.

Scene IV

It was from this scene that Poe thought he found "plagiarisms" in Act II, scene iv, of Longfellow's play *The Spanish Student*, which had appeared serially in *Graham's Magazine* late in 1842 and in book form in 1843. In the *Broadway Journal*, March 29, 1845, Poe printed what he called "parallel passages," those from *Politian* taken from the manuscript and not from the published text of the *Southern Literary Messenger* (1835), as is clear from the variants.

4 There is another reference to Lalage's humility in Scene VIII, 31.

5–6 Lalage reads (slightly inaccurately) from Milton's *Comus*, lines 632–633.

7–9 Lalage quotes these lines from an English version of Homer's *Odyssey*, IV, 566–568, which Poe presumably found in "Introduction to the Odyssey" in Henry Nelson Coleridge's *Introductions to . . . the Greek Classic Poets* (London, 1830), where they are ascribed to the pen of Abraham Moore in a note in his *Odes of Pindar* (London, 1822), Part I, p. 27. Coleridge discusses the Elysian plain as the abode of the dead, writes of the "Christian turn" given by Milton to the fable, and quotes the lines from *Comus* cited above as read by Lalage. See "Poe and H. N. Coleridge's *Greek Classic Poets*" by Palmer C. Holt, *American Literature*, March 1962. Apparently Poe's heroine thinks about Elysium as Heaven, and is almost on the verge of redemption under the benign influence of H. N. Coleridge, read anachronistically. Ironically, however, she soon chooses a path of unholy vengeance.

14–19 Lalage reads, slightly inaccurately, from John Webster's *Duchess of Malfi*, IV, ii, 264–265. Poe slips in writing of this "dame beyond the sea," for the scene of his own play is laid in Italy.

20–26 The sterner story is obviously that of Cleopatra, probably in Dryden's *All for Love*, V, 290ff., rather than in Shakespeare. In the introductory letter to his *Poems* (1831) Poe quotes from the prologue to Dryden's play. The names of Cleopatra's handmaidens are historical; they are given by Plutarch in his "Antony," lxxxv, 4. Dryden, like Plutarch, uses the form "Charmion." Poe's exact source for his spelling "eiros" is unknown. He used the two names again in the title of his tale "The Conversation of Eiros and Charmion," in 1839.

27 The meanings Poe gives of the names are somewhat fanciful. Iris means rainbow, but *eiros* is wool; Charmion seems rather to be connected with joy, grace, or charm than with "dove."

30–31 The "balm of Gilead," from Jeremiah 8:22, is mentioned again in "The Raven," line 89.

33–34 Lalage quotes from George Peele's *David and Bethsabe* (1599), lines 46–47; Poe repeats the quotation in his "To Marie Louise," about 1847. The passage is based on Psalm 133:3.

57 The story of the viper is from Aesop, but Poe here may echo Dryden's *All for Love*, IV, 467–469:

> . . . you serpents,
> Whom I have in my kindly bosom warmed
> Till I am stung to death.

66 Compare "A Dream," line 2, and see my notes, for "joy departed." Poe is careless of angelic ranks; he makes Hope an angel in *Politian*, VII, 81, and a cherub in "The Premature Burial."

67 Compare "To Zante" for "entombéd hopes."

73 The Monk reflects a remark of the "Mrs. Ellen R——n," to whom Ann Cook's *Letters* were addressed; at page 37 of the pamphlet she says: "I begged her to consult her Bible; for in that alone she would find happiness and peace; and to struggle to subdue her violent passions, which might yet lead her into the commission of dreadful errors."

77 The line is close to one in the canceled passage after *Politian*, I, 49, "To the frightful sounds of merriment below."

83–86 Beauchamp in his *Confession*, p. 99, says that Ann Cook's "father, brothers and friends, by a most strange succession of calamities had been swept into the grave." Poe used the phrase "the rivulet that ran by the very door" again in a letter of October 18, 1848, to Helen Whitman.

106ff. The use of a dagger as a cross recalls the action of Hamlet when he sees the Ghost and holds out his reversed sword as a cross.

107–108 Compare *King John*, III, iv, 43–44:

> *Pandulph.* Lady, you utter madness, and not sorrow.
> *Constance.* Thou art not holy to belie me so.

111   Lalage does not swear her own death but that of Castiglione.

Scene V

1ff.   The lost opening of this scene seems to have been of a serious kind.

36   Compare *Hamlet*, V, i, 210: "your flashes of merriment that were wont to set the table on a roar."

40   Compare with this *Midsummer Night's Dream*, V, i, 2: "More strange than true."

78   This line is the same as the last line of the third scene of Poe's play.

Scene VI

Henry W. Wells told me he thought Poe may have had in mind the end of the first scene of Dryden's *All for Love*, where Ventidius urges Antony to activity.

21   Compare "Murders in the Rue Morgue": "we then busied our souls in dreams" and "Colloquy of Monos and Una": "we wrapped our spirits, daily, in dreams."

22   Killis Campbell (*Poems*, page 232) compared the beginning of Moore's poem "Go Where Glory Waits Thee."

23   The expression "trumpet-tongued," Campbell points out (*Poems*, page 232), appears in *Macbeth*, I, vii, 19. Poe used it also in "The Imp of the Perverse" and in his sketch of Caroline Kirkland in *Godey's* for August 1846.

24   Roderick Usher, in "The Fall of the House of Usher," was "listening to some imaginary sound," and in "The Assignation" the protagonist "seemed to be listening to sounds which must have had existence in his imagination alone."

25   Sarah Helen Whitman used the second half of this line, together with lines 56–57, as a motto for her poem "The Phantom Voice," which concerns Poe. The poem first appeared in *Graham's Magazine* for January 1850 (36:91) and is collected in all editions of her poems.

29   Compare the opening of "The Pit and the Pendulum": "I was sick — sick unto death with that long agony."

31   "Bear with me" is said by Mark Antony in *Julius Caesar*, III, ii, 110.

34   Eternal City (*Urbs Aeterna*) as a name for Rome is first found in Tibullus, II, v, 23, and in Ovid's *Fasti*, III, 72, but is a commonplace since ancient times.

40   Compare "when the winds are breathing low" in Shelley's "Indian Serenade," which Poe quoted in "The Poetic Principle." See also "The City in the Sea," line 49: "The hours are breathing faint and low."

41   Opportunity "took for a cravat an hour-glass with golden grains" in "The Palace of Love," in *The Visions of Quevedo*, translated by William Elliott (Philadelphia, 1832), page 73. I once saw a copy of this little book supposed to have belonged to Poe, and I believe that it probably influenced a passage in his tale "Bon-Bon." For Poe's other references to the sands of

time as golden, see "To ———" ("Sleep on"), line 15, and "A Dream Within a Dream," lines 14–15. A close parallel in Tennyson's "Locksley Hall" (1842), lines 31–32, must be fortuitous.

55 The phrase "oppressed me as a spell" is found in Poe's tale "Morella."

57 In *Hamlet*, III, ii, 78, there is the phrase "heart of heart." Poe has "heart of hearts" also in *Politian*, VII, 51; in "To my Mother," in the tale "Landor's Cottage," and in a letter he wrote to Mrs. Whitman, October 1, 1848.

60–69 Judge Beverley Tucker wrote to Thomas W. White, proprietor of the *Southern Literary Messenger*, on November 29, 1835, complaining of the irregularity of the meter in Poe's play. The letter was shown to Poe, who on December first wrote Tucker that the "dischords" (resolved feet) were intentional, the result of careful study of prosody in several languages, and especially of the poems of Thomas Moore and the later works of Alexander Pope. Said Poe, "I especially pride myself on the accuracy of my ear." This did not silence Judge Tucker, who cited this speech of Baldazzar, in a letter to Poe of December fifth, as "lines that cannot by any reading be forced into time." Few, now, will agree with the judge's objections.

70ff. Lalage's song is from the second stanza of "A Suit to His Unkind Mistress Not to Forsake Him," by the Tudor poet, Sir Thomas Wyatt, who died in 1542. Wyatt's poetry is often printed together with that of his contemporary, Henry Howard, Earl of Surrey, from whom Poe's Baldazzar takes part of his title.

97–98 As in III, 35–36, "your" and "thee" clash.

103–104 The passage has no quotation marks in the manuscript and in the *Southern Literary Messenger*; it may well be rather a reminiscence than a direct quotation. No satisfactory source has been suggested.

Scene VII

This scene is largely founded on fact. Compare the following from Ann Cook's *Letters*, pages 74–75:

"I felt myself driven from society, and an object of scorn and derision . . . He offered me his hand. Yes, forlorn and abandoned as I was, he was willing to become my husband as he had been my friend. What could I do? I addressed him candidly and openly.

" 'You know my history,' said I, 'and my shame, if you are willing to receive to your bosom a poor outcast, whom the world has stigmatised as guilty and polluted, with a wounded heart and a blighted name, then take me. I am yours forever.'

" 'My dear Ann,' he replied, 'I regard you as the innocent victim of the most detestable treachery . . . I have long admired the cultivation of your mind, and the proud dignity and elevation of your soul. You were calculated to grace the most elevated circles of society . . . I am proud to be the object of your choice, humbled as you may be in your own estimation, or . . . in that of an unfeeling world. I have never felt for any woman what

I feel for you; my attachment is deep, sincere, and ardent, and while we live it shall never become extinct' . . .

"He had given me sufficient proofs of the truth of what he asserted."

Confirmation of this is to be found in a statement "To the Public" signed by Mrs. Eliza T. Sharp, printed in the Frankfort *Argus*, March 22, 1826, and copied in other Kentucky newspapers of the time. Sharp's wife there declared:

"Beauchamp married Miss Cook with a full knowledge of all the circumstances of her shame and of the charges which had been so widely circulated against my husband. It is said that he laughed at the delicacy of his family who would have dissuaded him from forming this connection, and . . evinced the most perfect indifference upon the subject of her character."

20f. Compare Moore's "Come rest in this bosom," quoted in "The Poetic Principle" — "I know not, I ask not if guilt's in that heart,/I but know that I love thee, whatever thou art" — and slightly misquoted in a letter to Mrs. Whitman on October 18, 1848.

28 The phraseology recalls Poe's "Happiest Day," line 2, and Byron's "Fare thee well," line 63: "Sear'd in heart, and lone, and blighted."

32 Poe here uses "ideal" in the unusual sense of "unreal."

38 Compare "Tamerlane" (*H*, 1845), line 178: ". . . of all we hope in heaven."

43-45 See Job 7:9: "he that goeth down into the grave."

54-56 Compare "The Masque of the Red Death" for "this spectral image, which with a slow and solemn movement . . . stalked to and fro," and a canceled passage in "The Imp of the Perverse," for "a vast and formless shadow . . . with a . . . stealthy pace." In "William Wilson" there is mention of a "step slow and solemn."

57-63 Compare "The Tell-Tale Heart" for "It is nothing but the wind in the chimney," and "The Raven" for " 'Tis the wind and nothing more." Killis Campbell (*Poems*, p. 233) remarks on lines 21-22 of "Dreams": ". . . the chilly wind/Came o'er me in the night."

63 Compare *As You Like It*, II, vii, 111: "Under the shade of melancholy boughs."

65 This is surely reminiscent of the opening line of Byron's *Bride of Abydos*: "Know ye the land where the cypress and myrtle," which Poe chose to scan carefully in his essays, "Notes Upon English Verse" and "The Rationale of Verse." Byron's indebtedness to "Mignon's Song" in Goethe's *Wilhelm Meister* is well known.

67 The allusion is obviously to Columbus and is the most important bit of evidence that Poe wished to lay his scene not long after 1492.

69 Compare "To One in Paradise," line 5: "All wreathed with fairy fruits and flowers."

78 This is reminiscent of Baldazzar's reproach in VI, 4-5.

78–79ff. Here Poe is using material from the Lexington *Kentucky Reporter* of July 7, 1826, quoted in an appendix to the *Confession*, where Beauchamp's dramatic farewell to his dying wife is thus described: " 'Farewell,' said he, 'child of sorrow — Farewell child of misfortune and persecution — you are now secure from the tongue of slander — for you I have lived; for you I die!' "

83 Compare Poe's letter to Helen Whitman of October 18, 1848: "whom I *love* — by one at whose feet I knelt — I *still* kneel — in deeper worship than ever man offered to God."

100 Poe may here echo *King Lear*, II, iv, 22–23: "They durst not do't;/They could not, would not do't."

Scene VIII

18 Compare *The Tempest*, I, ii, 389: "Sitting on a bank."

41 "Took" in this construction is of course vulgar English, but Jacinta is a low character, and Poe probably wished her to use an incorrect phrase here, although he corrected another of her solecisms, "all them jewels," in line 38 above. In the manuscript Poe canceled the word but supplied no substitute.

52 Genoa velvet was of excellent quality; Poe mentions it in "Bon-Bon," in the third chapter of "The Journal of Julius Rodman," and in "Landor's Cottage."

77 The spelling "ideot" was tolerated in Poe's day; in *The Yankee*, October 1829, there is an unsigned poem called "The Ideot-Boy," in which both "ideot" and "idiot" occur several times.

Scene IX

1 Compare *King Lear*, V, iii, 105, "My sickness grows upon me."

4 Azrael is the angel of death in Jewish and Mahometan lore; he is mentioned in the first version of "Metzengerstein," in "Ligeia," and in "Mesmeric Revelation."

38 Killis Campbell (*Poems*, p. 233) compared Addison's *Cato*, IV, iv, "Plato, thou reasonest well."

57–93 Poe here follows rather closely Beauchamp's description (in his *Confession*, pages 15–17) of an encounter with Sharp:

"[Sharp said] 'My friend . . . I never can fight the friend of that worthy injured lady . . . I never will raise my hand against you' . . .

"[I replied] 'Now, sir, tell me, will you fight me a duel,' (again raising my dagger.)

"He then stepped back a step, and I thought from the turn of his eye, was preparing to run. I sprang forward and caught him by the breast of his coat, and said, 'Now you damned villain, you shall die.' He then fell upon his knees and said, 'My life is in your hands, my friend I beg my life' . . . I then said, 'Get up, you coward, and go till I meet you in the street to-morrow . . . go arm yourself, for to-morrow I shall horsewhip you in the streets, and repeat it daily till you fight me a duel . . . You are about such a whining coward, as I was told you were . . .'

"[Sharp replied] 'You are the favored possessor of that great and worthy woman's love? Be it so, then. Here take my life. I deserve it. But do not disgrace me in the streets . . .'

"I bade him begone from me, or I would abide his offer in one moment (starting towards him.)"

74 At page 124 of the *Confession* there are some verses by Beauchamp called "The Death Scene," from which I quote two lines, "I pause — but short as lightning's gleam/The flash of Pity through my soul."

75 Describing the actual murder, in the *Confession*, p. 35, Beauchamp says, "I muttered in his face, 'Die, you villain.'"

Scene X

The macabre humor of this scene will please few readers, but good acting might make it tolerable.

48–49 There are two meanings for "flat." Ugo means "That's final." San Ozzo plays on the other meaning, "stupid."

58–63 Some people have, of course, fancied they were dead. It is said that King George III revealed his madness by talking to a courtier of having attended his own funeral.

113 The word "Paugh" is clearly written in the manuscript; more usual forms are "pah," "poh," and "faugh."

115–118 Compare "Bon-Bon," where the Devil says to the philosophic hero: "You must know that in a climate so sultry as mine . . . after death, unless pickled immediately, (and a pickled spirit is *not* good), they will — smell — you understand, eh?"

Scene XI

1–53 The author presumably chose the locale of this scene to permit his protagonist to deliver as a soliloquy Poe's own prize poem "The Coliseum," already slightly revised from the first version printed in 1833.

54–62 The idea of killing the bridegroom at the altar may have been taken from the climax of Victor Hugo's sensational play *Hernani* (1830), where the hero, losing a duel, must wait until his enemy chooses to sound a horn and kill him. The horn sounds as Hernani is about to wed his sweetheart Elvira. There was much discussion of Hugo's play at the time, even in America; Poe later names it in "The Masque of the Red Death." A bloody struggle at an altar in St. Peter's concludes the second act of Byron's *Deformed Transformed* (1824), a play echoed by Poe in "Al Aaraaf."

56 This line may echo *Paradise Regained*, I, 257: "Before the altar and the vested priest."

61–62 Here Poe seems to recall something in Ann Cook's *Letters*, p. 84. That lady wrote on July 4, 1826: "I . . . suggested that it would be better to plunge the dagger into his heart while folded in the arms of her for whom he deserted me."

POLITIAN

63–64   These last lines may be taken as an indication that Lalage (unlike her prototype in real life), repents although too late. I believe that Poe planned to have her rush between Politian and Castiglione, and herself be slain in a vain attempt to separate the two men in mortal combat. Poe did not write a final scene, and there really was nothing more to say. A playwright today might think the rest could be left to the imagination; a director might have the twelfth scene played in dumb-show.

POEMS OF 1836-1844

THE RAVEN

PARODY ON DRAKE

This is found in a critical article headed "Drake-Halleck" in the *Southern Literary Messenger*, April 1836 (2:326–336). Poe complains that the imagination of Joseph Rodman Drake's *Culprit Fay* has been overrated, and cites (p. 330) a passage from stanza xxv of the poem:

> He put his acorn helmet on;
> It was plumed of the silk of the thistle down:
> The corslet plate that guarded his breast
> Was once the wild bee's golden vest;
> His cloak of a thousand mingled dyes,
> Was formed of the wings of butterflies;
> His shield was the shell of a lady-bug queen,
> Studs of gold on a ground of green;
> And the quivering lance which he brandished bright
> Was the sting of a wasp he had slain in fight.

Poe offers to "accoutre" a fairy as well himself. His parody follows. In view of the technically incorrect use of a "beam from a maiden's eye" as a "lance," I cannot think that Poe did as well as Drake on this occasion, but the little impromptu verses contain the phrase "velvet violet," which was to reappear in "The Raven." Earlier editors of Poe's poetry have not collected this parody.

TEXTS

(*A*) *Southern Literary Messenger*, April 1836 (2:331), in "Drake–Halleck"; (*B*) *Complete Works of Edgar Allan Poe*, ed. Harrison (1902), VIII, 294. *The text followed is A.*

> His blue-bell helmet, we have heard,
> Was plumed with the down of the humming-bird,
> The corslet on his bosom bold
> Was once the locust's coat of gold,
> His cloak, of a thousand mingled hues,
> Was the velvet violet, wet with dews,
> His target was the crescent shell
> Of the small sea Sidrophel,

5

And the glittering beam from a maiden's eye
10   Was the lance which he proudly wav'd on high.   [1836]

NOTES

7-8 Sidrophel derivatively means a star lover, and is the name of a human astrologer in Butler's *Hudibras*. Lexicographers record no other usage, but Dr. Mairé Weir Kaye of the staff of G. & C. Merriam Company writes that Poe must mean the paper nautilus or argonaut (*Argonauta argo*) of the Mediterranean. Its shell is like a crescent in profile; the animal is given to navigation on the surface at night, and so should love the stars. Poe alludes to it in "The 1002nd Tale of Scheherazade."

MAY QUEEN ODE

This charming fragment is all that has reached us of a poem Poe composed about April 1836 for a schoolgirl in Richmond. She was Harriet Virginia Scott, who lived on Main Street, near the office of the *Southern Literary Messenger*. Her school was to have a May Day celebration, and she went in company with her cousin, a lawyer and friend of Poe, to ask him to compose a poem for her to recite to the Queen of the May. He complied by writing four or five stanzas. As a nonagenarian Mrs. Thomson of Austin, Texas, she remembered one of them and sent it to J. H. Whitty, sometime in the second decade of the present century. She thought that the stanzas might have been published in some periodical without Poe's name about 1836, but they have not been discovered. There is no reason to doubt the authenticity of these graceful lines.

Whitty published them in the second edition of *Complete Poems* (1917), page 164, and his text is followed. See also Phillips, I, 516.

[MAY QUEEN ODE]

Fairies guard the Queen of May,
Let her reign in Peace and Honor —
Every blessing be upon her;
May her future pathway lie
All beneath a smiling sky.   [1836]

POEMS: 1836–1844

SPIRITUAL SONG

This "most striking fragment," as its discoverer called it, was found by J. H. Whitty. It was written in Poe's hand, on the second page of an unsigned manuscript sent by William Maxwell to the owner of the *Southern Literary Messenger* when Poe was its editor. The missive is addressed to "Mr. Thomas W. White. / Publisher of the Southern Lit. Messenger. / Richmond." It is handstamped "STEAM" and marked "Pd" by a postmaster, and docketed by the recipient, "Anonymous / composition for Messenger." On the first page of the manuscript is a poem "Sacred Song" of sixteen lines beginning and ending:

> Oh! strike the Harp, while yet there lies
> In Music's breath the power to please; . . .

> Then strike the Harp in Zion's strains,
> And she shall soar at once to heaven.

Occupying the upper half of the second page is another poem, "Madrigal. The Wreath" — eight lines — in which Poe showed no interest. Lower on this page is the tiny piece, a title and three lines in Poe's hand. It is reasonable to suppose Poe thought about rewriting the first piece and then decided to seek out the author instead; the postal markings gave a clue to its being sent "by steam" from Norfolk. In the *Messenger* of August 1836 (2:554), "Sacred Song" appeared, as "By W. Maxwell," verbally like the manuscript quoted.

William Maxwell (1784–1857) was the author of *Poems*, issued at Philadelphia, of which there are editions, "Printed by William Fry, 1812," and "Published by M. Thomas, 1816." He resided at Norfolk in 1836, and made several contributions to the *Southern Literary Messenger*. In later years he was secretary of the Virginia Historical Society.

Whitty brought himself into disrepute by farfetched claims to "discoveries about Poe," but he made some real finds, and this fragment I am sure was one of them.

TEXTS

(*A*) Manuscript (1836), once in the Koester Collection; (*B*) *Complete Poems of Edgar Allan Poe*, ed. J. H. Whitty (1911), pp. 138–139, including facsimile.

The manuscript (*A*), of which the late William H. Koester sent me a photograph, is followed verbally, but I normalize the punctuation.

SPIRITUAL SONG

Hark, echo! — Hark, echo!
  'Tis the sound
Of archangels, in happiness wrapt.　　　　[1836]

BRIDAL BALLAD

This poem, although not usually considered one of Poe's major efforts, has the merit of an extremely original subject. Romantic literature is full of ladies forced into marriage against their will by cruel relatives or circumstances beyond their control. But it is hard to name another story in which the compulsion came only from a misunderstanding of a chance remark made earnestly and honestly by the heroine. The story is simple enough. A lady whose lover was killed in battle happens to faint. She revives in the arms of a friend, and momentarily thinks him her lost lover. She says that she is "happy now," and her rescuer, who is in love with her, believes that she wishes to marry him. The poem is the lady's soliloquy immediately after the wedding.

Poe's primary inspiration was almost surely a poem that had been printed in the *Southern Literary Messenger* of August 1835, in a brief article which deserves quotation in full.

For the Southern Literary Messenger

Mr. White: The subjoined copy of an old Scotch ballad, contains so much of the beauty and genuine spirit of by-gone poetry, that I have determined to risk a frown from the fair lady by whom the copy was furnished, in submitting it for publication. The ladies sometimes violate their promises — may I not for once assume their privilege, in presenting to the readers of the Messenger this "legend of the olden time," although *I promised not?*

BRIDAL BALLAD

Relying on the kind heart of the lady for forgiveness for *this breach of promise*, I have anticipated the pardon in sending you the lines, which I have never as yet seen in print. SIDNEY.

BALLAD.

They have giv'n her to another —
They have sever'd ev'ry vow;
They have giv'n her to another,
And my heart is lonely now;
They remember'd not our parting —
They remember'd not our tears,
They have sever'd in one fatal hour
The tenderness of years.
    Oh! was it weal to leave me?
    Thou couldst not so deceive me;
    Lang and sairly shall I grieve thee,
      Lost, lost Rosabel!

They have giv'n thee to another —
Thou art now his gentle bride;
Had I lov'd thee as a brother,
I might see thee at his side;
But *I know with gold they won thee*,
And thy trusting heart beguil'd;
Thy *mother* too, did shun me,
For she knew I lov'd her child.
    [Refrain.]

They have giv'n her to another —
She will love him, so they say;
If her mem'ry do not chide her,
Oh! perhaps, perhaps she may;
But I know that she hath spoken
What she never can forget;
And tho' my poor heart be broken,
It will love her, love her yet.
    [Refrain.]

Nothing else signed "Sidney" appeared in the magazine. His identity has never been plausibly suggested, nor has that of the lady who gave him the copy of the "Scotch" verses.[1] The names

---

[1] It has been suggested implausibly that Poe was "Sidney" and that he wrote the anonymous "Ballad" himself. This idea seems to have come from Woodberry, who in his *Life*, II, 415, wrote that "the poem given in S. L. M. Aug. 1835 as an unpublished Scotch ballad is connected with ["Bridal Ballad"], probably the first draft of the theme, and if this conjecture be accepted . . .," et cetera. Killis Campbell, impressed no doubt by Woodberry's "authority," did accept this conjecture almost unreservedly, as his discussions in the *Poems* (1917), p. 301, and in his *Mind of Poe*

are of little importance, for the magazine occasionally accepted anonymous or pseudonymous contributions from persons of whose names the proprietor admitted he was ignorant.

What is important is that Poe was moved by the poem to write an answer reversing the situation, and that he cast it in a form he considered that of a ballad. The first version is in regular stanzas of six lines, with rhyme scheme *a b a a a b*. This form is decidedly unusual in English poetry but resembles one — *a a a b a b* — that Burns used often, notably in "To a Mouse." The regular "Scottish" form seems not to have been hitherto a subject of comment.

In the first revision Poe made the stanzas of irregular length and in the second revision abandoned the stanzaic form, although he later returned to irregular stanzas.

It is not impossible that Poe had other sources of inspiration besides the "old Scotch ballad." In a review of William D. Gallagher's *Erato* in the *Messenger* of July 1836, Poe copied three stanzas of "The little ballad 'They told me not to love him,' " of which one seems pertinent.

> But they forc'd me to discard him!
> Yet I could not cease to love —
> For our mutual vows recorded were
> By angel hands above.
> He left his boyhood's home, and sought
> Forgetfulness afar;
> But memory stung him — and he fought,
> And fell, in glorious war.

Those who seek for Poe's personality in all his poems have suggested that "Bridal Ballad" concerns Elmira Shelton, and compare the early "Song" beginning "I saw thee on thy bridal day" — but this has little in common with "Bridal Ballad," which seems to me a poem of pure literary art. More to the point is A. H.

(1933), p. 206, reveal. Campbell considers the introductory note by Sidney "paralleled" by Poe's "attribution (by implication) of his 'Letter to B———' to another [writer] . . . in the *Messenger* for July, 1836." This is no real parallel. In 1836 Poe was an editor filling his columns, but wishing not to have too much appear to be from his own hand. In August 1835 the "mystification" would have involved hoaxing the proprietor of the magazine from whom he hoped for permanent employment, and giving away an article that as a contributor he might have sold for space rates. I think that is incredible.

BRIDAL BALLAD

Quinn's remark (p. 260), that it is the only example in Poe's poetry of "a lyric in which the speaker is a woman."

TEXTS

(A) *Southern Literary Messenger*, January 1837 (3:5); (B) *Saturday Evening Post*, July 31, 1841; (C) *Saturday Museum*, March 4, 1843; (D) *Broadway Journal*, August 2, 1845 (2:58); (E) *The Raven and Other Poems* (1845), p. 7; (F) J. Lorimer Graham copy of *The Raven . . .* with changes (1849); (G) *Works* (1850), II, 52–53.

Texts *A* and *F* are given here in full. In a letter of September 18, 1841, to Lewis J. Cist, Poe mentions arranging for the publication of *B* because he wished "to procure a printed copy" — an interesting sidelight on his method of revision.

BALLAD [A]

The ring is on my hand,
   And the wreath is on my brow —
Satins and jewels grand,
And many a rood of land,
5   Are all at my command,
   And I am happy now!

He has loved me long and well,
   And, when he breathed his vow,
I felt my bosom swell,
10 For — the words were his who fell
In the battle down the dell,
   And who is happy now!

And he spoke to re-assure me,
   And he kissed my pallid brow —
15 But a reverie came o'er me,
And to the church-yard bore me,
And I sighed to him before me,
   "O, I am happy now!"

And thus they said I plighted
   An irrevocable vow —

And my friends are all delighted
That his love I have requited —
And my mind is much benighted
   If I am not happy now!

25   Lo! the ring is on my hand,
   And the wreath is on my brow —
Satins and jewels grand,
And many a rood of land,
Are all at my command,
30   And I must be happy now!

I have spoken — I have spoken —
   They have registered the vow —
And though my faith be broken,
And though my heart be broken,
35   Behold the golden token
   That proves me happy now!

Would God I could awaken!
   For I dream — I know not how!
And my soul is sorely shaken,
40   Lest an evil step be taken,
And the dead who is forsaken
   May not be happy now!   [1836]

BRIDAL BALLAD [F]

The ring is on my hand,
   And the wreath is on my brow;
Satins and jewels grand
Are all at my command,
5   And I am happy now.

And my lord he loves me well;
   But, when first he breathed his vow,
I felt my bosom swell —

BRIDAL BALLAD

For the words rang as a knell,
10   And the voice seemed *his* who fell
In the battle down the dell,
   And who is happy now.

But he spoke to re-assure me,
   And he kissed my pallid brow,
15   While a reverie came o'er me,
And to the church-yard bore me,
And I sighed to him before me,
(Thinking him dead D'Elormie,)
   "Oh, I am happy now!"

20   And thus the words were spoken;
   And this the plighted vow;
And, though my faith be broken,
And, though my heart be broken,
Here is a ring, as token
25   That I am happy now! —
Behold the golden token
   That *proves* me happy now!

Would God I could awaken!
   For I dream I know not how,
30   And my soul is sorely shaken
Lest an evil step be taken, —
Lest the dead who is forsaken
   May not be happy now.   [1836–1849]

NOTES

18   D'Elormie is first mentioned in the text of 1841 and seems to be Poe's
spelling of De l'Orme, name of a French noble family. One of the almost

innumerable novels of George Payne Rainsford James (1799–1860) is called *De l'Orme* (1830); it was reviewed in the Philadelphia *Casket* for October 1830, and it is named in the heading of Poe's review of the English author's *Memoirs of Celebrated Women*, in *Burton's Magazine*, July 1839. There is also a man named De L'Orme, probably a wigmaker, mentioned in "The Man That Was Used Up" (1839).

32–33 Wilbur (*Poe*, p. 140) points out that this passage reflects an idea found in "The Sleeper," that "the dead sleep happily so long as the living are faithful to their memory," and compares also "For Annie," lines 85–87: "I lie so composedly . . . Knowing her love."

TO ZANTE

The occasion of the composition of this Shakespearean sonnet is almost surely a meeting of Poe and his first fiancée about 1836, while Poe was editor of the *Southern Literary Messenger*.

Elmira Shelton — signing only her first name — wrote Mrs. Clemm on September 22, 1849, after becoming re-engaged to Poe, a gentle and lovely letter. What is pertinent follows: "I remember seeing Edgar, & his lovely wife, very soon after they were married — I met them — I never shall forget my feelings at the time — They were indescribable, almost agonizing — However in an instant, I remembered that I was a married woman, and banished them from me." The manuscript of this letter is now in the Enoch Pratt Free Library, Baltimore, and was first completely published in *Edgar Allan Poe: Letters and Documents* (1941), edited by A. H. Quinn and Richard H. Hart.

The allegory may be interpreted as a continuation of that of "Tamerlane" and is possibly transitional to that of "Annabel Lee."

"To Zante" is partly based, as Woodberry observes (*Life*, I, page 167), on a passage in the *Itinéraire de Paris à Jérusalem* of Chateaubriand, that had already inspired several lines in "Al Aaraaf."

In "A Reviewer Reviewed" Poe began to point out an imitation in his verses "To Zante" of a "minor classic," but in the unfinished manuscript he did not complete his comment or name the poem — from the context either Greek or Latin — that he had

TO ZANTE

in mind. In view of this I reject the suggestion of a friend that
Poe was inspired by a very well-known sonnet by Ugo Foscolo,
published in 1803. It begins "Nè mai più toccherò le sacre
sponde," and laments Foscolo's inability again to touch the sacred
soil of Zante, the island where he was born.

TEXTS

(A) *Southern Literary Messenger*, January 1837 (3:32); (B) manuscript, in
a letter of November 6, 1840, to Richard Henry Stoddard, facsimiled in
Scribner's Magazine, February 1891 (9:224); (C) Philadelphia *Saturday Museum*, March 4, 1843; (D) *Broadway Journal*, July 19, 1845 (2:21); (E) *The
Raven and Other Poems* (1845), p. 20; (F) manuscript, in "A Reviewer Reviewed" (1849); (G) Griswold's *Poets and Poetry of America*, tenth edition
(1850), p. 419; (H) *Works* (1850), II, 43. The manuscripts (B and F) are both
owned by Mr. H. Bradley Martin.

TO ZANTE [H]

Fair isle, that from the fairest of all flowers,
    Thy gentlest of all gentle names dost take!
How many memories of what radiant hours
    At sight of thee and thine at once awake!
5   How many scenes of what departed bliss!
    How many thoughts of what entombéd hopes!
How many visions of a maiden that is
    No more — no more upon thy verdant slopes!
No more! alas, that magical sad sound
10   Transforming all! Thy charms shall please *no more* —
Thy memory *no more!* Acccurséd ground
    Henceforth I hold thy flower-enamelled shore,
O hyacinthine isle! O purple Zante!
    "Isola d'oro! Fior di Levante!"   [1836]

VARIANTS

Title: Sonnet. To Zante (A, C, D, E, F)   6 entombéd/entombed (A, D, F)
3 memories/mem'ries (B, C)   11 Accurséd/Accursed (A, B, C, D, F)

NOTES

1-2 Here again Poe uses Chateaubriand as source for the derivation of the
island's name from the flower called hyacinth by the Greeks. It has been

pointed out, however, that the early name of the island, Zacynthus, was derived from a hero of that name, said to have been a companion of Hercules, who was brought to the island for burial.

10 Poe was fond of the words "no more," as have been many poets. Here he perhaps had in mind Pope's first "Pastoral," lines 75–76: "If Sylvia smiles, new glories gild the shore,/And vanquish'd nature seems to charm no more." Compare also Crabbe's *Village*, II, 167–168: "Calmly to dwell on all that pleased before,/And yet to know that all shall please no more." Poe used the expression also in "To One in Paradise" and "Sonnet – Silence."

14 See note to "Al Aaraaf," I, 76–77.

THE HAUNTED PALACE

This is one of Poe's finest poems, pre-eminent in melody and symbolism of the highest order. It is an allegory, very exact in detail. The protagonist has golden hair and — at first — intelligent eyes, fine teeth, and lips whence flows intellectual conversation. But madness seizes him, his eyes are bloodshot, and there come from his lips only raving and insane laughter. This prosaic synopsis of the elaborate "conceit," worthy of the metaphysical poets of the seventeenth century, may serve to emphasize the artistic mastery of the author, for the success of the poem is undeniable. Poe's only other poem that is a single conceit, "To [Elmira]" ("The bowers") of 1829, is far less elaborately worked out.

Poe wrote Griswold on May 29, 1841, that by the palace he meant "to imply a mind haunted by phantoms — a disordered brain." [1] "Afterwards," Poe goes on to say, he "embodied the poem in a tale called 'The House of Usher' in Burton's Magazine." The verses are there called a ballad and placed in the mouth of the protagonist, Roderick Usher. The poem had something to do with the genesis of the story; the converse is impossible. C. Alphonso Smith well says that to call the ballad "self-portraiture" of Edgar Allan Poe "is to deal flagrantly with both literature and life." [2]

[1] This simple explanation can escape few readers, but J. L. O'Sullivan, editor of the *United States Magazine and Democratic Review* is said to have refused the poem because he did not understand it.

[2] *Edgar Allan Poe: How To Know Him* (Indianapolis, 1921), p. 216. Smith is replying to Woodberry, who, in the *Life*, II, 174, wrote of "The Haunted Palace" as

THE HAUNTED PALACE

The principal source of "The Haunted Palace" can now be confidently pointed out in one of the *New-Old Ballads* of John Wolcot (1738–1819), in his own time very widely known under his pseudonym, "Peter Pindar." It reads:

BALLADE

Couldst thou looke into myne harte,
 Thou wouldst see a mansion drear;
Some old haunted tower aparte,
 Where the spectre bands appear;
Sighing, gliding, ghostly forms,
'Mid the ruin shook by storms.

Yet my harte, which Love doth slighte,
 Was a palace passing fair;
Which did hold thyne image bright,
 Thee the queen of beauty rare;
Which the laughing pleasures filled,
And fair Fortune's sunne did gild.

When shall my poor harte, alas,
 Pleasure's palace be againe?
That, sweete made, may come to pass,
 When thou ceasest thy disdaine:
For thy smiles, like beams of day,
Banish spectre forms away.

The similarity of this playful imitation of an Elizabethan lyric to Poe's "Haunted Palace" was actually pointed out in the New York *Literary World* of September 28, 1850, by an anonymous contributor who thought the resemblance probably fortuitous. The article seems to have attracted no attention for decades, although Killis Campbell mentioned it without discussion in *Poems* (1917), p. 238. This neglect is not surprising, since Wolcot is generally known only for comic verses, usually coarse satires on everybody from George III to the biographers of Dr. Johnson.[3]

"intense, imaginative self-portraiture." This unfortunate phrasing of Woodberry's has led to misunderstandings. Poe was so temperamental that his friends and he himself, perhaps, feared he might go mad, and in later life he had brief periods of mental aberration. But he never had an extreme attack of madness before he wrote this poem, any more than he had blonde hair.

[3] Few who have enjoyed excerpts from *Bozzy and Piozzi* know who wrote them, and fewer know the story that the King forbade a prosecution for libel because he "laughed at Peter" himself.

But there is proof that Poe, at precisely the time when he composed "The Haunted Palace," did show an interest in Wolcot, a collected edition of whose poems had appeared in Philadelphia in 1835. In an article called "Literary Small Talk" in the Baltimore *American Museum* of January 1839, Poe wrote:

> City verses was an appellation applied . . . to the effusions of certain bards (Constantine Manasses, John Tzetzes, &c.) who flourished in the latter end of Rome, then so miscalled. Their verses . . . usually consisted of fifteen feet, but like those of Peter Pindar, made laws for themselves as they went along.

This note is taken in substance from a passage and footnote near the end of the fifty-third chapter of Gibbon's *Decline and Fall of the Roman Empire*, but the comparison to Wolcot is Poe's own. Though apt enough, since many of Wolcot's compositions are in lines of irregular length, it is somewhat unexpected. "Literary Small Talk" also has a good deal more from the same chapter of Gibbon, including something about the Byzantine Emperor Constantine VII Porphyrogenitus, who is clearly referred to in lines 21–24 of Poe's poem.

There may also have been in Poe's mind a description of a madman in Shelley's *Julian and Maddalo*, lines 224–225: ". . . like weeds on a wrecked palace growing,/Long tangled locks flung wildly forth, and flowing."

Other suggested sources have little to be said for them. An anonymous motto for the eleventh chapter of James Fenimore Cooper's *Wing-and-Wing* (1842), pointed out by Richard Beale Davis in the London *Notes and Queries*, September 1959, has not been found in print before Poe's poem.

John Forster's idea in a review of Griswold's *Poets and Poetry of America* in the London *Foreign Quarterly* of January 1844 that Poe imitated Tennyson must refer to the Laureate's "Deserted House." It does not much resemble "The Haunted Palace."

Poe's notion that Longfellow's "Beleaguered City" was plagiarized from "The Haunted Palace" may be dismissed here. It will be discussed in the volume containing Poe's criticisms of 1845. Another charge by Poe in the *Broadway Journal* of May 24, 1845, that William W. Lord plagiarized "The Haunted Palace" in "The New Castalia" was an ironic jest. Lord's poem was a deliberate parody, which Poe pretended to take seriously.

TEXTS

(A) Baltimore *American Museum of Science, Literature and the Arts*, April 1839 (2:320); (B) *Burton's Gentleman's Magazine*, September 1839 (5:148–149), in "The Fall of the House of Usher"; (C) *Tales of the Grotesque and Arabesque* (1840), I, 88–90, in "The Fall of the House of Usher"; (D) PHANTASY-PIECES (a copy of *Tales of the Grotesque and Arabesque*, with manuscript changes made for a revised edition projected in 1842 but not published until it was facsimiled in 1928); (E) Griswold's *Poets and Poetry of America* (1842), p. 388; (F) Philadelphia *Saturday Museum*, March 4, 1843; (G) *Graham's Magazine* for February 1845 (27:52–53), in Lowell's sketch of Poe; (H) *Tales* (1845), pp. 73–74, in "The Fall of the House of Usher"; (J) *The Raven and Other Poems* (1845), pp. 29–30; (K) Griswold, *Prose Writers of America* (1847), p. 527, in "The Fall of the House of Usher"; (L) Griswold, *Gift Leaves of American Poetry* (1849), pp. 277–278; (M) J. Lorimer Graham copy of *The Raven . . .* with changes (1849); (N) manuscript sent to Griswold about 1848 (lines 1–44 preserved at Harvard); (P) *Richmond Examiner* proof sheets, summer 1849 (Whitty, *Complete Poems*, 1911, pp. 38–39); (Q) *Works* (1850), I, 300, in "The Fall of the House of Usher"; (R) *Works* (1850), II, 29.

My text follows N, except for the last four lines, now missing from that manuscript, for which R is followed. The status of the proof sheet text P is uncertain but it contains a unique reading. Poe's quotation of the first dozen lines of the poem in a review of William W. Lord's *Poems* in the *Broadway Journal* of May 24, 1845, reprinted in *Works* (1850), III, 175, and quoted in "Marginalia," number 214, shows no variants from N.

THE HAUNTED PALACE [N, R]

In the greenest of our valleys
　　By good angels tenanted,
Once a fair and stately palace —
　　Radiant palace — reared its head.
5　In the monarch Thought's dominion —
　　It stood there!
Never seraph spread a pinion
　　Over fabric half so fair!

Banners yellow, glorious, golden,
10　On its roof did float and flow —

(This — all this — was in the olden
   Time long ago)
And every gentle air that dallied,
   In that sweet day,
15   Along the ramparts plumed and pallid,
   A wingéd odor went away.

Wanderers in that happy valley,
   Through two luminous windows, saw
Spirits moving musically,
20   To a lute's well-tunéd law,
Round about a throne where, sitting,
   Porphyrogene,
In state his glory well befitting
   The ruler of the realm was seen.

25   And all with pearl and ruby glowing
   Was the fair palace door,
Through which came flowing, flowing, flowing,
   And sparkling evermore,
A troop of Echoes whose sweet duty
30   Was but to sing,
In voices of surpassing beauty,
   The wit and wisdom of their king.

But evil things, in robes of sorrow,
   Assailed the monarch's high estate.
35   (Ah, let us mourn! — for never morrow
   Shall dawn upon him, desolate!)
And round about his home the glory
   That blushed and bloomed,
Is but a dim-remembered story
40   Of the old-time entombed.

And travellers, now, within that valley,
   Through the encrimsoned windows see
Vast forms that move fantastically

THE HAUNTED PALACE

To a discordant melody,

45   While, like a ghastly rapid river,

Through the pale door

A hideous throng rush out forever

And laugh — but smile no more.   [1838–48]

VARIANTS

Title: *This is given only in context in* B, C, D, H, K, Q

4 Radiant/Snow-white (*A, B, C, E, L*); reared/rear'd (*E, F, G*)

7 a/his (*A*)

15 ramparts/rampart (*A*)

16 wingéd/winged (*A, B, C, E, G, H, K, L, Q, although accent was added in D*)

17 Wanderers/All wanderers (*A*)

20 well-tunéd/well-tuned (*A, G, J, K, M*)

24 ruler/sovereign (*A, B, C, changed in D*)

29 sweet/sole (*B*)

34 Assailed/Assail'd (*E, F, G, L*)

35 morrow/sorrow (*misprint in F and J, corrected in M*)

38 blushed/blush'd (*E, F, G, L*); bloomed/bloom'd (*E, F, G, L*)

39 dim-remembered/dim remember'd (*F, G*); dim-remember'd (*E, L*)

40 entombed/entomb'd (*E, F, G, L*); old-time/old time (*all others except P*)

42 encrimsoned/encrimson'd (*P*); red-litten (*all others*)

45 ghastly rapid/rapid ghastly (*A, B, C, E, H, K, L, Q*)

NOTES

8 "Fabric" here means edifice, from Latin *fabrica*, as Richard Wilbur (*Poe*, p. 141) points out.

12 In "Time long ago" Poe characteristically turned a dialect phrase about, and made something magical of it. "Long time ago" is the title of an old minstrel song, containing the words "Down to Shinbone Alley, long time ago," and extremely popular, even in New Orleans, according to the Philadelphia *Saturday Evening Post*, January 16, 1841, although Shinbone Alley was then what is now Washington Mews in New York. The tune was "Comin' thro' the Rye," played slowly, according to an article on the Ethiopian Minstrels in the *Broadway Journal* of July 12, 1845. George P. Morris composed a song to "a Southern refrain" with the phrase "long time ago," published as *Near the Lake* (New York: James L. Hewitt, 1836). Poe is said to have been enraged when Henry B. Hirst wrote a parody on "The Haunted Palace" called "The Ruined Tavern," including the lines "Never negro shook a shinbone/In a dance-house half so fair," according to a letter from Thomas H. Lane in the New York *Independent* of November 5, 1896, quoted by Woodberry, *Life*, II, 420. The parody, which describes a fracas that led to a police raid at a Philadelphia tavern frequented by tough Negroes, was printed in *Sartain's Union Magazine* for May 1852, but the offending lines were omitted.

15 Pallid here, and in "The Raven," means yellow (from Latin *pallidus*) as Wilbur pointed out in *Poe*, page 141.

17 The subtitle of Dr. Johnson's *Rasselas* is "The Happy Valley."

· 3 1 7 ·

18 In "The Fall of the House of Usher" mention is made of the house having "vacant eyelike windows."

20 The lute is here the heart, as in "Israfel." The difficulty of keeping a lute in tune is proverbial.

22 No earlier use of the form "Porphyrogene" seems to be recorded. The reference is to the surname of Constantine VII Porphyrogenitus, "born to the purple." Gibbon, in the forty-eighth chapter of *The Decline and Fall of the Roman Empire*, explains it thus:

"An apartment of the Byzantine palace was lined with porphyry: it was reserved for the use of the pregnant empresses: and the royal birth of their children was expressed by the appellation of *porphyrogenite*, or born in the purple . . . but this peculiar surname was first applied to Constantine the Seventh. His life and titular reign were of equal duration."

This is clearly what Poe has in mind. Constantine VII was himself a man of letters, composer of an elaborate treatise, *On the Ceremonies of the Court at Constantinople*, which Gibbon mentions in his fifty-third chapter. Poe gave a reference to this work as "a pompous . . . book" in his essay "Literary Small Talk."

29 Echo was originally a nymph deprived by Juno of all save repetitive speech. See Ovid's *Metamorphoses*, III, 356.

30f. Professor W. P. Trent compared to these lines Lovelace's "To Althea from Prison":

> With shriller throat shall sing
> The sweetness, mercy, majesty,
> And glories of my King.

And note a prose parallel in Poe's "Literary Life of Thingum Bob": "the rich wit and wisdom which continuously flowed from their mouths."

42 (Earlier texts) "Red-litten" is paralleled by "gas-litten" in Poe's "Philosophy of Furniture" in *Burton's* for May 1840.

44 Robert Blair's poem was so well known that it is possible that Poe was here contrasting lines 545–547 of *The Grave*:

> Sound was the body, and the soul serene;
> Like two sweet instruments ne'er out of tune,
> That play their several parts.

COUPLET
(from "The Fall of the House of Usher")

These lines are seen inscribed "on a shield of shining brass" by the hero of an imaginary "antique volume" called *The Mad Trist* of Sir Launcelot Canning. From this book the narrator of

"The Fall of the House of Usher" reads to the distraught protagonist. All the other books named as in the library of Roderick Usher are genuine, but *The Mad Trist* is made up by Poe as part of the plot of his tale. Sir Launcelot Canning is purely a figment of Poe's imagination, his surname probably from the William Canynge of Thomas Chatterton's "Rowley" poems, his title and given name from the knight of Arthurian legend. Lines attributed to Sir Launcelot Canning were used by Poe in a prospectus he published in 1843 for his projected magazine, THE STYLUS, and were of course composed by Poe himself. See page 328.

TEXTS

(A) *Burton's Gentleman's Magazine*, September 1839 (5:151); (B) *Tales of the Grotesque and Arabesque* (1840), I, 99; (C) *Tales* (1845), p. 80; (D) Griswold, *Prose Writers of America* (1847), p. 530; (E) *Works* (1850), I, 307.
Text E is followed; there are no variants.

Who entereth herein, a conqueror hath bin;
Who slayeth the dragon, the shield he shall win.

[1839]

MOTTO
(for "William Wilson")

This scrap of verse appears at the beginning of all versions of the tale "William Wilson." Poe each time ascribed it to "Chamberlaine's *Pharronida*," in which the lines do not appear, although there is much said of conscience. However, William Chamberlayne's *Pharronida* of 1659 was reprinted in 1820 in an edition of three volumes which also included the author's play *Love's Victory* of 1658. In the play (V, 2746f.), Dr. Kenneth S. Rothwell found the following: "Conscience waits on me, like the frightening shades/ Of ghosts when ghastly messengers of death . . ." This is, to judge from the similar case of Poe's motto to "The Gold-Bug," obviously what Poe vaguely remembered and rewrote. Nothing else so close to the motto is found in the seventeenth-century bard's lines. (See note on *Politian*, I, 43, and *Modern*

Language Notes, April 1959; and compare also Politian, VII, 55f.:
"A spectral figure . . ./ Like the grim shadow, Conscience."

TEXTS

(A) The Gift for 1840 (1839), p. 229; (B) Burton's Gentleman's Magazine, October 1839 (5:205); (C) Tales of the Grotesque and Arabesque (1840), I, 27; (D) Broadway Journal, August 30, 1845 (2:113); (E) Works (1850), I, 417.

The text here adopted is C, which is verbally like A and B. By an obvious mistake the second "of" was omitted in D, and this error was followed in E.

What say of it? what say of CONSCIENCE grim,
That spectre in my path?

Chamberlaine's Pharronida

SONNET — SILENCE

This sonnet is one of Poe's most enigmatic poems, and has troubled the few commentators who have ventured to discuss it. It has some relation to the prose tale, "Silence — a Fable," written in 1833. I think it is primarily a poem of nature, with which Poe loved to commune alone, especially in wildly beautiful scenery. In his "Tale of the Ragged Mountains" he writes of a man's emotion when he believes himself the first human being ever to tread some remote spot in the virgin wilderness. As do hymns of the church, Poe also contrasts the death of the body, which is inevitable, and that of the soul, which is not.

John Phelps Fruit said, "Poe was deeply impressed with the idea of Silence as the eternal voice of God, as the music of the spheres" — which we mortals cannot hear. This impression is supported by an early canceled line after "Al Aaraaf," I, 125, "Silence is the voice of God," itself reminiscent of the "still small voice" heard by Elijah. Richard Wilbur also refers to the music of the spheres, and thinks Poe wished to contrast "death of the body (which is not the end of being)" with "death of the soul (or non-being)." Quinn saw a contrast between the silence that "hovers over those resting places of human souls we have loved, and that shadow cast by silence upon the soul, which is an active breeder of terror." [1]

The sources are clearly to be found in two sonnets of Thomas Hood; Poe answers the first with material from the second. They appeared with the signature "T." in the *London Magazine* of February and June 1823 (5:215, 636), respectively, and Poe copied the first as a filler in *Burton's* for September 1839 (5:144).[2] They follow.

SILENCE

There is a silence where hath been no sound,
   There is a silence where no sound may be,
   In the cold grave — under the deep, deep sea,
Or in wide desert where no life is found,
Which hath been mute, and still must sleep profound;
   No voice is hush'd — no life treads silently,
   But clouds and cloudy shadows wander free,
That never spoke — over the idle ground
But in green ruins, in the desolate walls
   Of antique palaces, where Man hath been,
Though the dun fox, or wild hyena, calls,
   And owls, that flit continually between,
Shriek to the echo, and the low winds moan,
There the true Silence is, self-conscious and alone.

SONNET: — DEATH

It is not death, that some time in a sigh
This eloquent breath shall take its speechless flight;
That some time the live stars, which now reply
In sunlight to the sun, shall set in night;
That this warm conscious flesh shall perish quite,
And all life's ruddy springs forget to flow; —
That verse shall cease, and the immortal spright
Be lapp'd in alien clay, and laid below: —
It is not death to know this, but to know
That pious thoughts, which visit at new graves,
In tender pilgrimage will cease to go

---

[1] Fruit, *The Mind and Art of Poe's Poetry*, p. 54; Wilbur, *Poe*, pp. 141–142; Quinn, p. 294. Killis Campbell told me that he wanted to withdraw a suggestion he had proposed in *Poems*, p. 241, that Poe's sonnet had some relation to Shelley's *Prometheus Unbound*, I, i, 195–209.

[2] Poe almost surely did not know that the author was Hood, but merely gave a copy of the sonnet, signed "T.," to his printer. In Poe's usually very legible hand, capital *T* is very much like *P*, and the poem appeared in *Burton's* signed "P." — a matter of little interest had it not led some scholars to suppose that Poe claimed the authorship.

So duly and so oft, and when grass waves
Over the past-away, there may be then
No resurrections in the minds of men!

In December 1839 Poe sent a copy of his poem to Joseph B. Boyd, a watchmaker of Cincinnati, for his autograph collection, probably before he gave another copy to the *Saturday Courier* for a first issue of the new year, to which all prominent Philadelphia authors were asked to contribute. The Boyd manuscript was sold by the American Art Association on April 21, 1921; I examined it at the time. The partial file of the *Saturday Courier* at the New York Public Library contains the issue of January 4, 1840, and was consulted for the readings of *B*.

TEXTS

(*A*) Manuscript, in a letter to Joseph B. Boyd, December 25, 1839; (*B*) Philadelphia *Saturday Courier* for January 4, 1840; (*C*) *Burton's Gentleman's Magazine*, April 1840 (6:166); (*D*) Philadelphia *Saturday Museum*, March 4, 1843; (*E*) *Broadway Journal*, July 26, 1845 (2:45); (*F*) *The Raven and Other Poems* (1845), p. 26; (*G*) *Works* (1850), II, 39.

SONNET – SILENCE   [*F*]

There are some qualities — some incorporate things,
   That have a double life, which thus is made
A type of that twin entity which springs
   From matter and light, evinced in solid and shade.
5 There is a two-fold *Silence* — sea and shore —
   Body and Soul. One dwells in lonely places,
   Newly with grass o'ergrown; some solemn graces,
Some human memories and tearful lore,
Render him terrorless: his name's "No more."
10 He is the corporate Silence: dread him not!
   No power hath he of evil in himself;
But should some urgent fate (untimely lot!)
   Bring thee to meet his shadow (nameless elf,
That haunteth the lone regions where hath trod
15 No foot of man,) commend thyself to God!

[1839–1845]

THE CONQUEROR WORM

Title: Silence, a Sonnet (*A, B, C*); Silence (*G*)

2   which thus is/life aptly (*A, B, C*)

3   A type/The type (*A, B, C*)

6   lonely/desert (*A*)

8   and/a (*A*)

14 That haunteth the lone/Who haunteth the dim (*A, B, C*)

NOTES

1–15 The form of "Sonnet — Silence" is a *deliberate* experimental variation of the Italian sonnet, although its fifteen lines have annoyed some criticasters. In the earliest form (in a manuscript) and in the publication in *Burton's* Poe divided the piece plainly into three stanzas of four, five, and six lines respectively, and in the notice he wrote of the magazine for *Alexander's Weekly Messenger* of April 1, 1840, he remarked laconically, "Mr. Poe has a clever Sonnet." Poe was not fond of sonnets and wrote only four others, two of which are Shakespearean and the others of varied Italian rhyme schemes.

9   Poe, like many poets of his day, was pleased with the sonorous phrase "no more." The most familiar use of it before Poe's is probably in "A Lament" by Shelley, with the refrain, "No more — oh, never more."

THE CONQUEROR WORM

This major poem, first published in *Graham's Magazine* for January 1843, is unsurpassed in its power and pessimism. Kent has pointed out that the five stanzas symbolize the five acts of a tragedy.[1] In 1845 it was put into the second version of Poe's tale "Ligeia" as a hint that the heroine of that story would not succeed in permanently returning to life. This nuance had been discussed by Philip Pendleton Cooke and Poe in letters of September 16 and 21, 1839, but the poem was probably not written with this specific purpose.

One inspiration may have come, as Ingram observed, from a little verse romance, *The Proud Ladye* (1840), by an obscure New York poet, Spencer Wallace Cone, who is not even given a place in Poe's "Literati" papers or in Griswold's *Poets and Poetry of America*. Poe reviewed Cone's poem in *Burton's* for June 1840 and there quoted the pertinent lines from the beginning of Part III, which I find at page 6 of the original volume:

[1] Harrison, ed., *Complete Works*, VII, 204.

· 3 2 3 ·

> Lay him upon no bier
> But on his knightly shield;
> The warrior's corpse uprear,
> And bear him from the field.
> Spread o'er his rigid form
> The banner of his pride,
> And let him meet the conqueror worm,
> With his good sword by his side.

It is more likely that Poe's impulse to write his poem came from a passage in a review in *Graham's Magazine* for February 1841 of Dr. James McHenry's epic, *The Antediluvians* (Philadelphia, 1840). Poe did not write that review,[2] but the discussion of McHenry can hardly have escaped his eye. The reviewer quoted a passage from *The Antediluvians*, page 202:

> Such scenes of cruelty and blood,
> Exhibited before appalled heaven,
> To make the angels weep, to look on earth!

This he calls a feeble imitation of Shakespeare. He gives, slightly abridged and misquoted from *Measure for Measure*, II, ii, 117–122:

> But man, frail man,
> Drest in a little brief authority,
> Plays such fantastic tricks before high heaven,
> As make the angels weep.

Poe seems to take ideas from both quotations, and especially the *frailty* of man is significant. In the play, Shakespeare wrote of "proud man" and likened him to "an angry ape." Neither pride nor anger has a place in Poe's poem.[3]

---

[2] Harrison thought he did, and collected it in *Complete Works*, X, 105f., but we now know that Poe did not join the staff of *Graham's* until March, and the review is inconsistent with his kindly remarks in "Autography," in *Graham's* for December 1841, on McHenry as the victim of a clique.

[3] Lest it be supposed overlooked, I mention a "suggested source" of Poe's poem in a piece called "Death of Time," which appeared in a volume called *Nacoochee . . . With Other Poems* by T. H. Chivers, M.D. (1837) — it is "a play, with God as dramatist, and Christ as leading man"(!) and "the setting for the end of the world." See S. Foster Damon, *Thomas Holley Chivers* (1930), p. 216, and Charles Henry Watts II, *Thomas Holley Chivers* (1956), p. 158. I can find no similarities in the two poems, nor did Chivers himself ever think there were any.

THE CONQUEROR WORM

TEXTS

(A) *Graham's Magazine* for January 1843 (22:32); (B) Philadelphia *Saturday Museum*, March 4, 1843; (C) New York *New World*, February 15, 1845 (10:100), in "Ligeia"; (D) *Broadway Journal*, May 24, 1845 (1:331); (E) *Broadway Journal*, September 27, 1845 (2:173), in "Ligeia"; (F) *The Raven and Other Poems* (1845), pp. 27–28; (G) manuscript sent to Griswold, mentioned by Whitty; (H) R. W. Griswold, *The Poets and Poetry of America*, 8th edition (1847), pp. 433–434; (J) J. Lorimer Graham copy of *The Raven* . . . with changes in lines 31 and 37 (about 1849); (K) *Works* (1850), I, 459, in "Ligeia"; (L) *Works* (1850), II, 31.

The text is that of the J. Lorimer Graham volume (J). Whitty's confusing discussion in *Complete Poems* (1911), page 224, mentions examination of a manuscript copy of the poem originally sent to Griswold, docketed "Last poem sent by Poe." Whitty gave no collation, and I have never seen the manuscript, hence I assign it a letter (G) but can give no variants.

THE CONQUEROR WORM [J]

Lo! 'tis a gala night
    Within the lonesome latter years!
An angel throng, bewinged, bedight
    In veils, and drowned in tears,
5   Sit in a theatre, to see
    A play of hopes and fears,
While the orchestra breathes fitfully
    The music of the spheres.

Mimes, in the form of God on high,
10   Mutter and mumble low,
And hither and thither fly —
    Mere puppets they, who come and go
At bidding of vast formless things
    That shift the scenery to and fro,
15   Flapping from out their Condor wings
    Invisible Wo!

That motley drama — oh, be sure
    It shall not be forgot!
With its Phantom chased for evermore,
20   By a crowd that seize it not,

Through a circle that ever returneth in
   To the self-same spot,
And much of Madness, and more of Sin,
   And Horror the soul of the plot.

25   But see, amid the mimic rout
   A crawling shape intrude!
A blood-red thing that writhes from out
   The scenic solitude!
It writhes! — it writhes! — with mortal pangs
30   The mimes become its food,
And seraphs sob at vermin fangs
   In human gore imbued.

Out — out are the lights — out all!
   And, over each quivering form,
35   The curtain, a funeral pall,
   Comes down with the rush of a storm,
While the angels, all pallid and wan,
   Uprising, unveiling, affirm
That the play is the tragedy, "Man,"
40   And its hero the Conqueror Worm.

[1842–1849]

VARIANTS

Title: None (*C, E, K*)
  3 An angel/A mystic (*A, B, D*); be-
   winged/bewing'd (*B, D, H*)
  4 drowned/drown'd (*B, C, D, H*)
13 formless/shadowy (*A*)
19 chased/chas'd (*B, C, D*)
31 seraphs/the angels (*A, B, D, F, H,*

   L); the seraphs (*C, E, K*)
34 quivering/dying (*A*)
37 And the seraphs, all haggard and
   wan (*A*); And the angels, all pallid
   and wan (*B, C, D, E, F, H, K, L*)
40 And its/Its (*A, B, D, H*)

NOTES

Title: See also Poe's tale "The Premature Burial," for the phrase "con-
queror worm" in 1844.

2 See the phrase "the lonesome latter days" in Poe's "Addenda" to *Eureka*.
This probably alludes to I Timothy 4:1: ". . . in the latter times some shall
depart from the faith." According to a note by Richard Wilbur (*Poe*, p. 142),
Poe here suggests that the end of the world approaches.

THE CONQUEROR WORM

3-6 Compare Henry Hart Milman's "Hymn for Palm Sunday," beginning "Ride on, ride on in majesty," stanza 3:

> The winged squadrons of the sky
> Look down with sad and wondering eyes
> To see the approaching sacrifice.

7 The music of the spheres is fitful because of the disharmony of the degenerate world, Wilbur explains (*Poe*, p. 142).

9 See also "The Black Cat" for "a man, fashioned in the image of the High God." The reference is to Genesis 1:27 — "So God created man in his own image."

15 All the known condors are confined to the Americas and inhabit the mountains near the western coasts. There are several species of these birds, the best known being the Andean condor, generally said to be the largest living bird capable of flight, the wing expanse sometimes exceeding twelve feet. Their plumage is almost wholly black, and after flapping their wings to gain altitude, they seem to soar almost without wing movement. Their voracity is proverbial, and although they occasionally attack living prey, they usually subsist on dead animals. In "Romance" Poe speaks of "eternal condor years" that devour the dead past. In the story "The Assignation" he compares a Venetian gondola at night to "some huge and sable-feathered condor." Poe seems to have had both of the foregoing ideas in mind in "The Conqueror Worm."

17 Motley is the costume of fools; the allusion is to them, both natural and professional.

19 The phantom is Happiness.

21-22 The division of the word "into" between two lines in a rhymed poem is as unusual as it is effective. An opinion of Croesus, the Lydian king, is recorded in Herodotus, I, 207, that "there is a wheel in human affairs, which continually revolving, does not suffer the same men always to be successful."

33-36 Compare the fifth and sixth stanzas of Thomas Campbell's "Last Man":

> Go, let oblivion's curtain fall
>   Upon the stage of men,
> Nor with thy rising beams recall
>   Life's tragedy again . . .
> The eclipse of Nature spreads my pall, —
> The majesty of darkness shall
>   Receive my parting ghost.

36 The curtain comes down with the rush of a storm of which the audience is unaware unless there is no applause. Those who have seen John Drinkwater's *Abraham Lincoln*, where applause is withheld by request until the final curtain, will recall the effect.

   Possibly Poe had in mind a well-known remark of Augustus Caesar, who, "on the last day of his life, received a number of his friends, and said 'Do you think that I have acted my part on the stage of life well?' and quoted two lines of Greek, meaning 'If I've played well, applaud me.'" See the ninety-ninth chapter of his *Life* by Suetonius.

MOTTO FOR THE STYLUS

In January 1843, Poe persuaded Thomas Cottrell Clarke to join him in a scheme of publishing the long-planned Penn Magazine under a new punning name, The Stylus. For the projected magazine Poe composed a three-line motto in verse, ascribed to "Launcelot Canning" — a person wholly unknown to historians and bibliographers, to whom, however, Poe ascribes an imaginary work, *The Mad Trist*, in "The Fall of the House of Usher." This Canning is, of course, Poe himself, and the motto for The Stylus is Poe's own.

The "Prospectus of The Stylus," with the motto and a woodcut by Felix O. C. Darley after a design by Poe, showing a hand writing *Alēthe[ia]*, the Greek word for "truth," was published in Clarke's paper, the Philadelphia *Saturday Museum*, on February 25, 1843; Poe sent a copy with a letter of the same date to his friend F. W. Thomas. Unfortunately, no copy of that issue now survives, but the paper carried the Prospectus regularly for several weeks more, with the verses but without the woodcut.

TEXTS

(*A*) Philadelphia *Saturday Museum* [February 25], March 4 (and later dates), 1843; (*B*) *Laurel Leaves*, edited by William F. Gill (1876), p. 372; (*C*) Gill's *Life* (1877), p. 115, with illustration "engraved from the original drawing by the poet."

The text used is *A*, from a copy of the issue of March 4, now at the University of North Carolina.

[THE STYLUS]

———— unbending that all men
Of thy firm TRUTH may say — "Lo! this is writ
With the antique *iron pen.*"

     — Launcelot Canning.
      [1843]

NOTES

3 The narrator of Poe's tale "Shadow" (1833) writes "with a stylus of iron" like those pens mentioned in Job 19:24 and Jeremiah 17:1. Horace Binney Wallace in *Stanley* (1838), I, 51, remarks, "Paulus Jovius said of his own, sometimes a pen of gold and sometimes a pen of iron." The reference is to a remark of the Italian historian Paolo Giovio (1483–1552). Poe referred to it in "Marginalia," number 255; and gave it in Latin, "Aureus aliquando STYLUS, ferreus aliquando" on the design for a title page for the magazine which he sent to E. H. N. Patterson in a letter of May 23, 1849. This design is reproduced by Phillips, II, 1405—the hand differs slightly from that in Gill's *Life*, showing only the thumb and two fingers where Gill's cut shows the full count.

MOTTO FOR "THE GOLD-BUG"

The lines given below appear in all versions of "The Gold-Bug," which was written in 1842.

Poe ascribes the verses to a comedy of 1761 by Arthur Murphy, *All in the Wrong*, in which nothing at all similar is to be found. However, as I pointed out in *Notes & Queries*, February 1953, in another comedy, *The Dramatist* (1789) by Frederick Reynolds, a character named Floriville, who has visited Italy and never forgets it, says (IV, ii): "I'm afraid you've been bitten by a tarantula . . . the symptoms are wonderfully alarming. —— There is a blazing fury in your eye—a wild emotion in your countenance." In his review of *Robinson Crusoe* in the *Southern Literary Messenger* for January 1836, Poe quoted inaccurately a speech of the character Vapid from the same scene of that play. It seems clear that this motto for "The Gold-Bug" is an amplification in verse of Reynolds' prose similar to the free rendering found in the motto to "William Wilson." The bite of the large spider was believed to be cured by dancing.

TEXTS

(*A*) Philadelphia *Dollar Newspaper*, June 21, 1843; (*B*) *Tales* (1845), page 1; (*C*) *Works* (1850), I, 52. Text *B* is used; there are no variants.

What ho ! What ho ! this fellow is dancing mad;
He hath been bitten by the Tarantula.

[1842]

LENORE

No other poem of Poe's gave him so much trouble as "Lenore." He himself regarded it as the same poem as "A Paean," the poorest thing in his *Poems* of 1831. He reworked that a little in 1836. Then late in 1842 he changed it greatly in content and cast it into a form called in the seventeenth and eighteenth centuries a "Pindarick Ode." By this time he had virtually a new poem, which he titled "Lenore." Not yet satisfied, he again recast it in long-line stanzas without much change of content. In the last summer of his life he was still altering that form.

Usually Poe's revisions were improvements, but many critics wish he had let "Lenore" stand as it was first published in 1843. Thomas Wentworth Higginson said in his *Short Studies of American Authors* (Boston, 1880), p. 15: "Never in American literature . . . was such a fountain of melody flung into the air as when 'Lenore' first appeared in 'The Pioneer'; and never did fountain so drop as when Poe rearranged it in its present form." [1]

The form in long lines with internal rhymes — the one usually known to modern readers — was arrived at in 1844. It seems possible that Poe was influenced by reading "Lady Geraldine's Courtship" by Elizabeth Barrett, in whose work he took great interest at the time. Her poem certainly influenced "The Raven," of which the heroine is also named Lenore, and for many of us the chief interest of "Lenore" in long lines lies in the fact that it is a steppingstone to "The Raven." [2]

There is an interesting explanation of what Poe was trying to accomplish, written at about the time when he recast the poem for the second time. In his "Marginalia," number 103, printed in the *Democratic Review*, December 1844, he has a long critique of a poem by Amelia Welby called "The Departed." He discusses

---

[1] J. P. Fruit in *The Mind and Art of Poe's Poetry* (1899), p. 101, defended the long lines as suggesting "a chant, a dirge, a requiem."

[2] For all that Poe occasionally wrote of "Lenore" as one of his best poems, and for all its undeniable melody, the poem, especially the third stanza, exemplifies the faults of which Poe's less friendly critics complain. The rhythm is too marked, the story too plainly told.

several attitudes appropriate in elegiac poems, and concludes, "Better still, [they should] utter the notes of triumph. I have endeavored to carry out this latter idea in some verses which I have called 'Lenore.'"

The heroine's name first appeared as Lenore in the wholesale reworking of the early "Paean" into the new poem late in 1842. In the 1836 version of "A Paean" the heroine had been named Helen, perhaps an allusion to Mrs. Jane Stanard. On the copy of the *Broadway Journal* Poe gave to Sarah Helen Whitman in 1848, he wrote, "Helen, Ellen, Elenore, Lenore." These names, like the title name in "Eleonora," a tale of 1841, all are generally supposed to mean "light" or "bright."

Poe's exact form of the name was, I suspect, from "Lenore," the title of the longest poem of the once very well known child poet, Margaret Miller Davidson (1823–1838). In reviewing, in *Graham's Magazine* for August 1841, Washington Irving's *Biography and Poetical Remains* of that young lady, Poe accorded some rather limited praise to Margaret's little romance with a happy ending, and he discussed the poem at length in his lecture on "The Poets and Poetry of America."

Poe also must have known Felicia Hemans' *Forest Sanctuary* (1825), her own favorite among her poems and once very widely read. In canto II, lix, she writes of her heroine, buried at sea:

> Gentlest Leonor!
> Once fairest of young brides! — and never more,
> Loved as thou wert, may human tear be shed
> Above thy rest!

This presumably had a place in the genesis of Poe's "Lenore" and "The Raven" too, in both of which "Lenore" and "nevermore" rhyme.[3]

---

[3] It has been generally supposed, as by Killis Campbell (*Poems*, p. 215), that Poe's heroine is a namesake of the heroine of the famous ballad "Lenore" by the German romantic Gottfried August Bürger. In reviews of Captain Basil Hall's *Skimmings* and of Henry F. Chorley's *Memorials of Mrs. Hemans*, both in the *Southern Literary Messenger*, October 1836, Poe tells about the admiration felt for that poem by Mrs. Hemans and by Sir Walter Scott, who wrote an adaptation of it called "William and Helen." The heroine, refusing to be reconciled to the loss of her lover Wilhelm in the Crusades, uttered such impious words as led his ghost to come and carry her off to his grave. What has this precious pair to do with Guy

Poe said that Elmira Shelton was his "lost Lenore," as John M. Daniel told in the *Southern Literary Messenger*, March 1850. But this was the remark of a gallant gentleman seeking a lady's hand, and one suspects that his reference was to "The Raven." "Lenore" seems to me in its later forms as impersonal a thing as Poe ever wrote.

Poe on December 25, 1842, sent in a letter to James Russell Lowell "a brief poem," which presumably was some form of "Lenore," and two days later a manuscript that surely was. In the second letter he quoted two phrases from "Lenore" in suggesting a permissive change, which Lowell decided against, in the arrangement of the line beginning "To friends above." Unhappily the manuscripts referred to are lost. The poem Lowell published at Boston in *The Pioneer* for February 1843 was signed in full "By Edgar Allan Poe." A somewhat revised version was included in Hirst's sketch of Poe in the Philadelphia *Saturday Museum* of March 4.

Exactly when Poe decided to put "Lenore" into the stanzaic form in which it is generally known is uncertain, since the first printing is probably *introuvable*. Soon after reaching New York on April 7, 1844, Poe went to work on the *Sunday Times*, edited by Major Mordecai M. Noah, and the poem was probably published in its columns; but only one number of Noah's paper for the proper period is known, and that number (April 14) is damaged. However, Poe's poem was popular and was copied in various papers, of which some do survive.

One curious publication in the *Evening Mirror*, November 28, 1844, deserves special mention:

To the Editors of the Evening Mirror

Dearest Mirror: I copy the subjoined lines "By Mr. Willis", from an old number of the Jackson (Tenn.) *Advocate*, where they are evidently out of place, and at all events so grossly misprinted that I must ask you to replenish them, and more especially as they do not appear in the late collection of Mr. W. It can scarcely be possible that there are *two Dromios*. *Amelia.*

De Vere and his gentle sweetheart? In his reviews Poe expresses no admiration for Bürger's ballad, nor even indicates that he knew its theme. I cannot regard it as a model for his own "Lenore."

LENORE

Here there follows the text of Poe's "Lenore" in twenty-four long lines, and Willis remarks:

We thank our friend, *the* "Amelia", for supposing us capable of the authorship of these majestic-paced stanzas. They are not ours — we wish they were! But, (if they are not "Amelia's" — and they are very much in the measure of the "Step-son"), we do not know whose they are . . .

Amelia Welby's best-known poem (on her stepson) is misquoted in Poe's "Rationale of Verse." Although Poe was on the *Mirror* staff, apparently he did not read the paper carefully and took no notice of the Willis article.[4]

A long-line version of the poem was included in Lowell's sketch of Poe in *Graham's* for February 1845; Poe reprinted the verses in the *Broadway Journal* of August 16 and collected them in *The Raven and Other Poems*. The following paragraph appeared in the *Broadway Journal* of September 13, 1845:

The "Chambersburg Times" does us the honor to make up the whole of its first page from a single number of "The Broadway Journal.["] This would be all very well, had it not forgotten to give us credit for our articles, contributed and editorial — and had it not forgotten *not* to make certain improvements in our compositions to suit its own fancy. Copying, for example, a little poem of our own called "Lenore," the Chambersburg editor alters "the damnèd earth" into "the cursed earth." Now, we prefer it damned, and will have it so.[5]

Mention may be made here of other echoes. A story signed "Lilla Herbert" in the *Columbian Magazine* for December 1845 is called "The Withered Heart," and in it Poe's poem is used as a theme. On a manuscript of a letter Poe wrote him on August 11, 1845, Dr. Chivers wrote some verses about one "false Guy de Vere," who somewhere in France betrayed a lady whose name was Hortense, but Chivers' lines have little in common with Poe's "Lenore" save the hero's name.[6] "Lenore" by George H. Thurs-

[4] No issues of the Jackson *Advocate* can now be located. Poe's occasional correspondent, John Tomlin, lived in Jackson, Tennessee, and may have been connected with the paper.

[5] No issue of the *Times* of Chambersburg, Pennsylvania, between August 16 and September 13, 1845, can be located. The piratical editor was either Franklin F. May or Enos R. Powell, who became May's partner some time in 1845, according to I. H. McCauley, *Historical Sketch of Franklin County*, second edition (1878), p. 68.

[6] The manuscript has been cut down so that almost no line of Chivers' poem is

ton in the *Home Journal* of April 27, 1850, is based on "The Raven" rather than its namesake poem by Poe.

Poe thought that Henry B. Hirst in his *Penance of Roland,* written about 1847, plagiarized a passage from lines 10–12 of the long-line version. Poe made the charge in a manuscript written about 1849 but not printed until Griswold included a text in the *Works* (1850), III, 211.

TEXTS

PINDARIC VERSION: (*A*) *The Pioneer* for February 1843 (1:60); (*B*) Philadelphia *Saturday Museum,* March 4, 1843.

LONG-LINE VERSION: (*C*) Uncertain periodical (probably New York *Sunday Times*) prior to October 1844, known only from unauthorized reprints in (*Ca*) New York *Evening Mirror,* November 28, 1844, and (*Cb*) *Oquawka Spectator,* September 13, 1848; (*D*) *Graham's Magazine* for February 1845 (26:53) in Lowell's sketch of Poe; (*E*) *Broadway Journal,* August 16, 1845 (2:81); (*F*) *The Raven and Other Poems* (1845), pp. 14–15; (*G*) *The Poets and Poetry of America,* tenth edition (dated 1850, issued in December 1849), p. 421; (*H*) letter to R. W. Griswold, late June 1849 (lines 20–26); (*J*) manuscript revisions in J. Lorimer Graham copy of *The Raven . . . ,* summer 1849 (lines 20–26); (*K*) *Richmond Daily Whig,* September 18, 1849; (*L*) *Works* (1850), II, 12–13.

The earliest version (*A*), and the final revised form (*K*) with a misprint corrected in the last line, are given in full.

The text of Griswold's anthology (*G*) was put back into short lines by him. It shows late readings, although Poe's letter to him (*H*) is ignored.

The version (*K*) printed in the *Richmond Daily Whig,* September 18, 1849, was obviously arranged for by the author in connection with announcement of his last lecture on Monday evening, September 24. It alone shows in print the line order of both late manuscripts (*H, J*). The paper had a semiweekly edition called *Richmond Whig and Public Advertiser,* in which the poem appeared from the same types in a number also dated September 18, probably issued in the afternoon. Files of both editions were examined at the New-York Historical Society.

LENORE [*A*]

AH, broken is the golden bowl!
The spirit flown forever!
Let the bell toll! — A saintly soul
Glides down the Stygian river!

---

complete. The fragments will presumably appear in a forthcoming volume of the *Complete Works* of Thomas Holley Chivers, now in course of publication by Brown University Press.

LENORE

And let the burial rite be read —
The funeral song be sung —
A dirge for the most lovely dead
That ever died so young!
And, Guy de Vere,

Hast *thou* no tear?
Weep now or nevermore!
See, on yon drear
And rigid bier,
Low lies thy love Lenore!

"Yon heir, whose cheeks of pallid hue
With tears are streaming wet,
Sees only, through
Their crocodile dew,
A vacant coronet —

False friends! ye loved her for her wealth
And hated her for her pride,
And, when she fell in feeble health,
Ye blessed her — that she died.
How *shall* the ritual, then, be read?

The requiem *how* be sung
For her most wrong'd of all the dead
That ever died so young?"

Peccavimus!
But rave not thus!

And let the solemn song
Go up to God so mournfully that *she* may feel no wrong!
The sweet Lenore
Hath "gone before"
With young hope at her side,

And thou art wild
For the dear child
That should have been thy bride —
For her, the fair
And debonair,

40　　　　　That now so lowly lies —
　　　　　The life still there
　　　　　　Upon her hair,
　　　　　The death upon her eyes.

　　　"Avaunt! — to-night
45　　　My heart is light —
　　　　No dirge will I upraise,
　　But waft the angel on her flight
　　With a Pæan of old days!
　　　Let *no* bell toll!
50　　Lest her sweet soul,
　　　Amid its hallow'd mirth,
　　　　Should catch the note
　　　　As it doth float
　　Up from the damned earth —
55　　To friends above, from fiends below,
　　　　⌊th' indignant ghost is riven —
　　　From grief and moan
　　　To a gold throne
　　Beside the King of Heaven!"

VARIANTS

3　*Printed as two lines in B*　　　23　blessed/bless'd (*B*)
4　Glides down/Floats on (*B*)　　54　damned/damnéd (*B*)
20　loved/lov'd (*B*)

LENORE　[*K*]

Ah, broken is the golden bowl! — the spirit flown forever!
Let the bell toll! — a saintly soul floats on the Stygian river: —
And, Guy De Vere, hast *thou* no tear? — weep now or never
　　more!
See! on yon drear and rigid bier low lies thy love, Lenore!
5　Come, let the burial rite be read — the funeral song be sung! —
An anthem for the queenliest dead that ever died so young —
A dirge for her the doubly dead in that she died so young.

"Wretches! ye loved her for her wealth and ye hated her for
　　her pride;

And, when she fell in feeble health, ye blessed her — that she
  died: —
10 How *shall* the ritual then be read — the requiem how be sung
By you — by yours, the evil eye — by yours the slanderous
  tongue
That did to death the innocence that died and died so young?"

Peccavimus: — yet rave not thus! but let a Sabbath song
Go up to God so solemnly the dead may feel no wrong!
15 The sweet Lenore hath gone before, with Hope that flew
  beside,
Leaving thee wild for the dear child that should have been
  thy bride —
For her, the fair and debonair, that now so lowly lies,
The life upon her yellow hair, but not within her eyes —
The life still there upon her hair, the death upon her eyes.

20 "Avaunt! — avaunt! to friends from fiends the indignant
  ghost is riven —
From Hell unto a high estate within the utmost Heaven —
From moan and groan to a golden throne beside the King
  of Heaven: —
Let *no* bell toll, then, lest her soul, amid its hallowed mirth
Should catch the note as it doth float up from the damnéd
  Earth!
25 And I — tonight my heart is light: — no dirge will I upraise,
But waft the angel on her flight with a Pæan of old days!"

[1844–1849]

VARIANTS

(The symbol *C* indicates that *Ca* and *Cb* are alike.)

Title: Dirge (*Cb*)
5 Come/Ah (*D*)
7 *Not in C; printed from broken type,
  losing first word, in E*
8 ye hated/hated (*all others except C*)
9 that/when (*Cb*); blessed/bless'd (*G*)
12 died and died/perished (*C*)
13 yet rave/but rave (*D, E, F, G, L*);
  but let/and let (*C, D, E, F, G, L*)

15 The sweet/She — sweet (*C*)
18 within/upon (*C*)
19 *Not in C*
20–26 *The order of the lines in all
  other texts except H and J is* 25–26,
  23–24, 20–22
20 Avaunt! . . . fiends/To friends above,
  from fiends below (*C, D, E, F, G, L*);
  Avaunt! avaunt! from fiends below

(*J*); the indignant/th' indignant (*Ca*)
21 unto/into (*Cb*); within the utmost/ far up within the (*all others*)
22 moan and groan/grief and groan (*F, G, J, L*); grief and moan (*C, H*); golden/gold (*C*)

23 then, lest her/lest her sweet (*C, D, E, F, G, L*); hallowed/hallow'd (*G*)
24 damnéd/damned (*C*)
25 And I/Avaunt! (*C, D, E, F, G, L*)
26 Pæan/Pœan (*misprint, E, K; here corrected from all others*)

NOTES

1–2   The allusion is to Ecclesiastes 12:5–7, "the mourners go about the streets . . . the silver cord is loosed . . . the golden bowl is broken . . . and the spirit returneth unto God who gave it," a passage used more fully in the third paragraph of Poe's tale, "The Premature Burial" (1844). Compare also the opening of "A Hero of the Revolution" by General George P. Morris:

> Let not a tear be shed!
> Of grief give not a token!
> Although the silver thread
> And golden bowl be broken.

Mr. Cortland P. Auser tells me that Morris's poem was written in memory of General Daniel Delavan in 1837.

3   The name of the hero, Guy De Vere, first appears at the same time as that of Lenore, about 1842. It is a somewhat conventional aristocratic name, implying "true," but Poe probably took the surname from John Plumer Ward's novel, *DeVere, or the Man of Independence* (1827). Poe mentioned this novel in a review of Bulwer's *Poems* in the *Broadway Journal*, February 8, 1845, and again in 1849 in "Marginalia," number 220. Tennyson's "Lady Clara Vere de Vere" seems to have no connection with Poe's hero.

9   In Southern speech, "bless" still sometimes means "curse"; compare French *blesser*, to injure.

11   The superstition about the "evil eye" is the basis of Poe's tale "The Tell-Tale Heart" (1843).

11–12   On a leaf on which Poe wrote down favorite passages from Shakespeare, he gives from *Much Ado About Nothing*, V, iii, 3: "Done to death by slanderous tongues."

13   *Peccavimus* (we have sinned), from the Vulgate of Psalm 106:6, is in the Burial Service.

15   The phrase "gone before" was given as a quotation in some, but not all, versions of the poem. Arthur Ransome, *Edgar Allan Poe* (1912), p. 40, objected to it as infelicitous. But Poe probably considered it quaint. Compare Ben Jonson's "Epigram xxxiii": ". . . gone before/Whither the world shall follow."

17   The word "debonair" is now rarely used in highly serious context, but Poe must have recalled that in "L'Allegro" Milton called Mirth "buxom, blithe and debonair."

18   (1843) In the old bestiaries there occurs a story that crocodiles cannot resist killing people, but seeing their human prey prostrate, think them so

like themselves that they weep, although they still eat them. Crocodile tears come of a shallow grief.

HEXAMETER

This single line in Poe's essay "Notes Upon English Verse" is described as "an unintentional instance of a perfect English hexameter formed upon the model of the Greek." In 1845 he gave it in one of his installments of the series now called "Marginalia" where he introduces it, remarking that "no one has seemed to suspect that the natural preponderance of spondaic words in Latin and Greek must, in the English, be supplied by art — that is to say, by a careful culling of the few spondaic words which the language affords," and adds: "This, to all intents, is a Greek Hexameter, but then its spondees are spondees, and not mere trochees." The two statements seem somewhat inconsistent, but the second seems to me a claim to Poe's invention of the line. The word "unintentional" may have been carelessly used because the line came into his head spontaneously. It expresses a complete and serious idea.

TEXTS

(A) Boston *Pioneer*, March 1843 (1:111), in "Notes Upon English Verse"; (B) *Godey's Magazine and Lady's Book* for August 1845 (31:51), in "Marginal Notes"; (C) *Works* (1850), III, 582, in "Marginalia," number ccvi. The latest text (C) is followed; the surviving fragments of the manuscript from which the first form (A) was printed do not include the section in which the monostich occurs. The title is from the context; there are no variants.

Man is a | complex, | compound, | compost, | yet is he | God-
born.   [1843]

[TO ELIZABETH WINCHESTER — IMPROMPTU]

In 1940 Professor William Starkweather of Hunter College told me the following family tradition. He was an adopted child whose foster mother was Elizabeth Winchester Starkweather, daughter of Samuel Winchester of Baltimore and niece of Oliver Winchester, maker of rifles.

One day when Elizabeth Winchester was about twelve years old, while out walking with her father, she dropped a glove. A passerby picked it up and handed it to her with a little impromptu speech in rhyme. Her father recognized the gallant gentleman as Poe, but the rhymes were not remembered.

Elizabeth was born about 1831, but was not too sure how old she was when she saw Poe, who visited Baltimore not infrequently. However, he lectured there on the evening of January 31, 1844, and that date may be suggested for the lost scrap of verse.

[1844]

FRAGMENT OF A CAMPAIGN SONG

This is all that survives of a song written impromptu by Poe during the presidential campaign early in 1844. Its authenticity is beyond doubt, although the verses were long preserved only in the memory of Poe's friend Gabriel Harrison.[1] Harrison gave at least two accounts of his meetings with Poe, differing only in slight details. The first was in a letter to the Brooklyn *Eagle*, November 18, 1875 (quoted in part by Phillips, II, 926), the second in an interview published in the *New York Times Saturday Review* of March 4, 1899 (quoted in part by Woodberry, *Life*, II, 422).

In the *Eagle* alone it is mentioned that the song was to the tune of "The Star-Spangled Banner," but only in the *Times* are recorded any of the words Poe composed. What follows is based primarily on the later source.

Gabriel Harrison is known chiefly as an artist and actor, but in 1843 he quit the stage for a while and opened a "tea store" at 568 Broadway, on the southeast corner of Prince Street. There on a chilly evening he saw "a small man with a large head looking

---

[1] Harrison was born on March 25, 1818, and died on December 15, 1902, according to his obituary in the New York *Dramatic Mirror* of December 27, 1902.

in rather wistfully at some beautiful plugs of tobacco [Harrison] had displayed . . . He entered and asked the price," but, Harrison continues,

made no move to buy, and started to leave . . . I was struck by . . . his manner, by his voice and by his fine articulation . . . so I offered the man a piece of tobacco. He accepted, thanked me and departed. Two or three weeks afterwards he came in again. At the time I happened to be in the throes of composing a campaign song for the White Eagle Club, a political organization of which I was President . . . I began to explain the matter to him . . . "Let me have your pencil," he said . . . In about fifteen minutes . . . I saw written a song of five stanzas with chorus . . . I can remember only a few lines, which ran thus: [Our text is given] . . . I was delighted, and wanted to pay him something for his trouble, but the only thing he would accept was a bag of my best coffee . . . I said that I should like to know his name . . . "Certainly," he answered with a faint smile, "Thaddeus K. Perley, at your service."

On a later occasion, Fitz-Greene Halleck met and recognized Poe at the store, and an explanation ensued. Soon afterward, Poe moved to New York. About 1846, Poe and Harrison saw a good deal of each other, and after Poe's death the actor became a good friend of Mrs. Clemm.

In the Brooklyn source the surname Poe used is printed as "Peasley," but this has no point, and Thaddeus Perley seems to be mildly jocular. In the Gospels the Apostle Thaddeus is referred to by varied names, and the subtitle of Horne Tooke's grammatical work, *Epea Pteroenta*, to which Poe referred with respect on occasion, is "The Diversions of Purley," from the place where it was composed. Poe's verses for the marching club were a diversion.

TEXTS

(*A*) *New York Times Saturday Review*, March 4, 1899, p. 144, in Gabriel Harrison's "Song which Poe wrote in 1844"; (*B*) Woodberry, *Life* (1909), II, 422; (*C*) *The Poems of Edgar Allan Poe*, edited by Killis Campbell (1917), p. 141. The text used is *A*; the title is Campbell's, given in *C*.

[FRAGMENT OF A CAMPAIGN SONG] [*A*]

See the White Eagle soaring aloft to the sky,
Wakening the broad welkin with his loud battle cry;

Then here's the White Eagle, full daring is he,
As he sails on his pinions o'er valley and sea.

[1844]

NOTES

1-4 Poe almost surely echoed the opening lines of a once widely known
poem, "The Gray Forest Eagle" by Alfred B. Street: "With storm-daring
pinion and sun-gazing eye,/The gray forest eagle is king of the sky." This
was first published in the *Knickerbocker* for November 1841 and was included
in Griswold's *Poets and Poetry of America* (1842). Street lived at Albany and
was for many years State Librarian of New York.

DREAM-LAND

This is one of Poe's most famous poems, a favorite with an-
thologists; it includes one of his most quoted lines, "Out of Space,
out of Time." Quinn (pp. 415f.) says it has "inevitability," and
"produces the effect of vastness and desolation by . . . denying
limitations." Like "Lenore" and many other poems of Poe's later
years, it adopts an elaborate metrical scheme, including the re-
frain — a feature made less striking in the first revision.

It seems to me to be founded on experience, and it is exactly
what its title suggests, a description of the world of dreams. There
all of us meet phantoms of the real and unreal, of the dead and
the living. Nothing is inconsistent with this in the poem. Notable
is the absence of true color: the lilies are white, the woods are
gray; in dreams by night many sleepers see no colors.

Richard Wilbur suggests to me that Poe's inspiration was in
Paradise Lost, II, 890–896:

> Before their eyes in sudden view appear
> The secrets of the hoary deep, a dark
> Illimitable Ocean without bound,
> Without dimension, where length, breadth, and highth,
> And time and place are lost; where eldest Night
> And Chaos, ancestors of Nature, hold
> Eternal anarchy . . .

There are at least two foreshadowings of "Dream-Land" in
descriptions of dreams in Poe's tales, the first in "Hans Pfaall"
(1835):

DREAM-LAND

Now there were hoary and time-honored forests, and craggy precipices, and waterfalls tumbling with a loud noise into abysses without a bottom . . . still noonday solitudes where no wind of heaven ever intruded, and where vast meadows of poppies, and slender, lily-looking flowers spread themselves out . . . all silent and motionless for ever . . . [Elsewhere] it was all one dim and vague lake, with a boundary-line of clouds.

The other is in the second chapter of "Arthur Gordon Pym" (1838): "Immensely tall trunks of trees . . . rose up . . . as far as the eye could reach . . . in wide-spreading morasses, whose dreary water lay intensely black, still, and altogether terrible, beneath. And the strange trees . . . were crying to the silent waters. . ." There are close similarities also in "Fairyland," "The Sleeper," and "Ulalume." [1]

TEXTS

(A) *Graham's Magazine* for June 1844 (25:256); (B) *Broadway Journal*, June 28, 1845 (1:407); (C) *The Raven and Other Poems* (1845), pp. 18–20; (D) Griswold's *Poets and Poetry of America*, 10th edition (1850), p. 420; (E) J. Lorimer Graham copy of *The Raven* . . . with changes of the summer of 1849; (F) *Richmond Examiner*, October 23, 1849; (G) *Works* (1850), II, 41–43.

The *Examiner* text (F), which is a companion piece to the final text of "The Raven," is followed. Its reading in line 42 seems to me a definite improvement, although the J. Lorimer Graham changes (E), which are also very late, differ slightly. J. H. Whitty, who discovered the *Examiner* text, in *Complete Poems* (1911), p. 217, gave its date incorrectly, and described a misprint in line 50 not to be found in the original paper in the Virginia Historical Society, which I follow. A manuscript in the Huntington Library, wherein Night has a "red throne," is not regarded as authentic.

DREAM-LAND [F]

By a route obscure and lonely,
Haunted by ill angels only,
Where an Eidolon, named Night,
On a black throne reigns upright,

[1] In *Scribner's Monthly* for October 1875, F. G. Fairfield absurdly declared the source of Poe's "Dream-Land" to be in Lucian of Samosata's "Island of Dreams." By this he clearly meant a famous passage in *Vera Historia*, II, 33–35. There are no close similarities at all. The chief divinities of "The Island of Dreams" are Night and the Cock, and its king is Sleep. The word "eidolon" is not used in the original Greek.

5   I have reached these lands but newly
From an ultimate dim Thule —
From a wild weird clime that lieth, sublime,
Out of Space — out of Time.

10   Bottomless vales and boundless floods,
And chasms, and caves, and Titan woods,
With forms that no man can discover
For the dews that drip all over;
Mountains toppling evermore
Into seas without a shore;

15   Seas that restlessly aspire,
Surging, unto skies of fire;
Lakes that endlessly outspread
Their lone waters — lone and dead, —
Their still waters — still and chilly

20   With the snows of the lolling lily.

By the lakes that thus outspread
Their lone waters, lone and dead, —
Their sad waters, sad and chilly
With the snows of the lolling lily, —

25   By the mountains — near the river
Murmuring lowly, murmuring ever, —
By the grey woods, — by the swamp
Where the toad and the newt encamp, —
By the dismal tarns and pools

30   Where dwell the Ghouls, —
By each spot the most unholy —
In each nook most melancholy, —
There the traveller meets aghast
Sheeted Memories of the Past —

35   Shrouded forms that start and sigh
As they pass the wanderer by —
White-robed forms of friends long given,
In agony, to the Earth — and Heaven.

For the heart whose woes are legion
40   'Tis a peaceful, soothing region —
For the spirit that walks in shadow
O! it is an Eldorado!
But the traveller, travelling through it,
May not — dare not openly view it;
45   Never its mysteries are exposed
To the weak human eye unclosed;
So wills its King, who hath forbid
The uplifting of the fringed lid;
And thus the sad Soul that here passes
50   Beholds it but through darkened glasses.

By a route obscure and lonely,
Haunted by ill angels only,
Where an Eidolon, name NIGHT,
On a black throne reigns upright,
55   I have wandered home but newly
From this ultimate dim Thule.

[1844–1849]

VARIANTS

6 Thule/Thulé (*D*)
12 dews/tears (*E*)
13 Mountains/Fountains (*B*)
21 *Before this lines 1–4 are repeated,*
followed by:
    I have reached my home but newly
    From this ultimate dim Thule. (*A*)
25 mountains/mountain (*A, B*)
38 the Earth/the worms (*A, B*); earth
(*D*)
39 *Before this lines 1–4 are repeated,*

followed by:
    I have journeyed home but newly
    From this ultimate dim Thule. (*A*)
42 O! it is/'Tis — oh 'tis (*all others*)
45 mysteries/mysterics (*misprint B*)
46 unclosed/enclosed (*misprint B*)
47 its King/the King (*A, B*)
48 fringed/fringéd (*A, E*)
50 darkened/darken'd (*D*)
55 wandered/wander'd (*D*)
56 Thule/Thulé (*D*)

NOTES

3 An eidolon is a phantom; there is no reason to identify Night with Death here.

6 Thulé was the Greek name for an island north of Britain. Its stock epithet is from Vergil, *Georgics*, I, 30, "ultima Thule." Poe's use is purely figurative here and in "The Pit and the Pendulum."

8 The phrase "out of space, out of time" is a familiar quotation, sometimes applied with partial justice to Poe's poetry. Oddly enough, I find the expression in transposed order — "out of time, out of space" — in the fifth paragraph of Emerson's "Divinity School Address" (1838), where Poe may have seen it, if he glanced at that celebrated document. Whether he did or not, the form Poe used is more memorable in a striking way.

10 The Titans were gigantic predecessors of the Olympian gods, whom they vainly defied. The word "titanic" conveys the ideas of age, great size, and struggle. There are Titanic cypress trees in "Ulalume."

12 In text *E*, the change makes the line identical with "Fairyland" (1829), line 4.

14 "Seas without shore" are a commonplace in poetry.

21–27 Killis Campbell (*Poems*, p. 245) compares to these lines the song of the Echoes in Shelley's *Prometheus Unbound*, II, i, 200–202:

> By the forests, lakes, and fountains
> Thro' the many-folded mountains;
> To the rents, and gulphs, and chasms . . .

29–30 Ghouls are haunters of graveyards in Eastern lore; they appear again in "Ulalume" and "The Bells."

34 There is an interesting parallel in the forty-fifth stanza of the first canto of Henry B. Hirst's "Endymion" (first published in the *Southern Literary Messenger* for July 1844):

> The sheeted shadows of old stories, buried
> Long in his memory, weird, and wan, and pale,
> Rose, and with solemn wail
> Told how of Old were demons, who had hurried
> At night from blackest caves, with spells to win
> Man's erring soul to sin.

These lines may be the result of Poe's "collaboration" — for Poe and Hirst were much together when "Dream-Land" and "Endymion" were probably composed.

37 See Revelation 6:11, "And white robes were given unto every one" of the saints.

39 See Mark 5:9, where the unclean spirit said, "My name is Legion, for we are many."

41 Reference is made to the Twenty-third Psalm. Poe used as motto to his story "Shadow," the phrase "Yea, though I walk through the valley of the shadow," the translation preferred by many of the learned.

41–42 The rhyming of "Eldorado" and "shadow" again occurs in Poe's poem "Eldorado" of 1849. He used the name Eldorado for "the place of heart's desire" in his "Letter to B———" of 1831.

44 Compare the last paragraph of "Shadow," for "But we . . . having seen the shadow . . . dared not steadily behold it."

50 See I Corinthians 13:12, "For now we see through a glass darkly, but then face to face."

EULALIE

This is certainly not a major effort, and surely is hardly to be taken too seriously. Poems about girls with pretty names were the fashion, and what more should one ask of them than grace? Vincent Buranelli calls it "such stuff" and adds, "Poe simply had Wordsworth's talent for writing heroically bad verse." [1] But on this occasion he had also Wordsworth's virtue of close observation of nature. There is considerable originality in his use of the visibility by day of Venus, the planet of love. The poem does not seem to have been written for an album, but it is not impossible that it was composed to please Virginia Poe. It was on a manuscript of "Eulalie" that Poe wrote the touching fragment "Deep in Earth" after her death. And "Eulalie" seems to have some relation to "Ulalume," which concerns (among other things) the planet Venus and the loss of Poe's wife.

The inspiration of "Eulalie," I believe, came from three items found together in the *New Mirror* of October 14, 1843 (2:20–21). Two of these were noticed by Ingram (*Edgar Allan Poe*, p. 226), but he presented his material so casually that its importance has been overlooked.

The first of these items is a story reprinted from *The Gift for 1844* (apparently just out), called "Revenge of Leonard Rosier," with a heroine named Eulalie, an uncommon name. Second, on the page facing the beginning of the story, is a poem by Albert Pike, called "Isadore" (reprinted without credit from the *Magnolia* for February 1843), including the lines:

> When first thy love for me was told and thou didst to me cling,
> Thy sweet eyes radiant through their tears, pressing thy lips to mine
> In that old arbour, dear, beneath the overarching vine —
> Thou art lost to me forever, Isadore!
> The moonlight struggled through the vines, and fell upon thy face,

[1] *Edgar Allan Poe* (1959), p. 105. Wilbur, *Poe* (1959), p. 145, based a cryptic interpretation on the readings of a manuscript of doubtful authenticity.

Which thou didst lovingly upturn with pure and trustful gaze . . .
The southern breezes murmured through the dark cloud of thy hair . . .

Third, is a note initialed by N. P. Willis prefacing Pike's poem: "Here is an imagination — we are happy to say *only* an imagination for he has an admirable wife, living and well . . . These lines were written after . . . the thought of losing her . . . suddenly crossed his mind in the stillness of the midnight."

Poe seems to have taken up a challenge (as he did in his stories "Berenicë," "Descent into the Maelstrom," and "William Wilson") and to have written a poem about a marriage with a wife alive and happy.

The poem was composed probably before Poe left Philadelphia early in 1844. His closest friend there at the time, Henry B. Hirst, owned a manuscript in a state earlier than the first printed version, and there is other evidence that he knew of the poem before it was published. Although the name Eulalie was decidedly unusual in America and England before the appearance of Poe's poem in print about July 1, 1845, Hirst has a poem called "Eulalie Vere" — a doubly Poesque title — in his volume *The Coming of the Mammoth*, which was published in time for a presentation copy from the author to Poe to be inscribed "June 1845." Poe's review of the book was in the *Broadway Journal* of July 12. An earlier version of Hirst's poem had been published in *Snowden's Ladies' Companion* for June 1843, but its title was then "Elenor Long."

TEXTS

(*A*) Manuscript (1844), once belonging to Henry B. Hirst; (*B*) *American Review*, July 1845 (2:79); (*C*) *Broadway Journal*, August 9, 1845 (2:65); (*D*) manuscript (about 1845), facsimiled in the Yale List (1959), number 50; (*E*) *The Raven and Other Poems* (1845), p. 24; (*F*) manuscript (1846) facsimiled in the *Bulletin of the New York Public Library*, December 1914 (18:1462); (*G*) J. Lorimer Graham copy of *The Raven* . . . with one change (from "vapour") in spelling (1849); (*H*) *Works* (1850), II, 44; (*Y*) doubted manuscript in a letter in the Lilly Collection at Indiana University; (*Z*) manuscript in the Koester Collection at the University of Texas, probably identical with *A*.

The text followed is the manuscript (*F*) in the New York Public Library since 1892 from the collection of Robert L. Stuart. The first manuscript (*A*) was listed as lot 563 in the sale of Hirst's papers at the Anderson Gallery, May 11, 1921; I noted the variants in the auction room at that time. The

EULALIE

manuscript at Yale (*D*) is in the Aldis Collection. The doubted manuscript (*Y*) is in a letter "to Robert Carter," dated "February 16, 1843," offering it for publication in *The Pioneer*. If it is a forgery it is a skillful one, but the language of the letter is horribly inflated (even for Poe!), and would show that Poe had difficulty in selling this uncontroversial poem. The text is very much like the genuine early manuscript (*A*) — especially in the cancellations in lines 4, 20, and 21. Observe also the extraordinary non-classical form "Astart" for "Astarte" in *Y*.

EULALIE [*F*]

I dwelt alone
In a world of moan,
And my soul was a stagnant tide
Till the fair and gentle Eulalie became my blushing bride —
5   Till the yellow-haired young Eulalie became my smiling bride.

Ah, less, less bright
The stars of the night
Than the eyes of the radiant girl,
And never a flake
10   That the vapor can make
With the moon-tints of purple and pearl
Can vie with the modest Eulalie's most unregarded curl —
Can compare with the bright-eyed Eulalie's most humble
and careless curl.

Now Doubt — now Pain
15   Come never again,
For her soul gives me sigh for sigh
And all day long
Shines bright and strong
Astarté within the sky,
20   While ever to her dear Eulalie upturns her matron eye —
While ever to her young Eulalie upturns her violet eye.

[1844–1845]

VARIANTS

Title: Eulalie — A Song (*B, C, D, E*)   6 Ah, less/And ah (*A, Y, Z*)
4 blushing/*first written* smil (*A, Z*)   10 That the vapor/Their lustre (*A, Z*)

11 With the moon-tints of purple/Of the vapor and gold (*A, Y, Z*); With the morn-tints of purple (*B*)

12 modest/sweet young (*A, Y, Z*); unregarded/humble and careless (*Y*)

13 humble/vagrant (*Y*)

17 And/While (*B, C, D*)

19 Astarté/*first written* The Moon *and changed to* Astart (*Y*); within the/in the purple (*Y*)

20, 21 While/And (*B, C, D*); to her/to it (*A, Z*); *first written* to it *but changed to* to her (*Y*)

NOTES

Title: The name Eulalie seems to be a "bright variant" of Ulalume.

5 Both Mrs. Albert Pike and Virginia Poe were brunettes, like Isadore, but unlike Eulalie.

16 In his unfinished satire on himself, "A Reviewer Reviewed," Poe about 1849 pointed out the parallel in Thomas Moore's "Last Rose of Summer":

> No flower of her kindred,
> No rosebud is nigh,
> To reflect back her blushes
> And give sigh for sigh.

19 Astartë is the Phoenician goddess sometimes identified with the moon and sometimes with the planet Venus. Poe had read a good deal about her, and alludes in "Ulalume" and the tale "Ligeia" to some of her less favorable aspects. Here he refers to her only as the benign patroness of love, the planet Venus. In "To Helen [Whitman]", line 66: "Venuses, unextinguished by the sun," Poe again refers to the planet as visible in the daytime. This phenomenon is far more common than is usually supposed; Venus is often visible to the naked eye on a clear day, if one knows where to look, and I assume that Poe (like me) had seen it for himself.

20 See the introductory note for a parallel in Pike's "Isadore."

THE RAVEN

"The Raven" is Poe's most famous composition. Like the short stories, it was written to please all kinds of readers, and it was immediately successful. Not only was it copied in countless newspapers at once, but it soon was to be found in textbooks and anthologies. Since it is, despite all its elaborate metrical ornamentation, a straightforward narrative, it can be and has been translated into every major language. Woodberry wrote of it: "No great poem ever established itself so immediately, so widely, and so imperishably in men's minds." [1]

[1] *Edgar Allan Poe* (1885), p. 222. In 1922 Woodberry told me he considered it

THE RAVEN

The subject is of universal appeal, for every mature person has lost someone beloved, and even for the firm believer in immortality death is a separation from the living. Poe himself said (in his "Philosophy of Composition") that his poem was emblematic of undying remembrance. The best comment I have seen is the remark of Charles Fenno Hoffman: "It is greater than we know — it is Despair brooding over Wisdom." [2]

There can be no doubt that Poe himself regarded it as a masterpiece. In the *New-York Tribune* of November 26, 1845, Margaret Fuller, who had certainly discussed the poem with him, called it "a rare and finished specimen . . . intended to show [his] artistic skill." On December 15, 1846, he wrote to George Eveleth that while "in the higher qualities of poetry ['The Sleeper'] is better than 'The Raven' . . . The Raven, of course, is far the better as a work of art." He told Frederick Saunders, later for many years chief librarian of the Astor Library, that he was sure that "future generations will be able to sift the gold from the dross, and then 'The Raven' will be beheld, shining above them all as a diamond of purest water." [3] On the other hand, he wrote to his close friend, F. W. Thomas, on May 4, 1845: " 'The Raven' has had a great run . . . but I wrote it for the express purpose of running — just as I did 'The Gold-Bug' . . . the bird beat the bug, though, all hollow."

Evidence of the interest excited by "The Raven" is to be found not only in its innumerable reprintings and many translations but

---

Poe's greatest poem. Curiously enough, no translation was printed in Poe's lifetime. The poem did in time find an ideal translation in France. Stéphane Mallarmé's line-by-line version in rhythmic prose, "Le Corbeau," preserves the spirit of the original, but is a masterpiece of a great French poet, too. It has had since 1875 immense influence on the writers of what we now call free verse.

[2] Quoted in *Selections from the Autobiography of Elizabeth Oakes Smith*, edited by Mary Alice Wyman (Lewiston, Maine, 1924), p. 123.

[3] See Woodberry, *Life*, II, 425. Saunders' unpublished autobiography has recently been found in the New York Public Library. He also mentioned that Poe, on another occasion, when not quite sober, declared his intention to read his poem before Queen Victoria. Poe was also perhaps not sober when he told William Ross Wallace that he thought "The Raven" the "greatest poem that ever was written." (See Joel Benton in *The Forum*, February 1897, p. 733.) There is no reason to doubt that Elmira Shelton wrote, "When Edgar read 'The Raven' he became so wildly excited that he frightened me — when I remonstrated he replied that he could not help it, that it set his brain on fire." (See Phillips, II, 1445.)

also in the imitations that continue to appear. More than a dozen circulated during Poe's lifetime; [4] one of them so pleased him that he polished it, and hence part of "To the Author of the Raven" by Harriet Winslow appears in this volume among the Collaborations below.

The great popularity of "The Raven" gave rise to many stories concerning its genesis. In many cases the development of Poe's poems can be traced through several successive versions, but in the case of "The Raven" no early forms are known. Legend, however, and some remarks by Poe himself indicate that there may have been, in the poet's mind if not on paper, at least two precursors. I give here what is firmly or with some probability known about these.

[4] All those that can be dated before 1850 are listed here: (1) "The Owl," by "Sarles," in the *Evening Mirror* of February 17, 1845 (reprinted in the *Weekly Mirror* of February 22), is the earliest parody yet found. (2) "The Veto," by "Snarles," is in the New York *New World* of February 22, 1845. (3) "The Black Cat" was anonymously contributed to the *Knickerbocker Magazine* for April, issued about March 15, 1845. (4) "The Craven," by "Poh!" in the *Evening Mirror* of March 25, 1845, advertises Gouraud's Medicated Soap. (5) "A Vision," by "Snarles," in the *New World* of April 15, was copied in part by Poe in the next week's *Broadway Journal*, with an introductory note headed "A Gentle Puff." (6) "The Gazelle," by C. C. Cooke, in the *Weekly Mirror* of May 3, in the *Broadway Journal* of May 10, had a complimentary notice by Poe, who said that the author was a boy of fifteen. (7) "The New Castalia," in William W. Lord's *Poems* (1845), parodies "The Raven" and other works of Poe; in a notice of the book in the *Broadway Journal* of May 24, Poe ironically called it plagiarism. (8) "The Whippoorwill," signed "I.," is in the *Weekly Mirror* of June 7, 1845. (9) "The Turkey" appeared in the Boston *Jester* in time to be copied into *Alexander's Weekly Messenger* of Philadelphia for June 25, 1845. The Boston paper's first number is acknowledged in the *Broadway Journal* of June 21 as a "slender imitation" of *Punch*; no copy of this ephemeral magazine has been located. (10) "The Pole Cat," by a "Mr. Johnston," is mentioned in a letter of Abraham Lincoln dated April 18, 1846. The poem probably was not printed. (11) "The Dove," by J. J. Martin, D.D., was copied from an unnamed source into the Brooklyn *Eagle* of January 11, 1847, with a brief note by Walt Whitman, who praised "its graceful spirit of Christianity." (12) Harriet Winslow's poem is in *Graham's* for April 1848. (13) "Moral II," in *The Moral for Authors* (1849), by J. E. Tuel, is discussed by Poe in a letter of June 16, 1849, to Mrs. Richmond as aimed at himself. (14) "The Voices of the Night — a Poe-um, by Professor Shortfellow" is in the Boston *Flag of Our Union* of April 28, 1849. (15) "Oquawka Turning Works for Sale," by J. Chickering, is in the *Spectator* of Oquawka, Illinois, for October 3, 1849. The editor of the paper was Poe's correspondent E. H. N. Patterson.

In compiling the foregoing catalogue, which may not be complete, I gratefully acknowledge the help of Joseph Jackson, Dr. John W. Robertson, Cleveland Rodgers, and Lewis M. Stark.

When wit, and wine, and friends have met
And laughter crowns the festive hour
In vain I struggle to forget
Still does my heart confess thy power

    And fondly turn to thee!

But Octavia do not strive to rob
My heart, of all that soothes its pain
The mournful hope that every throb
Will make it break for thee!

        May the 1st 1827—

TO OCTAVIA

(Written in Octavia Walton's album)

Columbia University Libraries

A PAGE OF THE WILMER MANUSCRIPT

("Dreams" and "The Lake")

Pierpont Morgan Library

Politian - a Tragedy

Scene - Rome in the ___ century.

Characters.

Lalage, an orphan of illustrious family, last of her race, and ward of Di Broglio.
Alessandra, niece of Di Broglio, and betrothed to Castiglione.
Jacinta, servant maid to Lalage.

Duke Di Broglio
Castiglione his son and heir.
San Ozzo, a companion of Castiglione.
Politian, ~~a young noble Roman~~.
Baldazzar his friend.
A Monk.
Ugo
Benito } servants in the family of Di Broglio.
Rupert

Act I. Scene I.

An apartment in the Palazzo of Di Broglio. Traces of a protracted revel. On a marble table some candles burnt to the socket. Masks, a lute, a lady's slipper, cards, a broken bottle are strewn about the floor and on the table. Enter Benito meeting Ugo intoxicated.

Ugo: Oh! is that you Benito (hiccup) are they gone?

Benito: Faith that's a question, Ugo, hard to answer,
But are the bottles empty? — then they're gone.
As for the count San Ozzo who knocked me down
Just now on the staircase as I came up hither
I can with more precision speak of him —
He's gone, I'm sure of that — pretty far gone.

Ugo: Is the bravo gone? (hiccup) where is the buffo-singer?
Did you say his Excellency had departed?
Are all the fiddlers (hiccup) the devil go with them!
I'm positively stupid for ~~a bound of~~ sleep!

Ben: (eying him) Oh you are right — quite right — being as you say
Ugo, a most confounded stupid man.

Ugo: I swear I did say not so, or else I (hiccup) lied.

Ben: I have no doubt, good Ugo, that you lied
Being as you observe, a most notorious liar —
(Ugo sits, and helps himself to wine. Enter Rupert)
Well, master Rupert, what have you done with the count?

Rupert: What should I do with any drunken man?
I spilled liquor from under the table where he lay
And tumbled him into bed.

Ben: I say good Rupert!
Can it be the Duke de Broglio is acquainted
With these unseemly revels of his son?
'Tis a pity in so proper a man
'Tis not a pity in so young a man
And of so gentle blood! Here is a change
I had not look'd to see — he is sadly altered!

Ugo: He is drunk Benito, — did you not say so, Rupert!
Most men are sadly altered when they're drunk
Oh, I am sadly altered when I'm (hiccup) drunk.

Rupert to Ben: You think the Count Castiglione altered —
I think so too — He was, not long ago,
Barring some trivial improprieties
A very nobleman in heart and deed.

EARLY CORRECTIONS FOR "THE RAVEN"

(Poe's letter to Shea, February 3, 1845)

Pierpont Morgan Library

VALENTINE SENT TO MRS. OSGOOD (1846)

Harvard College Library

VALENTINE FOR MARIE LOUISE SHEW

Annabel Lee.

By Edgar A. Poe.

It was many and many a year ago,
    In a kingdom by the sea,
That a maiden there lived whom you may know
    By the name of Annabel Lee; —
And this maiden she lived with no other thought
    Than to love and be loved by me.

I was a child and she was a child,
    In this kingdom by the sea;
But we loved with a love that was more than love —
    I and my Annabel Lee —
With a love that the winged seraphs in Heaven
    Coveted her and me.

And this was the reason that, long ago,
    In this kingdom by the sea,
A wind blew out of a cloud, chilling
    My beautiful Annabel Lee;
So that her high-born kinsmen came
    And bore her away from me,
To shut her up in a sepulchre,
    In this kingdom by the sea.

ANNABEL LEE

Harvard College Library

New York Public Library

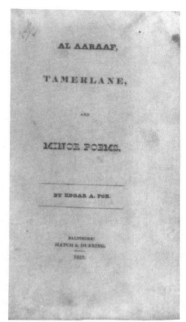

Yale University Library

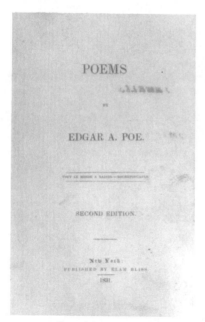

Harvard College Library

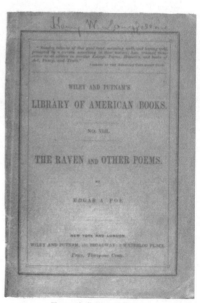

Harvard College Library

POE'S FOUR VOLUMES

THE RAVEN

The Parrot

In his "Philosophy of Composition," which includes a partly fictional account of the planning of "The Raven," Poe said that as a pretext for the repetition of the word "Nevermore," there "arose the idea of a non-reasoning creature capable of speech; and very naturally, a parrot, in the first instance, suggested itself, but was superseded forthwith by a Raven, as equally capable of speech." The word "forthwith" is part of the fictional element. As early as 1829, Poe wrote in "Romance" of "a painted paroquet" who "taught me my alphabet to say." And in Roderick Usher's library (in "The Fall of the House of Usher" of 1839) Poe placed the poem *Ver-Vert* (1734) by Jean Baptiste Louis Gresset, which concerns a parrot to whose remarks more meaning is attached than the poor bird understands.

The parrot as a precursor of the Raven is given support in the otherwise almost valueless *Edgar Allan Poe* (1901), by Colonel John A. Joyce, who tells a story (p. 78) that has a ring of truth about it. Joyce says:

> [Mathew] Brady, the noted photographer, told me in 1866 that he met Poe [in Washington] in March, 1843, at the house of the widow Barrett, where he was rooming on New York Avenue, south side, near the junction of H and Thirteenth Streets, adjoining the "Halls of the Ancients" . . . In one of his "moody moments," as Brady expressed it, he wrote the first draft of "The Raven."

Now the same Colonel Joyce, in the book just referred to (p. 207), claimed that Poe "plagiarized" his "Raven" from an Italian poem called "The Parrot" by Leo Penzoni in the Milan *Art Journal* of 1809. Penzoni and the periodical are unknown to bibliographers, and the English "translation" presented is obviously a concoction by Joyce. But did he get an idea of a parrot from some remark of Brady's?

The Owl

During his stay in Richmond in 1849, Poe discussed the composition of "The Raven" with Susan Talley:

His first intention, he said, had been to write a short poem only, based upon the incident of an *Owl* — a night-bird, the bird of wisdom — with its ghostly presence and inscrutable gaze entering the window of a vault or chamber where he sat beside the bier of the lost *Lenore*. Then he had exchanged the Owl for the Raven, for the sake of the latter's "Nevermore"; and the poem, despite himself, had grown beyond the length originally intended.[5]

She thought several phrases in "The Raven" were possibly survivors from the verses on the Owl, for they were more appropriate for the glaring-eyed bird of Pallas Athena: in particular "the bust of Pallas," "the grave and stern decorum of the countenance it wore," and "his eyes have all the seeming of a demon's."

In this connection it may be noticed that Poe must have seen "The Old Night Owl" by James Rees, dated June 20, in the Philadelphia *Dollar Newspaper* of June 28, 1843, the very same issue in which appeared the first part of Poe's own "Gold-Bug" — of which Rees was to write a dramatization produced on August 8, 1843. In the following extracts I have italicized the parts that may have impressed Poe.

> The old night owl sat in the hollow tree,
> While the winds they passed him fearfully
> *His eye like a demon's glar'd* around,
> *And from his throat came this mournful sound* —
> > Ha, woo! ha, woo! . . .
>
> Far, far aloft, *on the night-wind* floats —
> > Ha, woo! ha, woo! . . .
>
> He courts no kin, in his woody *haunt,*
> But to himself all night doth *chaunt* . . .
> > Ha, woo! ha, woo! . . .

SOURCES

Poe obviously took considerable interest in stories and legends about ravens, and in real birds of the species too. Few little boys sojourning in the British metropolis fail to see the ravens stalking about the Tower of London. The story may not be wholly fabulous that Poe once said to Cornelius Mathews: "That bird [a raven], that imp bird pursues me, mentally, perpetually; I cannot rid

---

[5] Weiss, *Home Life*, p. 185.

myself of its presence; . . . I hear its croak as I used to hear it at Stoke Newington, the flap of its wings in my ear." [6]

Poe's friend Henry B. Hirst kept a bird store and owned a tame raven, and Poe apparently studied it to good purpose.[7] The artist George W. Peck, reviewing Poe's *Works* in the *American Review*, March 1850, wrote (p. 310):

> There is not, in all poetry . . . a more vivid *picture* . . . than in this poem . . . The "tapping," the appearance of the Raven, and all his doings and sayings are . . . perfectly in character (we were once the "unhappy master" of one of these birds) . . . Poe . . . considered what motions a bird of that species would . . . make, and concluded to choose the most natural, as the most fantastic.

In reviewing Dickens' *Barnaby Rudge* in *Graham's* for February 1842, Poe wrote: "The raven . . . might have been made . . . a portion of the conception of the fantastic Barnaby. Its croakings might have been *prophetically* heard in the course of the drama." Dickens' raven Grip is fond of saying "I'm a devil," and on one occasion when Barnaby says, "Grip hopes, but who cares for Grip?" the raven answers, "Nobody." Barnaby's mother warns that dreams and ghosts are abroad, and Dickens mentions a bright red light shining in the raven's eye as he and his owner

[6] This comes from an article by Frances Aymar Mathews in the magazine *Bachelor of Arts* for September 1896, largely reprinted in Phillips, II, 936ff. Cornelius Mathews told his niece about Poe when she was twelve years old. Some of the article concerns a discussion at the Park Theater about putting a raven in Mathews' play *Witchcraft*, and how the playwright later met Poe in the street in the rain, writing his poem by the light of a street lamp. I think Mathews overly imaginative. See also Margaret Alterton, *Origins of Poe's Critical Theory* (Iowa City, 1925), p. 29, for a later account by Miss Mathews, who believed her uncle.

[7] William Sartain, son of the publisher John Sartain, mentions Hirst's bird in a letter dated May 6, 1919, published in the *New York Times* of May 13. In a poem called "To a Ruined Fountain in a Grecian Picture," first published in *Snowden's Ladies' Companion* for September 1842, Hirst wrote of

> Forms of chiefs and maidens bright
> Whom the never-dying raven
> Hath forgotten, nameless even
> In the poet's lay of might.

This stanza may account for Hirst's notion in later years, when harmlessly insane, that he wrote "Poe's Raven." Dr. Matthew O. Woods (Ingram List, no. 898) thought that Hirst's "Unseen River" inspired Poe, but it has nothing about a raven in it and was first printed in the *Broadway Journal* on May 31, 1845, months after the publication of Poe's poem.

look out at the buildings burning during the Gordon riots. It is perhaps significant that Poe began his "Philosophy of Composition" with a reference to a letter he had received from Dickens, and he made his own raven a prophet.[8]

A number of poems have been mentioned as possible contributory sources for "The Raven." Some have been discussed in connection with "Lenore" and "Eulalie" (which like the tale "Eleonora" are akin to the more famous poem), and others are mentioned in my notes on individual parts of the poem below. I relegate some other decidedly peripheral things to a footnote here.[9] But unquestionably the cardinal source of the final stanzaic form of Poe's poem was Elizabeth Barrett's "Lady Geraldine's Courtship" (1844). A few of the lines that probably influenced him follow, from the original first American edition; some were revised in later publications.

> "Eyes," he said, "now throbbing through me! are ye eyes that did undo me?
> Shining eyes, like antique jewels set in Parian statue-stone!
> Underneath that calm white forehead, are ye ever burning torrid,
> O'er the desolate sand-desert of my heart and life undone?
> With a rushing stir, uncertain, in the air, the purple curtain
> Swelleth in and swelleth out around her motionless pale brows;
> While the gliding of the river sends a rippling noise forever
> Through the open casement whitened by the moonlight's slant repose.
> .   .   .   .   .
> Ever, evermore the while in a slow silence she kept smiling . . .

Miss Barrett used the last line quoted as a kind of refrain.

In his review in the *Broadway Journal* of January 11, 1845, of Miss Barrett's *Drama of Exile and Other Poems*, Poe said that "Lady Geraldine's Courtship" combined "the fiercest passion . . . with the most ethereal fancy" but that it was a "palpable imitation" of Tennyson's "Locksley Hall." Poe's dedication of his vol-

---

[8] See Harry T. Baker in *The Nation* for December 22, 1910.

[9] John H. Ingram, in his special edition of *The Raven* (London, 1885) reprinted in full Tennyson's eight lines called "No More," first printed in *The Gem* for 1831, and some lines from Albert Pike's "Isadore" (see my comments on "Eulalie" above). Poe must have known Shelley's wonderful lines called "A Lament," with the refrain "No more — Oh, never more!" And he had seen Philip Pendleton Cooke's "Lady Lenore and Her Lover" in the *Southern Literary Messenger* of January 1836; its possibly significant lines are "What balm sought I? — Forgetfulness" and "Kind Heaven hath sent this gentle one."

ume *The Raven and Other Poems* (1845) to Miss Barrett seems to be a tacit recognition of his own similar debt to her.[10]

The acknowledged source of Poe's metrical form rules out mere alternative suggestions, but one of them is so well known that it must be noticed. Dr. Thomas Holley Chivers had a notion that Poe "plagiarized" from a poem in memory of the doctor's little daughter, "To Allegra Florence in Heaven." In the Macon *Georgia Citizen* of July 12, 1850, he claimed he had sent Poe the following stanza:

> Holy angels now are bending
> To receive thy soul ascending
> Up to Heaven to joys unending,
> And to bliss which is divine;
> While thy pale cold form is fading
> Under Death's dark wing now shading
> Thee with gloom which is pervading
> This poor broken heart of mine!

This does not seem to me much like Poe's poem, but a surprising number of people have thought it so.[11]

COMPOSITION

Since the metrical form of "The Raven" as we have it seems to place its composition not earlier than 1844, the poem must be ascribed to that year. The date of publication very early in 1845 makes such an ascription sure. Nevertheless, various stories about its composition persist.

Susan Archer Talley Weiss recalled that in Poe's conversation with her about the poem in 1849 he told her that it "had lain for

[10] J. H. Ingram says in his edition of *The Raven* (p. 12): "The late [Thomas] Buchanan Read even informed Mr. Robert Browning that Poe had described to him the whole construction of his poem and had stated [that] the suggestion of it lay wholly" in the line about the purple curtain. The debt was observed by Thomas Dunn English in *The Aristidean* for December 1845 and referred to in the *Southern Literary Messenger* for November 1857.

[11] Landon C. Bell demolished the theory in his *Poe and Chivers* (1931). For defenses of Chivers' belief see Joel Benton, *In the Poe Circle* (1899); S. Foster Damon, *Thomas Holley Chivers, Friend of Poe* (New York, 1930); and Charles Henry Watts II, *Thomas Holley Chivers, His Literary Career and His Poetry* (Athens, Ga., 1956). Chivers' letter does not survive, but some of "To Allegra Florence in Heaven" was in print (in the rejection columns) in a Georgia magazine, *The Orion*, for March–April 1843.

more than *ten years* in his desk unfinished, while he would at long intervals work on it, adding a few words or lines, altering, omitting, or even changing the plan or idea of the poem in the endeavor to make of it something which would satisfy himself." [12]

At the Yaddo Artists' Colony near Saratoga, New York, there is a tradition that Poe composed a version of "The Raven" while visiting the Barhyte Trout Pond there in 1843. He is said to have discussed the poem with Ann Van Riper Gillespie Barhyte, wife of the owner, John Barhyte, and herself a poet. Their children, James and Mary, remembered Poe, and the former claimed to have heard Poe reciting parts of the poem aloud in the open air. Poe did sometimes compose aloud, and the story is well witnessed. Since Mrs. Barhyte died in April 1844, the date is fixed as prior to the time Poe composed a version of his poem he finally published. [13] Woodberry (*Life*, II, 113) suggested that it was this (Saratoga) version of the poem that was rejected by Graham in Philadelphia, as described below.

The story told at the General Wayne Inn, Merion, Pennsylvania, that Poe wrote part of "The Raven" there seems to me due to the zeal of a local historian.

We do have a definite story, indubitably true, of how Poe wrote another version of the poem, probably the one he actually submitted for publication. While boarding at the farm of Mr. and Mrs. Patrick Henry Brennan near the Hudson River late in 1844, Poe one day (it is said) sat down and began to write steadily; as he finished a sheet of paper he laid it on the floor. The eldest daughter of the family, fifteen-year-old Martha Susannah (whom Poe called "the little lady"), picked up the sheets and arranged them, and found the work was a poem called "The Raven." The

---

[12] *Home Life*, p. 185.

[13] James Barhyte told his story, about 1881, to the Reverend William Elliot Griffis, a pastor in Schenectady, and to Acosta Nichols, brother of Mrs. Katrina Trask, a founder of the artists' colony. The fullest account is in Marjorie Peabody Waite, *Yaddo Yesterday and Today* (Saratoga Springs, 1933), pp. 16–23; but see also Woodberry's *Life*, II, 112. Griffis published accounts in newspapers in 1884 and 1924. Mary Barhyte, who became a Mrs. Waddell, was in direct communication with Miss Phillips (see *Edgar Allan Poe the Man*, I, 764). Poe's visit is confirmed by an apparently independent reminiscence of Peter Pindar Pease in the *Outlook* of September 1, 1920. Some of the story cannot be confirmed; I find no evidence that Mrs. Barhyte wrote for the New York *Mirror* under the pen-name "Tabitha," and an earlier visit of Poe in 1842 may be an accretion.

fullest account comes from Martha's husband, General James R. O'Beirne, in the New York *Mail and Express* of April 21, 1900. Other members of the family told the story without important discrepancies. Mary Brennan, Martha's mother, told Gill she heard Poe composing viva voce on occasion, and there is family tradition that Poe read his famous poem to her before its publication.[14]

Poe admitted freely that his "Philosophy of Composition," published in *Graham's Magazine* for April 1846, was not expected to be taken as literal truth, but it is a dramatized account of the actual writing of the earliest published version. Poe's descriptions of his intentions are serious, and that he planned the antepenultimate stanza first may be true.

Wholly irresponsible stories of Poe writing his masterpiece after 1845 have been told.[15] And there have been claims that Poe's poem is either largely or in part a translation,[16] and even that it was composed by somebody else.[17]

PUBLICATION

When Poe had decided that the poem was in a form fit for publication in a magazine, he took his manuscript to Philadelphia,

[14] See also Harrison, I, 223; Phillips, II, 883; and Winwar, p. 255. I have myself heard the story from my lifelong friend Henry Mott Brennan, a great-grandson of Patrick and Mary Brennan.

Another story, that Poe wrote "The Raven" when he was drunk, has been heard by almost everybody, but has rarely been printed. It is absurd, for Poe was on his best behavior at the Brennan home. However, he probably had heard the rumor, for he made a sardonic remark to Mary Jane Poitiaux Dixon that he "wrote 'The Raven' when on the verge of delirium tremens." She records this directly in a letter of July 2, 1875 (Ingram List, no. 237).

[15] At Fordham (necessarily 1846–1849), according to Francis Gerry Fairfield in *Scribner's Monthly* for October 1875; at Richmond (1848 or 1849), according to James K. Galt in Harrison's edition, VII, 211; after meeting one Leonora Bouldin in Baltimore (1847 or later), given only as a query in the reminiscences of R. D. Unger, M.D. (Ingram List, no. 402).

[16] From the Italian of "Leo Penzoni" (discussed above); the Chinese of Kia Yi (Chia I); the Persian of an author unnamed. See Ingram's edition of *The Raven*, p. 84; Killis Campbell's *Poems*, p. 232; and Phillips, II, 1646.

[17] In addition to the notion of poor Henry B. Hirst (see footnote 7, above), there is a story that Poe merely polished a piece by an inmate of an asylum, both found never to have existed, according to Appleton Morgan, quoted by Harrison, I, 260. A malicious story that Poe received the poem as a contribution from one Samuel Fenwick (unknown to researchers) and purloined it when Fenwick died — a story refuted by J. H. Ingram in his edition of *The Raven* — is discussed in *American Notes and Queries* for January 1943.

where he tried to sell it. Horace Wemyss Smith related that he was in George R. Graham's office when the poem was offered, and declared that he carried to Poe fifteen dollars, "contributed by Mr. Graham, Mr. Godey, Mr. [Morton] McMichael and others, who condemned the poem, but gave the money as charity." [18] Mrs. Weiss in her *Home Life of Poe* (p. 107) records that William Johnston, Graham's office boy, said he was present when Poe read the poem, but that he saw no subscription taken up. She sensibly remarks that this was probably done when the office boy was not in the room. In his still unprinted "Literary America" manuscript, Poe himself refers to a rejection of his "Raven."

He had better luck with George Hooker Colton, a young man who was establishing *The American Review: A Whig Journal* as a "five-dollar monthly" in New York. For its second number (February 1845) he bought "The Raven," probably for fifteen dollars, fair compensation at space rates.[19] The piece was printed with a pseudonym, "—— Quarles," appropriate to an emblematic popular poem since the best-known work of Francis Quarles is called *Emblems* (1635) and his verses were long treasured by people who read little else save the Bible. Some doubts of the success of the poem led Colton to print the following introduction, in which it is thought Poe had a hand.

The following lines from a correspondent — besides the deep quaint strain of the sentiment, and the curious introduction of some ludicrous touches amidst the serious and impressive, as was doubtless intended by the author — appear to us one of the most felicitous specimens of unique rhyming which

[18] See Edwin Wolf 2nd, "Horace Wemyss Smith's Recollections of Poe," *The Library Chronicle* (Philadelphia, 1951), 17:90–103. This important article shows that the reminiscences were related to Hyman Polock Rosenbach, and not recollected by him as many Poe scholars have thought.

[19] Fifteen dollars is the sum known from family tradition, according to Cullen B. Colton, who pointed out in *American Literature* for November 1938 that his great-uncle wrote James Russell Lowell on April 7, 1845, that it was less than twenty dollars. R. H. Stoddard gave the sum in his *Poems by . . . Poe* (1877) from "recollection of the publisher," as ten dollars, and this striking story is repeated constantly by biographers. Thomas Dunn English, writing in *The Independent* of November 5, 1896, thought it was thirty dollars; it is possible that a bonus was given later. The story in *The South* for November 1875 that "the late David W. Holley" bought the poem for five dollars is pure fiction. For J. H. Whitty's statement that Poe told F. W. Thomas he signed the poem "Quarles," "for a whim" and planned originally not to acknowledge it if it were a failure, see Phillips, II, 940.

has for some time met our eye. The resources of English rhythm for varieties of melody, measure, and sound, producing corresponding diversities of effect, have been thoroughly studied, much more perceived, by very few poets in the language. While the classic tongues, especially the Greek, possess, by power of accent, several advantages for versification over our own, chiefly through greater abundance of spondaic feet, we have other and very great advantages of sound by the modern usage of rhyme. Alliteration is nearly the only effect of that kind which the ancients had in common with us. It will be seen that much of the melody of "The Raven" arises from alliteration, and the studious use of similar sounds in unusual places. In regard to its measure, it may be noted that if all the verses were like the second, they might properly be placed merely in short lines, producing a not uncommon form; but the presence in all the others of one line — mostly the second in the verse — which flows continuously, with only an aspirate pause in the middle, like that before the short line in the Sapphic Adonic, while the fifth has at the middle pause no similarity of sound with any part beside, give the versification an entirely different effect. We could wish the capacities of our noble language, in prosody, were better understood. — ED. AM. REVIEW.

If Poe had doubts about his poem, they vanished before publication. "The Raven" is in the third sheet of the magazine, not the last, and was printed off before the issue was complete. Poe showed the poem to N. P. Willis, and they decided that it should be first published with the author's name. In the *Evening Mirror* of January 29, 1845, it was so published with Willis' famous introduction:

We are permitted to copy (in advance of publication) from the 2d No. of the American Review, the following remarkable poem by EDGAR POE. In our opinion, it is the most effective single example of "fugitive poetry" ever published in this country; and unsurpassed in English poetry for subtle conception, masterly ingenuity of versification, and consistent, sustaining of imaginative lift and "pokerishness." It is one of these "dainties bred in a book" which we *feed* on. It will stick to the memory of everybody who reads it.[20]

Poe also sent the poem to Benjamin B. Minor of the *Southern Literary Messenger*, who published it in the March number with the following introduction, of which the second paragraph is quoted from the New York *Morning Express* of February 5, 1845.

The following poem first appeared, we think, in the Evening Mirror; though intended for the American Review. It has since been frequently republished with the highest approbation. Still we take pleasure in presenting

[20] Willis' quotation is from *Love's Labours Lost*, IV, ii, 25; "pokerish" means spooky — I have heard it used.

it to our readers, who must remember with delight many of the contributions of Mr. Poe to the Messenger.

Mr. Brooks, editor of the New York *Express*, says:

There is a poem in this book, (The American Whig Review,) which far surpasses anything that has been done even by the best poets of the age: — indeed there are none of them who could pretend to enter into competition with it, except, perhaps, Alfred Tennyson; and he only to be excelled out of measure. Nothing can be conceived more effective than the settled melancholy of the poet bordering upon sullen despair, and the personification of this despair in The Raven settling over the poet's door, to depart thence "Nevermore." In power and originality of versification the whole is no less remarkable than it is, psychologically, *a wonder*.

Within a week of the poem's first publication, Poe eliminated its most obvious fault, the "bad rhyme" in the eleventh stanza, sending the changes to J. A. Shea for the *New-York Tribune*, but he made other changes occasionally until the last months of his life, and even then was not satisfied with a few words and phrases. We know which these are because he talked them over with Susan Talley, who gives a record of what he pointed out to her. She comments that she knew he discussed the poem with at least two other persons in Richmond.[21]

When the latest version of "The Raven" was published in the Richmond *Semi-Weekly Examiner* of September 25, 1849, the editor, John M. Daniel, one of those who had discussed the poem with Poe, added a long introduction.[22] This is here abridged, but

[21] Weiss, *Home Life*, pp. 186–193. I think discussions of this kind are the basis of reminiscenses by some persons who long afterward thought their opinions had been sought while the poem was being composed. One of these was the witty Philadelphia editor, John Stevenson DuSolle, who wrote Mrs. Weiss that he and other "writers for the press" had been consulted (Weiss, *Home Life*, pp. 99, 184). Poe seems even to have discussed the poem with Sarah Anna Lewis (!), who, in her sonnet "First Meeting," reprinted from the *Home Journal* of February 11, 1880, in J. H. Ingram's *Edgar Allan Poe* (II, 262), wrote: ". . . to teach to me poetic art/Thy 'Raven', piecemeal, thou didst take apart." One pleasant — even if fabulous — tale describes the poet as reading the poem, stanza by stanza, to several friends at the tavern of Sandy Welsh in Ann Street, and accepting their assistance. This story was first printed in *Scribner's* for October 1875 by Francis Gerry Fairfield, who fathered it on DuSolle. It has been usually completely rejected by biographers; even Hervey Allen, *Israfel* (1926, p. 597; 1934, p. 478), calls it "fancy run wild." But no one has considered the possibility of a consultation after publication, and the story persists among newspapermen in New York. Directories list Alexander Welsh's restaurant in the vicinity named, and once his place is described as a terrapin-bar, which might well attract a Baltimorean.

[22] The full text is reprinted by Whitty in *Complete Poems* (1911), p. 197.

THE RAVEN

so as to include the statements most probably inspired by the poet's conversation:

Mr. Edgar A. Poe lectured again last night . . . and concluded . . . with . . . The Raven . . .[23] we furnish our readers, to-day, with the only correct copy ever published — which we are enabled to do by the courtesy of Mr. Poe himself . . . To build theories, principles, religions . . . is the business of the argumentative, not of the poetic faculty. The business of poetry is to minister to the sense of the beautiful . . . That sense is a simple element in our nature . . . the art which ministers to it may . . . be said to have an ultimate end in so ministering. This the "Raven" does in an eminent degree. It has no allegory in it, no purpose — or a very slight one . . . In the last stanza is an image of settled despair . . . which throws a gleam of meaning and allegory over the entire poem — making it all a personification of that passion — but that stanza is . . . unconnected with the original poem. The "Raven" itself is a mere narrative of simple events. A bird . . . taught to speak by some former master, is lost in a stormy night, is attracted by the light of a student's window . . . and flutters against it. Then against the door. The student fancies it a visitor, opens the door, and the chance word uttered by the bird suggests to him memories and fancies connected with . . . his dead sweetheart or wife. Such is the poem. The last stanza is an afterthought . . . the "Raven" is a gem of art.

TEXTS

(A) *American Review*, February 1845 (1:143–145); (B) New York *Evening Mirror*, January 29, 1845, reprinted from same types in the weekly *New-York Mirror* for February 8; (C) *Southern Literary Messenger*, March 1845 (11:186–188); (D) letter to J. Augustus Shea, February 3, 1845, now in the Pierpont Morgan Library (lines 60–66); (E) *New-York Tribune*, February 4, 1845; (F) *Broadway Journal*, February 8, 1845 (1:90); (G) *Broadway Journal*, May 24, 1845 (1:330; lines 3–4 in a review); (H) London *Critic*, June 14, 1845; (J) *The Raven and Other Poems* (New York, 1845; copyright September 12), pp. 1–5; (K) manuscript written as an autograph, late 1845 (lines 103–108); (L) New York *Literary Emporium*, December 1845 (2:376–378); (M) *Graham's Magazine* for April 1846 (28:165–167; many lines quoted in "The Philosophy of Composition"); (N) Philadelphia *Saturday Courier*, July 25, 1846; (P) Rufus W. Griswold's *Poets and Poetry of America* (8th edition, published May 29, 1847) pp. 432–433; (Q) *Southern Literary Messenger*, January 1848 (14:34–35; lines 1–6, 9–18, 37–108, in Philip Pendleton Cooke's "Edgar A. Poe"); (R) manuscript "Inscribed to Dr. S. A. Whittaker of Phoenixville [Pennsylvania]," September 1848; (S) J. Lorimer Graham copy of *The Raven* (1845) with manuscript revisions, 1846–1849; (T) Richmond *Semi-Weekly Examiner*, September 25, 1849; (U) Philadelphia *Saturday Courier*, November 3, 1849; (W) *Works* (1850), II, 7–11.

[23] For an account of Poe's public reading of "The Raven" in Boston, see the Annals for 1845.

POEMS: 1836–1844

The first printing is certainly that of the *American Review* (*A*); the first publication, that in the *Evening Mirror* (*B*), as described in Willis's introduction. Poe arranged for the printing (from the early version) in the *Southern Literary Messenger* (*C*), and in his letter to Shea (*D*) he sent the first important changes, which were followed in the *New-York Tribune* (*E*). Poe's known connection with the *Broadway Journal* validates the texts there (*F, G*). The London printing (*H*) probably was arranged by Richard Hengist Horne. The text in Poe's volume of 1845 (*J*) is the first edition in a book by the author; but the poem's first appearance in a book was an unauthorized reprint in the second edition of *A Plain System of Elocution* by George Vandenhoff, a work advertised in the *Broadway Journal* of April 19, 1845.

The readings suggest that the text in the *Literary Emporium* (*L*) was authorized. That in Griswold's anthology (*P*) is in half-lines; Poe approved of it in a letter postmarked merely "New York, April 19," preserved in the Boston Public Library; the book was advertised in the *Literary World* of May 29, 1847. Both *Saturday Courier* texts (*N, U*) are validated by an introduction to the second.

The manuscript version of lines 103–108 (*K*) is certainly genuine; it was in the collection of Thomas McKee before 1900, and is now in the William H. Koester Collection at the University of Texas. The genuine complete manuscript (*R*) is now owned by Colonel Richard Gimbel, who recently issued a facsimile. It is obviously referred to in Poe's letter of October 18, 1848, to Eli Bowen, published in *American Notes and Queries*, January 1965.

Alexander McKelly's statement that he had set up "The Raven" and preserved the manuscript and sold it, recorded in *The Bookman* (New York) for June 1898, is unreliable; he was head printer for Graham, and probably set up "The Philosophy of Composition," and he did save some manuscripts of Poe; I think he did not really save that of bits of "The Raven" but only liked to think he did. A "complete manuscript" reproduced in *Muse: Anthology of Modern Poetry* (New York, 1939) is generally regarded as a recent concoction. "Poe's" letter of "May 10, 1849," promising an autograph transcript of the poem, is a forgery.

The text here followed is that of the Richmond *Semi-Weekly Examiner* (*T*), the last authorized version published during Poe's lifetime. The introduction accompanying it indicated that Poe had arranged for its publication in final form.

THE RAVEN [*T*]

Once upon a midnight dreary, while I pondered, weak and
    weary,
Over many a quaint and curious volume of forgotten lore —
While I nodded, nearly napping, suddenly there came a tap-
    ping,
As of some one gently rapping, rapping at my chamber door —

5   " 'Tis some visiter," I muttered, "tapping at my chamber
door —
        Only this and nothing more."

Ah, distinctly I remember it was in the bleak December;
And each separate dying ember wrought its ghost upon the
floor.
Eagerly I wished the morrow; — vainly I had sought to borrow
10 From my books surcease of sorrow — sorrow for the lost
Lenore —
For the rare and radiant maiden whom the angels name
Lenore —
        Nameless *here* for evermore.

And the silken, sad, uncertain rustling of each purple curtain
Thrilled me — filled me with fantastic terrors never felt be-
fore;
15 So that now, to still the beating of my heart, I stood repeating
" 'Tis some visiter entreating entrance at my chamber door —
Some late visiter entreating entrance at my chamber door; —
        This it is and nothing more."

Presently my soul grew stronger; hesitating then no longer,
20 "Sir," said I, "or Madam, truly your forgiveness I implore;
But the fact is I was napping, and so gently you came rapping,
And so faintly you came tapping, tapping at my chamber door,
That I scarce was sure I heard you" — here I opened wide the
door; ——
        Darkness there and nothing more.

25 Deep into that darkness peering, long I stood there wonder-
ing, fearing,
Doubting, dreaming dreams no mortal ever dared to dream
before;
But the silence was unbroken, and the stillness gave no token,
And the only word there spoken was the whispered word,
"Lenore?"

This I whispered, and an echo murmured back the word,
"Lenore!"
30   Merely this and nothing more.

Back into the chamber turning, all my soul within me
burning,
Soon again I heard a tapping somewhat louder than before.
"Surely," said I, "surely that is something at my window
lattice;
Let me see, then, what thereat is, and this mystery explore —
35 Let my heart be still a moment and this mystery explore; —
'Tis the wind and nothing more!"

Open here I flung the shutter, when, with many a flirt and
flutter,
In there stepped a stately Raven of the saintly days of yore;
Not the least obeisance made he; not a minute stopped or
stayed he;
40 But, with mien of lord or lady, perched above my chamber
door —
Perched upon a bust of Pallas just above my chamber door —
Perched, and sat, and nothing more.

Then this ebony bird beguiling my sad fancy into smiling,
By the grave and stern decorum of the countenance it wore,
45 "Though thy crest be shorn and shaven, thou," I said, "art
sure no craven,
Ghastly grim and ancient Raven wandering from the Nightly
shore —
Tell me what thy lordly name is on the Night's Plutonian
shore!"
Quoth the Raven "Nevermore."

Much I marvelled this ungainly fowl to hear discourse so
plainly,
50 Though its answer little meaning — little relevancy bore;

For we cannot help agreeing that no living human being
Ever yet was blessed with seeing bird above his chamber
    door —
Bird or beast upon the sculptured bust above his chamber
    door,
           With such name as "Nevermore."

55   But the Raven, sitting lonely on the placid bust, spoke only
That one word, as if his soul in that one word he did outpour.
Nothing farther then he uttered — not a feather then he
    fluttered —
Till I scarcely more than muttered "Other friends have flown
    before —
On the morrow *he* will leave me, as my Hopes have flown
    before."
60   Then the bird said "Nevermore."

Startled at the stillness broken by reply so aptly spoken,
"Doubtless," said I, "what it utters is its only stock and store
Caught from some unhappy master whom unmerciful Disaster
Followed fast and followed faster till his songs one burden
    bore —
65   Till the dirges of his Hope that melancholy burden bore
          Of 'Never — nevermore.' "

But the Raven still beguiling my sad fancy into smiling,
Straight I wheeled a cushioned seat in front of bird, and bust
    and door;
Then, upon the velvet sinking, I betook myself to linking
70   Fancy unto fancy, thinking what this ominous bird of yore —
What this grim, ungainly, ghastly, gaunt, and ominous bird
    of yore
          Meant in croaking "Nevermore."

This I sat engaged in guessing, but no syllable expressing
To the fowl whose fiery eyes now burned into my bosom's
    core;

75 This and more I sat divining, with my head at ease reclining
On the cushion's velvet lining that the lamp-light gloated
o'er,
But whose velvet-violet lining with the lamp-light gloating
o'er,
She shall press, ah, nevermore!

Then, methought, the air grew denser, perfumed from an
unseen censer
80 Swung by seraphim whose foot-falls tinkled on the tufted
floor.
"Wretch," I cried, "thy God hath lent thee — by these angels
he hath sent thee
Respite — respite and nepenthe from thy memories of Lenore;
Quaff, oh quaff this kind nepenthe and forget this lost
Lenore!"
Quoth the Raven "Nevermore."

85 "Prophet!" said I, "thing of evil! — prophet still, if bird or
devil! —
Whether Tempter sent, or whether tempest tossed thee here
ashore,
Desolate yet all undaunted, on this desert land enchanted —
On this home by Horror haunted — tell me truly, I implore —
Is there — *is* there balm in Gilead? — tell me — tell me, I
implore!"
90 Quoth the Raven "Nevermore."

"Prophet!" said I, "thing of evil! — prophet still, if bird or
devil!
By that Heaven that bends above us — by that God we both
adore —
Tell this soul with sorrow laden if, within the distant Aidenn,
It shall clasp a sainted maiden whom the angels name Lenore —
95 Clasp a rare and radiant maiden whom the angels name
Lenore."
Quoth the Raven "Nevermore."

THE RAVEN

"Be that word our sign of parting, bird or fiend!" I shrieked,
   upstarting —
"Get thee back into the tempest and the Night's Plutonian
   shore!
Leave no black plume as a token of that lie thy soul hath
   spoken!
100 Leave my loneliness unbroken! — quit the bust above my
   door!
Take thy beak from out my heart, and take thy form from off
   my door!"
          Quoth the Raven "Nevermore."

And the Raven, never flitting, still is sitting, *still* is sitting
On the pallid bust of Pallas just above my chamber door;
105 And his eyes have all the seeming of a demon's that is dream-
   ing,
And the lamp-light o'er him streaming throws his shadow on
   the floor;
And my soul from out that shadow that lies floating on the
   floor
       Shall be lifted — nevermore!

                [1844–1849]

VARIANTS

1 while/as (*U*)
3 nodded/pondered (*G*); tapping/
rapping (*G*)
4 rapping, rapping/tapping, tapping,
(*G*)
9 sought/tried (*A, B, C, E, F, H, L, P*)
11 name/named (*Q, U*)
18 This it is/That it is (*C, L, N, U*);
Only this (*Q*)
26 mortal/mortals (*W*)
27 stillness/darkness (*A, B, C, E, F,
H, J, L, N, P, U*)
28 Lenore?/Lenore! (*A, B, C, E, F, H,
J, L, N, P, U*)
31 Back/Then (*A, B, C, E, F, H, L,
P*)
32 again I heard/I heard again (*A, B,
C, E, F, H, J, L, N, P, U*); somewhat/
something (*W*)

39 a minute/an instant (*A, B, C, E, F,
H, J, L, N, P, Q, U*); a moment (*M*)
43 ebony/ebon (*Q*)
51 living human/sublunary (*A, C, E*)
55 the placid/that placid (*R*)
60 Then the bird said/Quoth the raven
(*A, B, C*)
61 Startled/Wondering (*A, C*)
64 till his songs one burden bore/so,
when Hope he would adjure (*A, B,
C*); songs/song (*H*)
65 that melancholy/the melancholy
(*D, E, F, H, L, P*; melancholy *changed
in S, but the change erased; only*
sa[d] *can be read*)
65 Stern Despair returned, instead of
the sweet Hope he dared adjure — (*A,
B, C*)
66 Of 'Never — nevermore.'/That sad

answer, "Nevermore!" (*A*, *B*, *C*);
'Nevermore — ah, nevermore!' (*D*, *E*);
Of "Nevermore" — of "Nevermore."
(*F*, *H*, *L*, *P*, *Q*)
67 my sad fancy/all my sad soul (*A*,
B, *C*, *E*, *F*, *H*, *J*, *L*, *N*, *P*, *Q*, *R*, *U*,
W); all my fancy (*S*)

73 This/Thus (*H*, *U*)
80 seraphim whose/angels whose faint
(*A*, *B*, *C*, *E*, *F*, *H*, *J*, *L*, *N*, *P*, *Q*, *U*)
83 Quaff, oh quaff/Let me quaff (*A*,
C, *E*)
105 demon's/demon (*A*, *B*, *C*, *E*, *F*, *H*,
K, *L*, *P*)

Except for the punctuation after "Lenore" in line 28, where the introduction of the interrogation mark by Poe in *R* and *S* seems a significant change, no record is made here of the many variations in punctuation, capitalization, spelling — Griswold's text (*P*) is peppered with apostrophes, e.g., "ponder'd" — or the use of italics.

NOTES

1 The opening of Poe's poem resembles the Thirty-third Ode of the *Anacreontea*; some lines in Thomas Moore's version read:

> 'Twas noon of night, when round the pole
> The sullen bear is seen to roll . . .
> An infant at that dreary hour
> Came weeping to my silent bower . . .
> I heard the bitter night-wind blow; . . .
> I trimm'd my lamp and op'd the gate.
> 'Twas Love! the little wandering sprite . . .
> Fondly I take him in and raise
> The dying embers' cheering blaze.

Moore quoted the first line of the ode in the original Greek, which is more strikingly like Poe's first line than is Moore's English version. The parallel has been thrice reported independently: by John Patterson in *Poet-Lore* for July–September 1897, by Ernest Riedel in *Classical Weekly* for February 14, 1927, and by Gilbert Highet in *The Classical Tradition* (1947), p. 629.

1–2 The hair of the heroine of Poe's tale "Ligeia" was "blacker than the raven wings of the midnight," as Richard Wilbur (*Poe*, p. 144) points out; Frances Winwar (p. 75) remarks on the foreshadowing in the tiny couplet of 1824, called "Poetry."

2 Poe questioned Susan Talley about the propriety of the "many" volumes rather than one (Weiss, *Home Life*, p. 187). But a scholar often turns from one volume to another and back again.

7 The following is from "The Gamester," the thirty-third chapter of William Wirt's *Old Bachelor* (Richmond, 1814), page 230: "It was a few weeks after the death of my mother, that on the dark and stormy night in December, I was awakened by a loud knocking, and the cries of children at my door." The chapter was contributed to Wirt's book by David Watson and seems to have inspired an incident in Poe's "William Wilson." (See Richard Beale Davis, "Poe and William Wirt," *American Literature*, November 1944, p. 218n.) The reader will perhaps recall the "Stanzas" by Keats, beginning:

> In a drear-nighted December,
> Too happy, happy tree,
> Thy branches ne'er remember . . .

THE RAVEN

No earlier notice has been taken of this by commentators; the poem was not published in England until 1848, but it was in the famous Galignani edition (of Coleridge, Keats, and Shelley), from which American reprints were made in the early 1830's.

7–12 Mrs. Weiss noticed that the arrangement of the rhymes in this stanza is different from that in the others (*Home Life*, p. 188).

10 See notes above on "Lenore." The heroine is almost surely an imaginary person, as Henry H. Harper argues well in his rather slight introduction to a special edition of *The Raven* (Boston, 1927), for Poe was concerned from his youth with the loss of beautiful ladies, but some writers see Virginia Clemm Poe as the lady's prototype. William Fearing Gill (*Life*, 1877, p. 140), suggested that Poe saw his wife "cold and breathless" — probably in a faint — and thought she had died. Another more incredible fancy is that of H. Alois Biedy, who decided the poem concerned the relations of the zodiacal Virgo (Virginia and Lenore for him) and the constellation Corvus, which is not zodiacal. See his *Mysteries of Poe's "Raven"* (New York, 1936), *passim*.

12 "Nameless here" means "not called on by name or spoken to in this world."

13–14 These lines were called fanciful by George W. Eveleth, writing Poe on January 19, 1847. Poe commented on the rhyme scheme in "Marginalia," no. 146. Purple may be a symbol of wealth and of mourning.

20 A parrot is addressed as "Sir, or Madam" and a talking raven appears on the next page in the forty-first of the *Noctes Ambrosianae*, contributed to *Blackwood's Magazine* for March 1829 by "Christopher North" (John Wilson). This correspondence was noticed in the *Southern Literary Messenger* of November 1857. Poe's visitor is not so addressed after it is known to be a bird. Poe told Thomas H. Lane that he wrote his poem "to see how near to the absurd I could come without over-stepping the dividing line" (see Phillips, II, 896).

26 Compare "Ligeia": "a melody more than mortal . . . aspirations which mortality had never before known."

27 In the *Saturday Evening Post* of April 2, 1842, there is copied a free translation of Ferdinand Freiligrath's "Gesicht des Reisenden" (1835), called "The Spectre Caravan," of which lines 9, 10, and 17 may be pertinent:

And the stillness was unbroken, save at moments by a cry,
From some stray belated vulture, sailing blackly down the sky . . .
On they came, their hueless faces towards Mecca, evermore!

Compare also *Politian*, VI, 18: "I heard not any voice except thine own."

28–29 Compare Keats, "Lamia," II, 269–270: " 'Lamia!' he shriek'd; and nothing but the shriek/With its sad echo did the silence break."

36 See *Othello*, IV, iii, 53: "Hark, who is't that knocks? — It's the wind." See Poe's "Tell-Tale Heart" for "It is nothing but the wind in the chimney."

37 Poe told Mrs. Weiss he thought "shutter" too commonplace. George W. Peck in the *American Review* for March 1850 (p. 310) cites Dr. Johnson as giving one meaning of "flirt" as "a quick, elastic motion."

38–47 "The Dying Raven" of the elder Richard Henry Dana has "black plumage . . . like the armor of steeled knight of Palestine." The poem was very well known and is mentioned in the controversy known as "The Long-fellow War" as having no relation to Poe's poem. There is little in Dana's poem, lamenting a raven, a prophet of spring, slain by a farmer's snare, that resembles Poe's. But the controversy between Poe and "Outis" (who may have been Poe himself) is complicated, and the disclaimer of any relation may not be candid.

41 General O'Beirne (cited in the introductory commentary above) said that in the big room of the Brennan farmhouse there really was a plaster cast of a bust of Minerva on a shelf above the casing of the door. Such hel-meted busts of the goddess of wisdom, the patroness of scholars (as Poe pointed out in his "Philosophy of Composition"), were popular; Mrs. Browning in her letter of April 1846 to Poe (quoted by Woodberry, *Life*, II, 164) said an acquaintance of hers had one and, after reading the poem, could not "bear to look at it in the twilight."

45 A cowardly knight sometimes had his head shaved. The pun on "knightly" is surely deliberate; it is one of the humorous touches referred to in the *American Review* introduction. Ravens may indeed be knightly. Patricia Ann Edwards points out that in the thirteenth chapter (pt. I, bk. II, ch. v) of *Don Quixote* there is a reference to the tradition that King Arthur never died, but was turned into a raven (*cuervo*) by enchantment. It was this story, no doubt, that led the Duchess of Kendal to think the soul of her lover, George I, flew to her window, in the form of a raven after his death. Byron, crediting Horace Walpole, mentions this legend in a footnote to his *Bride of Abydos,* II, xxviii, 48

46 Ravens are proverbially long-lived. See, for example, Pliny's *Natural History*, VII, xlvii.

47 Compare Horace, *Carmina*, I, iv, 16f., "Iam te premet Nox fabulaeque Manes,/et domus exilis Plutonia." In *Harper's Latin Dictionary*, the adjec-tive from which Poe's word is derived is cited only from this passage. See W. P. Trent's edition of *The Raven* (1894), page 5.

48 The word "nevermore" is commonplace in English poetry. See many examples collected by Robert S. Forsythe in *American Literature* for January 1936, especially from Shelley, Tennyson, and Mrs. Hemans, who, as is men-tioned in the notes to "Lenore" above, rhymes it with "Leonor." Henry E. Shepherd, in a speech at the unveiling of the Poe Monument, quoted by Gill (*Life*, 1877, p. 300), thought Poe had in mind Shakespeare's *King Henry IV*, Part One, I, iii, 224f.: "I'll have a starling shall be taught to speak/Nothing but 'Mortimer.' " Professor Joseph Jones, in *American Literature* for May 1958, called attention to an anonymous poem, "The Raven, or the Power of

Conscience," in *Fraser's Magazine* of March 1839, where a bird (who is called a prophet) speaks only the name of his master, "Sir Hildebrand."

50 Compare "The Gold-Bug," where a piece of parchment has a device which "suggested some meaning — some relevancy."

53 Mrs. Weiss (*Home Life*, p. 189) said that Poe worried about what beast could assume the position described, and smiled "one of his rare humorous smiles" when she suggested a mouse could do it.

54 According to James Barhyte's recollections, as a boy at Saratoga he heard Poe composing some of "The Raven" aloud and remarked, "Who ever heard of a bird named 'Nevermore'?" — whereupon Poe exclaimed, "Just the thing . . . I need!" This story (from Marjorie Peabody Waite's *Yaddo*, p. 21) is too amusing to omit — but I am not sure that I believe it.

58 Lambert A. Wilmer's *Merlin* (1827), I, iv, 19, reads: "Like other friends he leaves thee in thy need." Since the play concerns Poe's romance with Elmira Royster, this may well be something he recalled.

64 Compare *Midsummer Night's Dream*, III, ii, 416: "I followed fast, but faster did he fly."

76f. Poe considered "lining" here a blunder, but told Mrs. Weiss he was unwilling to sacrifice the whole stanza. He had used "velvet violet" in his parody on Drake in 1836. The word "gloated" has a rare meaning, "reflected light from," but, as in "The Bells," line 22, has usually some sinister implication.

79ff. There are parallel passages in "Eleonora," in which the heroine promised that she would "give . . . indications of her presence . . . with perfume from the censers of the angels," and in "Ligeia," where in "the rich lustre thrown from the censer" there was "a gentle foot-fall upon the carpet." See Richard Wilbur, *Poe*, p. 144.

80 The tinkling has been unduly criticized. Professor William Gravely tells me that in an unprinted manuscript Thomas Dunn English said that he infuriated Poe by asking if the angels "had bells on their toes." Poe wrote Eveleth on December 15, 1846, that he wanted the angels' feet to do something supernatural. Whitty (in *Complete Poems*, 1911, p. 195) reports that F. W. Thomas said Poe referred him to Isaiah 3:16, which describes the daughters of Zion "making a tinkling with their feet." If so, Poe ignored the unpleasant context.

82 Nepenthe is described in Spenser's *Faerie Queene*, book IV, canto iii, stanza 43, as

> . . . a drink of sovereign grace,
> Deviséd by the Gods, for to assuage
> Heart's grief . . .
> . . . Sweet peace and quiet age
> It doth establish in the troubled mind.

This is the draught (from Egypt) which Helen gave her guests in *Odyssey* IV, 219–220, but the form there, as in *Comus*, line 675, is "Nepenthes."

85 The passage may echo Agamemnon's speech to the seer Chalcas in *Iliad*, I, 106f., in Pope's version, "Augur accurst! denouncing mischief still,/Prophet of plagues, forever boding ill."

There are many ancient, medieval, and even modern stories about ravens as prophetic — they were sacred to Apollo. Pliny has much to say of them in his *Natural History* — in VII, lii, he says, "It is stated that in Proconnesus, the soul of Aristeas was seen to fly out of his mouth in the form of a raven (a most fabulous story)," and in X, xv, that ravens are "the only birds that comprehend their auspices, for when the guests of Medus were assassinated [a crime of which no more is known] they [the ravens] all took their departure" from the Peloponnesus and Attica.

87–88 The rhyme was almost surely not imperfect for Poe; the old pronunciation "ha'nt" survives today in Tennessee and Kentucky.

89 Compare Jeremiah 8:22: "Is there no balm in Gilead . . . ?" In Genesis 37:25 we read of Ishmaelites "from Gilead . . . bearing spicery and balm and myrrh," but Poe's reference, as in *Politian*, IV, 30–31, and "The Angel of the Odd," is purely figurative.

92 Compare Henry Cary's translation of Dante's *Inferno*, I, 127f.: " 'Bard! by that God whom thou dids't adore,/I beseech thee.' "

93 Poe uses the unusual spelling "Aidenn" (Arabic *Adn*: Eden) also in "The Conversation of Eiros and Charmion" and "The Power of Words." Edna B. Triplett in *American Literature* for November 1938 pointed out a poem in *Graham's* for July 1841 (when Poe was the editor), called "The Dervish, an Eastern Legend," by W. Falconer. In it the dervish, in a mosque, prayed, "Prophet of God! . . . /Grant me a token" and saw "a lovely bird/ . . . The light of Aden bringing." Poe uses "Eden" for heaven in "The Lake" and "To F[rances]."

97f. John Leslie Dameron points out to me a poem by "G. F. W." in *Bentley's Miscellany* of May 1, 1838, called "The Raven," in which we are told "that raven's hollow croak/. . . As though the voice of a demon spoke" is "the token/Surely spoken" of death.

106 The line troubled Poe, who told Mrs. Weiss it was "hopeless, and . . . the chief cause of his dissatisfaction with the poem." On December 15, 1846, Poe wrote George W. Eveleth that he had in mind a "bracket candelabrum, high up above the door and bust." Mrs. Weiss (*Home Life*, p. 191) said that she later thought of a large fanlight, opening on a galleried hall such as is often found in old colonial mansions, with a lamp hanging from the hall ceiling. Patricia Ann Edwards suggests to me that there are steps down to the doorway within the room. There is still a clash with the darkness of the twenty-fourth line that might have disturbed the meticulous author.

107–108 In "The Philosophy of Composition" Poe said that here the intention of making the bird "emblematical of *Mournful and Never-ending Remembrance* is permitted distinctly to be seen." C. Alphonso Smith (*Poe, How to Know Him*, p. 220) well says that "there is not a scintilla of remorse," which some less acute critics have sought to find here.

POEMS OF 1845-1847

LINES AFTER ELIZABETH
BARRETT

These lines first appeared in an elaborate study of the poems of the future Mrs. Browning. The criticism, finished during the last fortnight of 1844, is in two parts, of which the first appeared in the *Broadway Journal* of January 4, presumably published on January 2, 1845. In it Poe seems to allude to a criticism by E. P. Whipple in *Graham's* for January 1845, issued about December 15, 1844. The verses are in the second part, published in the *Broadway Journal* for January 11.

Poe thought his verses had improved upon Miss Barrett's "Drama of Exile," lines 1653–1656:

> Hear the steep generations, how they fall
> Adown the visionary stairs of Time,
> Like supernatural thunders — far, yet near,
> Sowing their fiery echoes through the hills!

Poe quoted his lines again in his essay "About Critics and Criticism," finished early in 1849 — according to an implication in a letter to Mrs. Richmond about January 21 — but not published until after his death.

TEXTS

(*A*) *Broadway Journal*, January 11, 1845 (1:18), in "Reviews — The Drama of Exile"; (*B*) manuscript, early 1849, of "About Critics and Criticism," once owned by Henry B. Hirst; (*C*) *Graham's Magazine* for January 1850 (36:51), from *B*; (*D*) *Works* (1850), III, 388, from *C*, with Griswold's title, "E. P. Whipple and Other Critics"; (*E*) *Works* (1850), III, 417, from *A*, with the title, "Elizabeth Barrett Barrett."

The text is that of *B*. It was kindly verified by Mr. Herbert C. Schulz, Curator of Manuscripts at the Huntington Library, where the original, sold at Anderson's on May 11, 1921 (lot 562), is now preserved. *A* and *E* differ slightly from the other texts in the use of commas.

Hear the far generations — how they crash
From crag to crag down the precipitous Time,

In multitudinous thunders that upstartle
Aghast, the echoes from their cavernous lairs
In the visionary hills!

[1845]

EPIGRAM FOR WALL STREET

This bit of punning verse appears in the New York *Evening Mirror* of January 23, 1845, with the following comment: "This is decidedly one of the best *jeux d'esprit* we have met in a year. Who did it? — *who?*"

In the *Evening Mirror* of January 14, there had appeared this paragraph:

The Southern Literary Messenger. — A broadly satirical article, oddly entitled "The Literary Life of Thingum Bob, Esq., late Editor of the Goosethereumfoodle," and which appeared originally in the "Southern Literary Messenger" for December, has been the subject of much comment, lately, in the Southern and Western papers, and the query is put to *us* especially, here in the North — "who wrote it?" Who *did?* — can any one tell?

Since Poe wrote "Thingum Bob," and no other parallel articles are met in the *Mirror*, I assume that Poe wrote the "Epigram," which resembles the "Lines on Joe Locke" and the "Impromptu to Kate Carol." It follows an article on grasshoppers, obviously Poe's. The scrap was not gathered into the weekly edition of the *Mirror* and was first noticed by the present editor.

EPIGRAM FOR WALL STREET

I'll tell you a plan for gaining wealth,
  Better than banking, trade or leases —
Take a bank note and fold it up,
  And then you will find your money in *creases*!
This wonderful plan, without danger or loss,
Keeps your cash in your hands, where nothing can trouble it;
And every time that you fold it across,
  'Tis as plain as the light of the day that you *double* it!

[1845]

IMPROMPTU—TO KATE CAROL

Poe met the popular poetess Frances Sargent Osgood early in March 1845, very soon after he had praised her verses in his lecture on "The Poets and Poetry of America" on the evening of February 28, 1845. The lady was at the time not living with her husband, the painter Samuel S. Osgood, although she desired a reconciliation. A literary romance with the author of "The Raven" soon began, and a good many verses were exchanged by the two poets. During the year Poe was to rededicate two of his early poems of compliment ("To F[rance]s S. O[sgoo]d" and "To F[rances]") to her. But there were some wholly new pieces composed by each of them. Mrs. Osgood, who was extremely facile, often had more than one article in a single issue of a magazine, and used several pen names.

In the notes "To Correspondents" in the *Broadway Journal* of March 29, 1845, we find "A thousand thanks to Kate Carol," and in the next issue of April 5 appears "Kate Carol's" poem "The Rivulet's Dream" with an introduction:

> We might guess who is the fair author of the following lines, which have been sent to us in a MS. evidently disguised — but we are not satisfied with guessing, and would give the world to know. We think the "Rivulet's Dream" an exceedingly graceful and imaginative poem, and our readers will agree with us. Kate Carol will do us the justice to note that we have preferred her "sober second thought" in the concluding line. — *Eds. B. J.*

Despite the plural signature, this is surely by Poe, whose colleagues, Briggs and Watson, had little interest in poetic ladies. Mrs. Osgood's authorship of the poem is sure for it appears in her *Poems* (1850),[1] pages 449–450, with its first line, "A careless rill was dreaming," as title.

In the paper of April 26, in the "Editorial Miscellany," three puns from a recent issue of the *Boston Post* are printed, immediately followed by "Impromptu — To Kate Carol." No fairminded scholar should doubt they were Poe's, but the discoverer was

---

[1] *Poems by Frances Sargent Osgood* (Philadelphia, 1850), copyrighted 1849, actually issued in December 1849.

Whitty, whose discussion was rambling and inept.[2] The puns in "The Impromptu" probably pleased the Virginia poet, who presumably pronounced the words "deah eye," and the New England poetess who probably said "idear."

TEXTS

(A) *Broadway Journal*, April 26, 1845 (1:271); (B) *Complete Poems*, ed. J. H. Whitty (1911), p. 147.
The original printing (A) is followed.

IMPROMPTU. TO KATE CAROL

When from your gems of thought I turn
To those pure orbs, your heart to learn,
I scarce know which to prize most high —
The bright *i-dea*, or bright *dear-eye*.

[1845]

TO [VIOLET VANE]

This poem — another piece in the Poe-Osgood literary romance — was recently discovered in the *Broadway Journal* of May 24, 1845, by Professor James B. Reece of the College of William and Mary, who has kindly communicated it to me. The title is mine; Poe called it merely "To ———."

In the *Broadway Journal*, March 29, 1845, receipt is recorded of a poem from "Violet Vane," which appeared in the issue of April 5. The author was Mrs. Osgood, in whose *Poems* (1850) it appears at pages 403-404.

---

[2] He misprinted a word; and in his notes in *Complete Poems* (1911), p. 287, called "Love's Reply," in the *Broadway Journal* of April 12, 1845 (1:231), a "response." That set of verses is about three female friends of Mrs. Osgood bidding her farewell on her departure for England. More confusion was added when the playful Fanny copied Poe's verses out for her friend Elizabeth Oakes Smith, with a new title, "To the Sinless Child"! See an article in *American Literature*, March 1936, and Mary A. Wyman, *Two American Pioneers* (1927), p. 123. Mrs. Osgood's manuscript of the four lines is now at the University of Virginia.

"SO LET IT BE"
To ———

Perhaps you think it right and just,
  Since you are bound by nearer ties,
To greet me with that careless tone,
  With those serene and silent eyes.

So let it be! I only know
  If I were in your place tonight,
I would not grieve *your* spirit so,
  For all God's worlds of life and light!

I could not turn, as you have done,
  From every memory of the past;
I could not fling, from soul and brow,
  The shade that Feeling should have cast.

Oh! I think how it must deepen all
  The pangs of wild remorse and pride,
To feel, that *you* can coldly see
  The grief, *I* vainly strive to hide!

The happy star, who fills her urn
  With glory from the God of Day,
Can never miss the smile he lends
  The wild-flower withering fast away;

The fair, fond girl, who at your side,
  Within your soul's dear light, doth live,
Could hardly have the heart to chide
  The ray that Friendship well might give.

But if you deem it right and just,
  Blessed as you are in your glad lot,
To greet me with that heartless tone,
  So let it be! I blame you not!

VIOLET VANE.

Poe's reply appeared with "M." as signature; his unusual discretion in delaying publication for several weeks has caused students to overlook the relation of the poems to each other. Once pointed out, this is unmistakable.

TEXT

The text given here is that of the *Broadway Journal*, May 24, 1845 (1:325); the poem has not, so far as I know, been hitherto reprinted.

TO ——

I would not lord it o'er thy heart,
    Alas! I cannot rule my own,
Nor would I rob one loyal thought,
    From him who there should reign alone;
5   We both have found a life-long love;
    Wherein our weary souls may rest,
Yet may we not, my gentle friend
    Be each to each the *second best?*

A love which shall be passion-free,
10   Fondness as pure as it is sweet,
A bond where all the dearest ties
    Of brother, friend and *cousin* meet, —
Such is the union I would frame,
    That thus we might be doubly blest,
15   With Love to rule our hearts supreme
    And Friendship to be *second best*.

[1845]

THE DIVINE RIGHT OF KINGS

This and "Stanzas [to F.S.O.]" are companion pieces, and they may most profitably be discussed together. Both were first published with the printed signature "P.," in separate issues of the "twenty-seventh" volume of *Graham's Magazine* — that for July to December 1845. A bound copy of this volume, with pencil markings made by a former owner who has been identified as Mrs. Osgood, was found about fifty years ago by J. H. Whitty. He said that in the signature of both poems she filled in the letters missing from Poe's name and marked some passages in her own contributions to the magazine. Whitty at once announced his discovery in the press, and reprinted both pieces, with his reasons for their inclusion, in his second edition of Poe's *Complete Poems* in 1917.[1] But Whitty mingled fact and fancy in a confusing way, and avoided showing anyone the marked copy of *Graham's*. Hence Killis Campbell remarked, "Further evidence must be forthcoming . . . before we can be sure that these two poems are Poe's."[2]

New evidence has been found. In the volume of *Graham's* for 1845 acquired by the Boston Public Library before 1890, a manuscript note ascribes "The Divine Right of Kings" to Poe. The existence of the tradition independent of Whitty seems to me sufficient for acceptance of the poems. They fit well with all now known of the relations of Mrs. Osgood and Poe. That Poe had a ready market for such innocuously graceful poems goes almost without saying.

"The Divine Right of Kings" was thought by Whitty to be a reply to a passage marked by Mrs. Osgood in her rather indiscreet story "Ida Grey," published in *Graham's* for August 1845. Poe sometimes used "Edward S. T. Grey" as a pseudonym, and the hero of the story is a married man described as very like him. The passage to which the poem may allude reads: "He bids me tell him that I love him, as proudly as if he had a right . . . a divine right to demand my love."

There is good reason to agree with Whitty that Mrs. Osgood sometimes used "Ellen" as a nom de plume. It was the given name of her eldest daughter, and among the notices "To Readers and Correspondents" (obviously by Poe) in the *Broadway Journal* of March 22, 1845, we find: "Is there *no* hope of our hearing from *Ellen* of the C.M.?" In the *Columbian Magazine* for March 1845 (3:133) is a poem "To the Evening Star," signed "Ellen," which is very much in the manner of Mrs. Osgood. She had a signed

[1] See New York *Sun*, November 21, 1915; *Nation*, January 27, 1916; *Complete Poems* (1917), pp. 148–150, 320–321. Whitty does not repeat in his book all that he said in the *Nation*. He suggests that R. W. Griswold and he himself had owned the volume marked by Mrs. Osgood, but William H. Koester did not find it in the Poeana he bought from Whitty's family. Whitty's texts in the *Complete Poems* show bad misprints.

[2] *The Mind of Poe* (1933), p. 209. Miss Helen I. Tetlow, great-niece of Mrs. Osgood, told me of a family tradition that there was an uncollected Poe poem relating to that poetess, in *Graham's* in 1845; and that there was an article about it in the *Springfield Republican*. An undated clipping once owned by Miss Tetlow has been lost.

poem, "To Amelia Welby," in the same issue (3:110), which would have been a good reason to use a pseudonym for the second poem. "Ellen's" verses do not concern Poe, but are about spirits who "soar upward to" a star and "gaze . . . upon the friends they love."

TEXTS

(A) *Graham's Magazine* for October 1845 (27:189); (B) *Complete Poems,* edited by J. H. Whitty (second edition, 1917), p. 150, where in line 10 "with" appears instead of "and."

Our text follows that of the original publication (A).

THE DIVINE RIGHT OF KINGS [A]

The only king by right divine
Is Ellen King, and were she mine
I'd strive for liberty no more,
But hug the glorious chains I wore.

5   Her bosom is an ivory throne,
Where tyrant virtue reigns alone;
No subject vice dare interfere,
To check the power that governs here.

O! would she deign to rule my fate,
10   I'd worship Kings and kingly state,
And hold this maxim all life long,
The King — *my* King — can do no wrong.

[1845]

NOTES

2 No satisfactory explanation of the second name of "Ellen King" has as yet been offered.

4 In "Ida Grey" the heroine addresses to her lover a poem beginning "Had we but met in life's delicious spring," which also may be seen in Mrs. Osgood's *Poems* (1849), pp. 115–118. In it she says that, because she met her true love too late, she feels that she is "a soul-worn slave in Custom's iron chain." This may well be an allusion to Hiram Powers' celebrated statue, "The Greek Slave," which received a great deal of publicity in 1845 and about which

Mrs. Browning was to write a poem. The statue represents a girl exposed for sale in a Turkish slave market, nude and manacled.

STANZAS [TO F.S.O.]

This poem is clearly a companion piece to "The Divine Right of Kings" and the reasons for its ascription to Poe are discussed in the comment on that poem. Whitty said that Frances Sargent Osgood, in her own copy of *Graham's Magazine* for December 1845, expanded the signature "P." to "E. A. Poe" and added "To F.S.O." to the title.

The lady's "Echo Song," beginning "I know a noble heart that beats/For one it loves how 'wildly well,' " had appeared in the *Broadway Journal* of September 6, 1845, and may have called forth Poe's lines. Mrs. Osgood's "To ——," beginning "Oh, they never can know that heart of thine,/Who dare accuse thee of flirtation," published in the *Broadway Journal* for November 22, may — or may not — be her reply to Poe's "Stanzas," which had appeared about November 15. These pieces of Mrs. Osgood's were collected in her *Poems* (1850), pp. 464 and 364 respectively.

TEXTS

(*A*) *Graham's Magazine* for December 1845 (27:251), issued in mid-November; (*B*) *Complete Poems*, edited by Whitty (second edition, 1917), p. 148.

The original published text (*A*) has been followed, but Mrs. Osgood's subtitle has been added.

STANZAS [*A*]
[To F.S.O.]

Lady! I would that verse of mine
    Could fling, all lavishly and free,
Prophetic tones from every line,
    Of health, joy, peace, in store for thee.

5   Thine should be length of happy days,
    Enduring joys and fleeting cares,

Virtues that challenge envy's praise,
    By rivals loved, and mourned by heirs.

Thy life's free course should ever roam
10   Beyond this bounded earthly clime,
No billow breaking into foam
    Upon the rock-girt shore of Time.

The gladness of a gentle heart,
    Pure as the wishes breathed in prayer,
15 Which has in others' joys a part,
    While in its own all others share.

The fullness of a cultured mind,
    Stored with the wealth of bard and sage,
Which Error's glitter cannot blind,
20   Lustrous in youth, undimmed in age;

The grandeur of a guileless soul,
    With wisdom, virtue, feeling fraught,
Gliding serenely to its goal,
    Beneath the eternal sky of Thought: —

25 These should be thine, to guard and shield,
    And this the life thy spirit live,
Blest with all bliss that earth can yield,
    Bright with all hopes that Heaven can give.

                        [1845]

A VALENTINE

This is a puzzle poem concealing a lady's name. Poe wrote it out on February 13, 1846, keeping the draft, which was later found among Mrs. Clemm's papers and is now in the Enoch Pratt Free Library, Baltimore. He made a copy with slight changes (substituting "comprehend" for "understand" in line 12 and omitting a superfluous comma in line 20), dated it the fourteenth, and sent it to the St. Valentine's Day party given by Anne Charlotte Lynch at 116 Waverly Place, New York. Poe did not attend, but I think the recipient was identified, for the manuscript was found among the papers of Rufus W. Griswold, Mrs. Osgood's literary executor; it is now in the Harvard College Library. Whether Poe knew that his piece was published in the *Evening Mirror* a week after the party cannot be certainly known.

Finding that he had misspelled the lady's middle name, the author later reworked the piece to introduce the correct spelling, preparing a manuscript which he dated "Valentine's Eve, 1848," and presumably hoped to have published that year in some magazine. In this he did not succeed. But, undaunted, he made ready again for the proper season in 1849, with unexpected and embarrassing double success.

On February 5, 1849, Poe told Frederick Gleason, publisher of *The Flag of Our Union* (Boston), that he was leaving with Mr. French, Mr. Gleason's New York agent, a short poem. Another letter written about the same time told an uncertain correspondent that "A Valentine" came out "in *The Flag* dated 3rd March, but which was issued the Saturday previous — Feb. 24." Poe seems to have been unaware that the Osgood verses had appeared in *Sartain's Union Magazine* for March, which came out on February 15. In *The Flag* for March 17, 1849, Killis Campbell (*Poems*, pp. 261–262) found the following paragraph.

THAT VALENTINE BY POE.

Having received a poem from our regular contributor, Edgar A. Poe, Esq., and having paid for the same as *original*, we were not a little surprised to see the poem appear in Sartain's Union Magazine for March, uncredited, and as original, though in the table of contents on the cover it is omitted. We at once addressed Mr. Poe, for an explanation, lest it should appear that we had taken the Valentine from the Magazine without credit. His answer to us is full and satisfactory. The said poem was written and handed to Mr. De Graw, a gentleman who proposed to start a magazine in New York, but who gave up the project and started himself for California. Mr. Poe, learning of this, thought, of course, his composition was his own again, and sent it to us as one of his regular contributions for the Flag; and was himself as much surprised as we could be, to see it, not long afterwards, in the Magazine, though the publisher does not say there that it was written for his pages.

It was doubtless handed by Mr. De Graw to Sartain, and published thus without any intent to wrong any one. We make this statement, as in duty bound to Mr. Poe, and ourselves.

De Graw was certainly connected with the *Union Magazine* and his name, James L. DeGraw, Agent, appears on the title page of Volume III, which indicates that when Israel Post disposed of the magazine, De Graw arranged to sell the bound volumes. In matters of this kind Poe was not always candid, and since Sartain's text is close to that of the manuscript of 1848, I suspect Poe had tried to get publication early in that year. In the first sixteen lines *The Flag* text preserves some readings of the original draft of 1846.

Poe later composed "An Enigma" in which were concealed in similar fashion the names of his patroness Sarah Anna Lewis.[1]

TEXTS

(*A*) Manuscript, "Valentine's Eve, 1846" (in Enoch Pratt Free Library, Baltimore; facsimile in Quinn and Hart, 1941, p. 2); (*B*) manuscript, "Saturday, February 14, [18]46," from Griswold's papers (now in Houghton Library, Harvard University; text printed by Harrison, VII, 217); (*C*) New York *Evening Mirror*, February 21, 1846; (*D*) manuscript, "Valentine's Eve, 1848," from Griswold's papers (now in Houghton Library; facsimile in Woodberry, II, 182); (*E*) *Sartain's Union Magazine* for March 1849 (4:173); (*F*) *Flag of Our Union* for March 3, 1849; (*G*) *Works* (1850), II, 14.

The first manuscript (*A*) was obviously retained by the poet (*pace* Quinn and Hart), for it comes from the papers of the poet's relatives. The second (*B*) was that sent to the party, for the *Mirror* text (*C*) was based on it. For convenience I call texts *A, B,* and *C* the "Sergeant versions" and *D, E, F,* and *G* the "Sargent versions."

We give the first text (*A*) and Griswold's (*G*) with one misprint corrected.

[*A*]

Valentine's Eve. 1846
For her these lines are penned, whose luminous eyes,
Bright and expressive as the stars of Leda,

---

[1] See page 424 below. In the volume of passages from his father's correspondence, issued by W. M. Griswold in 1898, there may be seen a poem by Mrs. Osgood on a similar but more elaborate plan. A second name is concealed in the last letter of the first line, the penultimate letter of the second, and so on. Thus linked are the names of the lady and the elder Griswold.

Shall find her own sweet name that, nestling, lies
Upon this page, enwrapped from every reader.
5 Search narrowly these words, which hold a treasure
Divine — a talisman, an amulet
That must be worn *at heart*. Search well the measure —
The words — the letters themselves. Do not forget
The smallest point, or you may lose your labor.
10 And yet there is in this no Gordian knot
Which one might not undo without a sabre
If one could merely understand the plot.
Upon the open page on which are peering
Such sweet eyes now, there lies, I say, *perdu,*
15 A musical name oft uttered in the hearing
Of poets, by poets — for the name is a poet's too.
In common sequence set, the letters lying,
Compose a sound delighting all to hear —
Ah, this you'd have no trouble in descrying
20 Were you not something, of a dunce, my dear —
And now I leave these riddles to their Seer.

E. A. P.

VARIANTS ("SERGEANT" VERSIONS)

Heading: [*added at a later time*] To
—— —— —— (*A*); To —— (*B*); To Her
Whose Name is Written Below (*C*)
12 understand/comprehend (*B, C*)
16 for/[*above this, written later*] as
(*A*)

19 Ah/All [*an obvious misprint, spoil-
ing the hidden name*] (*C*)
20 Were you not something of a dunce,
my dear: — (*B, C*)
B is dated at the bottom Saturday
Feb. 14. 46 *and has no signature*

A VALENTINE [G]

For her this rhyme is penned, whose luminous eyes,
    Brightly expressive as the twins of Læda,
Shall find her own sweet name, that, nestling lies
    Upon the page, enwrapped from every reader.
5 Search narrowly the lines! — they hold a treasure
    Divine — a talisman — an amulet
That must be worn *at heart*. Search well the measure —
    The words — the syllables! Do not forget

· 389 ·

The trivialest point, or you may lose your labor!
10   And yet there is in this no Gordian knot
Which one might not undo without a sabre,
    If one could merely comprehend the plot.
Enwritten upon the leaf where now are peering
    Eyes scintillating soul, there lie *perdus*
15   Three eloquent words oft uttered in the hearing
    Of poets, by poets — as the name is a poet's, too.
Its letters, although naturally lying
    Like the knight Pinto — Mendez Ferdinando —
Still form a synonym for Truth. — Cease trying!
20   You will not read the riddle, though you do the best
        you *can* do.

[1846–1849]

(To translate the address, read the first letter of the first line in connection with the second letter of the second line, the third letter of the third line, the fourth of the fourth, and so on to the end. The name will thus appear.)

VARIANTS ("SARGENT" VERSION)

Heading: A Valentine By Edgar A. Poe.
To ——— ——— ——— (*D, E*)
1 this rhyme is/these lines are (*F*)
2 Læda [*corrected from the manuscript D; it is misprinted* Lœda *in E, F, and G*]
3 that, nestling lies/that, nestling, lies (*D, F*)
4 the page/this page (*F*)
5 the lines/these lines (*D*); this rhyme (*F*); they hold/which holds (*F*)
7 *at heart*/at heart (*F*)

8 the syllables/the letters themselves (*F*)
11 sabre,/sabre [*no comma*] (*D*)
13 the leaf/this page (*F*); where now/ whereon (*F*)
14 Such eager eyes, there lies, I say, perdu, (*F*)
15 Three eloquent words/A well-known name (*F*)
18 [*Line enclosed in parentheses, D*]; Like the knight Pinto (Mendez Ferdinando) — (*F*)

[*The terminal note appears only in G*]

NOTES

2 The twins of Leda are Castor and Pollux, who became a constellation, Gemini, which governs a sign of the Zodiac. Poe compares the eyes of the heroine of "Ligeia" to the "twin stars of Leda." He perhaps had in mind some "Lines on Harvey's Death" by Cowley:

> Say, for ye saw us, ye immortal lights,
> How oft unwearied have we spent the nights
> Till the Ledaean stars, so famed for love,
> Wond'red at us from above.

He surely had seen them in the chapter on "Literary Friendships" in the *Curiosities* of one of his favorite writers, Isaac D'Israeli.

9 In his later years Poe was developing a rather complicated theory of scansion, for which the interested reader is referred to "The Rationale of Verse." Basically his system is quantitative, but he thought English syllables to be of several sizes, not merely long and short, and he wished to have no elisions save those made in ordinary speech. Since (in order to substitute "a" for "e") he deliberately change *smallest* to *trivialest* in this line, he obviously regarded *trivial* and *small* as metrical equivalents. Thus, the line is meant to be an iambic pentameter. See also the notes on "Ulalume," line 41.

10 The Gordian knot was that most cunningly tied on the cart of Gordius, a Phrygian peasant. In accordance with an oracle, Gordius was made king and the knot was preserved in the temple at Gordium. It was prophesied that whoever loosened it would conquer Asia. Alexander the Great drew his sword and cut it. In his manuscript selections from Milton, Poe quoted from "At a Vacation Exercise in the College," lines 89–90: "What power, what force, what mighty spell, if not/Your learned hands, can loose this Gordian knot?"

14 To lie *perdu* is to lie hidden. Poe used the French expression several times in articles about Mrs. Osgood, and elsewhere at least as early as in the first chapter of the "Journal of Julius Rodman," which was written late in 1839.

16 Poe also believed that certain words or syllables in a line, because of repetition of sound or for some other reason, receive special emphasis. Here a natural reading is "Of *poets* — by *poets* — as the *name* — is a *poet's* — *too*."

17–19 The lines will be understood as founded on a punning Spanish joke on the Spanish form of the name of a famous traveler, renowned as a teller of tall tales, Ferdinando Mendez Pinto (1509–1583). The name was regarded as a question and answer — "Mendez Ferdinando? Minto" means "Ferdinand are you lying? — I lie." When he admitted he was a liar he was not lying — and his name became a synonym for truth. Incidentally, in 1846, Charles F. Briggs (Poe's sometime associate on the *Broadway Journal*) wrote a series of letters to the *Evening Mirror* which he signed "Ferdinand Mendoza Pinto." Poe in his "Literati" sketch of Briggs in *Godey's* for May 1846, called the signature "apt." Far earlier, reviewing Thomas Campbell's *Life of Petrarch* in *Graham's* for September 1841, he coupled Pinto's name (in the Spanish form) with Baron Munchausen's. I am told that the Peregrinação of Fernãs Mendes Pinto, published posthumously in the original Portuguese in 1614, is undeserving of the incredulity it has long received.

19 Poe's Hungarian translator, Dr. György Radó, wished to see another pun, on "argent" and "O's good" here, but I think this is gilding the lily. See his *Edgar Allan Poe Összes Versei* (Budapest, 1959), p. 406.

POEMS OF 1845–1847

MODEL VERSES

At Fordham late in 1846 Poe recast and expanded his "Notes Upon English Verse" of 1843 into a new essay, which he called "The Rationale of Verse." It was not finished until after November 15, for it includes a quotation from a poem by Mary A. S. Aldrich published on that day, but on December 15, 1846, Poe wrote of it to George W. Eveleth as in the hands of George Hooker Colton for publication in the *American Review*. He later took it back in exchange for "Ulalume" (see the comment on that poem).

In the new essay Poe gave a number of examples of good and bad versification, some actually quoted from other authors, a few ostensibly so, and others that he made up himself. Those of the second and third kinds it seems well to give here, for at least two of the original pieces are of some poetic merit as well as purely metrical interest.

Six pages of the manuscript are known to survive, scattered in several collections, but only one page, numbered 18, includes any of the verses, the second line of the third item. Poe divided the metrical feet by virgules and marked the quantities in most of them, but these marks are here omitted; they will appear in "The Rationale" in a later volume of this edition.

Some months after the publication of the essay, which appeared in the *Southern Literary Messenger* late in 1848, Poe recast and expanded the last example — at the foot of a sheet of paper headed "Mem: for Philadelphia" containing items that relate to his journey south late in June 1849. The middle of the sheet is occupied by some rather full notes on versification, followed by the word "Evangeline" on a line by itself (Longfellow's poem had been published in 1847), with the hexameters below. This is certainly the final version, but it is a rough draft, without punctuation though with the metrical feet set off by virgules. I reproduce it in full from the manuscript in the Griswold papers at the Boston Public Library.

MODEL VERSES

TEXTS

(*A*) Manuscript of "The Rationale of Verse" (late 1846), now imperfectly preserved; (*B*) *Southern Literary Messenger*, October and November 1848 (14:577–585, 673–682); (*C*) *Works* (1850), II, 215ff.; (*D*) manuscript "Mem: for Philadelphia" (1849) at the Boston Public Library (the hexameters).

The texts given are *C* (which does not differ from *B*) and *D*.

[MODEL VERSES]   [*C*]

[i. "Triple-rhymed natural-dactylic lines"]

> Virginal Lilian, rigidly, humblily, dutiful;
> Saintlily, lowlily,
> Thrillingly, holily
> Beautiful!

[ii. An "iambic line" in which "there are no natural feet"]

> The unimaginable might of Jove.

[iii. "Dactylic lines in which we find natural feet" — that is, feet made up of undivided words]

> Can it be fancied that Deity ever vindictively
> Made in his image a mannikin merely to madden it?

[iv. A "trochaic line"]

> See the delicate footed rein-deer.

[v. Line illustrating the "error . . . of commencing a rhythm . . . with a 'bastard' foot"]

> Many a thought will come to memory.

[vi. Line illustrating (in the syllable *son*) a "variable foot" with "the value of three short syllables"]

> I have a little stepson of only three years old.

[vii. Line illustrating (in the last word) a foot with the value of four short syllables]

> Pale as a lily was Emily Gray.

[viii. Lines to show that "a truly Greek hexameter" *can* be composed in English]

Do tell! when may we hope to make men of sense out of
the Pundits

Born and brought up with their snouts deep down in the
mud of the Frog-pond?

Why ask? who ever yet saw money made out of a fat old

Jew, or downright upright nutmegs out of a pine-knot?

[Revision of example VIII (text D)]

Evangeline

Do tell | when shall we | make common | sense men | out
of the | pundits

Out of the | stupid old | God-born | Pundits who | lost
in a | fog-bank |

Strut about | all along | shore there | somewhere | close
by the | Down East

Frog Pond | munching of | pea nuts and | pumkins and |
buried in | big-wigs |

Why ask | who ever | yet saw | money made | out of a | fat
old

Jew or | downright | upright | nutmegs | out of a | pine-
knot |

[1846–1849]

VARIANTS

1 Pundits/*first written* owl-eyed   4 Frog/*first written* Duck
2 Out of the/*first written* Frog-faced

NOTES

I. These lines were probably suggested by Tennyson's "Lilian," which begins, "Airy, fairy Lilian,/Flitting, fairy Lilian."

II. This line is close in thought to "Al Aaraaf," I, 133f., but I think it is verbally an echo of Wordsworth's *Ecclesiastical Sonnets*, III, xxxiv, 14: "Or the unimaginable touch of time."

III. These lines are obviously Poe's own, and are given in some editions of *Bartlett's Familiar Quotations*. They allude to Genesis 1:27.

IV. Probably Poe's own.

V. This is surely Poe's; immediately after it he quotes from Christopher P. Cranch's *Poems* (1844) the opening of "My Thoughts," which is "Many are the thoughts that come to me."

MODEL VERSES

VI. Poe implies that this line is from a poem by Mrs. Welby, but the opening of her famous "Stepson" in *Poems by Amelia* (1846) is really: "I have a little stepson, the loveliest thing alive,/A noble sturdy boy is he, and yet he's only five."

VII. In reviewing Henry B. Hirst's volume, *The Coming of the Mammoth*, in the *Broadway Journal* of July 12, 1845, Poe had praised the lines:

> Time it has passed: and the lady is pale —
> Pale as the lily that lolls on the gale: . . .
> Years will she tarry — for cold is the clay
> Fettering the form of her Everard Grey.

Hirst's poem, "Everard Grey," which had first appeared in *Snowden's Ladies' Companion* for October 1843, is obviously the basis for Poe's line.

VIII. This example follows a paragraph condemning "Longfellownian" and "Feltonian" hexameters "as having been committed in a radical misconception of the philosophy of verse." Comments on specific expressions used are keyed to the lines of the expanded version.

Title: To this second example of hexameters, Poe definitely gave the title of "Evangeline."

1 The term "pundits," primarily meaning East Indian scholars, was often used for their supposed spiritual kin, the intellectuals of Boston.

3 In Poe's day "Down East" meant New England in general; it is now almost wholly confined to the shoreline of the state of Maine.

4 The "Frog Pond" is still a feature of Boston Common. Poe called Boston "Frogpondium" and Bostonians "Frogpondians." Such jokes were commonplace. Isaac Starr Clason wrote "Young Boston Bards croak worse than Boston waites" and added a note " 'Boston-waites' is an old nickname for frogs." See his *Horace in New York* (1826), pages 28 and 45.

In the *Broadway Journal*, November 1, 1845, discussing his recent reading of "Al Aaraaf" in Boston, Poe wrote: "We like Boston. We were born there . . . The Bostonians are very well in their way. Their hotels are bad. Their pumpkin pies are delicious. Their poetry is not so good. Their common is no common thing — and the duck-pond might answer — if its answer could be heard for the frogs." In the issue of November 22, he reprinted from the Charleston (South Carolina) *Southern Patriot* of November 10 a defense of his conduct, written by William Gilmore Simms but obviously inspired by Poe himself. In it Simms remarked that in a poem for delivery before the Boston Lyceum "You must not be mystical. You must not task the audience to study. Your song must be such as they can read running, and comprehend while munching peanuts." Lastly, in the same issue of the *Broadway Journal*, addressing Miss Cornelia Walter, who as literary editor of the Boston *Transcript* began on October 17, 1845, a series of articles attacking Poe and "Al Aaraaf," Poe said: "You are a delightful creature and your heart is in the right place — would to Heaven that we could always say the same thing of your wig!"

6 In his tale "The Business Man," Poe says, "You cannot make money out of a Jew, or the best nutmegs out of pineknots." A Jew meant, of course, a

· 395 ·

moneylender of any religion. Whether the good people of Connecticut made wooden nutmegs or not, the place called the Nutmeg State never has grown any real nutmegs.

DEEP IN EARTH

This tiny gem is worthy of the Greek Anthology; it is simple, direct, lofty, and complete. It is faintly penciled on a manuscript of "Eulalie," a cheerful poem about a happy marriage, which may have pleased Virginia Poe. "Deep in Earth" was presumably written soon after the funeral of the poet's wife on February 2, 1847. The late Victor H. Palsits found the manuscript in an autograph album and published the items in the New York Public Library's *Bulletin*. The album had reached the library in 1892 from the collection of R. L. Stuart.

TEXTS

(*A*) Manuscript, now in the New York Public Library; (*B*) *Bulletin of the New York Public Library*, December 1914 (18:1462); (*C*) J. H. Whitty, ed., *The Complete Poems of Edgar Allan Poe*, 2nd edition (1917), p. 152.

The text used here is *A*, but the title is mine. Whitty called the piece "Couplet."

["DEEP IN EARTH"] [*A*]

Deep in earth my love is lying
And I must weep alone.

[1847]

TO MISS LOUISE OLIVIA HUNTER

This poem was surely written, very shortly before the date it bears, for Miss Lynch's annual Valentine Soirée. Poe did not attend, but the identity of the author of these verses cannot have been uncertain, as he did not disguise his hand.

The date has been needlessly called in question. After his

wife's death Poe was very ill, and Marie Louise Shew urged him to rest but apparently thought writing some poetry would be of therapeutic value. She may have suggested that he might like to send a poem to a very young poetess at the party. Such compliments were not supposed to be taken seriously, of course, but there is a strangely wry quality of thoughtfulness in these lines of impersonal gallantry.

The circumstances of the poet's meeting with Miss Hunter are now fully known. In a volume compiled by Charles W. Kent,[1] there is a reminiscence by Charles E. West:

My acquaintance with Poe began in New York sixty years ago. Our boarding houses were opposite each other in East Broadway. I had just entered upon my duties as Principal of Rutgers Female Institute. Mr. Poe was writing for the New York papers and making a very scanty living. He soon moved to Fordham, where I called to see him. He was holding a loaf of bread, and said, "Here is all the food I have in the world for myself and family." He was almost in a state of despair. I did what I could to cheer him, assuring him that there was something of good in life for him. In 1845 he served as chairman of a committee to examine the compositions of the collegiate department of my institution and award the gold medal to the writer of the prize composition, which he read at the sixth commencement of the Institute.

Poe's letter to West has been found, and in 1944 it was presented by Mr. Christian Zabriskie to the New York Society Library. It is now first published, by permission of Miss Sylvia C. Hilton, Librarian of that institution:

Office of the Broadway Journal
June 20th, 1845

Dear Sir;

The previous letter to which you allude did not reach me. I trust, therefore, that you will exonerate me from the charge of discourtesy.

I shall be very happy to oblige you in any way — and it will give me very great pleasure to act as one of a Committee in which I shall be associated with two gentlemen whom I so highly respect as Drs. Griswold and Snodgrass.[2]

[1] *The Unveilng of the Bust of Edgar Allan Poe, October 7, 1899* (Lynchburg, Virginia: J. P. Bell Company, n.d.; preface signed May 1, 1901), p. 67.
[2] W. D. Snodgrass was an inactive committeeman, and Joy Bayless, *Rufus Wilmot Griswold* (1943), pp. 99, 275, records that when that editor decided not to go to the committee meeting, Henry T. Tuckerman took his place. Tuckerman and Poe met on the evening of July 10, for the first time. The next day Charles Fenno Hoffman wittily wrote Griswold, "Odd . . . that the women, who divide so many,

My time is entirely at your disposal — whenever you will be kind enough to let me know that you require it.

Very respectfully,
Yr. ob. Svt.
Edgar A. Poe.

Charles E. West, Esqr.

The commencement exercises were held on July 11 in the Rutgers Street Presbyterian Church at the northwest corner of Rutgers and Henry Streets and Poe read Miss Hunter's poem, of about one hundred lines. It was printed in a long article on the ceremonies in the *New-York Mirror* of July 19, 1845. The poem is without title; it begins, "Deep in a glade by trees o'erhung."

Poe met Miss Hunter at this time, and perhaps on later occasions. She greatly admired Mrs. Osgood. Griswold published in the *International Magazine* of December 1, 1850 (2:133), a letter dated March 6, 1850, to Mrs. Osgood from the girl. In it Miss Hunter wrote, "You know how, from childhood I have worshipped you, that since our first meeting you have been my idol." Perhaps Poe thought that a compliment to Louise Hunter might be taken as an indirect one to Mrs. Osgood.

Miss Hunter composed both poetry and fiction for *Godey's, Graham's, Sartain's, Peterson's Ladies' National,* and the *American Metropolitan Magazine.* Of her later career I have no details.

TEXTS

(*A*) Manuscript, dated February 14, 1847, now in the Koester Collection at the University of Texas; (*B*) *New York Times,* February 21, 1932; (*C*) *Colophon,* Autumn 1935 (n.s. 1:185), with facsimile, in an article by Sydney P. McLean.

Text *A,* which shows no changes, is given here by courtesy of Mr. William H. Koester. It was first published when the manuscript was owned by Dr. A. S. W. Rosenbach. The poem is collected here for the first time.

TO MISS LOUISE OLIVIA HUNTER

Though I turn, I fly not —
I cannot depart;

should bring these two together!" See Homer Barnes, *Charles Fenno Hoffman* (1930), p. 264.

I would try, but try not
To release my heart.
5 And my hopes are dying
While, on dreams relying,
I am spelled by art.

Thus the bright snake coiling
'Neath the forest tree
10 Wins the bird, beguiling
To come down and see:
Like that bird the lover
Round his fate will hover
Till the blow is over
15 And he sinks — like me.

February 14, 1847

NOTES

Title: The lady's name was given as "Louisa" in the *Mirror*, but her printed works are usually signed "Louise."

7f. The reference is to the supposed fascination of a serpent's bright eyes for its prey.

TO MARIE LOUISE SHEW

Marie Louise Shew was the daughter of a physician, Dr. Lowrey Barney, of Hendersonville, Jefferson County, New York. She had married and had moved to New York City, where she lived in two pleasant homes in Greenwich Village. She was deeply religious and given to good works. During the last illness of Virginia Poe, Mrs. Mary Gove, one of Poe's Literati, introduced her to the poet's family, and she went to Fordham every other day to nurse first the dying wife and then the husband, who became desperately ill after Virginia died. Mrs. Shew was little interested in literature, but for her Poe wrote three poems and probably planned a fourth.

"To M. L. S——" was written soon after the death of Virginia

Poe, and in time to be given to Mrs. Shew on Valentine's Day, 1847.

The piece was first published in the *Home Journal* with an introductory note, presumably by Willis: "The following seems said over a hand clasped in the speaker's two. It is by Edgar A. Poe, and is evidently the pouring out of a very deep feeling of gratitude."

TEXTS

(*A*) Poe's manuscript, dated February 14, 1847, now in the Henry E. Huntington Library; (*B*) *Home Journal*, March 13, 1847; (*C*) *Works* (1850), II, 111.

The text given here is C. No file of the *Home Journal* for 1847 is at present accessible; the publisher's file has been for many years in storage. I did see it myself nearly forty years ago at the office of *Town and Country*, the periodical's successor, and I am sure that the text (*B*) is verbally exactly like the Griswold text (*C*) here adopted.

TO M. L. S—— [*C*]

Of all who hail thy presence as the morning —
Of all to whom thine absence is the night —
The blotting utterly from out high heaven
The sacred sun — of all who, weeping, bless thee
5   Hourly for hope — for life — ah! above all,
For the resurrection of deep-buried faith
In Truth — in Virtue — in Humanity —
Of all who, on Despair's unhallowed bed
Lying down to die, have suddenly arisen
10   At thy soft-murmured words, "Let there be light!"
At the soft-murmured words that were fulfilled
In the seraphic glancing of thine eyes —
Of all who owe thee most — whose gratitude
Nearest resembles worship — oh, remember
15   The truest — the most fervently devoted,
And think that these weak lines are written by him —
By him who, as he pens them, thrills to think
His spirit is communing with an angel's.

[1847]

THE BELOVED PHYSICIAN

VARIANTS

Title: To Mrs. M. L. S. (*A*)
2 thine/thy (*A*)

9 Lying/Laying them (*A*); arisen/
risen (*A*)
14 resembles/approaches (*A*)

NOTES

3–4 There is a similar locution in "The 1002nd Tale of Scheherazade": ". . . the sun was entirely blotted out from the heavens, and it became darker than the darkest midnight."

6–7 In his last letter to Mrs. Shew, *circa* June 1848, Poe credits her with renewing his "hopes and faith in God . . . and in humanity" (transcript by M. L. S. Houghton, sent to Ingram April 3, 1875; see Ingram List, no. 213).

7–12 Compare lines in the third stanza of "To a Face Beloved," by N. P. Willis: "A lamp is lit in woman's eye/That souls, else lost on earth, remember angels by."

10 The quotation is from Genesis 1:3, but the manuscript version seems also to allude to the child's prayer from the *New England Primer*, beginning "Now I lay me down to sleep."

THE BELOVED PHYSICIAN

This is another poem written for Marie Louise Shew. We know it only through fragments. The following extract is from a long letter (Ingram List, no. 197), begun on January 23, 1875, from the former Mrs. Shew (who had married the Reverend Roland S. Houghton) to John H. Ingram, then collecting materials for his biography of Poe.

I came up a country doctor's only daughter, with a taste for painting and a heart for loving all the world. I saved Mr. Poe's life at this time, having been educated medically . . . I made my diagnosis, and went to the great Dr. [Valentine] Mott with it. I told him that *at best*, when he was well Mr. Poe's pulse beat only ten regular beats, after which it suspended or *intermitted* (as Doctors say) . . . He [Poe] talked to me *incessantly*, of the past, which was all new to me, and often he begged me to write for him his fancies for he said he had promised so many greedy publishers his next efforts that they would not only say he did not keep his word but they would revenge themselves by writing "all sort of evil of him" if he should die. I have a great many pages of these . . . somewhere, part of them have been published, I think. One poem of touching pathos "The Beloved Physician" he revised and prepared for publication . . . As he said he had been offered twenty dollars for it, I gave him twenty-five, and asked him to wait as every body

would know *who it was,* and it was so very personal and complimentary
I dreaded the ordeal . . .

The Poem was written in a singular strain, a verse describing the Doctor,
watching the pulse, etc. etc. and ending the refrain of two lines describing
the Nurse. It was very curious as it was a picture of a highly wrought brain
in an over-excited state.

There was in every verse a line "The Pulse beats ten and intermits" —
and in the refrain of the last verse (where he describes me holding my watch
and counting

"so tired, so weary"

and after I find that I have brought the pulse to the desired eighty beats —
as low as I dare give sedatives — I rested *and he did also,* trying his best to
sleep for my sake) in the refrain, as I said before, he adds

"The soft head bows, the sweet eyes close

"The large heart (or faithful heart) yields to sweet repose." You can imag-
ine it was a perfect thing as he revised it afterwards.

The date of the original composition was, according to another
letter to Ingram (Ingram List, no. 215), "two months or more
after Virginia's death," perhaps April 1847.

On June 7, 1875, Mrs. Houghton wrote (Ingram List, no. 232)
that her son, the Reverend Henry Houghton, said that both the
manuscript of the poem and a letter in which Poe referred to it
were in a desk at Pierrepont Manor, three hundred miles away
from Whitestone, Long Island, where the lady then was. Mr.
Houghton added that Poe had cut the poem to nine stanzas when
he prepared it for publication.

Poe's letter is presumably that of about June 1848. He said:

I place you in my esteem in all solemnity beside the friend of my boy-
hood, the mother of my schoolfellow [Mrs. Stanard] of whom I told you,
and as I have repeated in the poem the "Beloved Physician," as the truest,
tenderest of the world's most womanly souls, and an angel to my forlorn
and darkened nature . . .

Although Mrs. Houghton quoted portions of this poem to In-
gram in 1875, he did not publish the fragments until 1909. He
must have had some further information from her, for he gives
lines not found in the correspondence preserved at Charlottes-
ville. Perhaps the lines were given in letters (now missing) from
the lady to Ingram in 1876 and 1877.

Happily for us, the title is mentioned in Poe's letter of June
1848 to Mrs. Shew, quoted above, for Ingram chose to call it

THE BELOVED PHYSICIAN

"The Beautiful Physician," a title sometimes used by Mrs. Houghton in her letters to him. Whitty expressed the opinion that the name might be "The Great Physician." Mrs. Houghton was uncertain about the last line; I follow Ingram in giving the best reading to be extracted from what she wrote. There were nine stanzas in the final version, but we do not know their length; the opening and conclusion seem to survive.

Nothing has been known of the manuscript since 1875, and diligent search by the family in later years was in vain, I was assured by relatives of Mrs. Houghton. She cared little for poetry, and I have an intuitive suspicion that her Victorian delicacy led her to suppress the poem effectively by destroying it — something far easier to do than to admit having done.

TEXTS

(*A*) Manuscript, about April 1847, now lost; (*B*) manuscript letter of Mrs. Houghton, January 23, 1875 (Ingram List, no. 197); (*C*) New York *Bookman*, January 1909 (28:452–454); (*D*) *Selected Poems* . . . , edited by T. O. Mabbott (1928), p. 105.

Ingram's text (*C*) is my source.

[THE BELOVED PHYSICIAN]   [*C*]

I

The pulse beats ten and intermits.
God nerve the soul that ne'er forgets
In calm or storm, by night or day,
Its steady toil, its loyalty. [. . .]

***

5   The pulse beats ten and intermits.
God shield the soul that ne'er forgets. [. . .]

***

The pulse beats ten and intermits.
God guide the soul that ne'er forgets. [. . .]

IX

[. . .] so tired, so weary,

10   The soft head bows, the sweet eyes close;
        The faithful heart yields to repose.

                                        [1847]

NOTES

Title: An echo of Colossians 4:14, where St. Paul says, "Luke, the beloved physician, and Demas, greet you."

1 Physicians inform me that an intermittent pulse is somewhat terrifying and might be connected with Poe's drinking.

9 The last stanza related to the heroine's taking the patient's pulse with a watch after sedation.

[HOLY EYES]

It is not certain that a poem with this title was ever actually written down by Poe. But he obviously planned such a poem, and the title fits two passages (lines 37–47 and 51–65) of the poem of 1848 addressed to Mrs. Whitman.

The former Mrs. Shew, on April 9, 1875, wrote to Ingram an account of an elaborate story Poe had told her when his nurse noticed that he had a scar on his shoulder. This, he said, was the result of a wound received years before in a quarrel over a girl in a foreign port. There, he said, he lay ill for thirteen weeks. A kindly charwoman summoned a Scottish lady of good family, who came daily to see him, in company with her brother. Poe said he had promised never to reveal her name. Mrs. Houghton wrote:

> He described her as a plain looking, large featured, maiden lady, with no beauty but her eyes, which were heavenly blue with long dark lashes. That the magnetism and intense trust, deep, honest heart of sympathy, and trusting faith in God's ever present help to those who believed in and asked for mercy, was so expressed in this Lady's eyes, that he wrote a poem for her in parting called "Holy Eyes."

Poe may not have been delirious when he told this story, for he loved to quiz his friends, and found Mrs. Shew delightfully gullible. No serious student now believes that Poe wrote the poem about a lady's eyes for a Scottish lady in a foreign port, although

TO MARIE LOUISE

Ingram in his *Life* (1880), I, 65–68, told the tale as if he believed it. However, Mrs. Shew herself was rather plain, with beautiful eyes, and she had the same character as the lady of Poe's story. The matter-of-fact Mrs. Shew seems never to have thought of herself as possibly the model of Poe's heroine.[1]

A tradition that Poe composed a poem called "Holy Eyes" or "The Eyes" survives independently in the Houghton family and reached me directly through the Reverend Leonard Twynham. This and the presence in "To Helen [Whitman]" of lines (37–47 and 51–65) fitting the "Holy Eyes" title have led me to discuss "Holy Eyes" seriously.

TO MARIE LOUISE

Poe composed these verses at the request of Mrs. Shew, as the eighteenth line reveals. He rarely used blank verse, and had written none since "The Coliseum" of 1833 and the unfinished play *Politian* of 1835, save a few lines inspired by Elizabeth Barrett in 1845. He used the form in 1847 and 1848 for the present piece, for "To M. L. S——," and for the poem "To Helen [Whitman]," but for nothing thereafter. He seems to have concluded that un-rhymed verse was not a medium for which he was gifted, and although he handled it with something more than competence, most of his admirers will not regret his general avoidance of it.

When Poe prepared the piece for publication he omitted some of the lines, obviously as too personal, but the version he sent to Mrs. Shew is the more interesting.

The exact date of composition of the piece is somewhat uncertain. In a letter of March 28, 1875, to John H. Ingram, described in the Ingram List as number 210, Mrs. Houghton wrote somewhat confusedly about this poem and a poem she referred

[1] In the letter of April 9, 1875, to Ingram (Ingram List, no. 215), the then Mrs. Houghton recounted to the biographer that Poe also had told her that he had written a poem called "Humanity," which was afterward credited to George Sand, and a sensational novel, "Life of an Artist at Home and Abroad," later credited to Eugène Sue! This is obviously pure nonsense, or perhaps banter. See Woodberry, *Life* (1909), I, 170, for a complete refutation of the story of the novel.

to as "To Mrs. M. L. S." She said that they were valentines to
her, in succeeding years. The poem that follows is surely the later
of the two, but as it was published by February 15, 1848, it must
have been written considerably before Valentine's Day of that
year. I do not think it possible to be quite sure whether the per-
sonal version or the published one was composed first. But a
date in the period between December 1847 and January 1848
may be confidently assigned as that of the poem's composition.

TEXTS

(*A*) Manuscript given to Mrs. Shew (the original is now lost, but the
text is preserved in a tracing — no. 32 — in the Ingram Collection at the
University of Virginia); (*B*) *Columbian Lady's and Gentleman's Magazine*
for March 1848 (9:138); (*C*) *Works* (1850), II, 19.
The manuscript text (*A*) and the first publication (*B*) are given in full.
In the latter, changes from the manuscript are found in the title and in lines
8, 12, 13, 15, 16, 17–21 (which are entirely omitted), 24 and 26. Griswold's
text (*C*) followed that of the magazine (*B*) but shortened the title to "To
— —," and introduced a misprint, "unpurpled," in line 26.

TO MARIE LOUISE [*A*]

   Not long ago, the writer of these lines,
   In the mad pride of intellectuality,
   Maintained the "Power of Words" — denied that ever
   A thought arose within the human brain
5   Beyond the utterance of the human tongue:
   And now, as if in mockery of that boast,
   Two words — two foreign, soft dissyllables —
   Two gentle sounds made only to be murmured
   By angels dreaming in the moon-lit "dew
10   That hangs like chains of pearl on Hermon hill"
   Have stirred from out the abysses of his heart
   Unthought-like thoughts — scarcely the shades of thought —
   Bewildering fantasies — far richer visions
   Than even the seraph harper, Israfel,
15   Who "had the sweetest voice of all God's creatures,"
   Would hope to utter. Ah, Marie Louise!
   In deep humility I own that now

TO MARIE LOUISE

All pride — all thought of power — all hope of fame —
All wish for Heaven — is merged forevermore
20 Beneath the palpitating tide of passion
Heaped o'er my soul by thee. Its spells are broken —
The pen falls powerless from my shivering hand —
With that dear name as text I *cannot* write —
I cannot speak — I cannot even think —
25 Alas! I cannot feel; for 'tis *not* feeling —
This standing motionless upon the golden
Threshold of the wide-open gate of Dreams,
Gazing, entranced, adown the gorgeous vista,
And thrilling as I see upon the right —
30 Upon the left — and all the way along,
Amid the clouds of glory, far away
To where the prospect terminates — *thee only*.

[1847]

TO — — — [B]

Not long ago, the writer of these lines,
In the mad pride of intellectuality,
Maintained the "power of words" — denied that ever
A thought arose within the human brain
5 Beyond the utterance of the human tongue;
And now, as if in mockery of that boast,
Two words — two foreign soft dissyllables —
Italian tones made only to be murmured
By angels dreaming in the moonlit "dew
10 That hangs like chains of pearl on Hermon hill" —
Have stirred from out the abysses of his heart,
Unthought-like thoughts that are the souls of thought,
Richer, far wilder, far diviner visions
Than even the seraph harper, Israfel,
15 Who has "the sweetest voice of all God's creatures,"
Could hope to utter. And I! my spells are broken.
The pen falls powerless from my shivering hand.
With thy dear name as text, though bidden by thee,

I cannot write — I cannot speak or think,
20 Alas, I cannot feel; for 'tis not feeling,
This standing motionless upon the golden
Threshold of the wide-open gate of dreams,
Gazing, entranced, adown the gorgeous vista,
And thrilling as I see upon the right,
25 Upon the left, and all the way along
Amid empurpled vapors, far away
To where the prospect terminates — *thee only.*

NOTES

1-3 Poe published a story called "The Power of Words" in 1845, but his reference here is clearly to a passage in "Marginalia," number 149, published in *Graham's* for March 1846: "I am aware of these 'fancies' only when I am upon the very brink of sleep, with the consciousness that I am so . . . It is as if the five senses were supplanted by five myriad others alien to mortality. Now, so entire is my faith in the *power of words*, that, at times, I have believed it possible to embody even the evanescence of fancies such as I have attempted to describe."

7-8 The foreign dissyllables are the lady's personal names, "Marie Louise," but these are French, and not "Italian tones," as in the version Poe published. Frances Winwar (p. 321) observes that the Italian phrase for "I love you" is two dissyllables, "Io t'amo."

9-10 This inaccurate quotation from Peele's *David and Bethsabe*, lines 46-47, was used earlier in *Politian*, IV, 33-34.

12 With reading of versions B and C, compare, in the early "Stanzas," "Of a thought/The unembodied essence," and several passages in *Eureka*: "That class of terms . . . representing *thoughts of thought* . . . These ideas — conceptions such as these — unthoughtlike thoughts — soul-reveries rather than conclusions or even considerations of the intellect . . . That merest of words, "Infinity" . . . is by no means the expression of an idea — but an effort at one."

15 This quotation, used by Poe in "Israfel," is discussed in the notes to that poem, above.

16 In printed versions, B and C, compare the first line of Shakespeare's epilogue to *The Tempest*: "Now my charms are all o'erthrown."

26-28 Fred Lewis Pattee (*Side-Lights on American Literature*, New York, 1922, page 334) cited these lines as indication that "Ulalume" referred to Mrs. Shew. But compare the passage in "Ligeia": "With how vast a triumph . . . did I *feel* . . . in studies but little sought . . . that delicious vista by slow degrees expanding before me, down whose long, gorgeous, and all untrodden path, I might at length pass onward to the goal of a wisdom too divinely precious not to be forbidden."

27 For the gates of dreams see Vergil, *Aeneid*, VI, 893ff.

31 The reading "clouds of glory" is from Wordsworth's ode "Intimations of Immortality." There is plenty of evidence that Poe admired much of Wordsworth's poetry. Wilbur (*Poe*, p. 148) compares to this line (in *B* and *C*) "The Domain of Arnheim," where Ellison's bride's "loveliness and love enveloped his existence in the purple atmosphere of paradise."

ULALUME

"Ulalume" is by many considered the greatest of all Poe's poems. The vocal music by itself conveys one emotion after another, like the lapping of a river against a shore — steady, quiet, and resistless. It must be read aloud or sounded to the "inner ear," and indeed it was composed for recitation.

E. C. Stedman said, "It is so strange . . . and . . . full of meaning, that of itself it might establish a new method." Mrs. Whitman called it "perhaps the most original and the most strangely suggestive of all Poe's poems," and Theodore Watts-Dunton once said that Poe expressed himself "in the same way that the . . . musician would . . . by monotonous reiterations . . . 'Ulalume' properly intoned would produce something like the same effect upon a listener knowing no word of English that it produces upon us." [1] It is certainly possible to read it as a tuneful expression of the poet's own inner emotions; it is that. But it has a wholly explicable story, although some readers may prefer the indefinite effect and choose to skip the minute analysis that follows.[2] Yet it seems to me that when the parts are explained and the plot is understood, the poem remains as a whole inexplicably powerful, an unparalleled evocation of mystery.

The story of how Poe came to write "Ulalume" can at last be

[1] E. C. Stedman, *The Poets of America* (1885), p. 246; Sarah Helen Whitman, *Edgar Poe and His Critics* (1860), p. 29; [Theodore Watts-Dunton], "Poetry," *Encyclopaedia Britannica*, 11th ed. (1910–11), XXI, 880.

[2] My friend the late Professor Marjorie Anderson told me she regretted learning that the poem had a *definite* meaning, and I promised her I would put in my book the suggestion that one need not seek it unless one wished.

completely told.[3] The Reverend Cotesworth P. Bronson, an ordained Episcopal minister, became a famous teacher of public speaking whose book, *Elocution, or Mental and Vocal Philosophy* (copyright 1845), went through many editions. He gave lectures at various colleges, was usually addressed as "Professor," and had a wide acquaintance among politicians. In June 1847 he visited New York with his young daughter, Mary Elizabeth, partly to "hunt lions." Some lady (probably Mrs. Shew, who was a devout Episcopalian) suggested a trip to Fordham to meet a really big lion, Mr. Poe. He proved to be charming, assured his guests that a print of a lovely girl on the wall was not "the lost Lenore," and apologized for not having a pet raven. The Bronsons called several times before leaving the city for a while. When they returned in September (the young lady wrote in 1860) they found that "Mr. Poe had grown thin" and seemed unusually nervous. Mrs. Clemm "spoke hopefully of what Eddie could do if he could only obtain some regular employment worthy of his abilities." In 1888 our informant explained that her father, "knowing Poe's genius and poverty . . . urged him to write something suitable for recitation embodying thoughts that would admit of vocal variety and expression. He recited to the Poet in illustration Collins' Ode to the passions and assured Poe that he would gain both fame and profit for any suitable poem of this kind. Ulalume, Annabell [*sic*] Lee, and The Bells were written as the result of this suggestion and subsequent encouragement."

Poe took nothing from Collins except the idea of presenting varying emotions in a single poem. The impulse finally came to

[3] In the New York *Home Journal* of July 21, 1860, some of the facts were given in an article, "Recollections of Edgar A. Poe," signed only "Mrs. — —," quoting a letter from Poe to the writer's father, whose name appeared as a blank. That article was overlooked by scholars until Carroll D. Laverty reprinted it in *American Literature*, May 1948. The actual letter, with a brief description including the recipient's name — Professor C. P. Bronson — was sold by Dodd, Mead and Company in 1901, but was untraced until 1962. It then entered the collection of William H. Koester, accompanied by a manuscript of authentication signed by M. E. LeDuc as daughter of the recipient, with a new account of her acquaintance with Poe dated "Hastings, Minnesota, Nov. 1888." In my discussion I quote the letter from the original manuscript and use both accounts by Bronson's daughter. Some information is added from the manuscript autobiography of the lady's husband, William Gates LeDuc, examined for me by Miss Lucile Kane in the Minnesota Historical Society at St. Paul.

compose a version of "Ulalume" after a walk to Mamaroneck, New York, on the mainland a dozen miles from Fordham. There he saw the private cemetery of the Guion family, of Revolutionary stock. The tomb of Thomas Guion is approached by an avenue of pine trees, which gave Poe his setting. I heard the story myself from a lady resident of Mamaroneck over twenty years ago, and it is still told locally.[4]

Poe took his basic plot from a piece called "The Summons Answered," by his friend Elizabeth Oakes Smith, printed first in *The Token for 1844* and reprinted in her *Poetical Writings* (1845), which Poe reviewed in *Godey's* for December 1845. There he wrote:

Of the miscellaneous poems included in the volume . . . we greatly prefer "The Summons Answered." It has more of *power*, more of genuine imagination . . . It is a story of three "bacchanals," who, on their way from the scene of their revelry, are arrested by the beckoning of a white hand from the partially unclosing door of the tomb. One of the party obeys the summons. It is the tomb of his wife. We quote the two concluding stanzas.

"This restless life with its little fears,
  Its hopes that fade so soon,
With its yearning tenderness and tears,
And the burning agony that sears —
  The sun gone down at noon —
The spirit crushed to its prison wall,
  Mindless of all beside —
This young Richard saw, and felt it all —
  Well might the dead abide!

"The crimson light in the east is high,
  The hoar-frost coldly gleams,
And Richard chilled to the heart well-nigh,
Hath raised his wildered and bloodshot eye
  From that long night of dreams.
He shudders to think of the reckless band
  And the fearful oath he swore —
*But most he thinks of the clay-cold hand,
  That opened the old tomb door.*"

The germ of "Ulalume" was there, but what Poe did with so crude a story was amazing.

[4] Local inhabitants point out the rock on which they say Poe sat, and sometimes say that the poem was "Annabel Lee" — a slight confusion that tends to confirm the tradition. I have found no printed reference to the story earlier than that in my *Selected Poetry and Prose of . . . Poe* (1951), p. 412.

Mrs. LeDuc reports that a few weeks after the Bronson visit to Fordham she saw Mrs. Clemm, who told her that Poe had written a beautiful poem; the following day the professor received a note from Poe:

> Monday —
>
> My Dear Sir,
>
> I am anxious to see you for many reasons — not the least of which is that I have not seen you for so long a time — but among other things, I wish to ascertain if the poem which, at your suggestion, I have written, is of the lenth [*sic*], the character &c you desire: — if not I will write another and dispose of this one to Mrs Kirkland. Cannot Miss Bronson and yourself, pay us a visit at Fordham — say this afternoon or tomorrow?
>
> Truly your friend
>
> Poe
>
> Prof. C. P. Bronson

The Bronsons could not accept the invitation, and Poe took the poem to them the next day, but found only the young lady at home. She asked if she might read it, and, she says, "He not only assented, but opened the roll . . . It was the 'Ballad of Ulalume.' He made one or two remarks in regard to the ideas intended to be embodied, answering my questions while he read it to me, and expressing his own entire satisfaction with it."

It is not entirely clear whether Bronson paid Poe something for the poem he had commissioned. In any case he did not oppose the poet's selling the piece to a magazine. I doubt that Poe thought his retelling of a ghost story especially obscure; Auber and Weir, whose names have puzzled later readers, were both well known at the time. But when Poe approached Mrs. Kirkland of the *Union Magazine*, she sought advice from young Richard Henry Stoddard! They "could not understand it," and the poem was rejected.[5] Poe then went to his friend George Hooker Colton, who had purchased "The Rationale of Verse," but had been hesitant to publish it in his *American Review*. "I gave him 'a song' for it," Poe wrote to George W. Eveleth on January 4, 1848, "and took

---

[5] See James C. Derby, *Fifty Years Among Authors*, etc. (New York, 1884), p. 597. Stoddard seems never to have printed any candid account of this incident, although he wrote much about Poe.

it back. The song was 'Ulalume a Ballad' published in the December number of the Am. Rev." [6] As Poe had already been paid for the essay — probably seventy-five or a hundred dollars, at space rates for prose — he was for once decently compensated for a poem.

In a bid for publicity, he had the poem printed anonymously in Colton's magazine, but wrote Willis on December 8, 1847, asking that he reprint the poem in the *Home Journal* with a query about its authorship. Willis did this in the issue of January 1, 1848, calling his introduction "Epicureanism in Language." In Providence, Poe wrote his name as author in the copy of the *American Review* at the Athenaeum — the actual copy is preserved there. He also discussed the poem with Helen Whitman, and finally arranged to have it reprinted as his own in the *Providence Journal* of November 22, 1848, with an introduction embodying that of Willis and a second paragraph he obviously composed himself:

> We do not know how many readers we have who will enjoy as we do, the following exquisitely piquant and skillful exercise of rarity and niceness of language. It is a poem that we find in the *American Review*, full of beauty and oddity in sentiment and versification, but a curiosity, (and a delicious one, we think,) in its philologic flavor. Who is the author?
>
> In copying the paragraph above from Willis' "Home Journal," the "Saturday Courier," of Philadelphia gave the usual credit by appending the words *"Home Journal,* N. P. Willis." A Southern paper mistook the words, however, as a reply to the query just preceding — "Who is the author?" and thus, in reprinting the ballad, assigned it to the pen of Willis: — but, by way of rendering unto Caesar the things that are Caesar's, we now correct the mistake — which would be natural enough but for the wide difference of *style* between "Ulalume" and anything by Willis. "Ulalume," although published anonymously in the "American Review," is known to be the composition of EDGAR A. POE.

Poe sent this for republication in the New York *Literary World* where the editor, E. A. Duyckinck, in the issue of March 3, 1849 (4:202) gave the poem a brief introduction of his own, remarking that "in peculiarity of versification, and a certain cold moonlight

---

[6] Mary Gove Nichols, in the *Sixpenny Magazine* for February 1863, told a story of how Colton was induced to buy what she supposed was "Ulalume" from Poe. From Poe's statement to Eveleth it seems that it was actually the highly technical essay on verse which Colton bought only after hesitation.

witchery, it has much of the power of the author's 'Raven.' "
Meanwhile one dull parody had appeared.[7]

The surface story of "Ulalume" may be thus told. In October
of a year when recollection is difficult, in the imaginary realm of
music and painting the protagonist and his soul walk through a
strange landscape. It is Hallowe'en (when the dead have power),
and as dawn approaches they see the planet of love in the sky.
She is seen as warmer than the moon and as having escaped from
the turmoil of lust. The soul distrusts Venus but is calmed by
reasoning until stopped by a tomb, now seen to be that of the
protagonist's lost love. The question is asked if the ghouls (friendly
to living people) have called up a phantom of hope to save the
walkers from memory of an irreparable loss.

More poetically but less completely Mrs. Whitman, in a
letter dated September 29, 1875, published in the *New-York
Tribune* of October 13, wrote:

> . . . The *geist* of the poem . . . is . . . "Astarte" — the crescent star of
> hope and love, that after a night of horror was seen . . .
> The forlorn heart [was] hailing it as a harbinger of happiness yet to
> be, hoping against hope . . . when the planet was seen to be rising over
> the tomb of a lost love, hope itself was rejected as a cruel mockery . . .

She also indicates that Poe told her there was some autobiographi-
cal allegory in it, for she wrote Mrs. Clemm in April 1859: "Vir-
ginia died in January, did she not? . . . Perhaps the correspon-
dence in *time* was purely *ideal* — I know he described the emotions
themselves as *real*." [8]

Poe later sometimes refused to discuss the poem. In a charm-
ing but slightly ironic letter of September 10, 1849, sent to Miss
Susan Ingram in Norfolk with a manuscript copy of "Ulalume,"
which she had heard him read the night before, he said, "I would
endeavor to explain to you what I really meant — or what I
fancied I meant by the poem, if it were not that I remember Dr.
Johnson's bitter and rather just remarks about the folly of ex-
plaining what, if worth explanation, should explain itself." [9]

[7] "Sophia Maria," in Thomas Dunn English's Philadelphia magazine, *The John-
Donkey*, of January 29, 1848.
[8] See Quinn and Hart, p. 49.
[9] Miss Ingram's recollections and the letter were printed in the *New York Herald*,

ULALUME

There is also a tradition that after Poe recited "Ulalume" at the Mackenzies' home, Duncan Lodge, in Richmond, his hostess said, "Mr. Poe, why don't you write your poems so that everyone can understand them?" He replied, "Madam, I write so that *every* body can *not* understand them." [10] Real lovers of poetry usually can. Even in his first biography Woodberry wrote, "The criticism that finds in the ballad . . . merely a whimsical experiment in words has little to go on . . . we have, in this poem, the most spontaneous, the most unmistakably genuine utterance of Poe." [11]

TEXTS

(A) *American Review*, December 1847 (6:599); (B) *Home Journal*, January 1, 1848; (C) *Providence Journal*, November 22, 1848; (D) *Literary World*, March 3, 1849 (4:202); (E) manuscript about Henry B. Hirst, 1849 (lines 30–38); (F) R. W. Griswold, *Poets and Poetry of America*, tenth edition, p. 419; (G) *Works* (1850), II, 20; (H) *Works* (1850), III, 211 (lines 30–38); (J) *Richmond Examiner* proof sheets, summer, 1849, reprinted by Whitty (1911), p. 82; (K) manuscript written for Susan Ingram, September 10, 1849, now in the Pierpont Morgan Library.

I give *K* as text, by permission of the Pierpont Morgan Library; the closing quotation marks at the end of line 50 have been supplied; they do not appear in the manuscript. *E* (lines 30–38) is in a brief critical article (replying to an absurd charge of plagiarism by Henry B. Hirst) in the collection of William H. Koester, now at the University of Texas. Poe, since he and Hirst were reconciled in July 1849, may have wished to suppress the article, but Griswold included it in the third volume of his edition in 1850. For the complete poem (*G*) in his second volume, Griswold apparently used a slightly corrected clipping, but omitted the final stanza. It is certainly an earlier version than *J* and *K*.

ULALUME – A BALLAD [*K*]

The skies they were ashen and sober;
  The leaves they were crispéd and sere —
  The leaves they were withering and sere:

February 19, 1905, and are liberally quoted by Woodberry, II, 329f., and Miss Phillips, II, 1468f. Miss Phillips learned from Miss Ida Thurston of the Pierpont Morgan Library that Susan Ingram said Poe slipped the note and manuscript under her door at the Hygeia Hotel, and Miss Phillips gives a daguerreotype of Miss Ingram.

[10] I do not recall seeing the Mackenzie story in print; I was told it in Richmond.

[11] *Edgar Allan Poe* (1885), p. 282.

It was night, in the lonesome October
5   Of my most immemorial year:
It was hard by the dim lake of Auber,
   In the misty mid region of Weir: —
It was down by the dank tarn of Auber,
   In the ghoul-haunted woodland of Weir.

10   Here once, through an alley Titanic,
      Of cypress, I roamed with my Soul —
      Of cypress, with Psyche, my Soul.
These were days when my heart was volcanic
   As the scoriac rivers that roll —
15   As the lavas that restlessly roll
Their sulphurous currents down Yaanek,
   In the ultimate climes of the Pole —
That groan as they roll down Mount Yaanek,
   In the realms of the Boreal Pole.

20   Our talk had been serious and sober,
   But our thoughts they were palsied and sere —
   Our memories were treacherous and sere;
For we knew not the month was October,
   And we marked not the night of the year —
25   (Ah, night of all nights in the year!)
We noted not the dim lake of Auber,
   (Though once we had journeyed down here)
We remembered not the dank tarn of Auber,
   Nor the ghoul-haunted woodland of Weir.

30   And now, as the night was senescent,
   And star-dials pointed to morn —
   As the star-dials hinted of morn —
At the end of our path a liquescent
   And nebulous lustre was born,
35   Out of which a miraculous crescent
   Arose with a duplicate horn —

ULALUME

Astarte's bediamonded crescent,
 Distinct with its duplicate horn.

And I said — "She is warmer than Dian;
40   She rolls through an ether of sighs —
 She revels in a region of sighs.
She has seen that the tears are not dry on
 These cheeks where the worm never dies,
And has come past the stars of the Lion,
45   To point us the path to the skies —
 To the Lethean peace of the skies —
Come up, in despite of the Lion,
 To shine on us with her bright eyes —
Come up, through the lair of the Lion,
50   With love in her luminous eyes."

But Psyche, uplifting her finger,
 Said — "Sadly this star I mistrust —
 Her pallor I strangely mistrust —
Ah, hasten! — ah, let us not linger!
55   Ah, fly! — let us fly! — for we must."
In terror she spoke; letting sink her
 Wings till they trailed in the dust —
In agony sobbed; letting sink her
 Plumes till they trailed in the dust —
60   Till they sorrowfully trailed in the dust.

I replied — "This is nothing but dreaming.
 Let us on, by this tremulous light!
 Let us bathe in this crystalline light!
Its Sibyllic splendor is beaming
65   With Hope and in Beauty to-night —
 See! — it flickers up the sky through the night!
Ah, we safely may trust to its gleaming
 And be sure it will lead us aright —
We surely may trust to a gleaming

70   That cannot but guide us aright
        Since it flickers up to Heaven through the night."

        Thus I pacified Psyche and kissed her,
            And tempted her out of her gloom —
            And conquered her scruples and gloom;
75   And we passed to the end of the vista —
            But were stopped by the door of a tomb —
            By the door of a legended tomb: —
        And I said — "What is written, sweet sister,
            On the door of this legended tomb?"
80   She replied — "Ulalume — Ulalume! —
            'T is the vault of thy lost Ulalume!"

        Then my heart it grew ashen and sober
            As the leaves that were crispéd and sere —
            As the leaves that were withering and sere —
85   And I cried — "It was surely October,
            On *this* very night of last year,
            That I journeyed — I journeyed down here! —
            That I brought a dread burden down here —
            On this night, of all nights in the year,
90   Ah, what demon hath tempted me here?
        Well I know, now, this dim lake of Auber —
            This misty mid region of Weir: —
        Well I know, now, this dank tarn of Auber —
            This ghoul-haunted woodland of Weir."

95   Said we, then — the two, then — "Ah, can it
            Have been that the woodlandish ghouls —
            The pitiful, the merciful ghouls,
        To bar up our way and to ban it
            From the secret that lies in these wolds —
100   From the thing that lies hidden in these wolds —
        Have drawn up the spectre of a planet
            From the limbo of lunary souls —

ULALUME

This sinfully scintillant planet
From the Hell of the planetary souls?"

[1847–1849]

VARIANTS

Title: To − − −. Ulalume: a Ballad (*A*); Ulalume (*G*)
1 they/*omitted* (*C*)
2 crispéd/crispèd (*A, J*); crisped (*B, C, G*)
13 days/the days (*D*)
28 We/*omitted* (*C, F, G*); remembered/Remember'd (*F*)
31 And/As (*C*)
32 As/And (*C*)
33 our/my (*H*)
35 Out/Ont (*misprint, D*)
40 an/on (*misprint, B*)
51 uplifting/uplifted (*C*)

54–55 Ah . . . ah . . . Ah/Oh . . . oh . . . Oh (*A, B, C, D, F, G*)
57 Wings/Plumes (*C*); till/until (*G*)
59 Plumes/Wings (*C*)
69 surely/safely (*A, B, C, D, F, G*)
75 the vista/a vista (*K*)
76 But were/And were (*A, B, D*) But we (*C*)
83 crispéd/crispèd (*A, K*); crisped (*B, C, G*)
90 Ah/Oh (*A, B, C, D, F*); hath/has (*A, B, C, D, F, G*)
94 This/In the (*A, B, D, F*)
95–104 *Last stanza omitted* (*C, G*)
101 Have/Had (*A, B*)

NOTES

Title: The name is Poe's creation, and is what may be called a sorrowful form of "Eulalie," the title of the poem's cheerful companion piece. This is supported by Poe's pronunciation, "You-la-loom," which is certainly known, from the way Susan Ingram, who had heard the author's reading, said it to Belle da Costa Greene at the Pierpont Morgan Library. Miss Greene told me she recalled it distinctly, because she had been uncertain about what Miss Ingram said and asked her to repeat the name. It seems probable that the sound of the last syllable is meant to suggest the verb *to loom*. But no completely satisfactory explanation of the etymology of Poe's word as a whole has been found, hence all with which I have met must be discussed.

(1) One simple explanation seems the most probable: that the name combines the elements of the Latin verb *ululare*, to wail (the English cognate), and *lumen*, a light — Light of Sorrow. (2) Other explanations do not fit so well with the pronunciation, which many readers have not known. George Arms points out to me that William Dean Howells printed "Ullalume" (in dialogue) three times in *Indian Summer* (1886). (3) "Ul-ul-loo" — variously spelled — is a Gaelic phrase of wailing. (4) Thomas Holley Chivers suggested in his *Life of Poe* (edition of 1952, p. 76): "Ullalume [*sic*] signifies the . . . luminous guiding star of love, as Ul-Erin signifies the guiding star of Ireland." I am told that Chivers' Gaelic is wrong, but his notion that something Irish was intended is of interest. (5) A Turkish word of wailing is mentioned in the form "Wul-wullah" in Byron's *Bride of Abydos*, II, xxvii. (6) In the *Bulletin of the New York Public Library*, September 1959, Palmer C. Holt suggests that *ulu* is a Turkish word for dead, and part of a name of the Dead Sea taken by Poe from Chateaubriand in a note on "Al Aaraaf," II, 38. See a note below

on line 37, for a possible allusion to Chateaubriand, and observe the strange name "Tophet-Nour" given to Poe's "Al Aaraaf" on one occasion; Holt's suggestion cannot be wholly dismissed. (7) In Turkish *ulu* has another meaning, "high" or "elevated," recorded by Barthélemy d'Herbelot, *Bibliothèque Orientale* (1687), p. 914. (8) There is a suggestion, in an eccentric article by Diana Pittman printed in the revived *Southern Literary Messenger* for August 1941, that there is some connection with *Ulema*, a Turkish term for ecclesiastical hierarchy. Dedication (Version *A*): The three blanks probably stand for "C. P. Bronson" or "M. E. Bronson." Earlier suggestions have been "Frances Sargent Osgood" or "Marie Louise Shew."

3 Nelson Adkins in London *Notes and Queries*, January 14, 1933 (pp. 30–31), points out a parallel in a poem "To the Autumn Leaf" by W[illis] G[aylord] C[lark] in an anthology, *Autumn Leaves* (New York, 1837); the second and third lines read: "Last of a summer race, withering and sere/And shivering — wherefore art thou lingering here?" Another parallel was cited to me by the late Kenneth Daughrity in a poem "To — — —," by "Cassius" (N. P. Willis), reprinted from the Boston *Statesman* in the *New-York Mirror* of March 28, 1828, where "The bank on which I knelt" and "the grass" were "sere and withering."

4 Astrologically speaking, October is the month of hope; Poe almost surely finished his poem in that month in 1847.

5 "Immemorial" most usually refers to what cannot be remembered; the phrase "from time immemorial" is used in law for something true for as long a time as anyone can recall. The narrator of the poem cannot recall something that he knows it is important that he should recall. Complaint of a celebrated critic that Poe merely echoes Tennyson's "immemorial elms" is pointless; the Laureate used the word in a different, though correct, sense of "very old."

6 Daniel-François-Esprit Auber (1782–1871), composer of some forty operas, wrote a ballet, *Le Lac des Fées*, in 1839. It was presented at the Olympic Theater, New York, on December 1, 1845, and was part of the repertoire of the celebrated *danseuse*, Hermine Blangy, at about the time when Poe wrote his poem. (See G. C. D. Odell, *Annals of the New York Stage*, volume V, *passim*.) The rhyme with "October" agrees with the usual pronunciation of the surname when it is borne by Americans. In his parody "The Willows" Bret Harte joked about "the sweet music of Auber," but academic critics long thought it a made-up name. None of them seems to have referred to one slightly similar real place name: a small river Awber, on the east boundary of Derbyshire, is mentioned in the second chapter of Charles Cotton's continuation (1676) of Izaak Walton's *Compleat Angler*.

7 Robert Walter Weir (1803–1889) was a prominent painter of the Hudson River School who painted in glowing and magic colors the kind of scenery that surrounded Poe when he composed his poem. (See an article by Lewis Leary and my response in *Explicator*, February and June 1948.) Poe is capable of puns in serious poetry (as were Milton and Shakespeare) and

ULALUME

"weir" means a trap. The word also may suggest weird, as James E. Miller remarked in the *Philological Quarterly*, April 1955, p. 203.

10 See note on "Dream-Land," line 10.

11 The cypress is emblematic of mourning.

12 *Psyche* means both "butterfly" and "soul" in Greek. But it is also the name of the beautiful maiden in classic fable, whose story is most fully told by Apuleius. She became at first the secret wife of Cupid, whose mother, Venus, disapproved of, but later accepted, her daughter-in-law. Because of the old quarrel Psyche distrusts Venus. Soul–body dialogues occur frequently in literature, but Poe shows no dependence on others. Psyche in "Ulalume" is not a *Doppelgänger,* as has sometimes been suggested, for she is not of the same sex as the narrator.

14 "Scoriac" is an adjective connected with scoriae, jagged blocks of loose lava; in the twenty-fourth chapter of "Arthur Gordon Pym" Poe wrote of Antarctica, "Scoria [*sic*] were abundant." No use of the adjective earlier than Poe's is known, but it may someday be found in the literature of Antarctic exploration.

16–19 William P. Trent, in his textbook, *The Raven* . . . (1897), p. 13, says: "Generally speaking *boreal* means *northern,* from Boreas, the north wind. But Poe's imagination usually turned to the South Pole, so that it seems possible that he was following the French terminology, in which 'boreal pole' is that pole of the magnetic needle which points to the South. The whole expression would then be equivalent to 'Antarctic regions.'" Since no active volcano was known in Poe's time within the Arctic Circle — Mount Hecla in Iceland is south of it — this is necessarily correct. Poe is by no means the only writer of English to use the French term, which applies generally to magnets but only infrequently to geography.

There is one active volcano in the Antarctic: Mount Erebus, discovered in 1840 by the expedition of Sir James Clark Ross and named for one of his warships — appropriately, since the word means the infernal regions. It was first pointed out by Howard P. Lovecraft in a story in his volume *The Outsider* (1939), p. 445, that this *must be* Poe's Mount Yaanek. But *why* Poe called it so is a crux to which no quite satisfactory answer, as yet, is forthcoming. The double vowel suggests that Poe had something Arabic in mind. The following tentative explanations have been offered: (1) There is an Arabic execration, *yanak,* of uncertain meaning (probably obscene), but if Poe (in polyglot New York) asked what was the Arabic term for "hell," he might have been given the expletive and supposed it to be a place name. (2) Campbell, *Poems* (1917), p. 274, cited Yanik, a district in Trebizond (a country in which Poe in "Al Aaraaf" placed "the unforgiven"), but it is in the northern hemisphere and is not a mountain, let alone a volcano. (3) "Janik" (equivalent to "Jack") is sometimes used by Polish Jews for an unkindly Christian. (4) *Ya Neyk* is said to be Arabic for "O, thou fool." (5) *Yal anak* is said to be Arabic for "May God curse you." (6) Joseph Auslander told me he thought Poe changed slightly, for the rhyme, *Gehinnom,* the vale of Hinnom of Joshua 15:8 — the modern Arabic pronunciation is "Yahannam."

(7) An acquaintance of mine thought it rather like a word he had heard in Turkey meaning "Let it burn."

25   The "night of all nights" is Hallowe'en, when the dead have power.

31   "Star dials" I take to be the heavenly spheres regarded as horologues; the position of the stars shows that morning is near. Although time can be told scientifically by the stars, an astronomer assures me that no instruments that could be called star dials exist in fact.

37   Astarte is here as in "Eulalie" identified with the planet Venus. A star or planet can have diamond-like brilliance; the moon cannot. In the article quoted in our note on the poem's title, Palmer Holt points out a passage in Shoberl's translation of Chateaubriand's *Travels in Greece* (Philadelphia, 1813), p. 220:

"On the 12th [of October] at four in the morning, we weighed anchor . . . Aurora dawned on our right behind the highlands . . . the Eastern sky . . . grew paler as the light increased; the morning star sparkled in the empurpled radiance; and below that beautiful star the crescent of the moon was scarcely discernible . . . the ancients would have said that Venus, Diana and Aurora had met to announce . . . the most brilliant of the gods."

Poe quoted from Chateaubriand's book in notes on "Al Aaraaf," and used the rare word "empurpled" in his poem "To Marie Louise" of 1847. Compare also Fitz-Greene Halleck's "Twilight," lines 35–36: ". . . the dim evening star/That points our destined tomb."

39   Diana has the title Triplex, for she has power in heaven, earth, and hell, but as a virgin is not a patron of marriage. Observe that Diana is here definitely distinct from the star; the moon is contrasted with the planet of love, as she had been in Poe's early poem "Evening Star."

41   Some critics have found this line hard to scan. Poe's intention I think he would have expressed thus, "She *revels* in a *region* of *sighs*."

42   See Isaiah 66:24 and Mark 9:48 for the transgressors whose "worm shall not die." But Wordsworth in "Guilt and Sorrow," line 590, has "Say that the worm is on my cheek." See J. P. Blumenfeld in the London *Notes and Queries*, March 29, 1952, p. 147.

44   Venus in Leo signifies lust or trouble in love, as is mentioned in "E.K.'s" gloss to Spenser's *Shepheards Calender*, "December." Acting on a hint from Floyd Stovall, I have learned from an astronomer something of the aspect of the heavens in 1847. Venus left the sign of Leo and entered Virgo on July 30 and (partly because of a retrograde motion) remained in it until December; the latter sign is unfavorable to marriage. Venus was also in Virgo on Hallowe'en in 1846, but not in 1845.

46   Lethe is the river of Hades that brings forgetfulness. See Dryden's translation of Vergil, *Aeneid*, VI, 1016ff., where purified souls

". . . drink the deep Lethaean flood
. . . to steep the cares
Of their past labors . . ."

before reincarnation.

ULALUME

56–60 Drooping wings in sorrow is as old as the sixteenth fragment of Sappho. Poe had quoted with approval in the *Broadway Journal* of August 9, 1845, from Thomas Hood's "Ode to Melancholy":

> . . . the secret soul's mistrust,
> To feel her fair ethereal wings
> Weigh'd down with vile degraded dust.

Henry B. Hirst, in the Philadelphia *Saturday Courier* for January 22, 1848, pointed out a parallel in Thomas Buchanan Read's "Christine," lines 19–22:

> Then my weary soul went from me, and it walked the world alone,
> O'er a wide and brazen desert, in a hot and brazen zone!
>
> There it walked and trailed its pinions, slowly trailed them in the sands,
> With its hopeless eyes fixed blindly, with its hopeless folded hands.

The poem first appeared in *Graham's* for December 1846 (29:314), and Campbell, *Poems* (1917), p. 275, remarks that the parallel is evident.

63 The word "crystalline" refers to the sphere of the fixed stars according to N. Bailey's *Dictionary* (1721). See "Al Aaraaf," I, 143.

64 "Sibyllic" means prophetic; the Sibyls were inspired by Apollo.

75 "Vistas" and "sisters" are rhymed by Mrs. Osgood in her "Dying Rosebud's Lament." For many New Englanders, New Yorkers, and Southerners the rhyme is good.

77 "Legended" means "inscribed with something legible."

78 The protagonist is the brother of the soul; as in "The Fall of the House of Usher" the man represents reason, the sister intuition. In *Eureka* (1848), p. 70, Poe wrote, "The body and the soul walk hand in hand."

87 There is no reason to accept a suggestion of a few critics that there is any remorse for a crime here; it is at variance with the rest of the poem and its sources.

90 Poe "disliked the dark . . . He said to me, 'I believe that demons take advantage of the night to mislead the unwary . . . although you know . . . I don't believe in them.' " This is from a letter George R. Graham wrote William Fearing Gill on May 1, 1877, quoted in Harrison's edition of Poe, XVII, 437.

95–104 Poe's omission of the last stanza in some versions was at Mrs. Whitman's suggestion. See the Ingram List, numbers 138 and 303. The sentiment is obviously ungraceful for a fiancé. But the lady later felt she had made a mistake, and Poe was to come to the same conclusion.

96–97 The ghouls are here friendly; they do not harm living people.

101–104 Here, as in "Fairyland," the poet has in mind ancient notions that every moon is a monthly or even a daily new creation. Since Venus has phases like the moon, Poe applies the idea to her too. Limbo, "the easiest room in hell," is chiefly peopled by those lacking baptism.

AN ENIGMA

[Sarah Anna Lewis]

Sarah Anna Blanche Robinson Lewis, a Baltimorean who in signing her verses preferred "Estelle" or "Stella" to her given name, was the wife of Sylvanus D. Lewis, a Brooklyn lawyer who had met Poe in 1845. Particularly in the difficult period after the death of Virginia Poe in 1847, the Lewises befriended Poe and Mrs. Clemm, and Mrs. Lewis or her husband gave Poe (or more probably Mrs. Clemm) a hundred dollars for Poe's services as her press agent. He puffed her far from brilliant verses in various magazines, and revised at least one of her poems, "The Prisoner of Perotè" (see Collaborations, below). She permitted him to address her as "sister Anna," and this Vergilian nickname led Mrs. Clemm to tell her she was "Annabel Lee."

There is no doubt that she often bored Poe, who sometimes slipped out of the Fordham cottage when he saw her coming (see Mrs. Houghton's letter of April 3, 1875, described in the Ingram List, no. 213, and other references in the Ingram List). But Poe and Mrs. Clemm spent a good deal of time at the Lewis home at 125 Dean Street in Brooklyn. Mrs. Clemm took up her chief residence there after Poe's death and lived there until late in 1858, when the Lewises were divorced.

The reminiscences of Sylvanus Lewis are in *Edgar Allan Poe: A Memorial Volume* (1877), edited by Sara Sigourney Rice, p. 87. Whatever the Lewises quarreled about, they agreed completely in their admiration of the poet.

"Estelle" assisted Griswold in compiling the two volumes of Poe's *Works* (1850), and she later supplied Ingram with information. She died in 1880, and Ingram contributed an obituary to the London *Athenaeum* of December 4. Mrs. Lewis gave her portrait by Charles Loring Elliott to the New-York Historical Society, presumably so that it would be with Poe's. It was painted shortly before she and Poe met, and shows what Poe calls "a poetical face" and her chestnut hair in ringlets.

On November 27, 1847, Poe wrote to Mrs. Lewis thanking

her for her "repeated kindness" and enclosing a sonnet "too light in tone," embodying "a riddle." (As in "A Valentine" the first letter of the first line, the second of the second, and so on spell out the name of the recipient.) This he said he had sent "a day or two ago" to one of the magazines. Griswold was in close touch with Mrs. Lewis while preparing the second volume of the *Works*, and we need not doubt that Griswold's text in the *Works* (1850) followed the manuscript sent to Mrs. Lewis.

TEXTS

(*A*) *Union Magazine of Literature and Art* for March 1848 (2:130); (*B*) *Works* (1850), II, 26.

Griswold's text (*B*) is followed.

AN ENIGMA   [*B*]

"Seldom we find," says Solomon Don Dunce,
　　"Half an idea in the profoundest sonnet.
Through all the flimsy things we see at once
　　As easily as through a Naples bonnet —
5　　　Trash of all trash! — how *can* a lady don it?
Yet heavier far than your Petrarchan stuff —
Owl-downy nonsense that the faintest puff
　　Twirls into trunk-paper the while you con it."
And, veritably, Sol is right enough.
10　　The general tuckermanities are arrant
Bubbles — ephemeral and *so* transparent —
　　But *this* is, now, — you may depend upon it —
Stable, opaque, immortal — all by dint
Of the dear names that lie concealed within 't.

[1847]

VARIANTS

Title:　Sonnet (*A*)
10　tuckermanities/Petrarchanities (*A*)

NOTES

1　Solomon Don Dunce must be our poet himself, as one who said wise things but was stupid enough to write sonnets — a form Poe deprecated. In

Burton's Magazine for September 1839, he reviewed a book, *Solomon Seesaw*, by J. P. Robertson, and in *Eureka* (1848), he wrote of "as simple a thing as a sonnet by Mr. Solomon Seesaw." Some personal joke understood by Poe and the Lewises may have been intended.

4 By a "Naples bonnet," Poe means a "net à la Napolitaine," which encased the back hair and was made of strings of pearls finished with fringe and tassels. To this Mrs. Gertrude W. Markell of the staff of the Boston Museum of Fine Arts has found references from about 1855 to 1860. Bonnets were sometimes made of "gros de Naples," but this was a "most durable silken tissue," and Leghorn bonnets, though well known, were of straw; one could not *see through* either.

5 In his tale "The Literary Life of Thingum Bob" Poe has the phrase "trash of trash."

10 The reading adopted in the *Works*, "tuckermanites," is typically Poesque, from Henry Theodore Tuckerman. In his "Rationale of Verse" Poe used a similar word, "hudsonizing," derived from the name of Henry Norman Hudson, the lecturer on Shakespeare. Poe often referred to Tuckerman's work as dull, even as early as 1841 in "A Chapter on Autography," and Campbell points out (*Poems*, pp. 276–277) that Tuckerman contributed sonnets to the *Democratic Review* about 1845, and wrote for the *American Review* of May 1845 an article on Petrarch. Poe and Tuckerman seem to have liked each other personally, and Poe wisely used "Petrarchanities" in the version he sent to the *Union Magazine*. His opinion of Petrarch was not a high one, as is evident in his review in *Graham's* for September 1841 of Thomas Campbell's biography of the Italian poet.

LAST POEMS

1848–1849

THE BELLS

"The Bells," a great popular favorite, is one of the finest specimens of onomatopoetic verse in English. Although it was one of the two major poems of Poe that did not appear during his lifetime, it was begun in 1848, and the circumstances of its genesis and growth are known in great detail.

It has been shrewdly conjectured that the impulse to write the piece came from a copy of the *Union Magazine* for April 1848 (current after March 15), where the editor, Mrs. Caroline Kirkland, quoted with approval a paragraph from the *Literary World*: "A poem of twenty lines, spirited, intense, and exuberantly suggestive alike to feeling and to thought, is . . . of a higher order than an epic of twenty books." The lady, for all that she had rejected "Ulalume," sometimes bought Poe's verses, and he seems to have wished to take up her challenge.

Marie Louise Shew Houghton told the story to Ingram in a long letter written between January 23 and February 16, 1875.[1] According to her account, one day the poet came to visit her in New York where she lived, as a widow, at 47 Bond Street, the home of her brother-in-law, Dr. Joel Shew, and said, "I have to write a poem; I have no feeling, no sentiment, no inspiration." Tea was "served in the conservatory"[2] and the poet remarked, "I so dislike the noise of bells to-night, I cannot write. I have no subject — I am exhausted." His hostess then "took up the pen, and, pretending to mimic his style, wrote, 'The Bells, by E. A. Poe'; and then . . . 'The Bells, the little silver Bells,' Poe finishing off the stanza. She then suggested for the next verse, 'The heavy iron

[1] Ingram List, no. 197; recounted by J. H. Ingram, *Poe* (1880), II, 155–156. There is no reason to doubt any of this, although dislike of Ingram led some of his contemporaries to minimize its importance.

[2] This remark helps to date the poem: the Shews moved during the first fortnight of May 1848 from 47 Bond Street to 51 Tenth Street (now 17 West Tenth), where there was no conservatory. See the discussion by a relative, Chauncey C. L. Ditmars, quoted in Phillips, II, 1269. Both houses were still standing in 1968.

Bells'; and this Poe also expanded into a stanza. He next copied out the complete poem, and headed it, 'By Mrs. M. L. Shew,' remarking that it was her poem; as she had suggested and composed so much of it." Poe then went to bed and slept for twelve hours.

It is generally assumed that the day on which there was much ringing of bells was a Sunday. But it was the custom when there was a fire to toll all neighboring church bells simultaneously, and it has been suggested that such an occasion was what jarred on Poe's nerves.[3] At any rate, we are on firmer ground in locating some of the bells near the home of Mrs. Shew.[4] There were nearby bells at Bartholomew's (of which Mrs. Shew was a communicant), St. Luke's, St. John's, St. Mark's in the Bowery, and the Bleecker Street Presbyterian Church. But there was (and is) an outstandingly important bell, actually called the Silver Bell, in the belfry of the Middle Collegiate Church at 50 East Seventh Street at Second Avenue. This bell was cast in Amsterdam in 1729, and citizens of the Dutch city contributed silver coins for its alloy. It was given to the Old Middle Dutch Church by the family of Abraham De Peyster. When the church moved uptown to Seventh Street, the bell was for several years kept in the vestibule, until Samuel Ward, banker and poet, defrayed the cost of hanging it in time for its tolling on Easter 1848. It is still used.[5] Other bells, sometimes called Poe's inspiration, have less valid claims (although he heard most of them before writing the final version of his poem).[6] The bells at the chapel of what is now Fordham University are called Poe's bells in local tradition.

[3] A writer stated in *Our Town* (New York), March 1961, that there was such a fire on April 30, 1848; but I cannot verify this, and since there was a great fire at Hudson and Bond Streets on April 30, 1833, I suspect some confusion in the matter.

[4] I am greatly indebted to the research of Robert Hunter Paterson, who placed his notes, some unpublished, at my disposal.

[5] "Silver bells" are in all versions of Poe's poem. In the first version the purpose is not specified, in the second they are wedding bells, in the last they are finally sleigh bells.

[6] Those of the Church of the Ascension, Fifth Avenue and Tenth Street, may be mentioned. Those of Trinity Church, where Poe attended a midnight service on Christmas Eve, 1847, are too far from Bond Street to enter the picture. The bells of Grace Church at Broadway and Tenth are still often pointed out as "Poe's in-

THE BELLS

Later Poe revised the little poem, expanding it slightly, and sold it to the *Union Magazine* for fifteen dollars. On February 8, 1849, he wrote to Mrs. Richmond that two days previously he had written a poem longer than "The Raven" called "The Bells," which might appear in the *American Review*. Since "The Raven" has 108 lines, this version of "The Bells" must have been practically complete. When Poe visited Mrs. Richmond in Lowell during the last week of May, he recited it to a Reading Club (including Annie's sister Sarah Heywood) at nearby Westford, Massachusetts.[7] Poe returned with his new version to what had now become *Sartain's Union Magazine,* and received twenty-five dollars more. He got the poem back again some time later, revised it slightly, and received five dollars as final payment — a total of forty-five dollars.[8]

In *Sartain's* for December, John S. Hart printed an editorial account of the history of "The Bells," headed "Edgar A. Poe," in which he said, "There is a curious piece of literary history connected with this . . . It illustrates the gradual development of an idea in the mind of a man of original genius. The poem came into our possession about a year since. It then consisted of eighteen lines!" He then proceeded to publish them as I give them in the present edition, and explained how he had received two later enlarged versions.

There is no doubt that Mrs. Shew's suggestion had prompted the writing of the first little versions of "The Bells." But at most she had only awakened an idea dormant in Poe's mind. He had long been interested in bells and chimes, which have an important part in his grotesque sketch "The Devil in the Belfry" and in his highly poetic tale of "The Masque of the Red Death." There

---

spiration" but the ones he may have heard there in 1848 were long since replaced by a new set of chimes.

[7] See Ingram, *Poe* (1880), II, 188, 189, for statements of Mrs. Sarah Heywood Trumbull. Woodberry's statement in his *Life* (1909), II, 308, that Poe wrote a draft at Lowell is probably based on a confused version of this story. A reference by Phillips, II, 1295, to a manuscript of "The Bells" in Annie's family also probably represents confusion of memory.

[8] I follow John Sartain's *Reminiscences* (1899), p. 220: he was discussing prices he had paid authors in a way that suggests he was consulting his books. His statements about the intervals between receipt of the versions are not absolutely consistent with those of his editor, John S. Hart, in *Sartain's* for December 1849.

is a pertinent remark in his review in *Burton's Magazine*, August 1839 (5:116), of William Wallace's poem, *The Triumphs of Science*; from it Poe quotes a line, "Six thousand years the Bell of Time had tolled," and adds "An every-day poetaster . . . would never have dared to dream that there existed . . . the spirit-lifting and memory-stirring *bell*." This interest is what led to the expansion of Poe's little song into a long poem, in which Poe seems to me to have followed the plan suggested by Professor Bronson, as Mrs. LeDuc said (in her memorandum quoted above in the notes on "Ulalume") — a composition for recitation to exemplify the most varied emotions.

There had been countless poems on the subject. Who can forget "Those Evening Bells" by Thomas Moore, or "The Bells of Shandon" by Francis Mahony ("Father Prout")? And the subject was popular with Poe's contemporaries in America.[9] Like A. H. Quinn (*Poe*, p. 564) I think Poe owed little or nothing to them.

Some readers may recall seeing a very different account from the foregoing of how Poe wrote "The Bells." It is certainly fictitious, but of so pleasant a kind that it is synopsized here in a footnote.[10]

[9] Campbell in *Poems* (1917), pp. 280–281, gives an extensive list, with references and quotations — which could easily be expanded. Woodberry cited a passage in Chateaubriand's *Génie du Christianisme*, suggesting that a poet should not despise as a subject "a bell tolled by phantoms in the old chapel of the forest"; but the rest of the passage has little in common with Poe, who never mentioned *that* book of the rhetorical French author. Whitty claimed that Poe told F. W. Thomas he had *The Chimes* by Dickens in mind, though when and where Poe could have discussed "The Bells" with Thomas is not easy to imagine. Campbell himself quoted unimpressively from "Bells" in the New York *Mirror*, March 19, 1836. Some resemblance might be found in emphasis on the same bells tolling for wedding and burial in "The Old Chapel-Bell" by John G. Saxe in the *Union Magazine* for March 1848. And there is an account of a special bell, rung by the angels whenever the unpardonable sin is committed, in chapter xiii of George Lippard's *Quaker City* — a novel Poe probably glanced through before giving it a perfunctory friendly notice in the *Broadway Journal* of June 7, 1845.

[10] See Phillips, II, 1278–80, following "an old newspaper." It is said that in Baltimore a young lawyer, later Judge A. E. Giles, was called upon late one evening in November 1848 by the poet, who asked him for pen, paper, and a place to write. Next morning the author presented his host with a duplicate copy of what he had written during the night — "The Bells." There was a Baltimorean Judge Giles, but his initials were not "A. E." Two other stories ascribing to other persons the composition of poems by Poe are the Fenwick canard about "The Raven" (see p. 359, n. 17, above) and the tale about the Widow Meagher (p. 511, below). See discussions in *American Notes and Queries*, August and October 1942 and January 1943.

THE BELLS

When "The Bells" was published in *Sartain's* for November, issued about October 15, 1849, little more than a week after the author's death, the poem was an instantaneous success. N. P. Willis wrote, for a reprint in his *Home Journal*, October 27, 1849, one of those introductions the poet valued so highly:

Poe's Last Poem. The *Union Magazine* for November contains the following remarkable poem by the late *Edgar A. Poe*. We do not know of a piece of fugitive poetry in the English language that will be more likely to be more generally read. Its rhythmical harmony is perfect, and its tone, throughout, fit and sustained.

TEXTS

(*A*) Manuscript written in early May 1848 in the hands of Marie Louise Shew and Poe, probably lost but presumably like the next item; (*B*) the holograph fair copy made immediately by Poe, printed by J. H. Ingram in Chandos Classics *Poetical Works of . . . Poe* (London and New York, 1888), page 31, facsimiled in auction catalogue of Frank J. Hogan Collection (New York, January 23–24, 1945), lot 566, and now in the Koester Collection at the University of Texas; (*C*) manuscript, sold late in 1848, now presumably lost but text printed in *Sartain's Union Magazine* for December 1849 (5:386–387); (*D*) manuscript of a long version, written February 6, 1849, sold to Sartain, possibly lost, but in my opinion actually the next item before final changes; (*E*) manuscript in final revised form, sold to Sartain in summer of 1849, facsimiled by J. H. Ingram in the London *Bibliophile* of May 1909 (3:129, 131, 133), and now in the Pierpont Morgan Library; (*F*) *Richmond Examiner* proofsheets, summer 1849, reprinted by J. H. Whitty, *Complete Poems* (1911), pages 63–66; (*G*) *Sartain's Union Magazine* for November 1849 (5:304); (*H*) New York *Home Journal*, October 27, 1849; (*J*) *Works* (1850), II, 23–26.

Both short versions (*B*) and (*C*) are given in full. The long version, by permission of the Trustees of the Pierpont Morgan Library, follows the now incomplete holograph (*E*) through line 99. This manuscript is somewhat damaged, restored and silked; some of Poe's changes in pencil are now almost illegible. Facsimiles are misleading, since they do not show Poe's final changes in pencil. The rest of the poem is taken from the first printed version (*G*). When using (*E*) as copy the printers of *Sartain's Magazine* took many liberties such as using British spelling for words like "clamour" — which Poe did not use in his later years — and misunderstood some of his changes. The authorized version of Poe's de facto literary executor, Griswold (*J*), and that (*H*) of Willis (authorized by implication, since Poe always asked Willis to reprint his major poems), follow the *Sartain's* text verbally, but with minor emendations in spelling and punctuation. The text presented is very close to that of the "*Examiner* proof-sheet" as reproduced by Whitty (*F*), but the anomalous character of that document (which nobody now can find) is notorious.

THE BELLS [B]
By Mrs. M. L. Shew.

The bells! — ah, the bells!
The little silver bells!
How fairy-like a melody there floats
From their throats —
5   From their merry little throats —
From the silver, tinkling throats
Of the bells, bells, bells —
Of the bells!

The bells! — ah, the bells!
10   The heavy iron bells!
How horrible a monody there floats
From their throats —
From their deep-toned throats —
From their melancholy throats!
15   How I shudder at the notes
Of the bells, bells, bells —
Of the bells!

        [May 1848]

THE BELLS. — A SONG [C]

The bells! — hear the bells!
The merry wedding bells!
The little silver bells!
How fairy-like a melody there swells
5   From the silver tinkling cells
Of the bells, bells, bells!
Of the bells!

The bells! — ah, the bells!
The heavy iron bells!
10   Hear the tolling of the bells!
Hear the knells!

THE BELLS

How horrible a monody there floats
From their throats —
From their deep-toned throats!
15   How I shudder at the notes
From the melancholy throats
Of the bells, bells, bells —
Of the bells —

[1848]

THE BELLS   [*E/G*]

1.

Hear the sledges with the bells —
Silver bells!
What a world of merriment their melody foretells!
How they tinkle, tinkle, tinkle,
5   In the icy air of night!
While the stars that oversprinkle
All the Heavens, seem to twinkle
With a crystalline delight;
Keeping time, time, time,
10   In a sort of Runic rhyme,
To the tintinabulation that so musically wells
From the bells, bells, bells, bells,
Bells, bells, bells —
From the jingling and the tinkling of the bells.

2.

15   Hear the mellow wedding bells —
Golden bells!
What a world of happiness their harmony foretells!
Through the balmy air of night
How they ring out their delight! —
20   From the molten-golden notes
And all in tune,

·435·

What a liquid ditty floats
To the turtle-dove that listens while she gloats
On the moon!
25 Oh, from out the sounding cells
What a gush of euphony voluminously wells!
How it swells!
How it dwells
On the Future! — how it tells
30 Of the rapture that impels
To the swinging and the ringing
Of the bells, bells, bells! —
Of the bells, bells, bells, bells,
Bells, bells, bells —
35 To the rhyming and the chiming of the bells!

3.

Hear the loud alarum bells —
Brazen bells!
What tale of terror, now, their turbulency tells!
In the startled ear of Night
40 How they scream out their affright!
Too much horrified to speak,
They can only shriek, shriek,
Out of tune,
In a clamorous appealing to the mercy of the fire —
45 In a mad expostulation with the deaf and frantic fire,
Leaping higher, higher, higher,
With a desperate desire
And a resolute endeavor
Now — now to sit, or never,
50 By the side of the pale-faced moon.
Oh, the bells, bells, bells!
What a tale their terror tells
Of despair!
How they clang and clash and roar!
55 What a horror they outpour

In the bosom of the palpitating air!
    Yet the ear, it fully knows,
       By the twanging
       And the clanging,
60   How the danger ebbs and flows: —
    Yes, the ear distinctly tells,
       In the jangling
       And the wrangling,
    How the danger sinks and swells,
65 By the sinking or the swelling in the anger of the bells —
      Of the bells —
    Of the bells, bells, bells, bells,
      Bells, bells, bells —
    In the clamor and the clangor of the bells.

4.

70   Hear the tolling of the bells —
       Iron bells!
What a world of solemn thought their monody compels!
      In the silence of the night
      How we shiver with affright
75   At the melancholy meaning of the tone!
      For every sound that floats
      From the rust within their throats
       Is a groan.
      And the people — ah, the people
80   They that dwell up in the steeple
       All alone,
    And who, tolling, tolling, tolling,
      In that muffled monotone,
      Feel a glory in so rolling
85   On the human heart a stone —
They are neither man nor woman —
They are neither brute nor human,
      They are Ghouls: —
And their king it is who tolls: —

90 And he rolls, rolls, rolls, rolls
   A Pæan from the bells!
  And his merry bosom swells
   With the Pæan of the bells!
   And he dances and he yells;
95 Keeping time, time, time,
  In a sort of Runic rhyme,
    To the Pæan of the bells —
    Of the bells: —
  Keeping time, time, time,
100 In a sort of Runic rhyme,
    To the throbbing of the bells —
  Of the bells, bells, bells —
    To the sobbing of the bells: —
  Keeping time, time, time,
105   As he knells, knells, knells,
  In a happy Runic rhyme,
    To the rolling of the bells —
  Of the bells, bells, bells: —
    To the tolling of the bells —
110 Of the bells, bells, bells, bells,
    Bells, bells, bells —
To the moaning and the groaning of the bells.

                        [July 1849]

VARIANTS AND TEXTUAL NOTES

3 *The word* What *here, and in lines 17, 26, 38, and 72, is italicized plainly in the manuscript (E), but in no printed text save F.*
11 *The spelling* tintinabulation *is clear in the manuscript (E) and is used in Griswold's text (J); the spelling* tintinnabulation *appears in F, G and H.*
12–13 *Originally* bells *was written five times in line 12, and twice in line 13. Poe changed this in ink in the manuscript (E). There are similar changes in lines 33–34, and 67–68.*
41 Too much/*originally* Much too *but changed by Poe in ink (E).*
56 In/On *(F, G, H, J)*
61 Yes,/*misprinted* Yet *(G, H, J) but correct in F*
63 wrangling/rangling *(H)*
65 anger/*first written* clamor *but changed by Poe in ink (E)*
69 clamor/*first written* anger *but changed by Poe in ink (E)*
75 meaning *was the first reading, changed by Poe to* menace *in ink but changed*

THE BELLS

back to meaning *in pencil (E); this change was overlooked by his printers, hence* menace *appears in F, G, H, and J.*

77 the rust within their/*first written* out their ghostly *and altered in ink (E)*

80 They that dwell/*first written* Who live, *altered in ink to* They that sleep, *and back, in pencil, to the present reading, which is followed in F, G, H, J. The final pencil alteration is now practically illegible.*

88 They are Ghouls/*originally written as two lines*:

> But are pestilential carcases disparted from their souls —
> Called Ghouls: —

but altered in pencil by Poe (E) and correctly printed in F, G, H, J.

90–91 *All printed versions (F, G, H, J) print* rolls three times in line 90 *and* Rolls *alone as the next line, but the manuscript (E) does not support this arrangement, and in "The Rationale of Verse" Poe declared a verse of one syllable to be incorrect.*

99–112 *These lines are not preserved in E, hence G is followed; other printed versions (F, H, J) show no verbal changes.*

NOTES

1–3 One of the several poems Poe must have seen is a song by "J. D. K." called "The Merry Sleigh Bell" in the *Union Magazine* for February 1848, but it shows no close parallels.

5–7 Compare Spenser, "An Hymne in Honour of Beautie," line 257, where eyes "Doe seeme like twinckling starres in frostie night."

10 By Runic rhyme, Poe meant a magic spell. Compare Thomas Gray's "Descent of Odin" for mention of the "runic rhyme . . . that wakes the dead." The phrase "Runic rhymes" was also used in "Ode, Addressed to H. Fuseli" by Henry Kirke White. The runes — the earliest alphabets of northern Europe — were often used in magic and divination.

11 Compare Cowper's "Table Talk," lines 528–529: "Beating alternately, in measured time,/The clockwork tintinabulum of rhyme." There is a paragraph on bells in the compilation "Omniana" in *Burton's* for June 1840 (6:289) which mentions that the Romans called bells "Tintin-nabula." I cannot accept this article as from Poe's pen. The spelling of the English word tintinnabulation has not manuscript authority, and Poe's is the earliest use of the word usually cited in dictionaries, but it has been found (in the form tintinnabulations) in a private letter of William W. Lord, June 11, 1845, published in David A. Randall's "Footnote on a Minor Poet" (*Colophon*, Autumn 1938, p. 592). I suspect it may come from the publicity of "The Swiss Bell-Ringers" about whom Poe published a skit in the *New York Evening Mirror*, October 10, 1844.

44–46 and 69 Compare the following lines from "The Bell Song," based on Schiller's "Lied von der Glocke," in James Nack's *Earl Rupert* (New York, 1839), p. 57:

> The clamour of dismay
> Higher swells and higher;
> Loud and loud the bell is rung,
> Flies the cry from tongue to tongue,
> "Fire! fire! fire!"

Curiosity may well have prompted Poe to look at Nack's version, for the translator was almost completely deaf.

56 Compare *Romeo and Juliet*, II, ii, 32: "upon the bosom of the air."

72–75 Compare "An Indian Serenade," by William Gilmore Simms:

> Yet they wake a song of sorrow,
> Those sweet voices of the night
> Still from grief a gift they borrow,
> And hearts shiver, as they quiver,
> With a wild and sad delight.

Poe quotes this ballad in full in *Burton's* for November 1839, from the ninth chapter of *The Damsel of Darien*.

75 Compare the end of Thomas Hood's sonnet, "Midnight" (1822): "Only the sound of melancholy bells —/The voice of Time — survivor of them all."

77 Cowper's *Task*, IV, 104, has (of guns): "Hear the faint echo of those brazen throats."

80–88 Compare Pope's "Ode for Music on St. Cecilia's Day," lines 99ff.:

> Or where Hebrus wanders,
> Rolling in meanders,
> All alone,
> Unheard, unknown,
> He makes his moan;
> And calls her ghost,
> For ever, ever, ever lost!

88f. In the canceled line following this in the final manuscript, "disparted" is used. Poe may have recently seen his former friend Lambert A. Wilmer's *Somnia* (1848), on the opening page of which we read "And from the lowering and disparted mass/Came down the messenger of the Most High."

89f Compare Poe's "Devil in the Belfry": "There he sat in the belfry upon the belfry-man, who was lying flat upon his back. In his teeth the villain held the bell-rope, which he kept jerking about with his head . . . On his lap lay the big fiddle at which he was scraping out of all time and tune." Poe's story owes a good deal to William Maginn's "The Man in the Bell," first published in *Blackwood's*, November 1821, and often reprinted. Poe names it in a letter of April 30, 1835, and in his "How to Write a Blackwood Article." In it, the narrator, caught in a bell in a steeple, becomes delirious and fancies he sees demons about him.

113 Since Poe's bells were inspired by church bells, it may be appropriate to mention that as early as in *McMakin's Model American Courier*, Philadelphia, December 15, 1849, a correspondent published a reverent little sequel called "The Sabbath Bells: A Stanza omitted by Edgar A. Poe." It begins:

> Hear the holy Sabbath bells —
> Sacred bells!
> Oh, what a world of peaceful rest
> Their melody foretells!

and continues for twenty-three lines more. It is signed by H. S. Nolen. A copy was sent me by the discoverer, my friend Clarence S. Brigham.

TO HELEN [WHITMAN]

This major poem celebrates one of the great romances of literary history, the brief engagement of Poe and Sarah Helen Power Whitman of Providence. The poem was "worthy of himself, of her, and of the most exalted passion," as Griswold well said.[1] It is Poe's best accomplishment in blank verse, a medium in which he was never completely at ease.

When it was printed in the *New-York Tribune* of October 10, 1849, the editor said that the poem had been omitted from Griswold's "Ludwig" article of the previous day "by want of room," and added, "We know the scene, a neighboring city; and we know that the incident of his seeing the person under such circumstances is literally true." At any rate, it was *almost* literally true!

Poe first saw Mrs. Whitman when he and Mrs. Osgood, whom he had joined at Providence for Mrs. Osgood's lecture there early in July 1845, walked past the Whitman house at 76 (now 88) Benefit Street in Providence. (The house was still standing in 1962, at the northwest corner of Church Street.) Mrs. Whitman later stated that she was really standing on her doorstep, and not, as in the poem, in her garden; but she did have a rose garden, and she always in summer wore white. Poe learned who she was but did not meet her at the time, although Mrs. Osgood called upon her.

Some years later, on February 14, 1848, Mrs. Whitman sent to a valentine party given by Miss Lynch in New York a poem addressed to Poe. She revised the piece completely for her verses "The Raven," printed in her *Hours of Life* (Providence, 1853), pp. 66–69. Since the valentine is the known inspiration of Poe's poem, the original version is given here in full, as it appeared in the *Home Journal* for March 18, 1848.

[1] Griswold, "Memoir," *Works* (1850), I, xlv.

LAST POEMS

BEAUTIFUL ORIGINAL POEM

The following Valentine, by one of America's most justly distinguished poetesses, was among the number received at the Valentine *soiree*, commemorated in our paper of the 4th instant. A *poem*, however, whose intrinsic beauty takes it quite out of the category of ordinary Valentines, seemed to demand the honor of separate publication:

To Edgar A. Poe.

"— A raven true
As ever flapped his heavy wing against
The window of the sick, and croaked, 'Despair.' "
Young's "Revenge."

Oh, thou grim and ancient Raven,
From the Night's Plutonian shore,
Oft, in dreams, thy ghastly pinions
Wave and flutter round my door —
Oft thy shadow dims the moonlight
Sleeping on my chamber floor!

Romeo talks of "white doves trooping
Amid crows, athwart the night;"
But to see thy dark wing swooping
Down the silver path of light,
Amid swans and dovelets stooping,
Were, to me, a nobler sight.

Oft, amid the twilight glooming,
Round some grim, ancestral tower,
In the lurid distance looming,
I can see thy pinions lower —
Hear thy sullen storm-cry booming
Thro' the lonely midnight hour.

Midst the roaring of machinery,
And the dismal shriek of steam,
While each popinjay and parrot,
Makes the golden age his theme,
Oft, methinks, I hear thee croaking,
"All is but an idle dream."

While these warbling "guests of summer"
Prate of "Progress" evermore,
And, by dint of *iron foundries*,
Would this golden age restore,
Still, methinks, I hear thee croaking,
Hoarsely croaking, "Nevermore."

Oft, this work-day world forgetting,
From its turmoil curtained snug,

· 4 4 2 ·

TO HELEN [WHITMAN]

By the sparkling ember sitting,
   On the richly broidered rug,
Something, round about me flitting,
   Glimmers like a "Golden-Bug."

Dreamily its path I follow,
   In a "bee-line," to the moon,
Till, into some dreary hollow
   Of the midnight, sinking soon,
Lo! he glides away before me,
   And I lose the golden boon.

Oft, like Proserpine, I wander
   On the Night's Plutonian shore,
Hoping, fearing, while I ponder
   On thy loved and lost Lenore,
Till thy voice, like distant thunder,
   Sounds across the lonely moor.

From thy wing, one purple feather
   Wafted o'er my chamber floor,
Like a shadow o'er the heather,
   Charms my vagrant fancy more
Than all the flowers I used to gather
   On "Idalia's velvet shore."

Then, oh! grim and ghastly Raven!
   Wilt thou, "to my heart and ear,
Be a Raven true as ever
   Flapped his wings and croaked, 'Despair?' "
Not a bird that roams the forest
   Shall our lofty eyrie share!

Providence, R. I., Feb. 14.

Poe at first acknowledged this only by sending Mrs. Whitman anonymously the printed "To Helen" of 1831, torn out of his 1845 volume. But he apparently composed his long blank-verse reply to her valentine early in the year, and sent it to her about June 1.[2] On September 5, 1848 (under the pseudonym "Edward S. T. Grey"), he wrote asking her autograph, and soon thereafter went to see her. The poem was to some extent part of a campaign to win the beautiful if eccentric poetess, whom he had not yet met.

[2] According to Caroline Ticknor (*Poe's Helen*, pp. 224–225), Mrs. Whitman lent the manuscript of Poe's poem to a clairvoyant, Dr. Joseph R. Buchanan of Cincinnati, who lost it. Mrs. Whitman quoted line 22 in her poem "To Arcturus" in *Graham's* for June 1850. The leaf torn out of *The Raven* . . . is now in the Lilly Collection.

LAST POEMS

Mrs. Whitman, in *Edgar Poe and His Critics* (1860), pp. 70–71, tells us that on the manuscript of the poem Poe gave her he had penciled the following note:

> All that I have here expressed was actually present to me. Remember the mental condition which gave rise to "Ligeia" — recall the passage of which I spoke, and observe the coincidence. I regard these visions even as they arise, with an awe which in some measure moderates or tranquillizes the ecstacy — I so regard them through a conviction that this ecstasy, in itself, is of a character supernal to the human nature — *is a glimpse of the spirit's outer world.*

In the file of the *Broadway Journal* which he gave Mrs. Whitman, Poe wrote on the issue of September 27, 1845, "N. B. — The *poem* which I sent you contained all the events of *a dream* which occurred to me soon after I knew you [. . .] Ligeia was also suggested by *a dream*. Observe the eyes in both tale & poem." The lacuna is occasioned by cutting away of the page. This is interesting, but we must remember that Mrs. Whitman loved mystical things, as Poe surely knew; the dream element may have been very slight indeed.

It has been complained that Poe's verses lack warmth, but how could it be otherwise? The whole romance of "Poe's Helen" and "The Raven" was partly play-acting from start to finish; there was some genuine respect on both sides, some intellectual affinity, a good deal of consciously rhetorical correspondence, and a poem of distinction. (See also the notes to "Annabel Lee.") [3]

TEXTS

(*A*) Manuscript sent to Mrs. Whitman June 1, 1848, now lost; (*B*) *Union Magazine* for November 1848 (3:200); (*C*) *New-York Tribune,* October 10, 1849, Supplement; (*D*) *Poets and Poetry of America,* 10th edition (dated 1850, issued late in 1849), p. 420; (*E*) *Works* (1850), II, 17.

[3] Despite our knowledge of the circumstances of the inspiration and composition of this poem, Whitty claimed to think Poe really had in mind a rose garden in Richmond. See Phillips, p. 178, and Agnes M. Bondurant, *Poe's Richmond,* p. 200. I have also seen an elaborate comment on the psychological significance of the heroine "clad all in white" by somebody who didn't know that she always dressed that way in summer. A letter purporting to be from Poe to Bayard Taylor, dated "June 15, 1848," asking the good offices of that gentleman to submit "the lines enclosed" (obviously meaning "To Helen [Whitman]") to the *Union Magazine* (with which Taylor had no known official connection) has been in print since 1909, but I cannot regard it as authentic.

TO HELEN [WHITMAN]

The text used here is Griswold's (*E*), almost certainly based on the lost original manuscript. Lines 26–27 were omitted from texts *B*, *C* and *D* because of their very personal nature. They are, *pace* Whitty, patently genuine. I have corrected a misprint — "way" for "away" — in line 51.

TO HELEN   [*E*]

I saw thee once — once only — years ago:
I must not say *how* many — but *not* many.
It was a July midnight; and from out
A full-orbed moon, that, like thine own soul, soaring,
5   Sought a precipitate pathway up through heaven,
There fell a silvery-silken veil of light,
With quietude, and sultriness, and slumber,
Upon the upturn'd faces of a thousand
Roses that grew in an enchanted garden,
10   Where no wind dared to stir, unless on tiptoe —
Fell on the upturn'd faces of these roses
That gave out, in return for the love-light,
Their odorous souls in an ecstatic death —
Fell on the upturn'd faces of these roses
15   That smiled and died in this parterre, enchanted
By thee, and by the poetry of thy presence.

Clad all in white, upon a violet bank
I saw thee half reclining; while the moon
Fell on the upturn'd faces of the roses,
20   And on thine own, upturn'd — alas, in sorrow!

Was it not Fate, that, on this July midnight —
Was it not Fate, (whose name is also Sorrow,)
That bade me pause before that garden-gate,
To breathe the incense of those slumbering roses?
25   No footstep stirred: the hated world all slept,
Save only thee and me. (Oh, Heaven! — oh, God!
How my heart beats in coupling those two words!)
Save only thee and me. I paused — I looked —

And in an instant all things disappeared.
30 (Ah, bear in mind this garden was enchanted!)
The pearly lustre of the moon went out:
The mossy banks and the meandering paths,
The happy flowers and the repining trees,
Were seen no more: the very roses' odors
35 Died in the arms of the adoring airs.
All — all expired save thee — save less than thou:
Save only the divine light in thine eyes —
Save but the soul in thine uplifted eyes.
I saw but them — they were the world to me.
40 I saw but them — saw only them for hours —
Saw only them until the moon went down.
What wild heart-histories seemed to lie enwritten
Upon those crystalline, celestial spheres!
How dark a wo! yet how sublime a hope!
45 How silently serene a sea of pride!
How daring an ambition! yet how deep —
How fathomless a capacity for love!

But now, at length, dear Dian sank from sight,
Into a western couch of thunder-cloud;
50 And thou, a ghost, amid the entombing trees
Didst glide away. *Only thine eyes remained.*
They *would not* go — they never yet have gone.
Lighting my lonely pathway home that night,
They have not left me (as my hopes have) since.
55 They follow me — they lead me through the years.
They are my ministers — yet I their slave.
Their office is to illumine and enkindle —
My duty, *to be saved* by their bright light,
And purified in their electric fire,
60 And sanctified in their elysian fire.
They fill my soul with Beauty (which is Hope,)
And are far up in Heaven — the stars I kneel to
In the sad, silent watches of my night;
While even in the meridian glare of day

TO HELEN [WHITMAN]

65   I see them still — two sweetly scintillant
Venuses, unextinguished by the sun!

[1848–1849]

VARIANTS

Title: *Not recorded* (*A*); To — — —
(*B, C, D*)
5 precipitate/precipitant (*B, C, D*)
8, 11, 14, 19, 20 upturn'd/upturned
(*C, D*)
18 saw/see (*B*)

19 upturn'd faces of the/faces of the
upturned (*C*)
22 name is also/earthly name is (*A*)
26–27 *Omitted from B, C, D*
51 away/*misprinted* way *in E, correct
in all other texts*

NOTES

Title: The poem is generally known as "the second 'To Helen'," but it seems unlikely that Poe would have used a duplicate title in a collected edition. His own publication was addressed to a triple blank, which I think stands for Helen Power Whitman. Ingram thought that Poe disliked the name Sarah, and Mrs. Whitman had told Poe she thought that his and her family names were both modifications of De la Poer. My title, "To Helen [Whitman]," is arbitrarily adopted to avoid confusion.

1 On June 19, 1848, Poe wrote of Mrs. Whitman to Miss Anna Blackwell, an English poetess, "I have never seen her — but once." Compare the opening of Walter Savage Landor's "Lines on the Death of Charles Lamb," "Once, and once only, have I seen thy face."

4 In *Eureka* Poe said the soul "loves nothing so well as to soar in those regions of illimitable intuition which are utterly incognizant of 'path.'" Note also R. H. Horne's *Orion*, II, ii: "The high Moon floated and her downward gleam/Shone on the upturned Giant faces." Poe quoted this in his review of Horne in *Graham's* for March 1844.

27–41 Gunnar Bjurman, *Edgar Allan Poe* (Lund, 1916), p. 155, compared Coleridge's "Hymn before Sunrise," lines 13–16:

> O dread and silent Mount! I gazed upon thee,
> Till thou, still present to the bodily sense,
> Didst vanish from my thought: entranced in prayer
> I worshipped the Invisible alone.

Also compare Shelley's "Queen Mab," I, 85f.:

> Those who had looked upon the sight . . .
> Saw not the yellow moon,
> Saw not the mortal scene,
> Heard not the night-wind's rush,
> Heard not earthly sound,
> Saw but the fairy pageant.

Poe quoted Shelley's lines in reviewing Moore's *Alciphron* in *Burton's* for January 1840.

Not quite surely coincidental is a passage in William W. Lord's "Hymn to Niagara," lines 6of., quoted below, which is immediately followed by a passage Poe quoted in his unfavorable review in the *Broadway Journal*, May 24, 1845, of Lord's *Poems*. Poe chose to treat the burlesque parodies of his own verses in Lord's "The New Castalia" as bold plagiarisms, and he might have decided to use some of Lord's improvements — for Poe seems to have felt nothing wrong in *improving* on things found, when he was the finder.

> With inward and external sight beheld:
> And thee and God alone I saw and felt; —
> Earth, heaven, and all things vanished, but alone
> One central stay, and all-pervading soul
> Of love, and beauty, and eternal calm,
> In which I rested, as upon the heart
> Of universal life, and in its depths
> Breathed immortality.

Poe, in the *Democratic Review* for April 1846, told of looking again at Lord's "Niagara." See my edition of Lord's *Poetical Works* (1938), pp. viii and 27.

29f. Poe probably alludes to the famous lines of Prospero in *The Tempest*, IV, i, 151–156:

> And, like the baseless fabric of this vision,
> The cloud-capped towers, the gorgeous palaces,
> The solemn temples, the great globe itself,
> Yea, all which it inherit, shall dissolve,
> And, like this insubstantial pageant faded,
> Leave not a rack behind.

34–35 In the *Home Journal*, November 25, 1848, "C.M." (Caroline May?) accused Poe of boldly plagiarizing from Sarah Josepha Hale's *Three Hours* (Philadelphia, 1848), p. 37, "The sound of it died in the arms of night." Poe wrote to Mrs. Whitman, November 24, 1848, that "Mrs. H's book was published three months ago . . . You had my poem about the first of June." But see also Hirst's *Endymion*, I, xliii, 1–2: "Flowing the fragrance rose as though each blossom/Breathed out its very life."

36–66 I believe that much of this passage was originally composed as "Holy Eyes."

36–37 Compare "For Annie," lines 101–102: ". . . the thought of the light/ Of the eyes of my Annie."

37 There is much about the eyes of the heroine of Poe's tale, "Ligeia," to which Poe refers in his own note.

42 Compare "The Man of the Crowd" (1840): "How wild a history is written in that bosom."

59 For Poe "electric fire" meant lightning, and there is nothing in his phrase properly to suggest the highly mundane ideas that may now make the line seem unpoetical to us.

62 Compare *Paradise Lost*, IV, 944: "High up in heaven."

63 Compare Psalm 90:4: "For a thousand years in thy sight are but as yesterday when it is past, and as a watch in the night."

65 Compare Henry B. Hirst's sonnet, "Astarté," in his *Coming of the Mammoth* (1845):

> Floats thy fair form before me . . .
>
> . . . argent eyes, —
>
> Twin planets, swimming through love's lustrous skies.

The sonnet was quoted with approval in Poe's review of Hirst's book in the *Broadway Journal* of July 12, 1845. See also my notes on "Eulalie," for the planet Venus visible by day.

LINES ON ALE

This stanza is said to have been written in 1848 or 1849 by Poe at the Washington Tavern (founded in 1836) at Lowell, Massachusetts. He visited Lowell more than once in the last two years of his life, but the most probable occasion of his visiting the tavern was before his lecture on "Poets and Poetry of America" at Wentworth Hall, July 10, 1848. Mrs. Weiss (*Home Life*, p. 162) repeats a not unlikely story that when going to talk in a large company Poe found "some little stimulant was necessary to him."

The manuscript long hung on the wall of the tavern and was seen in 1892 by my informant, Mr. Jerry Murphy, when he began to work there. It disappeared before 1920. Years later Mr. Murphy recited the lines to Ethel Flamma (Mrs. Ario Flamma), who consulted Belle da Costa Greene about the discovery. Put in touch with me, Mr. Murphy, retired and living in Boston, sent me for publication a copy of the poem as he recalled it. It was printed in the London *Notes and Queries* of July 29, 1939 (pp. 77–78), and is now first collected.

Absolutely complete authentication is not possible, but the piece comes in an unsuspicious way, and I regard it as authentic. Poe was given to making up harmless little rhymes, but the fact has never been widely known — not enough, at least, to suggest forgery of a piece like this — and traditions about places, when not extravagant, are proverbially reliable.

Mr. Murphy was not sure of all the words; in the first line he thought "Fill" might have been "Filled"; the second line, "Fill that glass again"; and that "Quaintest" in line 5 might have been "Faintest." Metrically that line would be better thus: "Quaintest thought and queerest fancies."

[LINES ON ALE]

Fill with mingled cream and amber,
   I will drain that glass again.
Such hilarious visions clamber
   Through the chamber of my brain —
Quaintest thoughts — queerest fancies
   Come to life and fade away;
What care I how time advances?
   I am drinking ale today.

[1848]

A DREAM WITHIN A DREAM

In the final form here presented, this is one of the best known and finest of Poe's shorter poems. It takes a good deal from "To — —" ("Should my early life seem") of 1829, which in turn borrows from "Imitation" (1827). Hence some editors have treated the three as a single entity. But in each case the revision is so complete — no line of the first poem remaining in the third — that it seems well to treat them as three separate compositions. "A Dream Within a Dream" is a mature poem, characteristic of Poe's later years, and is based on an idea more complicated than the one that inspired the two earlier poems.

In "Marginalia," number 230, in the *Southern Literary Messenger* for June 1849 (15:336), Poe wrote: "It is by no means an irrational fancy that, in a future existence, we shall look upon what we think our present existence, as a dream." The reader may recall Shelley's "Adonais" (line 344): "He hath awakened from the dream of life," and the title of Calderon's play *La Vida es sueño.*

I discussed the more complicated idea, "dream of a dream," in *Notes and Queries* (London) for August 29, 1925 (p. 159). Poe wrote in "A Tale of the Ragged Mountains" (*Godey's,* April

1844): "Novalis errs not in saying that 'we are near waking when we dream that we dream.' " Poe found the quotation in Sarah Austin's *Fragments from German Prose Writers* (New York, 1841), p. 21. For the original, see Novalis, *Schriften* (Jena, 1907), II, 141. Among the many literary parallels, Poe surely was familiar with a passage near the end of Shelley's "Sensitive Plant":

> . . . in this life
> Of error, ignorance and strife,
> Where nothing is but all things seem,
> And we the shadows of the dream.

And E. C. Pinkney has in *Rodolph*, I, 71–72: "Alas! that such a tale must seem/The fiction of a dreaming dream!"

But Poe's exact phrase, "a dream within a dream," occurs in the first chapter of Margaret Fuller's *Summer on the Lakes* (Boston, 1844), p. 7, in a passage Poe quoted in his "Literati" sketch of her (*Works*, III, 78–79). And I also find it in *Graham's* for October 1848, as the title of a sentimental story by C. A. Washburn which ends, "It was but a dream within a dream." It seems not unlikely that this last item set Poe to reworking his verses of 1829.

TEXTS

(*A*) Manuscript sent to Mrs. Richmond in 1849 — facsimile in London *Bookman*, January 1909 (35:190); (*B*) Boston *Flag of Our Union* for March 31, 1849; (*C*) *Richmond Examiner* proof sheets, summer of 1849 (Whitty, *Complete Poems*, 1911, p. 123); (*D*) Works (1850), II, 40.

The text used is *D*, not differing verbally from *B*. The doubtful character of the proof sheet text (*C*) is well known, but in this case the changes do seem to me to sound like Poe.

A DREAM WITHIN A DREAM [*D*]

> Take this kiss upon the brow!
> And, in parting from you now,
> Thus much let me avow —
> You are not wrong, who deem
> That my days have been a dream;
> Yet if hope has flown away
> In a night, or in a day,

In a vision, or in none,
Is it therefore the less *gone*?
10 *All* that we see or seem
Is but a dream within a dream.

I stand amid the roar
Of a surf-tormented shore,
And I hold within my hand
15 Grains of the golden sand —
How few! yet how they creep
Through my fingers to the deep,
While I weep — while I weep!
O God! can I not grasp
20 Them with a tighter clasp?
O God! can I not save
One from the pitiless wave?
Is *all* that we see or seem
But a dream within a dream?

[1849]

VARIANTS

Title: For Annie (*A*); To — (*C*)
1 the/thy (*C*) (*perhaps a misprint, but there is a similar clash of "thee" and "you" in Politian, III, 35–36 and VI, 97–98*)

1–9 *Not in A*
4 wrong, who/wrong, to (*C*)
19, 21 O God!/Oh, God! (*A*)
23 we see/I see (*A*)

NOTES

Title: The blank of the proof-sheet version should stand for "Annie," but Poe may have hoped that Mrs. Shelton and her friends would imagine that it was meant for "Elmira."

15 Campbell (*Poems*, p. 163) compared *Politian*, VI, 41: "The sands of Time are changed to golden grains."

FOR ANNIE

Poe's "For Annie" has been popular with anthologists and their readers for generations. It is a great accomplishment, un-

FOR ANNIE

deniably effective, although a tour de force.[1] The subject is quietude, but a most unquiet rhythm is employed, obviously suggested by Thomas Hood's "Bridge of Sighs" — a poem Poe recited in his lectures on "The Poetic Principle" in 1848 and 1849.

The poem is far more than a metrical exercise. To the world, as E. C. Stedman said, "for delicate . . . melody, it is one of Poe's truest poems," and Mme. Thérèse Blanc called it "le plus tendre de tous les poèmes de Poe." [2] From the author to his cherished friend it was a most personal poem *for* Annie. She was Mrs. Charles B. Richmond of Lowell and Westford, Massachusetts. Her maiden name was Nancy Locke Heywood, but Poe called her "Annie." She liked others to do so, and in 1873 after the death of her husband she had the change of the name made legally.[3]

Poe first met Mrs. Richmond when he came to lecture at Lowell on July 10, 1848. Her husband did not object to their Platonic relationship. Poe's letters to her have never been completely published, and before her death she destroyed the originals. In one of the unpublished passages Poe definitely said that he thought that more than Platonic friendship for them would be unwise.[4]

The personal experience upon which the poem is based Poe recounted in a somewhat hysterical letter to "Annie" from Fordham on November 16, 1848:

Why am I not *with* you now *darling* that I might . . . look deep down into the clear Heaven of your eyes . . . whisper in your ear the divine

[1] Quinn (p. 600) says it "is one of Poe's finest poems . . . He reproduced an emotional state by a short throbbing measure . . . the very incoherencies mirror perfectly the mood." N. P. Willis invented the word "individualesque" for it, in the introduction he wrote at Poe's request and published with "For Annie" in the *Home Journal* of April 28, 1849. This introduction, headed "Odd Poem," was reprinted by Killis Campbell (*Poems*, p. 288); most of it has little pertinence.

[2] Stedman, *Poets of America* (Boston and New York, 1885), p. 246. Campbell (*Poems*, p. 289) gives these and other favorable opinions, and some from critics who disliked the poem, because of the clinical details in some stanzas.

[3] Phillips, II, 1293ff., quoting directly a letter of December 18, 1915, from Mrs. George P. Lawrence, Mr. Richmond's niece.

[4] Complete copies of Poe's letters were made surreptitiously before the originals were destroyed. About thirty years ago my late friend, James Southall Wilson, read them under pledge not to make copies, a pledge which he kept. He did, however, tell me of the nature of the passage to which I refer. I have been unable to trace these transcripts myself.

emotion[s], which agitate me[?] . . . in Providence — I went to bed & wept through a long, long, hideous night of despair . . . I procured . . . laudanum [5] and . . . took the cars back to Boston . . . I wrote you a letter, in which I opened my whole heart to you . . . I then reminded you of that holy promise, which was the last I exacted from you in parting — the promise that, under all circumstances, you would come to me on my bed of death . . . Having written this letter, I swallowed about half the laudanum . . . A friend was at hand, who . . . saved me . . . After the laudanum was rejected from the stomach, I became calm, & to a casual observer, sane . . . I am so *ill* . . . in body and mind, that I feel I CANNOT live, unless I can feel your sweet, gentle, loving hand pressed upon my forehead — oh my *pure, virtuous, generous, beautiful, beautiful sister* Annie! — is it not POSSIBLE for you to come . . . until I subdue this fearful agitation . . . Farewell — here & hereafter — *forever your own* Eddy —

There has been disagreement among commentators as to whether the protagonist in the poem is alive or not. Stéphane Mallarmé referred to him as one who has been so ill that he has fancied himself in the first moments of death but has been revived by the presence and affection of Annie. C. Alphonso Smith said the French translator "did not understand it: he thought the speaker was a convalescent." [6] But Mallarmé was certainly right. The decisive passage is in line 16, "might *fancy* me dead," which is supported by the symbolism of rosemary (which means revival, explained in my note on line 63) and the invocation of the Blessed Virgin in line 84, "to *shield* me from harm."

On March 23, 1849, Poe wrote to Mrs. Richmond: "I enclose also some other lines 'For Annie' — and will you let me know in what manner they impress you?" He added that he had sent them to the *Flag of Our Union*. This mention clearly refers to the present poem; "A Dream Within a Dream" had been called "For Annie" in a manuscript previously sent to Mrs. Richmond.

Poe's relation with Gleason and Ballou's *Flag of Our Union* was not a happy one. On April 20, 1849, he wrote to Willis: "The poem which I enclose . . . has been just published in a paper

---

[5] In Poe's day laudanum was a specific remedy for toothache and diarrhœa, was sold without a prescription by all druggists, and was often taken for other maladies, real or imagined.

[6] Smith, *Edgar Allan Poe: How to Know Him* (Indianapolis, 1921), p. 232. Mallarmé's interpretation appeared (with Edouard Manet's illustrations) in the first edition of his famous book *Les Poèmes d'Edgar Poe: Traduction en Prose* (Paris, 1889), pp. 190–191.

for which sheer necessity compels me to write . . . It pays well as times go — but . . . whatever I send it I feel I am consigning to the tomb of the Capulets." He went on to ask Willis to reprint the lines as "From a late [Boston] paper" and to write an introduction in the *Home Journal*. The *Flag* regularly came out a full week before the date it bore, and Poe rightly assumed that "For Annie" would be in the issue appearing April 21. Willis sent the script Poe had given him to the printer at once, with the note: "Will Mr. Babcock please put this on the second page *this* week, & leave me twenty lines room for an introduction." The result was that even if the *Flag* actually reached dealers before the *Home Journal*, Poe's poem appeared in two papers bearing the same date. The *Flag*, not unnaturally, protested in the issue for May 12. Poe soon thereafter sent Mrs. Richmond word that the *Flag* had misprinted his lines — an accusation which (if true at all) can only mean that the editor refused to make changes in proof at the last minute. Poe added that the *Flag* still had two of his articles. These had been paid for and were printed, but the paper for which he felt such contempt purchased nothing more of Poe's.

On May 23 Poe sent a *Home Journal* clipping to E. H. N. Patterson, thus authorizing its publication in that young editor's paper, the *Spectator* of Oquawka, Illinois.[7] Poe sent to Griswold in June "perfect copies" of "Annabel Lee" and "For Annie" for use in *Poets and Poetry of America*; the former is a manuscript, but the latter may well have been a corrected clipping.[8] Griswold used the same text in the *Works* as in his anthology.

TEXTS

(*A*) Manuscript sent to Mrs. Richmond, March 23, 1849, facsimiled in London *Bibliophile*, May 1909; (*B*) Boston *Flag of Our Union* for April 28, 1849; (*C*) manuscript sent to N. P. Willis on April 20, 1849; (*D*) *Home Journal* for April 28, 1849; (*E*) *Oquawka Spectator*, May 16, 1849; (*F*) *Poets*

[7] Apparently Patterson had already received a copy of the *Home Journal* or a clipping from it, since he published an identical text in his paper for May 16. I have used the file in the library of Knox College, Galesburg, Illinois.

[8] A letter of "May 17, 1849," addressed to Mrs. Lewis, promising to make a copy of "For Annie" for her that day and signed "Edgar A. Poe," has no history prior to 1935 and I cannot regard it as authentic. It is hard to believe we should have no earlier trace of so important a manuscript if the Brooklyn poetess ever had it.

and *Poetry of America*, 10th edition (dated 1850, issued late in 1849), p. 422; (*G*) *Works* (1850), II, 48–51; (*H*) manuscript sent to Susan Archer Talley on September 26, 1849, now lost; (*Z*) *Richmond Examiner* proofsheets from Whitty, *Complete Poems* (1911), pp. 74–77.

The text adopted is Griswold's (*G*), which has a superior reading in line 97. The presentation manuscript (*A*), once lent to Ingram, was in the Harold Peirce Sale, Philadelphia, May 6, 1903, lot 958, and is now owned by Colonel Richard Gimbel. The manuscript given to Willis (*C*), now incomplete, was once in the collection of the late William H. Koester. The manuscript sent Miss Talley on September 26, 1849, is mentioned in the article "Last Days of Edgar A. Poe" by Susan Archer Talley Weiss in *Scribner's Magazine* for March 1878 (15:714) but was destroyed during the Civil War. The text in Griswold's *Poets and Poetry of America* (*F*) is verbally like that in *Works* (*G*), but the printer used apostrophes thus: in line 6, conquer'd; 28, madden'd; 29, burn'd; 70, Drown'd; 79, extinguish'd; 80, cover'd. The *Examiner* proofsheets (*Z*) are said to have had a unique reading, in line 45.

FOR ANNIE [G]

Thank Heaven! the crisis —
   The danger is past,
And the lingering illness
   Is over at last —
5   And the fever called "Living"
   Is conquered at last.

Sadly, I know
   I am shorn of my strength,
And no muscle I move
10   As I lie at full length —
But no matter! — I feel
   I am better at length.

And I rest so composedly,
   Now, in my bed,
15   That any beholder
   Might fancy me dead —
Might start at beholding me,
   Thinking me dead.

The moaning and groaning,

FOR ANNIE

The sighing and sobbing,
Are quieted now,
     With that horrible throbbing
At heart: — ah, that horrible,
     Horrible throbbing!

The sickness — the nausea —
     The pitiless pain —
Have ceased, with the fever
     That maddened my brain —
With the fever called "Living"
     That burned in my brain.

And oh! of all tortures
     That torture the worst
Has abated — the terrible
     Torture of thirst
For the napthaline river
     Of Passion accurst: —
I have drank of a water
     That quenches all thirst: —

Of a water that flows,
     With a lullaby sound,
From a spring but a very few
     Feet under ground —
From a cavern not very far
     Down under ground.

And ah! let it never
     Be foolishly said
That my room it is gloomy
     And narrow my bed;
For man never slept
     In a different bed —
And, to *sleep*, you must slumber
     In just such a bed.

My tantalized spirit
   Here blandly reposes,
55   Forgetting, or never
    Regretting its roses —
Its old agitations
   Of myrtles and roses:

For now, while so quietly
   Lying, it fancies
60 A holier odor
   About it, of pansies —
A rosemary odor,
   Commingled with pansies —
65 With rue and the beautiful
   Puritan pansies.

And so it lies happily,
   Bathing in many
A dream of the truth
70   And the beauty of Annie —
Drowned in a bath
   Of the tresses of Annie.

She tenderly kissed me,
   She fondly caressed,
75 And then I fell gently
   To sleep on her breast —
Deeply to sleep
   From the heaven of her breast.

When the light was extinguished,
80   She covered me warm,
And she prayed to the angels
   To keep me from harm —
To the queen of the angels
   To shield me from harm.

FOR ANNIE

85 And I lie so composedly,
   Now, in my bed,
  (Knowing her love)
   That you fancy me dead —
 And I rest so contentedly,
90   Now in my bed,
  (With her love at my breast)
   That you fancy me dead —
 That you shudder to look at me,
   Thinking me dead: —

95 But my heart it is brighter
   Than all of the many
  Stars in the sky,
   For it sparkles with Annie —
  It glows with the light
100   Of the love of my Annie —
  With the thought of the light
   Of the eyes of my Annie.

        [1849]

VARIANTS

(No account is taken here of changes in punctuation or lineation.)

19-30 *Fourth and fifth stanzas transposed (A, B)*
21 now,/now; with *(A)* ; now; and the *(B)*
22 With that horrible/The horrible *(A)* ; Horrible *(B)*
23 ah,/oh, *(A)*; O, *(B)*
31 oh/ah *(A, B)*
36 Passion/Glory *(A, B)*
41 spring but/fountain *(B)*

45 And/But *(Z)*
60-62 *A reads*:
  Lying, I fancy
  A holier odor about me,
  Of pansy —
64 and 66 pansies/pansy *(A)*
67 it lies/I lie *(A)*
69 truth/love *(A, B)*
97 in the sky/of the heaven *A, B)*; of the sky *(D, E)*
99 light/thought *(A)*; fire *(B)*

NOTES

Title: Poe used the same title for a manuscript version of "A Dream Within a Dream."

5 Compare Macbeth's phrase (III, ii, 22): "After life's fitful fever he sleeps well." This idea is a commonplace, used by Milton, Shelley, Kirke White, Mrs. Browning, and others. Said Poe, in "Mesmeric Revelation": "Our present incarnation is progressive, preparatory, temporary. Our future is

perfected, ultimate, immortal. The ultimate life is the full design." And in "The Colloquy of Monos and Una" he wrote: "The pulses were still . . . Volition had not departed but was powerless . . . The rose water . . . affected me with sweet fancies of flowers."

8ff. One of Poe's extremely rare errors of spelling is "lenth," in a letter quoted above at page 412. It is a clue to his pronunciation of "strength" and "length."

10, 12 Wilbur (*Poe*, p. 150), calls the double use of *length* "a lame pun . . . probably not so intended." It seems to me rather a successful use of "absolute rhyme," since it has been so rarely noticed.

22 See "The Beloved Physician" for a note on Poe's heart trouble.

25 Many readers may regret that Poe chose to be so clinically accurate here. He defended Shelley's use of "sicken" in a review of a book called *The Poetry of Life* (by Sarah Stickney) in the *Southern Literary Messenger*, January 1836.

35 "Napthaline" is better spelled "napthalene." Moore, in a note to *Lalla Rookh*, quotes Scott Waring as saying, "Naptha [*sic*] is used by the Persians (as we are told by Milton it was in Hell) for lamps." It is clear, combustible rock oil, procured by the ancients from asphaltum, usually brought from the Dead Sea. Wilbur (*Poe*, p. 150) points out the allusion to Phlegethon, the fiery river of Hades. See also line 53.

36 The early reading "Glory" suggests the vanity of pride rather than lust. Wilbur (*Poe*, p. 150) compares "The Poetic Principle," where Poe said: "Passion, alas! its tendency is to degrade rather than elevate the soul."

37 John 4:14: "But whosoever drinketh of the water that I shall give him shall never thirst, but the water that I shall give him shall be in him a well of water springing up into everlasting life." The unusual form of the participle *drank* is in all texts authorized by Poe.

39–44 Wilbur, p. 150, suggests an allusion to Lethe, the river of forgetfulness.

53 Tantalus was tortured by water he could not drink and fruit he could not reach; see also line 35.

56–58 Roses and myrtles are symbols of love.

62–64 The reader may be expected by the poet to recall Ophelia's words in *Hamlet*, IV, v, 175ff.: "There's rosemary, that's for remembrance; Pray, love, remember; And there is pansies, that's for thoughts . . . There's rue for you, and here's some for me. We may call it herb-grace o' Sundays." In "The Island of the Fay" Poe says: "All about them the rue and rosemary clambered." And in "The Power of Words" there is a reference to "pansies and violets, and heart's-ease." There is, however, another significance of rosemary, for which the meaning "Your presence revives me" is given by Frances Sargent Osgood in *The Poetry of Flowers* (New York, 1841), p. 263. Mrs. Osgood also interprets rue as "Grace or Purification."

66 The very unusual phrase "Puritan pansies" is appropriate, since Annie was a New Englander. It may be suggested by a conceit in Emerson's "To Ellen at the South" (1843): "The flowers, tiny sect of Shakers."

83 The Blessed Virgin is called *Regina angelorum* (queen of the angels). Compare Poe's "Hymn," addressed to Our Lady.

91 Poe wrote Mrs. Whitman on November 14, 1848: "I feel your dear love at my heart."

102 In "Landor's Cottage" we are told, "The eyes of Annie . . . were spiritual gray; her hair a light chestnut." The eyes of the lady in "To One in Paradise" were changed to gray in the last revised version, perhaps for Annie's benefit.

ELDORADO

This is the noblest of Poe's poems, the most universal in implication, and the most intensely personal. It is utterly simple, yet rich in suggestion and allusion. The moral — for it has one — is brought in so subtly, one hardly knows it is there. The subject, for all the references to the past, is still the present; the occasion is the gold rush to California. It is only on the surface a light-hearted lyric.[1] It is the song of discovery of those who seek for the true gold, for beauty, for truth, for the ideal. In the face of every adversity, even death itself, they ride boldly, singing a song. This is our poet himself at his best, and what we wish to be. Even in defeat, the gallant and bold find Eldorado.

Men of every kind went off to the gold fields, including many men of letters; one of Poe's publishers, Israel Post, found death on the way. Poe must, at least in imagination, have considered making the journey. But he wrote to F. W. Thomas on February 14, 1849: "I shall be a *littérateur*, at least, all my life; nor would I abandon the hopes which still lead me on for all the gold in California."

Poe's story "Von Kempelen and His Discovery" was one result

[1] See Campbell, *Poems* (1917), p. 286, for the older literature and Eric W. Carlson in *Modern Language Notes*, March 1961, on more recent articles by Oral S. Coad and others. Almost all criticism is favorable, but there has been some disagreement about whether the poem is pessimistic or cheerful. Since it seems to me that it is both, I see no reason for further reference to the discussion.

of his interest in the events of '49. On a higher level these events inspired "Eldorado." However immediate the occasion of Poe's composition, he also had in mind something he had read long before in a chapter called "Tom o' Bedlams" in Isaac D'Israeli's *Curiosities of Literature*.[2] Those harmless madmen who wandered about England begging we all know about from *King Lear*, III, iv, where Edgar pretends to be one of them.

D'Israeli quotes a "Tom-a-Bedlam Song," from *Wit and Drollery* (1661). The seventh stanza reads:

> With a heart of furious fancies,
> Whereof I am commander:
> With a burning spear,
> And a horse of air,
> To the wilderness I wander;
> With a knight of ghosts and shadows,
> I summoned am to Tourney:
> Ten leagues beyond
> The wide world's end;
> Methinks it is no journey!

D'Israeli adds, "The last stanza of this Bedlam song contains the seeds of exquisite romance; a stanza worth many an admired poem." Poe quoted the first half of it as the motto for his tale "Hans Pfaal" in the manuscript version of 1835 and again in the final revision in the *Works* of 1850 (I, 1). The second part inspired "Eldorado." A tourney is properly a fight to the death, and the journey is short, for it is performed "in the twinkling of an eye" (I Corinthians 15:52).

Also significant is the following from Poe's review, in the *Broadway Journal* of July 12, 1845, of Henry B. Hirst's *Coming of the Mammoth*. Discussing Hirst's "Unseen River" (which had been published first in the *Broadway Journal* of May 31), Poe says: "By the river always heard but never seen, until the traveller is overtaken by death, it is the poet's intention to typify happiness." Hirst's poem may have been a contributory inspiration for Poe.

The meter for "Eldorado" is that of "The Man for Galway," a

---

[2] This source seems to have been first pointed out in my article in the *London Mercury*, August 1923 (8:414).

ELDORADO

song quoted in Charles Lever's *Charles O'Malley* (Dublin, 1841), chapter cxii; Poe reviewed the book in *Graham's* for March 1842.

TEXTS

(*A*) Boston *Flag of our Union* for April 21, 1849; (*B*) *Works* (1850), II, 45. The text used is *B*. There are no verbal variants; *A* used single quotation marks in the last two stanzas, but that was merely because of the style sheet of the printers of the *Flag*.

ELDORADO [*B*]

Gaily bedight,
A gallant knight,
In sunshine and in shadow,
Had journeyed long,
5   Singing a song,
In search of Eldorado.

But he grew old —
This knight so bold —
And o'er his heart a shadow
10   Fell, as he found
No spot of ground
That looked like Eldorado.

And, as his strength
Failed him at length
15   He met a pilgrim shadow —
"Shadow," said he,
"Where can it be —
This land of Eldorado?"

"Over the Mountains
20   Of the Moon,
Down the Valley of the Shadow,
Ride, boldly ride,"
The shade replied, —
"If you seek for Eldorado!"

[1849]

LAST POEMS

NOTES

Title: According to a story current from the sixteenth century on, somewhere in the region of what is now Colombia in South America there was or had been a ruler who was covered with gold, and he was called El Dorado, "the gilded one." Reputedly, in his domain everything was made of gold and jewels. Naturally many explorers sought for the place, among them Sir Walter Raleigh. By Poe's day "Eldorado" had come to mean a place, the object of search, where gold (or good fortune) was to be found. J. F. Cooper mentioned "the El Dorado of the immigrant" in this sense in 1827, according to the *Oxford English Dictionary*. Poe used the term figuratively in the introduction to his *Poems* in 1831 and again in 1844 in "Dream-Land," where he rhymed it with "shadow." The term was familiar enough so that, as soon as the news arrived in 1848 of the recent discovery of gold at Sutter's Mill and adventurous men began to make the dangerous journey to the far west, "Eldorado" became the universal nickname for California.

Americans usually wrote the title, as Poe did, as one word. Bayard Taylor's book of 1850 on his visit to the gold fields is called *Eldorado*. An article in *Holden's Dollar Magazine* for February 1849 cited by Killis Campbell (*Poems,* p. 286), said: "This word [Eldorado] is in everybody's mouth just now, but we suppose that very few know what it means." Poe pretty surely did know the romantic story, for there is a reference to the wealth of Eldorado in the eighteenth chapter of Voltaire's *Candide*; and in *Paradise Lost*, XI, 409–411, Milton told of "Guiana, whose great city Geryon's sons [Spaniards]/Call El Dorado."

19–20 The Mountains of the Moon are a type of the utterly remote. They are referred to by Thomas Moore in a note on *Lalla Rookh* quoting James Bruce: "The Mountains of the Moon or *Montes Lunae* of antiquity, at the foot of which the Nile is supposed to rise." They were referred to by Ptolemy and other geographers for centuries, but often were supposed fabulous, since no traveler had visited or even seen them. In the twelfth chapter of his *Epicurean* (1827), Moore wrote of the "bright tranquillity, which may be imagined to light the slumbers of those happy spirits, who are said to rest in the valley of the Moon, on their way to heaven." Poe may possibly allude to that legend too.

The mountains were actually visited by Sir Henry Stanley in 1888. The snowy peaks were seen from afar by Johann Rebmann, linguist and missionary, on May 11, 1848, but no account of this that Poe could have seen has been found.

21 The phrase "valley of the shadow" comes from Psalm 23:4, where the King James version (like the Septuagint, the Aramaic Targum, and the Vulgate) has "valley of the shadow of death." But there is another possible translation, simply "valley of the shadow [or darkness]" which Poe seems to have known about and apparently preferred. (See notes to "Dream-Land.") In Hebrew what was anciently written is Z-L-M-V-TH (Tzadi, Lamed, Mem, Vau, Tau). The Masoretic punctuation, by which vowels are now indicated in Hebrew, was invented centuries after the composition of most of the Old

Testament. Poe in 1836 referred in his "Pinakidia," number 73, to Masoretic punctuation. Thus with the addition of vowels, the Biblical word may be a compound of *zel* (shadow) and *maveth* (death), or a single word, *zalmuth* (darkness), which is found as an Arabic root. Mr. Abraham Berger, Chief of the Jewish Division, New York Public Library, referred me to E. F. C. Rosenmueller, *Scholia in vetus testamentum* (Leipzig, 1822), part 4, Psalms, volume II, pages 659f., and other sources, on which this note is based. Many scholars (of all faiths) have preferred the second explanation as more in keeping with the simple pastoral imagery of the Twenty-third Psalm. I think Poe wished his valley in "Eldorado" to be that of life *and* death.

TO MY MOTHER

This is a difficult poem to discuss justly. For the man in the street it has been called, "the best tribute to a mother-in-law ever written." [1] But its sincerity has been questioned in view of the long lapse of time between Poe's loss of Virginia and the composition of the poem and in view of its publication at a time when Poe was about to court Elmira Shelton. It must be remembered, however, that the embarrassingly late publication was the result of the publisher's delay. Poe had composed the piece after what he may have regarded as a providential escape from Helen Whitman and when he felt the comfort of the protection of his faithful aunt. The poem I think is heartfelt, though it perhaps shows but one side of the medal. [2]

[1] This remark is attributed to Bronson Howard (Phillips, II, 1400). The poem was addressed to Maria Poe Clemm, Poe's aunt and mother-in-law, born in Baltimore on March 12, 1790. She became the second wife of William Clemm, Jr., on July 13, 1817. She bore three children: Henry, Virginia Marie (who died as a small child), and Virginia Eliza, who became Edgar Poe's wife. Mrs. Clemm became a widow on February 8, 1826. The poet made his home with her from sometime in 1833, or perhaps earlier, until his death. After 1849 and until 1858, Mrs. Clemm lived much of the time with Mr. and Mrs. Sylvanus Lewis in Brooklyn, but from time to time with other friends. She entered the Church Home Infirmary on Broadway, Baltimore, in 1863, and died there on February 16, 1871. She is buried beside the poet and her daughter in Westminster Churchyard in Baltimore.

[2] It has been customary for recent biographers to sing the praises of "Muddie." But there is a great deal on the record to give us pause. Griswold and Dr. English said unpleasant things of her, which I fear are true. The bad opinions held of her by Mrs. Shew and Mrs. Richmond are revealed in letters decribed in the Ingram List (*passim*, but especially items 79 and 213). Helen Whitman, who sometimes contributed to the old lady's comfort, wrote to an unidentified correspondent: "You ask what I think of Mrs. Clemm. I have never seen her . . . Mrs. Osgood told

LAST POEMS

On February 8, 1849, Poe told Mrs. Richmond in a letter that the *Flag of Our Union* offered to pay five dollars for a sonnet, and the form he so rarely used may have been chosen for the known market. It is unlikely that the *Flag* bought anything from Poe after April 28 (see the notes on "For Annie"); at some time before June 9 Poe said the paper had two of his compositions still unprinted, this sonnet and the tale "Landor's Cottage," which appeared in the issue for that date. "Sonnet — To My Mother" was published in the *Flag* for July 7.

TEXTS

(*A*) Boston *Flag of Our Union* for July 7, 1849; (*B*) *Works* (1850), II, 28; (*C*) *Leaflets of Memory* for 1850, p. 48.

Texts *B* and *C* are given in full; it is not absolutely certain which should be considered the final version; that in the *Works* is the one long generally known to the world. Griswold, who shortened the original title, probably used a revised clipping; the single internal change from *A*, "dear" for "sweet" in the fifth line, is obviously auctorial, but it was not made in *C*, which does have changes in lines 1, 2, 3, 7, 11, and 12. Presumably Poe gave the manuscript for *C* to Dr. Reynell Coates, who edited the *Leaflets*, in Philadelphia, about July 1849, but just possibly it was sent earlier. The texts in the Richmond *Examiner*, October 29, 1849, in *Sartain's Union Magazine* for December 1849, and in the *Southern Literary Messenger* of the same date are without independent authority, being merely reprinted from the *Leaflets* — the last two in reviews of that volume.

TO MY MOTHER [*B*]

Because I feel that, in the Heavens above,
　　The angels, whispering to one another,
Can find, among their burning terms of love,
　　None so devotional as that of "Mother,"

---

me that she had been a thorn in Poe's side — always embroiling him in difficulties . . . Mr. Wyatt [a clergyman instrumental in obtaining Mrs. Clemm's admission to the Church Home] thought that she was very impulsive and indiscreet and exasperating." But Mrs. Whitman continued: "Poe always spoke of her with grateful and affectionate consideration. I believe that she loved him devotedly" (Ticknor, *Poe's Helen*, p. 171). It must be acknowledged that Mrs. Clemm did take care of the poet, and the world must be grateful to her for that. But her capacities were limited by her selfish character. Her conduct toward the poet's sister was particularly ungenerous. Nothing is known to me that belies the severe and masculine look revealed by her photograph. She was obviously a dragon, though often, no doubt, a protective one.

TO MY MOTHER

5   Therefore by that dear name I long have called you —
      You who are more than mother unto me,
    And fill my heart of hearts, where Death installed you
      In setting my Virginia's spirit free.
    My mother — my own mother, who died early,
10   Was but the mother of myself; but you
    Are mother to the one I loved so dearly,
      And thus are dearer than the mother I knew
    By that infinity with which my wife
      Was dearer to my soul than its soul-life.

[1849]

SONNET TO MY MOTHER   [C]

Because the angels in the Heavens above,
    Devoutly singing unto one another,
Can find, amid their burning terms of love,
    None so devotional as that of "mother,"
5   Therefore by that sweet name I long have called you;
      You who are more than mother unto me,
Filling my heart of hearts, where God installed you,
      In setting my Virginia's spirit free.
My mother — my own mother, who died early,
10   Was but the mother of myself; but you
    Are mother to the dead I loved so dearly,
      Are thus more precious than the one I knew,
    By that infinity with which my wife
      Was dearer to my soul than its soul-life.

[1849]

NOTES

5 Compare a phrase in Poe's letter of October 18, 1848, to Helen Whitman: "let me call you . . . by that sweet name."

8 An account of Virginia Poe is given below at page 522 in the discussion of her only surviving composition, the valentine she wrote for her husband. Poe addressed no poems to her during her lifetime (perhaps because she did not care much for poetry), although "Eulalie" may concern her. The tiny poem, "Deep in Earth," was obviously written after her death. That Poe's

marriage was not an ideal one seems to me indubitable, but what he says about Virginia in the present sonnet is surely in earnest. Dr. R. D. Unger, who met Poe in Baltimore during the years 1846 to 1849, wrote to Chevalier Reynolds on October 29, 1899, that "the loss of his wife was a sad blow" to Poe and that "he did not seem to care, after she was gone, whether he lived an hour, a day, a week or a year." (I quote from the letter, not yet completely published, no. 402 in the Ingram Collection.)

9 Poe's real mother, who died when he was less than three years old, was Elizabeth Arnold Poe, the actress, about whom the little we know is synopsized in the Annals. The poet privately resented the poor opinion held by his Baltimore relatives of his real mother because of her profession, and once told Mrs. Shew that he thought he owed his abilities to Elizabeth Arnold Poe. (See letter of May 16, 1875, from Marie Louise Shew Houghton to Ingram, described in the Ingram List, no. 266.) Poe may have been delirious when he made his remarks, and also may have feared that Mrs. Clemm had overheard something of this kind. His sonnet may have been meant as a disclaimer.

14 The reference is to the devotion of Ulysses to Penelope; compare "that long wand'ring Greek/That for his love refusèd deity" in Spenser's *Faerie Queene*, I, III, xxi, 5–6.

ANNABEL LEE

Poe's "Annabel Lee" is "the simplest and sweetest of his ballads," [1] second only to "The Raven" in popularity, and is widely recognized as one of the great lyric poems of the English language. It has long and generally been regarded as a tribute to the memory of Virginia Poe, although that idea is rather in the realm of legend than demonstrable fact.

Other ladies have been thought to be the original of Annabel Lee, but from the beginning the opinion has been sometimes held that the personal element in the poem is subordinate. Its continued appeal lies not in its immediate inspiration but in its preeminence as a poem of young love, unconquered and unconquerable. It is significant that Mrs. LeDuc thought "Annabel Lee" and "The Bells" were composed as onomatopoetic expressions of varying emotions for recitation, as "Ulalume" had been written at the suggestion of her father, Professor C. P. Bronson. [2] The poet

[1] Woodberry, *Life* (1909), II, 351.
[2] See commentary on "Ulalume," above.

never gave a dedication (not even "To — —") to his "ballad." Perhaps we should regard the poem as primarily a conscious work of art based on different sources in literature and experience, and including several references the poet hoped more than one of his fair friends would take personally.[3]

"Annabel Lee" is certainly, though very subtly, onomatopoetic. One sensitive reader felt the rhythm to be dirgelike, recalling the tolling of a buoy in the ebb and flow of the sea.[4] Others hear the breaking of waves on the shore. The poem may be called anapestic by metrists, but Poe was successfully using a special kind of anapest that had long interested him. In a review of Bryant in 1837, he called attention to the peculiar metrical structure of Wordsworth's *"many and many a song"* in an early version of "Guilt and Sorrow," and in 1845 himself wrote *"many and many a marvelous shrine"* in an iambic poem.[5] In 1849 in "Annabel Lee" he boldly began, "It was *many and many a* year ago" — and continued the whole ballad in this unusual rhythm.

In May 1849, Poe wrote to Annie Richmond, "I have written a ballad called 'Annabel Lee,' which I will send you soon." [6] This certainly indicates that a form of the poem satisfactory to its author had just been completed. At least in the form in which Poe submitted it for publication, "Annabel Lee" was his last poem, and he seems to have thought it would be.[7] It may well be significant that, exceptionally for him, he circulated it in manuscript.

---

[3] Sarah Helen Whitman (who thought herself the heroine of Poe's lines) asked pertinently, "Is the subject of the poem living or dead?" But she also wrote, "I do not doubt that the poem may have had [for the author] . . . other shades of meaning and may have been in some way associated with other persons." See Caroline Ticknor, *Poe's Helen* (1916), pp. 130–131.

[4] Frances Winwar, *The Haunted Palace* (1959), p. 357.

[5] See my notes on "The City in the Sea," line 21. In "The Rationale of Verse" Poe called this kind of "resolved" iambus a "bastard anapest."

[6] The date of the letter is uncertain, but its contents show that it cannot be earlier than May 5 or later than May 23, 1849.

[7] See Woodberry, *Life* (1909), II, 295–296. Poe may have composed earlier versions of this ballad, but the evidence for anything of the kind is shadowy. The only significant testimony is that of Mrs. Weiss, who told James A. Harrison that "Poe showed her the poem in 1849, and said it was composed years before his wife's death and had no reference to her." See Charles W. Kent's editor's note in Harrison's edition of the *Complete Works* (1902), VII, 219. Mrs. Weiss also said in her *Home Life* (1907), p. 129, that Rosalie Poe spoke of hearing the poem at Fordham in 1846, but one cannot expect Poe's sister to be strictly accurate about which

Poe on occasion used factual material from personal experience. The following story seems pertinent to "Annabel Lee." Its heroine is Catherine Elizabeth Poitiaux (pronounced "Poycha"), a goddaughter of the first Mrs. Allan. As a grown man, the poet was certainly not in love with her, but she received him as a dear friend in 1849. On September 11, 1872, her sister, Mary Jane Dixon, wrote: "We had been playmates . . . In the nursery we played at marrying him to my little sister whom he called his sweetheart." [8] The context suggests that this was before the Allans went abroad in June 1815, when the poet was not yet seven years old.

Another possible source for the poem in a memory of the poet's boyhood is known from a newspaper story, usually regarded as a legend, but perhaps having an element of truth.[9] It begins with a quoted obituary. "Died — on Monday evening, Feb. 24, — Annabel Lee, only daughter of Mary J. and T. C. Leland, aged 9 months and 2 weeks." What follows says that Poe as a boy knew Mary as a schoolgirl of twelve. When he left school they were separated; he heard she was very ill and supposed her dead. "Bright dreams . . . remained . . . and . . . her angel often rose up before him" and inspired his "Annabel Lee." Later he met her as "the wife of T. C. Leland. She cherished a sympathy for the . . . genius; her husband befriended, and . . . loved him for his talents, his warm heart, and . . . his conversation." Their only child was named for the poem.

There is some confusion in the story, for its writer thought the child was born while Poe was living. But the obituary, as I discovered, is in the *New-York Tribune* of March 1, 1851, and the New York City Directories of 1850 to 1855 list Theron C. Leland

---

poems she heard where. There is no reason to doubt Griswold's statement in the obituary signed "Ludwig" in the *New-York Tribune* of October 9, 1849, that Poe described it to him as his latest poem just before he left New York in June.

[8] The original letter is preserved with other papers of R. H. Stoddard in the Anthony Collection at the New York Public Library. It contains reminiscences of Mrs. Dixon, addressed to the editors of *Harper's Magazine*.

[9] Woodberry, *Life*, I, 376, reprints it from an undated clipping from the *Green Mountain Gem* of Brandon, Vermont. I have another clipping crediting the story to the *Free Democrat* of "Milwaukie," Wisconsin — the old spelling suggests a date in the fifties.

as teacher, reporter, and phonographer (court stenographer): precisely the kind of minor intellectual with whom the poet consorted. Poe was certainly capable of telling the lady, if he had known her in youth, that she was Annabel Lee.[10]

Two probable literary sources for "Annabel Lee" have been pointed out. The first is a poem signed "D.M.C.," in the *Courier* of Charleston, South Carolina, December 4, 1807.

THE MOURNER

How sweet were the joys of my former estate!
   Health and happiness caroll'd with glee;
And contentment ne'er envy'd the pomp of the great
   In the cot by the side of the sea.

With my Anna I past the mild summer of love
   'Till death gave his cruel decree,
And bore the dear angel to regions above
   From the cot by the side of the sea!

But the smile of contentment has never return'd
   Since death tore my Anna from me;
And for many long years I've unceasingly mourn'd
   In the cot by the side of the sea.

And her sweet recollections shall live in the mind
   Till from anguish this bosom is free,
And seeks the repose which it never can find
   In the cot by the side of the sea!

Robert Adger Law, who found this poem, felt that the similarities to "Annabel Lee" in meter and wording are so many that it is hard to think them a matter of pure chance.[11] There is, of course, the question of how likely Poe was to have seen the paper. The issue contains an advertisement of Placide's company of players, to which both the poet's parents sometimes belonged (although not in 1807) — and it is not at all improbable that he glanced through a file when stationed near Charleston, or even had a copy of the paper. "D.M.C." has not been identified.

---

[10] Unfortunately we do not know Mary Leland's maiden name. She was certainly not Mary of Baltimore, for that Mary's husband was a merchant tailor. See notes on the lost poem, "To Mary [Starr]."

[11] *Journal of English and Germanic Philology*, April 1922 (21:341–346). Professor Law, a close friend of Killis Campbell, found "The Mourner" by chance when searching the Charleston paper for reasons unconnected with Poe.

The second literary source suggested for "Annabel Lee" resembles Poe's poem less strikingly, but there is no possible doubt that Poe knew it. The poem is one by Mrs. Sarah Helen Whitman.

STANZAS FOR MUSIC

Tell him I lingered alone on the shore,
Where we parted in anger, to meet never more;
The night wind blew cold on my desolate heart;
But colder those wild words of doom — "Ye must part!"

O'er the dark, heaving waters I sent forth a cry;
Save the moan of those waters, there came no reply.
I longed like a bird o'er those waters to flee
From my lone island-home and the moan of the sea.

Away, far away from the wild ocean shore,
Where the waves ever murmur "No more, never more."
Where I look from my lattice, far over the main,
And weep for the bark that returns not again.

When the clouds that now veil from us Heaven's fair light
Their soft, silver lining turn forth on the night,
When time shall the vapors of falsehood dispel,
He shall know if I loved him, but never how well.

This was first printed in the second number of the *American Metropolitan Magazine*, that for February 1849, from which the foregoing text is copied.[12]

Mrs. Whitman's story is this: Poe had urged her to send her lines "To Arcturus" to the new magazine. She thought them too personal, but being urged by Israel Post to contribute something, she added a final stanza to a song she had composed some years before for an air by a friend who was an Italian guitarist. She meant the verses as a reply to Poe's last letter to her, and felt that he accepted them "as a peace-offering" to which "Annabel

[12] The magazine, edited by William Landon, was published at 259 Broadway, New York, by Israel Post, who had recently sold his *Union Magazine* to John Sartain. Post failed signally; the second number of his periodical was the last and, despite its date, did not appear until the middle of March. The only file known to contain both issues, that in the New-York Historical Society, is used. Mrs. Whitman republished the poem as "Our Island of Dreams" but never exactly in the form in which Poe saw it. Discussions of the relation of Mrs. Whitman to "Annabel Lee" are based on her letters of February 19 and 20, April 24, May 1, and May 11, 1874, to J. H. Ingram (Ingram List, numbers 122, 123, 147, 149, 153) and various documents quoted from Mrs. Whitman's papers by Caroline Ticknor in her biography, *Poe's Helen*, pp. 128–133.

Lee" was a reply — "the veiled expression . . . of his undying remembrance." Mrs. Whitman's claim is the one hinted at by Griswold when first publishing the poem, in the phrase, after a reference to personalities in Poe's latest poems, "perhaps some of our readers . . . will understand the allusions." Charles F. Briggs asserted her claim in the unsigned "Original Memoir" in the first American illustrated edition of Poe's *Poetical Works* (New York, 1859, p. 33).[13]

Soon another lady entered the field. Sarah Anna Lewis claimed that the poem was for her. In his last letter to that lady, about September 18, 1849, Poe wrote, "My dear sister Anna (for so you have permitted me to call you) — never while I live shall I forget you." That was little to go on, but Mrs. Clemm, wishing to pay her hostess a special compliment, told her the poet had assured her that "Annabel Lee" was for Anna Lewis. This was in the presence of Mary E. Hewitt, who immediately went and told Mrs. Osgood. Mrs. Hewitt later wrote to Mrs. Whitman:

> Mrs. Osgood's lip curled and she at once sat down to pen her comments on the poem for Griswold's "Memoir," in the course of which she points out that Poe's ballad was written to his Virginia, *"the only woman Poe ever loved."*
>
> I knew . . . that Fanny (Osgood) could not for a moment have believed this statement, and I saw that the lines were dictated by pique . . . She wrote the comments . . . not with reference to you, dear Mrs. Whitman, but only hoping to "put Mrs. Lewis down." [14]

What Mrs. Osgood wrote for Griswold was at least extremely effective.[15] Her most pertinent remarks on Poe's last poem must be quoted:

> In spite of the many little poetic episodes, in which the . . . romance of his temperament impelled him to indulge; . . . I believe . . . [his wife] was the only woman he ever truly loved; and this is evidenced by . . . the little poem . . . called Annabel Lee, of which she was the subject . . .
>
> It is said that it was intended to illustrate a late love affair of the author;

[13] Briggs was once closely associated with Poe but is unlikely to have discussed "Annabel Lee" with him in 1849. Mrs. Whitman wrote Ingram that she did not authorize the statement, and she apparently did not know Briggs wrote it.

[14] See Ticknor, *Poe's Helen*, pp. 132–133.

[15] See the "Memoir," p. liii. This "Memoir" was published in the *International Magazine* of October 1, 1850, a little before inclusion in the third volume of Poe's *Works* late in that year.

but they who believe this, have . . . missed the beautiful meaning . . . where he says ". . . her high-born *kinsmen* came,/And bore her away from me." There seems . . . a disregard of the sacred purity and spiritual tenderness . . . in thus overlooking the allusion to the *kindred* angels and the heavenly Father of the lost and unforgotten wife.

Whatever Mrs. Osgood's motives, her explanation of "Annabel Lee," if not perfect, was ingenious and poetic.[16] Griswold accepted her explanation, as did Ingram (who in print would refer to no other), and in 1917 Killis Campbell could write (*Poems*, p. 295) that it was "the view universally held to-day among students of Poe." [17] No such authority would now go so far. However, identification of Virginia Poe as the original of Annabel Lee need not be wholly rejected. It is the most beautiful of the stories of a personal element in Poe's ballad.

Elmira Shelton believed that she herself was Annabel Lee, and undoubtedly Poe told her so — any gallant author would assure a lady whose hand he was seeking that she was the inspiration of his latest masterpiece.[18] Yet one may find in "Annabel Lee" an allegory continuing those of "Tamerlane" and "To Zante." In the first the heroine is symbolically dead in her betrothal to

[16] Mrs. Osgood's motives were certainly complicated. She wished to minimize the importance of all the women in Poe's life save Virginia Poe and herself, of whom Virginia approved. She does *not* account for the reference to Annabel and her lover as having been children at the same time; although in favor of that interpretation are the Bible texts, that only those enter the Kingdom of God who receive it as little children. See Mark 10:15, and Luke 18:17. See also an article in the *South Atlantic Quarterly*, April 1912, by Wightman F. Melton, who sought analogies in Poe's tale "Eleonora" (which does concern Virginia). Mrs. Osgood and many others seem oblivious of the fact that a great love poem is not necessarily based on a great love.

[17] Many as are the commentators who have accepted this interpretation, Woodberry always avoided decisive comment.

[18] Mrs. Shelton told Thomas Alfriend that Poe assured her that she was his "lost Lenore" and inspired "Annabel Lee"; see the article by Edward M. Alfriend (son of Thomas) in the *Literary Era* for August 1901. On February 27, 1882, Dr. J. J. Moran wrote Mr. Edward Abbott that he had just returned from lecturing on Poe at Richmond, "the home of his *Annabel Lee*, who yet lives . . . she was at the lecture . . . and she and I, met." The letter is printed in full in Hervey Allen's *Israfel* (1926), II, 895. Hence Moran's record in his *Defense* (Washington, 1885), p. 32, cannot be discounted as a product of his notoriously expansive memory for times long ago. I do discount Mrs. Shelton's remark to Edward V. Valentine on March 19, 1875, quoted by Quinn, p. 91, that "Poe never addressed any poems to her" (he never did by name), for I think she mistrusted Valentine as well as J. H. Ingram whose emissary he was.

Alexander Shelton; in the second, in her marriage to him. In the last of this trilogy the death of her husband (on July 12, 1844) has made her live again for her first lover. The highborn kinsmen would be Elmira Royster's family, who broke up her engagement to Poe.

We may take leave of these rival claimants with mention of Mrs. Richmond, who apparently never even suggested that she was the real Annabel Lee. Yet Poe called her "Annie," and she was the first person to whom he is known to have promised to show the poem. She must have wondered about it, as have many readers since.[19]

Poe circulated the poem among his friends far more widely than was usual for him, and five manuscripts are preserved. If he sent a copy to Mrs. Richmond, as he promised about May 1849, she may have returned it, for no manuscript from her papers has been found, and she did not destroy his poems when she burned his letters.

Not long before he left New York at the end of June he discussed the poem with Griswold and sent a copy to him with an undated letter.[20] This was for inclusion in the revised tenth edition of *The Poets and Poetry of America*, dated 1850, scheduled for publication and issued in December 1849.

Before he left New York, Poe also gave a manuscript to John W. Moore, head bookkeeper of the printing house of Joseph Russell, 79 John Street, who sometimes helped the poet financially. Said Poe, "Moore, I may never be able to repay you, but take this; some day it may be valuable." [21] In Philadelphia, in July, Poe also gave a copy to Henry B. Hirst, from a collection of whose papers

[19] Unfortunately most of what Poe wrote to Mrs. Richmond is still known only from what J. H. Ingram chose to publish, and he did not print anything that might weaken the claims of Virginia Poe. The idea that Annie Richmond *might* be Annabel was advanced by Caroline Ticknor in 1916 — see *Poe's Helen*, p. 133.

[20] See Griswold's obituary of Poe, signed "Ludwig," in the *New-York Tribune* of October 9, 1849, for Poe's statement that it was his last poem, which need not be doubted. In printing the letter with the "Memoir," Griswold interpolated a forged postscript, to indicate that Poe wanted him to sell the poem for fifty dollars. The actual letter is at the University of Texas. The manuscript poem (referred to below as *A*) was given to Harvard by Griswold's grandchildren.

[21] See the story in the *New York Times* of January 17, 1909, recounted in Phillips, II, 1414. This manuscript (*B*) is now owned by Colonel Richard Gimbel.

it was sold in 1921.[22] He also sold the poem for regular publication to *Sartain's Union Magazine*. He had almost surely arranged for this previously.[23]

In Richmond, where Poe had read the poem in his lectures, on "the day before he left" (September 26) he gave a manuscript to John R. Thompson, in payment of a five-dollar debt.[24] This was obviously given as an autograph, although Thompson later wanted it thought a sale for publication. The *Richmond Examiner* proof sheet may be from this manuscript or may represent one that has been lost — they do not differ verbally, but the *Examiner* has two additional words italicized: "my life" in line 39. References that have been made to a manuscript sent N. P. Willis are based on careless reading of what he wrote in the *Home Journal* of October 20, 1849.

Poe's actions were strictly honorable, but Sartain was unexpectedly dilatory in publication — the poem appeared in *Sartain's* for January 1850.[25] On hearing of Poe's death, Griswold "jumped the gun" and printed the poem in the *New-York Tribune* at once. The strict propriety of *his* action was more than questionable, but he gave a great poem to the world.

TEXTS

(*A*) Manuscript sent to R. W. Griswold, June 1849, now at Harvard; (*B*) manuscript given to John W. Moore, June 1849 (facsimile in *New York Times*, January 17, 1909), now owned by Colonel Richard Gimbel; (*C*) manuscript given to Henry B. Hirst, early July 1849, now in the Huntington Library; (*D*) manuscript sold to John Sartain, early July 1849, now in the Pierpont Morgan Library; (*E*) manuscript given to John R. Thompson, September 26, 1849 (facsimile in Woodberry, II, 352), now at Columbia University;

[22] Anderson Galleries Sale, number 1583, lot 564. This manuscript (*C*) is in the Henry E. Huntington Library.

[23] This manuscript (*D*) is in the Pierpont Morgan Library. It is marked "$5 paid," with a note by Sartain's editor, Professor John S. Hart, "paid when it was accepted." The very small sum suggests to me a final payment after an advance.

[24] I combine what Thompson wrote in the *Southern Literary Messenger*, November 1849 (15:694–697) and February 1854 (20:124–125) with a statement of W. F. Gill, *Life* (1877), p. 231. Gill knew Thompson, who was, in my opinion, a sensational journalist with no passion for exact truth. This manuscript (*E*) was recently bequeathed to Columbia University by Mrs. Alexander McMillan Welch.

[25] Statements (of Griswold and Thompson and even perhaps Hirst) led John Sartain to suppose Poe had sold the poem to three other publishers; see Sartain's *Reminiscences of a Very Old Man* (1899), p. 205.

ANNABEL LEE

(F) *Richmond Examiner* proof sheet, late summer 1849 (printed by Whitty, pp. 80–81), from *E*; (G) *New-York Tribune*, morning edition, October 9, 1849, from *A*; (H) *Southern Literary Messenger*, November 1849 (15:697), from *E*; (J) R. W. Griswold, *Poets and Poetry of America*, 10th edition (dated 1850, issued late in 1849), p. 418, from *A*; (K) *Sartain's Union Magazine* for January 1850 (6:99–100), from *D*; (L) *Works* (1850), II, 27–28, from *A*.

The earliest version (*A*) and the latest (*E*) are given in full. Although Poe's revisions were few, they were important; and one, made in a single manuscript (*E*), is generally considered unfortunate, since it marred the concluding line, widely regarded as one of the great lines of English verse.

The first version (*A*), through Griswold's edition (*L*), is very generally known. Whitty's notes (*Complete Poems*, 1911, page 242) are confusing, but he told me that *F* was verbally like *H*, and that his text of line 41 was altered at the request of his publishers. A version in a gift book, *The Present*, edited by F. A. Moore (Manchester, New Hampshire, 1850), can hardly be authorized.

ANNABEL LEE [*A*]

It was many and many a year ago,
 In a kingdom by the sea,
That a maiden there lived whom you may know
 By the name of Annabel Lee; —
5 And this maiden she lived with no other thought
 Than to love and be loved by me.

I was a child and *she* was a child,
 In this kingdom by the sea;
But we loved with a love that was more than love —
10 I and my Annabel Lee —
With a love that the wingéd seraphs in Heaven
 Coveted her and me.

And this was the reason that, long ago,
 In this kingdom by the sea,
15 A wind blew out of a cloud, chilling
 My beautiful Annabel Lee;
So that her high-born kinsmen came
 And bore her away from me,
To shut her up in a sepulchre,
20 In this kingdom by the sea.

The angels, not half so happy in Heaven,
  Went envying her and me —
Yes! — that was the reason (as all men know,
  In this kingdom by the sea)
25 That the wind came out of the cloud by night,
  Chilling and killing my Annabel Lee.

But our love it was stronger by far than the love
  Of those who were older than we —
  Of many far wiser than we —
30 And neither the angels in Heaven above,
  Nor the demons down under the sea,
Can ever dissever my soul from the soul
  Of the beautiful Annabel Lee: —

For the moon never beams, without bringing me dreams
35 Of the beautiful Annabel Lee;
And the stars never rise, but I feel the bright eyes
  Of the beautiful Annabel Lee: —
And so, all the night-tide, I lie down by the side
Of my darling — my darling — my life and my bride,
40 In her sepulchre there by the sea —
  In her tomb by the sounding sea.

                   [May 1849]

ANNABEL LEE   [*E*]

It was many and many a year ago,
  In a kingdom by the sea,
That a maiden there lived whom you may know
  By the name of Annabel Lee; —
5 And this maiden she lived with no other thought
  Than to love and be loved by me.

She was a child and *I* was a child,
  In this kingdom by the sea,
But we loved with a love that was more than love —

10   I and my Annabel Lee —
With a love that the wingéd seraphs of Heaven
      Coveted her and me.

And this was the reason that, long ago,
      In this kingdom by the sea,
15   A wind blew out of a cloud by night
      Chilling my Annabel Lee;
So that her highborn kinsmen came
      And bore her away from me,
To shut her up, in a sepulchre
20   In this kingdom by the sea.

The angels, not half so happy in Heaven,
      Went envying her and me: —
Yes! that was the reason (as all men know,
      In this kingdom by the sea)
25   That the wind came out of the cloud, chilling
      And killing my Annabel Lee.

But our love it was stronger by far than the love
      Of those who were older than we —
      Of many far wiser than we —
30   And neither the angels in Heaven above
      Nor the demons down under the sea
Can ever dissever my soul from the soul
      Of the beautiful Annabel Lee: —

For the moon never beams without bringing me dreams
      Of the beautiful Annabel Lee;
35   And the stars never rise but I see the bright eyes
      Of the beautiful Annabel Lee;
And so, all the night-tide, I lie down by the side
Of my darling, my darling, my life and my bride
40   In her sepulchre there by the sea —
      In her tomb by the side of the sea.
                              [September 1849]

·479·

LAST POEMS

Title: Annabel Lee — A Ballad. (D, K)
7   I . . . she/She . . . I (B, C, E, F,
   H); She . . . I (D, K)
11 wingéd/wingèd (B, F); wingëd (G);
   winged (L); in/of (C, D, E, F, G, H, J,
   K, L)
15 chilling/by night (E, F, H)
16 My beautiful/Chilling my (E, F, H)

17 kinsmen/kinsman (K, L; misprint?)
25 by night/chilling (E, F, H)
26 Chilling and killing/And killing
   (E, F, H)
36 feel/see (E, F, H)
40 her/the (misprint, L)
41 sounding/side of the (E, H)

NOTES

Title: The name probably comes from a combination of two titles Poe knew. On February 18, 1844, he wrote a letter to George Lippard praising his novel *The Ladye Annabel* (1842), and one of the two best-known lyrics of Poe's friend Philip Pendleton Cooke is "Young Rosalie Lee," first printed in the *Southern Literary Messenger* of March 1835 on a page facing Poe's tale "Berenicë." Compare also Dryden's *Absalom and Achitophel*, line 34, where Absalom "made the charming Annabel his bride." The name "Anna" is from the Hebrew for "gracious," but the name was borne by the sister of Queen Dido in the *Aeneid*, IV, 32–33.

1   For Poe's use of the phrase "many and many a," see introductory comment above.

2   Most kingdoms have seacoasts. Mrs. Whitman's reference in "Stanzas for Music" to her "home, and the moan of the sea" was literal, since Providence is a seaport. But Fordham and Richmond are near rivers.

7   In the *Literary Era* of August 1901, Edward M. Alfriend wrote: "Poe . . . was extremely fond of children . . . My father said that he would romp with them by the hour, and in their childish sports would become himself a child again."

11–16   R. M. Hogg (Phillips, II, 1392) suggested that Poe had in mind the beautiful Scottish legend that the soul was conducted to Heaven by the spirit of its last predeceased kinsman. This would be more cogent if the singular form "kinsman" had manuscript authority, but it need not be wholly given up. An objection to Mrs. Osgood's identification of the kinsmen with angels, who are not *born*, is weakened by a common usage of words like "angels" and "seraphs" for blessed human souls.

18   According to Caroline Ticknor (*Poe's Helen*, p. 131), Mrs. Whitman believed that Poe had seen a letter she wrote to Mrs. Osgood in the spring of 1849 saying that friends had "caught her up" and "borne her away to the . . . shores of Massachusetts."

21   Compare "Tamerlane" (G), lines 88–89, "angel minds . . . might envy" — the closest link to Elmira Shelton's story.

25   Compare "The night wind blew cold" in Mrs. Whitman's "Stanzas," above. Miss Winwar unpoetically sees a reference to what Mrs. Clemm called Virginia Poe's bronchitis (*The Haunted Palace*, p. 357).

ANNABEL LEE

26 Lewis S. Friedland told me he thought a line in Scott's "Young Lochinvar" was echoed — "There was racing and chasing on Cannobie Lea" (*Marmion*, V, XII, viii, 3) — and indeed that Scott's ballad influenced Poe's whole poem.

30–33 See Romans 8:38–39: "neither death, nor life, nor angels . . . nor powers . . . nor height, nor depth . . . shall be able to separate us from the love of God which is in Christ Jesus" — a familiar passage used in the Episcopal funeral service.

36 Comparison of stars to eyes is commonplace, but we may cite a passage by Poe's friend N. P. Willis — from "The Confessional": "Thy face looks up from every sea,/In every star thine eyes are set."

41 It is generally agreed that Poe's final phrasing "side of the sea" is inferior to the earlier "sounding sea" in this line. The reason for the change was probably to obtain greater metrical regularity. In "The Rationale of Verse" Poe said, "*That* rhythm is erroneous . . . which any ordinary reader *can*, without design, read improperly . . . the intention *must* be caught at once." The new reading is, as Miss Phillips once said to me, "more harmonious, but the older one is more melodious." The phrase "sounding seas" is in *Lycidas*, line 154.

APPENDIXES

SERIOUS RHYMES IN PROSE

In his prose Poe usually avoided rhyme except for comic effect. There are in the tales, however, three examples of rhyming prose of the most serious kind. These are here collected.

1. In all versions of "Morella," written about 1834 and first published in the *Southern Literary Messenger*, April 1835, the heroine says to her husband:

> The days have never been when thou couldst love me — but her whom in life thou didst abhor, in death thou shalt adore.

2. In all versions of "Eleonora," written in 1841 and first printed in *The Gift* for 1842, a rhyme is introduced thus:

> I wedded; — nor dreaded the curse I had invoked; and its bitterness was not visited upon me.

3. "The Masque of the Red Death," written in 1842 and first printed in *Graham's Magazine* for May of that year, has in all versions a highly wrought metrical and rhymed conclusion:

> And the life of the ebony clock went out with that of the last of the gay. And the flames of the tripods expired. And Darkness and Decay and the Red Death held illimitable dominion over all.

COMIC RHYMES

Discussing the works of John G. C. Brainard, Poe wrote in *Graham's Magazine* for February 1842, "Of the merely humorous pieces we have little to say. Such things are not *poetry* . . . Humor, with an exception to be made hereafter, is directly antagonistical to . . . the soul of the Muse . . . But it so happens that humor and . . . imagination are both essentially aided . . . by rhythm and . . . rhyme." The exception is made for humor combined with archness. In view of this, I have treated the playful poems in the main body of the present volume, and the early satires, too, since Poe probably thought of them as poems when he wrote them. In this appendix are given only the rhymes devoid of any serious purpose at all. Some of these were written and printed as prose, but there are so few items that subdivision seems needless. One scrap, number 21, is now printed for the first time. All are surely Poe's except number 23, which is preserved only by anonymous tradition, but is rather probably authentic. (Two rhymes, still of uncertain origin, occur in *Pinakidia*, numbers 20 and 140, but that series contains almost nothing original, and there is little reason to think them composed by Poe; the present reference seems sufficient here.)

1. In Poe's story, "How to Write a Blackwood Article," originally "The Psyche Zenobia," Mr. Blackwood gives Miss Suky Snobbs — alias "Psyche Zenobia" — a number of scraps of learning with which to ornament her projected horror tale. He reads her a quatrain "from Cervantes," actually an old rhyme quoted in *Don Quixote* (II, xxxviii) and quoted by Poe once before in "Pinakidia":

> Van muerte tan escondida,
> Que no te sienta venir;
> Porque el plazer del morir
> No me torne à dar la vida.

In Miss Suky's tale, "The Scythe of Time," later called "A Predicament," the authoress reproduces what she thinks she heard:

> Vanny Buren tan escondida,
> Query no te senty venny
> Pork and pleasure, delly morry
> Nommy, torny, darry widdy!

The third line seems to echo a bit from Dr. Johnson's poem on "A Lady Coming of Age": "Pride and pleasure, pomp and plenty." References to the "pork barrel" in politics had not yet become familiar.

The tales were first published in the Baltimore *American Museum* for November 1838 (1:301–309, 310–317). The nonsense verses, without verbal changes, appear in all versions.

APPENDIX II

2. Also in "The Scythe of Time" is the following line:

Andrew O'Phlegethon, you really make haste to fly.

This is Psyche Zenobia's version of a line given her by her advisor as from the Greek of Demosthenes, Ἀνὴρ ὁ φεύγων καὶ πάλιν μαχήσεται, which Poe transliterated "Aner o pheugon kai palin makesetai (*sic*)." It is literally "The man who flees will also fight again" and is proverbial in English as "He who fights and runs away." There seems to be an allusion to Phlegethon, the fiery river of Hades, in Poe's "For Annie."

3. In the same story Poe's Psyche Zenobia made the two lines

Il pover hommy che non sera corty
And have a combat tenty erry morty;

out of "Il pover 'huomo che non se'n era accorto,/Andava combattendo, e era morto." This means "The poor man, who did not know he was slain, kept on fighting, although he was already dead." Poe ascribes the lines here and in "Pinakidia" incorrectly to Ariosto.

4. From the same sources also comes the following:

Unt stubby duk, so stubby dun
Duk she! duk she!

This is Psyche Zenobia's version of Mr. Blackwood's quotation "from Schiller," thus, "Und sterb' ich doch, so sterb' ich denn/Durch sie — durch sie!" ("And if I die, at least I die for thee — for thee.") The original is in Goethe's ballad "Das Veilchen," which Poe thus misquoted but correctly ascribed in "The Visionary."

5. The following occurs only in the first two versions of "A Predicament" in the *American Museum* and *Tales of the Grotesque and Arabesque*

Is — *is* that the departed spirit, the shade, the ghost of my beloved puppy, which I perceive sitting with a grace and face so melancholy, in the corner?

6. In his tale "Von Jung" in the *American Monthly* for June 1837 and in the *Tales of the Grotesque and Arabesque* there is the following rhyming passage:

I have seen the college chapel bombarded — I have seen the college ramparts most distressingly placarded — I have seen the whole world by the ears — I have seen old Wertemuller in tears.

Later versions of the tale, called "Mystification," are emended to omit this jingle. At Charlottesville Poe had a friend and fellow-student, the librarian, named William Wertenbaker.

7. In all versions of "The Philosophy of Furniture" first printed in *Burton's* for May 1840 is the following sentence:

We are violently enamoured of gas and of glass.

8. Poe introduced rhyme into the account of a geologist in his story "Lionizing" in *Tales of the Grotesque and Arabesque* (1840):

There was a great geologist Feltzpar. He talked of internal fires and tertiary formations; of aëriforms, fluidiforms, and solidiforms; of quartz and marl; of schist and schorl; of gypsum, hornblende, mica-slate, and pudding-stone.

In the versions of the *Tales* (1845), the *Broadway Journal*, March 15, 1845, and that in the Griswold edition, the passage is much expanded:

There was Ferdinand Fitz-Fossillus Feltspar. He informed us all about internal fires and tertiary formations; about aëriforms, fluidiforms, and solidiforms; about quartz and marl; about schist and schorl; about gypsum and trap; about talc and calc; about blende and horn-blende; about mica-slate and pudding-stone; about cyanite and lepidolite; about haematite and tremolite; about antimony and calcedony; about manganese and whatever you please.

9. In all versions of "Never Bet the Devil Your Head," those in *Graham's* for September 1841, in the *Broadway Journal*, August 16, 1845, and in the second volume of the *Works* (1850) there are three passages in rhymed prose. The first is:

I remonstrated — but to no purpose. I demonstrated — in vain.

In the first version we read "but in vain."

10. The second jingle now reads:

There was something . . . in his *manner* of enunciation . . . which Mr. Coleridge would have called mystical, Mr. Kant pantheistical, Mr. Carlyle twistical, and Mr. Emerson hyperquizzitistical.

In the first version "Emerson's" term was "hyperfizzitistical."

11. The third passage is:

The best pigeon-winger over all kinds of style, was my friend Mr. Carlyle.

12. In a review of Rufus Dawes, probably written in 1839, but first published in *Graham's* for October 1842, Poe parodies two lines of "Geraldine," from the volume *Geraldine, Athenia of Damascus and Miscellaneous Poems* (1839), page 79: ". . . dare I tell!/'Tis Alice! — curse us, Geraldine! — farewell!". Poe says:

The whole passage, perhaps, would have read better thus —
"oh, my eye!
'Tis Alice! — d——n it, Geraldine! — good bye!"

Despite his cavalier treatment of "Geraldine," its ending influenced the climactic scene of Poe's "Premature Burial."

13. The following occurs in all versions of Poe's tale "Three Sundays in

a Week," first published in the Philadelphia *Saturday Evening Post*, November 27, 1841:

> "You hard-hearted, dunder-headed, obstinate rusty, crusty, musty, fusty, old savage!" said I in fancy, one afternoon, to my grand uncle Rumgudgeon.

There is a reflection here of Tennyson's "To Christopher North" (1833): "Crusty . . . Rusty . . . Musty . . . Fusty Christopher."

14. In *Graham's* for August 1843, Poe reviewed the recently issued *Poems* of William Ellery Channing the younger with extreme severity. Channing was a Transcendentalist and a friend of Emerson. He bore the same name as his uncle, the famous Unitarian divine, and later dropped the first name. His romantic contempt for conventions included those of grammar. Poe thus discussed two lines from Channing's "Thoughts," II, 17–18:

> Mr. Channing could never have meant to say: "Thou meetest a common man/With a delusive show of *can;*" for what *is* a delusive show of *can?* No doubt it should have been,
>
> > Thou meetest a little pup
> > With a delusive show of tin-cup."

15. In all versions of Poe's tale "Diddling," first published in the Philadelphia *Saturday Courier*, October 14, 1843, there is an account of an imaginary business firm:

> Boggs, Hogs, Logs, Frogs, & Co.
> No. 110 Dog Street.

In another of Poe's stories, "Thou Art the Man," there is a firm of similar name: "Hoggs, Frogs, Bogs & Co." Compare also some of the rhymes from "X-ing a Paragrab," number 22 below.

16. In the several versions of Poe's satire, "The Literary Life of Thingum Bob," first published in the *Southern Literary Messenger*, December 1844, the hero begins his career as a magazinist by composing a "poem" inspired by a hair tonic invented by his father, the barber Thomas Bob. It reads:

> To pen an Ode upon the "Oil-of-Bob"
> Is all sorts of a job.
>
> > > (Signed.) SNOB.

17. In a review of William Wilberforce Lord's *Poems* (New York, 1845), in the *Broadway Journal*, May 24, 1845, Poe ridicules a poem called "To a Lady about to take the Veil" and says:

> Mr. Lord winds up a dissertation on the subject with the patronizing advice — "Ere thou, irrevocable, to that dark creed/Art yielded, *think, Oh Lady, think again!*" the whole of which would read better if it were
>
> > Ere thou, irrevocable, to this d — d doggrel
> > Art yielded, Lord, think! think! — ah think again.

COMIC RHYMES

For the poem castigated see *The Complete Poetical Works* of W. W. Lord (New York, 1938), page 50.

18. In all versions of the story called "The Spectacles," first printed in the Philadelphia *Dollar Newspaper*, March 27, 1844, much is made of the rhyming names of the hero's ancestors. One sentence will suffice:

Here, however, are Moissart, Voissart, Croissart, and Froissart, all in the direct line of descent.

19. A brief nonsense rhyme is given in each text of "The 1002nd Tale of Scheherazade," first published in *Godey's* for February 1845. It is described as a specimen of what one of the "men-vermin" (the crew of a battleship) was "vain enough to denominate its language":

Washish squashish squeak, Sinbad, hey-diddle diddle, grunt unt grumble, hiss, fiss, whiss.

The extreme rarity of intentional pure nonsense, even in Poe's comic tales, should be observed.

20. The following jingle is from the story "Mellonta Tauta," written in 1848 and published in *Godey's* for February 1849:

Mob . . . set up a despotism, in comparison with which those of the fabulous Zeros and Hellofagabaluses were respectable and delectable.

The protagonist of this story of some thousand years in the future (A.D. 2848) is badly mixed up about history and refers to the Roman emperors Nero and Heliogabalus (more properly Elagabalus).

21. In "The Living Writers of America," a late manuscript in the Pierpont Morgan Library, there is the following passage on the credulity of the "Humanity party of Boston":

Never saw one of them who is not at once Mesmerist, Phrenologist, Homœopathist, Priessnitzian, Swedenborgian, Fourierite, and Fanny Wright.

I expand the eleventh to fifteenth words from abbreviations, and supply punctuation. This scrap apparently has not been previously published. In the "Literati" sketch of Mrs. Gove, Poe attributed most of these "advanced" opinions to *her*.

22. In Poe's story "X-ing a Paragrab," first published in the Boston *Flag of Our Union*, May 12, 1849, the hero, Touch-and-Go Bullet-head, an editor, reproached by John Smith, editor of a rival sheet, for too frequent use of the vowel *o*, composes the following defiant reply:

So, ho, John! how now? Told you so, you know. Don't crow, another time, before you're out of the woods! Does your mother *know* you're out? Oh, no, no! — so go home at once, now, John, to your odious old woods of Concord! Go home to your woods, old owl, — go! You won't? Oh, poh, poh, John, don't do so! You've *got* to go, you know! So go at once, and don't go slow; for nobody owns you here, you know. Oh, John, John, if you *don't* go you're no *homo* — no! You're only a fowl, an owl; a cow, a sow; a doll, a Poll; a poor, old, good-for-nothing-to-nobody log, dog, hog, or frog, come out of a Concord bog. Cool, now — cool! Do be cool, you fool! None of your crowing, old cock! Don't frown so — don't! hollo, nor howl, nor growl, nor bow-wow-wow! Good Lord, John, how you *do* look! Told you so, you know — but stop rolling your goose of an old poll about so, and go and drown your sorrows in a bowl!

Smith apparently came from Concord, the great center of Transcendentalism. Compare the rhymes on "bogs" in item 15 above.

23. In the New York *Cosmopolitan Art Journal* of December 1858 is a brief editorial article on Poe, which includes the following anecdote:

Poe was once dunned savagely for a grocer's bill, long overdue. He immediately sat down, penned one of his most savage onslaughts upon one of "the literati," and upon the *strength* of it borrowed the amount needed to free him from the grocer.

"There, sir!" said he, "*grow*, sir, you grocer puppy, into a dog, sir, and may you then be dogged sir, as you have dogged Poe, sir. Now, go sir, and be —— to you."

I am not sure of the identity of the editor of the rare periodical, but for various reasons suspect it was Prosper M. Wetmore. The magazine was friendly to Poe's memory, and called for a monument to him. It is very hard to say whether the grocer story represents something Poe said (or said that he said) or not, but the rhymes are very like the doggerel from "X-ing a Paragrab" given above, and it seems to me to deserve inclusion with a caveat. I think the word "so" may have fallen out between "dogged" and "sir," but refrain from emendation.

COLLABORATIONS

Like most professional men of letters, Poe occasionally polished verses for friends, as a matter of courtesy, or even for a fee.[1] We have several references to schemes to have Poe help other writers which came to little or nothing.[2] The most important plan, putting in shape a volume of poems for Mrs. M. St. Leon Loud, discussed by Poe in the summer of 1849, he did not reach Philadelphia to begin.

We do have one manuscript poem, revised for Mrs. Lewis; and three poems of friends, where Poe's suggestions about a few lines were accepted. These are discussed in the paragraphs that follow.

A REVISION FOR ALEXANDER T. CRANE, 1845

Alexander Taylor Crane, an office boy for the *Broadway Journal*, greatly admired Poe, who was a very kind employer. Crane's reminiscences are given in a letter to the *New York Tribune* of January 30, 1880, an article in the *Book-Lover*, November–December 1901, and a feature interview in the *Omaha Sunday World-Herald*, August 6, 1911 — this last when Crane, then a farmer from Little Sioux, Iowa, was eighty-two years old and visiting a friend in Omaha. I have a photostat of the interview from the Nebraska State Historical Society at Lincoln. Said Crane: "Poe's writings and poetry inspired me. I wanted to be able to write as he did. Even then, as a boy of 14, I used to try to write poetry. I still remember one little poem, a temperance poem, that I wrote at that time. I showed it to Poe, and he . . . only made a little change in correcting it . . . in the last line . . . necessary for meter." Crane said that at Poe's suggestion he took the poem to a Sunday School paper, *The Youth's Cabinet*, edited in New York by Myron Finch, who accepted it.

Mr. Robert H. Haynes of Harvard College Library has located the piece in the issue of Thursday, May 1, 1845 (8:67). It appears in a section headed "Temperance" and is described as "Written for the Youth's Cabinet."

Crane's version of the poem from memory in 1911 differed somewhat

---

[1] At least once he accepted suggestions for one of his own poems. Four lines of the first version of "The Bells" were written by Mrs. Marie Louise Shew.

[2] In a letter of about March 1845, Anna Cora Mowatt asked Poe to make suggestions for her comedy *Fashion*, but if she used any, we cannot identify them. A letter of Poe to Mrs. Sarah Josepha Hale on January 16, 1846, discusses possible help on a projected reprint of her play, *Ormond Grosvenor*, but nothing more is known about it. Poe's remark in an article on Henry B. Hirst, first printed posthumously in *Works* (1850), III, 212, that "he adopted my advice so implicitly, that his poems, upon the whole, are little more than our conversations done into verse" is obviously jocular, and points to nothing specific.

from the original publication, and his description of Poe's revision is confusing. However, since the last line in the *Cabinet* is metrically correct, I feel sure Poe revised it *from* (not *to*) "'Tis then the cold shower gives a proof of God's care." The printed original reads:

WATER
By Alex T. Crane, S.S. No. 26

Cold water so bright, cold water so free,
Of all other liquids, cold water for me;
It is heard in the torrent with thundering roar,
In low murmuring music, it springs at your door.

In the broad fields of ocean, it is seen in its might,
When the clouds lower above it with darkness of night;
When the tempest sweeps o'er it, in fury it raves,
Converting its depths to an ocean of graves.

In the day when oppressed by the summer sun's heat, —
When the pulse throbs within us with languishing beat;
When all nature seems drooping away in despair,
'Tis then the cool showers give proof of God's care.

REVISION FOR HARRIET WINSLOW, 1848

The serious parody "To the Author of 'The Raven,'" by Miss Harriet Winslow, is known in two forms, a manuscript in Poe's hand and a slightly revised and improved form in *Graham's Magazine* for April 1848. The manuscript was among the Poe documents sold by the younger Griswold through Bangs & Co., on April 11, 1896, and was listed and printed in the sale catalogue as a new, original composition of Poe. It is headed there:

TO THE AUTHOR OF THE RAVEN
By Miss Harriet Winslow

Author of "To the Unsatisfied" —
"Why thus longing, thus forever sighing —
"For the far-off unattained and dim?"

Its theme was that the raven was friendly.

Harriet Winslow was a real person, as Victor H. Paltsits pointed out to Miss Phillips (*Edgar Allan Poe*, II, 1004). She was born in Portland, Maine, on June 30, 1819; and her poem "Why thus longing" was printed by Longfellow in the *Waif* (1844). An expanded version of this poem, headed "To the Unsatisfied," appeared in Duyckinck's *Cyclopedia of American Literature* (1856), II, 689. Miss Winslow was married to Charles Liszt of Philadelphia in June 1848 and later resided in Boston. See also R. W. Griswold's *Female Poets of America* (1849), p. 354.

Poe apparently saw and copied out the poem she had addressed to him before it appeared in *Graham's*. The printed version has two emendations which I ascribe to Poe. Line 11 is changed from the grammatically faulty, "Knows he not the littlenesses that poor human nature presses" to "Knows he not the littlenesses of our natures — its distresses? In lines 24–25, "By the memories of Lenore,/Oh, renounce him nevermore" is improved by the substitution of "thy memories."

SUGGESTION FOR SARAH HELEN WHITMAN, 1848

In 1848 Mrs. Whitman sent Poe her poem "Arcturus," upon which, in a letter of November 24, he commented:

> The first note leave out: . . . 61 Cygni has been proved *nearer* than Arcturus and Alpha Lyrae is presumably so. Bessel, also, has shown six other stars to be *nearer* than the brighter ones of this hemisphere . . . There is an obvious tautology in "pale candescent." To be *candescent* is to become *white* with heat. Why not read . . . "To blend with thine its incandescent fire."

Mrs. Whitman did not use Poe's line in a printing of an obviously revised version (it mentions Poe's death) in *Graham's* for June 1850, nor in the much cut-down and divided "Arcturus Written in April" and "Arcturus Written in October" in her volume *Hours of Life* (1853) at pages 77–81. But she used Poe's line in her own revised copy of that book (now at Brown University), and it appears in the October piece in her posthumous *Poems* (1879) at page 86. Special thanks are due to Miss Marion E. Brown of Brown University Library for this note.

COLLABORATION WITH MRS. LEWIS, 1848 OR 1849

There is reason to believe that in 1848 and 1849 Poe polished many of the verses of his patroness, Mrs. Sarah Anna Lewis. Only one specimen of these revisions survives, "The Prisoner of Perotè." The manuscript is in her hand, with suggested changes and an unsigned note penciled by Poe. This fell into the hands of J. H. Ingram, who published it imperfectly in the *Albany Review* for July 1907; J. H. Whitty reprinted from this publication in *Complete Poems*, second edition (1917), pp. 210–211. The manuscript is now in the Ingram Collection at the University of Virginia, and from it I print the poem as Poe wished it to read; the original forms of the lines he changed appear at the foot of the page. Poe suggested all the occasional indented short lines.

The authoress published "The Prisoner" herself in *Poems by Estelle Anna Lewis* (1857), pp. 218–221. In that version she adopted most of Poe's changes, but corrected lines 7, 56, 59, and 69 in her own fashion, and did not change line 70.

THE PRISONER OF PEROTÈ

The only person, that shared the captivity of Santa Anna, in the cold and gloomy Prison of Perotè, was his young and beautiful Wife, who by a thousand little acts of kindness and affection, Soothed his Sorrows, and rendered less irksome the horrors of his prison house.

The troops of Parasites, who had fattened upon his bounty, and been loud in their "Vivas" to him in the Noon and tide of his Power, forgot their Benefactor in the Night of his Adversity, and cried "Death to the Tyrant!" but the affectionate wife clung closer to his bosom, the more the darkness gathered around him, and by her presence, and her smiles lit up the gloom of his dreary abode.

Translated from a Spanish Paper.

In the Prison of Perotè
Silently the warrior sate
With his eye bent sadly downward
Like one stricken sore by Fate;
5   Broken visions of his Glory
Quick before his spirit passed
Like clouds across the summer Heaven
    Hurtled by the Blast.
The sullen booming of the cannon,
10   And the clash of the blade and spear —
"Death — death unto the Tyrant!"
Still were ringing in his ear.
Much he sorrowed for the people,
For whose weal he fain would die —
15   On the Tablets of The Future,
    Sadly fell his eye:
There he saw his weeping country
Close beleaguerd by the foe,
Saw her chained and faint and bleeding.
20   Heard her shrieks of wo;
From the eastward and the westward
He beheld the Pilgrims come
To muse upon her wild ruins,
    As now they flock to Rome.
25   Then in thought afar he wandered
Unto Andalusia's shore,
To the cities of Abdallah,
And the valiant Compeador;
To the dark land of the Paynim,
30   Mecca's consecrated Shrine,
To Palmyra of the desert, —
    And to Palestine:

---

3 His eye bent sadly downward
6 Before his spirit passed./*Poe first altered* "Before" *to* "O'er."
7 Like clouds across the Heaven.
8 Driven onward by the Blast
9 The booming of the Cannon
13 **Sadly bent his mental eye**

19 He saw her chained and bleeding
20 He heard her shrieks of wo;
21 From the east and from the westward
23 To ponder o'er her Ruins,
32 And to the fallen Palestine:

COLLABORATIONS

Well he weighed the fate of Nations,
Well their glory and their Shame,
35   Well the fleetness of all Power,
Well the emptiness of Fame;
Well the wasting wrecks of Empires
Choking time's impatient stream,
Till Beauty with her gentle whispers
40   Woke him from his dream —
"Arouse thee, gallant soldier!"
In a heavenly voice she cried,
"Though forsaken by all others,
I am hovering by thy side;
45   Though thine own heroic Valor,
Turned against thy breast the dart,
As the feather of the Eagle
Guides the arrow to his heart;
Though the Tempest wildly rages,
50   Though the sky is dread and dark,
Steadfast keep thine eye on Heaven,
         And God will guide thy Bark —
Sorrow not! attendant angels
Thee to fate will ne'er resign,
55   Soon the storm will all pass over
         And the sun will shine —
Sorrow not! the proud and lofty
Sun and Sky I've left for thee.
The very dungeon of thy presence
60   Is a throne to me
Every gleam of thy Affection,
Every glance of thy dark eyes,
Deep into my aching bosom
         Pour a Paradise
65   And forever, as the flower,
Far away from Pleasure's sight
Close beside some stately Ruin
         Sheds its holy light:
As the faithful Woodbine twines
70   Still around the mouldering tree,

34–37 "Well" *was added by Poe in each
line.*
38 That choke Time's rapid stream
39–40 Till Beauty's gentle whispers
      Awoke him from his dream. —
45–48 *Poe wrote beside this,* "Very
fine."
50 The sky is dread and dark
51 Keep thine eye steadfast on Heaven
52 God will guide thy helmless Bark

55 The storm will all pass over
56 The Sun again will shine —
59 The dungeon in thy presence
60 Is a Palace unto me
63 Into my aching bosom
64 Pours the Peace of Paradise;
67 Beside some stately Ruin,
68 Sheds its meek and holy light;
69 As the faithful Woodbine twineth
70 Still around the fallen tree,

APPENDIX III

So, to cheer thy desolation,
Will I cling to thee.

NOTES

Title: Antonio López de Santa Anna (1795–1876), the adventurer, may seem an odd hero for a romantic poem. But he was personally courageous, and patriotic enough to come back from exile to command his own country's army in the Mexican War.

Santa Anna was twice married. Soon after the death of his first wife he married a very young girl, Maria Dolores Tosta, who wanted a wedding in the cathedral in Mexico City. El Presidente was detained by affairs at home, but the ceremony was performed by proxy on October 3, 1844, as the lady desired. The young wife did take care of him at Perotè, where he was a prisoner of state, from January 13 to June 3, 1845. The marriage continued to be a fairly happy one until Santa Anna died. See W. H. Callcott, *Santa Anna* (University of Oklahoma Press, 1936), pp. 203ff.

26 To this line Mrs. Lewis added a footnote: "The name of Andalusia was applied by the Arabs not only to the Province so called, but to the whole Peninsula." This she took verbatim from a note to the third canto of "The Abencerrage" in *Tales and Historic Scenes* by Mrs. Hemans. See her *Poems* (Boston, 1828, I, 114).

27–28 Abdallah (whose name means "Servant of God"), King of Granada, was defeated by the great Spanish hero, Rodrigo (or Ruy) Díaz de Bivar, called "El Cid Campeador" (The Lord Warrior), who flourished in the eleventh century.

69 In her *Poetry of Flowers*, Mrs. Caroline M. Kirkland says the woodbine means fraternal love. Mrs. Lewis later changed it to ivy.

---

71 To cheer its desolation,   72 So I'll ever cling to thee.

APOCRYPHA

I

The following poems have been ascribed to Poe plausibly but with insufficient evidence to warrant their inclusion in the canon. There is reason enough behind the ascriptions, however, to justify their presentation in an appendix. Further evidence may yet appear.

TO IRENË

This poem presents many problems, some of which are not completely soluble at present. John H. Hewitt, said that in Richmond he "found two manuscripts of Poe's, given me by ladies of that city." Hewitt said he sent them to Neilson Poe who said he did not receive them. Nothing is known of the second poem, but Hewitt, who was vague about dates, printed the poem "To Irenë" in the *Staunton Spectator*, March 23, 1869, with a note:

> Messrs Editors: The following lines, written by Edgar A. Poe, were copied from the fly-leaf of a music book, belonging to a lady of Richmond. I have every reason to believe that they are genuine, as they were in his hand-writing and over the initials of E.A.P. Of their merit I have nothing to say. CHIPS

The signature is one acknowledged by Hewitt, who preserved a clipping among his papers, now at Emory University in Atlanta, Georgia. See *Recollections of Poe* by John Hill Hewitt, edited by Richard Barksdale Harwell (Atlanta, 1949), especially pp. 20 and 29. The ascription cannot be lightly dismissed, but cannot be accepted without reservations. Hewitt was given to the uncritical use of legendary material, how well he knew the handwriting of Poe may be questioned, and the manuscript from which he copied the verses has never turned up, although Hewitt implies it had survived the Civil War. I do not think Hewitt himself would have perpetrated a hoax, but by 1869 hoaxers were busy with Poe. The echo in the second stanza of Moore's constantly quoted lines in *Lalla Rookh*, "I never loved a tree or flower . . . I never nursed a dear gazelle," means little. The verses, if genuine, must have been written about 1836. The text given here is from the file of the *Staunton Spectator* at the University of Virginia. I add a diaeresis in the title because of the difference in pronunciation in our day from Poe's.

TO IRENË

Thou wert alone — thy harp was mute,
And grief was written on thy face;

A sigh, it's tell-tale attribute,
  Stole softly from its native place.
5 Why fade the roses from thy brow?
  Art thou, too, wedded unto woe?
It is too true — thou grievest now,
  And scalding tears profusely flow.

'Tis so with me: my journey past
10   Has been o'er thorns of toil and grief;
My hours of youth were overcast,
  Tears blotted Fate's mysterious leaf.
I never lov'd or garner'd up
  A little bliss, but what some power
15 Would dash away the sweeten'd cup,
  Or blight and crush the cherish'd flower.

My heart's a charnel house, where sleep
  The bones of hopes, once fondly cherish'd,
What have I now to do, but weep
20   And groan o'er pleasures long since perish'd?
What — but to laugh when thou dost sigh?
  What — but to gloat o'er one so fair,
Whose glad star once shone proudly high,
  Only to set in dark despair?

25 Weep on, weep on — thy hot tears flow
  Like blood-drops oozing from the heart;
We've laugh'd together — now of woe
  Thou, surely, must receive thy part.
Together we will riot in
30   The carnival of sighs and tears,
Hugging the hooded form of Sin
  That haunts the tomb of perish'd years.

[1836?]

THE TRUMPET REVEILLEE

This piece, hitherto never reprinted, is ascribed to Poe with great reservation. I first heard of it from J. H. Whitty, who told me that F. W. Thomas said Poe wrote a poem for the second number of the *Military Magazine*. If Poe did contribute a poem to the periodical, "The Trumpet Reveillee," though signed "S." and in the seventh number (September 1839), must be the piece.

In its final form the magazine was issued in two bound volumes described thus by the catalogue at the Historical Society of Pennsylvania:

The Military Magazine: and record of the volunteers of the city and county of Philadelphia. Comprising authentic data of their Institution, Organization, and matters generally pertaining thereto, tending to foster the spirit of Patriotism so essential to the preservation of our social institutions, and to merit for Citizen Soldiery the approbation and applause of their fellow citizens. In 2 vols. royal quarto, 24 No.'s each. Embellished with 2 views to each number. Edited by William M. Huddy. Philadelphia. Published by William M. Huddy, No. 84 Noble Street.

Poe, in noticing two numbers favorably in *Burton's* (December 1839 and February 1840), in one issue calls it the *United States' Military Magazine* and in the other *The U.S. Military Magazine*. He names as publishers Huddy and Duval. The latter was Peter S. Duval, who made the plates for "Poe's" *Conchologist's First Book* in 1839. Woodberry says that in the *United States Military Magazine*, "at one time [Poe] had an article of considerable length." [1] I have, however, found nothing in the prose of the magazine to be identified stylistically as Poe's.

"The Trumpet Reveillee" is headed "For the U.S. Military Magazine" and occupies the lower half of page 51. It was perhaps written "to fill." Poe was obliging to friends in matters of this kind, as we know. Copies of the publication are very rare; the only complete files I have located are in the Historical Society of Pennsylvania and the Library at West Point; the latter is used here.

This information obviously is unsatisfactory, but the poem is melodious and correct enough to be authentic, and the chances of complete authentication some day seem to me to warrant inclusion of a text here, with a caveat.

THE TRUMPET REVEILLEE

Hark! Hark! Hark! to the trumpet's merry call,
    Loud through the dales and the ringing woods resounding;
Hark! how it floats amid the cedars tall,
    From the rough mountain's rocky breast rebounding.

5   Up! Up! Up! for the ruddy day is there,
    There, where the East with opal hues is glowing;
Up! for the steeds have snuff'd the morning air,
    Down from the hills in balmy freshness blowing.

Wake! Wake! Wake! for the booming morning gun,
10   Pours to the dawn a loud, exultant greeting;
Wake! the last star, its high guard-duty done,
    From the red sky is sullenly retreating.

March! March! March! ere the risen orb shall beam,
    Fierce on our path, its noontide fervor pouring!
15   March! till the flash of friendly steel shall gleam,
    Where the wild ocean's thousand waves are roaring.

                        S.

[1839]

[1] *Life* (1909), I, 265; in *Edgar Allan Poe* (1885), p. 143, he says "articles." His footnote in both cases cites — without directly quoting — "P. S. Duval to the author, August 4, 1884," and adds that the magazine was printed in Duval's shop.

APPENDIX IV

MONODY ON DOCTOR OLMSTED

The authenticity of this bitterly satirical epigram is not completely established and its date is largely a matter of conjecture. The manuscript was found about 1938 by workmen moving furniture from a downtown office in Baltimore, and it was acquired by Mr. Paul S. Clarkson, who felt so much doubt about it that he did not announce the discovery until 1942.

The manuscript consists of a single leaf, at the top of which is written "Edgar A. Poe," and at the bottom an extract from "Al Aaraaf," II, 100–109, both in a large hand. Between them, in a small, almost printlike hand, resembling one Poe sometimes used in the thirties, is the "Monody." In the extract from "Al Aaraaf," II, 102, "ideas" is put for "idea" (spoiling the rhyme), and in the words "toss" and "albatross" the penultimate letter is an old fashioned long *s* which is also used in "ass" in the first line of the "Monody." This usage is almost unparalleled in late manuscripts of Poe. Such freaks are not in the manner of forgers and hoaxers. It might be suggested that Poe was not sober when he produced the manuscript. His letter of March 11, 1843, facsimiled in W. F. Gill's *Life* (1878), facing p. 120, shows unusual handwriting, but includes no example of double *s*. No other manuscript surely written by Poe when he was inebriated is known.

The subject of the piece is undoubtedly Denison Olmsted (1791–1859), who was Professor of Mathematics and Natural Philosophy at Yale from 1825 to 1836, and who thereafter until his death held the chair of Natural Philosophy and Astronomy. He received his doctorate when the honorary degree of LL.D. was conferred upon him by New York University on July 2, 1845. Poe had been asked to read a poem in connection with the commencement of that year, and so must have taken some interest in it.[1]

It is not easy to explain why Poe should have disliked Professor Olmsted. Careful investigation reveals one possible reason for his contempt,[2] although the exact occasion that provoked the poem has not been found. Olmsted wrote on many subjects — including widely used textbooks — but he was particularly renowned for his publication (in the *American Journal of Science and Arts*, January–April 1834, January 1836) of papers on the Leonid shower (of meteors) in 1833, which had caused tremendous excitement, especially in Baltimore. The papers were referred to as a brilliant contribution to knowledge. But Olmsted declared that the meteors originated in "a body 2238 miles from the Earth." So minutely exact an estimate, in view of the obviously inexact data on which it was based, could come only from an extremely self-satisfied person, and Poe disliked pretentious scientists.[3]

[1] See *The New-York Daily Tribune*, July 1, 2, 3, 1845.

[2] This and the grim vigor of the piece induce me to accept the poem as Poe's, with only slight reservations. Observe the author's command of versification — the ninth line is a syllable short, but highly effective.

[3] Compare Poe's satirical use of Dionysius Lardner, LL.D., in "Three Sundays in a Week." Olmsted's papers were synopsized in Thomas Dick's *Atmosphere and Atmospherical Phenomena* (1848), of which I use the reprint (Cincinnati, 1855), p. 44. Dick, oddly enough, does not point out that Olmsted's estimate is too good to be true.

APOCRYPHA

The date I assign the poem is appropriate, for Poe was in Baltimore in about March and April of 1846, less than a year after Olmsted received his degree. He was there again (not always sober) in 1847 and 1848. However, since Olmsted as a prominent scientist was probably called "Doctor" long before he really was one, a far earlier date may be possible.

TEXTS

(A) Manuscript; (B) Baltimore *Sun*, August 18, 1942. The text used is *A*, from a photostat sent me by the owner.

MONODY ON DOCTOR OLMSTED – IF DEAD – DAMNED. (A)

If this prime ass is with his brother worms –
Forgive the license of the *clASSic* terms! –
I hope they'll make a "black-board" of his face
And make it minus all but its grimace,
That devilish simper which he frequent wore
When, with the glibness of a saint, he swore,
That, "His last work was plainer far than dirt" –
As tainting too, thou muddy-headed squirt!
Plain – dead level – flat – they are the same –
At him, ye worms! till appetite is lame.   [1846?]

VARIANTS

Title: if dead/*First written* dead and

8   As tainting/*First written* 'Tis famous *then changed to something illegible; third reading is that of text.*

NOTES

Title: Among the imaginary contributions to magazines listed in "The Literary Life of Thingum Bob," is "Monody in a Mud-puddle by Mr. Mumblethumb."

2   There is a triple pun here, on "classic," "class" (of students), and "ass."

7   The exact occasion of Olmsted's remark remains unknown and is difficult to search for, in view of the uncertainty of the date of the epigram. Some of his prefaces reveal his complacent satisfaction with the clarity of his exposition.

9   Compare *Politian*, X, 1–2: "that's flat/Extremely flat."

ADDENDUM

[LINES WRITTEN IN A CONTEST]

There is a strong tradition in Baltimore that Poe once engaged in a contest with John Lofland, the Milford Bard, to see which of them could write more verses in a given time — and that Poe was the loser. It comes to us in two very different forms, both told with probably imaginary details.

The earlier form encountered is in William Fearing Gill's *Life of Edgar Allan Poe* (1877), pp. 46–49, as "narrated by a Baltimore acquaintance of Poe." According to this story, Poe met in a bookstore (presumably that of Edward J. Coale) the very voluminous versifier, John Lofland, M.D.,[1] who took his sobriquet from his home in Milford, Delaware, where he was born in 1798. Lofland is said to have boasted to Poe that he could "write more stanzas in one hour than you can in a whole day." Poe accepted the challenge, and "the Bard . . . in *quantity* . . . tipped the scale." In this story both men were represented as authors of recent books. Lofland's *The Harp of Delaware* came out in 1828. A date soon after Poe's book of 1829 will fit the contest; no other is probable bibliographically.

The other version, clearly independent of Gill's, is in John Smithers' *Life of John Lofland* (1894), p. 108, and is largely quoted by Miss Phillips, *Edgar Allan Poe the Man* (1926), p. 457. Smithers has a number of poets meeting at the Seven Stars Tavern, and Poe as the challenger. It is less credible in details than Gill's story, but the survival of the tradition in these two romantically fictional versions seems to point to some basis in fact. Happily, nobody has claimed to recall any of the verses written in the contest.

II

The following is a descriptive catalogue of pieces in verse that have been ascribed to Edgar A. Poe for erroneous or insufficient reasons. They are numerous, and range from confessed hoaxes — and worse — to poems ascribed to him by reputable scholars. A few have some merit, many are harmlessly pedestrian, and others are trash. Some selectivity might seem desirable, but seems to me unwise. Anything omitted, no matter how trivial, would ere long be "discovered" and solemnly discussed. Hence I describe and comment on all the items known to me, in a chronological order.

Both external and internal evidence is considered dispassionately. What I know of the personalities of the attributors is taken into account.[1] We are often told that the merit of a poem is no criterion for judgment, but that is only a half truth. Poe could — and on occasion did — write undistinguished verses, but some faults were not his. He was an impeccable metrist; and, except for comic effect, did not write nonsense.[2]

[1] Lofland wrote an immense amount of prose and verse — a stanza of his is quoted among the sources of Poe's "Song," p. 67 above — under his sobriquet and as a ghost writer. He was for a time addicted to opium, and lived in a hospital at Baltimore, 1838–1846, to be cured. He was a kindly, harmless, and picturesque eccentric. When he died on January 22, 1849, he was literary editor of the weekly newspaper called *The Blue Hen's Chicken* in Wilmington, Delaware.

[1] Some were sanguine, and given to wishful thinking. Others were overcautious. Scholars who made firm or tentative ascriptions of poems to Poe, which are unacceptable in the present state of knowledge, include Ingram, Harrison, Woodberry, Killis Campbell, and myself.

[2] I use this word in the technical sense like critics of the eighteenth century. Poe's "echoes" do not "mutter."

REJECTED POEMS

The collection includes everything of which I have record. I describe poems "received from Poe's spirit" by mediums; at least one of them was later hoaxingly ascribed to Poe in this world. Paul G. Henderson, son of the editor who published James Whitcomb Riley's "Leonainie," kindly gave me a good deal of material collected by him for a study of that and the other hoaxes, and I include references to all. Regretfully, I mention everything first attributed to Poe in a pamphlet *Index* of 1941.[3] Every item ascribed to Poe by J. H. Whitty in print, or in correspondence known to me, is discussed here [4] — except, of course, his valid discoveries recorded among the accepted texts. Excluded from my list as not warranting discussion are twenty poems ruled out by Killis Campbell in a footnote on page 198 of his book *The Mind of Poe* (1933) — poems signed "P." found in old periodicals which, he thought, could not possibly have any connection with Poe.[5]

1. "Lines to Louisa" or "The Vital Stream," sixteen lines beginning "Flow softly — gently — vital stream" from a manuscript in Poe's hand, were assigned to him by J. H. Whitty in the New York *Sun*, November 21, 1915, and collected by Whitty in the second edition (1917) of *The Complete Poems of Edgar Allan Poe*, p. 151. Sylvia Townsend Warner in a comment on Dame Una Pope-Hennessy's *Edgar Allan Poe* in the *New Statesman*, November 17, 1934 (8:730, n.s.), pointed out that they are found in a novel by Thomas Skinner Surr, *George Barnwell*, published in 1798.

2–22. Twenty-one poems in a compilation by Elizabeth Chase, *Miscel-*

---

[3] The Pamphlet Distributing Company, New York, in 1941 issued *Index to American Literature*, part 2, "Edgar Allan Poe," with an introduction I wrote, being promised a sight of the proofs. The promise was not kept, and the work appeared, marred by many irresponsible attributions. Nothing it *first* ascribed to Poe can be accepted. This is not the first occasion on which I have repudiated that *Index*.

[4] Whitty sometimes ascribed pieces to Poe without revealing precisely where he found them. All but one of these, and that not firmly ascribed, have now been tracked down.

[5] Campbell's list is less detailed and accurate than might be expected. I have checked his material carefully, and the poems he had in mind must be the following: in *The Memorial* (1826), "A Voice is Heard," "Ye Come to Me," and "O! Sing to Me"; in the Philadelphia *Casket*, May 1827, "Morning in Spring"; in the Baltimore *Emerald*, June 21, 1828, "To Hope" (from the Danish), and June 28, 1828, "From Goethe's Faust"; in *The Token* for 1830, "The Wounded Bird" and "To —" ("When Love and Reason dwell"); in the Boston *American Monthly Magazine*, August 1830, "Ambition" ("There came"), and November 1830, "Changes"; in the *New England Magazine*, January 1832, "To Mary" and "The Employments of Death"; in the Providence *Literary Journal*, February 22, 1834, "Ambition" ("What is Ambition?"); in the *New England Magazine*, December 1834, a sonnet beginning "The hour — the place — the twilight"; in *The Casket*, November 1837, "Lines" "As I sat at eve"); in *Alexander's Weekly Messenger*, Philadelphia, December 13, 1837, "The Fairy Queen," and December 20, 1837, "Impromptu" (about a song of Miss C. H. Waterman); in the Philadelphia *Saturday Courier*, October 15, 1842, "Autumn Morning"; in the New York *New Mirror*, July 8, 1843, "Woman's Tactics" (a punning quatrain); and in the Philadelphia *Dollar Newspaper*, May 17, 1848, "To — (On Giving Her an Album)." There is nothing pertinent in *The Token* for 1829.

APPENDIX IV

laneous Selections (1821), pp. 204–222 and 129, are signed "Edgar." The
author is described as a "youth of eighteen" and a "very young gentleman
of Baltimore." He had a sister named Ellen. See Charles F. Heartman and
James R. Canny, *A Bibliography of the First Printings of the Writings of
Edgar Allan Poe* (1943), pp. 11–12, for the absurdity of an ascription to
Edgar Poe. The titles are: (2) "Absent Friends," (3) "Music," (4) "To a
Friend on his Departure for Europe," (5) "Ode to Contemplation," (6) "To
the Eagle," (7) "Martial Glory," (8) "To the Olive," (9) "To the Laurel,"
(10) "A Lily," (11) "To my Friend — —," (12) "A Dream," (13) "Lines on the
Death of Mr. John C. Clapham," (14) "Ode, for the Twelfth of September,"
(15) "To my Sister on her Birthday," (16) "To Sorrow," (17) "To a Female
Friend," (18) "A Smile," (19) "Female Virtue," (20) "Twilight," (21) "To
Despondency," and (22) "Monody on the Death of General Joseph Sterett."

23. "Lines by E. A. S.," presumably published about 1821, are mentioned
(without source) in Whitty's first edition of *The Complete Poems of Edgar
Allan Poe* (1911), p. 170, as "perhaps . . . Poesque." The quatrain quoted
begins "What clouds my brow, O, ask me not" and can be dismissed.

24. Thomas Hood's sonnet "Silence" has been mistaken for Poe's work.
It was originally published, signed "T.," in the *London Magazine* for Feb-
ruary 1823, and was copied in *Burton's* for September 1839 as a filler with
signature "P." It is quoted in full in the notes on Poe's own "Sonnet —
Silence" above.

25–27. "Isabel," thirty-one lines; "Mr. Po," twenty-five lines; and "Rich-
mond, or the Map of Virginia," forty-six lines, are found in the *Southern
and Western Songster* (1826), a compilation of J. Grigg. See Heartman and
Canny, pp. 21–22, on absurd ascriptions to Poe by an auctioneer.

28. "To Lucy," fifty-six lines beginning "The silver tones of woman's
tongue," in "Noctes Ambrosianae," no. xxviii, by Christopher North (*Black-
wood's*, October 1826, 20:636) was tentatively ascribed to Poe by Diana Pitt-
man in the revived *Southern Literary Messenger*, April 1942, for unreasonable
reasons.

29. "Enigma" appeared in the Philadelphia *Saturday Evening Post*,
March 10, 1827, and was reprinted in *The Casket* for May of that year and
by Killis Campbell in *The Mind of Poe*, p. 200. It was given in a new ver-
sion in "Omniana" in *Burton's Gentleman's Magazine*, May 1840. Whitty re-
printed the second version in his *Complete Poems* (1911), p. 146, because he
thought Poe had composed "Omniana," but that now seems most improbable.
The amusing poems (on palindromes) can be removed from the canon.

30. "In a Pocket-Book," signed W.H.P., in the Baltimore *North American*,
August 11, 1827, is certainly by Edgar Poe's elder brother Henry (see Appen-
dix VI). Frances Winwar in *The Haunted Palace* (1959), p. 63, insisted on
thinking it Edgar's work.

31. "The Sabbath Morning," thirty lines beginning "How calm comes

in the holy day!" and signed "P.," is in the Baltimore *North American*, August 11, 1827. It is wholly unlike the work of Edgar Poe or his brother.

32. "A Poor Scholar," thirty-six lines beginning "I saw him starting in his new career" and signed "E.P.," is in *The Forget Me Not*, a Philadelphia annual for 1828. Neither its finder, the Reverend Leonard Twynham, nor I can think this undistinguished piece is Poe's.

33. "The Three Meetings — To Eva," twenty lines signed "Edgar" and dated "Cambridge, Feb. 19, 1828," in *The Yankee* (published at Portland, Maine), February 27, 1828, was ascribed — in the face of the fact that Poe was in the South at the time of its publication — to Poe by Irving T. Richards in *Modern Language Notes*, March 1927.

34, 35. Two poems that appeared in 1829 in John Neal's monthly magazine, *The Yankee; and Boston Literary Gazette*, were ascribed to Poe by George Birdley in the Chicago *Current Opinion*, June 14 (reprinted in the *Richmond Dispatch* of June 15), 1884; J. H. Ingram refuted this ascription in a letter printed in the same paper for July 3. See the Ingram List — J. C. Miller, *John Henry Ingram's Poe Collection at the University of Virginia* (1960) — numbers 835, 836. The pieces are (34) "The Skeleton-Hand," sixty lines beginning "Lo! one is on the mountain side," in *The Yankee* for August 1829; and (35) "The Magician," forty-two lines beginning "Thou dark sea-stirring storm," in the magazine for December. Both are crude and incoherent, but they turn up like bad pennies. They may be seen in James A. Harrison's *Complete Works of Edgar Allan Poe* (1902), VII, 252–256.

36. "First of May," forty-two lines beginning "There is music on the breeze," is in the *Atlantic Souvenir for MDCCCXXX* and was assigned to Poe by one Charles Bromback in 1917 since Poe had mentioned the possibility of his contributing to the annual in a letter of July 28, 1829. The poem ends:

> Then how can I be gay
> On this merry first of May?
> Ah no! I am sad, I am sad.

It is to its unknown author's credit that no signature was affixed to this trash.

37. "Life," twenty lines beginning "Look back on life! years, how they pass," assigned to "Poe" and dated October 22, 1829, in the album of Miss Mary A. Hand of Baltimore, were copied for Ingram by William Hand Browne. See the Ingram List, no. 2. I assign the piece to William Henry Poe.

38. *The Musiad or Ninead, by Diabolus, edited by ME* (1830), was printed in Baltimore. It has 101 lines, some *referring* to Poe. I think attempts to ascribe the work to Edgar Poe are mere wishful thinking. See the Ingram List, numbers 292 and 293, and an extract in the Annals, below.

39–41. Three pieces signed "A.P." appeared in the New York *Euterpiad* in 1831. They are (39) "To Music," thirty lines in the issue of January 1;

(40) "To —" (beginning "Lady! forgive the uncourteous strain"), forty lines in that of February 15; and (41) "Sonnet[s] to Keats," twenty-five lines in that of April 1. The editor of that period, George W. Bleecker, said A.P. was a young man of twenty-seven. See Heartman and Canny, p. 182. My former ascription to Albert Pike is incorrect.

42. Some verses described as having been addressed by Poe to Miss Kate Bleakly are mentioned by Mary E. Phillips in *Edgar Allan Poe the Man* (1926), I, 421–423. The material strikes me as of doubtful reliability; but in any case, the verses described are said to have been burned.

43. "The Magic of Night," twenty-four lines in the Philadelphia *Saturday Courier*, January 28, 1832, I discussed in correspondence with J. H. Whitty long ago. I am now satisfied it is not Poe's.

44. "Woman's Heart," twenty-four lines beginning "First take a feather," is in the *Baltimore Times* of June 10 (misprint for 16), 1832. See Phillips, I, 435, where the poem is reprinted as perhaps the lost poem "To Mary." It seems to me not reproachful enough to be the poem described by Mary Starr Jenning, and it seems unnecessary to reprint it here from the unique file in the Enoch Pratt Free Library.

45. In the Bookfellows' *Step Ladder* (Chicago), October 1927 (13:226), J. H. Whitty told of finding some lines written in an old book as by Poe. He suggested that they were the lost poem "To Mary" and quoted the first four lines, beginning "What though the name be old and oft repeated." These are from "Mary" by Henry Theodore Tuckerman, to be seen in R. W. Griswold's *Poets and Poetry of America* (1842), p. 415.

46. "Extract from an Unfinished Poem," twenty-six lines beginning "There is a form before me now," is in the *Southern Literary Messenger*, March 1835. The piece was tentatively ascribed to Poe by Killis Campbell in *Modern Language Notes*, May 1917, and in his *Mind of Poe*, p. 206. I cannot accept it.

47. "Spring," twenty lines beginning "To see thy tiny songsters" and signed "A Prisoner," in the *Southern Literary Messenger* of May 1835, is tentatively ascribed to Poe by Heartman and Canny, p. 251. I cannot accept this ascription.

48. "To Sarah," twenty-four lines beginning "When melancholy and alone," signed "Sylvio" in the *Southern Literary Messenger*, August 1835, was collected by J. H. Whitty in *Complete Poems* (1911), p. 142. He admitted to me that a memorandum he found in a copy of the magazine that was once in Poe's hands did *not* specifically acknowledge authorship. The piece I firmly reject from the canon.

49. "Ballad," thirty-six lines in Scottish dialect, in the *Southern Literary Messenger* of August 1835 (1:705–706), is quoted in connection with Poe's "Bridal Ballad," above. Woodberry's suggestion in his *Life* (1909), II, 415, that Poe composed the dialect piece is wholly unacceptable.

50. "Hymn, in Honor of Harmodius and Aristogiton," is in an article entitled "Greek Song," signed "P.," in the *Southern Literary Messenger* of December 1835 (2:38). The verses were collected by J. H. Ingram in his *Complete Poetical Works . . . of . . . Poe* (1888), p. 106. They were composed by Lucian Minor. See Poe's letter of October 31, 1835; an article signed "M." in the *Southern Literary Messenger*, March 1848 (14:184–185); and Campbell's *Mind of Poe*, p. 194.

51. "The Great Man," twenty lines beginning "The great man lives," J. H. Whitty claimed to have found in an unsigned manuscript "in Poe's hand," and published in *Complete Poems* (1911), p. 143. Whitty's failure to show me the manuscript makes me think he came to doubt it, and the phrasing of the last lines, "Like the needle to the mariner amidst the tempest wrath / Let it fire your hopes," is too technically nonsensical for me to accept the piece as composed by Poe.

52. "To Ianthe" is discussed in Phillips, I, 616, as a poem addressed to one Miss Anne Savidge about 1838. A fragment of the manuscript, reading "never to forget . . . losing thee . . . Yet will love thee always," is said to have been worn by the lady in a locket and to have been buried with her. One may gravely doubt it.

53. "The First Day of May," thirty-six lines beginning "From the isles of the south," signed "E.P." and dated "Camden, S.C.," is in the *Southern Literary Messenger* of May 1840 (6:385). This was ascribed to Poe in the *Index to American Literature* in 1941.

54. "Lines to My Mother," beginning "By Thrasymené's lake," signed "P.E." and dated "Passignano, Italy, 1839," was printed in the *Knickerbocker Magazine* for July 1840, and was ascribed to Poe by the irresponsible compilers of the *Index* in 1941. The author was Dr. Pliny Earle and the verses may be seen in his *Marathon and Other Poems* (Philadelphia, 1841), pp. 86–87.

55. "Night," 104 lines beginning " 'Tis night," is signed "E.P." in the *Yale Literary Magazine* for February 1842. The only Yale student at that time having those initials was Eliphalet Parker, in the Divinity School.

56. "The Bridge of Sighs," a couplet reading, "Could it but read the nonsense on its stones, / The Bridge of Sighs would be a bridge of groans!" in *Blackwood's*, June 1842 (51:738), is in "Sketches of Italy," obviously by a Briton. The ascription by Miss Phillips, I, 751, is absurd.

57. "Rupert and Madelon," beginning "*Mad*. Why hast thou led me here" is from "Woman's Trust" by Frances Sargent Osgood, first published in her volume *A Wreath of Wild Flowers from New England* (London, 1842). Poe copied it out for a review of her work in the *Southern Literary Messenger* of August 1849 (15:510). The extract was facsimiled by John P. Kennedy in *Autograph Leaves of Our Country's Authors* (1864) as if composed by Poe.

58. "An Angel Face," eight lines from Mrs. Osgood's "Woman's Trust," beginning "An Angel Face; its sunny wealth of hair," was written as a "sentiment" and signed "Edgar A. Poe" in the album of one Sarah E. Turner, who died in 1855. It has, I believe, been thought Poe's composition on occasion. (The album is described in a letter to me from Richard Hart of the Enoch Pratt Free Library, Baltimore.)

59, 60. Two short poems are written in what is said to be Poe's hand in a copy of J. L. Comstock's *Conversations on Chemistry* (8th American ed., 1822) which once belonged to Henry Morton Partridge (1820–1893), who gave up a classical academy in Baltimore in 1842. The first item, (59) a dozen lines beginning "Is there a tear that scalds the cheek?" was published in the auction catalogue of the Parke-Bernet Galleries, January 16, 1941. Although signed "E.A.P.," the poem is in quotation marks. The second piece, (60) eight lines beginning "How mildly the sun of the even," is also in quotation marks, not signed. I now believe that neither item was composed by Poe. Mr. Freeman F. Hepburn and I gave the Comstock book to Princeton University Library in 1961.

61, 62. *English Notes for General Circulation* by "Quarles Quickens," a pamphlet published in Boston on December 6, 1842, was ascribed to Poe by Joseph Jackson in "Dickens in America Fifty Years Ago" (*World's Work*, January 1912, pp. 292–293). The pamphlet was reprinted in 1920. W. N. C. Carlton demolished the ascription in the *Americana Collector* for February 1926. See Heartman and Canny, p. 65. The pamphlet contains two "poems," each of twenty-four lines — (61) "A Poetical Epistle to Mr. Pickwick" and (62) "A Bachelor's Address to his Cane," which must be mentioned as erroneously ascribed to Poe.

63. "The Times" by "The Author of English Notes" is in the Boston *Daily Mail* of January 11, 1843, and was reprinted by W. N. C. Carlton in the *Americana Collector*, February 1926. It has more than 130 lines. Two extracts are enough: "From lip to lip, the ringing echo passed / Mounts on the breeze and mutters on the blast," and "Man wraps himself in narrowness of soul." Nevertheless, Phillips, I, 738f., discussed this stuff seriously as by Poe, and it must be mentioned here.

64. "The Maniac Lover," twenty-four lines, unsigned, is in *Snowden's Ladies' Companion* for March 1843. I discussed this piece in correspondence with J. H. Whitty, but now see no reason to connect it with Poe.

65. *A New Year's Address of the Carriers of the Columbia Spy* is a broadside, issued about January 1, 1844, that accompanied the file of the paper used by Jacob E. Spannuth and myself for our edition of Poe's *Doings of Gotham* (1929). We reprinted the lines with a query if they could be by Poe. I feel sure now that they are not.

66. "The Forsaken" by Mrs. Sarah Anna Lewis was printed in her *Records of the Heart* (1844) before she met Poe. He admired the poem excessively, and often quoted it in reviews. A detached fragment of a manuscript in his

handwriting was taken for his composition when auctioned by Bangs & Co., April 13, 1903, lot 346.

67. "The Departed," forty lines beginning "Where the river ever floweth," in the *Broadway Journal* of July 12, 1845, is signed with a broken printer's ornament. Dr. Thomas Holley Chivers attributed it to Poe in his manuscript "Life of Poe" — see the edition of Richard Beale Davis (1952), p. 74. Since Chivers admits that Poe disclaimed writing the poem, and it includes the bathetic line "Spirit, cooped in mortal bower," I do not think an ascription to him is justified. From the story as told I think Poe suspected "The Departed" was by Chivers. See also Killis Campbell, *Mind of Poe*, p. 201.

68. "Flora," twenty lines beginning "The snow lay thick upon the ground" and signed "P.," in *Graham's Magazine* for June 1845, I ascribe to Charles J. Peterson, since the single initial of his surname is usually an editor's prerogative. The conclusion, "But what to me is Spring or Love / Since Flora's gone to Heaven above?" is too flat for Poe. Mention must be made of "Flora" because two poems concerning Mrs. Osgood, signed "P." later in 1845 in *Graham's*, are accepted in this edition — see "The Divine Right of Kings" and "Stanzas to F.S.O."

69. In the "Editorial Miscellany" of the *Broadway Journal* for August 30, 1845, Poe said, "A very pretty poem, which (unfortunately for us) *we* did not write, appears in Wednesday's Tribune with the initials E.A.P. appended." It begins, "O, where shall our waking be?" and is assigned, with a query, to E. A. Stansbury by Killis Campbell in his *Mind of Poe*, p. 192.

70–73. Four poems signed "A. M. Ide" were published in the *Broadway Journal* in 1845. John H. Ingram thought "A. M. Ide" might be a pen name of Poe, and reprinted three of these four poems as possibly Poe's in *The Complete Poetical Works . . . of Edgar Allan Poe* (1888) — but Abijah M. Ide was a young New Englander who corresponded with Poe and with J. R. Lowell and wrote for the *Columbian Magazine* in 1844 and 1845. In 1865 he was an editor of the *Gazette*, in Taunton, Massachusetts. His poems in the *Broadway Journal* are: (70) "The Village Street" (September 13, 1845), (71) "The Forest Reverie" (September 27), (72) "To Isadore" (October 25), and (73) "Annette" (December 6).

74. "The Mammoth Squash" is an amusing burlesque in an article (also containing parodies on Whittier and others) in the *Aristidean* for October 1845. In the *Broadway Journal* of November 29, 1845, Poe said the article was "no doubt by the editor" — Thomas Dunn English. "The Mammoth Squash" has several times been reprinted, most conveniently by Harrison in *Complete Works* (1902), VII, 236.

75. Two lines without title reading, "I thought Kit North a bore — in 1824 —/I find the thought alive — in 1845," are in the *Broadway Journal* of January 3, 1846. They have been taken for Poe's by several writers (including myself), but Thomas Dunn English mentions writing them in his unpublished autobiography, as Professor William Graveley informs me. Christopher North was the pen name of John Wilson, editor of *Blackwood's*.

APPENDIX IV

76. An epigram, "P—, the Versifier, Reviewing his own Poetry," signed "W." in *Graham's Magazine* for December 1846, was used by Poe in his *jeu d'esprit* "A Reviewer Reviewed" (1849). Miss Phillips, II, 967, suggested that Poe wrote it himself — something I find no reason to believe.

77. "The Idiot Boy," 138 lines signed "E.P." in *Graham's Magazine* for June 1847, is probably by Emily Percival.

78. A valentine beginning "Like all true souls of noble birth," sent by Mary Gove Nichols to Marie Louise Shew probably in 1847 was copied out by Poe. He did not compose it. See the Ingram List, no. 39 and no. 213.

79. Poe told Mrs. Shew he wrote a poem called "Humanity" which was later credited to George Sand. See the Ingram List, no. 215. This was obviously mere banter which Mrs. Shew swallowed as fact.

80. *The Poets and Poetry of America* by Lavante, published as a pamphlet by W. S. Young (Philadelphia, 1847), was republished as Poe's by "Geoffrey Quarles" (Oliver Leigh) in 1887. Leigh supposed it Poe's "lost" projected work on the "American Parnassus." We now know the little done on the book Poe planned was in prose. Of the Philadelphia satire (479 heroic couplets) Harrison gives samples in *Complete Works*, VII, 246ff. I think ascription of this stuff to Lambert A. Wilmer as improbable as that to Poe.

81. "Gratitude," twenty lines beginning "As turns the eye," was signed "E.A.P." in a tiny octavo periodical called *The Symposia*, published in Providence, Rhode Island. Whitty reprinted the verses in *Complete Poems* (1911), p. 144. Campbell, in *The Mind of Poe*, p. 201, says *The Symposia* contained two poems signed "E.A.B."; he thought the signature to "Gratitude" might be a misprint for the initials of E. A. Brackett. Whitty dates the leaflet January 27, 1848: Campbell, "early in 1845." A copy was auctioned at Boston in 1896, but I cannot locate it. "Gratitude" certainly can be rejected from the canon of Poe's writings.

82. "To the Author of the Raven" by Harriet Winslow, in *Graham's Magazine* for April 1848, seems to have been polished by Poe. See Collaborations above, p. 492. A manuscript copy in his hand sold by Bangs in New York on April 11, 1896, was erroneously described as Poe's own composition.

83–85. Three poems signed "Henry Adams" appeared in the *Columbian Magazine*, June, July, and October 1848. They are: (83) "To Kate Karol" (forty-six lines); (84) "A Dream" (forty-eight lines), and (85) "Lunar Aspirations" (thirty lines). Whitty wished to ascribe them to Poe. His discussion in the *Step Ladder*, October 1927, is baffling, but with the clues he provided I was able to find the poems. The first begins "Will you, darling, dainty Kate/In your kindness please to state," and is addressed to Mrs. Frances S. Osgood, who had many admirers capable of such stuff. I cannot accept an ascription to Poe on the wishful thinking of Whitty.

86. On February 17, 1849, George W. Eveleth asked Poe if he had written a poem called "Ullahanna," and on June 26 Poe denied it. I find the gro-

tesque title coupled with "The Raven" in *Holden's Dollar Magazine* for December 1848 (2:719) in a way that convinces me that it is a misprint for "Ulalume."

87. "The Lady Hubbard" is in *Godey's Lady's Book* for December 1849 in an article called "Specimens of American Poets." It is given as by E. A. Poe, but other pieces are ascribed to Morris, Willis, John Neal, and Whittier. All are dated April 1, 1848, and are delightful burlesques. That assigned to Poe is about Mother Hubbard and her disappointed dog, whose "extremity caudal/Dropped slowly again." I once saw a manuscript of these verses in the hand of Thomas Dunn English, who is the probable author. But the poem has been seriously attributed to Poe on occasion, as by Ruth E. Finley in *The Lady of Godey's* (1931), p. 249.

88. "Verses for the Widow Meagher" were referred to by Eugene L. Didier in the Richmond *Critic*, January 20, 1889, and in *The Poe Cult* (1909), p. 175. The story is that Poe, when in Baltimore, frequented the Widow Meagher's oyster stand and liquor bar and composed "many a witty couplet and at times poems of some length" at the request of the widow. Didier credits "a former Baltimorean now living in San Francisco," who incidentally said Poe wrote "The Gold-Bug" at the tavern, and had just left it when nabbed by election hoodlums in 1849. This is a farrago of nonsense. Mary Meagher, widow of Patrick, is mentioned in Baltimore directories from 1829 to 1837, but was a "huckster." Nobody named Meagher kept a tavern in Baltimore during Poe's lifetime. See Phillips, II, 1496–1497, for an elaborate flight of fancy, "signifying nothing."

89. "Poe in Heaven," thirty-four lines beginning "O, the dark, the awful chasm!" were received by a medium, Mrs. Lydia M. Tenney of Georgetown, Massachusetts, in November 1851, according to her manuscript volume of poems at Brown University. The verses, headed "Message from Edgar A. Poe," were printed at Springfield, Ohio, in *The Spirit Messenger* for January 15, 1852. See also the Ingram List, no. 519.

90. Dr. J. J. Garth Wilkinson, a Swedenborgian who practiced "automatic writing," in his *Improvisations from the Spirit* (London, 1857), p. 178f. printed a poem called "Edgar Allan Poe." The third stanza includes lines he believed to be from Poe's spirit:

> He said: "How came you hither?
> You have no title here:
> My little eye could wither
> The fruits your eyes revere:
> They are my subject creatures;
> Created by my rays:
> They ripen through my features;
> And my smiles are their days"

The physician was a friend of the James family and godfather of Garth Wilkinson James, a brother of Henry James the novelist.

91. "The Fire-Fiend — A Nightmare," sixty lines beginning "In the

deepest dearth of midnight," is a hoax by Charles D. Gardette. It was first printed in the New York *Saturday Press*, November 19, 1859, with a note from the editor, Henry Clapp, indicating disbelief in its authenticity. Gardette in his pamphlet, *The Whole Truth in the Question of "The Fire Fiend"* (Philadelphia, 1864), stated that he considered it a "venial and harmless literary joke," and he collected it as his own in *The Fire Fiend and Other Poems* (New York, 1866). The piece is called "The Fire Legend" in the *Southern Literary Messenger* for July 1863, where it is ascribed to Poe; W. F. Gill, who also thought it was by Poe, calls it "The Demon of the Fire" in a letter dated June 1, 1901, to James A. Harrison. See Harrison's *Complete Works of . . . Poe* (1902), VII, 238–245. See also London *Notes and Queries*, September 17, 1864, and January 21, 1865.

92. "Dream: 'The Angel,'" in the *Knickerbocker Magazine* for April 1860, is signed "E.B." or "E.P." — the type is broken. The ascription to Poe in the notorious 1941 *Index* is laughable.

93–98. Elizabeth Doten, a medium and a poet of some talent, believed that she was sometimes inspired by the spirits of Shakespeare, Burns, Poe, and others. In the first edition of her *Poems from the Inner Life by Lizzie Doten*, issued before December 19, 1863, she gave five poems she believed Poe's; she added another in later editions. These poems are the following: (93) "The Streets of Baltimore," 100 lines beginning "Woman weak, and woman mortal" was "received" in Baltimore on January 11 and printed in the Boston *Banner of Light* for January 31, 1863; Brown University Library has a broadside separate edition. The conclusion reads:

> For my soul from out that shadow
> Hath been lifted evermore —
> From that deep and dismal shadow
> In the streets of Baltimore.

The last line has become a familiar quotation. (94) "The Prophecy of Vala," 118 lines beginning "I have walked with the Fates and the Furies," founded "on the Scandinavian mythology." (95) "The Kingdom," 104 lines beginning "'Twas the ominous month of October," first printed in the *Banner of Light*, April 4, 1863. (96) "The Cradle or Coffin," fifty-four lines beginning "The Cradle or Coffin, the robe or the shroud." (97) "Resurrexi," sixty-six lines beginning "From the throne of Life Eternal," "recited . . . Boston" and printed in the *Springfield Republican* of uncertain date. I have seen a copy "from a Poe manuscript" as made by "Thomas T. Latham . . . January 15, 1847." This copy has a new title, "The Spirit Ideal"; the text is printed in the *Mobile Chronicle*, March 5, 1882. (98) "Farewell to Earth," 139 lines beginning "Farewell! Farewell!" These verses were "given in New York, . . . November 2, 1863," and printed in the *Banner of Light*, January 2, 1864. They appear only in later editions of Miss Doten's collection. In this poem she was informed that it was to be Poe's last communication from heaven.

99. "Leonainie," beginning "Leonainie — Angels named her," is a hoax by James Whitcomb Riley. He wrote it and signed it "E.A.P." in a copy of

Ainsworth's Latin Dictionary (preserved in the Lilly Collection at the University of Indiana), and arranged for John Oscar Henderson, editor of the *Dispatch* of Kokomo, Indiana, to print it in his paper on August 2, 1877. The editor's son, Paul G. Henderson, assures me that Riley, who merely wanted to show he could write something that might be believed to be Poe's, also arranged for the exposé in the *Kokomo Tribune* of August 25, 1877. Riley published the poem as a song in 1879 and collected it in *Armazindy* (1894); it is in his *Complete Works* (1916), I, 216. Many persons — E. C. Stedman among them — were taken in.

100, 101. "Poe's Two Unpublished Poems" were described in the *Richmond State* of May 29, 1880. A clipping is catalogued in the Ingram List, no. 768. It states that in May 1874 a lady of Washington, who as a girl was engaged to Poe but broke her engagement and married another, had two manuscript poems (not quoted) on the broken engagement and her marriage. This is a typical newspaper canard. No sweetheart of Poe ever resided in Washington.

102. "Lilitha" or "Lilitha, Princess of Ghouls," sixty-four lines beginning "The night, it was misty, and phantasmagorical" (a bad imitation of "Ulalume"), is said to have been printed in the Washington *Sunday Gazette* in 1882; no file for the period is known. It was published as by Poe in the Louisville *Southern Bivouac*, April 1886 (1:655–657), but in the issue of October 1886 was claimed by Francis Gerry Fairfield, who said he had written it "as early as 1863." The name of N. J. Kent has also been suggested. Lilith is the demon first wife of Adam in many legends.

103. "A Wine Ballad" appeared, with Fairfield's letter dated July 19, 1886, in the *Southern Bivouac* for October (2:298–300), as something omitted from "Lilitha." The new part consists of seven lines beginning "They say these dwellers in palaces of shadow."

104. "A Sequel to the Raven," thirty-three lines beginning "Fires within my brain were burning," is said to have been dictated by Poe's spirit to "R. Allston Lavender Jr. . . . of an asylum in Raleigh, North Carolina." See the Ingram List, no. 840. The date is 1884, but the lines have not been traced in London *Funny Folks*, to which the clipping in the Ingram Collection has been questioningly credited.

105. "The Murderer," seventy lines beginning

> Ye glittering stars! how fair ye shine tonight,
> And O, thou beauteous moon! thy fairy light
> Is peeping thro' those iron bars so near me.

appeared as an uncollected poem by Poe in George W. Conklin's *Handy Manual* (Chicago, 1887), a work of which there are later editions. The ascription to Poe is baseless, but it is widely known.

106. "The Demon of the Doldrums," fifty-six lines beginning "One night I lay a-dreaming," is known from an undated clipping: "Frantic Jerry Foodle

sends to the Editor of the *Daily Graphic* a new poem said to be by Poe," described in the Ingram List, no. 844. Credit is given *The Looking Glass,* a weekly of Atlanta, Georgia, probably in 1892 or 1893 — years lacking in the unique file at the New York Public Library, which was searched for me by Gabriel Austin. The ascription cannot have been serious.

107. "My Soul," thirty-two lines beginning "Sailing over seas abysmal," a cleverly prepared hoax, was printed in *Corks and Curls* (1895), the annual of students of the University of Virginia. McLane Tilton has acknowledged authorship; but a forged separate edition, *Poem by a Bostonian* (dated "Boston, 1827") is described in Heartman and Canny's *Bibliography* (1943), p. 18.

108. "The Sea of Serenity," sixty lines beginning "From the Mountains of the Moon," was printed as Poe's in the literary supplement of the San Francisco *Examiner* on March 12, 1899. The author, Herman Scheffauer, was induced by Ambrose Bierce to publish it as a joke on James Whitcomb Riley, who was lecturing in California. See Carroll Douglas Hall, *Bierce and the Poe Hoax* (San Francisco, 1934).

109. "Kelah," seventy lines beginning "In my hermitage, I lingered," appeared in the *Baltimore Sun* of October 7, 1906. See the Ingram List, no. 928. This hoax is not connected with "The Murderer," as some have supposed.

110. Amelia F. Poe, on August 16, 1912, sent Ingram a copy of a stanza without title, said to be signed "E. A. Poe" in manuscript. The description in the Ingram List, no. 465, is inadequate. The "poem," which begins "Then the vessel, sinking, lifting," is the last stanza of "My Soul," no. 107 above.

111. "A Bowlegged Man," reading, "Yo ho, what manner of man is this,/ Who wears his pants in parenthesis?" was described as "written by Poe in a barroom" in an article by Joseph Maxwell in the New York *Evening Journal.* I have only an undated clipping, but the date was shortly before December 8, 1930. This is a jocular hoax — I have seen a blank verse version called Shakespeare's.

112. In the New York Times *Book Review* of September 3, 1950, "M.H." sought a very short children's prayer supposed to have been written by Edgar Allan Poe and containing the words, "Make me worthy." No reply was forthcoming, but Poe was capable of composing a prayer for children, whom he loved. We thus conclude with what, if it is a legend, is at least a charming legend.

POEMS BY MEMBERS OF POE'S FAMILY

Members of Poe's family were given to writing verses. His uncle Samuel is said to have been an eccentric wit — "wag" might be the better word (see the Ingram List, numbers 268, 414, and 418). A scrap of doggerel ascribed to him may be seen in Ingram's *Edgar Allan Poe* (1880), II, 252, though I think it is not original, but a traditional piece. Edgar's brother and sister wrote poems, and the only known composition of his wife is in verse. In the present section I give a brief biography of Poe's brother Henry and a catalogue raisonnée of his poems; a sketch of Rosalie Poe's life and texts of her two known poems, hitherto printed only in a decidedly obscure periodical; and a biography of Virginia Clemm Poe, together with the text of her only known poem, which is a valentine for her husband. I have never heard of any "poetry" ascribed to Mrs. Clemm or Neilson Poe.

I. POE'S BROTHER

William Henry Leonard Poe [1] was born in Boston, January 30, 1807, and was soon taken to Baltimore, where his grandfather had something to do with his upbringing. His godfather, Henry Didier,[2] helped to educate him and later took him into his counting house. In 1825 Henry Poe visited his brother and sister at Richmond. He went to sea, and in February 1827 wrote a travel letter from Montevideo, where he attended the carnival; his other travels are matters of somewhat vague tradition, but he probably did visit Russia. Edgar Poe adopted the sailor's yarns of his brother as adventures of his own.[3]

Henry was writing poetry as early as 1826. He probably knew the Baltimore poet Edward Coote Pinkney and he was a friend of Frederick W. Thomas, who years later, on August 3, 1841, wrote to Edgar that Henry and he had been "rather rivals in a love affair." Henry was at one time in love

---

[1] There is no doubt that this was his full name, but on May 2, 1912, Amelia F. Poe wrote to J. H. Ingram that she had no idea why he was named Leonard. He was usually called Henry, and signed his printed works W.H.P. or W. H. Poe. No personal letter from Poe's brother is known, but the text of one addressed to him by John Allan on November 1, 1824, is given in A. H. Quinn's *Edgar Allan Poe*, page 89.

[2] Father of Eugene L. Didier, whose statements in his *Life and Poems of Edgar Allan Poe* (1877) are based on information from people who remembered Poe's brother.

[3] Henry Poe's Montevideo letter was published in the Baltimore *North American*, September 22, 1827. His narrative "The Pirate" and two other prose pieces — all romantic fictions — also appeared during that year in the same periodical, as did a number of his poems.

with a lady whose name was Rosa Durham. Stoddard says that he was handsome and talented, but of irregular habits because of which his fiancée dismissed him.[4]

The brothers saw much of each other in 1827 and in 1829 and 1831. Edgar wrote to John Allan, August 10, 1829, that Henry was already hopelessly addicted to drink. He incurred debts that were later to embarrass Edgar, who wrote to Allan about them on November 18, 1831, after Henry's death.

Henry died, presumably of tuberculosis, on August 1, 1831, at the home of his aunt, Mrs. Clemm, and was buried the next day in the churchyard of the First Presbyterian Church, according to the Baltimore *American* of August 2. No portrait of him is known.

POEMS OF WILLIAM HENRY POE

Most of the few compositions of William Henry Poe known in 1926 were collected in that year by Hervey Allen and myself in a volume called *Poe's Brother*. Nothing can be added to the prose, but a slightly expanded list of the verses may now be offered. Texts of three have been inserted with commentary below. The first dozen listed are in the volume of 1926.

1. "Jacob's Dream," Philadelphia *Saturday Evening Post*, January 20, 1827; sixty-four lines, beginning, "Inspir'd by faith's illuming ray."

2. "Psalm 139th," Philadelphia *Saturday Evening Post*, February 3, 1827; thirty-two lines, beginning, "Lord! thou hast searched and scanned me through."

3. "On the Death of Miss E.S.B.," Baltimore *North American*, July 28, 1827; twelve lines beginning, "The eyes which once with sweetest beauty shone."

4. "Oh! Give that Smile," Baltimore *North American*, August 4, 1827; sixteen lines beginning, "Oh! give that smile — that smile again."

5. ["In a Pocket Book"], Baltimore *North American*, August 11, 1827:

FOR THE NORTH AMERICAN

(In a pocket book I lately found three locks of hair,
from which originated the following lines: —)

My Father's! — I will bless it yet —
For thou hast given life to me:
Tho' poor the boon — I'll ne'er forget
The filial love I owe to thee.

My Mother's, too! — then let me press
This gift of her I loved so well, —
For I have had thy last caress,
And heard thy long, thy last farewell.

---

[4] The surname comes from Amelia F. Poe in a letter to Ingram, February 28, 1911; the given name is revealed in Henry's poems. Stoddard's remarks are from his memoir, page xxxvii.

My Rosa's! pain doth dim my eye,
When gazing on this pledge of thine —
Thou wer't a dream — a falsity —
Alas! — 'tis wrong to call thee mine!

A Father! he hath loved indeed!
A mother! she hath blessed her son, —
But LOVE is like the pois'ning weed
That taints the air it lives upon.

The first two stanzas are self-explanatory. The third obviously concerns an unhappy love affair, surely that referred to by Stoddard in the passage mentioned above. In 1926 Hervey Allen and I, who knew nothing definite of Henry Poe's broken engagement, thought that "Rosa" might have some reference to his sister Rosalie, an opinion I reject now, since the next item (no. 6) here shows that Henry's lady love had the initial "R." Frances Winwar, in *The Haunted Palace* (1959), p. 63, suggests that the feeble quatrains on the three locks of hair are the work of Edgar Poe, but neither Hervey Allen nor I ever thought such a thing as that. The verses are certainly by one who remembered his mother, and Edgar said that he did not. (See *Annals*, p. 533.)

6. "To R.," Baltimore *North American*, September 22, 1827. This obviously also refers to the broken engagement, and to someone not yet married:

TO R.

Nay — 'tis not so — it cannot be —
Those feelings ne'er will come again;
I gave my heart — my soul to thee,
And madly clasped the burning chain.

'Tis sever'd now — and like the slave
When freed, will scorn the bars he wore,
And feels he would prefer the grave
Than wear those galling fetters more —

Yet not like him — for memory brings
A tear to joys — to pleasures fled —
A something which still fondly clings —
" 'Tis vainly mourning o'er the dead."

It cannot be! for pride will now
Relieve the anguish of my heart —
Thy faithless pledge! thy broken vow!
'Tis fit — 'tis meet — that we should part.

7. Sixteen lines without title, *North American*, September 29, 1827, beginning, "I've lov'd thee — but those hours are past."

8. Sixteen lines without title, *North American*, October 6, 1827, beginning, "Scenes of my love! of boyhood's thoughtless hour!"

9. Twenty-four lines, *North American*, November 3, 1827, beginning, "Despair! Despair! — oh what art thou?"

APPENDIX V

10. "LINES written extempore on a tombstone with a pencil," *North American*, November 10, 1827; twenty-two lines of blank verse, beginning, "There is something in this holy place."

11. "On Seeing a Lady Sleeping," *North American*, November 17, 1827; seventeen lines, beginning, "Dream'st thou of love?"

12. "Waters of Life," *North American*, November 24, 1827; sixteen lines, beginning, "There are thoughts so wild in our childhood's hours."

13. "To ——"; thirty-nine lines beginning, "A bitter tear for thee is shed." Reproduced (with no. 14) in W. F. Gill's *Life of Edgar Allan Poe* (1877), pp. 43–45, from the *Baltimore Minerva*, a literary paper conducted by John H. Hewitt. I think Gill used clippings for his sources.

14. "To Minnie"; five quatrains beginning, "The rose that gloried on your breast." Reproduced with number 13.

15. "Woman," written in Margaret Bassett's album in which Edgar wrote his cento "To Margaret" in 1827. The manuscript is now in the Lilly Collection, Indiana University, at Bloomington. I saw it in the Walpole Galleries Sale of March 25, 1930, and by permission of the late Mrs. Edward Turnbull copied it and gave a text in London *Notes and Queries*, May 21, 1932, p. 369:

WOMAN

Well then I will — altho' I like it not —
E'en stain this page with an attempt at rhyme —
But now indeed — I really have forgot —
And wish the book in other hands than mine —

Yet as I've promised — I must now begin,
Tho' lame and jaded as my Muse appears,
But as I hope some little praise to win,
I'll spur her on — although with many fears.

I cannot flatter — nor will not even say
More than I think when Woman is the theme,
But if the truth I speak — if truth I may —
They've been to me a dark and troubled dream.

I hate *the Sex* — not hate — to meaner thought —
They're fickle — tasteless — vain — without a heart —
And if they have — for Gold it can be bought,
A changing — giddy toy — yet often full of art.

Balt. 11th Sept. 1827.   W. H. Poe

16. Three stanzas, untitled, written in Edgar Poe's hand and ascribed to his brother in the album of Lucy Holmes, later Mrs. Balderston. In the same album Edgar wrote his own fine poem "Alone." The date is presumably 1829. Eugene L. Didier printed Henry's poem in his Baltimore *No Name Magazine* for August 1890. It was reprinted, from a copy sent me by the late Kenneth Rede, in London *Notes and Queries*, May 21, 1932, p. 369.

I have gaz'd on woman's cheek
    With a passion and a thrill,
Which my tongue would never speak —
    I have taught it to be still.

I have linger'd on a lip
    In an ecstasy of bliss —
I have thought it heaven to sip
    The luxury of a kiss.

Those kisses are all over
    With my deep love, and, so, then,
I will be no more a lover —
    Till I love as much again.

17. [Verses written in an album belonging to Miss Durham], mentioned by Amelia F. Poe in a letter to Ingram, February 28, 1911 (Ingram List, no. 446). The album is said to have been destroyed by fire. These verses were probably distinct from number 6 above.

18. "Life," from a copy sent by William Hand Browne to Ingram about 1875 and now preserved at the University of Virginia (Ingram List, no. 2). Browne, a respected scholar but something of an enthusiast when he dealt with Poe, said it was understood in Baltimore that the lines had been written by Poe in the album of Miss Mary A. Hand. The verses are surely too value-less to be the work of Edgar Poe, but Browne does not ascribe them firmly to Edgar, and they may well be a production of William Henry Poe. The lines are headed "Life (original)" in the manuscript. Because they seem not to have been published, they are here quoted in full:

LIFE

Look back on life! Years, how they pass away —
    Hopes, how they rise, and fade, and die: —
How transient bliss! how soon to feel decay,
    And wake the stings of grief and memory!

The blessed sunshine of the sportive child
    How soon obscured by manhood's clouds of care:
The cheeks with health that glowed — its lips that smiled —
    How soon the curl of scorn or grief may wear.

The dreams of Love, that soothed the swelling heart,
    Sweep by like dreams the chained captive knows,
Where thoughts run back to scenes that can impart
    Awhile — till broken — respite for his woes.

The changing world — the lost remembered friends —
    The urn decaying o'er a friend decayed —
Bring thoughts — and hopes — and fear that tends
    To pall the present and the past upbraid.

APPENDIX V

Oh Life! thou art a weary load indeed,
Yet one, though bitter, few would cast aside,
But bear the pangs that make the bosom bleed
And cling to thee — to woo thee and to chide.

P.

Baltimore, October 22, 1829.

II. POE'S SISTER

Rosalie Poe was born at Norfolk in 1810, possibly on December 20 in a boarding house run by Andrew Martin at 16 Brewer Street — a house sometimes called "the Forrest Home." [1] Her paternity has been questioned, but since it was never questioned in court this is mere gossip and she must be presumed legitimate under the laws of Virginia.[2] Very soon after the death of her mother in December 1811 the blue-eyed baby girl was taken into the home of Mr. and Mrs. William Mackenzie, close friends of the Allans. The child was very ill during August 1812, but on September 3, 1812, "Rosalie . . . was christened . . . and had Mackenzie added to her name." [3]

As a child Rosalie was sent to the fashionable school of Miss Jane Mackenzie, the sister of William, in Richmond. She was not thought to show much talent, and it is said that, after an illness when about twelve years of age, she showed no efforts to excel, except in penmanship. Of that she later became a teacher in the school. Many of Poe's biographers, however, have been misled in supposing her of subnormal mentality. Her letters are rare now, but several, including one rather long specimen, are known. These show her to have been a person of refinement, and respectably educated. She could play the piano nicely.

Edgar sometimes visited Rosalie and her schoolmates and read his satires and perhaps other poems to them. A copy of his verses about young Mr. Pitts ("Oh Tempora, Oh Mores!") was preserved by Rosalie.

Rosalie naturally saw something of her brother during his residence in Richmond from 1835 to 1837. It is clear that she and Mrs. Clemm disliked each other heartily. But Rosalie visited the family in Philadelphia in 1843,

[1] See Quinn, p. 40: the exact date comes only from J. H. Whitty, who cited a "Mackenzie family bible" that cannot be verified, but no other day has been suggested, and Whitty sometimes did not reveal his true sources for things he really knew.

[2] In Virginia, court decisions in favor of presumptive legitimacy are particularly clear. I am informed of this fact by Robert R. Parrish Esq., a prominent attorney of Richmond. For some of the gossip see Quinn, pp. 89–90, and the Ingram List, no. 236. Frances Winwar, in *The Haunted Palace* (1959), p. 66, remarks that Rosalie looked very much like John Howard Payne, whose leading lady Mrs. Poe had been. Mrs. Clemm professed to believe that Rosalie was really the child of the nurse who had charge of her in infancy (see a letter from Helen Whitman, described in the Ingram List, no. 156) — but "Muddie" had reason to wish that Rosalie was no relative of "Eddie" at all, since his sister was his presumptive heiress.

[3] See Quinn, p. 58; Poe's sister was often called both Rosie and Rose by her friends.

and at Fordham in 1846. During his last summer in Richmond in 1849, Poe saw a good deal of his sister. She attended his lectures and at times embarrassed him because of her complete disregard of fashion in dress, but regarded her brother as "far above her," and seems to have been fond of him. She carried to Susan Archer Talley the very last letter Poe ever wrote. Mrs. Weiss says enough about her friend to make it clear that Rosalie was something of a bore.[4]

Rosalie was certainly Poe's sole heiress at law, since Edgar died intestate. But she did not take out the letters of administration required by law in Virginia. Mrs. Clemm's lawyer, Sylvanus D. Lewis, raised technical claims.[5] Ultimately some kind of agreement was made; and I believe the publishers arranged to compensate Rosalie by the free gift of as many sets of Poe's *Works* as she could dispose of by private sale.

The Mackenzies suffered badly from the Civil War, and Rosalie was largely dependent, in Baltimore and Washington, on charity.[6] The only thing she wrote for publication is a letter of February 4, 1873, to the editors of the *Newark Advertiser*, who published it two days later, under the heading "A Case for Charity." [7]

Sometime about 1870 Rosalie was admitted to Epiphany Church Home (Episcopalian) in Washington, D.C. There she died suddenly ("of debility") on June 14, 1874. Mrs. Weiss believed she was holding an unopened letter containing a check from the Philadelphia philanthropist, George W. Childs. She was buried next day in Rock Creek Cemetery; the funeral was conducted by the Reverend N. R. Boss. Her tombstone is inscribed merely "Rosalie Mackenzie Poe / 1812–1874," the first date taken apparently from the date of her christening.[8]

POEMS BY ROSALIE POE

Two poems from the pen of Poe's sister are known. J. H. Whitty, according to Phillips, II, 1618, had "facsimiles" of them, by which I think he meant transcripts. In October 1927 he published them in the Chicago *Step Ladder*,

[4] See her "Last Days of Edgar A. Poe" in *Scribner's Monthly* for March 1878, pp. 713f.; and her *Home Life of Poe, passim.*

[5] See Joy Bayless, *Rufus Wilmot Griswold* (1943), pp. 169–180, and Rosalie's letter to Griswold of August 20, 1850, described in the Yale List, no. 131.

[6] Mrs. Weiss (*Home Life*, p. 215) reproduces the text of a letter of 1868 to her from Rosalie. See also Phillips, II, 1594f., for record of a hundred dollars from Arthur Corning Clark, and other details, including a photograph of Rosalie in her later years. Some of her letters on her needs survive; two to R. H. Stoddard, of May 9 and of uncertain date, 1873, which show he gave her something. Letters to Ingram, April 19 and June 9, 1874, say she knew little of Edgar Poe to tell him. My list of her letters is incomplete; the only long one I recall seeing is discussed below.

[7] The editors of the New Jersey paper were William B. and Thomas T. Kinney; the former was Edmund Clarence Stedman's stepfather. I reprinted the text in London *Notes & Queries*, December 28, 1935.

[8] I am indebted to Richard E. Shands, Esq., a trustee, for a search of the records; and to Mr. Thurlow Field Collier, who visited the grave in 1961.

an obscure journal, without revealing his source, and giving a date of "1827," which may be a guess.

However, the authenticity of one poem can now be fully confirmed by a long letter of June 7 [1873], from Rosalie to a Mrs. Jordan, of Washington, whose guest she had been. In this letter she gives the second stanza of the first piece as her own. I have preferred the manuscript reading of this, as the *Step Ladder* text shows a misprint. The letter, signed "Rosalie M. Poe" and docketed "Rosie M. Poe's letter," came to me from a colonel in the Army to whom descendants of the recipient gave it. It is surely authentic and I gave it to the Henry E. Huntington Library. I see no reason to doubt the second poem, and print both below. Neither has a title.

I

Fare thee well, may peace attend thee,
Hope each cheering influence lend thee,
May heaven from every ill defend thee
And bless the home that holds my friend.

Though we may never meet again
Thy image I will long retain
And whilst thy goodness I commend
My heart with pride shall call thee Friend.

II

Yon rose that wears the blush of morn
Which glittering drops of dew adorn
    Of various hue,
Whilst its chaste beauties I survey
Its fragrance sip as Zephyrs play
    I think of you.

Yon violet too, that gives delight
Presenting to the enraptured sight
    A matchless blue,
Whilst gazing mute it often brings
Upon my view on fancy's wings
    The form of you.

When each fair flower I behold
Which to mine eyes its charms unfold
    In shining dew,
Or wafted on the gentle gale
Its odors o'er the air prevail
    I think of you.

III. POE'S WIFE

Edgar Poe's future wife, Virginia Eliza Clemm, was the third child of William Clemm, Jr., and his second wife, the poet's aunt, Maria Poe Clemm.

POEM BY POE'S WIFE

Virginia was born in Baltimore on August 16, 1822, and baptized on November 15, the day her elder sister, Virginia Maria (or Sarah), was buried. As a child she called herself "Diddie"; later Poe called her "Sissie" or "Sis." We do not know when she first met her cousin Edgar; he was living at her mother's home in 1833, when she was ten or eleven. She adored him, carried notes from him to "Mary of Baltimore," and went on walks with him in the neighboring countryside, sometimes accompanied by Lambert A. Wilmer. Wilmer says that on one occasion they came to a churchyard where a funeral was in progress, the tender-hearted girl began to weep, and the poet joined in her tears although they were total strangers to the deceased.[1] She was never sent to school, but was taught at home partly by her cousin Eddie. Virginia played the piano and sang well. In later years there was talk of getting her a harp. However, she was not intellectual, although we hear of her husband trying to teach her algebra "to improve her mind" — the only unkindness he ever showed her.

When Poe went off to work in Richmond, Virginia's cousin, Neilson Poe, offered to take her into his home and educate her. This suited neither "Muddie" Clemm nor "Sissie," and Mrs. Clemm arranged for her daughter's marriage. Virginia and Edgar Poe were married publicly in Richmond in 1836.[2]

Poe told his best friend in Richmond, John Mackenzie (Rosalie Poe's foster brother), that the marriage had not been congenial. And he told at least two people that he and his young wife lived as brother and sister for two years after their wedding.[3]

Virginia cared little for poetry — her husband said she had never read half of his; but she knew one of his pieces well enough to write it out (and sign it as if it were her own) in the album of her cousin Mary E. Herring about 1841, the poem called in the present edition "To Frances S. Osgood." Poe never addressed any poetry to his wife while she was alive, although the poem "Eulalie" may concern her, as do the tales of "Eleonora" and "Three Sundays in a Week." Virginia was certainly tolerant toward Poe's affection for Mrs. Osgood, but she could be fretful and refuse to eat when Poe was away from home; this is mentioned in a letter from the poet of July 7, 1842, to Mrs. Elizabeth Tutt.[4]

Virginia's "ethereal beauty" has been described by the romantic pens of the bookseller William Gowans, Captain Mayne Reid, and others. Mrs. Weiss, however, says the real Virginia was described by those who knew her at the age of twenty-two as looking more like a girl of fifteen than a woman grown, with, notwithstanding her frail health, a round, full face and figure, full pouting lips, a forehead too high and broad for beauty, bright black eyes,

[1] See my edition of Wilmer's *Merlin* (1941), pp. 30ff.

[2] See Annals for 1835 and 1836.

[3] For the statement of Elizabeth Oakes Smith, see her letter of January 18, 1875, described in the Ingram List, no. 196; for the reminiscence of Amos Bardwell Heywood (brother-in-law of Mrs. "Annie" Richmond), who saw Poe in 1848 or 1849, see the *New England Quarterly*, September 1943.

[4] See Catalogue of the Anderson Galleries, January 18, 1922; the extract there given has as yet been only incompletely reprinted.

and colorless complexion. Her manner and expression were soft and shy, with something childlike and appealing. "She was liked by everyone," said George R. Graham. A decided lisp added to her childlikeness.

Virginia seems to have been in fair health until January 1842, when she burst a blood vessel in singing. After that she was always more or less an invalid, although she occasionally went out socially with her husband in New York in 1845. Poe treated her with great kindness, as friends and foes alike testify, and undoubtedly suffered terribly from his knowledge that she could not live long. At Fordham she grew weaker and weaker and there she died on January 30, 1847. Her husband, it is believed, never looked at her in death. She was first entombed at Fordham, but since 1885 her body has rested beside her beloved Eddie and "Muddie" in Baltimore. One can echo R. H. Stoddard's comment on it all — "Poor child!" [5]

A lady who knew Poe has remarked that Virginia and Edgar had affection for each other of a kind they could have had merely as cousins. She was neither a helpmeet nor an intellectual companion. R. D. Unger, who met Poe in Baltimore in 1846, says in his still unpublished reminiscences that the poet said to him that marriage "has its joys, but its sorrows overbalance them." And yet Unger adds: "The loss of his wife was a sad blow" to Poe; and "He did not seem to care, after she was gone, whether he lived an hour, a day, a week or a year."

A VALENTINE BY VIRGINIA ELIZA CLEMM POE

The only known composition by Virginia Poe is the following acrostic in verse written as her husband's valentine less than a year before her death:

> Ever with thee I wish to roam —
> Dearest my life is thine.
> Give me a cottage for my home
> And a rich old cypress vine,
> Removed from the world with its sin and care
> And the tattling of many tongues.
> Love alone shall guide us when we are there —
> Love shall heal my weakened lungs;
> And Oh, the tranquil hours we'll spend,
> Never wishing that others may see!
> Perfect ease we'll enjoy, without thinking to lend
> Ourselves to the world and its glee —
> Ever peaceful and blissful we'll be.

[5] The foregoing account differs a good deal from popular notions about Poe's marriage. It is based on my reading of all the sources accessible to me, but I have preferred to follow what comes from people close to the poet rather than the remarks of obviously romantic writers who hardly met or never saw him or his wife. Susan Archer Talley Weiss, in her "Last Days of Poe" (*Scribner's Monthly*, March 1878) and in her *Home Life of Poe* (1907), seems to me (despite occasional minor errors) a highly reliable witness. Woodberry (*Life*, 1909, II, 440) also records the Richmond traditional view, together with an admission from Mrs. Clemm that

POEM BY POE'S WIFE

This is dated "Saturday, February 14, 1846," and addressed outside "Mr. Edgar Allan Poe, 85 Amity St. New York." The verses have no title but the first letters of the verses spell out Poe's full name. References to the hoped-for retreat at Fordham and to gossip about Mrs. Osgood are clear enough.

Virginia's poem was published in facsimile by a distant cousin, Josephine Poe January, in the *Century Magazine* for October 1909 (78:893).

---

she made the match, and that Virginia was "frail and consumptive." Cothburn O'Neal's novel, *The Very Young Mrs. Poe* (1956), is fiction, and the author does not pretend to avoid a very free treatment of the factual sources.

ANNALS

ANNALS

This short biographical account of Edgar Allan Poe is written primarily for the convenience of readers who have not made an extensive study of his life. It is arranged by calendar years, since the principal events fall into them conveniently. Special emphasis has naturally been laid upon what Poe referred to in his writings, but much attention has also been given to problems that have troubled advanced scholars, for which I now can suggest solutions.

Many questions remain, and some may always remain, unanswered. Poe kept no diaries, had few intimate friends, and to only one (F. W. Thomas) in whom he did confide had he frequent occasion to write letters. Poe told romantic stories about himself and made ironic and jocular remarks that his hearers thought were in dead earnest, and his capacious memory was inaccurate. Many of his acquaintances, their friends, and their relations were likewise unreliable. They contradicted each other and even themselves. Some were burdened with Victorian delicacy, others with too-vivid imaginations.

Excellent scholars have written about Poe, but they have often liked or disliked the poet so much that they wrote like prosecutors or attorneys for the defense, and some disliked each other. Suffice it to say here that I am indebted to all of them, but especially to the works of George Edward Woodberry, Arthur Hobson Quinn, and Mary E. Phillips. I have often gone also to the sources they cite, and I have discovered others for myself.

Writing today I am aware of disadvantages, for I have met only one man, Edward V. Valentine, who remembered seeing Poe, and he did not talk to him. But I am not hampered by any desire to spare the feelings of living persons by suppressing anything pertinent and true. I have weighed the evidence and testimony in the light of considerable knowledge of the character, accuracy, and prejudices both of the witnesses who knew Poe and of the biographers.[1]

FOREBEARS

The remote ancestry of the poet greatly interested some of his biographers but need not concern us here. His paternal grandfather, David Poe, born at Dring, County Cavan, Ireland, about 1743, was brought as a child to Lancaster County, Pennsylvania. There he married Elizabeth Cairnes (born 1756), also of Protestant Irish descent. About 1775 they removed to Baltimore, where David Poe engaged in trade as a wheelwright and later had a drygoods store. He was active in the American Revolution and in 1779 was commis-

---

[1] For the poet's forebears and for the events of his life I follow, unless otherwise indicated, the well-documented narrative of Arthur H. Quinn, *Edgar Allan Poe: A Critical Biography* (1941), occasionally supplementing Quinn's account from his own and other sources.

sioned Assistant Deputy-Quartermaster General for the city of Baltimore, with the rank of major. This post gave him a courtesy title; he was usually called General Poe. He spent forty thousand silver dollars on the cause. He died in October 1816, and in 1824 his friend Lafayette visited his grave.

David and Elizabeth Poe had at least seven children, including David Poe, father of the poet; Maria, who became the second wife of William Clemm; and Elisabeth, who married Henry Herring on November 17, 1814.

Mrs. Clemm kept in touch with the families of two brothers of "General" Poe — William, who moved to Georgia, and George, who remained in Maryland. Neilson Poe — who knew the poet and, like Neilson's children, John Prentiss Poe and Amelia Fitzgerald Poe, was an informant of the biographers — was a grandson of "General" Poe's brother, George Poe.

Of Poe's maternal ancestors in England very little is known. His grandmother, as Mrs. Arnold, first appeared on the stage at Covent Garden on February 28, 1791. Her last appearance in London took place on June 13, 1795. On January 5, 1796, the Boston *Massachusetts Mercury* announced: "On Sunday [the third] arrived in . . . the ship *Outram* . . . from London, Mrs. Arnold and Daughter from the Theatre Royal, Covent Garden, and Miss Green. Both engaged . . . for the Boston Theatre . . . Mrs. Arnold is about in her four and twentieth year . . . Other passengers . . . [included] Mr. Tubbs . . ." Mrs. Arnold opened in Boston February 12, 1796.

After the Boston season ended on May 16, Mrs. Arnold gave concerts at Portsmouth, New Hampshire, and elsewhere, assisted by her daughter. At about this time the mother became the wife of Charles Tubbs, a pianist. On November 25 the Tubbs family opened the first season of the Portland (Maine) Theatre with David Garrick's farce, *Miss in Her Teens*, in which Miss Elizabeth Arnold played Biddy Bellair. In the Portland *Eastern Herald* of November 28, 1796, it was reported, "Miss Arnold, in Miss Biddy, exceeded all praise. Although a Miss of only nine years old, her powers as an actress would do credit to any . . . of maturer age." Quinn accepted this statement about her age, although others have felt some doubt of her extreme precocity.[2] Of her talent there can be no doubt. The poet was not unreasonable when, late in life, he said he thought he owed his mother every good gift of his intellect or heart.[3]

In April 1798, after several changes of theatrical company, Mr. and Mrs. Tubbs and Elizabeth Arnold appeared under the management of a leading man, Mr. Edgar, as members of the Charleston (South Carolina) Comedians. On May 2, 1798, Mrs. Tubbs sang in a concert at Charleston, and thereafter her name disappears from the record. The next year, Miss Elizabeth Arnold

[2] See Quinn, pp. 2–6, 16. Like George E. Woodberry in *Edgar Allan Poe* (1885), p. 6, and *The Life of Edgar Allan Poe* (1909), I, 7, I think that both mother's and daughter's ages were understated. Quinn quotes a London marriage record, May 18, 1784, of Henry Arnold and Elizabeth Smith as perhaps that of Poe's grandparents. The couple signed with their marks, and I cannot accept this identification for an *actress* as evidential of the given names of Poe's grandparents.

[3] See letter of May 16, 1875, from Marie Louise Shew Houghton to J. H. Ingram, described as no. 226 in the Ingram List — J. C. Miller, *John Henry Ingram's Poetry Collection at the University of Virginia* (1960).

made her Baltimore debut on May 31. On June 7, 1799, Mr. Tubbs had a small part in Miss Arnold's benefit there, and then his name, too, is found no more. Elizabeth Arnold was now under the protection of a young actress known as Miss L'Estrange, who later married the actor Luke Usher.[4]

By 1800, Miss Arnold had become a leading lady. On March 14 of that year, Charles D. Hopkins made his debut in Philadelphia with Wignell's company with which she appeared, and, before August 11, 1802, he married her. She took part on August 22 in the first theatrical performance given in the new capital, Washington.

Meanwhile, David Poe, Jr., born on July 18, 1784, had grown up in Baltimore and was destined by his family for the law. He had probably been a member of an amateur "Thespian Club" in Baltimore[5] before he escaped from a law office to the stage. He made his professional debut on December 1, 1803, with Alexandre Placide's company at Charleston, South Carolina, where he remained until April 19, 1804. On June 30, we find him in Green's Virginia Company at Richmond, together with Mr. and Mrs. Hopkins.

Charles Hopkins died on October 26, 1805. On March 14, 1806, "David Poe Jr." entered into a marriage bond with "Mrs. Eliza Hopkins widow."[6] The bridegroom's family is said to have disowned him, but a partial reconciliation ensued when a son was born to the young couple in Boston on January 30, 1807. The boy was taken to his grandfather in Baltimore, probably in the summer of 1808 when his parents went to Richmond, and christened William Henry Leonard Poe.[7] David Poe, Jr., and Elizabeth Poe were again in Boston with Powell's Company on October 19, 1808.

1809–1814

[1809] Edgar Poe, the poet, was born in Boston on January 19, 1809. On February 23 young David Poe in Baltimore wrote a letter trying in vain to borrow money from a cousin, George Poe, Jr.[1] He was back in Boston on April 17, playing Laertes to the Hamlet of John Howard Payne; Mrs. Poe played Ophelia — she was now leading lady for that youthful star. On June 6 the Poes were in New York, where an entertainment at Mechanics' Hall was postponed because of the "sudden disappearance" of Mrs. Poe. On September 6 both husband and wife appeared at the Park. David, on October 18, as Captain Cypress in Richard Leigh's *Grieving's a Folly*, made his last appearance. His career was finished at the age of barely twenty-six.

David Poe, rarely praised, was a mediocre actor. He was hot-tempered — he threatened to beat a critic who ridiculed his wife's costume[2] — and he had

[4] See Mary E. Phillips, *Edgar Allan Poe, the Man* (1926), II, 1611ff. I suspect that Mr. or Mrs. Usher was related to the Arnolds.

[5] Eugene L. Didier, *The Life and Poems of Edgar Allan Poe* (1877), pp. 23–24.

[6] Quinn, p. 23, gives a facsimile of this document, which contains the only authenticated signature of the poet's father. The lady is called Mrs. Hopkins in the *Virginia Patriot* on April 5, the day before Easter, but Mrs. Poe on April 9, 1806.

[7] See Appendix V for an account of Poe's brother.

[1] The letter is the only surviving composition of the poet's father. Quinn, *Edgar Allan Poe*, p. 32, published it from a transcript by the recipient.

[2] Quinn, pp. 34–35. The criticism was exceptional. Mrs. Poe was generally ad-

ANNALS

a reputation for drunkenness even when on the stage. From him the poet inherited little to commend.

[1810] In March 1810 Mrs. Poe again was John Howard Payne's leading lady at the Park, where she made her last New York appearance on July 4. She was at Richmond from August 18 to September 21. During this year her daughter Rosalie was born. Of the poet's father in 1810 nothing is known.

[1811] From January 23 to May 20, 1811, Mrs. Poe was at Charleston, and on July 26 at Norfolk. On September 20 she opened at Richmond and on October 11 made her last appearance on the stage. On November 29, 1811, the Richmond *Enquirer* carried a notice: "To the Humane Heart. On this night *Mrs. Poe*, lingering on the bed of disease and surrounded by her children, asks your assistance and *asks it perhaps for the last time.* The Generosity of a Richmond Audience can need no other appeal. For particulars, see the Bills of the day." The paper of December 10 announced the passing of Mrs. Poe "on last Sunday morning," December 8, and commented, "By the death of this lady the Stage has been deprived of one of its chief ornaments." She was buried in Old St. John's burial ground. Her funeral, at ten o'clock on December 10, was recorded in the *Virginia Patriot* of that day.

David Poe, Jr., died, I believe, on or about December 10, 1811. William Fearing Gill said in his *Life of Edgar Allan Poe* (1878), p. 20, "The poet's father did not long survive his wife, dying only three days later of consumption." My correspondent Frederick H. Howard had it from John P. Poe that David Poe, Jr., "was a widower only two days."[3] Edgar Poe himself wrote in a letter of August 20, 1835, to his kinsman William Poe, that his mother died "a few weeks before" her husband, and in a letter of December 1, 1835, to Judge Beverley Tucker, that his parents died "within a few weeks" of each other. That David Poe survived his wife is argued by the fact that she was never referred to as his widow. There are a number of other stories about the last days of Poe's father which I dismiss as incredible.

Mr. and Mrs. Luke Usher, the closest friends of Mrs. Poe (whom they called by her nickname "Betty"), took care of Edgar and Rosalie during their mother's last illness, and continued to do so for some time thereafter.[4] It is most improbable that so young a child as Edgar was taken to his mother's funeral or that he ever saw his mother after her death. In any case, in his

---

mired in hoydenish parts, and thought to look charming in boy's clothes. She may once have been allowed to play Hamlet, but the playbill for the performance (formerly owned by Guido Bruno) is not accessible for authentication. Quinn's records are not complete for some cities; for example, he gives nothing for Petersburg, Virginia, where Woodberry, *Life*, I, 8, places David Poe in November 1804.

[3] On December 28, 1908, however, Amelia F. Poe wrote to John H. Ingram that David Poe died "a short time *before*" his wife, in Norfolk (Ingram List, no. 414, incompletely described). Phillips, I, 77f., quotes an undated, unsigned newspaper article that said David Poe, Jr., was in New York on July 10 and died in Norfolk on October 19, 1810, but when I saw the clipping in the auction room I thought it to be later than 1850.

[4] I follow reminiscences of John P. Poe, given about 1890 to my correspondent, F. H. Howard.

letter of December 1, 1835, to Judge Beverley Tucker, the poet said he had no memory of his mother. His record of his pride in his mother's stage career, in a discussion of Mrs. Mowatt in the *Broadway Journal*, July 19, 1845, is quite impersonal. But Poe knew he looked like his mother, for he owned a picture of her.

On December 26, 1811, there occurred a disastrous fire at the Richmond Theater, in which seventy-two persons lost their lives, among them Governor George William Smith of Virginia.[5] A good many children were orphaned, and they were kindly taken into the families of their parents' friends. Edgar and Rosalie Poe, although not really sufferers from the fire, were also taken into good families: Rosalie into that of Mr. and Mrs. William Mackenzie (Mackenzie, McKenzie), and Edgar into that of Mr. and Mrs. John Allan.[6]

John Allan was a merchant. He was born in the parish of Dundonald, Ayrshire, Scotland, in 1780, arrived in Richmond before 1795, became the partner of Charles Ellis on November 23, 1800, and was naturalized on June 4, 1804. On February 5, 1803, he had married Frances Keeling Valentine, a lady of some beauty. Mrs. Allan's sister, Ann Moore Valentine, made her home with the Allans over the general store of Ellis & Allan — exporters of tobacco and importers of many kinds of merchandise — at the northeast corner of Main and Thirteenth Streets. The Allans were prosperous and entertained a good deal, although Mrs. Allan was often indisposed. They had no children.

[1812] On January 7, 1812, John Allan bought a crib. According to tradition, the child Edgar was baptized by the Reverend John Buchanan.[7] He was given the name Edgar Allan Poe; I assume from the name that John Allan was his godfather — Poe usually called him "Pa."

[1813] On May 14, Mr. Allan recorded that Edgar had caught the whooping cough; by July 26 he had recovered from the measles. Even in the nursery Poe showed great affection for a little playmate, Catherine Poitiaux. The two remained lifelong friends.

[1814] Poe was probably first sent to a dame school when he was about five years of age. Available information is slight and somewhat confusing. On January 20, Clotilda Fisher signed a receipt to John Allan for four dollars for "one quarter's Tuition of Edgar A. Poe." The lady was probably identical with, or a sister of, Elizabeth Fisher, listed in the Richmond City Directory of 1819 as a teacher. There is also a story that Poe attended the school of a Miss Elizabeth Miller, who taught him to read aloud with a

[5] The romantic story told by Didier in *Life and Poems*, p. 25, that Poe's father rushed into the theater and died trying to save his wife, is pure fiction; but I suspect it emanated from Edgar Poe himself.

[6] It has also been said that the boy was taken into the care of his foster parents before the disaster of December 26 and was with them at a friend's home in the country at the time. In this instance I have preferred the account suggested by Woodberry (*Life*, I, 16) as the more reasonable. John Allan had cousins by marriage named Poe, in Scotland. See Phillips, II, 1623. For more about Rosalie Poe, see Appendix V.

[7] Thomas Ellis, quoted by J. A. Harrison in *The Complete Works of Edgar Allan Poe* (1902), I, 23; see also Ingram List, no. 418.

Scottish burr, but it strikes me as a legend.[8] It is also told that for being naughty, a schoolmistress punished Poe by hanging a vegetable around his neck, that he went home wearing it, and that John Allan went to the teacher, rebuked her, and (perhaps) withdrew Poe from the school.[9] Poe is said to have been handsomely dressed by his foster parents.

In summer the Allan family visited the Blue Ridge Mountains of Virginia. It is said that there little Edgar was taken about on horseback by one of Mrs. Allan's relatives who had the child demonstrate his precocity by reading the newspaper to people they met. At home he was taught to stand on the table in his stocking feet and toast the ladies at a dinner party with a glass of sweetened wine. We are told, too, that Allan was a poor disciplinarian, alternately petting and scolding the child, who was often disobedient.[10] Some people thought him spoiled.

1815–1826

[1815] In the first part of 1815 Poe attended, in Richmond, the school of Mr. William Ewing, who in 1817 wrote of him as "a charming boy," who had liked his school. But John Allan had decided to go to England to establish a branch of his firm, and accordingly he and his family boarded the *Lothair* at Richmond on June 22, 1815, put to sea from Norfolk the next day, and landed after thirty-four days at Liverpool. From there the family went to Scotland, where they visited John Allan's relatives. They went to Irvine, Kilmarnock, Glasgow, Greenock, and Edinburgh. At Irvine, Poe may have observed archers shooting the popinjay on the cathedral.[1] He learned something about the Hebrides and the Isle of Syke, but he did not visit them. From Edinburgh the Allan family went by way of Newcastle and Sheffield to London, where in October they were at 47 Southampton Row, Russell Square, Bloomsbury.

[1816] In 1816 and 1817, in London, Poe went to the boarding school of the Misses Dubourg, 146 Sloane Street, Chelsea. The boy almost surely was taken to visit the Tower of London, where he must have seen the ravens; he may have been taken to the British Museum [2] and to Westminster Abbey.

[8] For this story see Phillips, I, 114–115; her "authorities" were imaginative persons. There is nothing of a teaching Miss Miller in the Richmond City Directory or any early document.

[9] I follow R. H. Stoddard's account in his "Life of Edgar Allan Poe," *Selected Works of Edgar Allan Poe* (1880), p. xxiv. The vegetable story is supported by Mary Jane Poitiaux Dixon in a letter dated July 2, 1875, now at the University of Virginia, described only in part in the Ingram List as no. 237; a complete copy is before me.

[10] William Fearing Gill, *The Life of Edgar Allan Poe* (1878), pp. 24–25, apparently following Edward V. Valentine.

[1] See note on line 5 of "Romance." A tradition that Poe went to school at Irvine is doubtful, though he may have spent a few days in school there. Phillips I, 132ff., gives some material that can hardly be considered reliable.

[2] It is extremely improbable that Poe was ever a reader at the British Museum as one biographer has fancied; admission of anyone under twenty-one was very rare. Poe's later knowledge of London slums came from the writings of Dickens rather than from experience.

[1817] In 1817, John Allan moved into 39 Southampton Row. His office was at 18 Basinghall Street, near St. Andrew's Stair.

[1818] In 1818, Poe went to the boarding school of the Reverend John Bransby at Stoke Newington, where he did well in French and Latin. The master said, long afterward, that the boy was spoiled with too much spending money. In August the Allan family visited the Isle of Wight, presumably on vacation. On the way Poe may have seen Stonehenge.[3]

[1819] In 1819 Allan's business was doing badly, but Edgar remained in school at Stoke Newington.

[1820] On June 8, 1820, the Allan party was in Liverpool on the way home. The New York *Daily Advertiser* of July 22 announced the arrival of the "ship *Martha*, [Captain] Sketchly, 31 days from Liverpool," and mentioned as among the passengers, "J. & F. Allan, E. A. Poe, Ann Valentine." This is Poe's first notice in the press.

On July 28 the family took the steamboat home by way of Norfolk, and by August 2 were in Richmond, where they lived for a while at the home of Charles Ellis. His son, Thomas Ellis, tells us of his admiration of Poe, who taught him to shoot, swim, and skate, and who incidentally joined him in shooting some domestic fowls at Bushrod Washington's estate, Belvidere — an act for which Poe received the only whipping the younger Ellis ever knew him to get from Mr. Allan.

Poe now entered the school (on Broad between Fifth and Sixth streets) of Joseph H. Clarke, a fiery Irishman from Trinity College, Dublin. Clarke examined him in Latin and found that Poe had proceeded so far as to decline the nouns *penna, domus, fructus,* and *rus* (all the declensions save the difficult third) and the regular adjective *bonus.* He also knew some French. He early read Ovid, Caesar, and Virgil under Clarke. Poe preferred poetry to prose, but was somewhat "averse from mathematics." He was ambitious to excel, although "not especially studious" (that is, did not labor over his lessons), and did rather well.[4]

[1821–22] At Clarke's, Poe was considered second as a classicist to Nat Howard, but he was the best reader of Latin verse. He at this time composed a series of poems to little girls of Richmond, which the master advised John Allan not to have printed. He also sent Clarke a letter in Latin verse during a summer vacation. In his last year with Clarke, Poe was reading Homeric Greek, and, in Latin, Horace and Cicero's *De Officiis.* When Clarke gave up his school, Poe read an ode in English at the farewell ceremonies. Clarke continued to be his friend as long as the poet lived.

[1823] On April 1, 1823, Allan entered Poe in the school in the old Atheneum Building, Marshall and Tenth streets, run by William Burke, another Irishman and classicist. Here the poet remained until March 1825; he was never whipped, according to his deskmate, Creed Thomas, who remained a lifelong friend. His other best friends there were Robert G. Cabell and Robert Stanard. The mother of the latter, Jane Stith Craig Stanard, was

---

[3] Letter of John Allan, dated August 18, quoted in Phillips, I, 165.

[4] Here I follow Stoddard's "Life" (1880), p. xxvii, in the main. Clarke gave many reminiscences of Poe. The curriculum was usual at the time. Clarke also indicated that Poe read Xenophon in Greek; the *Anacreontea* probably preceded that.

kind to Poe, who felt for her a pure affection, perhaps the strongest of his life.[5] Probably about this time Poe, dressed in a sheet and a mask, tried to scare the Gentlemen's Whist Club at the Ellis home. He was unmasked by General Winfield Scott and Dr. Philip Thornton of Rappahannock.[6]

[1824] On April 28, 1824, Mrs. Stanard died. Her mind was clouded in her last illness, and the poet grieved deeply at her death, which, more than any other incident of his life, turned his thoughts so often to the passing of fair ladies. Poe sometimes visited her grave in company with her son Robert.[7]

In school Poe practiced declamation and read his favorite part, the speech of Cassius in *Julius Caesar*, Act I, Scene 2, with unforgettable scorn and fire.[8] There are also references, but of a less definite kind, to his acting in amateur theatricals while he was a schoolboy. In June he swam some six or seven miles in the James River, from Ludlam's Wharf to Warwick, against a tide of three miles per hour. His schoolmates Stanard and Cabell accompanied him on the shore, and his schoolmaster, Burke, went along in a rowboat to rescue him in case of need. Poe boasted of the feat throughout his life.

In October, Poe was lieutenant of the Junior Richmond Volunteers, who acted as guard of honor for Lafayette when he came to the city.

Allan's business partnership was dissolved in this year. His relations with his godson, hitherto cordial, had become strained; it is thought that Mrs. Allan sometimes quarreled with her husband and that Poe sided with her. At about this time Poe composed several rhymed satires, one of which ("Oh, Tempora! Oh, Mores!"), ridiculing a socially minded drygoods clerk, Robert Pitts, survives. Another, now lost, was about the Junior Debating Society, of which the poet was a member.

[1825] Allan's financial worries were of short duration, for in March 1825 his uncle, William Galt, died and left his nephew the bulk of his fortune of several hundred thousand dollars. In this year Poe fell in love with Sarah Elmira Royster, the daughter of a neighbor, and they became engaged without parental approval.

During Poe's boyhood, the Allans, accompanied by Edgar, went regularly in the summers to the Virginia mountains. Poe's poem "The Lake" suggests that he may have visited the Dismal Swamp near Norfolk; just when is not known. Poe attended church with his foster mother frequently; the Allans had a pew in Monumental Church; and I think it probable that Poe was confirmed as an Episcopalian by Bishop Richard Channing Moore.[9]

---

[5] See the commentary on "To Helen."

[6] Reminiscence of Thomas Ellis. This and other details of Poe's boyhood are found in reminiscences of contemporaries cited by Harrison, I, 23–29.

[7] Poe's statement that he visited her tomb alone by night may be questioned. Cemetery gates were closed at night, and Poe disliked visiting such places in the dark, for all that he wrote in his fictions.

[8] Stoddard, "Life," p. xxix.

[9] See Phillips, I, 108; and George D. Fisher, *History and Reminiscences of the Monumental Church, Richmond, Va., from 1814 to 1878* (Richmond, 1880), where on p. 37 it is stated that in 1814 John Allan paid $340 to subscribe to pew number 80. It cannot be *proved* that Poe was confirmed, because if Bishop Moore, rector

The Allans presumably attended the theater often, and took Edgar with them. We know what he could have seen, although not what he did: he probably saw *Timour the Tartar*, a horse spectacle, and surely some Shakespeare, and doubtless he did not miss the Egyptian mummy exhibited at the Senate Chamber of the Capitol in 1823 and 1824.[10] John Allan is listed as a subscriber for Rees' *Cyclopaedia*, with which Poe shows familiarity. Allan admired Shakespeare and poetry in general, although not that of Byron. Edward M. Alfriend tells us that Allan walked with Poe and read with him and once said, "Edgar is wayward and impulsive. . . for he has genius . . . He will someday fill the world with his fame." [11] John Allan was to learn far more of the waywardness than he had reason to expect, but he did not live to see his prophetic words come true in 1845 when "The Raven" appeared.

[1826] On February 14, 1826, Poe entered the University of Virginia at Charlottesville.[12] There he attended the Greek and Latin classes of Professor George Long, and the classes of Professor George Blaetterman in French, Italian, and Spanish. The latter praised Poe's verse translation (now lost) of a passage in Tasso. The poet had high academic standing and in class could translate from all these languages at sight, or at least after reading a passage once.[13]

The first librarian of the University, William Wertenbaker, who was also a student in Poe's time, has left reminiscences and a list of books borrowed by Poe from June 13 to November 4, 1826: Robertson's *America*, Marshall's *Washington*, some volumes of Rollin's *Ancient History* in French, a historical work by Voltaire, the title of which is unknown, and Dufief's *Nature Displayed*, a textbook on learning the French language.

Poe was noted as a skillful draftsman and covered the walls of his room with pictures copied from an illustrated Byron — and according to statements he made long afterward, there were caricatures of his professors as well. In reminiscences of contemporaries mention is made of poems and stories he composed at this time, but unless some of the shorter pieces in *Tamerlane and Other Poems* of 1827 were among them, nothing of what Poe wrote at the University has reached us, save two letters to John Allan.

Poe was well liked at the University. Among his closer friends were William M. Burwell (later editor of *De Bow's Review*), Thomas S. Gholson, Philip Slaughter (later a distinguished Episcopal clergyman), Zaccheus Col-

---

and father of Poe's friend Channing Moore, kept a parish register, it has not survived.

[10] See Agnes M. Bondurant, *Poe's Richmond* (1942), p. 122ff.

[11] In "Unpublished Recollections of Edgar Allan Poe," *Literary Era*, August 1901.

[12] Almost all that we know of Poe at the University is given in Harrison's memoir in *Complete Works*, I, 35–63.

[13] Poe's favorite Latin poet was Horace. His later reading in the classics was desultory, but he had far more than "a smattering of Greek" (the phrase is Woodberry's); Poe could and did expand a rare Greek contraction in a review when he was over thirty and in his last years occasionally quoted Homer correctly. His ability to converse in French with his Jesuit friends at Fordham makes me sure that he spoke that language well.

lins Lee (who attended Poe's funeral), and Miles George. The last once had a fist fight with the poet, but they made up completely. The University was a disorderly place. Poe sometimes drank too much, taking off a tumbler of peach brandy at a draft. Worse, he gambled heavily at cards, losing two thousand dollars — so large a sum that one surmises he was cheated. During the year at the University, he surely wandered about the countryside. Classes ended in mid-December but Poe stayed on for a few days in order to testify in a faculty investigation on December 20 that he "never heard until now of any Hotel-Keepers playing cards or drinking with students." [14]

Upon returning to Richmond, Poe found Elmira Royster engaged to Alexander B. Shelton. Poe had been writing to her while he was at the University but her father had intercepted the letters; only one is said to have reached her.

1827–1829

John Allan refused to pay Poe's gambling debts and some others incurred at college. Allan's action was not wholly in consonance with the attitude of the best families, where a son was expected to be helped out of *one* serious scrape. But John Allan did not come of a "First Family of Virginia," and he had once been in serious financial trouble. Certainly, to a man of business, Poe's irresponsibility in money matters must have been hard to understand, as it was to the poet's friends throughout life. Poe did not return to the University.

In March, after a serious quarrel, Poe left his guardian's house and took a room in the Court-house Tavern. Within a few days, after appealing to John Allan for "the expence of my passage to Boston ($12) and a little to support me there until I shall be engaged in some business," he sailed from Richmond, probably on March 24, accompanied as far as Norfolk by his friend Ebenezer Burling.[1] Then Poe went on to Baltimore, where he almost certainly saw his brother Henry, became acquainted with Lambert A. Wilmer, and probably met the fine poet Edward Coote Pinkney.[2] Very little is

---

[14] Faculty Minutes, quoted by Quinn, p. 109.

[1] In a letter (now in my files) dated January 27, 1908, to William Peterfield Trent, Mary Rosalie Picôt says she often heard her mother mention "Aunt Burling" and her only child, Ebenezer, who was a friend and schoolmate of Poe's. See also Phillips, I, 292.

[2] The history of Poe's broken engagement not only inspired his own "Tamerlane" and "Song" ("I saw thee") but provided plots for two Baltimore writers. William Henry Poe made use of it in "The Pirate" (a violent prose tale with a hero named Edgar, published in the Baltimore *North American*, November 27, 1827), and Lambert A. Wilmer used it in *Merlin* (a three-act play printed in the *North American* of August 18 and 25 and September 1, 1827; a pamphlet edition was advertised for sale on September 22, but no copy is known). Wilmer gives a happy ending to the story, but his source is obvious; his hero is called Alphonso (from Allan?) and his heroine Elmira. In the *Southern Literary Messenger* of February 1835, in reviewing Wilmer's novel *Emilia Harrington*, Poe praised *Merlin* without reference to his personal connection with it. Hervey Allen and I reprinted "The Pirate" in *Poe's Brother* (1926), and I published an edition of *Merlin*, from the periodical text, in 1941.

known of this visit, which is not even mentioned by Poe's early biographers, but he evidently enjoyed some social life, for he wrote verses in the albums of Margaret Bassett and Octavia Walton.

We next find him in Boston, where for a short time he was probably clerk for a merchant, P. P. F. DeGrand, and market reporter for DeGrand's paper, *The Weekly Report.* On May 26, 1827, Poe enlisted in the United States Army as "Edgar A. Perry" and was assigned to Battery H of the First Artillery, then stationed at Fort Independence in Boston Harbor. While in Boston, he arranged to have his *Tamerlane and Other Poems* printed and published by Calvin Frederick Stephen Thomas, who was less than a year older than Poe himself.[3] Poe did not read proof on the later pages of the tiny pamphlet, but a few copies were circulated. It was noticed as received by two magazines — the *U. S. Review and Literary Gazette* for August and the *North American Review* for October — but no review has been found. The poetry is largely Byronic, but in the final poem, "The Lake," is first revealed the author's distinct and original genius.

On October 31, Poe's battery was transferred to Fort Moultrie at Charleston, South Carolina. He sailed November 8 on the brig *Waltham* and reached Charleston on November 18. While stationed at the fort, which is on Sullivan's Island in Charleston Harbor, he was made company clerk with the rank of artificer. He dealt much with the commanding officer, Colonel William Drayton, who became his lifelong friend. Another officer, one who wrote a recommendation for him, was Captain H. W. Griswold.[4]

[1828] Late in 1828, Poe's battery was ordered from Charleston to Fortress Monroe, Virginia. On December 11, the battery sailed on the ship *Harriet*; it arrived at Fortress Monroe on December 15. Poe had written a repentant letter to John Allan before this. Meanwhile, on December 6, 1828, Elmira Royster was married to Alexander B. Shelton.[5]

[1829] On New Year's Day, Poe was promoted to sergeant major. On February 28, 1829, Frances Allan died. Poe is said to have returned to Richmond on leave the day after her funeral. There was a partial reconciliation

---

[3] See my introduction to the 1941 facsimile of *Tamerlane and Other Poems*, where the Boston adventures of the poet and the printing of his little book are discussed in considerable detail.

[4] Poe's military record, turned up by Woodberry (*Edgar Allan Poe*, 1885), is documented in detail by Quinn. The hypothesis of Poe's meeting at Charleston with a famous naturalist, Dr. Edmund Ravenel, was merely advanced as "probable" by Quinn, p. 130, but Poe never mentioned Ravenel. There is no reason to think Poe took any interest in natural history so early as this.

[5] For my account of the Sheltons, I am largely indebted to Mrs. Ralph T. Catterall of the Valentine Museum and to Mr. Milton C. Russell of the Virginia State Library. Sarah Elmira Royster was born in 1810 or 1811; married December 6, 1828; baptized, "aged twenty-four," on July 1, 1835. She died in her seventy-eighth year, on February 11, 1888, at her residence, 1000 East Clay Street, Richmond, and was buried from the Grace Street Presbyterian Church. Her husband, Alexander Barret(t?) Shelton, was born in 1807. He died at the couple's home, "The Cottage," in Henrico County, Virginia, aged thirty-seven, on July 12, 1844. They had five children. Shelton left an estate worth about $50,000. Both Shelton and his wife were buried in Shockoe Hill Cemetery.

with John Allan. Poe was released from the Army on April 15, and Allan set about helping him get an appointment to West Point, which did not come until March of the next year.

Poe's time in the Army, where he had a good deal of leisure, was not wasted. He made a study of Shakespeare and of Milton (at least the minor poems). Extracts of his favorite passages, all very brief, survive in his handwriting. Abandoning the manner of Byron, he attempted to adopt something of Milton and Thomas Moore in a poem of several hundred lines, "Al Aaraaf." The piece is extremely difficult, containing much of the mysticism, curious lore, and wholly individual melody that were to distinguish his later work.

This, with a much shortened version of "Tamerlane," several other poems from the 1827 pamphlet, and a few new short lyrics, Poe brought together for a small volume. After going to Washington to push his quest for appointment to the Military Academy, and then to Baltimore where he called upon William Wirt, he went in May to Philadelphia and there met Joseph Hopkinson, the author of "Hail, Columbia," and Isaac Lea, the publisher. The firm of Carey, Lea & Carey consented to bring out the book if a hundred dollars were offered to back it. Allan refused to advance the money, but in Baltimore the book was accepted, and published in December by Hatch and Dunning,[6] two young men from New York who started in Baltimore with a small capital, and whose firm soon disappeared.

Poe's *Al Aaraaf, Tamerlane, and Minor Poems* had very little sale but it did receive some critical attention. A brief review, concluding, "The author, who appears to be very young, is evidently a fine genius, but wants judgment, experience, tact," was published in the Boston *Ladies' Magazine* of January 1830. In Baltimore, John H. Hewitt published in the *Minerva and Emerald* a review mildly praising the minor poems but denouncing "Al Aaraaf" as a "pile of brickbats." John Neal, to whom Poe had dedicated the new version of "Tamerlane," wrote enthusiastically of its "old-fashioned simplicity and power" and concluded, "If the young author now before us should fulfill his destiny . . . he will be *foremost* in the rank of *real* poets." [7] It was this praise which led Poe's cousin, Neilson Poe, on January 26, 1830, to write to his future wife, Josephine Clemm: "Edgar Poe has published a volume of Poems one of which is dedicated to John Neal the great autocrat of critics — Neal has accordingly published Edgar as a Poet of great genius

[6] See E. L. Didier's *Life and Poems of . . . Poe*, p. 39. The only known imprints of Hatch and Dunning are of 1829, when they also issued a *Maryland Spelling Book* by John Henry Shea.

[7] The review in the *Ladies' Magazine* was pointed out by J. H. Whitty in the New York *Evening Post Book Review*, August 13, 1921. It was not composed by the editor, Sarah Josepha Hale, but abridged from a slightly longer and more complimentary notice, of which the manuscript, in a hand I cannot identify, has survived and was reproduced in *Virginia Cavalcade* (Summer 1955). Hewitt's review long survived only in clippings, but was reprinted in full by Vincent Starrett in the *Saturday Review of Literature*, May 1, 1943. It is also in John Hill Hewitt's *Recollections of Poe*, edited by Richard Barksdale Harwell (Atlanta, 1949). Neal's comment is known only from a quotation in the Philadelphia *Saturday Museum*, March 4, 1843.

. . . *Our* name will be a great one *yet.*" [8] This I am sure was meant to be contemptuous. Still another colorless notice appeared in an unidentified newspaper and was reprinted in *Virginia Cavalcade* (Summer 1955) from a clipping. It may be one of those alluded to in the following lines:

> Next Poe who smil'd at reason, laugh'd at law,
> And played a tune who should have play'd at taw,
> Now strain'd a license, and now crack'd a string,
> But sang as older children dared not sing.
> Said Clio "by all the wise, who can admit
> "Beardless no goat a goat — no wit a wit,
> "Say! did not Billy Gwynn, the great, combine
> "With little Lucas to put down thy line?
> "And thou! thy very heart is on thy toy!
> "Thy red-hot lyre will burn thee — drop it, boy!" [9]

These lines suggest that there were reviews from William Gwynn of the Baltimore *Gazette*, who had printed a few lines from "Al Aaraaf" in his paper before Poe's book appeared, and from Fielding Lucas, Jr.,[10] bookseller and publisher, later a founder of the Maryland Historical Society. This is Poe's earliest appearance in a satire, and shows that the author (whom I cannot identify) had considerable respect for the youthful poet, who certainly "smiled at reason" in "Al Aaraaf."

At this time and perhaps in 1830 and 1831, Poe's Baltimore residence was with "his cousin, Mrs. Beacham, in a house then No. 9 (now No. 28) Caroline Street, corner of Bounty Lane. Some of their family, named Cairnes, were staying with her." [11]

---

[8] See Quinn, p. 165. Quinn thought this showed Edgar's "improved . . . standing with his relatives in Baltimore." I wish I could agree, but I have seen more than was accessible twenty years ago about Neilson Poe (1809–1884), himself a minor journalist who edited newspapers in Baltimore. In a letter of October 7, 1839, Edgar said he thought his cousin "jealous" of his literary reputation. As late as 1847 Neilson (whose name was pronounced and is often misspelled "Nelson") revealed his critical acumen by a remark that he thought Poe's brother Henry to be more of a genius than Edgar! See the Ingram List, no. 184.

[9] The verses are from *The Musiad or Ninead*, "a poem, by Diabolus, edited by ME" (Baltimore, 1830), p. 8. *The Musiad* is a small octavo of eight pages. It recounts a visit to America of the muses (with the approval of Wordsworth and Moore) to interview the poets N. P. Willis, Henry Pickering, Poe, and Sumner Lincoln Fairfield. I use the copy at Brown University. Mrs. Whitman, in 1874, thought that Poe was the author; I think it highly unlikely. The pamphlet (possibly a fragment) has recently been reprinted by David A. Randall in *The J. K. Lilly Collection of Edgar Allan Poe: An Account of Its Formation* (Lilly Library, Indiana University, 1964), pp. 55–62.

[10] See J. Thomas Scharf, *Chronicles of Baltimore* (1847), pp. 377, 381, and 510. Lucas was, with Gwynn, among the Managers who laid the cornerstone of the famous Washington Monument in Baltimore on July 4, 1815; on his publishing career, see *Proceedings of the American Antiquarian Society*, October 1955.

[11] See William J. High's "New Poeana" in the Baltimore *Sun*, June 26, 1921, quoted by Phillips, I, 439. High recorded this tradition from his grandfather, Joseph

ANNALS

[1830] Poe visited Richmond early in 1830. Late in June he entered West Point, where he stood third in French and seventeenth in mathematics in a class of eighty-seven. He roomed with Timothy Pickering Jones and Thomas W. Gibson; both have left reminiscences. Another friend, Allan B. Magruder, said that Poe's intimates were chiefly Virginians. The poet told fictional stories of his adventures including one of a visit really made by his brother to South America. He composed comic verses about his officers and probably about his companions; and sometimes visited the celebrated tavern of Benny Havens, of course.[1]

Before the end of the year Poe had no doubt seen a copy of the Galignani edition of the poems of Coleridge, Keats, and Shelley. Perhaps equally important to his literary development was the friendship of a civilian resident, the poet John Augustus Shea, whose fine lyric "To the Ocean" Poe seems to echo in "To Helen." [2]

[1831] Since John Allan sent him no allowance, Poe was in an uncomfortable position. He proceeded to get himself expelled. He absented himself from classes and roll calls, "disobeyed orders" (to go to church and class), and when court-martialed on January 27, 1831, he pleaded guilty to all charges save absence from roll call. He was expelled, but as of March 6, to allow him to receive his pay then due.

He was apparently already in touch with a New York publisher, Elam Bliss, and before leaving West Point on February 19 for New York was permitted to solicit subscriptions among the cadets for his forthcoming volume. *Poems by Edgar Allan Poe* (1831) was reviewed in the New York *Mirror* on May 7, 1831, and a very brief notice, presumably by L. A. Wilmer, appeared in the Philadelphia *Saturday Evening Post*, May 21, 1831, and was reprinted in the *Casket* for May, which came out at the end of the month. The book had little sale save to subscribers (for seventy-five cents a copy), and in 1836 Poe was to refer to it as "printed for private circulation." For it he had made extensive revisions in "Tamerlane," "Al Aaraaf," and a few earlier poems;

B. Jenkins, a friend of these relatives of Poe. I corresponded with Mr. High and think he was reliable, although perhaps inaccurate, since search of the directories does not confirm his statements. A Mrs. Mary Beastall lived on Caroline Street, near Pratt, in 1833; Edward Carnes, a stage driver, at 8 Caroline Street.

[1] Absurd stories were and still are told at West Point of the poet's frolics; that of roasting a goose named for an officer and "eating him in effigy" is possibly not made up. Poe, however, was in no serious trouble with the authorities for mischievous conduct. Gibson's article was published in *Harper's New Monthly* for November 1867; for Jones's, see Woodberry, *Life*, I, 369–372. In 1884 Magruder wrote letters to George E. Woodberry, who quoted from them in *Edgar Allan Poe* (1885), pp. 54–55.

[2] *The Poetical Works of Coleridge, Shelley, and Keats, Complete in One Volume*, Paris: A. and W. Galignani, 1829, was quickly available to American readers; see letter of George Keats written in November 1830, saying that the book was then "for sale in the eastern Cities" (Hyder E. Rollins, *The Keats Circle*, Cambridge, Mass., 1948, I, 331–332). For this and other references I am indebted to Mr. Eugene P. Sheehy. For Shea, see my note on lines 9–10 of "To Helen."

these changes he subsequently abandoned. There were also six wholly new poems, including the first version of the famous lyric "To Helen." One of them, "Israfel," even in its earliest form, is a masterpiece. According to Poe's roommate Gibson, some of the cadets, to whom Poe dedicated the volume, were disappointed because he omitted the comic squibs that had amused his companions at West Point.

Ill and in need of money, Poe remained in New York for a short while, appealing vainly to John Allan for financial help and considering ways to join the Polish Revolution; but by early May he was in Baltimore, perhaps living with his grandmother, "General" Poe's widow, and his aunt, Maria Clemm. His brother, William Henry Poe, died at the house of Mrs. Clemm on August 1. Sometime after July 16, Poe submitted some prose stories in a contest announced by the Philadelphia *Saturday Courier*; the closing date for entries was December 1, 1831. The award was announced in the issue of December 31, 1831, to "Love's Martyr," by Delia Bacon.

[1832] Miss Bacon's story was duly printed in the *Courier* issue of January 7, 1832.[3] Poe was apparently the runner-up, for, between January 14 and December 1, 1832, five of his stories were published in the *Courier* anonymously:[4] "Metzengerstein," "The Duc de l'Omelette," "A Tale of Jerusalem," "A Decided Loss" (now called "Loss of Breath"), and "The Bargain Lost" (a draft of "Bon-Bon"). Whether Poe ever heard of their publication is not known, but he never referred to any connection with the *Courier* contest and later printed the five stories in the *Southern Literary Messenger* as if they had not been published before.

Apart from the publication of these stories, the year remains almost completely obscure in Poe's biography. Only one thing is firmly established: in the Baltimore *Saturday Visiter*, August 4, 1832, the editor, Lambert A. Wilmer wrote that "Mr. Edgar A. Poe has favored us with the perusal of some manuscript tales, written by him."

The poet may have been, for part of the year, in the Army as a private soldier under an assumed name. The story is very old, and I incline, with some reservations, to accept it.[5] The stories of Poe's travels abroad in 1832 (or 1834) to Greece, Russia, or anywhere else, are all fiction.[6]

[3] Miss Bacon is remembered as the leading exponent of the notion that Francis Bacon wrote Shakespeare's plays.

[4] Killis Campbell announced in *The Dial*, February 17, 1916, his discovery of the texts. All essential documents were published in facsimile by John Grier Varner in *Edgar Allan Poe and the Philadelphia Saturday Courier* (Charlottesville, 1933).

[5] The source is Griswold's "Memoir," p. xxvii, in his edition of Poe's *Works*. Contrary to popular belief, it does not seem to be a confused account of Poe's earlier enlistment of 1827–28. The author of the "Memoir," who tended to present Poe in the worst light, says, "He was recognized by officers who had known him at West Point, and efforts were made privately . . . to obtain for him a commission, when it was discovered . . . he had deserted." The presence of a former cadet in the ranks was socially embarrassing to officers; the "private efforts" may be suspected (if the story has a factual basis) to have been contributions for the sum needed to obtain his "release by purchase."

[6] The stories are synoptically discussed by Edward Wagenknecht, *Edgar Allan Poe: The Man behind the Legend* (1963), pp. 22–23. A manuscript ascribed to

ANNALS

1833–1838

[1833] In 1833, Poe had completed eleven "Tales of the Folio Club." They were, as a careful reading of the introduction Poe wrote for them shows, literary exercises in the style of popular authors of the day. In addition to the five stories published in the *Saturday Courier*, they were "Lionizing," "The Visionary" (now called "The Assignation"), "Shadow," "Epimanes" (now called "Four Beasts in One"), "Silence" and "MS. Found in a Bottle." They are almost wholly literary or impersonal in that the author used little of himself or people he knew in them. The stories include some masterpieces, but the volume planned was never published. Poe submitted several of the stories in a contest held by the Baltimore *Saturday Visiter*, and his "MS. Found in a Bottle" won the first prize of fifty dollars.[1] His poem "The Coliseum," submitted at the same time, was placed second to one by "Henry Wilton," who turned out to be John H. Hewitt, who had succeeded Wilmer as editor of the *Visiter*.

Poe's story received some national attention, and the author came to the notice of the judges, Dr. James H. Miller, John H. B. Latrobe (who later gave highly inaccurate reminiscences), and John Pendleton Kennedy, who became a good friend to Poe. Late in the year Poe sold "The Visionary" to the *Lady's Book*, where it appeared, unsigned, in the number for January 1834. This was his first story to appear in a magazine of really wide circulation; the editor was Louis A. Godey, who later gave his name to that well-remembered periodical. Poe did not contribute to it again for about a decade.

In this year Poe was living with his grandmother, his aunt Mrs. Clemm, and his young cousin Virginia, in Amity Street.

[1834] Early in 1834 Poe made a visit to Richmond and called at the home of John Allan, who was extremely ill. Allan's second wife, the former Louisa Gabriella Patterson (whom he had married on October 5, 1830), said her husband was not well enough to receive him, and Allan himself shook his cane at Poe and ordered him to leave.[2] On March 27, 1834, John Allan died; he mentioned in his will his legitimate and illegitimate children, but not Edgar Allan Poe.

Alexandre Dumas is obviously fiction — it has Poe meeting Dumas in Paris through "une recommendation de . . . Fenimore Cooper." See the Ingram List, no. 215, for adventures in a foreign port recounted when Poe was delirious. That he sailed to Wexford in Ireland and came right back is so unromantic one might believe it, but it is a sailor's yarn of one James Tuhey, told to F. W. Thomas, according to Whitty's "Memoir," p. xxxiv.

[1] Rumors that Poe was the sole contestant are baseless. Timothy Shea Arthur is quoted in the Philadelphia *Saturday Museum*, March 4, 1843, as saying he had entered a story. For further details of the contest, see commentary on "The Coliseum."

[2] Thomas H. Ellis, quoted by Quinn, p. 205. See also the Ingram List, no. 222. Mrs. Allan apparently avoided later contact with Poe, but she is said to have sent his bride a reassuring letter blaming herself for the complete break between Allan and the poet. See the Ingram List, no. 210. The actual letter was undoubtedly among those unwisely destroyed by Mrs. Clemm.

Poe continued during 1834 to reside in Baltimore at the house on Amity Street. It is said that at this time Virginia Clemm used to carry messages from Poe to a girl named Mary Starr, with whom the poet was — or fancied himself — in love. In 1834 or early 1835, Poe was visited by Mary Winfree of Chesterfield, Virginia, to whom he first addressed the little poem of compliment he later addressed to several other ladies; in the present volume it is called "To Frances." [3]

The fiction Poe composed at this period is decidedly somber. "Berenicë" and "King Pest" are both in part inspired by unpleasant true stories; in "Morella" he returned to pure "Gothick" romance.

[1835] Early in 1835, Poe began to write his never-completed blank-verse tragedy *Politian*. He seems to have had some connection with the Baltimore *American*. Probably through John P. Kennedy he was put in touch with Thomas W. White, who, late in 1834, had begun to publish the *Southern Literary Messenger* at Richmond. [4] In the number for March there appeared Poe's grim story "Berenicë," and about this time he began to write book reviews for the magazine. He rivaled the severity of the British reviewers and became involved in a number of controversies. He sent the *Messenger* his fine tale of supernatural horror "Morella," and the poor grotesque "King Pest," and wrote especially for it "Hans Pfaal." On July 7 his grandmother died.

By August 18, Poe was in Richmond. It is reported that he drank too much at times and had fits of despondency. [5] He met the publisher's eighteen-year-old daughter, Eliza White (called "Lizzie"), and in the September *Messenger* published, addressed to "Eliza" the complimentary little poem originally written for his cousin Elizabeth Rebecca Herring and later addressed to Frances Sargent Osgood. It seems to me certain that Mrs. Clemm decided to "save" her nephew from Lizzie. [6] Neilson Poe had a plan to take Virginia into his home and to educate her. Poe's aunt wrote the poet a letter, which does not survive, apparently mentioning Neilson's plan, and Poe wrote a reply on August 29, 1835, asking Virginia's hand in marriage. The letter seems to me somewhat hysterical and concludes with a *postscript* addressed to the bride-to-be!

[3] See comments on the lost poem "To Mary [Starr]," and "To Frances."

[4] White conducted the magazine until his death on January 19, 1843. His middle name is given variously as Willis, Willys, and Wyllis; no full signature is known. White was somewhat secretive about his editors. The first was James Ewell Heath; the second was Edward Vernon Sparhawk, who, White said, began with the ninth number and "retired with the eleventh" (May to July 1835). There is evidence that Lucian Minor always assisted White behind the scenes, and so did Heath. The magazine did not always come out on time, and there were no issues dated October or November 1835 or December 1836.

[5] See the extracts from White's letters to Lucian Minor, in Whitty's *Complete Poems* (1911), pp. 178–179. The letters were owned by Oliver Barrett of Chicago. I have never seen the manuscripts but am confident of their authenticity.

[6] Mrs. Weiss, *Home Life of Poe*, p. 78, thought that there was an engagement; see also the Ingram List, numbers 196, 214, and 223. Elizabeth Oakes Smith is the authority for record about Maria Clemm's notions that Lizzie White was capricious and used morphine. Mrs. Whitman doubted the truth of the second idea, as do I.

ANNALS

On September 22, Poe was back in Baltimore, where he took out a marriage license for Virginia and himself. I am convinced that they were privately married by the Reverend John Owen of the First Presbyterian Church.[7] Virginia was barely thirteen. She and her mother soon went to Richmond, and in October were residing with Edgar at the boarding house of Mrs. James Yarrington on the corner of Bank and Eleventh Streets.[8] There was some talk of Mrs. Clemm opening a boarding house, but it came to nothing. In the issue of the *Messenger* for December 1835, which began volume 2, Poe was announced (without name) as assisting White.

[1836] Poe was editor of the *Southern Literary Messenger* throughout 1836, contributing chiefly reviews. Of the reviews that appeared, he wrote not quite all, though he "assumed responsibility" for all of them.[9] These reviews included two praising the early work of Dickens, one of Joseph Rodman Drake and Fitz-Greene Halleck, and a good many attacks on authors who would be wholly forgotten had not Poe disliked their work and said so with biting sarcasm. It is regrettable that these diatribes and a great deal of purely routine reviewing kept Poe too busy for his own imaginative work. He composed no tales during the year 1836, although he did publish a few of those previously written, including the wonderful prose poem "Shadow." His first series on "Autography" — less studies of handwriting than criticisms *in petto* — and the analysis of "Maelzel's Automatic Chess Player" appeared during the year. Two significant poems were written before it ended: "Bridal Ballad" and "To Zante."

On May 16, 1836, Poe and Virginia were publicly married by the Reverend Amasa Converse, editor of the *Southern Religious Telegraph*. The young couple went on a brief honeymoon to Petersburg, Virginia. There they visited Hiram Haines, proprietor of the local Democratic *Constellation*, and Dr. W. M. Robinson. Virginia was not yet fourteen, and the marriage

[7] The evidence is somewhat incomplete but to me seems conclusive. Eugene L. Didier, in *Life and Poems* (1877), p. 58, mentioned the marriage as on "September 2d" — an easy slip for "22d" — and Woodberry, *Life* (1909), I, 143, shrewdly pointed out that this allusion was made *before* the existence of the marriage license had been discovered, that return of the license was not obligatory, and that there are other incomplete records for this time. Didier had interviewed, and seems to have followed, Mrs. Clemm, who gave him the names of an impossible minister (one who became a bishop) and the wrong church, but she was capable of flourishes like these. My friend Robert Hunter Paterson tells me he has himself investigated the problems. John Owen had conducted the funeral of Poe's grandmother. He was a supply preacher and did not have access to the records of the church, for the regular minister, who preceded him, had died of an epidemic disease and the volume had been temporarily placed "in quarantine." Later, Owen's successor filled in *one* marriage entry; the proper pages are otherwise blank. This fact was unknown to previous students, who used a typescript made by the late L. H. Dielman. Quinn, p. 227, ignored Woodberry's subtle analysis.

[8] See Phillips, I, 515.

[9] The article defending "Slavery" (so headed), though reprinted by Harrison as Poe's, is the work of Judge Beverley Tucker. Lucian Minor wrote at least one review. Poe's salary was now $520 a year, with some pay for extra work; in a letter of January 22, he estimated his income at $800.

was frowned upon in Richmond by some of the ladies; but T. W. White and his daughter Lizzie are said to have attended the wedding.[10]

[1837] Poe's withdrawal from the *Southern Literary Messenger* was announced in the January number,[11] which contained two poems written in 1836, five book reviews including a long one of William Cullen Bryant's *Poems* and another of Washington Irving's *Astoria,* and the first installment of *The Narrative of Arthur Gordon Pym.* A second installment appeared in the February issue; thereafter Poe did not contribute anything to the magazine until after T. W. White's death in 1843.

The Poe family probably moved to New York in February. They there boarded at 113 1/2 Carmine Street with the eccentric and learned bookseller William Gowans, who has left reminiscences. From him Poe probably learned much — some facts and some legends. Poe attended a banquet at the City Hotel, 123 Broadway, tendered by the booksellers to the writers of the city on April 2, 1837, and met several distinguished guests: Irving, Bryant, Halleck, George P. Morris, and Noah Webster were present. He was also asked to be one of those who proposed toasts. Poe's, the only thing of the kind he is known ever to have composed, was:

> The monthlies of Gotham — their distinguished
> editors and their vigorous collaborators.[12]

To the June issue of the *American Monthly Magazine* (edited by Charles Fenno Hoffman), Poe contributed his story that was later called "Mystification." He also contributed to the *New-York Review* for October an unsigned review of John Lloyd Stephens' *Incidents of Travel in Egypt, Arabia Petraea, and the Holy Land* (New-York, 1837), in which there is a discussion, with which Professor Charles Anthon of Columbia College assisted, of the exact interpretation of a Hebrew text. Poe later used this material as if it were wholly his own, an act which has led to accusations of charlatanism. However, I am convinced that Poe knew a little Hebrew.

The winter of 1837–38 was severe in New York, and Poe at one time

---

[10] For some of these details see Allen, *Israfel* (1934), pp. 318–320. The marriage was announced in the Richmond *Enquirer* of May 20 and the *Whig* of the same date. The marriage bond is reproduced by Quinn, p. 253; in it a witness made affidavit that the bride was "of the full age of twenty-one years." But that is part of the printed form; no real deception was intended, and the signer probably was not even asked to read it. He was Thomas W. Cleland, said to have been the son-in-law of Mrs. Poore, at whose boarding house on Bank Street Poe had resided in 1835. She was presumably Mrs. Ann Poore, who died aged 68 on August 22, 1854, according to the records of Shockoe Hill Cemetery. See Phillips, I, 529f.

[11] White, in a notice "To the Patrons," dated January 26, said: "Mr. Poe, who has filled the editorial department for the last twelve months . . . retired . . . on the 3rd inst.; and the entire management of the work again devolves upon myself alone."

[12] My attention was called to this toast by Nelson Adkins. See William L. Keese, *John Keese, Wit and Litterateur* (1883; 2nd ed., 1884), p. 25. Keese was toastmaster at the banquet. Poe's words are quoted in the New York *American,* in the *Evening Post,* and in the *Commercial Advertiser,* all of April 3, 1837. The word "collaborators" was often used at the time for "contributors."

dropped in at the famous old Northern Dispensary at Christopher Street and Waverly Place in Greenwich Village and asked for medicine for a cold.[13] He renewed Baltimore contacts and contributed his fine prose poem "Siope" (now called "Silence") to *The Baltimore Book* for 1838.

[1838] Obscurity covers some of the year 1838 in Poe's life. His book, *The Narrative of Arthur Gordon Pym*, was published in July by Harpers. Some copies were sent to England, where the book was at once pirated; it sold better there than in America. Poe himself did not think highly of this work; its chief importance may be that it is supposed to have inspired to some extent Melville's *Moby-Dick*.

In this year Poe moved his family to Philadelphia. On July 19, 1838, he wrote from there to James K. Paulding, then Secretary of the Navy, vainly begging for any kind of clerkship "by land or sea." It was presumably at about this time that he said "he could not possibly live by literary labor" and "actually endeavored to acquire the art of lithography" under the tuition of Peter S. Duval.[14] It may be also that he worked for a time in a Philadelphia printing house with James Pedder, an Englishman. Pedder and his daughters Anna and Bessie became intimates of the Poes and Mrs. Clemm, who were for a while in very great need. Bessie reported that the poet's family lived on bread and molasses for weeks together, that Poe's gratitude toward the Pedder sisters was almost unbounded. At weekly meetings of the Needlewoman's Friend Society, of which Anna was secretary, Poe sometimes gave readings from his poems. James Pedder remarked long afterward that he had known Poe "too well" and had thought him "the most gentlemanly young man he ever saw" but so temperamental that he feared Poe might end his days in a madhouse.[15]

In any case, Poe's retirement from professional writing was brief, for a

[13] Phillips, I, 556–557. The superintendent, N. D. Luks, wrote me on September 23, 1920, confirming the recollections of a trustee, John R. Voorhis. The books were destroyed about 1890.

[14] Lambert A. Wilmer, "Recollections," reprinted in my edition of his *Merlin* (1941), p. 33. For a categorical denial by Duval in 1844 see Woodberry's *Edgar Allan Poe* (1885), p. 143. Duval is not directly quoted, and his original statement has not been found among Woodberry's papers at Harvard or Columbia. *The Conchologist's First Book* (see below) caused a scandal, and Duval may have remembered badly what he might have been glad to forget. I regard Wilmer as a more reliable witness than Duval.

[15] The period of the Poes' great destitution in Philadelphia can have been only in 1838, early 1839, or late 1840. I take much of my discussion from Dr. A. S. W. Rosenbach's note describing a copy, specially bound in one volume, of Poe's *Tales of the Grotesque and Arabesque*, marked "For Miss Anna and Miss Bessie Pedder, from their most sincere friend, the Author" (*A Catalogue of the Books and Manuscripts of Harry Elkins Widener* [1918], p. 56). Dr. Rosenbach seems to have drawn his information from either a letter or a clipping of an article written by Pedder at his home in Roxbury, Massachusetts, in 1852; neither, unhappily, now accompanies Poe's book, which is in the Widener Collection at Harvard. Rosenbach places Pedder's arrival in America "after 1840," during that year Pedder was editing the Philadelphia *Farmer's Cabinet*. This slight inaccuracy does not invalidate the other information in the catalogue.

poem in the *Saturday Evening Post,* August 11, 1838, addressed to Poe by "Horace in Philadelphia," his old friend Lambert A. Wilmer, welcomed him back to the field of letters.[16] And in the first number, that for September 1838, of a new Baltimore magazine, the *American Museum,* run by Poe's friends Nathan Covington Brooks and Dr. Joseph Evans Snodgrass, appeared the story "Ligeia," which Poe sometimes called his finest. It was followed in November by the pieces that were later called "How to Write a Blackwood Article" and "A Predicament."

On September 4, Poe wrote N. C. Brooks that he was just "leaving Arch Street for a small house" — presumably that at Sixteenth and Locust Streets. During the summer he may have made a walking tour in rural Pennsylvania.[17]

1839–1842

[1839] Early in 1839, Poe was associated with Peter S. Duval and Professor Thomas Wyatt, author of *A Manual of Conchology* (New York: Harpers, 1838), in producing *The Conchologist's First Book.* Poe was paid fifty dollars to permit his name to appear as its author.[1] The work, priced at a dollar and seventy-five cents, was issued before April 20, 1839; a second revised edition (dated 1840) in September, and a third (without any author's name) in 1845. Poe worked in like fashion on *A Synopsis of Natural History,* but this was signed by Wyatt; it came out in June 1839.

Meanwhile, to the *American Museum* for April Poe sent "The Haunted Palace," his only important poem of this period, and to the Philadelphia *Saturday Chronicle* of May 18, a story, "The Devil in the Belfry." He also wrote two unsigned reviews for the Pittsburgh *Literary Examiner,* edited by E. Burke Fisher, who had been a contributor to the *Southern Literary Messenger.*

In May, Poe became coeditor with the proprietor of *Burton's Gentleman's Magazine.* The owner was a fine comedian, William E. Burton, who wrote rather well and was later a great collector of Shakespeareana. Since Burton's theatrical engagements often called him for long periods to New York and elsewhere. Poe wrote most of the book reviews from July 1839 to June 1840. He was also expected to furnish a signed original feature every month. Two

[16] See Carroll D. Laverty, "A Note on Poe in 1838," in *Modern Language Notes,* March 1949.

[17] In July 1838 Poe may have gone to Povalley (named for his relatives) in Mifflin County. The stories about what he did there (Phillips, I, 601f.) are obviously made up, but traditions about places are proverbially reliable, and the visit itself may be a fact.

[1] The book was largely based on French sources and was really the work of Wyatt, who had assistance on lists of species from Isaac Lea, the well-known publisher. Poe revised the introduction and acted as textual editor. Without giving credit, Wyatt and Duval copied the dozen pages, "Explanation of the Parts of Shells," and four accompanying plates from a book by Captain Thomas Brown, *The Conchologist's Text-Book* (Glasgow, 1833, often reprinted). This borrowing was discovered in 1846 and led to a charge of plagiarism against the whole book — a charge that has been constantly repeated, even as recently as 1960, although the works are in general utterly dissimilar.

of these were the tales "The Fall of the House of Usher" (September) and "William Wilson" (October). Burton was associated from December 1839 to May 1840 with a newspaper called *Alexander's Weekly Messenger*, for which during those months Poe wrote a good deal, including his first series of solutions of cryptograms. In it he also published "Instinct vs Reason," an account of his sagacious pet, the remote inspiration of his tale "The Black Cat." Poe's "Sonnet — Silence" was sent off for the first number of the year 1840 of the *Saturday Courier*, which had contributions from almost every member of the Philadelphia *corps éditorial*. Late in 1839, the firm of Lea and Blanchard brought out his collected *Tales of the Grotesque and Arabesque* in two volumes, dated 1840. The work was dedicated to Colonel William Drayton, his old commander in the Army, who possibly backed the venture financially. Only 750 copies were issued; it received very few reviews and sold very slowly, although Sarah Josepha Hale noticed it favorably in *Godey's Lady's Book* for January 1840.

Poe was much in company at this time with James Pedder and with Henry B. Hirst, a poet who kept a bird store and owned a raven. Hirst was later a lawyer, an editor, and, finally, a harmless madman.[2] In 1839 Poe also met Thomas Dunn English, a young physician.

[1840] In 1840, besides many reviews, Poe contributed an anonymous serial, "The Journal of Julius Rodman," to *Burton's*. Late in May he drank too much, and was discharged after a quarrel with his employer, although I believe that later the two men became friends again.[3] In September we find Poe attempting to find a position in Richmond for C. Auguste Dubouchet — from whom came the unusual given names of our author's famous detective, C. August Dupin.[4]

About November, Burton sold his magazine to George Rex Graham, who united it with his *Casket* to form *Graham's Magazine*. To the new magazine's first number (for December) Poe contributed a fine tale, "The Man of the Crowd," in the manner of some of the *Sketches by Boz* of the youthful Dickens, who described in that series the less savory districts of London.

[1841] That Burton recommended Poe to Graham is a tradition in accord with what we know of the actor's good nature. On February 20, 1841, the Philadelphia *Saturday Evening Post* announced Poe as one of the editors

[2] Hirst was rather wild, drank absinthe, and got into fights about women. He seems, however, to have had no bad influence on Poe.

[3] Of Poe's unfortunate conduct when not sober we naturally know more from his foes than his friends, but that he was often difficult for both is unquestionable. The quarrel with Burton had something to do with Poe's plans for a magazine of his own. The story (usually rejected) told by R. W. Griswold, "Memoir," p. xxxiii, although probably overcolored, does not seem to me to be baseless, for it describes the kind of thing Poe did. According to Griswold, Burton, finding his editor inebriated, reproached him, and Poe replied, "Burton, I am the editor of the *Penn Magazine* — and you are a fool." In the New York *Independent* of October 22, 1896, Thomas Dunn English told of another incident of this period. English found Poe "struggling to raise himself from the gutter . . ." He continues, "I volunteered to see him home . . . I knocked at the door, and Mrs. Clemm opened it . . . she cried, 'You make Eddie drunk, and then you bring him home.'"

[4] See W. T. Bandy in *PMLA*, September 1964.

of *Graham's*, and the April number (published about March 15) contained some reviews by Poe. As with *Burton's*, Poe was expected to contribute a feature every month. In April the feature was "The Murders in the Rue Morgue," which, if not actually the first detective story every written, is the first consciously composed as such and the direct ancestor of all that have come after it. Later in *Graham's* came "A Descent into the Maelstrom" (May) and "The Island of the Fay" (June), a charming fantasy written to accompany a picture engraved by John Sartain after a painting by the once famous artist John Martin. In the June number of *Graham's* there was a fashion plate which some have supposed to represent Mrs. Clemm, Edgar and Virginia Poe, and Henry B. Hirst. Poe began in the August number a new series on secret writing, and in that for November, another series on Autography.

In this year Poe wrote for other periodicals, too. He demonstrated his analytic powers not only in his articles on secret writing, but also (in the *Saturday Evening Post* of May 1) by forecasting from the first few chapters the outcome of *Barnaby Rudge*. In the same periodical, in the issue of November 27, there appeared the first form of "Three Sundays in a Week," Poe's only simple love story. In it the hero wins the hand of his cousin, aged fifteen — surely a touch of autobiography. There is a little of the author's personality, too, in another piece from this time — the lovely and gentle, though enigmatic, fantasy "Eleonora," which concerns the love of two wedded cousins whose mutual happiness ends with the lady's death. This, however, is much less autobiographical than some critics have supposed, for it appeared in *The Gift for 1842*, an annual that was in print in the autumn of 1841, some months prior to the first known serious illness of Virginia Poe.

In the spring of 1841 Poe met Rufus Wilmot Griswold, who was preparing the first edition of his *Poets and Poetry of America*. To him Poe sent a highly inaccurate account of his life and some of his poems, three of which were chosen for the anthology that appeared the next year.[5]

[1842] In January 1842 Virginia Poe burst a blood vessel while singing, and her life was despaired of. She was never again in good health for long, although she lived for five more years. The poet himself had a brief illness and when he returned to his office found that Charles J. Peterson, Graham's other editor, had taken over. This so upset Poe that he quit at once,[6] ceasing

---

[5] A complete account of Griswold's career, which was one of amazing industry, would require a far larger work than the only biography, *Rufus Wilmot Griswold* (Nashville, 1943), by Joy Bayless. Griswold, often called "Reverend," was licensed to preach and delivered a few sermons but was not a pastor. He was the literary executor of Frances Sargent Osgood as well as of Poe. Although his tampering with the texts of Poe's letters cannot be excused, he did so many fine things — helping young authors such as Charles Godfrey Leland and rescuing from dispersal the famous Abbott Collection of Egyptian antiquities (now in the Brooklyn Museum) — that he must not be regarded as the complete villain some of Poe's later biographers have thought him.

[6] See John Sartain, *Reminiscences of a Very Old Man* (1899), p. 200. Many biographers have mistakenly supposed that Poe's immediate quarrel was with R. W. Griswold.

with the May number to be a regular editor. Griswold, whose *Poets and Poetry of America* [7] had just appeared, was called in to succeed Poe.

In March, Poe met Dickens in Philadelphia. The novelist had been impressed by Poe's analysis of *Barnaby Rudge*, but the acquaintance, from which Poe hoped much, resulted in no benefits for the poet. More pleasant was a visit from his friend F. W. Thomas. Poe also began in this year to correspond with James Russell Lowell and Thomas Holley Chivers. Poe's attempts to obtain a job in the Customs House at Philadelphia were frustrated by the "regular" politicians.

During the year Poe published important reviews, marred by charges of plagiarism but generally discerning, of Longfellow and Hawthorne. His new stories were: "Life in Death" (the first version of "The Oval Portrait"); "The Masque of the Red Death"; and "The Pit and the Pendulum." Inspired by the horticultural planning of A. J. Downing, Poe wrote a happy sketch of pure beauty, "The Landscape Garden," by which he set great store. He also composed "The Mystery of Marie Rogêt," a long study of the mysterious death of a cigar girl, Mary Rogers, in New York in the previous year. It was finished by June 4. In June, Poe went to New York on a business trip, which worried his wife; nothing else about it is surely known. Two more stories were written, though not printed, in 1842. One was "The Black Cat"; the other was "The Gold-Bug," which was designed originally for serial publication. In this year also he put together a new and enlarged collection of his short stories — PHANTASY-PIECES — but did not succeed in having it published.

His only verse appearing in 1842, not published until about December, was "The Conqueror Worm."

1843–1844

[1843] Late in 1842, Poe had been in touch with James Russell Lowell, who began to issue his magazine, *The Pioneer*, at Boston in January 1843. To it Poe contributed "Lenore" and "The Tell-Tale Heart," a tale of crime and retribution. In the third and last issue of *The Pioneer*, he published his "Notes Upon English Verse." He continued to write for Graham, with whom he did not quarrel even though some of his friends did so.

By now Poe had formed a partnership with Thomas Cottrell Clarke to publish Poe's long-projected magazine, now named THE STYLUS, which was to

[7] Poe reviewed the book very briefly in *Graham's* for June and at greater length in the *Boston Miscellany* for November. Griswold arranged for the second review and paid for it in advance. From Poe's letters we know that he thought (perhaps rightly) that Griswold meant to pay him for a "puff," that he thought it a great joke to review the book without special consideration, and that he wondered if his critique would appear. However, some biographers have misunderstood the affair. Griswold did have the review printed, and collected it in Poe's *Works* (1850), although he was disappointed, as a letter (which I have read in manuscript) to J. T. Fields of August 12, 1842, shows. Poe's joke was a mild one; his review was decidedly favorable but concluded with praise of Griswold's "taste, talent, *and* tact." The italics are Poe's and his "victim" cannot have missed the *double entendre*, although few readers of the time probably saw the point.

be illustrated by Felix O. C. Darley. Clarke published a weekly paper, the *Saturday Museum*, in Philadelphia; Poe was announced as an editor but denied that he was a member of the staff although he wrote for the paper regularly. Its columns for March 4, 1843, contain the earliest printed biography of Poe and reprints of most of his shorter poems. The life is full of inaccuracies and fictions undoubtedly emanating from Poe himself.[1] In this month Poe went off to Washington, seeking a government job and subscriptions to THE STYLUS. There he went on a spree, called on President Tyler with his cloak inside out, and got into a quarrel with Thomas Dunn English. Poe returned to Philadelphia jobless and penniless after a few days. Publication of THE STYLUS was again "postponed"; it never did appear, although Poe took subscriptions for it until the end of his life.

"The Gold-Bug," written in 1842, was submitted in a contest of the *Dollar Newspaper*, and won a prize of one hundred dollars. Published in the issues of June 21 and June 28, it was widely reprinted. It was Poe's first really national success. William H. Graham commenced "publication in parts" (at 12 1/2 cents each) of *The Prose Romances of Edgar A. Poe*; the first part, containing "The Murders in the Rue Morgue" and "The Man That Was Used Up," was on sale on July 22, but no second part was ever published. During the summer, Poe may have visited Barhyte's Trout Pond at Saratoga Springs, where he is said to have discussed with Mrs. John Barhyte a plan of "The Raven."[2] At some time in 1843, Poe visited New York City, where on March 11 he published pseudonymously in Park Benjamin's weekly, *The New World*, a bitter attack on "The Magazines."

On July 19, 1843, Poe registered in the District Court of Philadelphia to study law in the office of his friend Henry B. Hirst.[3] That Poe read much law beyond a chapter or two of Blackstone may be doubted. To *The Opal* for 1844 he contributed, to accompany a plate, his charming sketch, "The Elk," based apparently on what he saw when he visited the falls of the Wissahickon near Philadelphia. Poe and his family were then living at 2502

[1] The only surviving issues of the *Saturday Museum* during Poe's connection with it are those of February 4, March 4 and 18, April 1, and an undated "Extra No. 1." A letter of Poe's certainly implies that the biographical sketch, "by Henry B. Hirst," appeared a week before the date I give for it, but the possibility of an unexpected delay leads me to use only what information I can verify. Abridgements of the sketch were published in the *Boston Notion*, April 29, 1843, and the Baltimore *Saturday Visiter*, July 29, 1843. W. F. Gill (in his *Life of . . . Poe*, pp. 327–346) reprinted from a clipping from the *Saturday Museum* of January 28, 1843 (my date is from an advertisement in the Philadelphia *Public Ledger* of the day) a savage attack on Griswold's *Poets and Poetry of America* that has often been ascribed to Poe and is given as his in Harrison, *Works*, XI, 220. I am now satisfied that this is by Hirst, although it may include a few things Poe had said. A series of attacks on Griswold, Graham, and the latter's magazine in a periodical called *The Citizen Soldier* I am now sure is also not by Poe.

[2] For this and other traditions concerning "The Raven" see the commentary and notes on that poem.

[3] The relevant document has been seen in the present century, but is now said to be missing from the files. See Phillips, I, 838, for my record from the Philadelphia *Times*, July 20, 1901.

Coates Street (now Fairmount Avenue), on the outskirts of Philadelphia.[4] Poe's sister paid them a visit there.

On August 8 a dramatization by Silas S. Steele of Poe's "Gold-Bug" was performed on the last night of the season at the American Theatre in Walnut Street, Philadelphia — the only dramatization of a Poe story reported during his lifetime. And late in the year Poe began his career as a lecturer, delivering his "Poetry of America" in Philadelphia on November 21, 1843. He repeated this lecture in Wilmington, Delaware, on November 28, and at Newark in the same state on December 23.

[1844] In 1844, Poe published only one poem, "Dream-Land," but was busily composing short stories, of which several are important: "A Tale of the Ragged Mountains," "The Purloined Letter," "Thou Art the Man," "Mesmeric Revelation," "The Premature Burial," and "The Oblong Box."

On January 31 Poe gave his lecture on American poetry at Baltimore, and on March 13 at Reading, Pennsylvania.

Thomas Dunn English said that at this time Poe got into a scrape in Philadelphia, but never revealed its nature.[5] On April 6, Poe and his wife moved to New York.[6] They were soon followed by Mrs. Clemm and Catterina (or Kate), the cat, but not before Poe's mother-in-law had sold to Leary's bookstore, among Poe's own books, some copies of the *Southern Literary Messenger* belonging to William J. Duane — a mistake that later greatly embarrassed Poe.

In New York, Poe sold his "Balloon Hoax" for publication in *The Extra Sun* of April 13. It was reprinted the next day in the *Sunday Times*, edited by Major Mordecai M. Noah. This suggests that Poe had already joined Noah as subeditor. What Poe wrote for the *Sunday Times* is conjectural since no specimens of the paper for the proper period, save a fragment of the issue of April 14, 1844, are now known.

Poe also arranged to send a series of seven newsletters to Eli Bowen, an editor of *The Spy* of Columbia, Pennsylvania, between May 14 and June 25, 1844. They were collected in book form in 1929 as *Doings of Gotham*.

Poe left Noah to join the staff of the new *Evening Mirror* of George P. Morris and Nathaniel P. Willis, a daily "for the upper ten thousand," begun on October 7.[7] Poe wrote for it from the first. His work was that of a

[4] Poe moved several times in Philadelphia, on dates now uncertain — see Quinn, pp. 274, 361, 384f. His home at 234 (now 530) North Seventh Street was still standing in 1965.

[5] See the New York *Independent*, October 22, 1896. A suggestion that it concerned Mrs. Barhyte is absurd; she had no connection with Philadelphia.

[6] Poe first boarded with a Mrs. Morrison, 130 Greenwich Street, then with a Mrs. Foster at 4 Ann Street. While in lower Manhattan, Poe moved often.

[7] What are certainly Noah's reminiscences are quoted in "The Late N. P. Willis," an unsigned article in the *Northern Monthly* for January 1868, published at Newark, New Jersey. This article also quotes from one by Willis (which I find in the New York *Home Journal*, October 30, 1858) mentioning that neither he nor Morris knew Poe well when they engaged him. Poe got on well with the kindly Noah, and they remained friends for life. Noah said that Poe worked for him before joining Willis in October. Noah also said he printed a biographical sketch of Poe with a woodcut after a daguerreotype.

"mechanical paragraphist," or perhaps we may say subeditor, for he used the editorial "we." His contributions, when identifiable, were of slight importance during the first few months.

In 1844, Poe sometimes visited the tea store of Gabriel Harrison, from whom several literary men, including Halleck and Morris, bought tobacco. Harrison became Poe's friend, and for his political club Poe composed a marching song (p. 340, above) — whether in favor of Polk or Clay is not recorded. Poe's letters of this time reveal annoyance at finding Dr. English editing the New York *Aurora*, of which no issues of the proper period are known.

Perhaps the most amusing of Poe's satires (if the background is understood), "The Literary Life of Thingum Bob," appeared in the *Southern Literary Messenger* of December. The article made so much fun of Graham and other veteran magazine editors that Poe sent it for publication to a newcomer in the field, Benjamin Blake Minor, who had taken over the *Messenger* after Thomas W. White died. For *Graham's* Poe wrote a long appreciation — far too enthusiastic — of R. H. Horne's epic, *Orion*. Great hopes of this man's help in England proved vain. Poe also reviewed the poetry of J. R. Lowell appreciatively.

Before the end of the year, Poe had moved with his family to the farmhouse of Patrick Henry Brennan near what is now 84th Street and Broadway and not far from the big rock near the Hudson known as Mount Tom, where Poe and Virginia liked to sit and gaze on the river. Mr. Brennan was a man of culture; Mrs. Brennan, who did not usually take boarders, consented to have the poet stay with them, largely for the charm of his conversation. It is almost certain that "The Raven" was finally prepared for publication here.[8] Poe first offered the poem to Graham, who rejected it, but it was soon afterward accepted by George Hooker Colton (a friend of Lowell) for a new magazine in New York, *The American Review: A Whig Journal*. Poe and Colton remained good friends until the latter's untimely death on December 1, 1847.[9]

1845

[1845] Poe's *annus mirabilis* was 1845. About January 15, the February issue of *Graham's Magazine* came out with a sketch of his life by James Russell Lowell. On January 29, the *Evening Mirror* appeared with "The

[8] See commentary and notes on "The Raven." The Brennans never saw Poe under the influence of liquor. He from time to time made himself useful to the household, taking Thomas Brennan, a small son, to the shore of the Hudson River and drawing pictures in the sand. There is an anecdote (hitherto unprinted) from a descendant, Mary A. Farley, that his landlady once asked Poe to show himself at the door to scare off a chicken thief, which the poet refused to do. This fits in with Poe's remark that a brave man may sometimes choose "to seem or to be a coward," for which see "Marginalia," no. 184.

[9] Careless biographers' references to a quarrel between Poe and G. H. Colton are baseless. It was Walter Colton who disliked Poe; see *Passages from the Correspondence and Other Papers of Rufus Wilmot Griswold* (1898), edited by W. M. Griswold, p. 262.

Raven," copied from advance sheets printed for the February issue of Colton's magazine, *The American Review,* and preceded by an enthusiastic introductory note by Willis, in which the author's name was revealed.[1] Success was immediate; the poem was copied, parodied, recopied, and even anthologized in a schoolbook within a few weeks. Poe gave his lecture on the "Poets of America" at the New York Society Library at 348 Broadway on the last evening of February.[2] In this lecture, he praised the poems of Frances Sargent Osgood. She did not attend, but soon managed to meet him.[3] A romantic friendship resulted, furthered by the exchange of a number of poems. Frances Osgood wrote good verses, had great charm, and was probably a good influence on Poe — at any rate, Poe's wife thought so.[4]

[1] My statement is correct that the *first publication* was in the daily newspaper, the *Evening Mirror* of January 29, of which all known copies are now publicly owned, to the sorrow of private collectors.

[2] See the *New-York Tribune* for March 1, 1845, and the *Evening Mirror* of the same date; about three hundred persons were present. The New York Society Library was located (from 1840 to 1853) in its own building at the corner of Broadway and Leonard Street. The institution, chartered in 1754, has always been distinct from the New-York Historical Society, founded in 1804, which was in Poe's day housed in "the building of the University" on Washington Square. These institutions, which still flourish in new homes, are often confused by writers on Poe.

[3] On March 1, William M. Gillespie, then connected with a New York paper and soon to become a professor at Union College, wrote to Poe hinting that the lady would like to meet him. Mrs. Osgood later said that Poe had sought to meet her, and that N. P. Willis had introduced them at the Astor House.

[4] Frances Sargent Locke was born in Boston on June 18, 1811, but passed most of her childhood in Hingham, Massachusetts. At an early age she began to write verses for Lydia Maria Child's *Juvenile Miscellany.* She had too much facility for greatness, but wrote pleasantly always. In 1834 she met and soon after married the painter Samuel Stillman Osgood, and went to London with him. There she became a friend of the Honorable Mrs. Norton, one of the lovely granddaughters of Richard Brinsley Sheridan, and in 1838 published *A Wreath of Wild Flowers from New England.* The Osgoods returned to Boston in 1840 and settled soon after in New York. Mrs. Osgood was recognized as a leading contributor to *Graham's* and wrote for many other magazines; her contributions were often tales, into which she introduced poetry.

In 1844 I judge that there was a rift with her husband because of another woman. (Osgood's flirtation in 1842 with Elizabeth Newcomb, sister of Emerson's friend Charles King Newcomb, caused much gossip, Ellen B. Ballou informs me.) Fanny Osgood often used herself for copy, and she published a poem in the *Evening Mirror,* December 10, 1844, without title but with a foreword, probably by N. P. Willis: "The following heartfelt and womanly farewell to a faithless lover, is from the pen of Mrs. Frances Sargent Osgood — a true poet." The poem begins, "Yes, lower to the level / Of those who love thee now!" and the lover is reproached for pining " 'mid passion's madness" but is assured that he may yet return, if he will. It is clearly the errant husband who is addressed. (This poem is quoted in a review by Poe in the *Broadway Journal,* December 13, 1845, and may also be seen in Mrs. Osgood's *Poems* of 1849, p. 461.)

She met Poe in the early part of 1845 and proceeded to flirt with him, with R. W. Griswold, and with Edward J. Thomas, a merchant. She had a habit, mentioned by Thomas Dunn English, of sitting at gentlemen's feet at parties and look-

1845

Lowell had put Poe in touch with Charles F. Briggs, editor of a new literary weekly, *The Broadway Journal*, founded in January 1845, and Poe wrote for it from the first. In the issue of March 8, he was announced as coeditor with Briggs and Henry C. Watson, a music critic. In the paper Poe reprinted many of his poems and stories "to fill," but most of his original work was reviewing. A long study of Elizabeth Barrett, later Mrs. Browning, was an important contribution. More notorious is a series of five articles on the "plagiarisms" of Longfellow. (Willis said Poe believed that "Longfellow is asleep on velvet; it will do him good to rouse him. His friends will come out and fight his battle." [5]) It was a regrettable business, however, and I do not think it even increased the paper's circulation.

---

ing up at them; but despite this pretense of docility she seems to have been a woman of strong mind. She was certainly the most gifted and charming of the ladies among Poe's Literati of New York. She gave Poe intellectual companionship, and Virginia Poe encouraged the friendship, presumably deciding that it was better to have her husband charmed by a lady whom almost everybody, herself included, liked than by someone such as the malicious Mrs. Elizabeth F. Ellet. Few people, however, understood the situation, and Poe was widely criticized for "deserting a dying wife" for a playful poetess, and gossip led to quarrels and scandals of a most unfortunate kind.

The affair was certainly the most serious in Poe's life. Poe did not see Mrs. Osgood after 1847, but always referred to her with kindness. It appears that ultimately she was completely reconciled to her husband, as is suggested by a poem (collected in her *Poems* of 1849) "To S. S. Osgood," signed "F. S. O.," which appeared in the New York *Literary World*, October 23, 1847. Samuel Osgood went to California in February 1849 and prospered, and he returned some time before Mrs. Osgood's death at their home in New York on May 12, 1850.

It should be plainly said that Poe broke up no home, but was used by a clever woman as part of a successful campaign to win back an errant husband. If Poe and Mrs. Osgood were in love — and Poe did use the word "amour" to his friend Chivers — the matter was something to which neither Mrs. Osgood's husband nor Poe's wife objected. Samuel Osgood painted both his wife's portrait and that of Poe, and these were bequeathed by Griswold to the New-York Historical Society.

(The foregoing account is based on wide reading, for I have long believed it worthwhile to know more about this lady, for whom Poe felt a deep and lasting affection. See *Chivers' Life of Poe*, and my review of it in the *Quarterly* of the New-York Historical Society, October 1953. I have been aided by some personal letters of Ellen B. Ballou, who has been working at Brown University on a doctoral dissertation about Mrs. Osgood. Writing in the New York *Independent*, October 29, 1896, Thomas Dunn English said plainly that he told Mrs. Clemm, who "seemed rather unconvinced," she should tell Virginia Poe the "connection was purely Platonic, that Poe admired her [Mrs. Osgood's] ability and she admired him." But, English said, "The supposed intrigue became town talk." The paternity of Mrs. Osgood's third child, Fanny Fay, who was born about June 1846 and died on October 28, 1847, has been questioned — although perhaps not in print — but the date of the poem indicating complete reconciliation of the Osgoods — discovered by me only in the summer of 1962 — indicates that Samuel Osgood either believed himself the father or chose to accept that position.)

[5] See *The Prose Works of N. P. Willis* (1845), p. 768. That Poe himself wrote the defense of Longfellow signed "Outis" ("Nobody") published in the *Weekly Mirror*, March 8, 1845, is not certain; I incline to believe so.

ANNALS

Poe composed no important poems in 1845 but addressed a number of compliments in verse to Mrs. Osgood. New tales included "Some Words with a Mummy," "The 1002nd Tale of Scheherazade," "The Imp of the Perverse," and "The Facts in the Case of M. Valdemar."

Poe took an interest in the production of Mrs. Anna Cora Mowatt's comedy, *Fashion*, which opened at the Park Theater on March 25, and in a review on April 5 said that he attended every performance. In this year he for the first time entered largely into the society of literary pople. He met Miss Anne Charlotte Lynch, whose literary soirées at 116 Waverly Place in Greenwich Village were famous.[6] There, on July 19, he read "The Raven" at her request — in a very quiet way.[7] The charm and brilliance of his conversation are recorded, and his reticence, too. Few really came to know him, said Mary E. Hewitt, who mentioned rumors of his mesmeric powers — which he seems not to have denied in conversation, although he did, carefully, in print. To these salons came almost all the company we find mentioned in "The Literati of New York City," written the next year. There was a preponderance of female poets, but prominent men came, too, including Griswold, Halleck, Willis, George P. Morris, and the colorful Dr. John W. Francis, president of the Academy of Medicine.

The author of "The Raven" was asked by the Philomathean and Eucleian Societies of New York University to read a poem at commencement exercises on July 1, but he was unable to write a new poem and pleaded indisposition. The eccentric poet, Dr. Thomas Holley Chivers, who first met him about then, found him in bed but not sick.[8]

On July 10, Poe and Henry T. Tuckerman met to judge the poems of girls graduating from the Rutgers Female Institute. Poe read the winning poem the next evening at the commencement in the Rutgers Street Presbyterian Church, and in 1847 sent the winner, Louise Olivia Hunter, a valentine.

At the conclusion of the first volume of the *Broadway Journal*, Briggs sought to drop Poe and the publisher, John Bisco. But in the end Bisco won, and from July 12 the paper came out edited by Poe and Watson. Finally, Poe bought the *Broadway Journal*, and the issue of October 25 had "Edgar A. Poe, Editor and Proprietor" at the masthead. This achievement must have been a matter of great personal satisfaction to Poe, but he had been forced to borrow money from Halleck, Horace Greeley, and others including Thomas Dunn English and Griswold.

During the year a dozen of Poe's tales were selected by Evert A. Duyckinck, a new friend, and published by Wiley and Putnam in New York under the title *Tales*, about June 26. This volume was followed by *The Raven and Other Poems*, which appeared on November 19.

[6] Miss Lynch later married Professor Vincenzo Botta and continued to be a leading hostess throughout her life. Her *Memoirs* appeared in 1894. Some of my statements are based on quotations collected by Harrison, I, 241ff.

[7] The date comes from a newly found letter of July 17, from Miss Lynch to Poe, now in the Pierpont Morgan Library.

[8] See *New-York Tribune*, July 1, 2, 1845; *Chivers' Life of Poe*, p. 61; and Yale List, no. 59: "Engraved invitation . . . from the University of the City of New York for the Annual Oration and Annual Poem, before the Philomathean and Eucleian Societies on July 1, 1845."

Lowell was in New York and met Poe probably in May 1845, and neither was much pleased. Poe was, in Mrs. Clemm's words, "not himself." [9] But it was through Lowell's good offices that Poe was invited to deliver a poem before the Boston Lyceum on October 16 for a fee of fifty dollars. Unable to compose a new poem for the occasion, he read "Al Aaraaf," renamed "The Messenger Star of Tycho Brahe," before the Boston audience. Following a two-and-a-half-hour oration by Caleb Cushing, Poe discoursed for twenty minutes on the nature of poetry before delivering his poem. The reading was characterized by the Boston *Courier* of October 18 as "an elegant and classic production . . . containing the essence of *true* poetry, mingled with . . . a graceful delivery"; but "that it was not appreciated by the audience, was very evident, by their uneasiness and continual exits in numbers at a time." The Boston *Transcript* denounced the performance as a failure, and there were other unfavorable comments.[10] Poe retaliated by saying in the *Broadway Journal* that he had been drunk and had hoaxed his audience with a poem written when he was ten years old.[11] One statement is as reliable as the other: he did become inebriated after the reading. The whole affair was regrettable. There is a pleasanter side to the picture, however, far less well known. Thomas W. Higginson was present, and on several occasions described Poe's reading. He said, "I heard Poe read . . . in Boston in a voice whose singular music I have never heard equalled." [12]

During 1845, Poe was usually on good terms with Thomas Dunn English and contributed to his obscure magazine, *The Aristidean*. But he had also met the formidably dreadful Elizabeth F. Ellet, who advanced him fifty dol-

[9] See Woodberry, *Life*, II, 137.

[10] My chief sources for this unfortunate episode are those cited by Phillips, II, 1049ff., and Quinn, pp. 487ff. See also a discussion by Sidney P. Moss in *Poe's Literary Battles* (Durham, 1963). I differ with Mr. Moss on several matters of opinion, such as the reliability of some witnesses. The fee is named definitely in the Boston *Transcript* of November 4, 1845, and I find that a document that has been cited as evidence of a lower sum refers to what Poe's trip to Boston cost him. Griswold says that Poe appealed to Mrs. Osgood to write a poem for him and that she obliged with "Lulin, or the Diamond Fay," which she later published in the *Union Magazine* for May and June 1848. It was collected in her *Poems* (1849). I see no reason to doubt Griswold's account of this in the "Memoir."

[11] Later, Poe actually printed in the *Broadway Journal* of the sixth of December, ". . . we have a fine poem that we wrote at seven months — and an invitation to deliver it before the Lyceum." Whether or not Poe had thought in advance of his actions as a hoax is not clear, but things said by E. P. Whipple (in Gill's *Life*, p. 168) and by Thomas Dunn English in the *Independent* of November 5, 1896, makes me think he did. English thought, as I do, that Poe's glass of wine was taken after the lecture. The Boston *Star* reprinted the 1831 verison of "Al Aaraaf" on November 5.

[12] See a letter to Charles W. Kent, dated October 6, 1899, published in Kent's *The Unveiling of the Bust of Edgar Allan Poe . . . October 7, 1899* (Lynchburg, Va., n.d.), p. 64. There is another favorable article (hitherto unnoticed) in the Boston *Museum* of November 17, 1849. It is unsigned and may or may not be from Higginson. The writer says that Poe "with the most imperturbable sang froid" offered to recite "The Raven," and that "all was hushed at once, and Mr. Poe recited that remarkable poem in a manner that will never be repeated."

lars and pursued him — with poems in the *Broadway Journal* and by letters — all for literary advancement. Poe repulsed her, and a complicated quarrel resulted in which an embarrassing situation arose concerning the letters of Mrs. Osgood and Mrs. Ellet to Poe.[13] One ramification was that Poe, intoxicated, had a fist fight with Dr. English. In the fight, Poe received a black eye; this (according to English's reminiscences in the New York *Independent* of October 29, 1896) Poe ingeniously explained to friends as the result of an accidental collision with an Irish laborer carrying a board.

Late in the year Poe was on terms of friendship with a tragedian, James E. Murdoch, who contributed largely to the columns of the *Broadway Journal* on the drama. Poe's associate in the musical department of his magazine, Henry C. Watson, obtained a better paid position elsewhere; there had been no quarrel. Other contributors to the *Broadway Journal* included, in addition to several of the female poets, Dr. Chivers, William Gilmore Simms, and Poe's Virginian friend Philip Pendleton Cooke. In the issue of November 29 there appeared an essay, "Art Singing and Heart Singing," signed "Walter Whitman." Long afterwards Walt Whitman recalled meeting Poe at the office of the paper.

During the year Poe's residence was at one time 195 East Broadway (an entirely different thoroughfare from Broadway) and later at 85 Amity Street (now Third Street).

The *Broadway Journal* continued to lose money, and concluded with the issue dated January 3, 1846.

1846–1847

[1846] In 1846 Poe was selling criticisms to Graham and Godey. The former, in *Graham's Magazine* for April, published "The Philosophy of Composition" — Poe's imaginative story of how he wrote "The Raven," which he thought nobody would regard as literally true.[1]

In *Godey's* for May, Poe began his famous series called "The Literati of New York City." [2] The sketches were for the most part rather mild, which apparently surprised even some contemporaries. But Poe could not restrain himself from discussing men with whom he had quarreled. He made an all-out and unfair attack on Thomas Dunn English, which provoked the author of "Ben Bolt" to publish an angry reply.[3] Godey arranged to publish an even worse-mannered reply by Poe in the Philadelphia *Spirit of the Times* on

[13] See a synoptic account of the quarrel in Sidney Moss, *Poe's Literary Battles*, p. 207ff. My extremely unfavorable opinion of Mrs. Ellet is based on very wide reading of contemporary sources.

[1] See W. F. Gill, *Life* (revised edition, 1878), pp. 137 and 150, for statements of Graham and Mrs. Weiss.

[2] Among the authors treated, Halleck, Willis, and Margaret Fuller are remembered for other reasons, but most of the rest are saved from oblivion today by being "included in Poe's Literati." Poe did not reach Bryant or Morris.

[3] English was not "without the commonest school education," as Poe alleged, for his medical degree was awarded by the University of Pennsylvania and he had already published his celebrated poem, which Poe did not mention.

July 10, 1846. On July 23, Poe brought suit for libel against Hiram Fuller, the editor, and Augustus W. Clason, Jr., the proprietor of the New York *Evening Mirror*, which had printed several attacks on him, including that by English. The trial did not take place until February 17, 1847, when Poe was awarded damages of $225. Poe was cleared of English's charge that he had committed forgery but his reputation was not helped by the testimony of his own character witnesses; Freeman Hunt, editor of the *Merchant's Magazine*, and Major Noah both swore that the poet was "occasionally addicted to intoxication." [4] The hubbub led Godey to discontinue "The Literati" with the sixth installment. In the subsequent issue, for November, was "The Cask of Amontillado," a great story of revenge, in which many readers see a sublimation of Poe's bitter feeling at the time, although he used literary sources (Balzac and Joel T. Headley) for his plot.

In the spring of 1846 Poe made a trip to Baltimore where he met R. D. Unger, and was much in the company of printers and obscure newspapermen. Unger describes meeting Poe in unusually good spirits at a famous oyster house. During the visit Unger says Poe was drinking steadily, although less excessively than on some occasions. [5]

In this year Poe moved from Amity Street. He seems first to have gone back to the Brennan home, then for a time to a house owned by Mr. and Mrs. John C. Miller at Turtle Bay (now the foot of Forty-seventh Street) on the East River. There the poet enjoyed boating and would row out to the little uninhabited islets south of Blackwell's (now called Welfare) Island. [6] Chivers probably suggested Poe's retreat from town.

Finally the Poe family moved to the Fordham cottage, later to be idealized as "Landor's Cottage," which Poe rented from Mr. John Valentine for one hundred dollars a year. [7] Here Marie Louise Shew was brought to help Mrs. Clemm nurse Virginia, whose illness grew worse. A number of visitors have left records of visits to the Poe family at Fordham. Mrs. Osgood and Elizabeth Oakes Smith called there, and Mary Starr (Mrs. Jenning) and her

[4] See the *New-York Tribune*, February 18, 1847. Poe did *not* sue English. Actually, testimony brought out that Poe had induced English to invest thirty dollars in the *Broadway Journal*, which Poe claimed would be a great success. English's calling this action "obtaining money under false pretenses" was libel per se, although only because of the phraseology used.

[5] Letter to Chevalier Reynolds from Chicago, October 29, 1899, signed R. D. Unger, M.D., in the Ingram Collection (Ingram List no. 402). Ingram regarded this as a "pack of lies — perhaps some grains of truth," and James A. Harrison, who printed extracts from an incorrect transcript (as if by "R. D'Unger") in the *Independent*, November 1, 1906, put little faith in it. But neither Harrison nor Ingram knew that there was independent evidence for the Baltimore visit of 1846. In a letter to Poe, April 15, 1846, Mrs. M. E. Hewitt referred to his recovery from a recent illness in Baltimore. The letter, cited by Quinn, p. 506, is in the Griswold Collection in the Boston Public Library.

[6] See Phillips, II, 1109ff., for reminiscences of John LeFevre Miller and his sister Sarah, respectively nine and thirteen years old in 1846, when Poe was their parents' tenant.

[7] The cottage is preserved, but has been moved from its original position on Kingsbridge Road to nearby Poe Park.

husband sometimes came. Rosalie Poe stayed for some days at the cottage.[8]
Poe also visited nearby St. John's College, founded in 1841, the institution
which has now become Fordham University. He was there on terms of friend-
ship with Father Edward Doucet, S.J., and Father Thebaud. He conversed in
French with them, and sometimes played cards, and he had the privilege of
using the library.[9]

In this year Poe began to write to an admirer, George W. Eveleth, a
young medical student from Phillips, Maine, who may be called the first
special student of Poe. There is also a story, perhaps of this year, that Poe
stood sponsor in baptism for the child of a neighbor and gave him the name
Edgar Albert, because of the unhappy associations of his own middle name.[10]

[1847] On Saturday, January 30, 1847, Virginia Poe died. Her funeral
took place on February 2,[11] and was attended by Morris, Willis, Mrs. Ann
Stephens, Mrs. Shew, Mrs. Edmund Morton Smith (the Poes' cousin Elizabeth
Herring, on a visit to New York), Mary Starr Jenning, and Mary Valentine
(later Mrs. Briggs; she was an adopted daughter of Poe's landlord). It is be-
lieved that the poet never looked at his wife in death. The tiny poem "Deep
in Earth" was probably composed by him almost at once.

After his wife's death, Poe was extremely ill. Mrs. Shew came out every
other day to help Mrs. Clemm take care of him. She obtained from the
famous Dr. Valentine Mott the opinion that Poe had suffered from a brain
lesion early in life, and would not reach old age.[12] Her patient, although

[8] Phillips, II, 1137, 1183; Weiss, *Home Life*, 127–130. I have a record of a letter
from Charles Steele to Joseph Wood Krutch, dated April 9, 1935, telling of another
visitor. Mr. Steele said that his grandmother, Ellen Maria Keith Steele of Boston,
told him about 1887 that she had called on her cousin, Mrs. Edgar Allan Poe,
who was in great poverty at Fordham. I recall no other reference to this family
connection.

[9] See Quinn, p. 520, and Phillips, esp. II, 1115 and 1240ff. The card playing
was mentioned in a letter from J. H. Hopkins on February 9, 1875 (Ingram List,
no. 201). Father Doucet became president of the college, and Poe's association with
him and the institution as what would now be called a "visiting scholar" is well
known to this day on the campus.

[10] See the reminiscences of the child's sister, Mrs. Mary Andre Phelps, as copied
from a Chicago paper in the New York *Commercial Advertiser* of June 18, 1897.
(Unfortunately I do not know Mrs. Phelps's maiden name.) She says the poet some-
times played Dr. Busby (a card game resembling Old Maid) with her and her
brother.

[11] Identical obituaries, possibly composed by her husband, in the New York
Herald and in the *Tribune* of February 1, 1847, read: "On Saturday, 30th ult.
of pulmonary consumption in the 25th year of her age, VIRGINIA ELIZA, wife
of EDGAR POE. Her friends are invited to attend her funeral at Fordham,
Westchester County on Tuesday next (tomorrow) at 2 P.M. The cars leave New
York for Fordham, from City Hall at 12 M. — returning at 4 P.M." She was laid to
rest in the family vault of John Valentine in the churchyard of the Dutch Re-
formed Church at Fordham. On January 19, 1885, she was reinterred beside her
husband in Baltimore. See Woodberry, *Life* (1909), II, 225f., and Phillips, II,
1200–1207.

[12] A modern medical man who saw a photograph of Poe told my friend Robert
Hunter Paterson that a twist in the poet's face suggested to him a brain lesion,

his heart, too, gave him trouble, was strong enough to address several poems of compliment to her, and to send to Miss Lynch's annual St. Valentine's Day party another poem, written for Louise Hunter, to whom Poe's committee had awarded a school poetry prize in 1845.

During the year Poe wrote little prose — chiefly a revised review of Hawthorne and a story,"The Domain of Arnheim," an enlarged version of his "Landscape Garden" of 1842. The great event in 1847 was the composition of "Ulalume," the strangest and yet probably the most characteristic of his poems.

In February Poe won the libel suit begun in 1846, but he was disturbed by word from Eveleth that he was being attacked for "plagiarism" of *The Conchologist's First Book*, a charge that was not actionable, though untrue. In the summer he went South again, visiting Washington and its environs. With a party of friends from Alexandria he attended the commencement of the Episcopal High School in Virginia, and, being recognized, obligingly recited "The Raven." [13] He went back to Baltimore, and again saw Unger, who found him drinking rather steadily, and depressed.[14] After Poe's wife died, Unger said, Poe seemed not to care if he lived a year or a day. The younger man discussed with Poe his own recent reading. Poe said he too had read a new translation of Fouqué's *Sintram and His Companions*; Poe praised it highly, remarking that "every man had his own devil." [15] But he had nothing to say of Herman Melville's *Omoo*, of 1847.

Poe also went to Philadelphia. On August 6, Louis A. Godey wrote George W. Eveleth that Poe had called on him "quite sober," but that he had "heard from him elsewhere, when he was not." Apparently Judge Robert Conrad and George R. Graham befriended Poe on this trip.[16] Also some time after Virginia's death Poe went to Albany to see Mrs. Osgood, and seems to have acted irresponsibly.[17] Probably in this year he began to see

---

and Poe certainly had manic and depressive periods. Poe wrote of some kind of secret he concealed for reasons of family pride; aristocratic Baltimoreans (and Mrs. Clemm was one) considered any kind of insanity disgraceful. Woodberry's notion that Poe referred to drug addiction is nonsense; addiction was not especially disgraceful in 1849, and no doctor of medicine who knew Poe ever thought him an addict.

[13] See the account of Arthur Barksdale Kinsolving, D.D., in William A. R. Goodwin's *History of the Theological Seminary in Virginia* (1924), p. 420.

[14] The Unger letter has already been described in note 5 on the year 1846. Some details of Poe's drinking "like a gentleman" on these occasions are of interest. He usually preferred whiskey and enjoyed sitting in a room in John Boyd's establishment at 9 South Street, where there was a collection of theatrical mementoes on the wall. Poe sometimes went to Guy's Monument House. Unger mentions, as two friends of Poe, John M. Millington, a printer, and John Wills, a minor journalist, both connected with the Baltimore *Patriot*. I find them in directories.

[15] Sintram's chief "companion" is a demon. So far as I recall, there is nothing to show that Poe ever took any interest in Melville. *Moby-Dick* was not published while Poe was alive.

[16] See Phillips, II, 1228; and Poe's letter of August 10, 1847, to Conrad.

[17] He is said to have begged her to elope with him. The informant is Mrs. Osgood's brother-in-law (whose home she was visiting), the Reverend Henry F. Har-

a good deal of Sarah Anna Lewis (also called Estelle, and later Stella), a poetic lady of Brooklyn, to whom he was introduced by her husband, Sylvanus D. Lewis, an attorney whom he had known for some time.

1848

[1848] Early in 1848, Poe finished a long work on cosmology, and on the evening of February 3 he delivered it as a lecture, "The Universe," at the New York Society Library Lecture Room. He reworked and expanded this lecture to make a book called *Eureka*, which was published by Putnam in July.

More interesting to most of us are the pleasant visits he made to Mrs. Shew in Greenwich Village. She shared the home of her brother-in-law, Dr. Joel Shew, first at 47 Bond Street and after early May at what is now 17 West Tenth Street. At the former place Poe "collaborated" with her (she wrote four lines) on a first draft of "The Bells." For the second house, Dr. Shew allowed the poet to select some of the furnishings. Mrs. Shew, an Episcopalian, sometimes took Poe to church with her. She had a genuine and deep affection for him but she did not want to marry him, and after a while she ceased to see him. In this breaking off she was to some extent prompted by a young student of theology, John Henry Hopkins, Jr., who was horrified at a pantheistic tendency in *Eureka* and feared that Mrs. Shew's orthodoxy might be shaken by the author of that recondite treatise.

Meanwhile, through the offices of a relative of Mrs. Osgood, Jane Ermina Locke, a minor poetess of Lowell, Massachusetts, Poe was invited to lecture there on July 10. There he met Nancy Locke Heywood Richmond, wife of Charles Richmond, a prosperous local manufacturer of wrapping paper. Another romance began which was of very great emotional importance to Poe.[1]

After July 15, Poe went south and visited Richmond, where he spent three weeks. There he saw his sister and the Mackenzies, and called daily upon a pretty widow, Mrs. Jane Clark, who looked somewhat like Virginia Poe. She heard him recite "The Raven" to a small party, including Rosalie, in a voice "like Edwin Booth's."[2] Little else is firmly known of the visit.

---

rington, who published a long letter about the episode in the New York *Critic*, October 3, 1885 — a document to which few biographers save Miss Phillips refer. I am assured by Harrington's granddaughter that he was a lovable and kindly old gentleman. He was obviously shocked about Poe, but his letter refers to the poet as "breaking up a home," and this shows that he was unaware that the Osgoods were already separated in fact when Mrs. Osgood met Poe. I do not think Mrs. Osgood took her sister's husband into her confidence at all. (Edward Wagenknecht, *Edgar Allan Poe*, 1963, discussing Harrington's story, p. 256, says, "I do not trust Harrington . . . he published an hysterical attack.") I have read some unpublished statements of Mrs. Osgood, and, like Wagenknecht, I think Harrington prejudiced and ready to believe and exaggerate gossip having little basis in fact.

[1] See commentary and notes on "For Annie."

[2] Mrs. Clark's "Reminiscences" are given in an interview for the New York *Sunday World*, March 17, 1878, when she lived in Louisville, Kentucky. She was a native Virginian and first met Poe in 1835. Her maiden name is not known. Mrs. Clark stated that she never saw Poe intoxicated.

Poe claimed to have challenged John M. Daniel, editor of the Richmond *Examiner*, to a duel which did not take place,[3] and there is testimony that Poe met Charles M. Wallace, later a well-known Richmond historian, in company with the journalist, D. Hammersley, and others at Our Home Restaurant, where *Eureka* was discussed.[4] Poe certainly met John R. Thompson, who bought "The Rationale of Verse" for publication in the *Southern Literary Messenger* of October and November 1848 and "was responsible for a distressing picture of Poe's habits at that time." [5] That Poe recited parts of *Eureka* at some convivial gathering seems probable enough, although I do not believe the details of Thompson's account.

Poe went home by way of Baltimore, and there again saw R. D. Unger. Naturally he must have gone through Philadelphia. He was at home before September. Late in the summer he made a walking tour of two of the Hudson River counties of New York, which he mentioned in a letter of October 18, 1848, to Eli Bowen (formerly editor of the *Columbia Spy*), through whom he seems to have sold to a collector a manuscript of "The Raven." [6]

Back in New York, Poe returned to a romantic adventure that had begun early in the year. At a valentine party of Miss Lynch, a poem "To Edgar A. Poe" had been read, sent in from Providence, hence obviously by Sarah Helen Whitman.[7] To this Poe had replied by composing in blank verse the poem that I have called in this volume "To Helen [Whitman]" and sending it to her in manuscript about the first of June. He now arranged to go to Providence where, on September 21, he met his "Helen of a thousand dreams."

Mrs. Whitman was somewhat eccentric in dress and manner and was interested in things spiritual and romantic. Poe proposed marriage and after some time was accepted, with reservations. Mrs. Whitman told him that she would dismiss him if she ever saw him intoxicated, and she prudently transferred all her property to her mother and sister. Poe (wisely, I think, for once) after drinking called upon his fiancée.[8] A tradition reaches me directly from Mr. Alfred Hall-Quest of New York, a descendant of one of Mrs. Whitman's neighbors who saw the poet ride a horse down the street on this occasion.

Poe's letters to Mrs. Whitman are well known; they are extremely literary — he later expanded a paragraph of one of them into his story "Landor's

[3] Poe mentioned it as of "last year" in a letter of September 1849 to Mrs. Clemm.

[4] Phillips, II, 1302, quotes directly from a manuscript note by Wallace, dated "Sept. 18, 1875." Whitty's discussion, "Memoir," p. lxvi, may be partly conjectural.

[5] Quinn, p. 568. Quinn points out the shadowy nature of our sources, but does not mention Mrs. Clark. He makes clear that Thompson was self-contradictory. I would add that Thompson was a sensational writer given to self-glorification as a rescuer of Poe. Quinn gives most of the needed references, but we may add Mrs. Weiss, *Home Life of Poe*, pp. 163–168; Woodberry, *Life*, II, 443–446. There is a lurid article about Poe and Thompson in *Lippincott's Magazine* for May 1872.

[6] For a text of the letter to Bowen see *American Notes & Queries*, January 1965.

[7] Sarah Helen Power, born in 1803, was married July 10, 1828, to John Winslow Whitman, who died in 1833. Mrs. Whitman lived until June 27, 1878. There is a valuable biography, *Poe's Helen* (1916), by Caroline Ticknor.

[8] Quinn tells the story of the courtship in well-documented detail.

Cottage." One feels that the two poets (from the beginning "a pair of star-cross'd lovers") were at best in love with love. Yet there was much of nobility in Mrs. Whitman, who in later years was a staunch asserter of what was noble in Edgar Poe.[9]

In late October Poe again saw Mrs. Richmond at Lowell. Plans for another lecture there fell through, and Poe went from Lowell to Boston to Providence and then back to Boston. He was distraught, and later wrote Mrs. Richmond that he had taken a dangerous amount of laudanum.[10] This illness is of literary importance, for the poet's recovery is commemorated in his poem "For Annie." On December 20, he delivered his new lecture, "The Poetic Principle," before the Franklin Lyceum of Providence at the Earl House. He later claimed that his audience numbered sixteen hundred.[11] It was in the course of this visit to Providence that his engagement to Helen Whitman was definitely broken.

During 1848 Poe issued a *Prospectus of the Stylus*, dated January, promising a work to be called "Literary America." A later prospectus, dated April, omits mention of it. Some pages of a preface and fragmentary notes survive.

1849

[1849] Poe's last year was one of great activity. Godey, with whom he had quarreled, brought out one story purchased a year before, "Mellonta Tauta," a half-serious prophecy of the twenty-ninth century. It has a somber element; Poe feared that individuals' rights would come to be little regarded in the future.

He continued to write for *Graham's* and the *Southern Literary Messenger*, but his chief market was now the Boston *Flag of Our Union*, a cheap popular weekly, which he despised although it paid well. There appeared his horror tale "Hop-Frog," the charming "Landor's Cottage," and the highly original autobiographical verses "For Annie." Interest in the Gold Rush inspired both a hoax, "Von Kempelen and His Discovery," the short lyric "Eldorado," and the sonnet "To My Mother."

He fell into correspondence with E. H. N. Patterson, a young newspaperman of Oquawka, Illinois, with new plans to publish the chimerical *Stylus* magazine.

[9] Mrs. Whitman's *Edgar Poe and His Critics* (1860) was the first book to defend Poe's memory. A new edition with introduction and notes by Oral S. Coad appeared in 1949.

[10] Students have taken many views of this incident, some thinking it a serious attempt at suicide, others feeling that the whole episode was mere hallucination or even a made-up story. Poe said in his letter of November 16, 1848, that he procured two ounces of laudanum, went to Boston, swallowed "about half" of it, became violently sick, was rescued by a friend, and returned to New York. The crucial word is "about" — an ounce of laudanum could be a fatal dose to a man neither an addict nor in extreme pain. But how much *was* "about half"? Did the druggist, observing his customer's condition, give him a diluted potion? I incline to think that Poe's "attempted suicide" was not quite serious.

[11] See Providence *Manufacturers' and Farmers' Journal*, December 20, 1848; and *Richmond Whig*, August 17, 1849.

1849

Meanwhile, "The Bells" was expanded to its present form. It was sold in July, together with "Annabel Lee," written in May, to John Sartain for his *Union Magazine*. Poe seems to have thought "Annabel Lee" would be his last poem, and, contrary to his usual practice, he circulated it in manuscript, as if to be sure it would reach the world. His forebodings were not mere premonition; the symptoms of his heart trouble were of a terrifying kind.

At the end of June, Poe went south, stopped off in Philadelphia, drank a great deal too much, and for the first time had delirium tremens. John Sartain came to his rescue, as did C. Chauncey Burr, George Lippard, S. D. Patterson, and Godey, the last of whom sent him a kind message with five dollars. On July 13 Poe was on his way to Richmond, where he arrived on July 14 and put up at the Swan Tavern.[1]

In Richmond the poet spent more than two happy months, the Indian summer of his life. He was now received into society, and we have pleasant reminiscences of his attendance at the Mackenzies', where he saw his sister Rosalie and mingled with young people and even children, who usually liked him. Other friends were his childhood "little sweetheart" Catherine Poitiaux, Robert Stanard, Robert Sully the painter, Dr. Robert Henry Cabell and his wife Julia Mayo Cabell (a cousin of the second Mrs. John Allan), Dr. John F. Carter, and Thomas Alfriend and his son Edward. Poe called almost daily on Susan Archer Talley, a poetess of eighteen, whom he trusted and regarded with such affection that he instructed his friends to watch him to make sure she never saw him when he was not himself.[2] He also called often upon his early fiancée, Elmira Royster Shelton, then a widow. He proposed marriage and apparently was accepted, although Mrs. Shelton's son, Southall B. Shelton, and her daughter, Ann Elizabeth, who were apparently schoolchildren, did not approve of the match.[3]

Poe wrote little during the summer, leaving behind him only a few criticisms, the unfinished satire "A Reviewer Reviewed," and a fragment of an adventure story, now called "The Lighthouse." He delivered his lecture on "The Poetic Principle" at the Exchange Concert Rooms in Richmond on August 17 and again on September 24, and at Norfolk on September 14. A little earlier he had read "Ulalume" at the Hygeia Hotel, Old Point Comfort, and had given a manuscript copy of it to Miss Susan Ingram, who was present.

All was not completely happy, however. In Richmond Poe was intoxi-

[1] See Quinn, pp. 616ff., for references to Sartain's and other accounts. Sartain said that at Poe's request he clipped off the poet's mustache. Since Poe wore one a few weeks later, more than one critic has questioned Sartain's accuracy. However, a mature man can grow a mustache in three weeks.

[2] My principal sources are Susan Archer Talley Weiss, "Last Days of Edgar A. Poe," *Scribner's*, March 1878; her *Home Life of Poe* (1907); and the extremely important brief article by Edward M. Alfriend in the *Literary Era*, August 1901, which preserves several of Poe's *bons mots*. Harrison, *Complete Works* (1902), I, 310–337, is also useful on this period.

[3] See "Poe's First and Final Love" in the revived *Southern Literary Messenger*, March 1943, by F. Meredith Dietz, who interviewed a granddaughter of Mrs. Shelton. The extreme disapproval of her children accounts for Mrs. Shelton's contradictory statements about her friendship with the poet.

cated at least twice.[4] He called on John M. Daniel, who in the Richmond *Examiner* of August 21 had unfavorably criticized his reading of "The Raven." Daniel is said to have offered him a job as literary editor of the paper, but nothing came of the offer save that a number of Poe's poems were set up in type and the final version of "The Raven" was published in its pages on September 25, 1849.

Poe's last surviving letters are of September 18, 1849. He refers in one to a planned journey to Philadelphia, where he was to edit (for a fee of one hundred dollars) the poems of Margaret St. Leon Loud and where he hoped to see her on September 26. But he delayed, in order to deliver his last lecture, and left Richmond on the boat for Baltimore on the morning of September 26. He had said farewell to a friend, Dr. John F. Carter, leaving with him a copy of Moore's *Irish Melodies*, perhaps as a parting gift, and taking the doctor's malacca cane instead of his own. He left with his sister a letter (his last) for Miss Talley, with a manuscript copy of "For Annie." Neither letter nor manuscript survives. To John R. Thompson, who was among those who saw him off, he gave a holograph of "Annabel Lee" for five dollars, obviously as an autograph. Poe seemed in fair health.

Presumably on September 28, Poe reached Baltimore. The next few days are somewhat obscure, although it is certain that he began to drink. Bishop O. P. Fitzgerald said long afterward that Poe attended a birthday party and could not refuse to pledge his hostess in wine.[5] Poe also called on N. C. Brooks, but unfortunately did not find him at home. The poet may then have tried to take the train for Philadelphia.[6]

[4] On August 27, Poe joined the Sons of Temperance, Shockoe Hill Division, Number 54. See Rayburn S. Moore, "A Note on Poe and the Sons of Temperance," *American Literature*, November 1958.

[5] Bishop Fitzgerald, quoted by Harrison, *Complete Works*, I, 319, had an inaccurate memory, but it is unlikely that a Victorian bishop would make up the story, which fits in with Neilson Poe's reference, in 1849, quoted by Woodberry, *Life*, II, 447, to his knowledge of a "single indulgence." Neilson Poe's reticence may also result from some feeling that he had failed to rescue the poet in time. Elizabeth Ellicott Poe, in an otherwise horribly inaccurate article in the St. Louis *Globe-Democrat* of January 17, 1909, says one thing "from family tradition" — that her own grandfather, "the first cousin of the poet," saw Edgar Poe in a stupor "lying under the steps of the Baltimore Museum," on the corner of Baltimore and Calvert streets, and "sent a message to Neilson Poe." Since Edgar Poe had often recovered without aid, if Neilson neglected him on this occasion, who now can blame him? But he might have blamed himself.

[6] The story that Poe reached Philadelphia but returned in confusion to Baltimore is well witnessed, in manuscript reminiscences of Thomas H. Lane, cited by Phillips, II, 1498, and Quinn, p. 637. Apparent inconsistencies arise from the fact that Lane wrote four versions of what he recalled, all of which I have read in manuscript; but I now suspect that the date of Poe's adventure was 1848 instead of 1849. Another story is that Poe boarded the wrong train, and was sent back from Havre de Grace to Baltimore by the conductor, George W. Rollins. Several biographers tell this anecdote, without naming its source, which turns out to be the unreliable Dr. John J. Moran, in *A Defense of Edgar Allan Poe* (Washington, 1885), p. 60. Moran's statements in this pamphlet and elsewhere in his later years reveal an almost incredibly expansive imagination.

On October 3 (Election Day in Baltimore), Joseph W. Walker, a compositor, found Poe extremely ill at Cornelius Ryan's "4th Ward polls," at Gunner's Hall, 44 East Lombard Street, and summoned Dr. Joseph Evans Snodgrass, who, in company with Henry Herring, Poe's uncle by marriage, took the author in a carriage to Washington Hospital.[7]

There Poe was cared for by Dr. John J. Moran. The doctor wrote a brief account to Mrs. Clemm on November 15, 1849; and we have another from the doctor's wife, who helped to nurse the patient.[8] Poe was delirious or unconscious most of the time, but toward the end he had lucid intervals. He asked Mrs. Moran if she thought there was hope for him in the next world. She replied affirmatively, read him the fourteenth chapter of St. John, and left him. He died soon afterward, very early in the morning of Sunday, October 7, 1849.

No death certificate was required at the time, but the Baltimore *Clipper* of October 9 said that Poe had died "of congestion of the brain." [9]

Poe's funeral was held on Monday, October 8, at four o'clock, and he was buried in the Poe family lot in the Presbyterian Cemetery in Baltimore. The ceremony was conducted by a relative, the Reverend William T. D. Clemm; the coffin was made by Charles Suter; the sexton was George W. Spence. Dr. Snodgrass, Z[accheus] Collins Lee (a classmate at the University of Virginia), Henry Herring, and Neilson Poe attended, as did Edmund Morton Smith and his wife (Poe's cousin Elizabeth), Poe's schoolmaster, Joseph H. Clarke, and perhaps a few more.[10]

[7] The story that Poe was a victim of election violence is twaddle, as R. D. Unger remarked, in his letter in the Ingram Collection (no. 402). It first turned up in John R. Thompson's lecture, "The Genius and Character of Edgar Allan Poe," which Gill, *Life*, p. 267, says was delivered in Baltimore (obviously before April 30, 1873, when Thompson died). Thompson said that Poe was "seized by lawless agents of a political club, imprisoned in a cellar . . . and next day in a state bordering on frenzy made to vote in eleven different wards, as if in . . . compensation for never having exercised the right of suffrage before." See *Genius and Character*, ed. James H. Whitty and James H. Rindfleisch (Richmond, 1929), p. 42. Thompson cited no authority, and no real witness ever appeared, though cheap journalists in time supplied imaginary ones. See Woodberry, *Life*, II, 448. Dr. Unger noted that in Baltimore Poe was widely known by sight, and as a non-resident. Poe had the malacca cane; would lawless fellows have failed to purloin so salable an object?

[8] See Quinn and Hart, *Edgar Allan Poe . . . Documents*, pp. 32–34, for the complete letter of Dr. Moran. The statement of Mrs. Mary O. Moran was published by Harrison, *Complete Works* (1902), I, 337.

[9] Dr. Unger thought (from what he heard later) that the cause was "inflammation of the intestines, the diarrhoea preceding the fever." Unger knew that Poe's periods of drinking were followed by this condition. Dr. Moran made references to Poe's being "drugged." An opiate was the usual remedy — to be bought from any apothecary. Poe's weak heart made any illness or strong remedy dangerous for him.

[10] The date was established by John C. French, Baltimore *Sun*, June 3, 1949. For a list of those attending, see Phillips II, 1511; and Quinn, p. 643. Suter was a prominent and highly skilled cabinet-maker, who probably never built another coffin; I am told this by his great-grandson, Oscar S. Benson, D.D.S.

ANNALS

POE'S APPEARANCE AND MANNER

Poe's personal appearance is very well known from numerous portraits taken from life in several media. The more familiar image (which appears on a United States three-cent postage stamp, issued on October 7, 1949) shows that he wore a mustache. This is to be seen in all the daguerreotypes — one by Matthew Brady among them. But Poe, prior to some time in 1845 or 1846, wore slight chin whiskers and no mustache.[1] He had dark brown curly hair, and luminous hazel eyes, a very high forehead, and a somewhat weak chin. He was about five feet eight inches in height.[2] He always walked like a soldier and dressed plainly but neatly; in later years he usually wore a stock.

His conversation was fascinating, and he was assertive and positive in literary opinions but less contentious than might be supposed from his published criticisms. We have already recorded instances of his good relations with children. His Negro barber and his office boys, Alexander Crane and Ash Upson, bore witness to his affability.[3]

All this of course was when Poe was sober; liquor often brought out the worst in him, and he could be quarrelsome and even pugnacious after a glass or two of wine. He was certainly not addicted to drugs,[4] although like almost everyone of his time, he must have had medicinal doses of opiates.

Poe's attitude toward women was chivalrous to an extreme, although Mrs. Whitman said he was not a Sir Galahad.[5]

[1] The earliest fully authenticated picture is that used by J. H. Whitty as a frontispiece in *Complete Poems*; Whitty found the glass photographic plate made from a lost miniature that once belonged to Rosalie Poe. The engraved fashion plate in *Graham's* for June 1841, the woodcut in the Philadelphia *Saturday Museum* of March 4, 1843 (a very bad picture but not a deliberate caricature), the engraving in *Graham's* for February 1845, and the fine oil portrait by Samuel Stillman Osgood, who saw Poe only in 1845 and 1846, all show Poe without a mustache. Osgood's, which was bequeathed to the New-York Historical Society by Rufus Wilmot Griswold, is decisive on Poe's coloring, about which there has been debate.

[2] See his own letter to J. M. Field, June 15, 1846, and Hirst's sketch in the *Saturday Museum*, March 4, 1843. But even in medical examinations, a man's statement about his height is often accepted; and Eugene L. Didier's description in *The Life and Poems of . . . Poe*, pp. 123ff, certainly based on information from many people who saw Poe, said five feet, six inches. Poe may have been slightly bow-legged. Edward Wagenknecht, *Edgar Allan Poe*, pp. 44ff., has a discussion of Poe's appearance. The poet's voice was low and musical, and he spoke with a slight Southern drawl.

[3] See the Ingram List, no. 728, and Wagenknecht, pp. 79 and 237.

[4] See Woodberry, *Life*, II, 429f., for medical opinions of doctors — one was Thomas Dunn English — who knew Poe. I have consulted physicians who assure me that Woodberry (who held a contrary view to mine) was unaware of how decisive the testimony he quoted and dismissed really is.

[5] See the Ingram List, no. 283. Dr. Unger in the letter frequently cited tells a pertinent story he had from Mary Nelson, who kept a house in 1847 to 1851 at what was then 1 Tripolet's Alley. On one occasion Poe came there with William M. Smith, a printer of 72 French Street, who had a bottle of champagne to share in the parlor with two of the inmates. One girl, Leonora Bouldin (nicknamed "Lenore") was only sixteen. The poet kissed her and urged her to reform. The

AFTERWORD

The poet, although usually cheerful, was throughout his life occasionally subject to fits of almost hopeless gloom. Once he said to Thomas Alfriend, "God gave me a spark of genius, but He quenched it in tears." Not quite, one feels; Poe struggled against odds and suffered defeats, but he returned again and again to the fray. Like his own gallant knight, he never ceased to ride boldly, and to "seek for Eldorado."

AFTERWORD

There were several fairly kind short obituaries, and one long one of surprising malignity, signed "Ludwig" (really Rufus Wilmot Griswold), in the *New-York Tribune* on October 9, 1849.[6]

At the news of Poe's death, Mrs. Clemm gave up the Fordham cottage and moved to the home of the Lewises in Brooklyn.[7] Poe had died intestate, and his sole heir-at-law was really his sister Rosalie, but she was unable to put up the money required to take out letters of administration in Virginia. Sylvanus D. Lewis drew up some papers (of questionable legality), and Mrs. Clemm took over the estate of her son-in-law. She and the Lewises asked Griswold to assume the position of literary executor.[8] He accepted the invitation, found in J. S. Redfield a New York publisher, and in six weeks put together the first two volumes of the *Works* of Edgar Poe, including the poems and many of the tales, together with brief articles by James Russell Lowell and N. P. Willis. Advertisements in the *New-York Tribune* announced publication on January 10, 1850.

Griswold set to work on a "Memoir" for the third volume, which was to appear late in 1850. In this amazing document, Griswold found little about Poe to praise save his genius. He saw the poet's character in the worst possible light, twisted facts to fit his viewpoint, and even altered texts of letters. This is inexcusable, although there were extenuating circumstances.[9] The Suetonian biography ruined Poe's personal reputation for years, but it helped to sell the books. In 1856, a fourth volume was brought out, just before the editor's death, and the *Works* sold steadily. The editorial work, which was by no means bad on the rest, was particularly good on the stories. All

---

addresses have been found in the Directories, Smith's first in that for 1849, hence the most probable time of the incident is Poe's visit in 1848. (Dr. Unger's letter is that described in the Ingram List as no. 402.)

[6] See Quinn, p. 644, for some short notices; Harrison, I, 348ff., reprinted the "Ludwig" article and other early material.

[7] Catterina, the poet's cat, who had eaten little during her owner's absence, was found dead the last time Mrs. Clemm visited Fordham. See the Ingram List, no. 226.

[8] The appointment has led to much discussion; the most reasonable view is that Poe had wished Griswold, a very able man, to be his editor, and had even mentioned the possibility to him, but in a way that Griswold had not thought a firm commitment.

[9] In a letter of February 19, 1850, to John R. Thompson, Griswold said that the first two volumes were not selling well (see Thompson, *Genius and Character*, appendix). See also Ingram List, no. 197, on Griswold's remark that the work would sell best as it was, with the "Memoir."

subsequent editions of the prose works were largely based on Griswold until 1902, when James A. Harrison's *Complete Works of Edgar Allan Poe*, in seventeen volumes, appeared.

Usually an important author's standing is little enhanced by statues. But in the case of Poe, whose reputation had been so injured by his first biographer, a monument was of value. The idea was suggested in the columns of the New York *Cosmopolitan Art Journal* as early as 1856, but nothing came of it. However, on October 7, 1865, it was resolved by the Public School Teachers' Association of Baltimore to campaign for something appropriate.[10] Money for the monument was raised largely from teachers and students of the city, and of the Troy Female Seminary,[11] plus a large contribution from the philanthropist George W. Childs. The unveiling took place on November 17, 1875, before a large audience. Letters were read from Longfellow, Holmes, Whittier, Tennyson, and Poe's friends John Neal and Helen Whitman. Stéphane Mallarmé sent a sonnet in French. But only one important poet came from out of town. He was Walt Whitman.[12]

Poe's fame is established. It is that of an artist who, facing extreme difficulties, gave the best he could in the realms of exalted art. This has been in many ways a sad chronicle, but it is not a tragedy. A man who accomplished what he wished in his chosen fields of poetry and romance won a victory. "To him the laurels belong."

[10] See Sara Sigourney Rice, *Edgar Allan Poe: A Memorial Volume* (Baltimore, 1877), and Gill's *Life*, pp. 276ff., for full accounts.

[11] This is now the Emma Willard School at Troy, New York. As a girl Mrs. Lewis had been a special student there, and she presumably arranged for the donation. Her divorced husband, Sylvanus D. Lewis, sent a long letter to be read at the unveiling of the monument.

[12] The ceremony came too late for the poet's sister, Rosalie, whose death had occurred in Washington on July 21, 1874, and for Mrs. Clemm, who had died in Baltimore on February 16, 1871, and whose body now rests beneath the monument. But Neilson Poe spoke, W. F. Gill took part, and Poe's old schoolmaster, Joseph H. Clarke, attended, as did Dr. Snodgrass, John H. B. Latrobe, John H. Hewitt, and N. C. Brooks. A letter from the poet Swinburne came too late to be read at the unveiling but was facsimiled in Miss Rice's memorial volume.

SOURCES

SOURCES OF TEXTS COLLATED

MANUSCRIPT COLLECTIONS

Titles are given as in the source. Titles and text designations in square brackets are those under which the poems are discussed in this edition.

Boston Public Library: Griswold Papers
    Mem: for Philadelphia [Model Verses, *D*]

Columbia University Libraries
    Annabel Lee [*E*]
    To Octavia [*A*], in Octavia Walton's album

Enoch Pratt Free Library, Baltimore, Maryland
    Valentine's Eve, 1846 [A Valentine, *A*]

Harvard College Library
    To — (" I heed not") [To M — , *D*]
    A Valentine [*B, D*]
    The Haunted Palace [*N*]
    Annabel Lee [*A*]

Henry E. Huntington Library and Art Gallery
    To One Departed [To One in Paradise, *Z*]
    (Untitled hymn) in "Morella" [Hymn, *A*]
    To Mrs. M. L. S. [To Marie Louise Shew, *A*]
    (Untitled lines) in "About Critics and Criticism" [Lines after Elizabeth Barrett, *B*]
    Annabel Lee [*C*]
        Also the annotated copy of the *Broadway Journal* given to Helen Whitman

Indiana University Library: Josiah K. Lilly Collection
    Eulalie [*Y*]
    To Margaret [*A*], in Margaret Bassett's album
        Also the leaf (p. 91: "To Helen") torn out of *The Raven and Other Poems* (1845) and sent to Helen Whitman

Library of Congress: Ellis and Allan Papers
Poetry

The New York Public Library
    Manuscript Division: Eulalie [*F*] and Deep in Earth [*A*]
    Berg Collection: Poe's letter to Joseph B. Boyd, December 25, 1839 [Sonnet — Silence, *A*]
    Also Elizabeth Herring's copy of *Al Aaraaf* (1829)

SOURCES OF TEXTS COLLATED

Pierpont Morgan Library
Tamerlane (Wilmer manuscript, fragment) [B]
Dreams (Wilmer manuscript) [C]
The Lake (Wilmer manuscript) [B]
Politian [A]: leaves 1–4, 6–10, 12
The Raven [D]: lines 60–66 in letter to J. A. Shea, February 3, 1845
The Bells [E]
Ulalume [K]
Annabel Lee [D]

University of Texas: Miriam Lutcher Stark Library
Romance [B]: lines 11–15 in letter to John Neal, December 29, 1829
The Coliseum [D] in Mary Herring's album
Politian [A]: the last leaf, containing text B of "The Coliseum" and the
    end of the play
Eulalie [Z]
The Raven [K]: lines 103–108
To Miss Louise Olivia Hunter [A]
Ulalume [E]: lines 30–38 in manuscript about Henry B. Hirst
The Bells [B]
To – [To Frances S. Osgood, D], in Mary Herring's album
Lenore [H], lines 20–26 in letter to Griswold, June 1849
    Also the J. Lorimer Graham copy of *The Raven and Other Poems*
    (1845)

University of Virginia: Ingram Collection
The Beloved Physician [B]
To Marie Louise [A]

Williams College: Chapin Library
To – —— [To Frances S. Osgood, J]

Yale University: The Beinecke Rare Book and Manuscript Library, Aldis
Collection
Eulalie [D]

Collection of Colonel Richard Gimbel
The Raven [R]
For Annie [A]
Annabel Lee [B]

Collection of H. Bradley Martin, Esq.
Al Aaraaf [N]: extracts in "A Reviewer Reviewed"
Elizabeth [A], in Elizabeth Herring's album
An Acrostic [A], in Elizabeth Herring's album
The Spirits of the Dead (Wilmer manuscript) [B]
Latin Hymn [A], in "Epimanes"
Song of Triumph [A], in "Epimanes"
To Zante [B]

POE'S OWN COLLECTIONS

To Zante [F], in "A Reviewer Reviewed"
Also the copy of *The Raven and Other Poems* presented by Poe to Mrs.
Whitman

POE'S OWN COLLECTIONS
PUBLISHED VOLUMES

Tamerlane and Other Poems. By a Bostonian. Boston: Calvin F. S.
Thomas — Printer, 1827. 40 pp. (Issued in paper covers before the end of
August 1827.): Tamerlane [*A*]; To —— —— [Song, *A*]; Dreams [*A*]; Visit of
the Dead [Spirits of the Dead, *A*]; Evening Star; Imitation; (untitled) "In
youth have I known" [Stanzas]; (untitled) "A wilder'd being" [A Dream,
A]; (untitled) "The happiest day" [The Happiest Day, *A*]; The Lake [*A*].
I edited a facsimile edition, published for the Facsimile Text Society by
Columbia University Press, New York in 1941.

Al Aaraaf, Tamerlane, and Minor Poems. By Edgar A. Poe. Baltimore:
Hatch & Dunning, 1829. 72 pages. (Issued in boards in December; two copies
with Poe's manuscript changes are known.): (untitled) "Science! meet
daughter of old Time . . . " [Sonnet — To Science, *A*]; Al Aaraaf [*C*];
Tamerlane [*C*]; Preface [Romance, *A*]; To —— —— (" Should my early life
seem") [*C*]; To —— —— ("I saw thee on thy bridal day") [Song, *C*]; To ——
—— ("The bowers whereat") [To (Elmira), *A*]; To the River — To the River
(Po), *B*]; The Lake —— To —— [The Lake *C*]; Spirits of the Dead [*C*]; A
Dream [*B*]; To M —— [*B*]; Fairyland [*C*].

—— [The Herring copy, with revisions made in 1845]. When Poe was pre-
paring *The Raven and Other Poems* for publication in 1845, he made cor-
rections in a copy of *Al Aaraaf. . .* (1829) borrowed from his cousin Elizabeth
Herring (by now Mrs. Tutt) and gave it to the printers. This copy is now in
the Berg Collection at the New York Public Library. It is carefully described
in my 1942 facsimile reprint of *The Raven and Other Poems* of 1845. Poems
showing corrections are: Al Aaraaf [*J*, *J₂*]; Tamerlane; Preface [Romance,
E]; To —— —— ("Should my early life") — the whole poem is marked for
deletion; To —— —— [Song, *E*]; To —— —— ("The bowers whereat") [To
(Elmira), *B*]; To the River —— [To the River (Po), *E*]; A Dream; To M ——
[*C*]; Fairyland [*G*].
The changes in "Tamerlane" and "A Dream" are not verbal.

—— [John Neal's presentation copy]. This shows manuscript changes in
"Tamerlane" [*D*] and "To —— " [Song, *D*].

Poems by Edgar A. Poe . . . Second Edition. New York: Elam Bliss, 1831.
124 pp. (Issued about May 1, 1831. Killis Campbell supervised a facsimile edi-
tion, published for the Facsimile Text Society by Columbia University Press
in 1936.): Introduction [Romance, *C*]; To Helen [*A*]; Israfel [*A*]; The
Doomed City [The City in the Sea, *A*]; Fairy Land [II; Fairyland *E*]; Irene
[*A*]; A Paean [*A*]; The Valley Nis [The Valley of Unrest, *A*]; (untitled)

"Science! meet daughter of old Time thou art" [Sonnet – To Science, *D*]; Al Aaraaf [*E*]; Tamerlane [*F*; including The Lake, D].

Tales of the Grotesque and Arabesque. 2 vols. Philadelphia: Lea and Blanchard, 1840 (actually issued in November 1839): [To One in Paradise, *E*], in "The Visionary"; Catholic hymn [Hymn, *D*], in "Morella"; [Latin Hymn and Song of Triumph, *C*], in "Epimanes"; [The Haunted Palace, *C*, and Couplet, B], in "The Fall of the House of Usher"; motto for "William Wilson" [*C*]

Tales. New York: Wiley and Putnam, 1845 (brought out about June 15 under the supervision of E. A. Duyckinck): Motto for "The Gold-Bug" [*B*]; [The Haunted Palace, *H*, and Couplet, *C*] in "The Fall of the House of Usher."

The Raven and Other Poems. New York: Wiley and Putnam, 1845. 91 pages, in a paper wrapper. The London edition of 1846 is not a reprint, but American sheets bound up with a cancel title page.

The circumstances of the compilation and publication of this collection are dealt with at length in the introduction to my reprint (1942) of the J. Lorimer Graham copy noted below. In a letter to E. A. Duyckinck, September 10, 1845, Poe said: "I leave for you what I think the best of my Poems." He added that, if they could not be made to fill a book, "I can hand you some 'Dramatic Scenes' from the S. L. Messenger (2d Vol) and 'Al Aaraaf' and 'Tamerlane,' two juvenile poems of some length." Since the extra material was desired, he borrowed a copy of *Al Aaraaf* . . . from his cousin Elizabeth and volume 2 of the *Southern Literary Messenger* from R. W. Griswold and made corrections in them for printer's copy. The copyright copy of the book was deposited November 12, and on November 19 the *New-York Tribune* carried an advertisement announcing that the book was "this day published," at the price of thirty-one cents. Poe was to have received seventy-five dollars for the book in February 1846, but he settled for a lump sum on it, together with what was due him for the *Tales*, on November 13, 1845.

Reviews of the New York volume appeared in the following journals in 1845 (the list is perhaps not quite complete): *Evening Mirror* (New York), November 21, 1845, by N. P. Willis; *New-York Tribune*, November 26, by Sarah Margaret Fuller; *Evangelist* (New York), November 27; *Aristidean* for November, by Thomas Dunn English; *Democratic Review* for December, by John L. O'Sullivan; *Harbinger*, December 6, by John S. Dwight (this fulmination from Brook Farm was quoted and answered by Poe in the *Broadway Journal* of December 13); New York *Illustrated Magazine*, December 6, by Lawrence Labree; the *Golden Rule*, December 13, and the *Knickerbocker Magazine* for January 1846, by Lewis G. Clark. The English issue was reviewed in the London *Athenaeum*, February 28, 1846 (by Thomas Kibble Hervey), and in the *Literary Gazette*, March 14, 1846.

The dedication reads: "To the noblest of her sex — to the author of 'The Drama of Exile' – To Miss Elizabeth Barrett Barrett, of England, I dedicate this volume, with the most enthusiastic admiration and with the most sincere esteem. E.A.P."

PREFACE.

THESE trifles are collected and republished chiefly with a view to their redemption from the many improvements to which they have been subjected while going at random "the rounds of the press." If what I have written is to circulate at all, I am naturally anxious that it should circulate as I wrote it. In defence of my own taste, nevertheless, it is incumbent upon me to say that I think nothing in this volume of much value to the public, or very creditable to myself. Events not to be controlled have prevented me from making, at any time, any serious effort in what, under happier circumstances, would have been the field of my choice. With me poetry has been not a purpose, but a passion; and the passions should be held in reverence; they must not—they cannot at will be excited with an eye to the paltry compensations, or the more paltry commendations, of mankind.

E. A. P.

PREFACE TO *THE RAVEN AND OTHER POEMS* (1845)

with Poe's changes, marked in the Lorimer Graham copy now in the Miriam Lutcher Stark Library at the University of Texas. In the photographs supplied through the courtesy of the Library, Poe's faint pencilings were barely discernible; this reproduction therefore is made from the facsimile edition of 1942, by permission of Columbia University Press.

Poetry as a "passion" for truth, beauty, and power, was discussed by Leigh Hunt in his essay "What is Poetry?" prefixed to *Imagination and Fancy* (1844). Hunt's volume was reprinted in New York early in 1845 by Poe's publishers. Poe, however, in the "Letter to Mr. —" prefixed to his *Poems* of 1831, had said that poetry should be a passion.

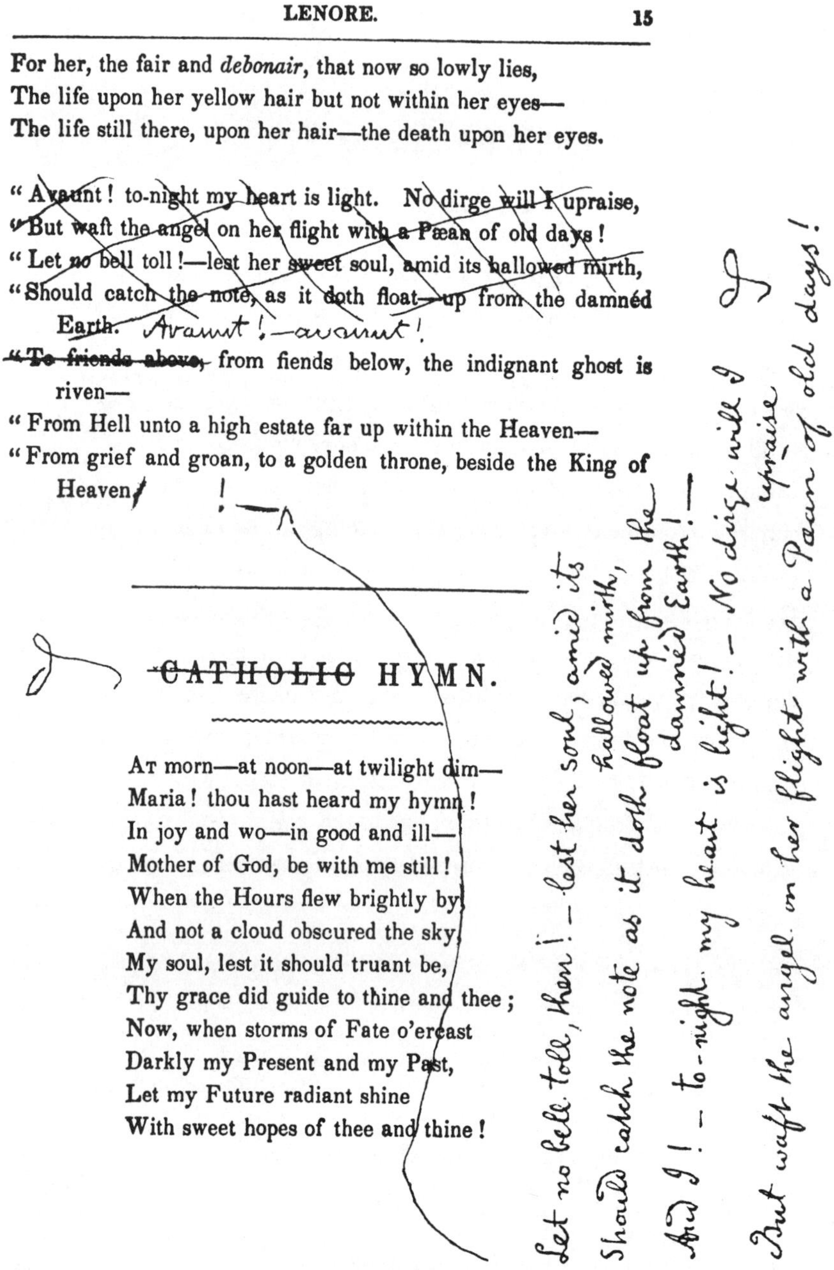

For her, the fair and *debonair*, that now so lowly lies,
The life upon her yellow hair but not within her eyes—
The life still there, upon her hair—the death upon her eyes.

" Avaunt ! to-night my heart is light.   No dirge will I upraise,
" But waft the angel on her flight with a Pæan of old days !
" Let no bell toll !—lest her sweet soul, amid its hallowed mirth,
" Should catch the note, as it doth float—up from the damnéd
    Earth. Avaunt !—avaunt !
" To friends above, from fiends below, the indignant ghost is
    riven—
" From Hell unto a high estate far up within the Heaven—
" From grief and groan, to a golden throne, beside the King of
    Heaven ! —

CATHOLIC HYMN.

At morn—at noon—at twilight dim—
Maria ! thou hast heard my hymn !
In joy and wo—in good and ill—
Mother of God, be with me still !
When the Hours flew brightly by,
And not a cloud obscured the sky,
My soul, lest it should truant be,
Thy grace did guide to thine and thee ;
Now, when storms of Fate o'ercast
Darkly my Present and my Past,
Let my Future radiant shine
With sweet hopes of thee and thine !

(handwritten marginalia):
Let no bell toll, then ! — lest her soul, amid its hallowed mirth,
Should catch the note as it doth float up from the damnéd Earth ! —
And I ! — to-night, my heart is light ! — No dirge will I upraise,
But waft the angel on her flight with a Pæan of old days !

A PAGE FROM THE LORIMER GRAHAM COPY OF *THE RAVEN*

This is an acknowledgment of Poe's debt in "The Raven" to Miss Barrett's "Lady Geraldine's Courtship." The dedication copy, now in the Berg Collection of the New York Public Library, is inscribed "To Miss Elizabeth Barrett, With the Respects of Edgar A. Poe." Her letter of thanks, dated "April 1846," is also in the Berg Collection. Dr. Saul Rosenzweig calls my attention to a passage in a letter of Elizabeth Barrett to Browning, December 1, 1845, indicating that she supposed Poe's preface would contain some reference, not wholly complimentary, to her poems. This almost surely was due to a misunderstanding of some communication, possibly from Cornelius Mathews, about Poe's notices in the *Evening Mirror* and *Broadway Journal*.

The preface, with Poe's changes made in 1849, is reproduced on page 579.

The pieces reprinted, all of which had previously been published in periodicals, are, in this order: The Raven [*J*]; The Valley of Unrest [*E*]; Bridal Ballad [*E*]; The Sleeper [*H*]; The Coliseum [*J*]; Lenore [*F*]; Catholic Hymn [Hymn, *G*]; Israfel [*F*]; Dream-land [*C*]; Sonnet — to Zante [To Zante, *E*]; The City in the Sea [*E*]; To One in Paradise [*M*]; Eulalie — A Song [*E*]; To F——s S. O——d [To Frances S. Osgood, *F*]; To F—— [To Frances, *E*]; Sonnet — Silence [*F*]; The Conqueror Worm [*F*]; The Haunted Palace [*J*]; Scenes from "Politian" [*D*]. POEMS WRITTEN IN YOUTH Sonnet — To Science [*J*]; Al Aaraaf [*K*]; Tamerlane [*H*]; A Dream [*E*]; Romance [*G*]; Fairyland [*H*]; To —— [To (Elmira), *D*]; To the River —— [To the River (Po) *G*]; The Lake —— To —— [The Lake, *F*]; Song [*F*]; To Helen [*F*]. Before POEMS WRITTEN IN YOUTH there is a note reading:

> Private reasons — some of which have reference to the sin of plagiarism, and others to the date of Tennyson's first poems — have induced me, after some hesitation, to republish these, the crude compositions of my earliest boyhood. They are printed *verbatim* — without alteration from the original edition — the date of which is too remote to be judiciously acknowledged. E. A. P.

The earlier poems were certainly not printed verbatim, although changes in the two longest were not numerous. The reference to plagiarism was called forth by John Forster's pointless remark, in reviewing Griswold's *Poets and Poetry of America* in the London *Foreign Quarterly Review*, January 1844, that "The Haunted Palace" was indebted to Tennyson's "Deserted House."

—— [Whitman copy]. This is the copy of *The Raven and Other Poems* (1845), bound with the *Tales* (1845) and issued by Wiley and Putnam in 1846, that Poe gave to Helen Whitman. It has a manuscript change, "Stannard" added, in the title of "To Helen" [*H*]. This copy is now owned by Mr. H. Bradley Martin.

—— [The J. Lorimer Graham copy with revisions as late as 1849]. This celebrated copy of *The Raven and Other Poems* (1845) contains manuscript revisions by Poe — some clearly very late — of the Preface and fourteen other pieces. The book came into Griswold's hands too late for use in his edition of the *Works*. It was sold by his estate and acquired by James Lorimer Graham, whose widow gave it to the library of the Century Club, New York; it is now in the Miriam Lutcher Stark Library at the University of Texas. I edited a reproduction for The Facsimile Text Society in 1942. The poems affected are: The Raven [S]; Bridal Ballad [F]; The Sleeper [J]; The Coliseum [L]; Lenore [J]; Hymn [H]; Israfel [G]; Dreamland [E]; The City in the Sea [F]; To One in Paradise [N]; Eulalie [G]; The Conqueror Worm [J]; The Haunted Palace [M]; *Politian* [D].

The revisions in "The Coliseum," "Israfel," "The City in the Sea," "Eulalie," "The Haunted Palace," and *Politian* were not verbal.

POE'S COLLECTIONS NOT IN BOOK FORM

Poe made several collections of his poetry that are not in the form of published editions. Descriptions of these follow.

[The Wilmer Manuscript]. About 1828 Poe made manuscript copies of "Tamerlane" and some of his other poems, including (from the volume of 1827) revised versions of the poems now called "Song" ("I saw thee"), "Dreams," "Spirits of the Dead," "The Lake," and 'To —— ——" ("Should my early life," completely rewritten from "Imitation"), as well as two new poems that were first printed in 1829, now called "To the River [Po]," and "To M——" ("I heed not"). The manuscript came into the possession of Poe's early friend, Lambert A. Wilmer, whose heirs made it accessible to G. E. Woodberry in 1895 for use in the tenth volume of the Stedman–Woodberry edition of Poe's works. Later the already imperfect manuscript was divided; most of it is now in the Pierpont Morgan Library, but one leaf was in the collection of Mr. William H. Koester, and another, described in the Yale List as number 10, is owned by Mr. H. Bradley Martin.

PHANTASY PIECES. In 1842 Poe planned a new collection of his tales. He drew up a table of contents and marked a number of changes in a copy of *Tales of the Grotesque and Arabesque* (1840), but he was unsuccessful in finding a publisher. The marked volume I is now owned by Mr. H. Bradley Martin. A limited facsimile edition issued by George Blumenthal is mentioned in the Yale List, under number 150. The poems showing changes are The Haunted Palace [D], in "The Fall of the House of Usher," and Hymn [E], in "Morella."

Saturday Museum collection (1843). Poe made a small collection of his poems early in 1843 for the *Philadelphia Saturday Museum,* and inserted it in a sketch of his life which he said was by Henry B. Hirst, but in which he himself obviously had a hand. It first appeared in the issue of February 25, was reprinted in the issue of March 4, and was also put out as an Extra. The University of North Carolina has the issue of March 4; the American Antiquarian Society has the Extra, but no extant copy of the issue of February 25 is known. I examined in a large photostatic reproduction what purported to be an exemplar of that issue once owned by J. H. Rindfleisch, a bookseller and associate of J. H. Whitty. It was made up of clippings.

For the pieces introduced in the *Museum* sketch see the list of Newspapers and Magazines, page 587, below.

For this couplet and other mention of a boyish collection, see pages 3–6 above.

TENTATIVE BEGINNING OF AN EARLY COLLECTION

From a document in the Ellis and Allan Papers at the Library of Congress. John Allan used both sides of the sheet for some personal figuring. For this couplet and other mention of a boyish collection, see pages 3–6 above.

POE'S OWN COLLECTIONS

THE "RICHMOND EXAMINER TEXTS," 1849

These texts purport to be from late drafts given by Poe to the *Richmond Examiner* during his last visit to Richmond. In the preface to his *Complete Poems of Edgar Allan Poe* (1911), pages viii–x, J. H. Whitty claimed that Poe's friend, F. W. Thomas, had access to proof sheets of several poems of Poe set up by the printers of the *Examiner* late in the summer of 1849. "The poems from proof sheets of the *Examiner* were compiled by F. W. Thomas," says Whitty, "with the intention of publishing a volume of Poe's poems. He wrote his *Recollections of Edgar A. Poe* for this,, but his death ended the project in 1866." Judge Robert W. Hughes, according to Whitty, later "placed the manuscript in my hands for publication in the Richmond, Virginia, Sunday *Times,* with which newspaper I was associated at the time, but it was found unavailable. A copy, however, was retained, and all the important facts and changes are incorporated in this volume." If we take Whitty at his word, he had a copy (presumably in his·own hand) of a document by F. W. Thomas which has long since disappeared, and Whitty's copy, too, has now disappeared. Whitty was evasive when I asked to see the *Examiner* material, although he freely showed me the manuscript of "Spiritual Song" (which survives) and allowed me to examine the changes Poe made (in his tales) in the Duane volumes of the *Southern Literary Messenger,* as he had done for Woodberry before 1894. (These changes are· certaintly authentic. Woodberry studied but did not record them; I have a complete record.)

To sum up, we have the report of a far from reliable person on the copy he had made of a lost manuscript. I am satisfied that Whitty had some kind of document; he quotes from it some passages of considerable length that are not in his own style. How he treated some of his briefer quotations, how far he quoted from memory and how accurately, cannot be answered at present. How reliable the memory of F. W. Thomas was after two decades cannot be answered at all.

The texts from the proof sheets present grave problems. We have a statement, independent of Whitty (and Thomas) that "Edgar A. Poe was induced to revise his principal poems for special publication in the Examiner" (Frederick S. Daniel, *The Richmond Examiner During the War,* 1868, p. 220). We know it was Poe's custom to have his poems in revised form occasionally set up for publication in newspapers. "The Raven" appeared in the *Examiner* while Poe was still in Richmond; "Dreamland" soon after his death.

The "Richmond Examiner proof-sheet texts" of a dozen other poems (Bridal Ballad, The Sleeper, Lenore, Israfel, The Conqueror Worm, The Haunted Palace, The Bells, For Annie, To My Mother, A Dream Within a Dream, Ulalume, and Annabel Lee) are known from the Whitty records alone, and hence through *two* manuscript copies. F. W. Thomas was not a meticulous scholar; his hand was none too legible; he sometimes wrote dashes and periods — and perhaps commas — alike. His punctuation is certainly unreliable. Some of the dozen Whitty texts are verbally extremely like (or even identical with) other printed old texts which differ from Griswold's texts. Did Thomas take *all* his versions from *Examiner* proof sheets, or did he take some from other clippings in his possession? We do not know even what Thomas himself said.

Some of these versions seem to me really independent and possibly final texts, if they could be authenticated; but the differences are usually of only a word or two. (The change of the title of "A Dream Within a Dream" to the meaningless "To —— " seems to me indubitably Poe's, for he was at his worst when it came to titles; but that text has a doubtful reading.) I have given the variants in my notes, but I adopt none of the proof-sheet versions as my final text.

ANTHOLOGIES PREPARED DURING POE'S LIFETIME
(in chronological order)

The Gift: A Christmas and New Year's Present for 1840 (Philadelphia: Carey and Hart, copr. 1839): Motto for "William Wilson " [*A*].

American Melodies, ed. George P. Morris (New York: Linen & Fennell, 1841; copr. 1840): To One in Paradise [*F*].

The Poets and Poetry of America, ed. Rufus Wilmot Griswold (Philadelphia: Carey & Hart, 1842; eighth edition, 1847; tenth edition, dated 1850 but issued late in 1849). The most important anthology of the time. Although never on the best of terms with Poe, Griswold consulted him on his selections and was supplied by Poe with authorized texts. The first edition (1842) contained The Sleeper [*E*], The Coliseum [*F*], and The Haunted Palace [*E*]. Although a new edition appeared in almost every year, the Poe selections were not changed until there was a major revision in the eighth edition (1847). In it, texts of The Conqueror Worm [*H*] and The Raven [*P*] were added. The tenth edition, dated 1850 but issued late in 1849, was again extensively revised. Griswold now omitted The Coliseum and added Israfel [*H*], The City in the Sea [*G*], To One in Paradise [*P*], To Zante [*G*], Lenore [*G*], Dreamland [*D*], Ulalume [*F*], To Helen [Whitman] [*D*], For Annie [*F*], and Annabel Lee [*J*]. In all subsequent editions Poe's poems are printed from the plates used for the tenth.

The Poetry of the Sentiments, ed Rufus Wilmot Griswold (Philadelphia: Uriah Hunt & Son, 1845. Stereotyped; reissued in 1846 and occasionally after 1850): The Coliseum [*K*].

The Missionary Memorial: A Literary and Religious Souvenir (New York: E. Walker, 1846; copr. 1845): The Lake [*E*].

The Prose Writers of America, ed. Rufus Wilmot Griswold (Philadelphia: Carey & Hart, 1847): The Haunted Palace [*K*] and Couplet [*D*] in "The Fall of the House of Usher".

The Lover's Gift, ed. Elizabeth Oakes Smith (Hartford: 1849; actually issued late in 1848). Since the editor was a good friend of Poe, the texts of the two poems selected are probably authorized. They are To Helen [*G*], its first appearance in an anthology; and To Frances S. Osgood [*G*].

Gift Leaves of American Poetry, ed. Rufus W. Griswold (New York: J. C. Riker, copr. 1849): The Haunted Palace [*L*].

Leaflets of Memory: An Illuminated Annual for MDCCCL, ed. Reynell Coates. (Philadelphia: E. H. Butler & Co., 1850; actually issued and reviewed in 1849): To My Mother [*C*].

GRISWOLD'S EDITION OF POE'S WORKS

The Works of the Late Edgar Allan Poe. Edited by Rufus W. Griswold. 4 vols. (New York: J. S. Redfield, 1850–1856). When Griswold edited the first two volumes of the *Works,* late in 1849, he did not make use of the J. Lorimer Graham copy of *The Raven and Other Poems* of 1845 because it came into his hands too late. Obviously he sent the printer the copy from which Poe had torn the final leaf — page 91, containing the early "To Helen" — to send to Mrs. Whitman. Of all the poems in the 1845 volume, only this one was not included in Volume II of the *Works* with the texts of the other poems. It did appear, however, in Volume I, in Lowell's sketch of Poe originally written for *Graham's Magazine.* To the poems from the 1845 collection Griswold added eleven poems of 1846–1849 (probably from corrected clippings). One poem of eight lines, "To —— " ("I heed not"), omitted from the 1845 *Raven,* though marked for abridgment, not omission, in the Herring *Al Aaraaf,* is also given in the *Works* in a new form, abridged and improved; Griswold used a manuscript which is now in the Harvard College Library.

Volume I. Tales (1850): To Helen [*J*] in Lowell's "Edgar A. Poe"; To One in Paradise [*Q*] in "The Assignation"; The Haunted Palace [*Q*] and (untitled) Couplet [*E*] in "The Fall of the House of Usher"; Motto for "William Wilson" [*E*]; (untitled) The Conqueror Worm [*K*] in "Ligeia"; (untitled) Motto for the Gold-Bug [*C*];

Volume II. Poems and Tales (1850): Preface as in *The Raven . . .* (1845), without the corrections marked in the Lorimer Graham copy; The Raven [*W*]; Lenore [*L*]; Hymn [*J*]; A Valentine [*G*]; The Coliseum [*M*]; To Helen [Whitman] [*E*]; To Marie Louise [*C*]; Ulalume [*G, H*]; The Bells [*J*]; An Enigma [*B*]; Annabel Lee [*L*]; To My Mother [*B*]; The Haunted Palace [*R*]; The Conqueror Worm [*L*]; To Frances S. Osgood [*H*]; To One in Paradise [*R*]; The Valley of Unrest [*F*]; The City in the Sea [*H*]; The Sleeper [*K*]; Sonnet — Silence [*G*]; A Dream Within a Dream [*D*]; Dream-Land [*G*]; To Zante [*H*]; Eulalie [*H*]; Eldorado [*B*]; Israfel [*J*]; For Annie [*G*]; To M—— [*E*]; Bridal Ballad [*G*]; To Frances [*H*]; Scenes from "Politian" [*F*]. POEMS WRITTEN IN YOUTH [with Poe's note as in *The Raven . . .*]: Sonnet — To Science [*K*]; Al Aaraaf [*P, Q*]; To the River [Po] [*H*]; Tamerlane [*J*]; To [Elmira] ("The bowers whereat") [*E*]; A Dream ("In visions of the dark night") [*F*]; Romance [*H*]; Fairyland [*K*]; The Lake [*G*]; Song [*H*]; To Marie Louise Shew [*C*]; Latin Hymn and Song of Triumph [*E*] in "Four Beasts in One."

Volume III. The Literati, Marginalia, etc. (1850): Extract from *Politian* [*G*] in "Mr. Longfellow and Other Plagiarists"; Lines after Elizabeth Barrett [*D, E*] in "E. P. Whipple and Other Critics" and "Elizabeth Barrett Barrett"; Ulalume (lines 30–38) [*J*]; Hexameter [*C*].

LATER BOOKS

William Fearing Gill, ed. *Laurel Leaves: Original Poems, Stories, and Essays, by Henry W. Longfellow* [and 34 others] (Boston: William F. Gill and Company. 1876): Motto for The Stylus [*B*].

William Fearing Gill. *The Life of Edgar Allan Poe* (New York: Dillingham, 1877): Lines on Joe Locke [*D*]; Motto for The Stylus [*C*].

Eugene Didier. *The Life and Poems of Edgar Allan Poe* (New York: W. J. Widdleton, 1877): Alone [*C*].

George Edward Woodberry. *The Life of Edgar Allan Poe.* 2 vols. (Boston and New York: Houghton Mifflin Company, 1909): Fragment of a Campaign Song [*B*].

J. H. Whitty. *The Complete Poems of Edgar Allan Poe* (Boston and New York: Houghton Mifflin Company, 1911): Elizabeth [*B*]; An Acrostic [*C*]; Spiritual Song [*B*]; The Haunted Palace [*P*]; Impromptu: To Kate Carol [*B*].

—— (1917): May Queen Ode [the only text listed]; The Divine Right of Kings [*B*]; Stanzas (to F.S.O.) [*B*]; Deep in Earth [*C*]; To Frances S. Osgood [*A*].

NEWSPAPERS AND MAGAZINES

(in alphabetical order)

American Monthly Magazine (Boston): Fairyland [*B*].

American Museum of Literature and the Arts (Baltimore): The Haunted Palace [*A*].

American Review: A Whig Journal (New York): The Valley of Unrest [*C*]; The City in the Sea [*C*]; Eulalie [*B*]; The Raven [*A*]; Ulalume [*A*].

Baltimore Gazette and Daily Advertiser: Al Aaraaf [*A*], extracts.

Baltimore Saturday Visiter: Enigma (on Shakespeare); Serenade; To —— ("Sleep on"); Fanny; The Coliseum [*A*].

Bookman (New York): The Beloved Physician [*C*].

Broadway Journal (New York): Song [*G*]; A Dream [*D*]; Sonnet — To Science [*H*]; Al Aaraaf [*H*]; Romance [*F*]; To [Elmira] [*C*]; To the River [Po] [*F*]; Fairyland [*J*]; Israfel [*E*]; The Sleeper [*G*]; The Valley of Unrest [*D*]; The City in the Sea [*D*]; To One in Paradise [*K, L*]; Hymn [*F*]; Latin Hymn [*D*]; Song of Triumph [*D*]; Coliseum [*H*]; Politian [*C*]; Bridal Ballad [*D*]; To Zante [*D*]; Motto for "William Wilson" [*D*]; Sonnet — Silence [*E*]; The Conqueror Worm [*D, E*]; To Frances [*D*]; To Frances S. Osgood [*E*]; Lenore [*E*]; Dream-Land [*B*]; Eulalie [*C*]; The Raven [*F, G*]; Lines after Elizabeth Barrett [*A*]; Impromptu: To Kate Carol [*A*]; To [Violet Vane].

Burton's Gentleman's Magazine (Philadelphia): Spirits of the Dead [*D*]; To the River [Po] [*C*]; Fairyland [*F*]; To One in Paradise [*D*]; Hymn [*C*]; The Haunted Palace [*B*]; Couplet from "The Fall of the House of Usher" [*A*]; Motto for "William Wilson" [*B*]; Sonnet — Silence [*C*]; To Frances S. Osgood [*C*].

Casket, The (Philadelphia): Sonnet — To Science [*C*].

Columbian Lady's and Gentleman's Magazine (New York): To Marie Louise [*B*].

NEWSPAPERS AND MAGAZINES

Critic (London): The Raven [H].

Dollar Newspaper (Philadelphia): Motto for "The Gold-Bug" [A].

Evening Mirror (New York): Lenore [Ca]; The Raven [B]; Epigram for Wall Street; A Valentine [C].

Flag of Our Union (Boston): A Valentine [F]; A Dream Within a Dream [B]; For Annie [B]; Eldorado [A]; To My Mother [A].

Godey's Magazine and Lady's Book (Philadelphia): Hexameter [B].
Graham's Magazine (Philadelphia): Sonnet — To Science [F]; Al Aaraaf [G]; To Helen [C, E]; Israfel [C]; The Haunted Palace [G]; The Conqueror Worm [A]; To Frances [B]; Lenore [D]; Dream-Land [A]; The Raven [M]; Lines after Elizabeth Barrett [G]; The Divine Right of Kings [A]; Stanzas (to F. S. O.) [A].

Harper's New Monthly Magazine: Lines on Joe Locke [C].
Home Journal (New York): To Marie Louise Shew [B]; Ulalume [B]; The Bells [H]; For Annie [D].

The Lady's Book (Philadelphia): To One in Paradise [B].
Literary Emporium: A Compendium of Religious, Literary, and Philosophical Knowledge (New York): The Raven [L].
Literary World (New York): Ulalume [D].

McMakin's Model American Courier (Philadelphia): see *Saturday Courier*.

New World (New York): The Conqueror Worm [C].
New York Times: To Miss Louise Olivia Hunter [B].
New York Times Saturday Review: Fragment of a Campaign Song [A].
New-York Tribune: The Raven [E]; To Helen [Whitman] [C]; Annabel Lee [G].
No Name Magazine (Baltimore): Oh, Tempora! [D]; Alone [B].
North American (Baltimore): Dreams [B]; The Happiest Day [B].

Oquawka Spectator (Oquawka, Illinois): Lenore [Cb]; For Annie [E].

Philadelphia Saturday Museum, Marcn 4, 1843: Sonnet — To Science [G]; Al Aaraaf (extracts) [F]; Romance [D]; To the River [Po] [D]; To Helen [D]; The Coliseum [G]; Israfel [D]; The Sleeper [F]; To One in Paradise [H]; Bridal Ballad [C]; To Zante [C]; The Haunted Palace [F]; Sonnet — Silence [D]; The Conqueror Worm [B]; To Frances [C]; Motto for the Stylus [A]; Lenore [B]; Lines on Joe Locke [A].
The Pioneer (Boston): Lenore [A]; Hexameter [A].
Providence Daily Journal: Ulalume [C].

Richmond Daily Whig: Lenore [K].
Richmond Semi-Weekly Examiner: The Raven [T].

Sartain's Union Magazine of Literature and Art (Philadelphia): A Valentine [E]; The Bells [C, G]; Annabel Lee [K].

SOURCES OF TEXTS COLLATED

Saturday Chronicle (Philadelphia): The Sleeper [D].

Saturday Courier (Philadelphia): Lines on Joe Locke [B]; Epigram from Pulci; Sonnet — Silence [B]; The Raven [N, U].

Saturday Evening Post (Philadelphia): Sonnet — To Science [B]; To One in Paradise [G]; Coliseum [E]; Bridal Ballad [B].

Scribner's Monthly (New York): Alone [B].

Southern Literary Messenger (Richmond): Sonnet — To Science [E]; Al Aaraaf [M]; To Helen [B]; Israfel [B]; Irene [B]; The Valley of Unrest [B]; The City in the Sea [B]; A Paean [B]; To One in Paradise [G]; Hymn [B]; Latin Hymn and Song of Triumph [B]; Coliseum [C]; Politian [B]; Parody on Drake [A]; Bridal Ballad [A]; To Zante [A]; To Frances [A]; To Frances S. Osgood [B]; The Raven [C, Q]; Model Verses [B]; Annabel Lee [H].

Southern Opinion (Richmond): Oh, Tempora! [C].

Spectator (London): To One in Paradise [A].

Sunday Times (New York): Lenore [C].

Union Magazine of Literature and Art (New York): An Enigma [A]; To Helen [Whitman] [B].

Virginia Cavalcade: Fairyland [D], reproduced from an unidentified Baltimore paper.

Yankee and Boston Literary Gazette: Tamerlane [E]; Al Aaraaf [B]; To —— ("Should my early life") [B]; Fairyland [A].

OTHER SOURCES FREQUENTLY CITED

Alfriend, Edward H. "Unpublished Recollections of Edgar Allan Poe," *Literary Era* (Philadelphia), August 1901. An important article by the son of Poe's friend Thomas Alfriend.

Allen, Hervey. *Israfel: The Life and Times of Edgar Allan Poe.* 2 vols. New York: George H. Doran, 1926. Revised, 1 vol., New York: Farrar & Rinehart, Inc., 1934. Planned as a novel, it retains fictional elements, but Allen did quote directly from traditions and previously unpublished documents.

Allen, Hervey and Thomas O. Mabbott. *Poe's Brother: The Poems of William Henry Leonard Poe,* etc. New York: George H. Doran Co. [1926].

Bondurant, Agnes M. *Poe's Richmond.* Richmond, Virginia: Garrett & Massie, [1942].

Booth, Bradford A., and Claude E. Jones. *A Concordance of the Poetical Works of Edgar Allan Poe.* Baltimore: The Johns Hopkins Press, 1941.

Braddy, Haldeen. *Glorious Incense: The Fulfillment of Edgar Allan Poe.* Washington, D.C.: The Scarecrow Press, 1953. A mine of information on Poe's sources and influence.

Buranelli, Vincent. *Edgar Allan Poe.* New York: Twayne Publishers, 1961. The best very short book on Poe.

Campbell, Killis. *The Mind of Poe and Other Studies.* Cambridge, Massachusetts: Harvard University Press, 1933. Seven important articles by the leading authority of his day; supplements his edition of the poems.

Campbell, Killis, ed. *The Poems of Edgar Allan Poe.* Boston [etc.]: Ginn and Company, [1917]. The first thoroughly annotated book of Poe's verses, with an extremely valuable Introduction. Generally authoritative.

Chateaubriand, François A. R., vicomte de. *Itinéraire de Paris à Jerusalem* (1811). In the translation by Frederic Shoberl: *Travels in Greece, Palestine, Egypt, and Barbary.* Philadelphia: M. Thomas, 1813.

Chivers, Thomas Holley. *Chivers' Life of Poe.* Edited with an Introduction by Richard Beale Davis. From the manuscripts [written before 1856] in the Henry E. Huntington Library. New York: E. P. Dutton & Co., Inc., 1952. Poe's eccentric friend was surprisingly matter-of-fact as a biographer.

Chivers, Thomas Holley. *The Complete Works of Thomas Holley Chivers.* Edited by E. L. Chase and L. F. Parks. Vol. I. Providence, R.I.: Brown University Press, 1957.

Coleridge, Henry N. *Introductions to . . . Greek Classic Poets.* London, 1830.

Didier, Eugene L. *The Life and Poems of Edgar Allan Poe.* New York, W. J. Widdleton, 1877; rev. ed., 1879. Didier's "New Memoir" presents some first-hand information but includes some legends. The injudiciously revised version in *The Poe Cult and Other Poe Papers* (New York: Broadway Publishing Company, [1909]) is of practically no value.

SOURCES FREQUENTLY CITED

D'Israeli, Isaac. *Curiosities of Literature.* 6 vols. London, 1791–1824.

English, Thomas Dunn. "Reminiscences of Poe," in *The Independent* (New York), Oct. 15, 22, 29, and Nov. 5, 1896. Important articles, unexpectedly unprejudiced.

Fagin, N. Bryllion. *The Histrionic Mr. Poe.* Baltimore: The Johns Hopkins Press, 1949. Valuable for understanding Poe's personal life and its relation to his work.

Fruit, John Phelps. *The Mind and Art of Poe's Poetry.* New York: A. S. Barnes & Co., 1899.

Gill, William Fearing. *The Life of Edgar Allan Poe.* Fourth edition, revised and enlarged. New York: W. J. Widdleton; London: Chatto and Windus, 1878. First issued in 1877 but corrected in later editions, it had much new material; but Gill's reputation for fair dealing is not of the best.

Gordan, John D. *Edgar Allan Poe . . . A Catalogue of First Editions, Manuscripts, Autograph Letters from the Berg Collection.* New York: The New York Public Library, 1949.

Graham, George R. "The Late Edgar Allan Poe," *Graham's Magazine* (Philadelphia), 36: 224–226, March 1850.

Graves, Charles Marshall. "Landmarks of Poe in Richmond . . . " *The Century Magazine,* 67: 909–920 (April 1904).

Griswold, Rufus Wilmot. The "Ludwig" article. So called from the pseudonymous signature, this is the vicious obituary of Poe that Griswold published in the evening edition of the *New-York Tribune* on October 9, 1849. It was widely reprinted and did immense damage to Poe's reputation.

Griswold, Rufus Wilmot, ed. *The Works of the Late Edgar Allan Poe, with a Memoir by Rufus Wilmot Griswold and Notices of His Life and Genius by N. P. Willis and J. R. Lowell.* New York: vols. I–III, 1850; vol. IV, 1856. The "Memoir" appeared first in vol. III, but was moved to vol. I in subsequent issues; it is notoriously biased, but more valuable than is often supposed.

Griswold, Rufus Wilmot. *Passages from the Correspondence and Other Papers of Rufus W. Griswold.* Cambridge, Massachusetts: W. M. Griswold, 1898. Most of the originals are now in the Boston Public Library, which issued a catalogue in its periodical *More Books* and its successor, *The Boston Public Library Quarterly,* between March 1941 and April 1951.

Harrison, James A., ed. *The Complete Works of Edgar Allan Poe.* 17 vols. New York: Thomas Y. Crowell & Company, [1902]: the "Virginia Edition." The first attempt at a complete edition of Poe and invaluable as such, although it contains a few things Poe did not write. Volume 1, biography, and volume 17, letters, were also issued as *Life and Letters of Edgar Allan Poe* (2 vols., New York: Crowell, 1902–03).

Heartman, Charles F., and James R. Canny, compilers. *A Bibliography of First Printings of the Writings of Edgar Allan Poe.* Revised edition. Hattiesburg, Miss.: The Book Farm, 1943.

SOURCES FREQUENTLY CITED

Hirst, Henry Beck. Biographical sketch of Poe, in *Philadelphia Saturday Museum*, March 4, 1843. Contains unreliable information, probably from Poe himself. Important because it presented presumably authorized texts of a number of poems.

Holt, Palmer C. "Poe and H. N. Coleridge's *Greek Classic Poets . . .* Sources," in *American Literature* 34:8–30 (March 1962).

Indiana List. "The J. K. Lilly Collection of Edgar Allan Poe," by David A. Randall, in *The Indiana University Bookman*, March 1960.

Ingram, John H. *Edgar Allan Poe: His Life, Letters and Opinions.* 2 vols. London, 1880. Ingram, Poe's English biographer, collected zealously and published many articles and an edition of Poe in four volumes. He was quarrelsome, given to concealing his sources, and prejudiced, but his contribution cannot be lightly dismissed.

Ingram, John H. "Memoir," in *The Works of Edgar Allan Poe.* 4 vols. Edinburgh: A. & C. Black, 1874–75. The first of many collections of Poe's writings published by Ingram.

Ingram List: *John Henry Ingram's Poe Collection at the University of Virginia: A Calendar . . .* by John Carl Miller. Charlottesville: University of Virginia Press, 1960. An extremely valuable checklist of manuscripts, clippings, etc.

Lowell, James Russell. "Edgar Allan Poe. With a Portrait." *Graham's Magazine*, 27:49–53 (February 1845). Reprinted with alterations and omissions in Griswold's edition, *The Works of the Late Edgar Allan Poe*, vol. I (1850).

Miller, John Carl. *John Henry Ingram's Poe Collection at the University of Virginia: A Calendar . . . .* Charlottesville: University of Virginia Press, 1960. Cited as the Ingram List.

Moran, John J. *A Defense of Edgar Allan Poe.* Washington: Wm. F. Boogher, 1885. The imaginative nature of this late account by the physician who attended Poe in his last illness is notorious.

Moore, Thomas. *Letters and Journals of Lord Byron with Notices of His Life.* 2 vols. London, 1830.

Osgood, Frances Sargent. *Poems by Frances Sargent Osgood . . . Illustrated by Huntington, Darley, Rossiter, Cushman, and Osgood.* Philadelphia: Carey and Hart, 1850. Dedicated to Griswold. Preface dated 1849. Entered for copyright 1849.

Ostrom, John Ward, ed. *The Letters of Edgar Allan Poe.* 2 vols. Cambridge, Massachusetts: Harvard University Press, 1948. Contains all Poe's letters, and a checklist of all letters to Poe, known at the time of publication. The work is textually excellent, although a very few highly doubtful and forged letters have been included.

Phillips, Mary Elizabeth. *Edgar Allan Poe: The Man.* 2 vols. Chicago-Philadelphia-Toronto: The John C. Winston Company, 1926. Miss Phillips spent decades in devoted research, and her work contains an immense amount of information and some misinformation. She was uncritical and wrote in a strange style, but reveals her sources, sometimes very important. The work is of great usefulness to trained and discriminative students.

Pinkney, Edward Coote. For his works, see *The Life and Works of Edward Coote Pinkney*. By Thomas O. Mabbott and F. L. Pleadwell, 1926.

Poe, Edgar Allan. (For further information on books by Poe, see Sources of Texts Collated, and Index.) His separately published volumes in chronological order, are:

    Tamerlane and Other Poems. Boston, 1827.
    Al Aaraaf, Tamerlane, and Minor Poems. Baltimore, 1829.
    Poems. Second Edition. New York, 1831.
    The Narrative of Arthur Gordon Pym. New York, 1838.
    The Conchologist's First Book. Philadelphia, 1839.
    Tales of the Grotesque and Arabesque. Philadelphia, 1840.
    Prose Romances No. 1. Philadelphia, 1843.
    Tales. New York, 1845.
    The Raven and Other Poems. New York, 1845.
    Mesmerism "In Articulo Mortis" (pirated). London, 1846.
    Eureka: A Prose Poem, New York, 1848.

Significant posthumous collections (for fuller information, see under the editor's names), are:

    Works, ed. Griswold. 4 vols. New York: 1850–56.
    Works, ed. Ingram. 4 vols. Edinburgh, 1874–75.
    Works, ed. Stoddard. 6 vols. New York, 1884.
    Works, ed. Stedman and Woodberry. 10 vols. Chicago, 1894–95.
    Complete Works, ed. Harrison. 17 vols. New York, 1902.
    Complete Poems, ed. Whitty. Boston and New York, 1911; 1917.
    Poems, ed. Campbell. Boston, New York, etc., 1917.
    Letters, ed. Ostrom, 2 vols. Cambridge, Mass., 1948.

Quinn, Arthur Hobson. *Edgar Allan Poe: A Critical Biography*. New York and London: D. Appleton-Century Company, 1941. A distinguished piece of scholarship, generally authoritative, but in his dedicated admiration of Poe Quinn sometimes ignored problems.

Quinn, Arthur Hobson, and Richard H. Hart, eds. *Edgar Allan Poe: Letters and Documents in the Enoch Pratt Free Library*. New York: Scholars' Facsimiles and Reprints, 1941.

Rice, Sara Sigourney. *Edgar Allan Poe: A Memorial Volume*. Baltimore: Turnbull Bros., 1877.

Stedman, Edmund Clarence, and George Edward Woodberry. *The Works of Edgar Allan Poe*. 10 vols. Chicago, 1894–95. There have been reprints. The editorial work was that of Woodberry, whose methods were typically "late Victorian."

Stoddard, Richard Henry. "Life of Edgar Allan Poe," in *Select Works of Edgar Allan Poe, Poetical and Prose, with a New Memoir*. New York: W. J. Widdleton, 1880. Reprinted as "Memoir" in *The Works of Edgar*

Allan Poe, 6 vols., New York, 1884. This is quite different from Stoddard's earlier memoir prefixed to *Poems by Edgar Allan Poe* (New York: Widdleton, 1875). Stoddard knew Poe and did not like him, but he contributes largely to our knowledge.

Stovall, Floyd, ed. *The Poems of Edgar Allan Poe.* Edited with an Introduction, Variant Readings, and Textual Notes. Charlottesville: The University Press of Virginia, 1965. Supplies what is not given in our edition, a complete record of the variants in punctuation.

Thompson, John R. *The Genius and Character of Edgar Allan Poe.* Edited from the manuscript by James H. Whitty and James H. Rindfleisch. Privately printed, 1926. A lecture delivered in Baltimore (according to Gill, *Life,* p. 267) some time before Thompson's death in 1874. Although Thompson knew Poe, his lecture seems to me a piece of sensationalism, unreliable in detail.

Trent, W. P., ed., *The Raven, etc.* Boston and New York, etc.: Houghton Mifflin, 1897.

Weiss, Susan Archer Talley. *The Home Life of Poe.* New York: Broadway Publishing Company, 1907. Should be supplemented by her article, "Last Days of Edgar A. Poe," *Scribner's Monthly,* 15: 707–716 (March 1878). The author knew Poe well at the end of his life.

Whitman, Sarah Helen. *Edgar Poe and His Critics.* New York: Rudd and Carleton, 1860. A well-informed defense. The original edition was reproduced, with an introduction and notes, by Oral S. Coad, New Brunswick: Rutgers University Press, 1949.

Whitty, J. H., ed. *The Complete Poems of Edgar Allan Poe; collected, edited, and arranged with memoir, textual notes and bibliography.* Boston and New York: Houghton Mifflin Company, 1911; second edition, enlarged, 1917. Whitty's "Memoir" is marred by a too-active imagination, and must be used with caution.

Wagenknecht, Edward. *Edgar Allan Poe: The Man Behind the Legend.* New York: Oxford University Press, 1963. Largely based on secondary sources, but sympathetic, sensible, and usually reliable.

Wilbur, Richard. *Poe: Complete Poems* [New York: Dell, 1959], contains an introduction and notes of unusual originality and perception.

Wilmer, Lambert A. *Merlin . . . together with Recollections of Edgar A. Poe.* Edited with an introduction by Thomas Ollive Mabbott. New York: Scholars' Facsimiles and Reprints, 1941. Wilmer's play was first published in Baltimore in 1827.

Wilmer, Lambert A. "Recollections of Edgar A. Poe." *Baltimore Daily Commercial,* May 23, 1866. Reprinted with *Merlin* (see above) in 1941.

Winwar, Frances. *The Haunted Palace: A Life of Edgar Allan Poe.* New York: Harper & Brothers, 1959. Interesting especially for its intuitive interpretations.

Woodberry, George Edward. *Edgar Allan Poe.* Boston: Houghton Mifflin and Company, 1885. (American Men of Letters series)

Woodberry, George Edward. *The Life of Edgar Allan Poe, personal and literary, with his chief correspondence with men of letters.* Boston and New York: Houghton Mifflin Company, 1909. A thorough revision and expansion of the 1885 biography, judicious, appreciative of Poe's genius, and beautifully written. Woodberry was not well informed about Poe's youth, but his book is a *sine qua non* for the serious student.

Yale List. " 'Quoth the Raven': an exhibition of the work of Edgar Allan Poe," etc., *The Yale University Library Gazette*, 33:138–189 (April 1959).

INDEXES

INDEX OF FIRST LINES

INDEX OF FIRST LINES

INDEX OF NAMES AND TITLES

Works of Poe and anonymous works are indexed by title, other works under the author's name. An asterisk following an entry indicates that the name or title will be found also in the list of Sources of Texts Collated; a small r following a title denotes a poem rejected from the Poe canon.

INDEX

INDEX

INDEX

INDEX

INDEX

INDEX

"Dream-Land," 342; and "Eldorado," 462; mentioned, 545

"The Happiest Day": 80–82; and "Romance," 129; and "To [Elmira]," 132; *Politian*, 295

Harley, Lady Charlotte: 125, 212

Harper, Henry H.: 371

Harper's New Monthly Magazine (New York)*: 156n, 232, 470n, 542n

Harrington, Reverend Henry F.: 563n

Harrison, Gabriel: 340, 555

Harrison, James A., *Complete Works* cited (for specific subjects see individual entries): xvii, 13, 92, 164n, 323n, 324n, 359n, 423, 469n, 505, 509, 510, 512, 533n, 537n, 553n, 558n, 567n, 568n, 569n, 571n, 572

Hart, John S.: 431, 476n

Hart, Richard H.: 310, 508

Harte, Bret: 420

Harvard: holdings, 3, 387, 475, 491, 548n

Harwell, Richard Barksdale: 497, 540n

Hatch and Dunning: 89, 98, 540

"Haunted Palace, The": xxix, 312–318; and "To Helen," 170; mentioned, 549

Havelock, E.A.: 169

Haviland, Thomas P.: xxvin, 137

Hawthorne, Nathaniel: 552, 563

Haynes, Robert H.: 491

Headley, Joel T.: 561

Heartman, Charles F., and Canny: 504, 506, 508, 514

Heath, James Ewell: 545n

"Heaven." See "Fairyland" [I]

Hebrides: 190

Hemans, Mrs. Felicia: xxix, 216, 331, 496

Henderson, John Oscar: 513

Henderson, Paul G.: 503, 513

"Henry Wilton" (John H. Hewitt): 227, 544

Hepburn, Freeman F.: 508

Heraclitus of Ephesus: 12

Herbelot, Barthélemy d': 23, 90, 420

Herodotus: 327

Herring, Elizabeth Rebecca: Poe poems addressed to, 147–149, 233; Poe's letter, 523; mentioned, 130, 545, 562, 569

Herring, Henry: 569

Herring, Mary Estelle: 136, 213, 216, 234, 523

Hewitt, John Hill: *Recollections of Poe*, 497, 540n; mentioned, 137n, 227, 518, 544, 572

Hewitt, Mrs. Mary E.: 473, 558, 561

"Hexameter": 339

Heywood, Amos Bardwell: 523n

Heywood, Sarah. See Trumbell, Sarah Heywood

Higginson, Thomas W.: 330, 559

High, William J.: 541n

Highet, Gilbert: 370

Hill, George: 178

Hilton, Miss Sylvia C.: 397

Hirst, Henry B.: 355, 550; biographical sketch of Poe, 123, 124, 150, 165n, 332, 553n, 570n; owned manuscripts of "Eulalie," 348, of "Annabel Lee," 475; Poe's review of his "The Coming of the Mammoth," 395, 462; his parody of "The Haunted Palace," 317; his poems quoted, 346, 355, 448, 449; mentioned, 334, 359, 491

Hoffman, Charles Fenno: on "The Raven," 351; editor of *American Monthly Magazine*, 547; mentioned, 243, 245, 397n

Hogan, Frank J.: 433

Hogg, R.M.: 83n, 129, 190, 198n, 480

Holden's Dollar Magazine (New York): 464, 511

Holley, David W.: 360n

Holmes, Lucy. See Balderston, Lucy Holmes

Holmes, Oliver Wendell: 572

Holt, Palmer C.: 90n, 167, 171, 291, 419, 422

[Holy Eyes]: 404–405; and "To Helen [Whitman]," 448

Home Journal (New York)*: Miss Bronson's recollections, 221, 410; Mrs. Whitman's poem to Poe, 441; Poe accused of plagiarism, 448; Poe's poems, 400, 413, 433, 453n; mentioned, xxvi, 334, 362n, 455, 476, 554n

Homer: 166, 221; *Odyssey* 167 291, 373

Hood, Thomas: xxix, 321, 423, 440, 453, 504

"Hop-Frog": 566

Hopkins, Charles D.: 531

Hopkins, J.H.: 562n

Hopkins, John Henry Jr.: 564

Hopkinson, Joseph: 97, 540

Horace: xxvi, 288, 372, 535, 537n

Horne, R.H.: 447, 555

Hotten, John Camden: 13

Houghton, Reverend Henry: 402

INDEX

INDEX

INDEX

INDEX

INDEX

INDEX

INDEX

White, 227, 245; Mrs. Whitman, 125, 164, 292, 295, 296, 443, 448, 493; Willis, 413, 454; last letters, 568
Lectures given: "Poets and Poetry of America," 449, 554, 556, 564; introduction to "Al Aaraaf," 559; "The Universe," 564; "Poetic Principle," 566, 567
Poe, Mrs. Edgar Allan (Virginia Eliza, Clemm): 522–525; and Edgar Poe, 467, 546, 555; and Poe's poems, 234, 371, 414, 468, 474; and Mrs. Osgood, 557; illness and death, 561, 562; mentioned, 232, 347, 350, 396, 399, 402, 424, 544n, 545, 551
Poe, Elizabeth (Mrs. Henry Herring): 530
Poe, Elizabeth Ellicott: 568n
Poe, George: 530
Poe, George, Jr.: 531
"Poe in Heaven" r: 511
Poe, John Prentiss: 530, 532n
Poe, Josephine: 525
Poe, Neilson: 541, 568n; offers home to Virginia, 523, 545; mentioned, 497, 530, 540, 569
Poe, Mrs. Neilson (Josephine Clemm): 540
Poe, Rosalie: 520–522; in Mackenzie home, 7, 8, 533; Poe's heir, 571; mentioned, 4, 469n, 517, 532, 564, 567, 570n, 572n
Poe, Samuel: 515
Poe, William: 530, 532
Poe, William Henry Leonard: 515–520; his "The Pirate," 65, 538; mentioned, 14, 81, 145, 504, 505, 531, 541, 543
Poem by a Bostonian r: 514
Poems (1831)*: xxviii, 150, 155–156, 542; and "To Helen," 168; and *Politian*, 292; mentioned, 26, 80, 127, 139, 159, 161, 190, 204, 330
Poe's pseudonyms: "Edward S.T. Grey," 383, 443; "Tamerlane," 221, 223, 225; "Edgar A. Perry," 539; "Thaddeus Perley," 341; "Quarles," 360
"Poe's Two Unpublished Poems" r: 513
"Poetic Principle, The": xxviii; and "Irenë," 179; and "To One in Paradise," 216; and "For Annie," 460; as a lecture, 566, 567; mentioned, 83n, 133, 293, 295, 453
"Poetical Epistle to Mr. Pickwick, A" r: 508

"Poetry": 6, 370
Poets and Poetry of America, The r: 510
"Poets and Poetry of America" ("Poetry of America, Poets of America"), lecture: 331, 449, 554, 556, 564
Poitiaux, Catherine: 470, 533, 567
Politian: 241–298; and "A Dream," 80; and "Happiest Day," 82; and "Al Aaraaf," 119; and "To – ," 225; and "Coliseum," 227, 231; and "The Raven," 371, 374; and "Marie Louise," 408; and "Dream Within a Dream," 452; mentioned, 319, 320, 405, 501, 545
Poliziano, Angelo (Politian): 212, 216, 289
Pollard, Henry Rives: 8
Polybius: 218
"Poor Scholar, A" r: 505
Poore, Mrs. Anne: 547n
Pope, Alexander: xxv, xxvii, 294; and "To Margaret," 15, 16; and "Tamerlane," 64; and "Al Aaraaf," 119, 121; and "To Helen," 170; and "Irenë," 186; and "To Zante," 312; and "The Raven," 374; and "The Bells," 440; mentioned, 22, 61, 116, 221
Pope-Hennessy, Dame Una: 503
Porphyrogenitus, Constantine VII: 314, 318
Portland Advertiser: 98
Post, Israel: 388, 461, 472n
Pouder, William P.: 227
Pound, Louise: 198n
Povalley: 549n
Powell, Enos R.: 333n
"Power of Words, The": 125, 374, 408, 460
Powers, Hiram: 384
"Predicament, A": 485, 486, 549
"Preface," *See* "Romance"
"Premature Burial, The": 292, 326 338, 487
Preston, Colonel John T.L.: 5
Princeton University Library: holdings, 508
"Prisoner of Perote, The," collaboration: 424
"Prophecy of Vala, The" r: 512
Prose Romances, The: 553
"Prospectus of The Stylus": 319, 328, 566
Proverbs: 290
Providence: Poe, and Mrs. Osgood, 441, and Helen Whitman, 565, lectures, 566

INDEX

INDEX

Rogers, Samuel: 221
Rolfe, John C.: 169
Rollins, George W.: 568n
Rollins, Hyder E.: 542n
"Romance": 127–129; and "Introduction," 156, 158; and "Israfel," 177; and "Conqueror Worm," 327; and "The Raven," 353; mentioned, 534n. *See also* "Introduction"
Romans: 481
Rosenbach, Dr. A.S.W.: 398, 548n
Rosenbach, Hyman Polock: 360n
Rosenmueller, E.F.C.: 465
Ross, James: 126
Ross, Sir James Clark: 421
Rossetti, W.M.: 167
Rothwell, Dr. Kenneth S.: 319
Rowe, Nicholas: 23
Royster, Elmira (Mrs. Alexander B. Shelton): 536, 539n; inspiration of, poems by Poe, 24, 65, 79, 80, 132, of Wilmer's *Merlin*, 373, 538, of W.H. Poe's "The Pirate," 538; Poe's "lost Lenore," 332; connection with "Annabel Lee," 62, 474, 480; her letter to Mrs. Clemm quoted, 310; on Poe's reading of "The Raven," 351n; mentioned, 67, 70, 76, 82, 159, 212, 236, 306, 452, 465, 567
Rufus, William: 180, 288
"Rupert and Madelon" r: 507
Russell, Milton C.: 539n
Ryan, Cornelius: 569

"Sabbath Morning, The" r: 504
Sādi: 126
St. Athanasius: 169
St. John: 216, 569
St. John's College (Fordham): 562
Saintsbury, George Edward: xxixn
Sale, George: his version of the Koran cited, 95, 96, 119, 177
Salmasius, Claudius: 218
Samuel, Bunford: 67
Sand, George: 405n, 510
Sanderson, Adam: 191
Santa Anna, Antonio Lopez de: 496
Sappho of Eresus: 116
Sappho of Mitylene: 116
Sartain, John: 431n, 472n, 476, 551, 567
Sartain, William: 355n
Sartain's Union Magazine (New York)*: 317, 387, 398; and "The Bells," 431, 433; and "Annabel Lee," 476, 567.

See also *Union Magazine*
[Satire on Junior Debating Society]: 6–7
Saturday Chronicle (Philadelphia)*: 179n, 549
Saturday Courier (Philadelphia)*: poems by Poe, 211, 322, 550; tales by Poe, 211, 488, 544
Saturday Evening Post (Philadelphia*): tales by Poe, 488, 551; Poe forecasts outcome of *Barnaby Rudge*, 551; poems by W.H. Poe, 516; review of *Poems* (1831), 155, 542; other mention, 67, 317, 371, 504
Saunders, Charles: 24
Saunders, Frederick: 351
Saxe, John G.: 432n
Scharf, J. Thomas: 541
Scheffauer, Herman: 514
Schiller: 439, 486
Schulz, Herbert C.: 377
Scotland: 533, 534
Scott, Harriet Virginia (Mrs. Thomson): 302
Scott, Sir Walter: his poems, and "Tamerlane," 62, and "Al Aaraaf," 124, and "Valley of Unrest," 194, and "Annabel Lee," 481; mentioned, 331
Scott, General Winfield: 536
Scribner's Monthly (New York)*: 145n, 343n, 359n, 362n, 521n, 524, 567n
"Sea of Serenity, The" r: 514
Seip, Miss Elizabeth Cloud: 221, 222
"Selections from Milton": 137
Seneca: 120
"Sequel to the Raven, A" r: 513
"Serenade": 222–223; 63, 141, 150
"Shadow — A Fable": 158, 329, 346, 544
Shakespeare: xxvi, xxvii, xxix, 220–222; Poe studied, 540; mentioned, 73, 537
  Specific plays: *Hamlet*, and "To Margaret," 16, and "Tamerlane," 64, and "Al Aaraaf," 125, and *Politian*, 291, 293, 294, and "For Annie," 460; — *Julius Caesar*, and "Al Aaraaf," 125, and *Politian*, 293, Poe's favorite speech, 536; — *King Lear*, and *Politian*, 296, and "Eldorado," 462; — *Macbeth*, and "Al Aaraaf," 119, and "Introduction," 159, and Fairy Land," 163, and "Irene," 181, 186, and *Politian*, 293, and "For Annie," 459; — *Midsummer Night's Dream*, and "Fairyland," 142, and "Mysterious

INDEX

INDEX

INDEX

INDEX

White, Thomas W.: publisher of *Southern Literary Messenger*, 303, 545; Poe's letter, 227; Kennedy's letter, 245; his death, 547; mentioned, 243, 294, 555

White, William A.: 171

Whitman, John Winslow: 565n

Whitman, Mrs. Sarah Helen: 441–444, 469n, 565, 566; letters from Poe cited, 125, 164, 292, 295, 296, 443, 448, 493; file of *Broadway Journal*, 331, 444; and "Ulalume," 413, 414, 423; her poems, 95, 293, 472, 480, 493; mentioned, 465n, 520n, 545n, 572; *Edgar Poe and His Critics* cited, 409

Whitman, Walt: 560

Whittier, John Greenleaf: 572

Whitty, J.H.: cited, on "Spiritual Song," 303, on other poems, 67, 360n, 432n, 540n; on a garden in Richmond, 212, 444n; on Rosalie, 520n, 521; mentioned, 129, 242n, 498, 569n

Complete Poems (1911): on Poe's poems, 8n, 198, 362n, 373; discovery of "Kate Carol," 381; on doubtful poems, 504, 506, 507, 510; quotes White's letters to Minor, 545n; reproduces Poe's earliest portrait, 570n; "Memoir" cited, 544n, 565n

Complete Poems (1917): discoveries printed in, 302, 382, 493, 503

Wieland, Christoph Martin: 172

Wilbur, Richard: on inspiration for "Dream-Land," 342

Poe: Complete Poems, cited: on "Tamerlane," 62, 63; on "Dreams," 69; on "Stanzas," 76; on "Al Aaraaf," 118; on "Romance," 129; on "To —," 133; on "Fairy-Land" [I], 139, 142; on "To Helen," 169, 170; on "Israfel," 177, 178; on "Coliseum," 226; on "To F —," 237; on "Bridal Ballad," 310; on "Haunted Palace," 317; on "Sonnet — Silence," 320, 321; on "Conqueror Worm," 326, 327; on "Eulalie," 347n; on "The Raven," 370, 373; on "To Marie Louise," 409; on "For Annie," 460

Wiley and Putnam: 558

Wilkinson, Dr. J.J. Garth: 511

Willard, Miss Helen: 12n

"William Wilson": and *Politian*, 288, 290, 295; mentioned, 329, 348, 370, 550

Willis, Nathaniel P.: 554; introductory remarks on Poe's poems, 333, 361, 400, 413, 433, 453n, 455, 556; his poems cited, 203, 401, 420, 481; rejects "Fairy-Land" [I], 139; *Prose Works* quoted, 557; mentioned, xviiin, 348, 454, 476, 541n, 558, 560n, 562, 571

Wills, John: 563n

Wilmer, Lambert A.: editor, *Baltimore Saturday Visiter*, 543; poem addressed to Poe, 549; Poe manuscripts owned by, 25, 66, 70, 84, 130, 134, 136; *Merlin* (Mabbott edition) cited, 62, 123, 373, "Recollections" in, 523, 548n, plot of, 538n; mentioned, 15, 155, 198, 440, 510, 542

Wilmington, Delaware: Poe lectures in, 554

Wilson, James Southall: 241n, 453n

Wilson, Professor John: 181, 371, 504, 509

Winchester, Elizabeth: 340

Winchester, Samuel: 340

"Wine Ballad, A" r: 513

Winfree, Mary: 136, 236, 545

Winslow, Harriet: 492, 510

Winwar, Frances, *Haunted Palace*: on "Poetry," 6; on "Fairy-Land" [I], 139; on "Valley of Unrest," 194; on "To One in Paradise," 211; on "The Raven," 370; on "Marie Louise," 408; on "Annabel Lee," 469; mentioned, 480, 504, 517, 520n

Wirt, William: 97, 370, 540

Wissahickon, The: 553

Wolcot, John ("Peter Pindar"): xxix, 313, 314

Wolf, Edwin (2nd): 360n

"Woman's Heart" r: 506

Woodberry, George Edward: 242n, 529; on "The Raven," 350n; *Edgar Allan Poe* (1885) on Poe's life, 530n, 539n, 548n, 563n, on Poe's poems, 3, 350, 415

Life of . . . Poe (1909)*: on poems, 3, "Spirits of the Dead," 70, "Fairy-Land" [I], 139, "To One in Paradise," 211, "Bridal Ballad," 305n, 506, "To Zante," 310, "Haunted Palace," 312n, 317, "The Raven," 351n, 358, 372, "The Bells," 431n, "Annabel Lee," 468, 469n, 470n; on Poe's life, 524n, 532n, 533n, 542n, 546n, 562n, 565n, 568n, 569n, 570n; mentioned, 233, 340, 405n, 499

INDEX

University of Illinois Press
1325 South Oak Street
Champaign, IL 61820-6903
WWW.PRESS.UILLINOIS.EDU